COUNTY
STREET ATLAS

EAST SUSSEX

COUNTY STREET ATLAS

EAST SUSSEX

3½ INCHES TO 1 MILE

2nd edition

COUNTY STREET ATLAS
EAST SUSSEX

First Edition published 1988
2nd Edition published 1990 by

Ordnance Survey and George Philip Ltd
Romsey Road
Maybush
Southampton SO9 4DH

George Philip Ltd
59 Grosvenor Street
London W1X 9DA

ISBN 0 540 05573 5 (George Philip)
ISBN 0 319 00267 5 (Ordnance Survey)

Reprinted 1991

Printed in Great Britain by
Butler & Tanner Ltd, Frome and London

CONTENTS

Key to map pages	vi-vii
Administrative boundaries	viii
Street maps	1-190
Index explanation and abbreviations	192
Index of towns, villages and rural localities	193
Index of street names	194-210

KEY TO MAP SYMBOLS

British Rail Station

London Transport Station

Private Railway Station

Bus or Coach Station

Police Station
(may not be open 24hrs)

Hospital with Casualty Facilities
(may not be open 24hrs)

Post Office

Place of Worship

Important Building

P Parking

120 Adjoining page indicator

Motorway and Dual Carriageway

Main or through road

A 27(T) Road numbers (Dept of Transport)

Gate and obstruction to traffic
(restrictions may not apply at all times and to all vehicles)

Footpath
Bridleway
} The representation in this atlas of a road, track or path is no evidence of the existence, of a right of way.

Amb Sta	Ambulance Station	Liby	Library
Coll	College	Mus	Museum
FB	Foot Bridge	Sch	School
F Sta	Fire Station	TH	Town Hall
LC	Level Crossing		

The large letter and numbers around the edge of the maps form the referencing system.
An explanation of how to use the system for locating the position of street names appears on page **192**.

The small numbers identify the 1 kilometre National Grid lines.

Scale of Map is 3½ inches to 1 mile (1 : 18103)

0 ¼ ½ ¾ 1 Mile

0 250m 500m 750m 1 Kilometre

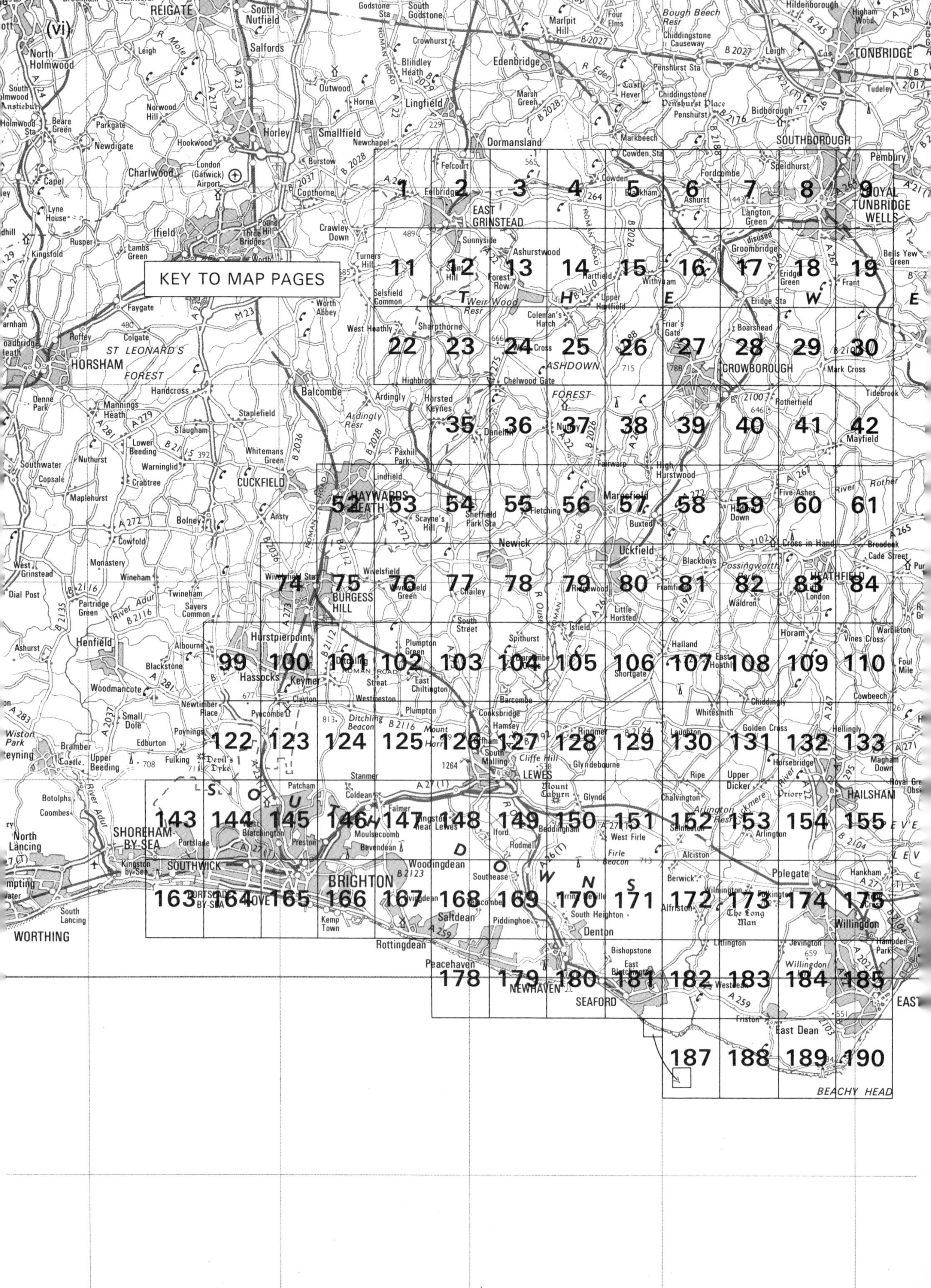

KEY TO MAP PAGES
1 2 3 4 5 6 7 8 9
11 12 13 14 15 16 17 18 19
22 23 24 25 26 27 28 29 30
35 36 37 38 39 40 41 42
52 53 54 55 56 57 58 59 60 61
74 75 76 77 78 79 80 81 82 83 84
99 100 101 102 103 104 105 106 107 108 109 110
122 123 124 125 126 127 128 129 130 131 132 133
143 144 145 146 147 148 149 150 151 152 153 154 155
163 164 165 166 167 168 169 170 171 172 173 174 175
178 179 180 181 182 183 184 185
187 188 189 190
REIGATE
South Nutfield
Salfords
North Holmwood
Horley
Smallfield
Lingfield
Edenbridge
Dormansland
TONBRIDGE
SOUTHBOROUGH
ROYAL TUNBRIDGE WELLS
Pembury
Charlwood
London (Gatwick) Airport
Copthorne
Felbridge
EAST GRINSTEAD
Crawley Down
Ifield
Three Bridges
Turners Hill
Ashurstwood
Forest Row
Groombridge
Frant
Faygate
HORSHAM
ST LEONARD'S FOREST
Colgate
Sharpthorne
West Hoathly
ASHDOWN FOREST
CROWBOROUGH
Balcombe
Handcross
Ardingly
Horsted Keynes
Danehill
Nutley
Mayfield
Rotherfield
Lindfield
HAYWARDS HEATH
CUCKFIELD
Sheffield Park Sta
Fletching
Maresfield
Buxted
Five Ashes
Newick
Uckfield
Blackboys
Cross in Hand
HEATHFIELD
Wivelsfield
BURGESS HILL
Chailey
Framfield
Waldron
Horam
Henfield
Hurstpierpoint
Hassocks
Keymer
Ditchling
Plumpton Green
Barcombe
Shortgate
Halland
East Hoathly
Steyning
Bramber
Upper Beeding
Devil's Dyke
Pyecombe
Ditchling Beacon
Cliffe Hill
LEWES
South Malling
Ringmer
Glyndebourne
Hellingly
HAILSHAM
SHOREHAM-BY-SEA
Portslade
SOUTHWICK
Patcham
Preston
Stanmer
Falmer
Moulsecoomb
Kingston near Lewes
Iford
Rodmell
Beddingham
Glynde
Mount Caburn
West Firle
Firle Beacon
Chalvington
Arlington
Alciston
Polegate
Hankham
BRIGHTON
Kemp Town
Woodingdean
Rottingdean
Saltdean
Southease
Piddinghoe
South Heighton
Denton
Berwick
Alfriston
Wilmington
The Long Man
Willingdon
Lancing
WORTHING
Peacehaven
NEWHAVEN
SEAFORD
Bishopstone
East Blatchington
Litlington
Westdean
Friston
Jevington
East Dean
BEACHY HEAD
SOUTH DOWNS
THE WEALD

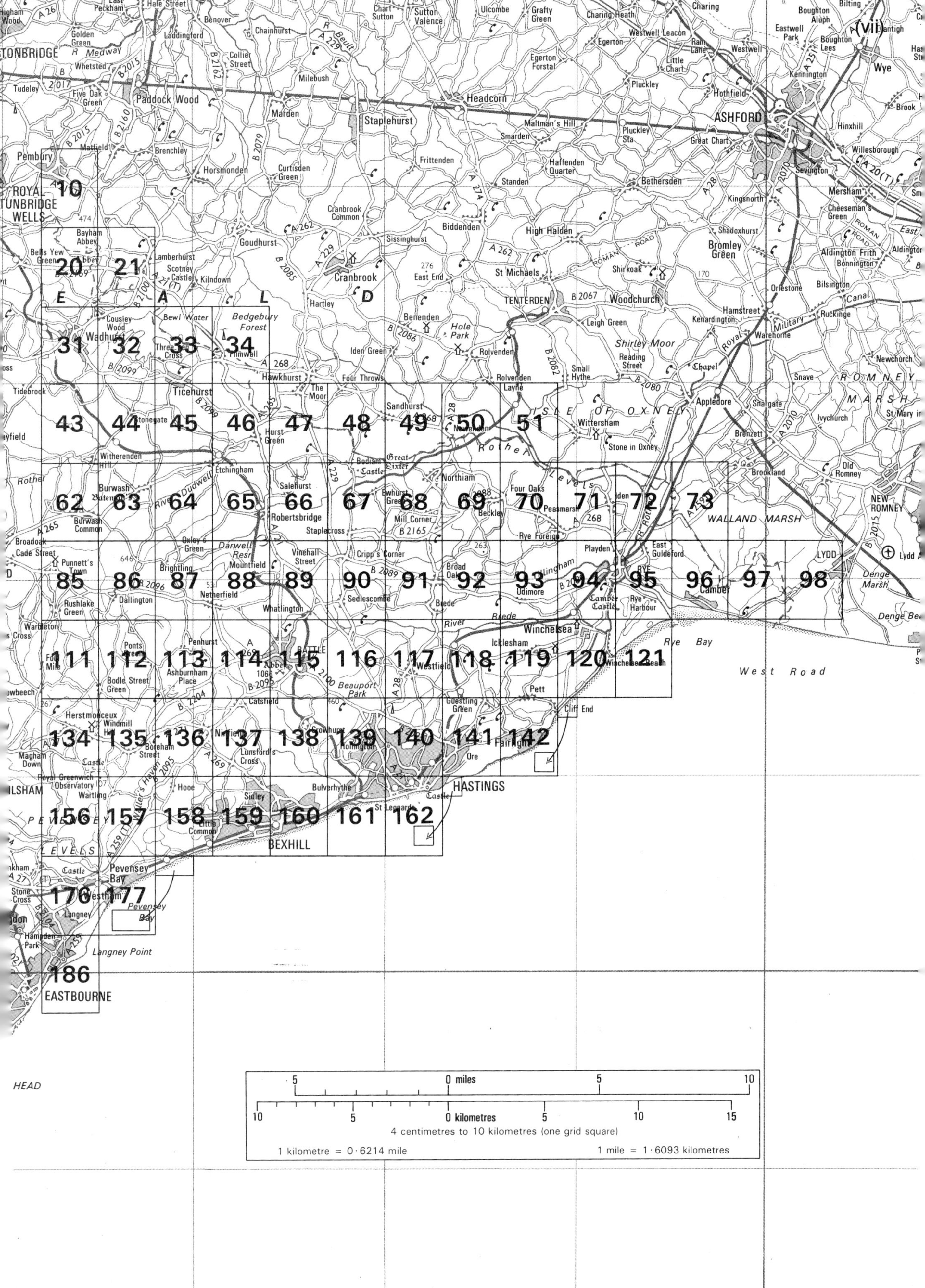
TONBRIDGE
Paddock Wood
Staplehurst
Headcorn
ASHFORD
Wye
Pembury
ROYAL TUNBRIDGE WELLS
Goudhurst
Cranbrook
Biddenden
High Halden
Bethersden
Woodchurch
TENTERDEN
Wadhurst
Ticehurst
Hawkhurst
Robertsbridge
Etchingham
Burwash
Northiam
Appledore
Hamstreet
NEW ROMNEY
LYDD
Rye Bay
Winchelsea
Icklesham
BATTLE
Westfield
Fairlight
HASTINGS
St Leonards
BEXHILL
Pevensey Bay
EASTBOURNE
Langney Point
West Road
HEAD
10
20
21
31
32
33
34
43
44
45
46
47
48
49
50
51
62
63
64
65
66
67
68
69
70
71
72
73
85
86
87
88
89
90
91
92
93
94
95
96
97
98
111
112
113
114
115
116
117
118
119
120
121
134
135
136
137
138
139
140
141
142
156
157
158
159
160
161
162
176
177
186
5 0 miles 5 10
10 5 0 kilometres 5 10 15
4 centimetres to 10 kilometres (one grid square)
1 kilometre = 0·6214 mile
1 mile = 1·6093 kilometres

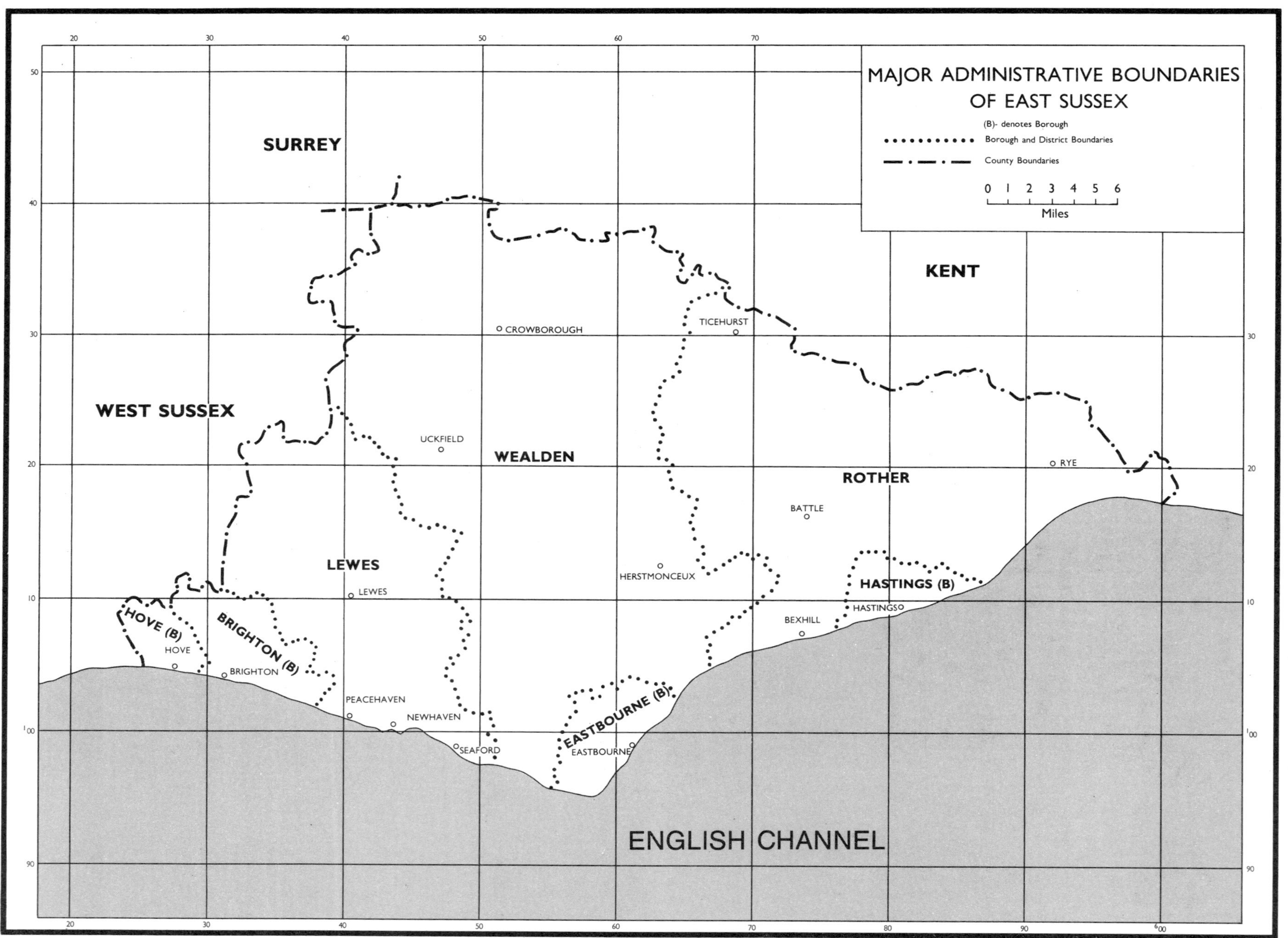
MAJOR ADMINISTRATIVE BOUNDARIES
OF EAST SUSSEX
(B)- denotes Borough
Borough and District Boundaries
County Boundaries
0 1 2 3 4 5 6
Miles
SURREY
KENT
WEST SUSSEX
WEALDEN
ROTHER
LEWES
HOVE (B)
BRIGHTON (B)
EASTBOURNE (B)
HASTINGS (B)
ENGLISH CHANNEL
CROWBOROUGH
TICEHURST
UCKFIELD
RYE
BATTLE
HERSTMONCEUX
LEWES
HOVE
BRIGHTON
PEACEHAVEN
NEWHAVEN
SEAFORD
EASTBOURNE
BEXHILL
HASTINGS

not continued, see key diagram

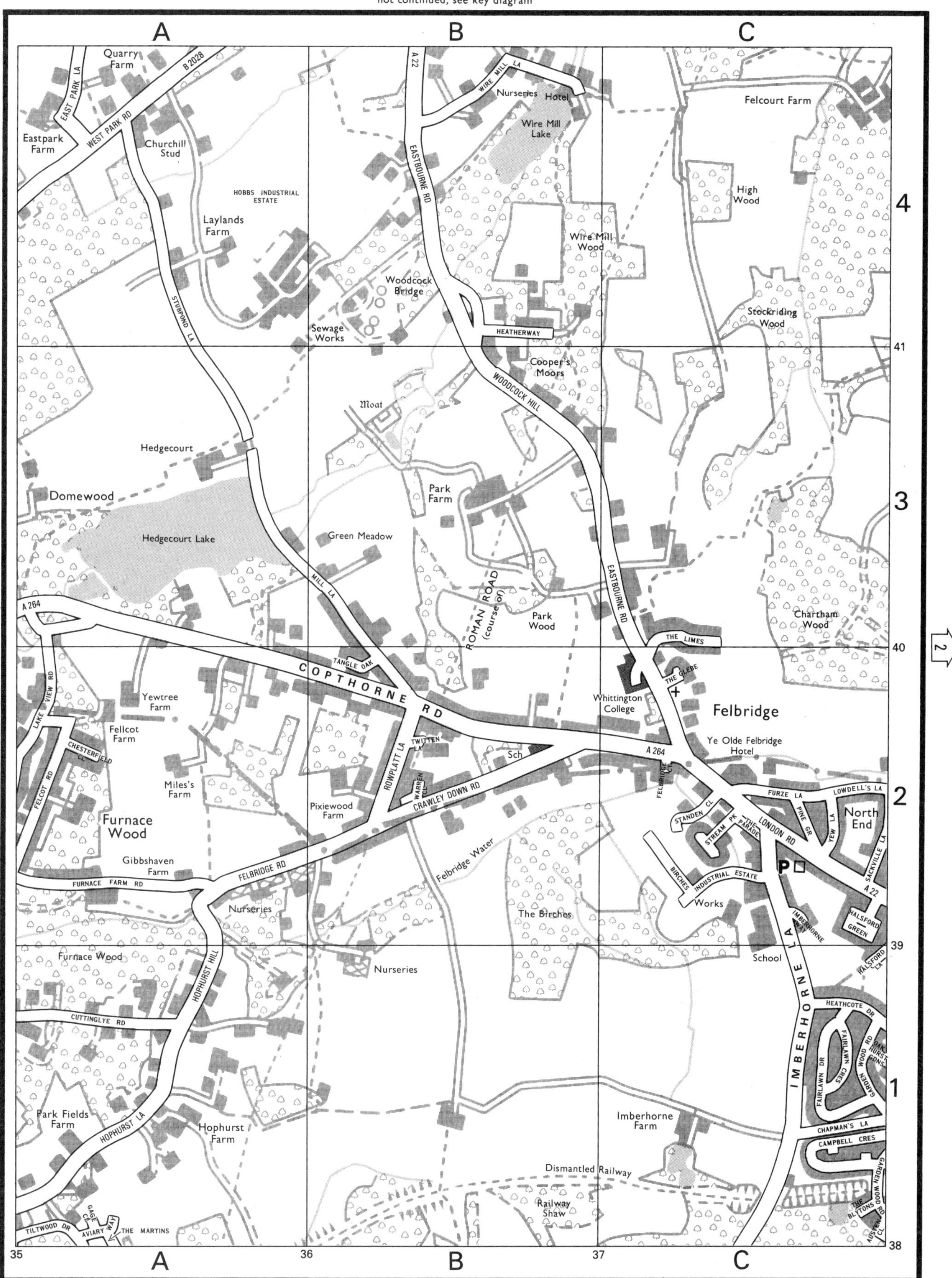

not continued, see key diagram

2

11

not continued, see key diagram

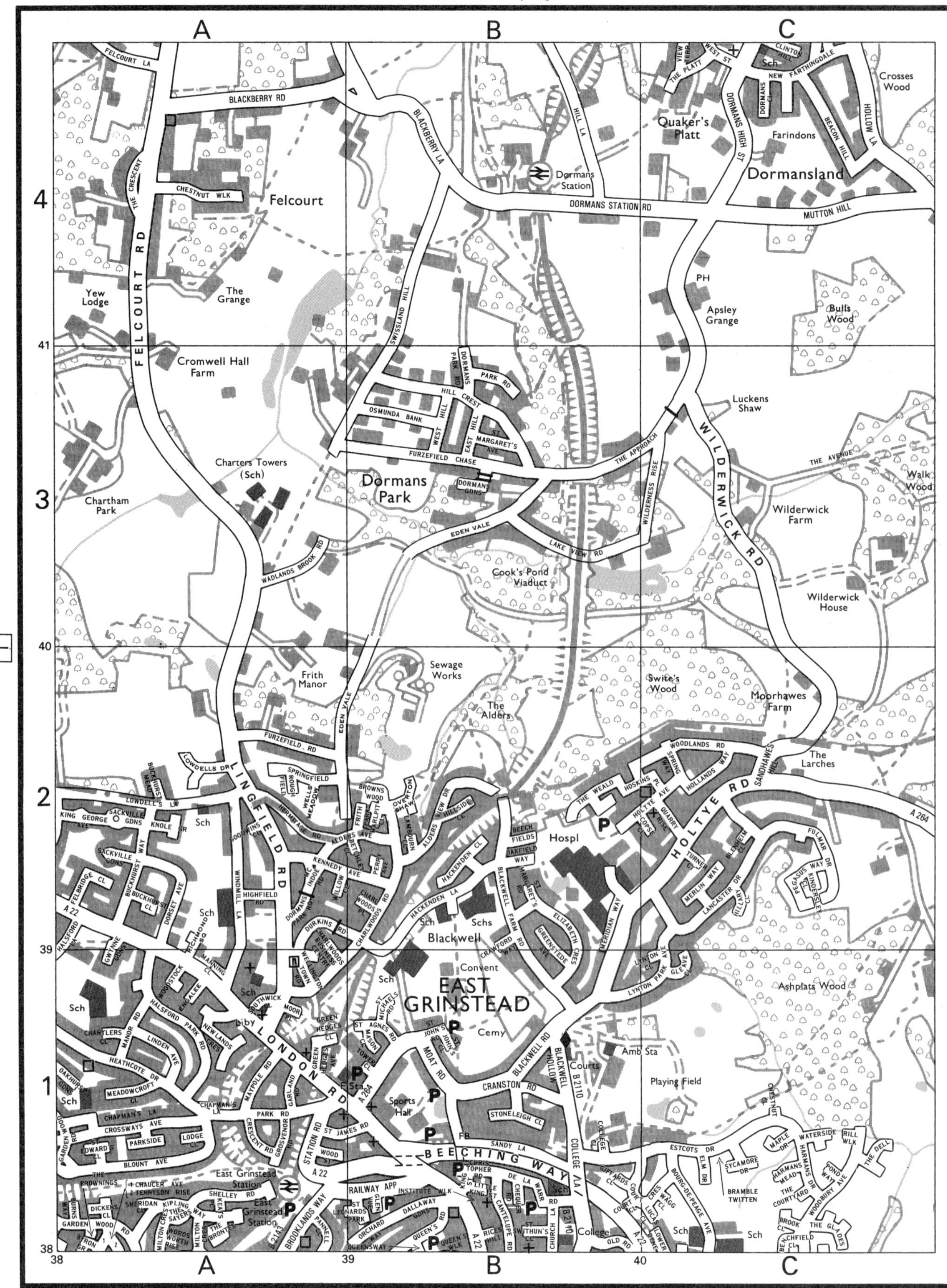

1

not continued, see key diagram

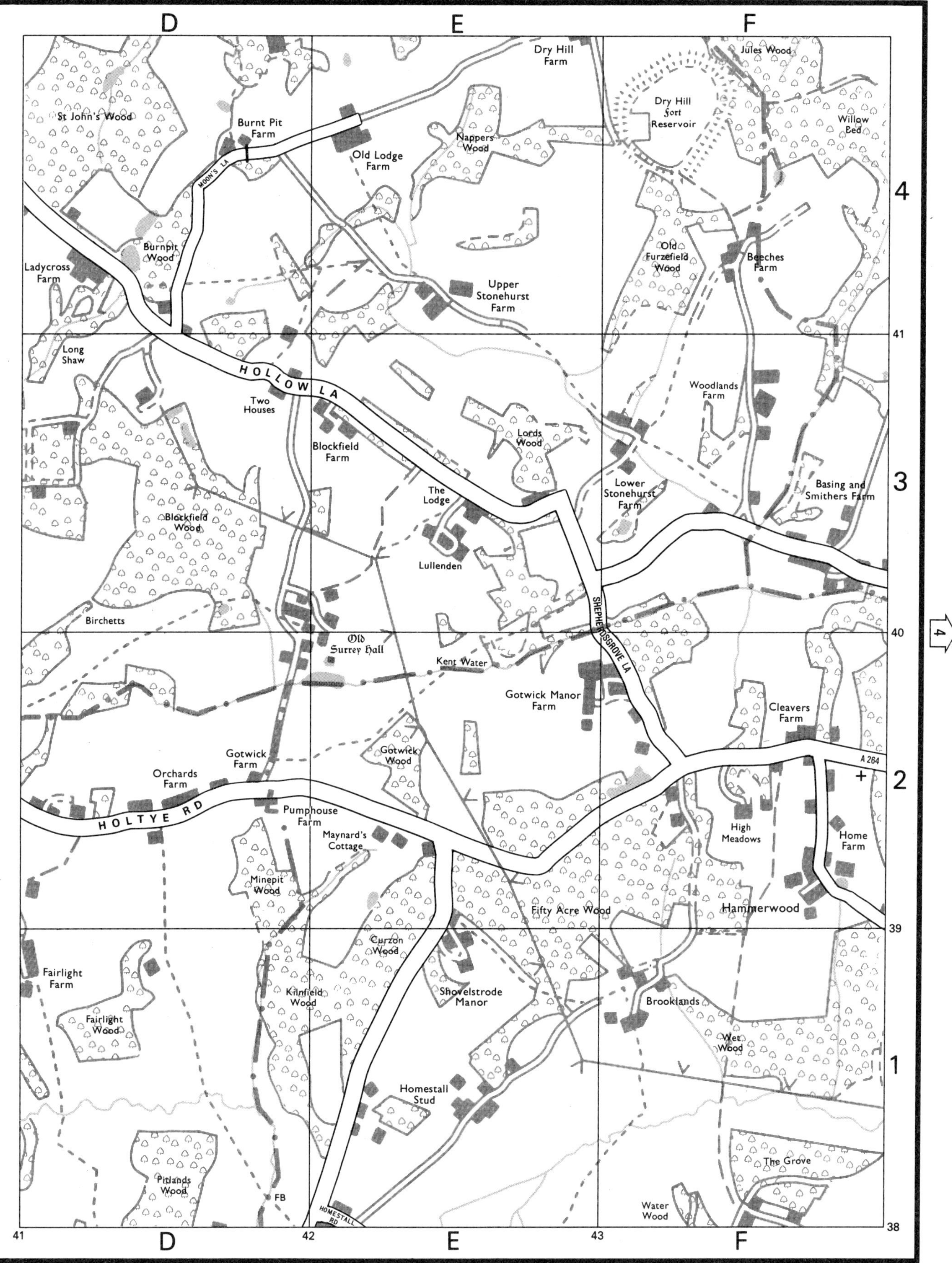

4

13

not continued, see key diagram

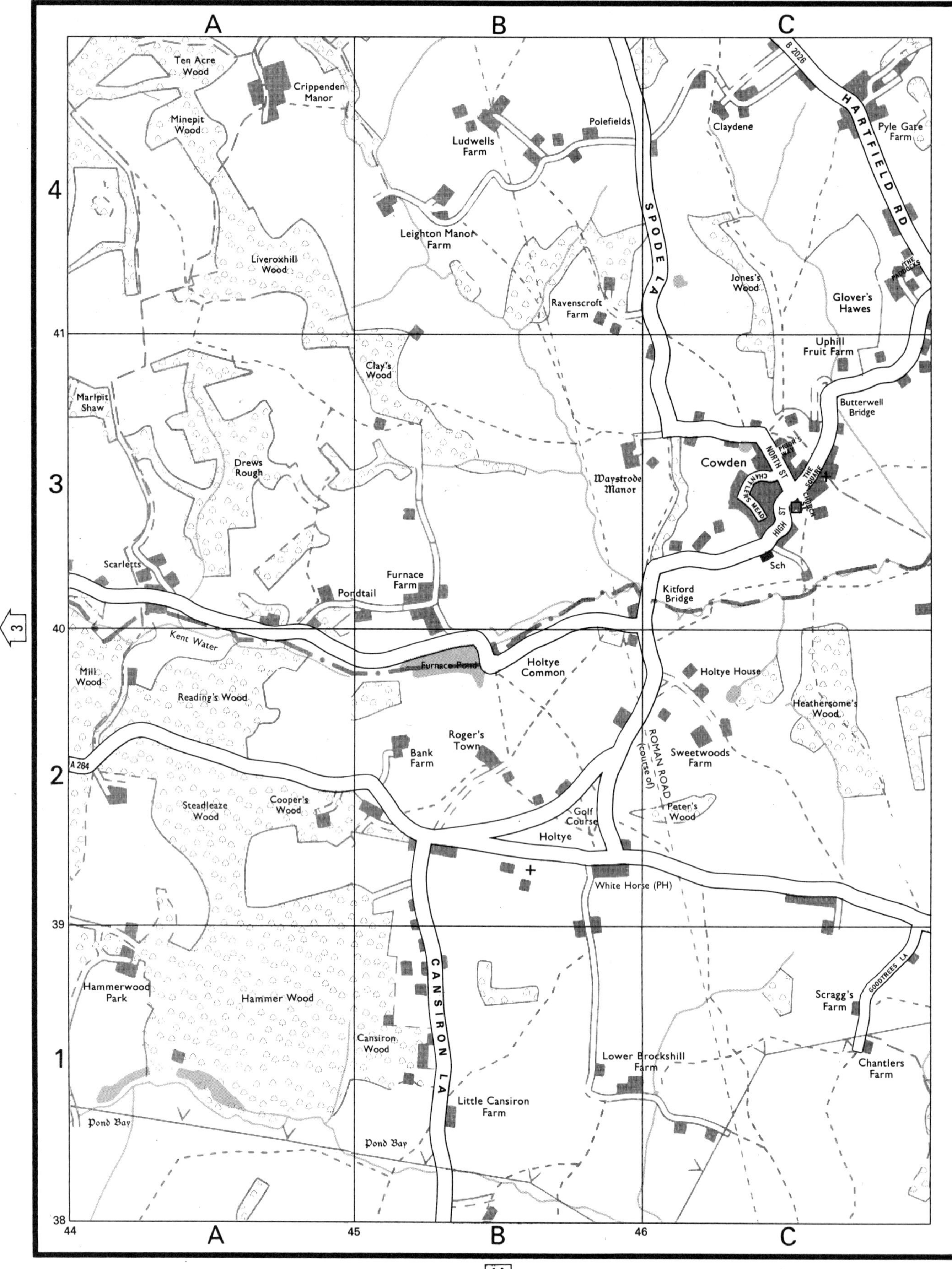

3

14

not continued, see key diagram

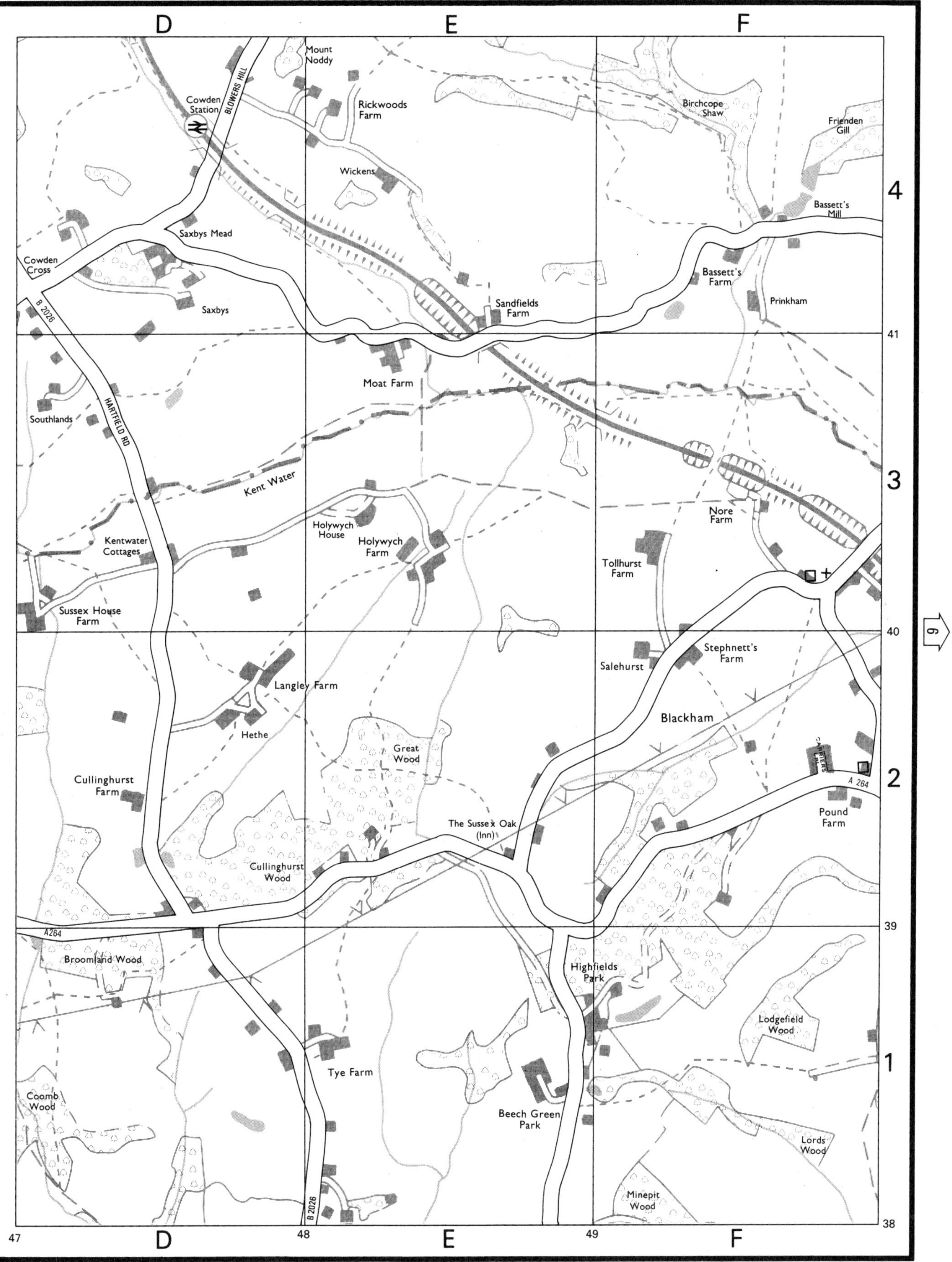

6

15

not continued, see key diagram

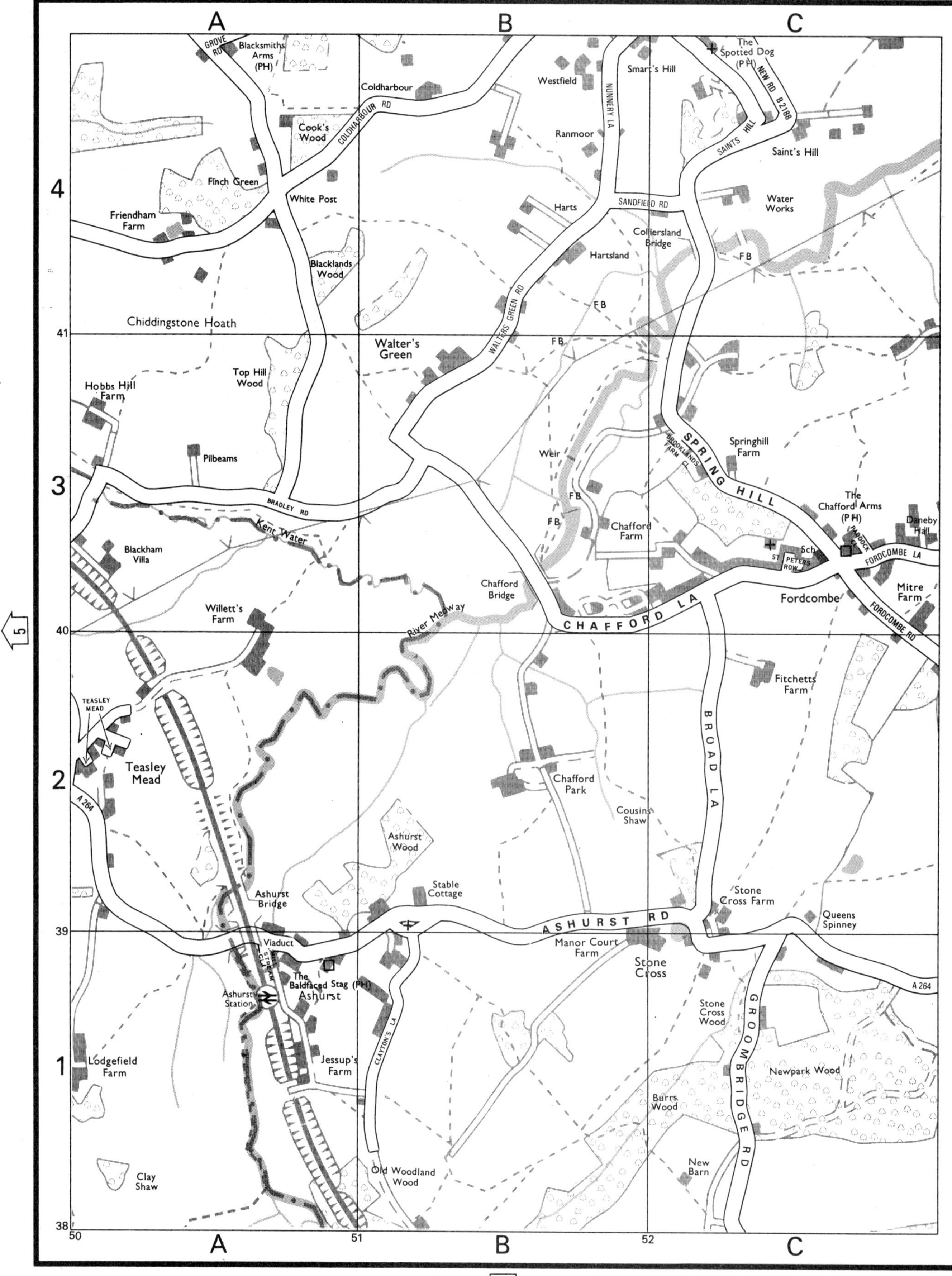

not continued, see key diagram

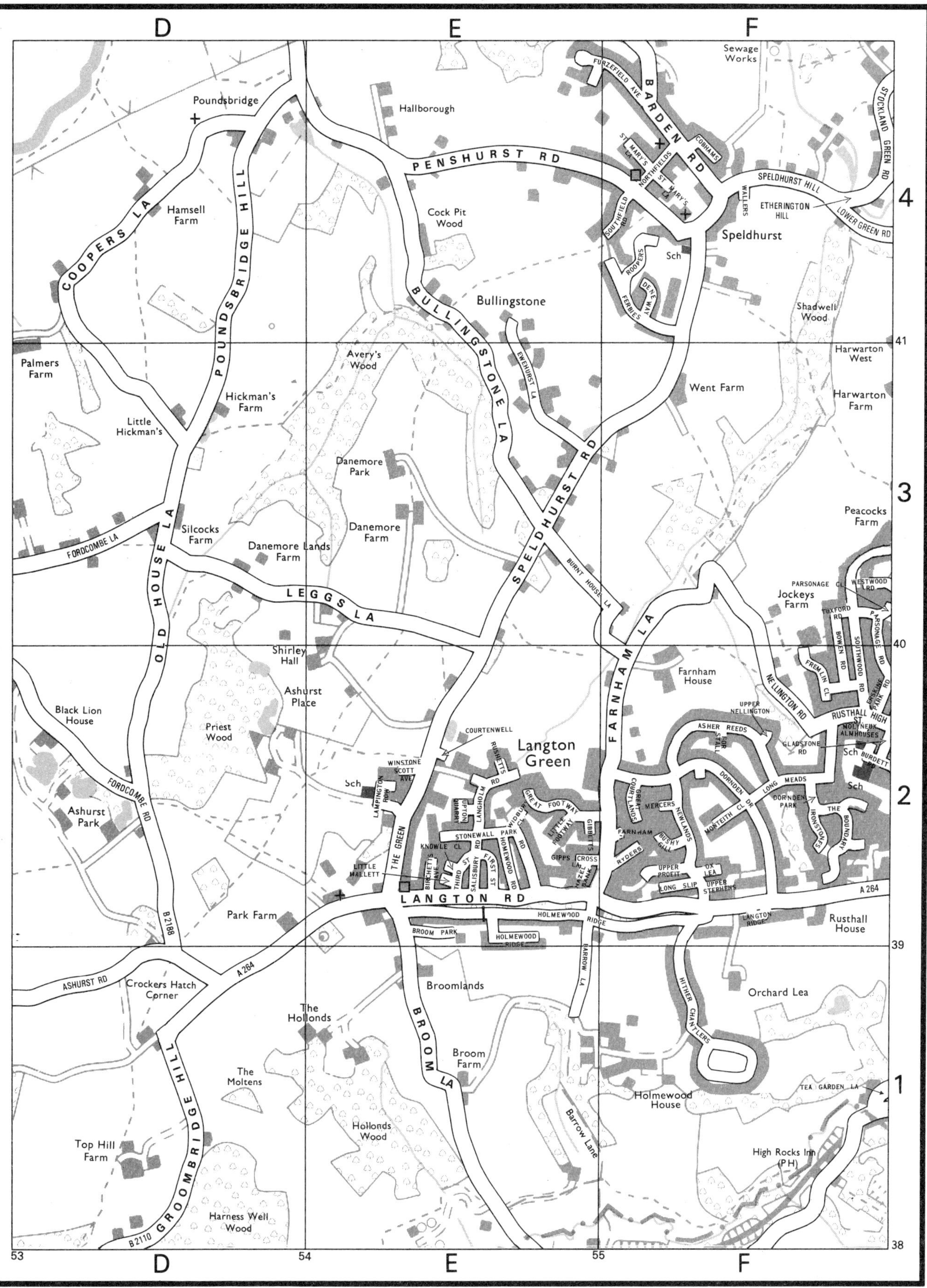

8

17

not continued, see key diagram

7

not continued, see key diagram

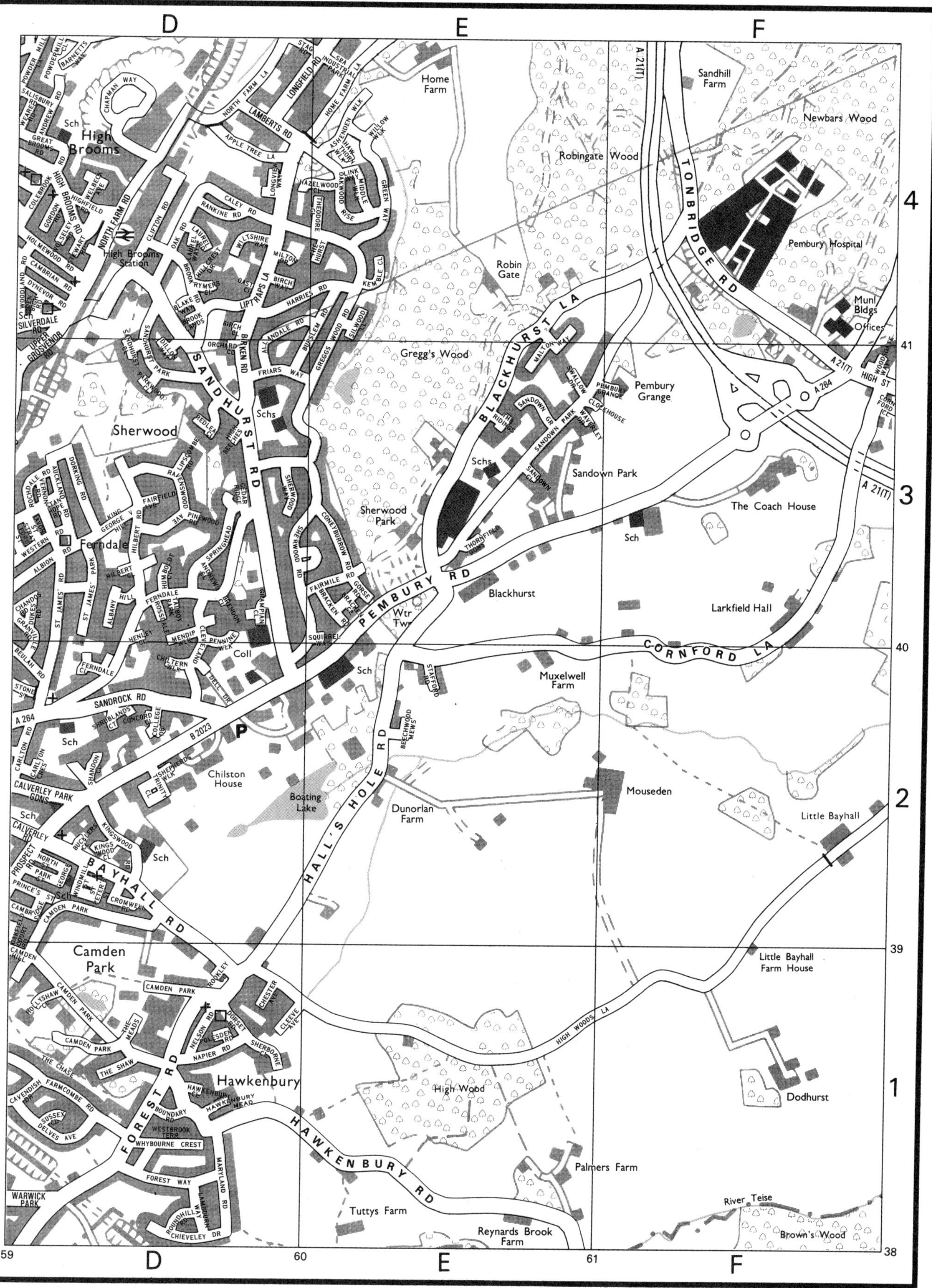

10

not continued, see key diagram

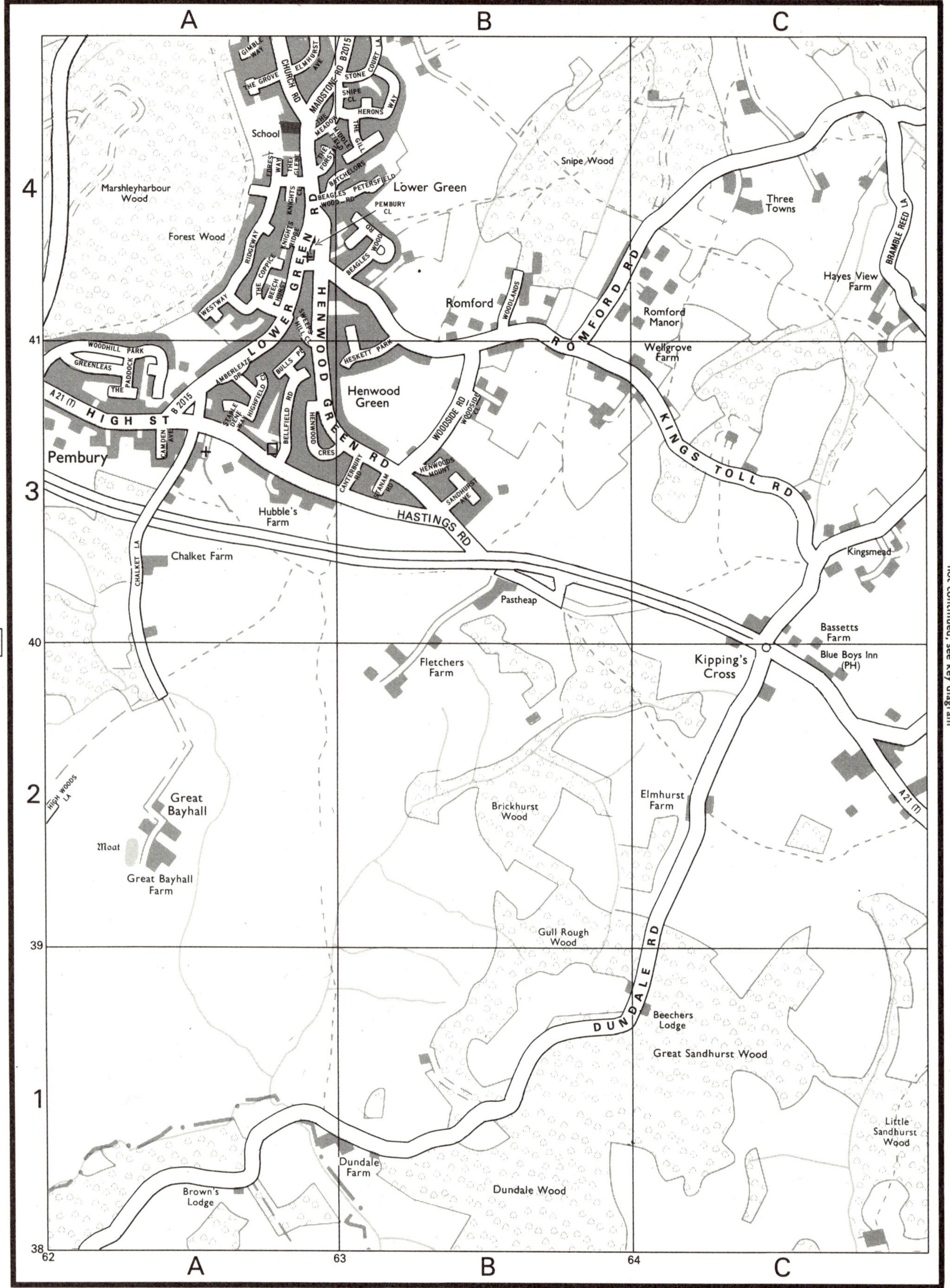

not continued, see key diagram

9

20

1

D
E
F
4
3
2
1
37
36
35
34
Crawley Down
Rushetts Wood
Gulledge Wood
Great Wood
Coles Wood
French Wood
IMBERHORNE LA
High Grove
BURLEIGH LA
Burleigh House Farm
Tilkhurst Farm
Crockshed Wood
Sandhill Farm
ROMAN ROAD (course of)
Peartree Shaw
Fen Place Mill
Hazleden Farm
B2110
ST HILL RD
Home Wood
Mobile Home Park
Mill Wood
Moat Shaw
Hurley Farm
Ash Lea Farm
The Plantation
Fen Place
EAST ST
Furze Field
TURNER'S HILL RD
High Wood
Furzewood Farm
The Rough
Dismantled Railway
River Medway
Tickeridge Farm
Ridge Hill Manor
Hen Robin Wood
Holstein Wood
South Wood
Mary Wood
Rookery Wood
Stone Wood
VOWELS LA
Mill Place Wood
Mill Place Farm
Bushy Wood
Drive Shaw
Home Farm
Moatlands
Duckell's Wood
Pine Wood
Hastings Wood
Birch Farm Nursery
GRINSTEAD LA
Lower Lake
Gravetye Manor (Hotel)
not continued, see key diagram

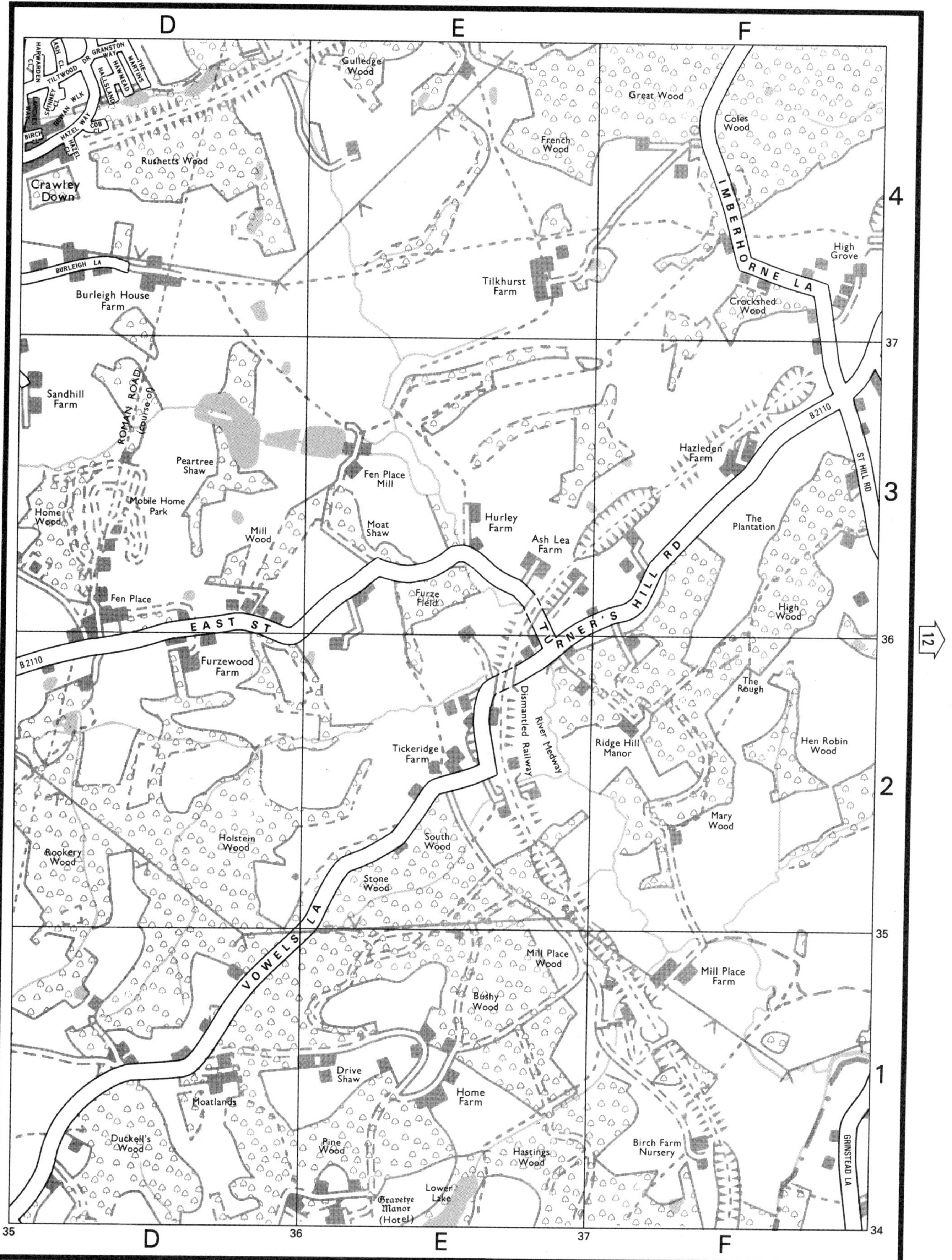

12

22

2

A
B
C
4
3
2
1
37
36
35
34
38
39
40
Hill Place Farm
Brook House Farm
Brook House
Coombe Hall
Bulrushes Farm
Coombe Hall Farm
Imberley
Dunning's Wood
School
Fonthill
The Beachcroft Towse
Saint Hill Green
Saint Hill Manor
Saint Hill Farm
Cock Robin Wood
Stone Hill Farm
Neylands Farm
Rockingshill Wood
Jenkin's Wood
Standen Farm
Standen
Millfield Farm
Rushett's Shaw
Busses Farm
Jenhurst Wood
Busses Wood
Botley Wood
Weir Wood Reservoir
Charlwood Farm
Sunnyside
Herontye
Home Farm
Luxford's
Luxford's Farm
Forest Way Country Park
Sewage Works
Horseshoe Farm
Water Works
Weir Wood
South Park Farm
Nature Reserve
Spring Hill Farm
Mudbrooks House
Sch
HIGH ST
A 22
B 2110
WEST ST
WEST HILL
B 2143
BROOKLANDS WAY
GARDEN WOOD RD
TURNER'S HILL RD
COMBE HILL RD
WEST HOATHLY RD
ST HILL RD
STONE HILL
ADMIRAL'S BRIDGE LA
GRINSTEAD LA
LEGSHEATH LA
LEWES RD
LUXFORD'S LA
SHIP ST
DUNNING'S RD
MORTON RD
CORONATION RD
FOREST VIEW RD
STOCKWELL RD
LISTER AVE
FARADAY AVE
STEPHENSON DR
HARWOOD'S LA
FAIRFIELD RD
HERONTYE DR
STUART WAY
VICTORIA WAY
HURST FARM RD
MUSGRAVE AVE
SOUTH LANDS
MILL WAY
PORTLAND RD
HERMITAGE LA
WORSTED LA
OAKLEY CL
WOODBURY AVE
FARM CL

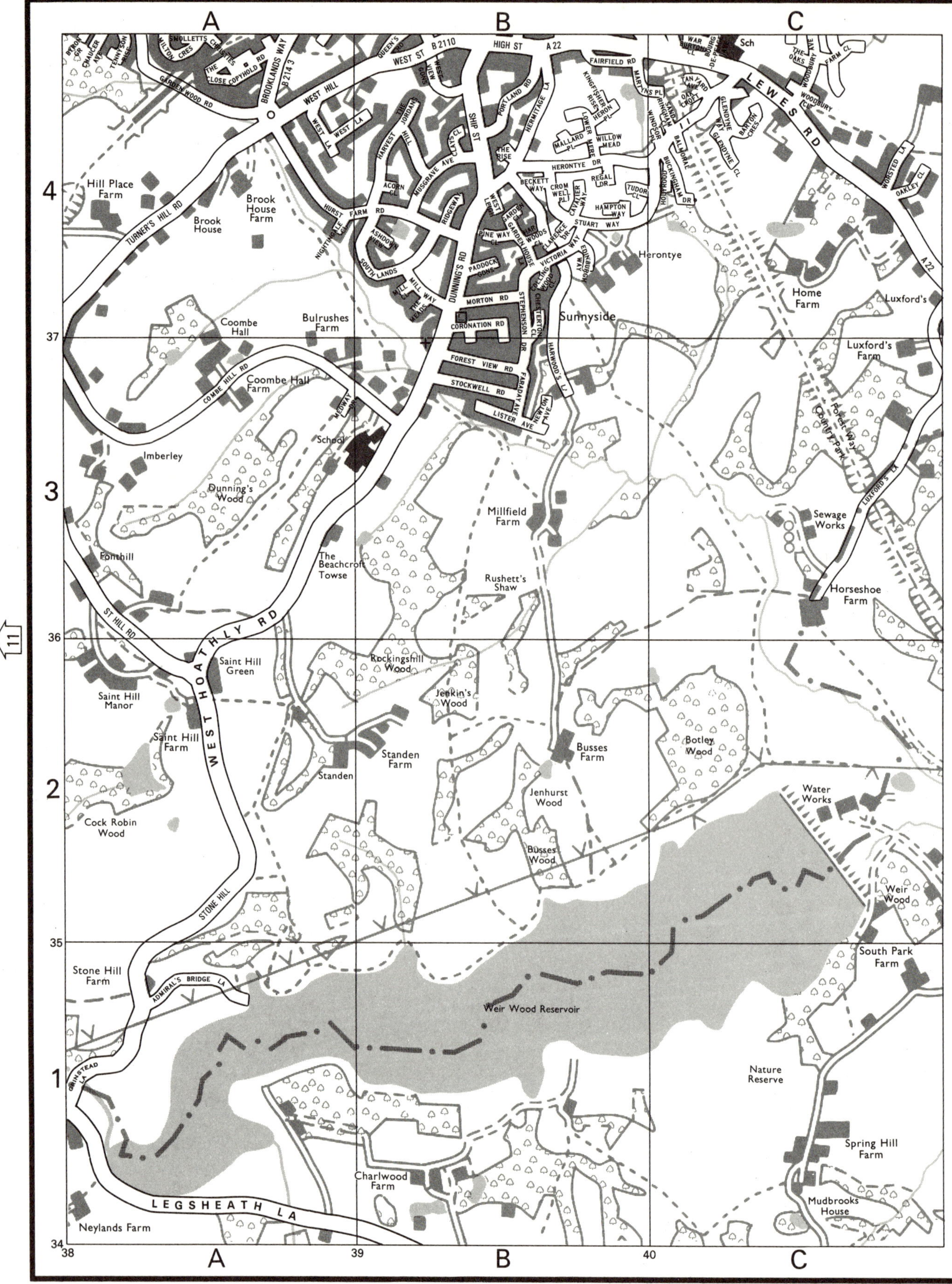

11

23

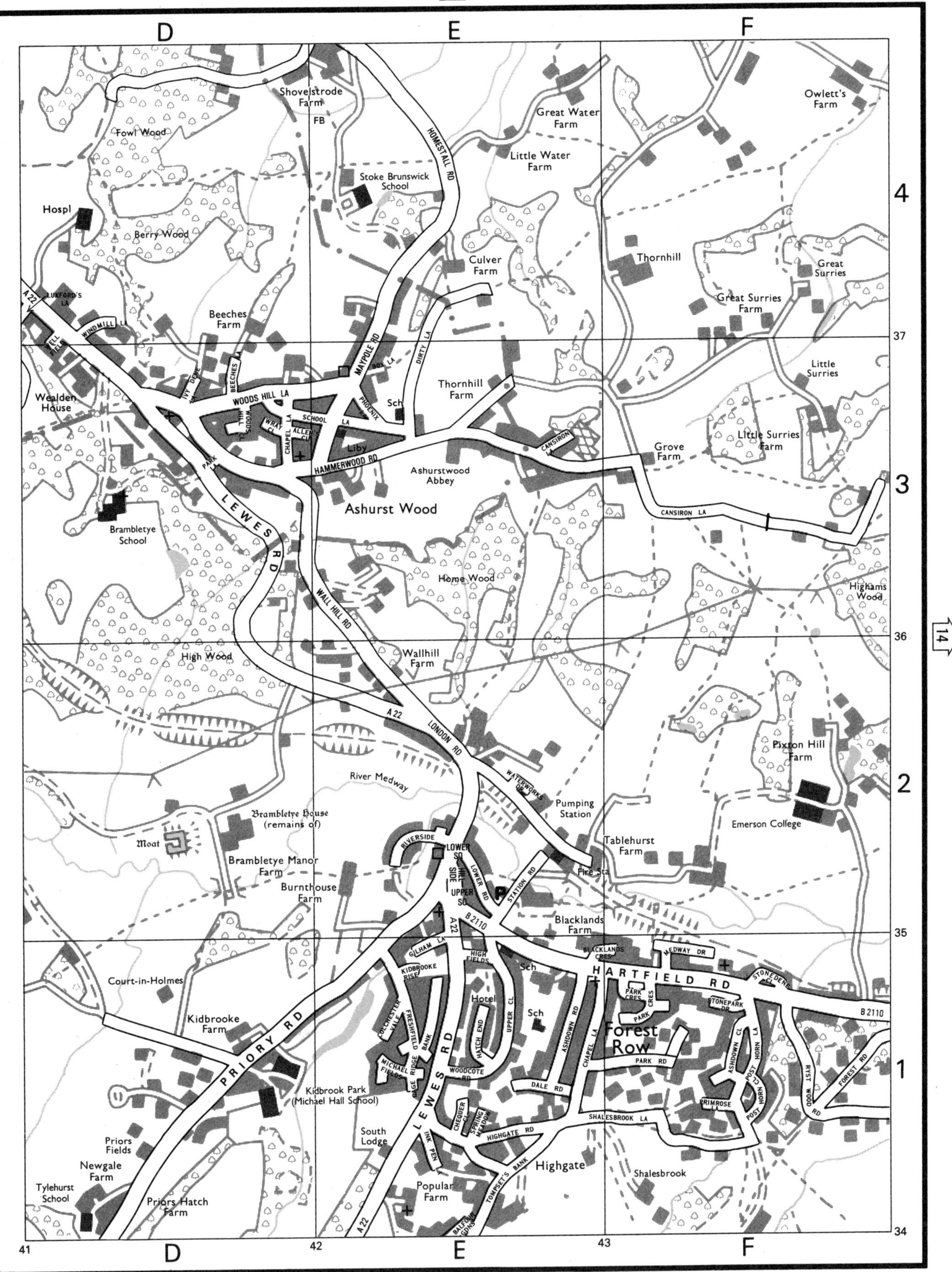
3
D
E
F
Shovelstrode Farm
FB
Fowl Wood
Great Water Farm
Little Water Farm
Owlett's Farm
HOMESTALL RD
Stoke Brunswick School
Hospl
Berry Wood
Culver Farm
Thornhill
Great Surries
Great Surries Farm
Beeches Farm
LUXFORD'S LA
WINDMILL LA
Little Surries
Thornhill Farm
Wealden House
WOODS HILL LA
MAYPOLE RD
DIRTY LA
SCHOOL LA
Sch
Liby
CANSIRON LA
Grove Farm
Little Surries Farm
HAMMERWOOD RD
Ashurstwood Abbey
Ashurst Wood
LEWES RD
CANSIRON LA
Brambletye School
Home Wood
Highams Wood
WALL HILL RD
High Wood
Wallhill Farm
A22
LONDON RD
Pixton Hill Farm
River Medway
WATERWORKS RD
Pumping Station
Emerson College
Brambletye House (remains of)
Moat
RIVERSIDE
LOWER SQ
Tablehurst Farm
Brambletye Manor Farm
Burnthouse Farm
UPPER SQ
LOWER RD
STATION RD
Fire Sta
B2110
Blacklands Farm
BLACKLANDS CRES
MEDWAY DR
HARTFIELD RD
STONEDENE CL
GILHAM LA
HIGH FIELDS
Sch
Court-in-Holmes
KIDBROOKE RISE
Hotel
STONEPARK DR
B2110
Kidbrooke Farm
PRIORY RD
Sch
Forest Row
ASHDOWN RD
CHAPEL LA
PARK RD
DALE RD
LEWES RD
HATCH END
UPPER CL
WOODCOTE RD
PRIMROSE LA
POST HORN CL
POST HORN LA
RYST WOOD RD
FOREST RD
Kidbrook Park (Michael Hall School)
SHALESBROOK LA
HIGHATE RD
South Lodge
Priors Fields
Newgale Farm
Highgate
Shalesbrook
Tylehurst School
Priors Hatch Farm
Popular Farm
TOMPSET'S BANK
A22
4
3
2
1
37
36
35
34
41
42
43
14
24

4

A
B
C
Cansiron La
Bassett's Manor
Church Wood
Acre Wood
Great Cansiron Farm
Beeches Farm
Butcherfield La
Holden Wood
4
Roughfield Wood
Butcher's Cross
Cansiron Lane
37
Pollard Wood
Paupersdale Wood
Marlpit Shaw
North Clays
St Ives Farm West
St Ives Farm East
3
Collingsbush Wood
Wick Wood
Clay Wood
36
Lower Parrock
Roman Road (course of)
Ashdown Farm
Ashdown House
Sawpit Wood
Hodore Farm
2
River Medway
Dismantled Railway
Forest Way Country Park
Sewage Works
Alder Shaw
Penfield Shaw
35
Gassonsfield Wood
Upper Parrock Farm
Parrock La
B 2110
Lines Farm
Upper Hartfield
Hartfield Rd
1
Ryst Wood Rd
Little Parrock Farm
Rystwood Farm
Paternoster Wood
Cotchford Wood
Cat St
Quabrook
Cabbagestalk
Ryecroft Farm
34
44
45
46

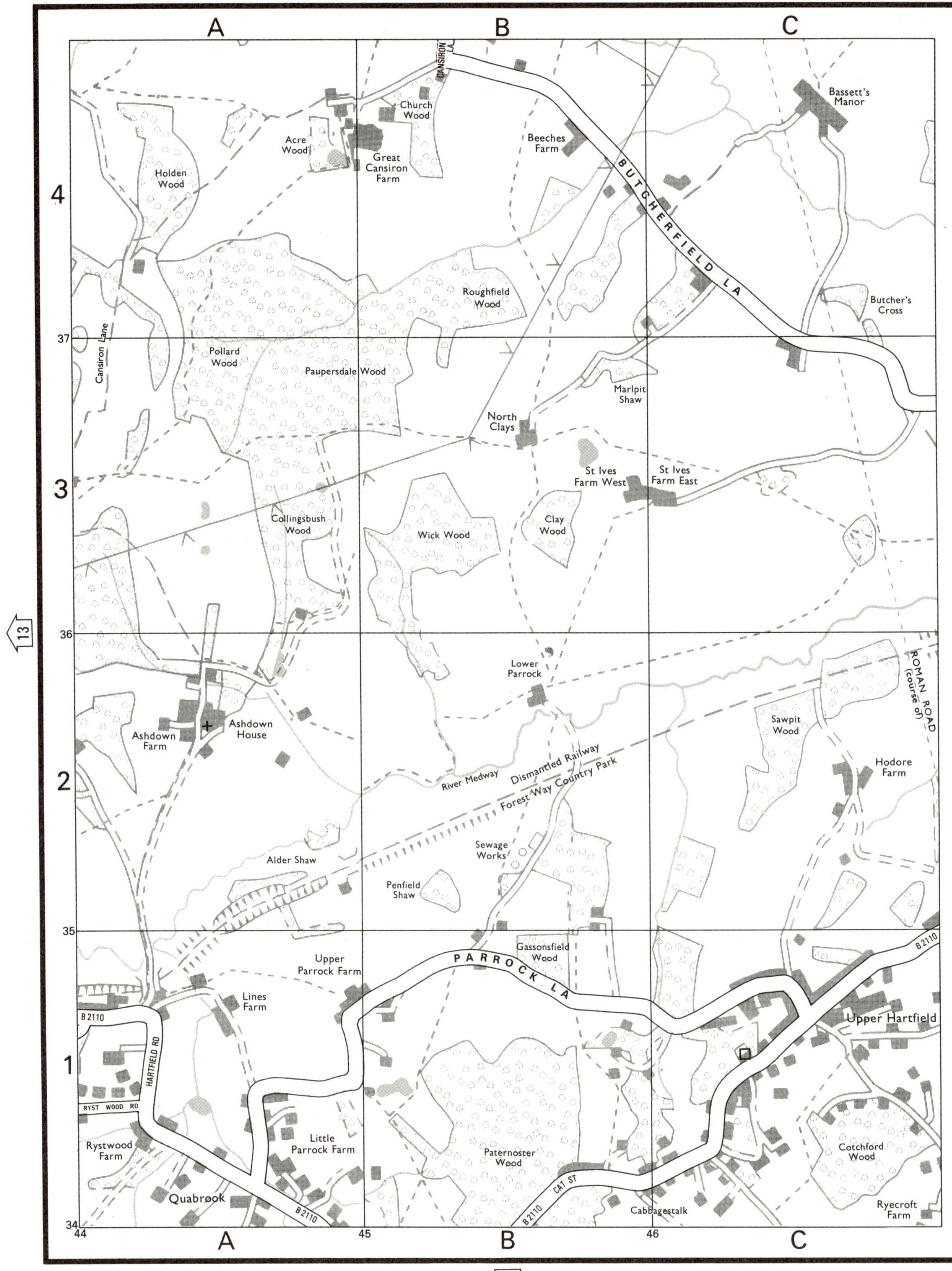

13

25

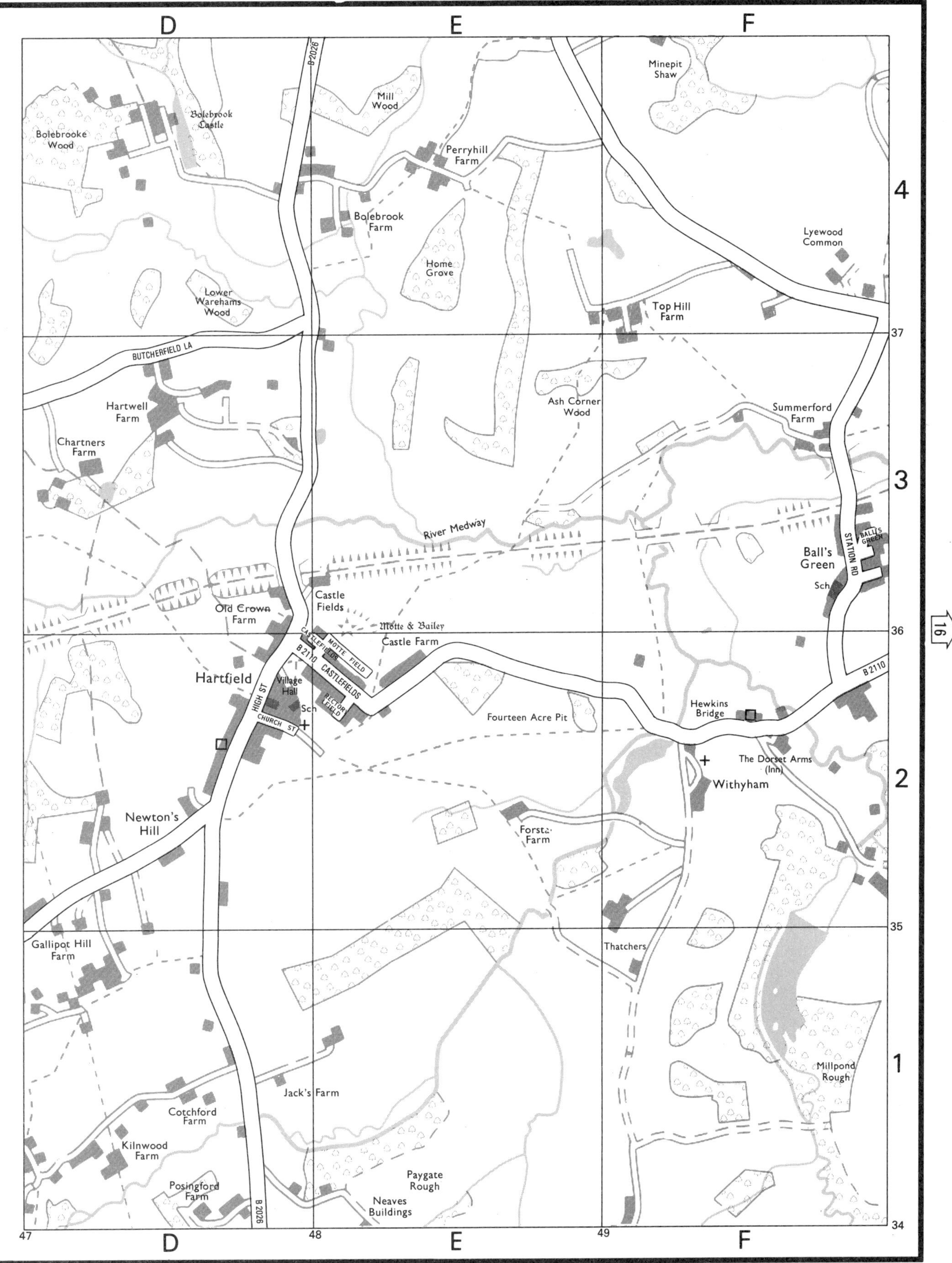
5
D
E
F
Bolebrooke Wood
Bolebrook Castle
Mill Wood
Perryhill Farm
Minepit Shaw
Bolebrook Farm
Home Grove
Lower Warehams Wood
Lyewood Common
Top Hill Farm
B2026
BUTCHERFIELD LA
Hartwell Farm
Chartners Farm
Ash Corner Wood
Summerford Farm
River Medway
Ball's Green
STATION RD
BALLS GREEN
Sch
Old Crown Farm
Castle Fields
Motte & Bailey
Castle Farm
CASTLEFIELDS
MOTTE FIELD
B2110
Hartfield
HIGH ST
Village Hall
Sch
RECTORY FIELD
CHURCH ST
Fourteen Acre Pit
Hewkins Bridge
The Dorset Arms (Inn)
Withyham
Newton's Hill
Forsta Farm
Gallipot Hill Farm
Thatchers
Millpond Rough
Jack's Farm
Cotchford Farm
Kilnwood Farm
Posingford Farm
Paygate Rough
Neaves Buildings
47
48
49
34
35
36
37
1
2
3
4
16
26

6

15

A
B
C
4
3
2
1
37
36
35
34
50
51
52
Blackham Court
Fish Ponds
Hale Court Farm
Lyewood House
River Medway
Pond Wood
Burrswood Home Farm
Burrswood
Beech Wood
GROOMBRIDGE RD
BIRD IN HAND ST
River Grom
Florence Farm
Ham Farm
Groombridge
Tithe Barn
Old Farm
The Ridge
ORCHARD RISE
OAKLANDS RD
WITHYHAM RD
B 2110
B 2188
CORSELEY RD
Ham Bridge
Stoneland's Farm
Hendal Bridge
Hendal Wood
Hendal Farm
Alksford Farm
Sherlock's Wood
Hunt's Farm
B 2110
Sherlock's Farm
Mottsmill Stream
Glen Andred
The Warren
Cherrygardens Farm
The Plain
Old Birchden Farm
Bullen's Wood
Mott's Mill
Motts Down
Rocks Wood
Leyswood
Buckhurst Park
Plumyfeather Farm
Leyswood Farm
Rocks Farm
Coppice Wood
Jockey's Wood
Penns in the Rocks
Bullfinches
Marchant Wood
Lye Green House
Park Grove Farm
Lye Green
Big Wigsell
Bingles
Badbrook Wood
Millpond Wood
B 2188

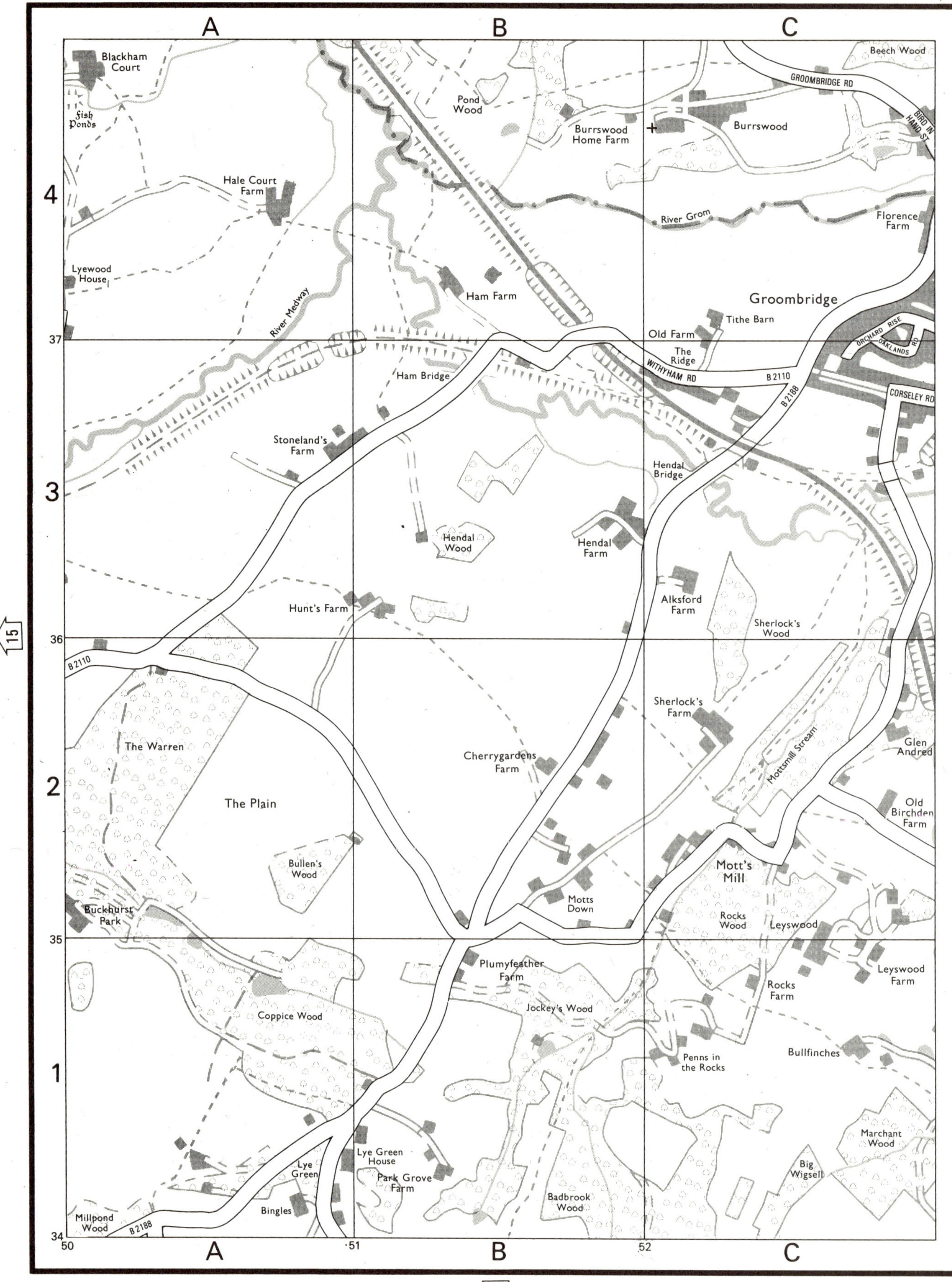

27

7

D
E
F
Pokehill
Adam's Well Crossing
GROOMBRIDGE HILL
B2110
Groombridge Place
Moat
Southern Sewage Works
South Farm
Broadwater Forest
The Firs
Railway (disused)
STATION RD
MEADOW RD
SPRING FIELD RD
CROMENFIELD
Lealands Farm
Broadwater Bridge
BROAD OAK
CORSELEY RD
THE CLOSE
LEALANDS CL
Sch
Little Quarry Farm
Birchden Farm
Aytton's Wood
Birchden
The Warren
Park Corner
Birchden Wood
PH
A26
Bridgers
Warren Farm
Pinstraw Farm
Harrison's Rocks
Birchett's Wood
Eridge Green
Forge Farm
Cobbarn Farm
Cobbarn
Sch
THE FORSTAL
Crown House
Hamsell Wood Farm
Ligg's Wood
Steel Bridge
Mott's Farm
Square Shaw
Holden Wood
Eridge Station
Hamsell Shaw
Hamsell Bridge
Steel Bridge Farm
Renby Farm
Little Wigsell
Hollybridge Wood
Bushy Wood
Hamsell Farm
Great Robbins Shaw
A26
4
37
3
36
2
35
1
34
53
54
55

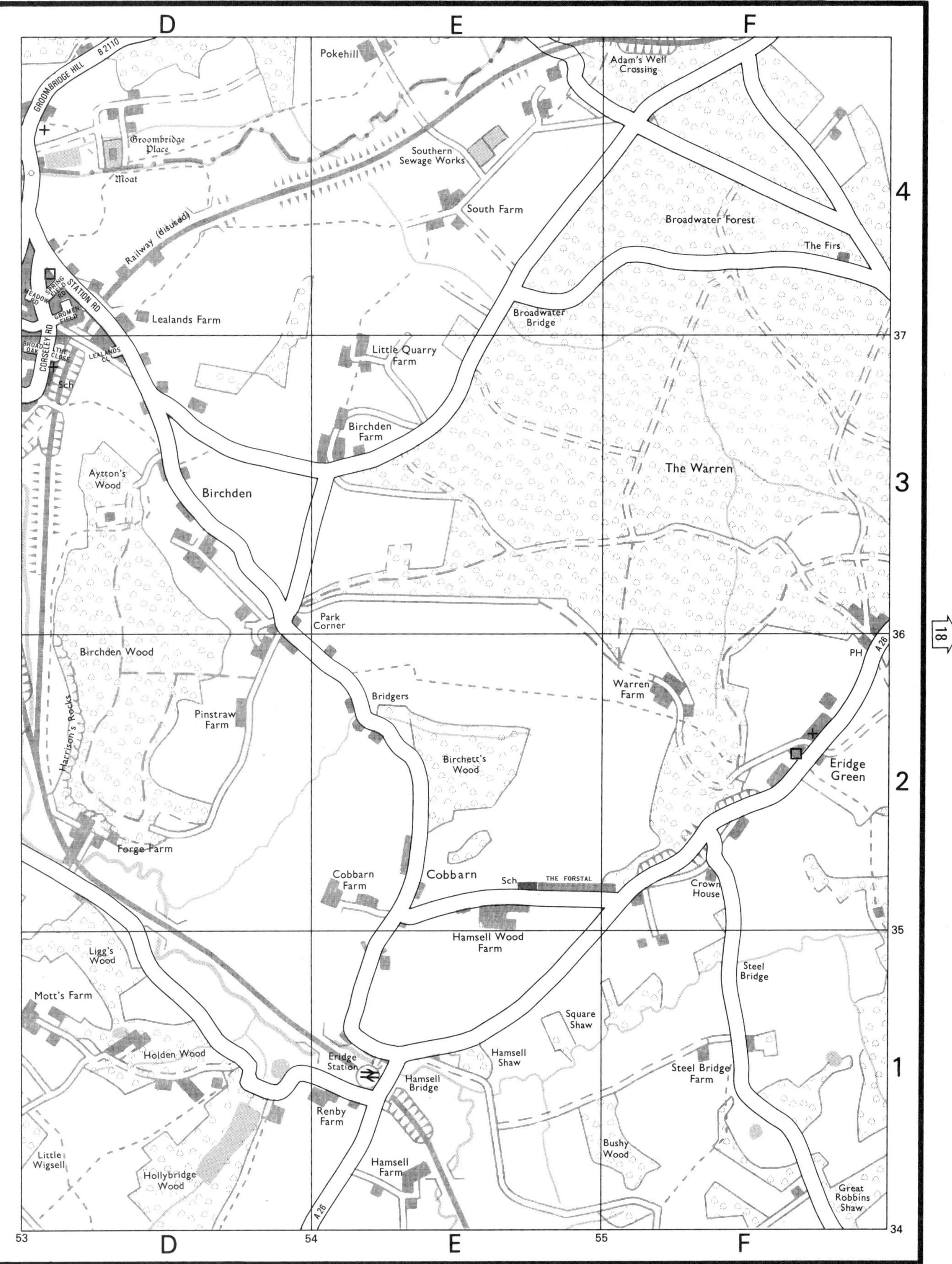

18

28

8

A
B
C
Ramslye Wood
Strawberry Hill
Ruffet Wood
Broadwater Down
BROADWATER DOWN
ERIDGE RD
FRANT RD
FOREST RD
Rumbers Hill
Town Court
Stone Farm
Quarry Farm
Strawberry Hill Farm
Spratsbrook Farm
Sprat's Brook
Hargate Forest
Pinewood Farm
Broadwater Lodge
Firtree Plantation
TANGIER LA
Tangier Farm
Tangier Lodge Farm
The Roundabouts
Chase Farm
Chase Wood
Bohemia
Kennels
Whitehill Wood
Martin's Farm
Eridge Park
CHURCH LA
Abergavenny Arms (PH)
St Laurence
Mill Wood
Eridge Old Park
Keepers' Cottages
SLEECHES CROSS
Saxonbury House
Forge Wood
The Platt
Bushy Shaw
DOWN LA
A 26
A 267
B 2169
B 2099
ST MARK'S RD
Sch
4
3
2
1
37
36
35
34
56
57
58

17

29

9

D
E
F
Benhall Wood
HAWKENBURY RD
Windmill Farm
CYPRESS GR
ACER AVE
Cemy
BENHALL MILL RD
Benhall Mill Farm
Coker's Down
Rushlye Down
BAYHAM RD
Golf Course
Court Lodge Down
Oxpasture Wood
Brickhouse Farm
Park Wood
Brook Farm
Rushlye Farm
Court Lodge
Frant Station
Bells Yew Green
Village Hall
RUSHLYE CL
Highfield
Abbots Down
Stubbygrove Wood
B2169
MIDDLE RD
The Brecknock Arms (PH)
Ely Grange
Kennels
Works
B2169
Higham Wood
Higham Farm
HOME FARM CT
HIGH ST
WARREN RIDGE
Village Hall
Churchfield Wood
Manor Farm
Frant
Barelands Farm
Crowhurst Wood
Brookland Wood
Grigg's Wood
Hollow Wood
Shernfold Park
Morgan's Wood
Clay's Wood
Camden Wood
Henley Wood
Knowle
Glebe Farm
Frant Place
Woodside
Great Wood
B2099
Down Wood
4
3
2
1
37
36
35
34
59
60
61
D
E
F

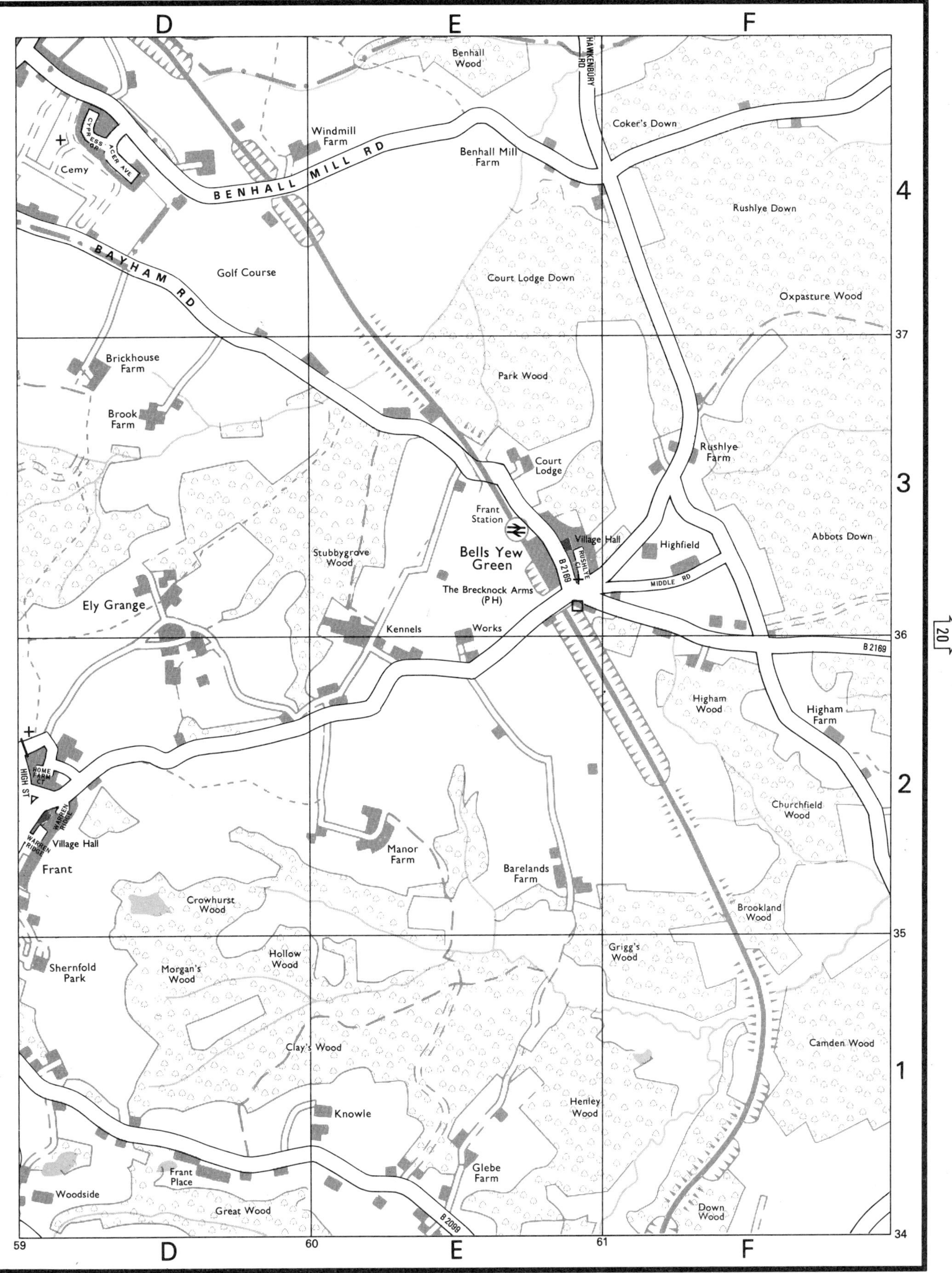

20

30

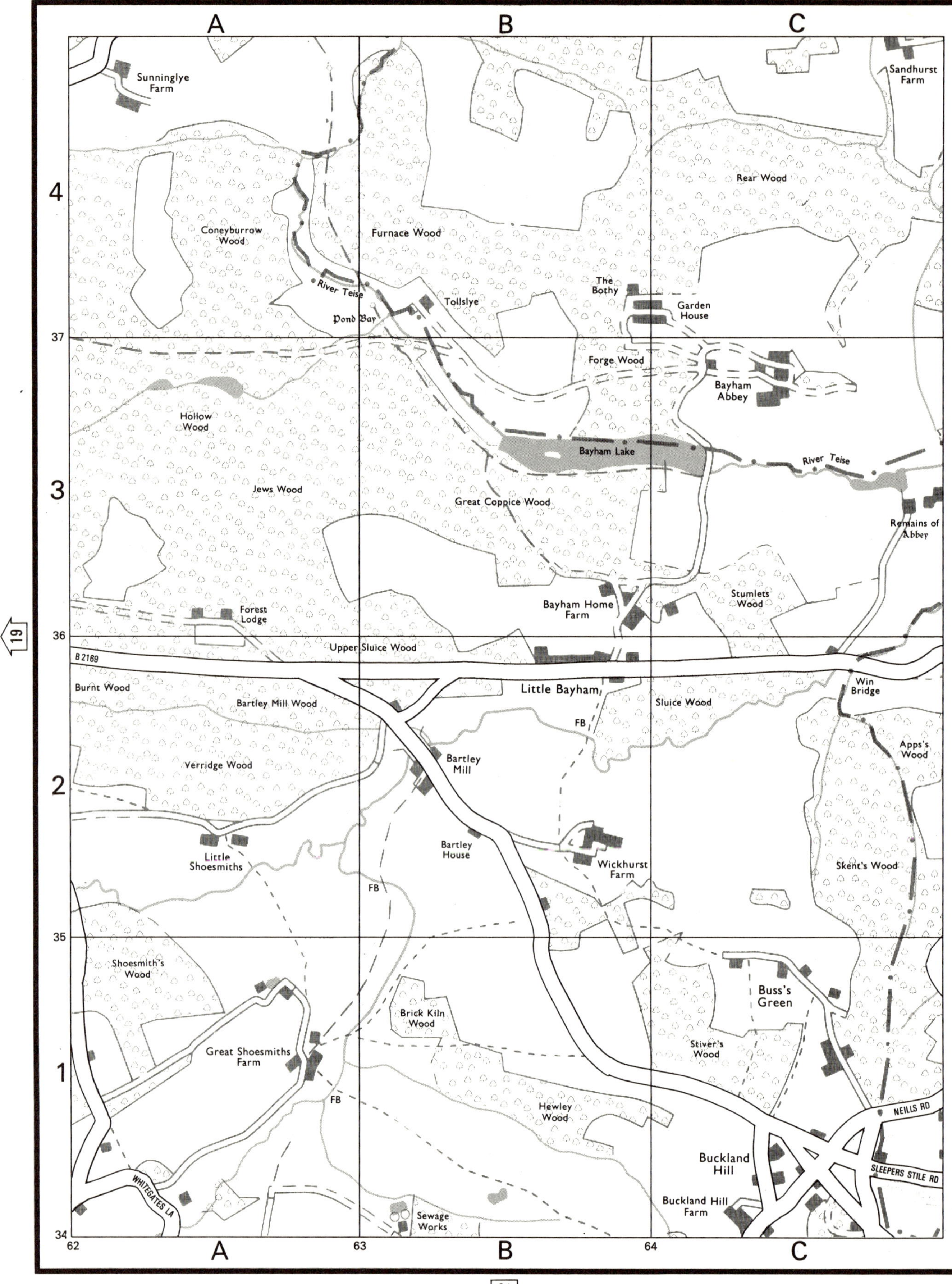
10
A
B
C
Sunninglye Farm
Sandhurst Farm
Rear Wood
4
Coneyburrow Wood
Furnace Wood
River Teise
Pond Bay
Tollslye
The Bothy
Garden House
37
Forge Wood
Bayham Abbey
Hollow Wood
Bayham Lake
River Teise
3
Jews Wood
Great Coppice Wood
Remains of Abbey
Forest Lodge
Bayham Home Farm
Stumlets Wood
19
36
Upper Sluice Wood
B 2169
Burnt Wood
Little Bayham
Win Bridge
Bartley Mill Wood
Sluice Wood
FB
Apps's Wood
Verridge Wood
Bartley Mill
2
Bartley House
Little Shoesmiths
Wickhurst Farm
Skent's Wood
FB
35
Shoesmith's Wood
Buss's Green
Brick Kiln Wood
Great Shoesmiths Farm
Stiver's Wood
1
FB
Hewley Wood
NEILLS RD
Buckland Hill
SLEEPERS STILE RD
WHITEGATES LA
Buckland Hill Farm
Sewage Works
34
62
63
64
31

not continued, see key diagram

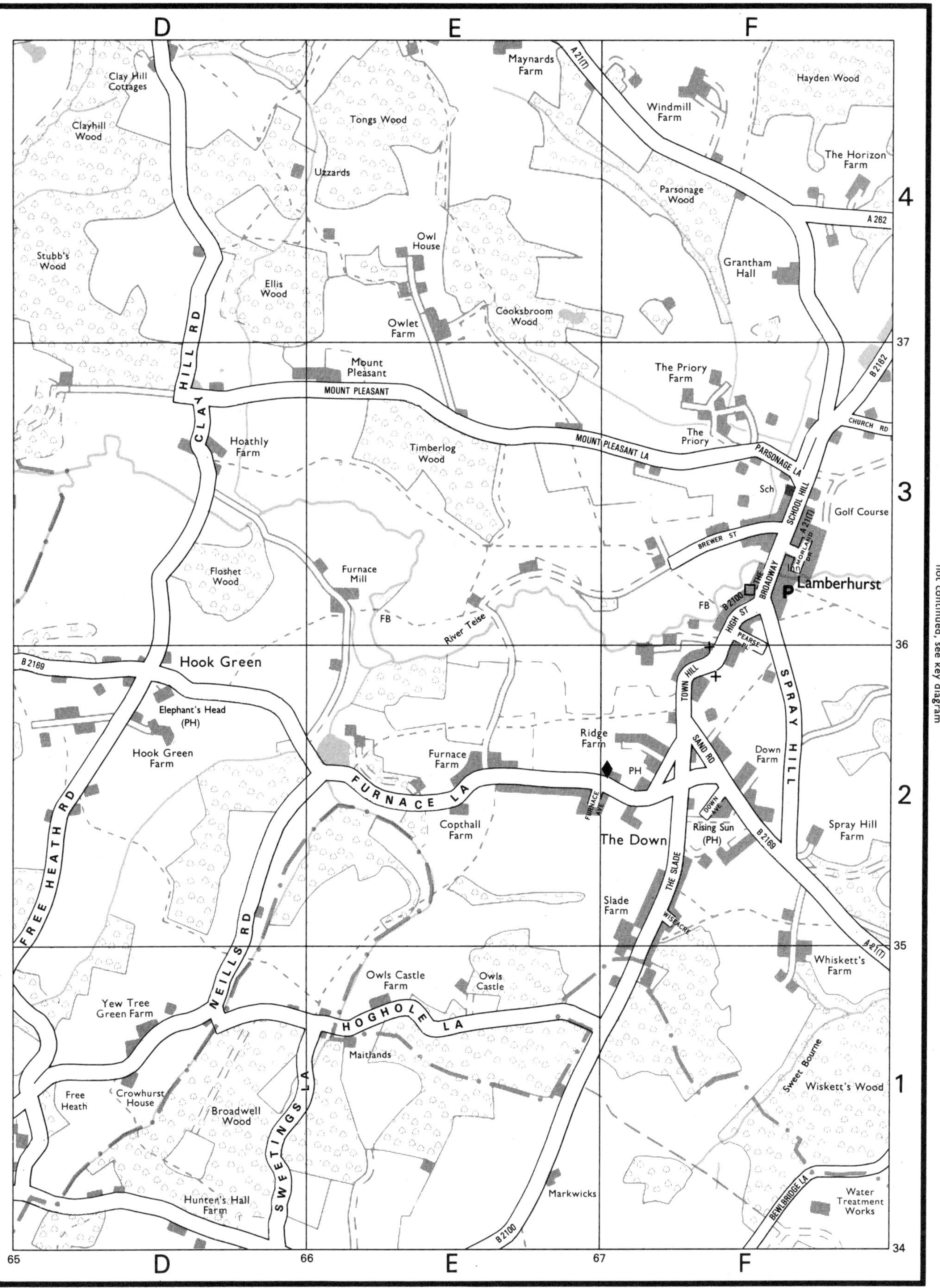

not continued, see key diagram

11

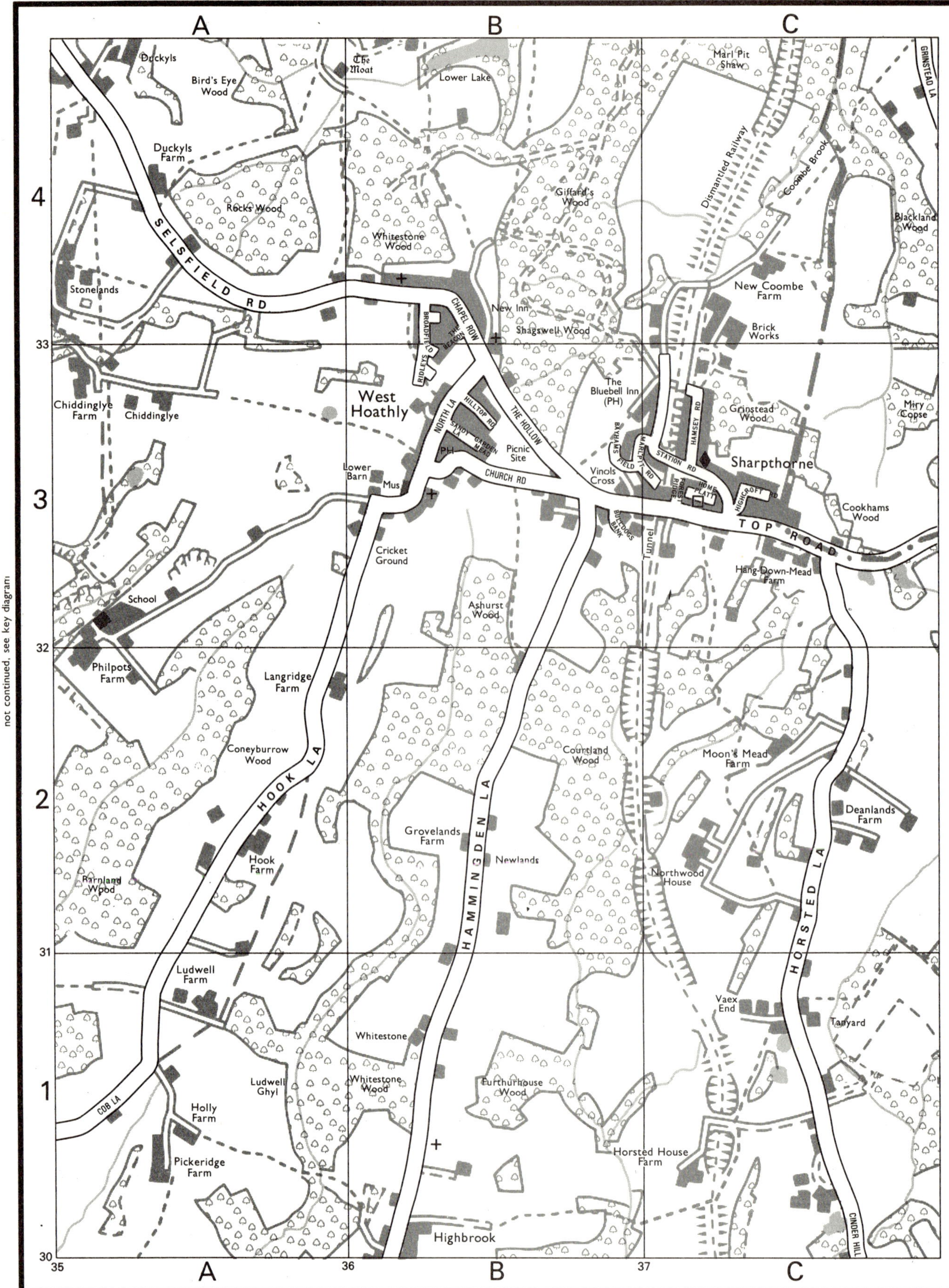

not continued, see key diagram

not continued, see key diagram

12

D
E
F
Marlpit Wood
Monkshill Farm
Round Wood
Hollow Shaw
Mayes
Mayes Farm
Blackland Farm
Legsheath Farm
Plaw Wood
LEGSHEATH LA
PRIORY RD
Tits Wood
GRINSTEAD LA
Mayes Wood
Lavender Platt
Dodges Farm
Blackdog Wood
Coldharbour Manor
Plawhatch Hall
Front Wood
The Farm
P
Tyes Cross
Goat Farm
Hindleap Farm
Dodge's Wood
TOP RD
PLAW HATCH LA
Picnic Area
Courtlands
Horncastle
Courtlands Farm
Dalingridge Farm
Wickenden Manor
Cripps Manor
Smockfarthing
Dalingridge Place
Horncastle Wood
Sandpit Wood
Balcombe Farm
Wickenden Farm
Wych Cross Place Farm
Hang Wood
Suttons Farm
CHILLING ST
BALCOMBE LA
Twyford Farm
Twyford Lodge
Grinstead Wood
Restlands
Ford
Stumblewood Common
Round Wood
Piplye Wood
BIRCHGROVE LA
Westlands
Ford
HURSTWOOD LA
Gosses Farm
Broadhurst Manor
Ass Wood
Hurstwood Farm
4
3
2
1
33
32
31
30
38
39
40

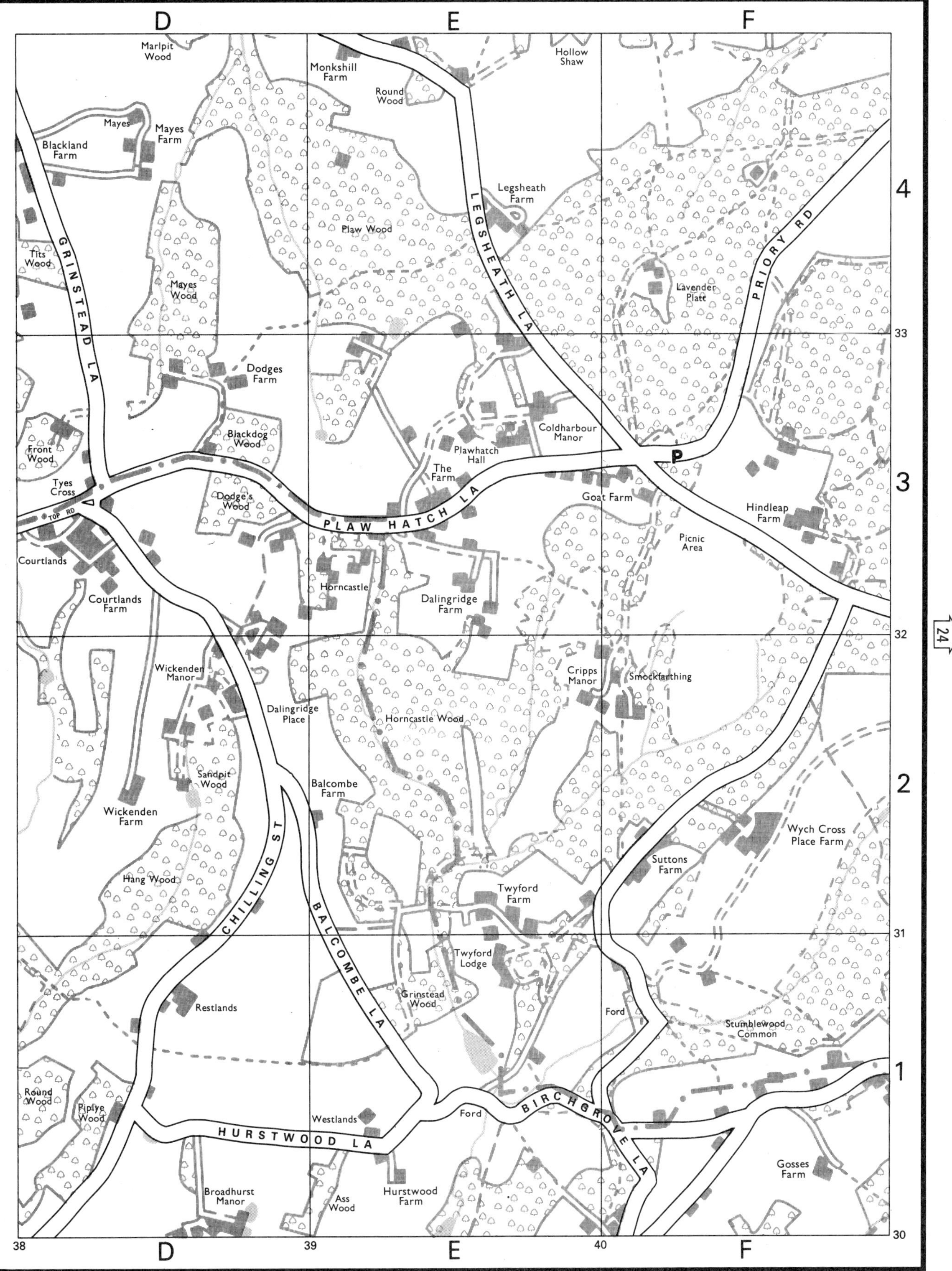

24

35

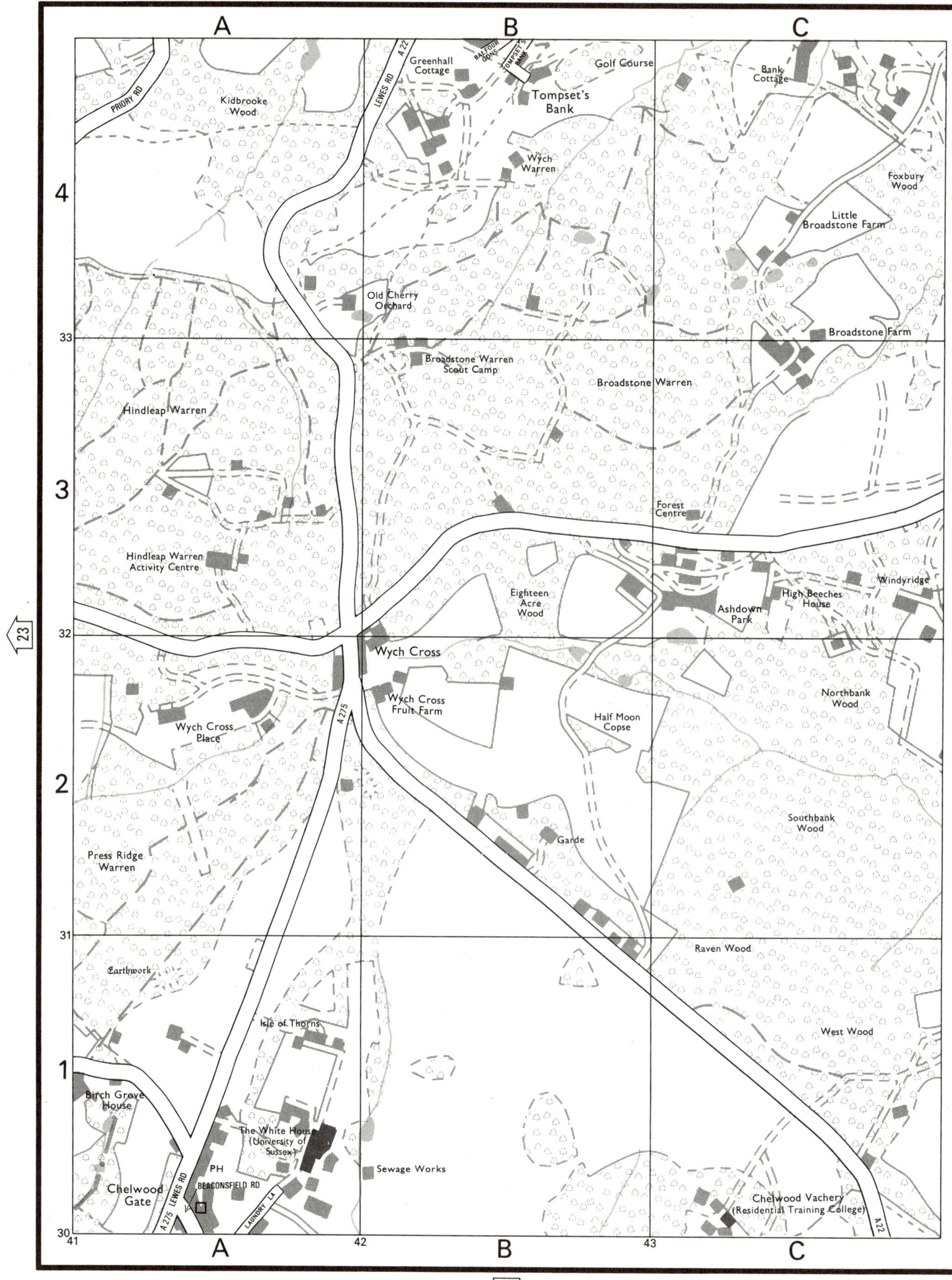
13
A
B
C
4
3
2
1
33
32
31
30
41
42
43
23
36
PRIORY RD
Kidbrooke Wood
LEWES RD
A 22
Greenhall Cottage
BALFOUR GDNS
TOMPSET'S BANK
Tompset's Bank
Golf Course
Bank Cottage
Wych Warren
Foxbury Wood
Little Broadstone Farm
Old Cherry Orchard
Broadstone Farm
Broadstone Warren Scout Camp
Broadstone Warren
Hindleap Warren
Forest Centre
Hindleap Warren Activity Centre
Eighteen Acre Wood
Windyridge
High Beeches House
Ashdown Park
Wych Cross
Wych Cross Fruit Farm
Northbank Wood
Wych Cross Place
A 275
Half Moon Copse
Southbank Wood
Garde
Press Ridge Warren
Raven Wood
Earthwork
Isle of Thorns
West Wood
Birch Grove House
The White House (University of Sussex)
Sewage Works
PH
Chelwood Gate
BEACONSFIELD RD
A 275 LEWES RD
LAUNDRY LA
Chelwood Vachery (Residential Training College)
A 22

14

D
E
F
Coleman's Hatch
B2110
SHEPHERD'S HILL
Hollycroft
Fincham Farm
Little Shepherd's Farm
Holly Hill
Water Farm
Shepherd's Gate
Marsh Green
4
The Birches
The Hatch Inn (PH)
Hart's Farm
Shawhurst Farm
South Hartfield House
Jumpers Town
Podlea Flock Farm
33
Peculiar's Farm
Sunting's
Newbridge Mill
SANDY LA
Spring Farm
Stone Cottage
Furnace Farm
Newbridge
P
The Rough
3
End House
New Lodge Farm
32
KIDD'S HILL
Cobbers Farm
B 2026
The Park
Birch Wood
Kidd's Hill Farm
Ironworks (site of)
P
2
North Wood
Triangle Wood
31
B 2026
Pippingford Park
1
Home Farm
East Wood
Old Lodge Farm
30
44
45
46
D
E
F

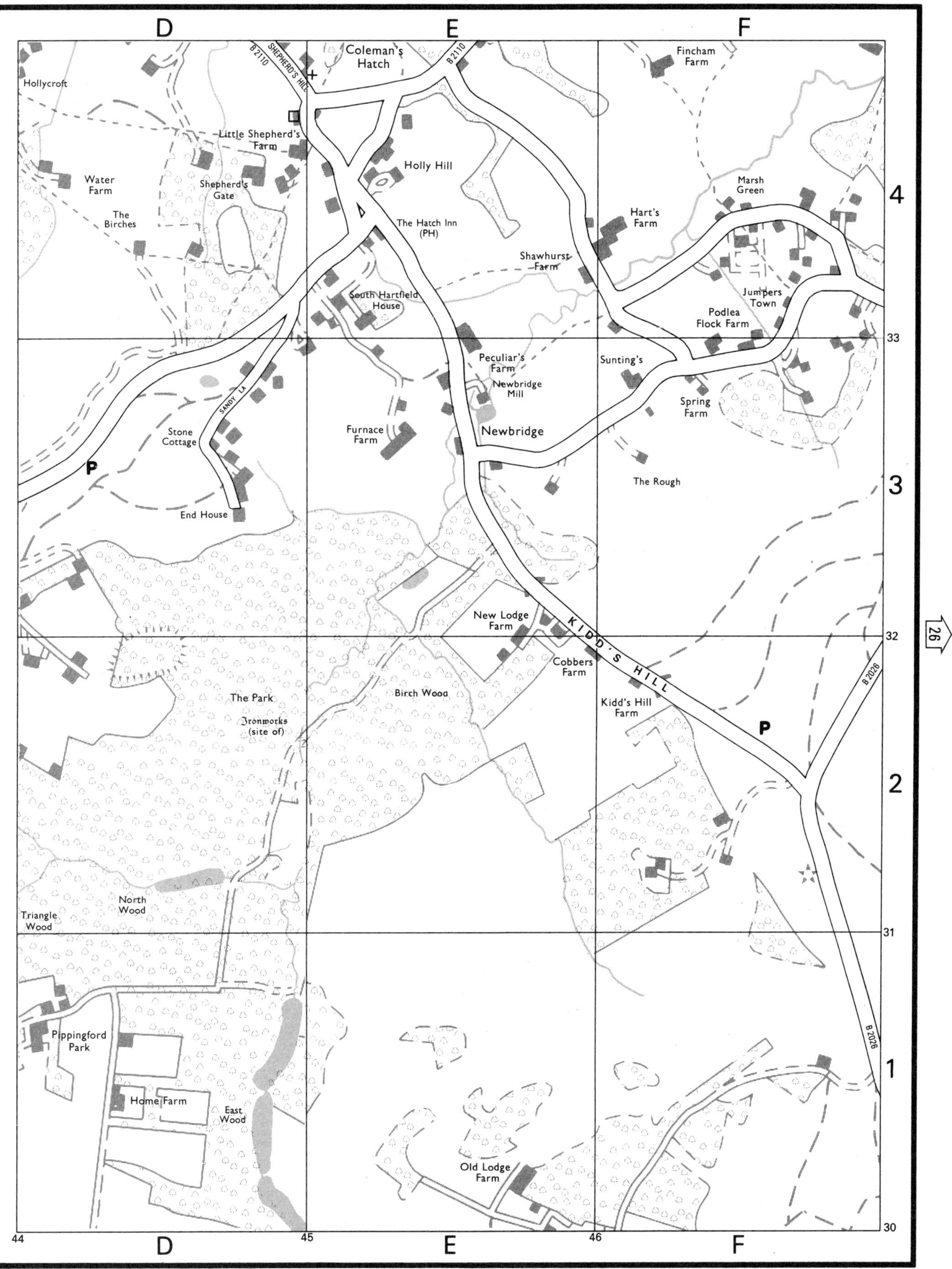

26

37

15

A
B
C
Pond Bay
B 2026
Tile Barn Farm
Neaves Farm
Posingford Wood
Buckhurst Farm
Fisher's Gate
Oak Plat
Half Moon Inn
Chuck Hatch
Pimp Barn Cottages
Sewage Works
Friar's Gate
Moorlands
Forest Lodge Farm
Five Hundred Acre Wood
Lone Oak Hall
Five Hundred Rough
Wren's Warren
ROMAN ROAD (course of)
Church Hill
MARDEN'S HILL
Marden's Hill
Fagot Stack Corner
Pond Bay
Wood Eaves
Bunker's Hill
Cow Field
Jack Daw
Sand Holes
Enclosure
Heasman's Lodge Farm
Greenwood Gate Clump
Green Wood Gate
Black Hill
Warren Chimney
Deerswood Farm
The Orchard
Home Farm
WARREN RD
The Nursery
King's Standing
B 2188
Old Mill Farm
Brownknoll Gill
Old Mill House
B 2026
4
3
2
1
33
32
31
30
47
48
49

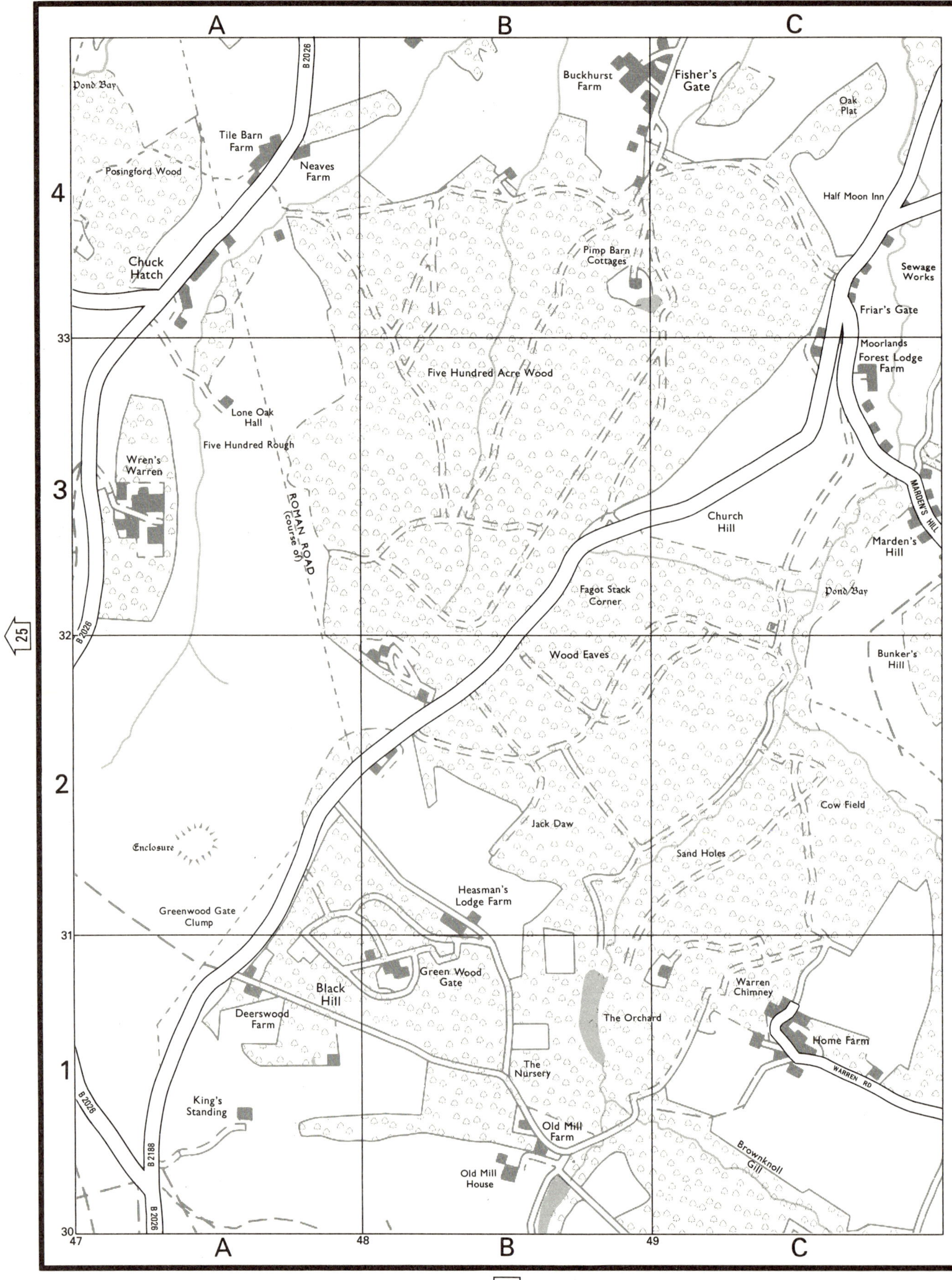

25

38

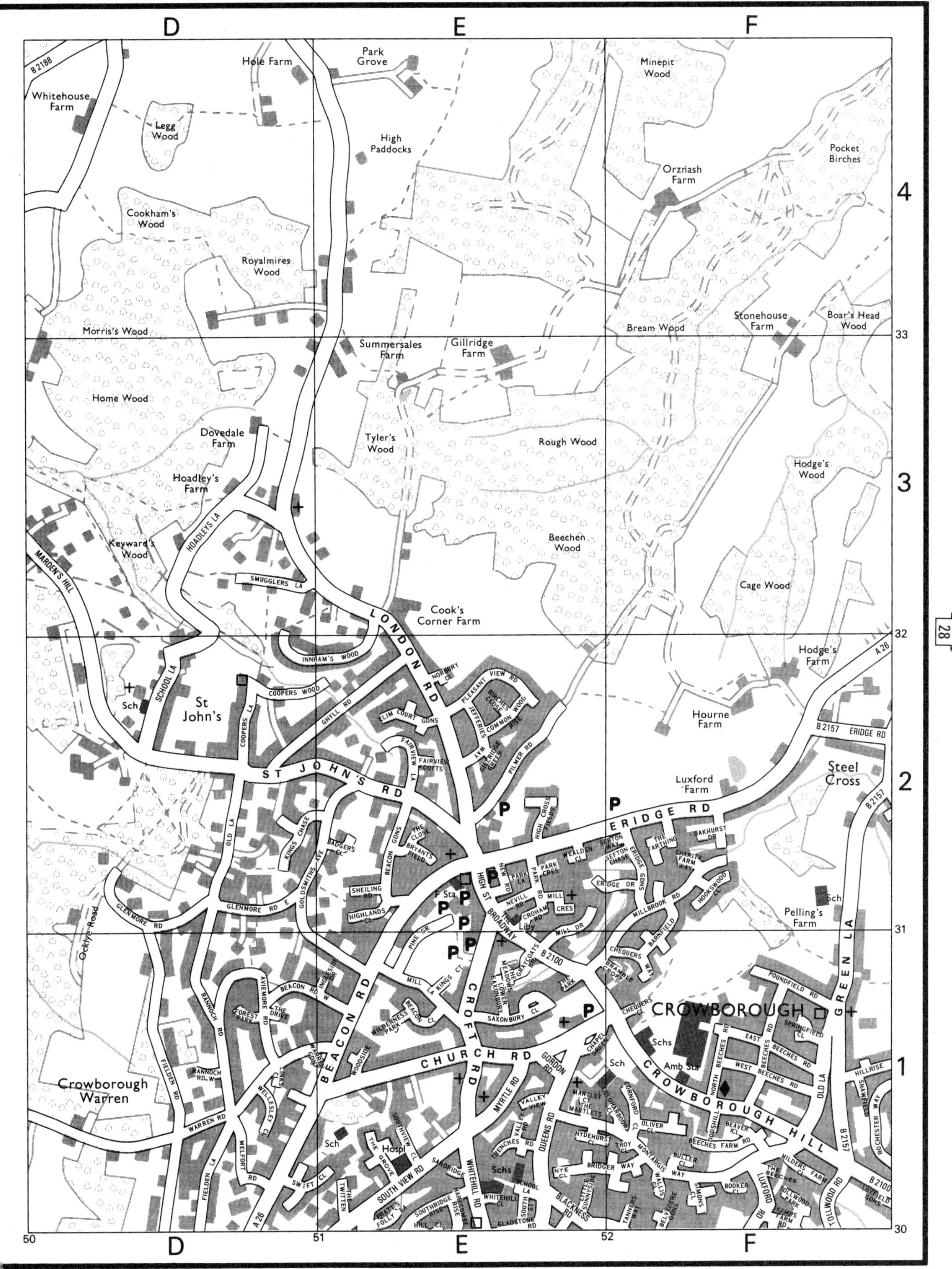
16
39
28
D
E
F
4
3
2
1
50
51
52
33
32
31
30
Hole Farm
Park Grove
Minepit Wood
Whitehouse Farm
Legg Wood
High Paddocks
Pocket Birches
Orznash Farm
Cookham's Wood
Royalmires Wood
Morris's Wood
Summersales Farm
Gillridge Farm
Bream Wood
Stonehouse Farm
Boar's Head Wood
Home Wood
Dovedale Farm
Tyler's Wood
Rough Wood
Hodge's Wood
Hoadley's Farm
Keyward's Wood
Beechen Wood
Cage Wood
Cook's Corner Farm
Hodge's Farm
St John's
Hourne Farm
Steel Cross
Luxford Farm
Pelling's Farm
CROWBOROUGH
Crowborough Warren
LONDON RD
ST JOHN'S RD
ERIDGE RD
CHURCH RD
CROWBOROUGH HILL
BEACON RD
CROFT RD
GREEN LA
HIGH ST
BROADWAY
B 2188
B 2157
B 2100
A 26
Sch
Schs
Hospl
Liby
F Sta
Amb Sta

17

A
B
C
Hamsell Manor
Renby Farm
Copyhold Farm
Rowland Wood
Crooked Wood
Slab Wood
Stonewall Ghyll
Silverlands
Sandhill Cottages
Renby Grange
SANDHILL LA
Stitches Farm
Sandhill Farm
Bowle's Rocks
Laurel Tree Farm
Bowles Outdoor Pursuits Centre
Roughets Wood
Marchant's Wood
Boarshead
Aldwick Grange
Rocks Farm
ERIDGE RD
Boar's Head Farm
The Boar's Head (inn)
Burnt House Wood
Redgate Mill Farm
Mead Farm
Blackdon Hill Farm
BLACKDON HILL
Cherrytree Farm
Rocky Bank
Newhouse Farm
A 26
B 2157
Sewage Works
GREEN LA
Limekiln Wood
The Cants
Black Acre Forest
Steel Cross Farm
Park Wood
Hornshurst Wood
Limekiln Forest
LIMEKILN CT
Byeways
Little Millhole Wood
PALESGATE RD
Jeffery's Wood
The Warren
Old Lodge Warren Farm
Lime Kiln Oast
Burial Ground
Highgate Farm
SHEPHERDS WLK
Chant Lane
MEDWAY
ROCHESTER WAY
BROOK CL
St Denys' Lodge
Rochester's Forest
HORNSHURST RD
CROWBOROUGH HILL
BRACKEN CL
B 2100
BURDETT RD
FOREST RISE
HEATHER WLK
FOREST DENE
Old Forest Lane
4
3
2
1
33
32
31
30
53
54
55
27

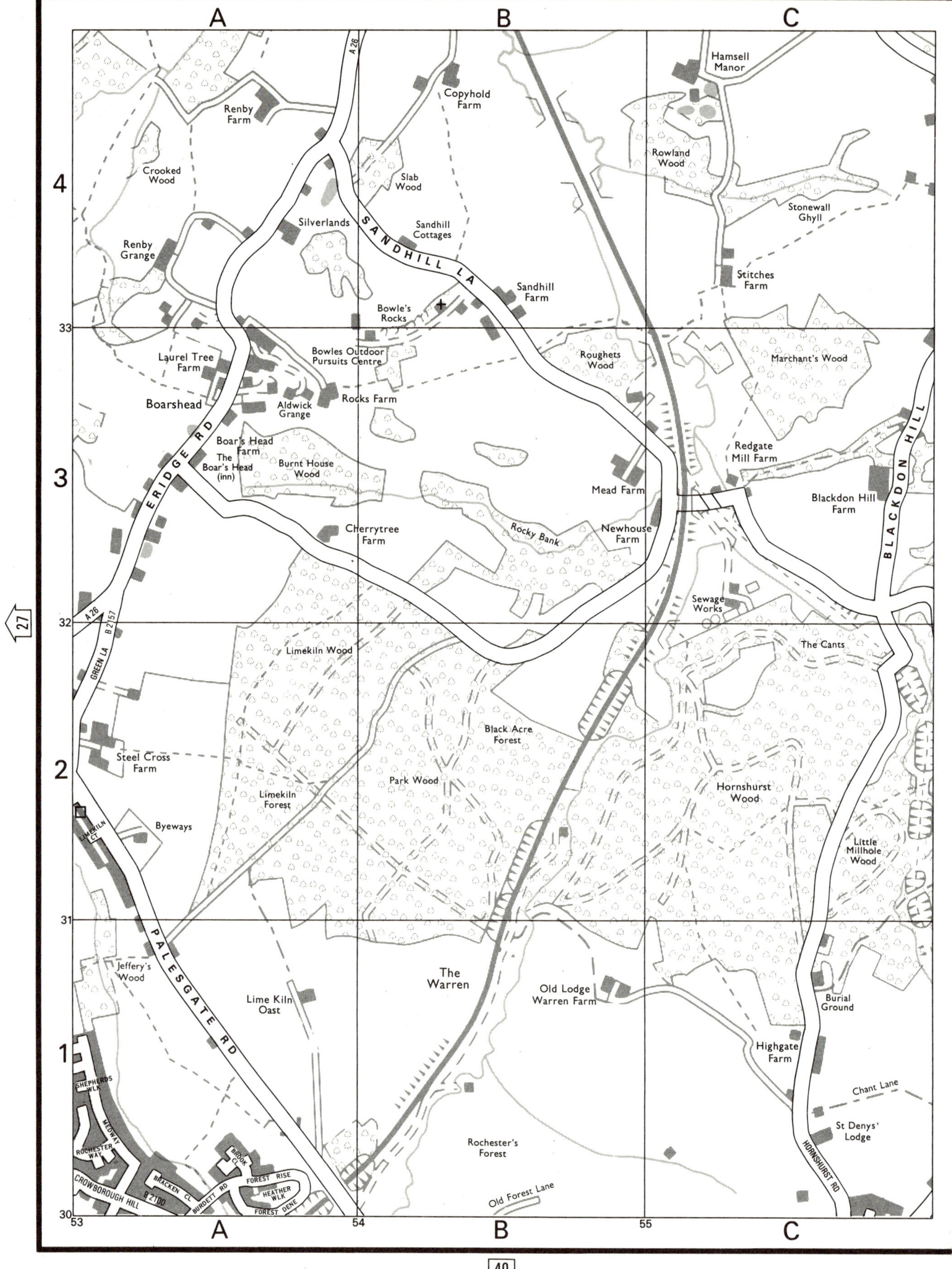

40

18

D
E
F
Sham Farm
Danegate
Long Wood
tonewall
Rocks Wood
Rowden House Farm
Pococksgate Farm
4
Spring Wood
Saxonbury Wood
Great Danegate
Whitehouse Farm
Saxonbury Hill
Fort
Nap Wood
33
Ashets
Hoth Farm
Saxonbury Farm
Ellen Gray
3
Green Hedges Farm
Towsers Lodge Farm
Saxonbury Farm
Lords Wood
Entryhill Wood
Card's Wood
BRICKYARD LA
32
Hoth Wood
Entry Hill
Forest Farm
Strood Wood
Stone House Farm
Catts Farm
2
Strood House
Beechglade Farm
B 2100
Mark Cross
Sch
PH
Sandyden House
The Gill
Lodge Farm
Law Court
Greenhouse Farm
Big Millhole Wood
Town Row Green Farm
Markhouse Farm
31
Orphanage Wood
Heathfield Hall
CATT'S HILL
St Joseph's College
Renhurst Farm
1
Ashley Farm
DOUGLAS RD
Bletchingley Wood
Chant Lane Farm
Town Row
Medway Farm
Stile House Farm
Stilehouse Wood
Little Trodgers Farm
CHANT LA
STATION RD
BAINDEN CL
B 2100
Bletchinglye Farm
LAKE ST
B 2100
NEW RD
YEWTREE LA
BLETCHINGLYE LA
A 267
A 267
30
56
57
58
D
E
F

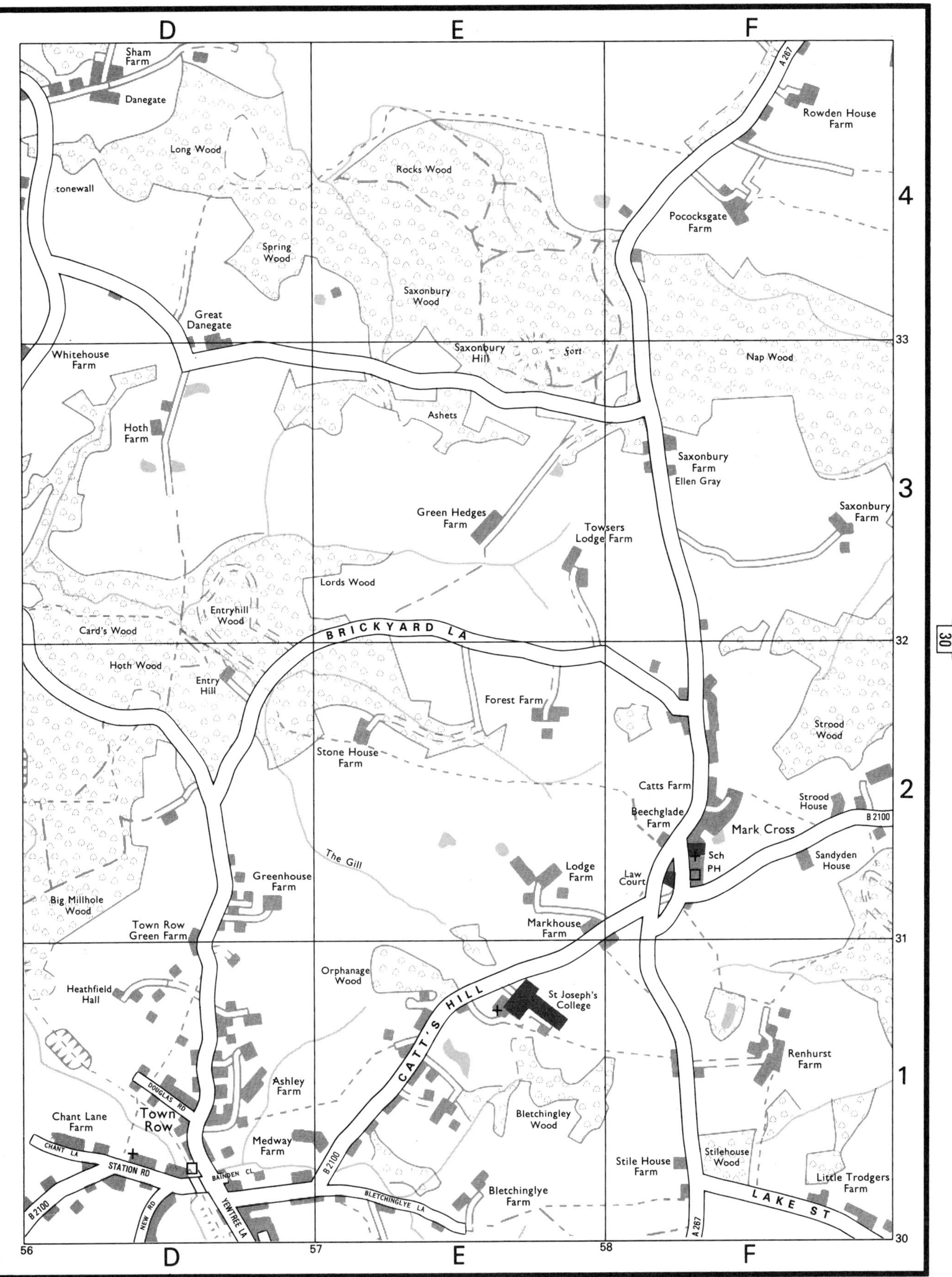

30

41

19

A
B
C
DOWN LA
Comptons
B 2099
Dewhurst Farm
LC
Dewhurst Lodge
4
Furnace Wood
Lightlands
Greenman Farm
Riverhall
STATION RD
33
FAIRCROUCH LA
Mount Farm
Colesgrove Wood
Earlye Farm
Hillyfields Farm
PARTRIDGES LA
BUCKHURST LA
Groomden Farm
Buckhurst Place
3
The Mount
Alder Shaw
Lorien Arboretum
Partridges
BIRD LA
32
Frankham Wood
Steel's Farm
Frankham Farm
Wessons
FAIRGLEN RD
FAIRCROUCH LA
Little Frankham
Frankham Dene
2
Frankham
MAYFIELD LA
B 2100
Beggars Bush
Best Beech Hotel
Houndsell Place
Houndsell Farm
Skinner's Farm
Best Beech Hill
St Benedict's Priory
31
Bensfield Farm
Earl's Farm
Sandyden Wood
1
Newhouse Farm
RISEDEN RD
Riseden
Bassetts
Rocks Wood
Tide Brook
Devil's Gill
Badgers Hill
Highfields Farm
30
59
60
61

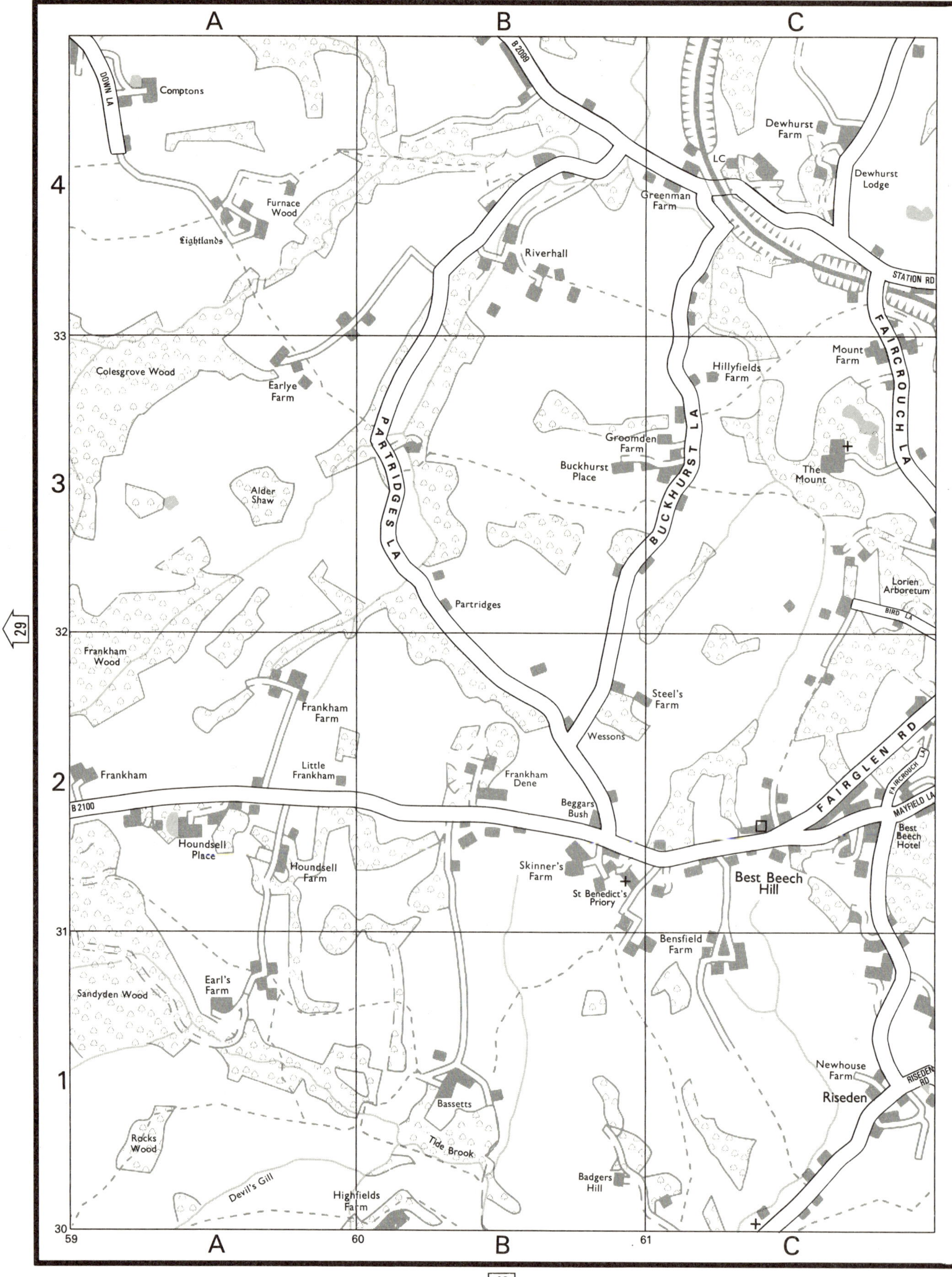

29

42

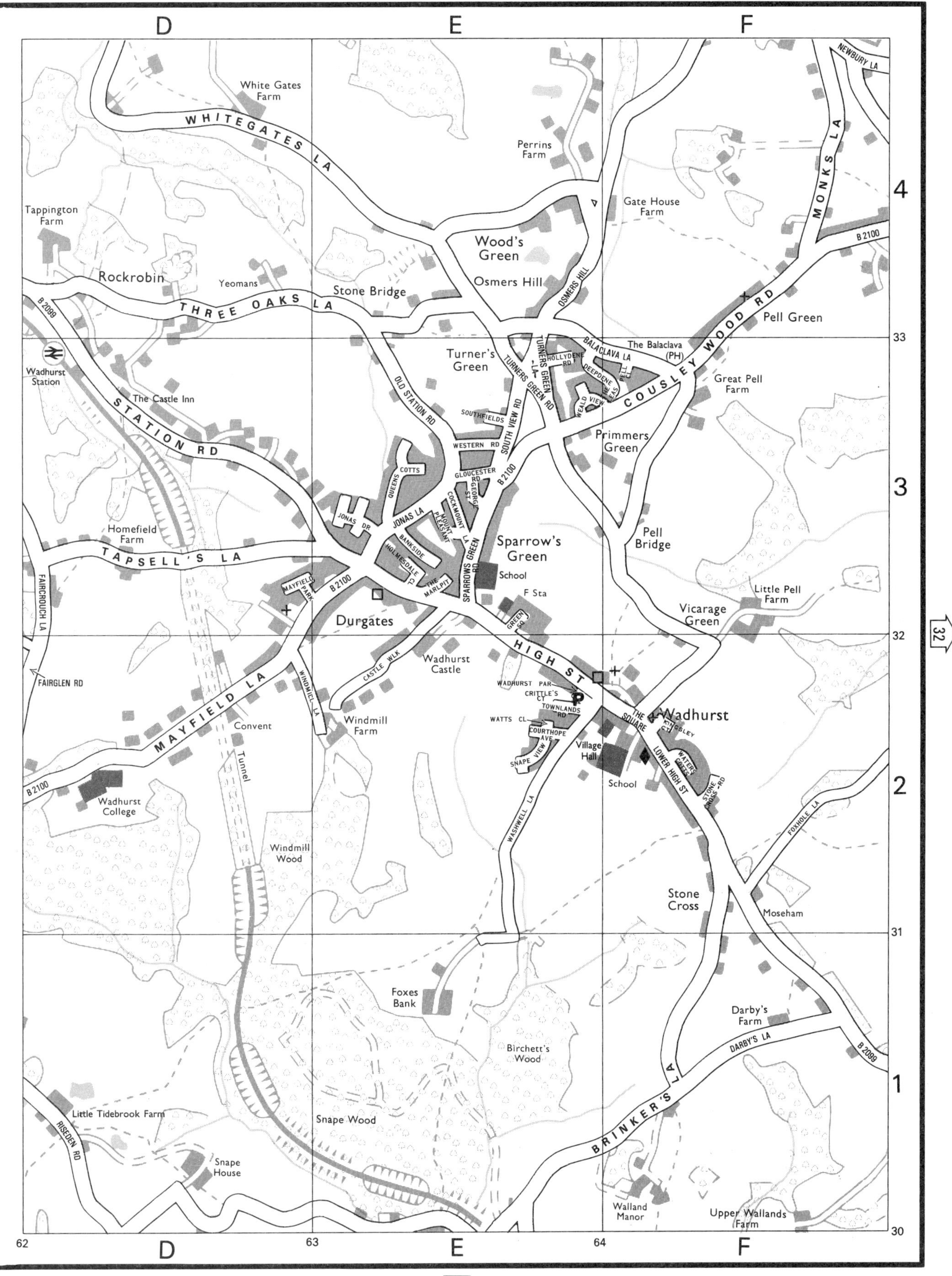
20
D
E
F
White Gates Farm
WHITEGATES LA
Perrins Farm
NEWBURY LA
MONKS LA
Tappington Farm
Gate House Farm
Wood's Green
Osmers Hill
OSMERS HILL
Rockrobin
Yeomans
Stone Bridge
THREE OAKS LA
B 2099
B 2100
COUSLEY WOOD RD
Pell Green
Wadhurst Station
Turner's Green
TURNERS GREEN LA
TURNERS GREEN RD
HOLLYDENE RD
BALACLAVA LA
The Balaclava (PH)
DEEPDENE
PELL CL
WEALD VIEW
THE LEAS
Great Pell Farm
OLD STATION RD
SOUTHFIELDS
SOUTH VIEW RD
The Castle Inn
STATION RD
WESTERN RD
Primmers Green
COTTS
QUEENS
GLOUCESTER RD
GEORGE ST
COCKMOUNT LA
MOUNT PLEASANT
JONAS DR
JONAS LA
Homefield Farm
BANKSIDE
HOLMESDALE CL
Sparrow's Green
SPARROWS GREEN RD
Pell Bridge
TAPSELL'S LA
School
THE MARLPIT
MAYFIELD PARK
F Sta
Little Pell Farm
FAIRCROUCH LA
Durgates
GREEN SQ
Vicarage Green
CASTLE WLK
Wadhurst Castle
HIGH ST
FAIRGLEN RD
WINDMILL LA
WADHURST PAR
CRITTLE'S CT
TOWNLANDS RD
THE SQUARE
Wadhurst
KINGSLEY CT
MAYFIELD LA
Convent
Windmill Farm
WATTS CL
COURTHOPE AVE
Village Hall
WATERS CROFT
Tunnel
SNAPE VIEW
LOWER HIGH ST
School
STONE CROSS RD
Wadhurst College
WASHWELL LA
FOXHOLE LA
Windmill Wood
Stone Cross
Moseham
Foxes Bank
Darby's Farm
DARBY'S LA
Birchett's Wood
Little Tidebrook Farm
RISEDEN RD
Snape Wood
BRINKER'S LA
Snape House
Walland Manor
Upper Wallands Farm
4
3
2
1
33
32
31
30
32
62
63
64
43

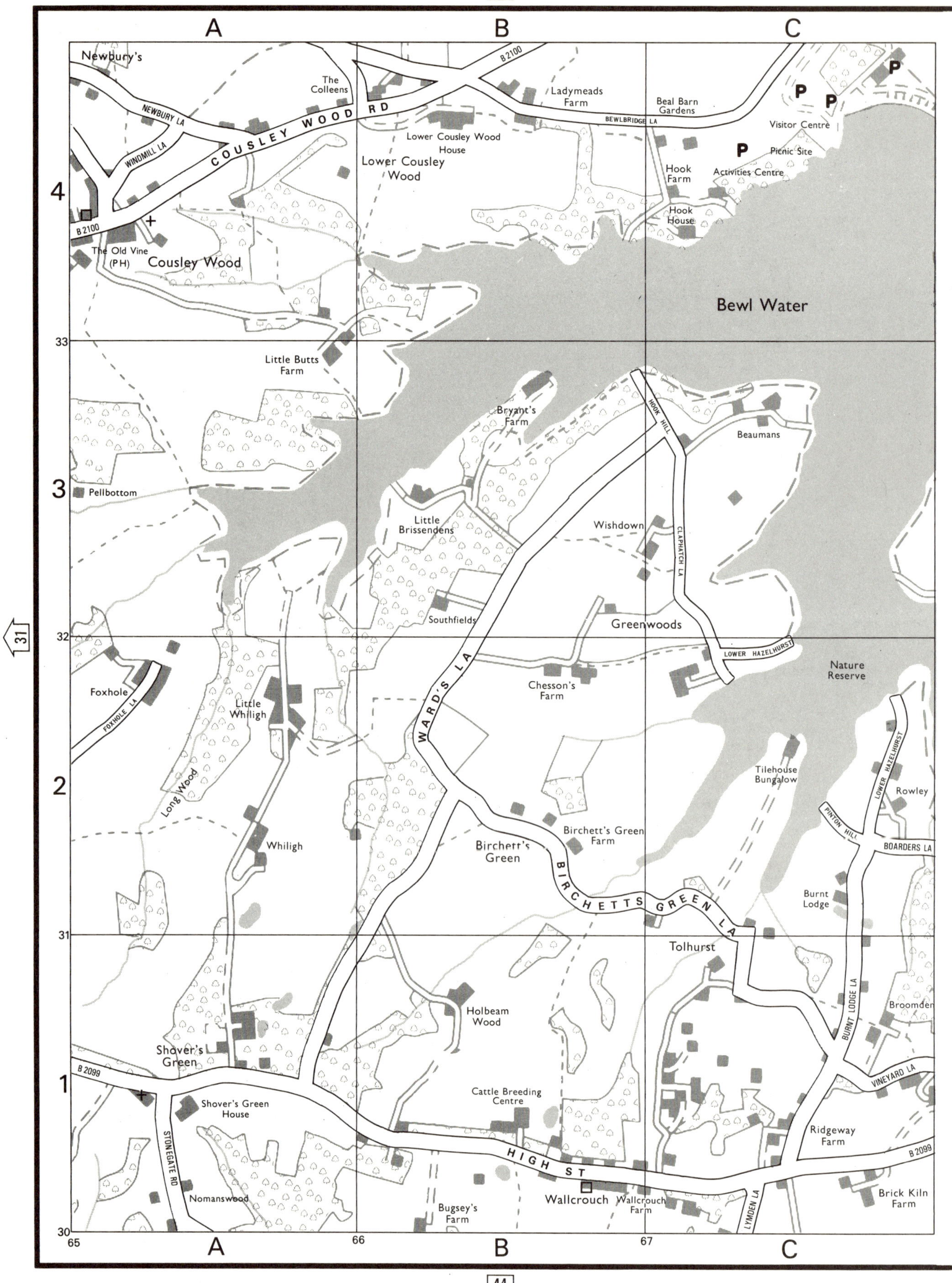
21
A
B
C
Newbury's
The Colleens
B 2100
Ladymeads Farm
Beal Barn Gardens
NEWBURY LA
COUSLEY WOOD RD
BEWLBRIDGE LA
Visitor Centre
Lower Cousley Wood House
WINDMILL LA
Lower Cousley Wood
Picnic Site
Hook Farm
Activities Centre
4
Hook House
B 2100
The Old Vine (PH)
Cousley Wood
Bewl Water
33
Little Butts Farm
Bryant's Farm
HOOK HILL
Beaumans
3
Pellbottom
Little Brissendens
Wishdown
CLAPHATCH LA
Southfields
Greenwoods
31
32
LOWER HAZELHURST
Nature Reserve
Chesson's Farm
Foxhole
FOXHOLE LA
Little Whiligh
WARD'S LA
Tilehouse Bungalow
2
Long Wood
LOWER HAZELHURST
Rowley
PINTON HILL
Birchett's Green Farm
Whiligh
Birchett's Green
BOARDERS LA
BIRCHETTS GREEN LA
Burnt Lodge
31
Tolhurst
BURNT LODGE LA
Broomden
Holbeam Wood
Shover's Green
1
B 2099
VINEYARD LA
Cattle Breeding Centre
Shover's Green House
STONEGATE RD
HIGH ST
Ridgeway Farm
B 2099
Nomanswood
Wallcrouch
Wallcrouch Farm
Bugsey's Farm
LYMDEN LA
Brick Kiln Farm
30
65
66
67
44

not continued, see key diagram

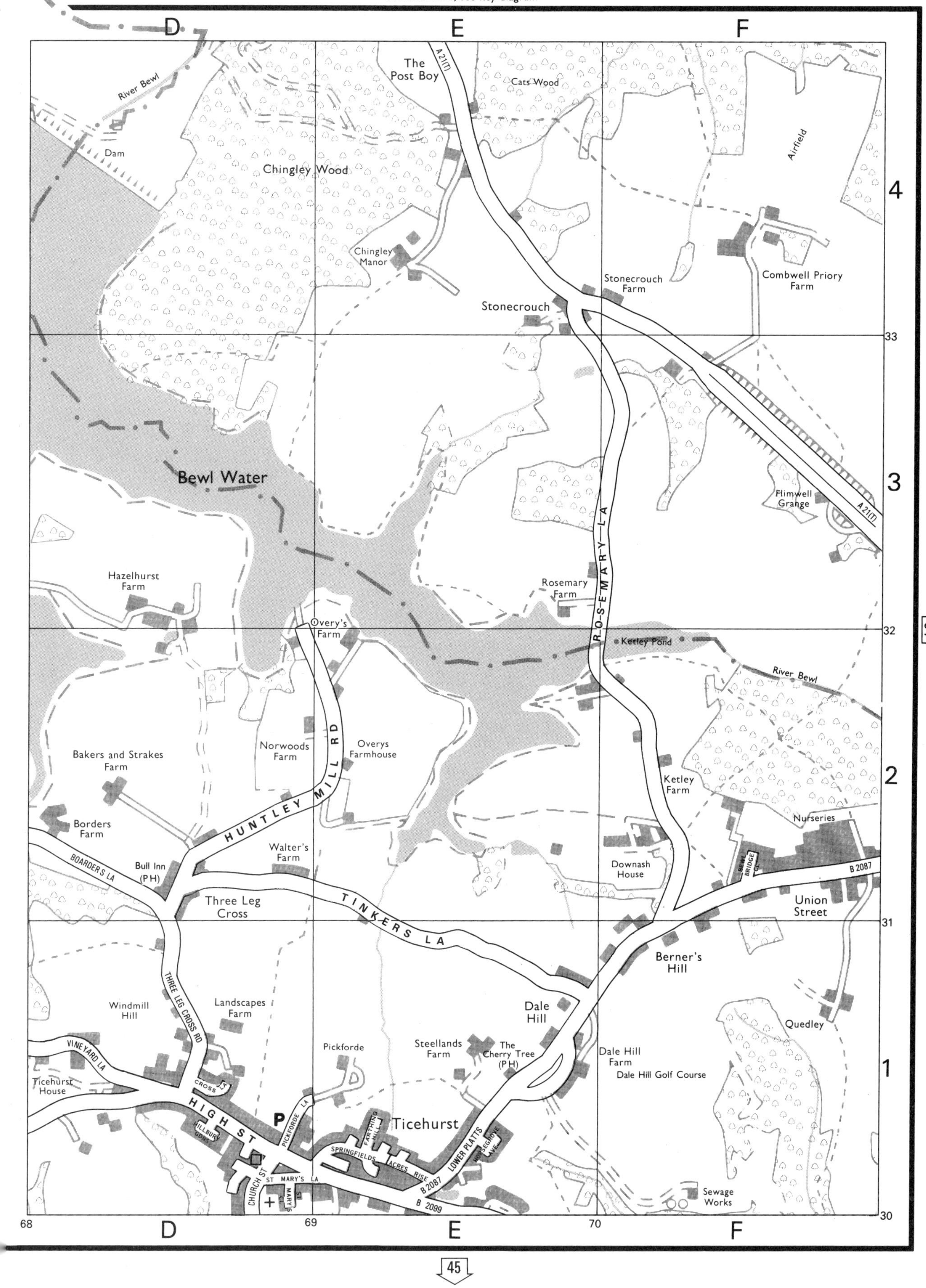

D E F

River Bewl
Dam
Chingley Wood
The Post Boy
A 21(T)
Cats Wood
Airfield
Chingley Manor
Stonecrouch
Stonecrouch Farm
Combwell Priory Farm
Bewl Water
Flimwell Grange
A 21(T)
ROSEMARY LA
Hazelhurst Farm
Rosemary Farm
Overy's Farm
Ketley Pond
River Bewl
Norwoods Farm
Overys Farmhouse
HUNTLEY MILL RD
Bakers and Strakes Farm
Ketley Farm
Borders Farm
Nurseries
Walter's Farm
BOARDERS LA
Bull Inn (PH)
Downash House
BEWL BRIDGE CL
B 2087
Three Leg Cross
TINKERS LA
Union Street
Berner's Hill
THREE LEG CROSS RD
Windmill Hill
Landscapes Farm
Dale Hill
Quedley
VINEYARD LA
Pickforde
Steellands Farm
The Cherry Tree (PH)
Dale Hill Farm
Dale Hill Golf Course
Ticehurst House
CROSS LA
HIGH ST
P
PICKFORDE LA
HILLBURY GDNS
Ticehurst
FARTHING HILL
SPRINGFIELDS
ACRES RISE
LOWER PLATTS
HORSEGROVE AVE
B 2087
CHURCH ST
ST MARY'S LA
ST MARY'S CL
B 2099
Sewage Works

4
3
2
1

33
32
31
30

68 69 70

D E F

34

45

not continued, see key diagram

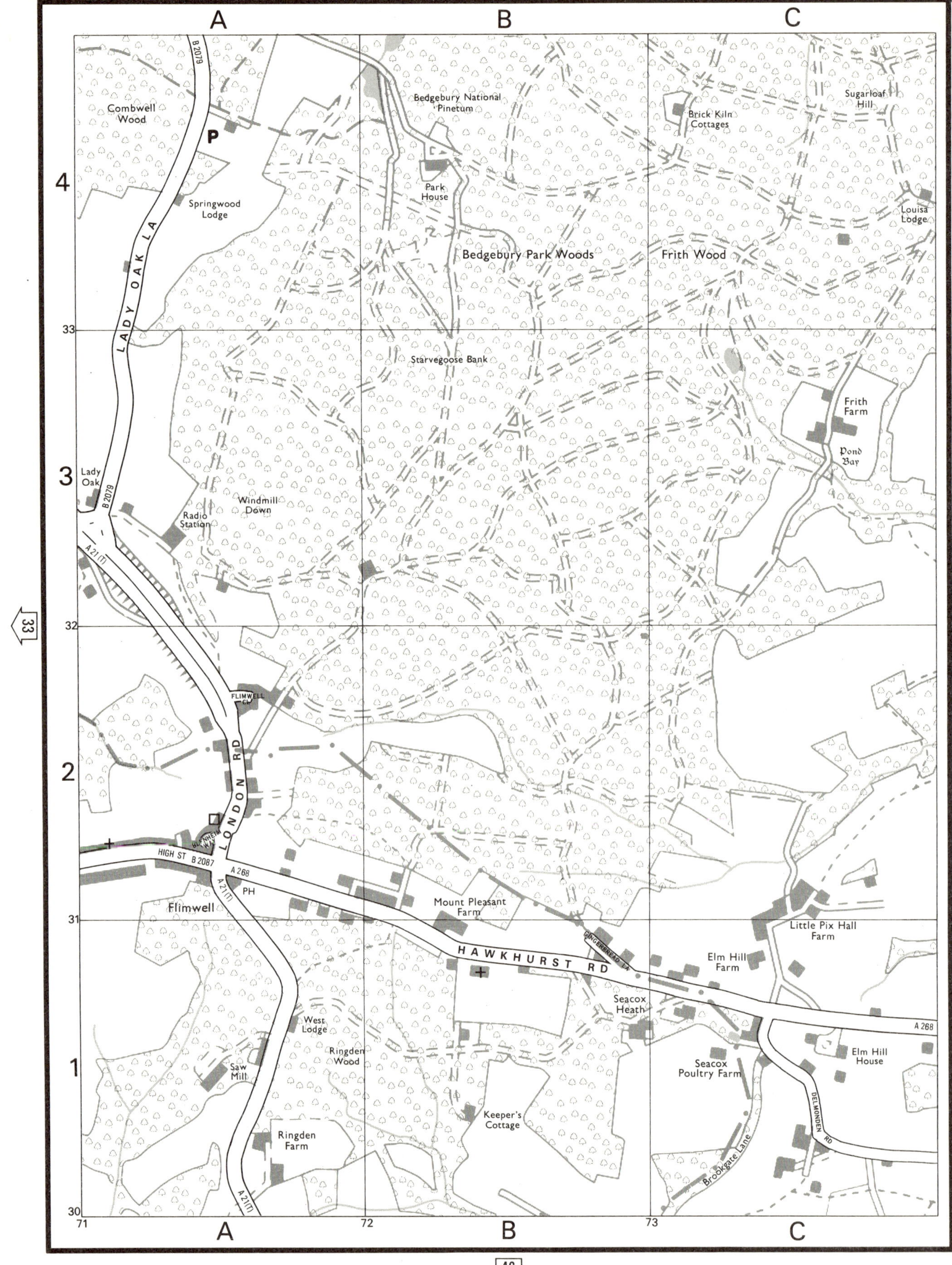

46

23

D
E
F
Birchgrove
Forest Farm
Gitlands Wood
A275
Wickens
Oaken Wood
Sussex Border Path
Birchgrove Wood
Wheeler's Wood
Newnham's Wood
Warren Farm
BIRCHGROVE RD
New Barn Farm
Sch
The Old Rectory
CHURCH LA
Woodgate Farm
Cumnor House School
CHEELEYS
LEIGHTON RD
LUCAS
STATION RD
Ovenden Wood
High Wood
Withy Wood
BONFIRE LA
DANEHILL LA
BOXES LA
LEWES RD
WYATTS LA
Valley Farm
CHALLONERS
Withy Farm
HORSTED LA
LONDON RD
SCHOOL LA
SUGAR LA
HAMSLAND
Horsted Keynes
Sch
Wyatts
Swithe Wood
Enholm's Wood
Danehill Farm
OAK TREE COTTS
COLLINGFORD LA
Collingford Farm
Danehill
TREEMANS RD
Sandpits Wood
LEWES RD
Hole Ho
North Northlands Farm
CHURCH LA
Down Wood
Moaps Farm
Cowstocks
Latchetts
FRESHFIELD LA
East Wood
Cowstocks Wood
TANYARD LA
Otye Wood
Works
Stoaches Farm
Butchers Barn
Kidborough Farm
Northland Wood
SLIDER'S LA
A275
29
28
27
26
4
3
2
1
38
39
40
D
E
F
36
not continued, see key diagram

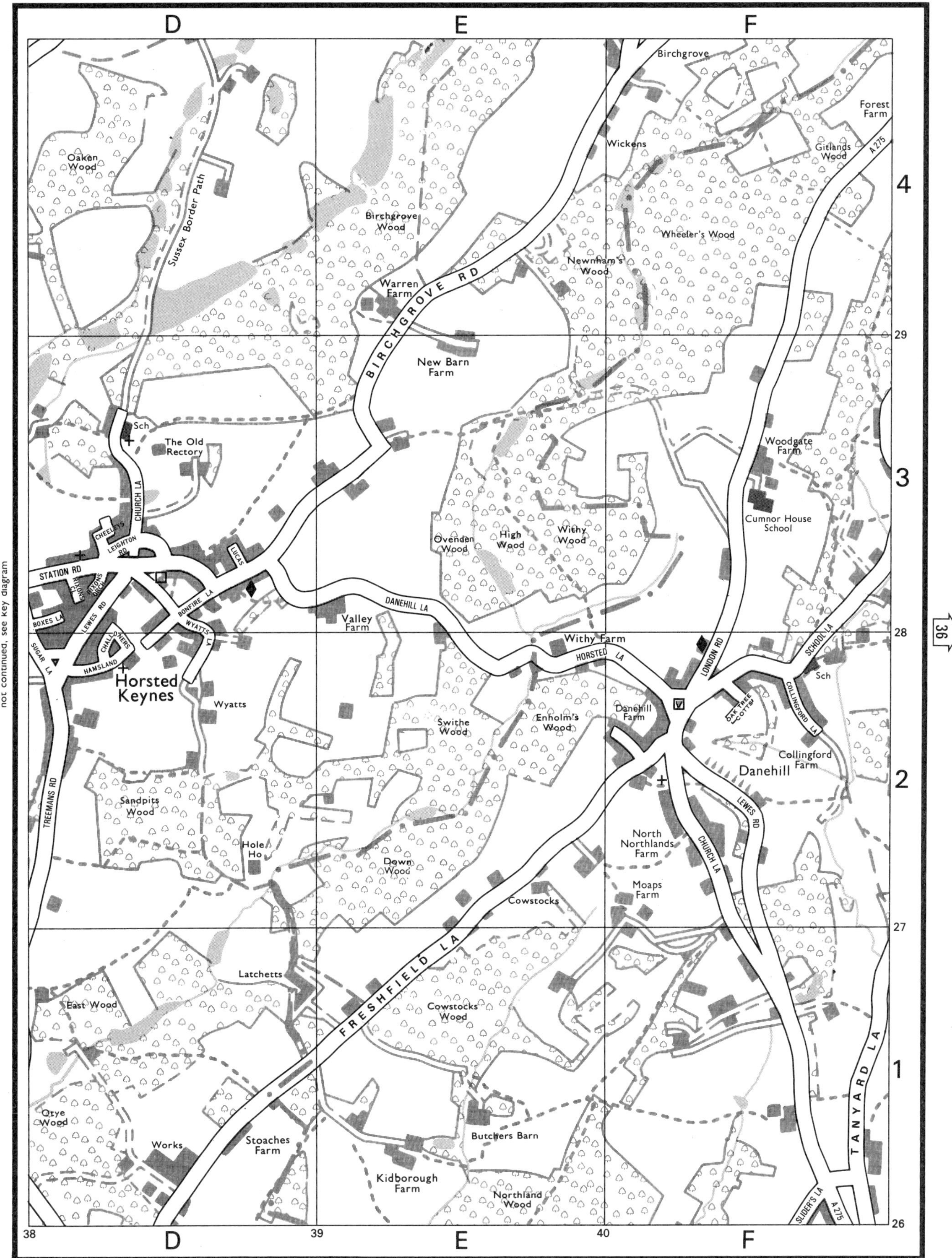

54

24

A
B
C
4
3
2
1
29
28
27
26
41
42
43
Chelwood Gate
Village Hall
P
Braberry Hatch
FBs
Ford
Chelworth
The Ridge
BEACONSFIELD RD
LEWES RD
LAUNDRY
A 275
A 22
Small's Wood
Beacon Wood
STONE QUARRY RD
The Quarry (PH)
Dovecote Farm
Beaconwood Farm
Chelwood Beacon
Streeter's Rough
Millbrook Farm
Stonemead
BOX'S LA
BAXTERS LA
Chelwood Corner
The Clock Tower
Chelwood Common
Coach & Horses Inn (PH)
Chapelwood Manor
Chapelwood Court
Mill Wood
Chelwood Farm
COACH AND HORSES LA
Upperstone Farm
COACH LA
Maskett's Farm
SCHOOL LA
Avenings Farm
TANYARD LA
Ashdown House
Lamb's Rough
Maskett's Wood
Danehill Lodge
Grindfield Farm
Carr's Wood
Burntwood Farm
Allin's Farm
Annwood Farm
Juniper Wood
Jessop's Hill
Annwood Brook
Ann Wood
BROOKHOUSE BOTTOM
Perryman's Hill
Hole and Alchorne Farm
BELL LA
PERRYMAN'S LA
Tanyard Farm
Pollardsland Wood
Mark Street
Colin Godmans Farm
Hollybush Wood
Lane Wood
Wilmshurst
Stephens Farm
Bowyer's Wood
Woolpack Farm
Wet Wood
Searles Wood
Portmansford
Brooker's Rough
Sheffield Forest

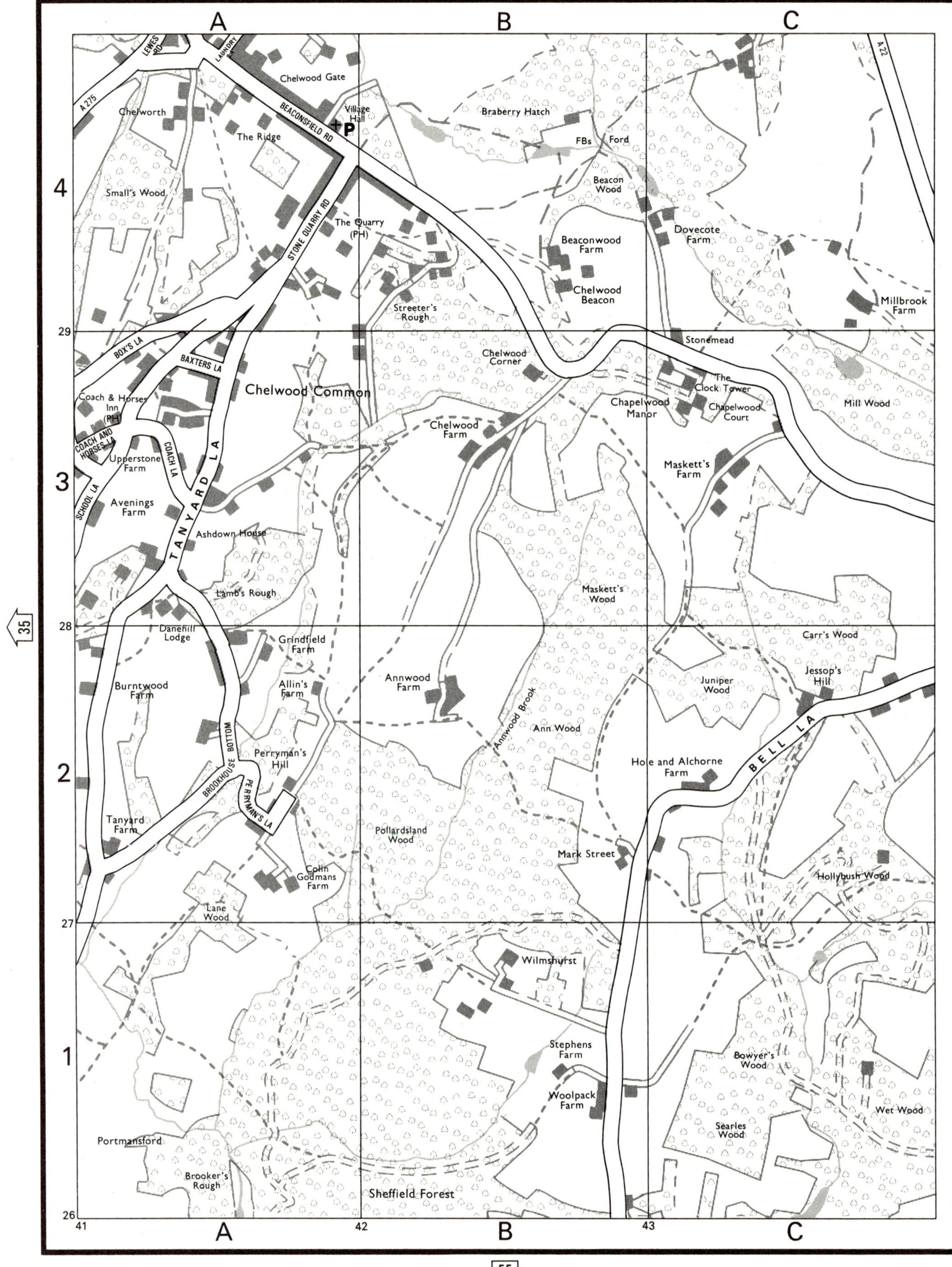

35

55

25

D
E
F
Old Lodge
Mill Brook
A 22
Londonderry Farm
Marlpitts Farm
Camp Hill
Millbrook
Beech Hill
Marlpits
Duddleswell Manor
Ashdown Forest Riding Centre
B 2026
Outback Farm
Ashdown Forest Gardens
Morrisfield
The Shelley Arms Hotel
Court House
School La
Ashdown View
Ridge Cl
Sch
Oakwood Park
Churchfields
Bell La
High St
Clock House La
Nutley Hall
Nursery La
Upper Misbourne Farm
Yew Tree Farm
Nutley
Duddleswell
Roman Road (Course of)
Lower Misbourne Farm
Chestnut Farm
Putland's Farm
Forest View
Nether La
William IV (PH)
Chantersell
Ford's Green
Dodd's Hill
Great Birch Wood
Spring-garden
Pleasant Farm
Prickets Hatch
Dodd's Bottom
Hole Farm
Dodd's Bank
Cackle Street
Funnell's Farm
Courtlands
Boringwheel Lake
Down St
Cackle St
Hunter's Farm
Boringwheel Mill Farm
Fairwarp
Hop Gdns
Marlpits
Fairwarp Village Hall
Nursery La
Paddock Farm
Forest Lodge
Cophall Farm
Woodcock Farm
Tylers La
Old Forge La
Ford's Bank
Picketts La
Normans Land
4
3
2
1
29
28
27
26
44
45
46

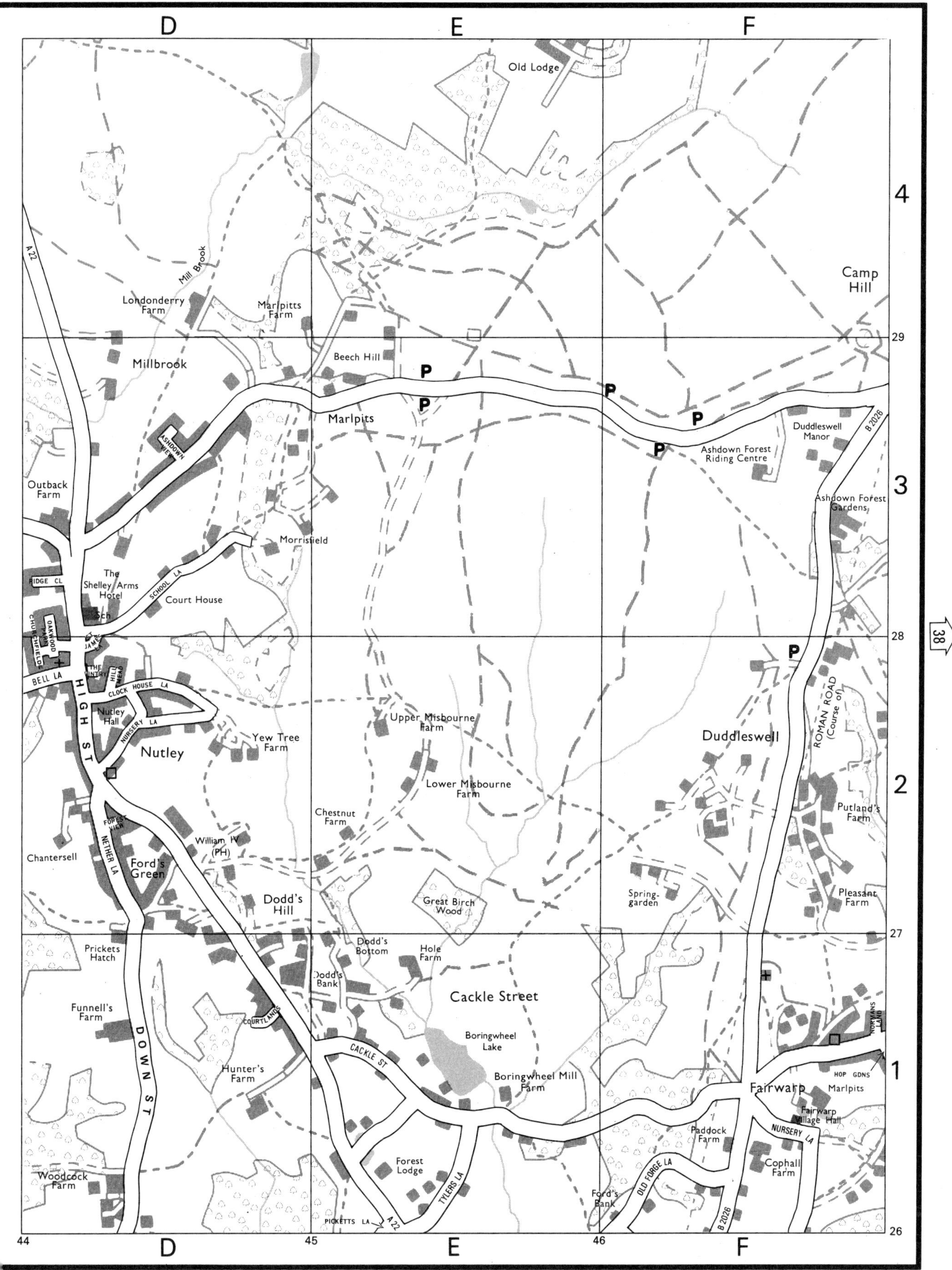

38

56

26

A
B
C
4
3
2
1
29
28
27
26
47
48
49
ROMAN ROAD (Course of)
B 2026
Crowborough Training Camp
Crabtree Farm
Brown Knoll
Birchfield Farm
New Pond Cottages
Wt Sta
Poundgate
UCKFIELD RD
A 26
Crow & Gate (PH)
Broomhill
The Crow's Nest
Newnham Park Farm
Bartons
Poplar Farm
Broom Farm
Crest Farm
Barnsgate
Moulden Wood
Newnham Park Wood
Campfields Rough
Barnsden
Lodge
Brown's Brook
Oldlands Wood
Chillies
CHILLIES LA
Chillies Farm
Stroods House Farm
Oldlands Hall
Broadfield Wood
Heron's Ghyll
Payne's Hill Cottages
Temple Grove (School)
Greystones Farm
Shadwell Farm
Quarry Wood
OLDLANDS HILL
Oldlands Farm
Home Farm
Holly Cottage
Holly Mount
Perryman's Farm
Oldhall Farm
Sch
High Hurstwood
Furnace Wood
Claygate Farm
Mount Pleasant Farm

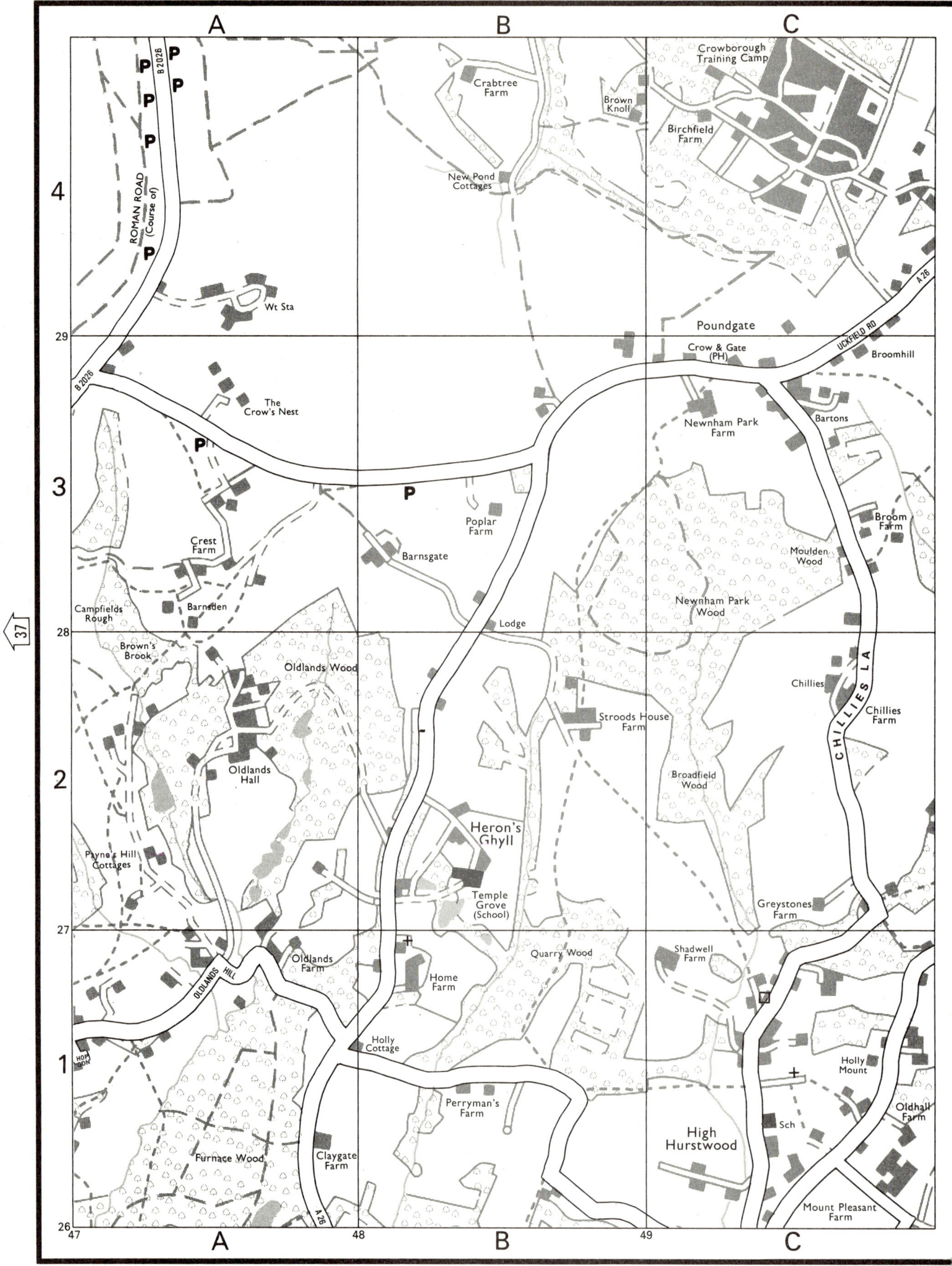

37

57

27

D
E
F
Little Warren Farm
Crowborough Common
The Ghyll
Golf Course
Hurtis Hill
Brook Farm
Alderbrook Farm
Cemy
Sch
Recn Gd
Luxford
Kemp's Farm
Plough and Horses (PH)
High Broom
Allfrey's Farm
Sweethaws
Sweethaws Wood
Redbridge Farm
Sweethaws Farm
Sinnock's Rough
Stone Cross
Perryman's Farm
Rockman's Farm Cottage
Lotmans Farm
Pick Pale
Walsh Manor
Moat
Tunnel
Adam's Farm
Piping Wood
Ketches Farm
Owlsbury Farm
Mabb's Farm
Grovehurst Farm
Marlpit Wood
Scaland Wood
Stumletts Pit Wood
Welchwood Farm
Oaky Wood
Oxley Wood
Brook House
Burnt Oak
Sparrow Cottages
Burnt Oak Farm
Inchreed Farm
Grey Burchetts Wood
Pickreed Wood
Fordbrook Farm
Wilding Wood
Lodge Wood
Hurstwood Farm
The Rough
Kiln Farm
Viaduct
Hastingford Cottage
SHEEP PLAIN
UCKFIELD RD
BEACON RD
HEAVEGATE RD
FIELDEN RD
FIELDEN LA
A 26
WHINCROFT PARK
SOUTH VIEW RD
OSWELL LA
HARLEQUIN LA
HARLEQUIN PL
SOUTHRIDGE RD
SOUTHRIDGE RISE
SPRINGHEAD WAY
MANOR WAY
HARECOMBE RISE
HARECOMBE RD
COMBE END
WILLOW MEAD
HURTIS HILL
WHITEHILL RD
GLADSTONE RD
FERMOR ROW
QUEENS RD
HUNTINGDON RD
FIGG LA
HERNE RD
HERNE RD
WOLFE CL
BLACKNESS RD
ROCKINGTON WAY
ST MICHAEL'S CL
TOLLWOOD RD
LUXFORD LA
LUXFORD DR
LUXFORD RD
WOODLAND WAY
FERMOR WAY
WAYLANDS AVE
ROTHERHILL RD
HERNE DOWN
ROTHER CL
ST RICHARDS RD
BROOKLANDS AVE
FERMOR RD
ALDERVALE COTTS
WALSHES RD
MOUNT PLEA
HIGH BROOM RD
HIGH BROOM LA
ALICE BRIGHT LA
STONE CROSS RD
ALDERBROOK CL
ALDERBROOK PATH
ALDERBROOK WAY
SWEETHAWS LA
REDBRIDGE LA
TIBBS MILL LA
FOWLY LA
4
3
2
1
29
28
27
26
50
51
52

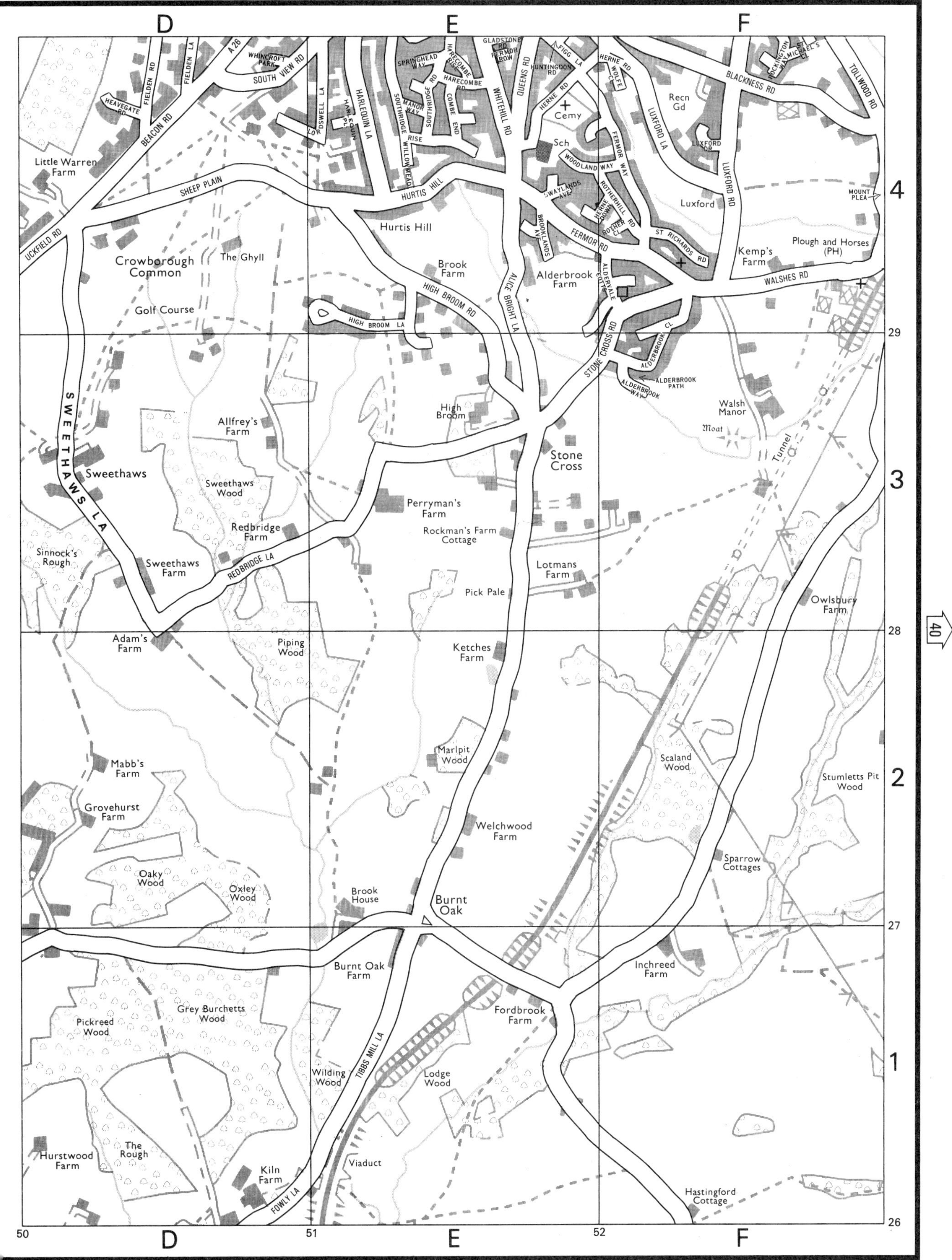

40

58

28

A
B
C
Jarvis Brook
Millbrook Industrial Estate
Crowborough and Jarvis Brook Station
Works
PH
Sch
WESTERN RD
TUBWELL LA
MOTTINS HILL
CLACKHAMS LA
PALESGATE RD
OLD FOREST LA
ROTHERFIELD RD
CHURCH ST
Village Hall
Milk Lodge Farm
Rotherfield
NORTH ST
HIGH ST
SOUTH ST
STATION RD
B2100
B2101
Horsegrove Farm
Cottage Hill Shaw
Tubwell Farm
Cottage Hill
Yewtree Wood
Peeps Lane
Hayward's Farm
Lodgeland
TREBLERS RD
Rotherhurst Farm
Rotherhurst
Haywards Grange
Castle Hill Farm
Steep Hill Farm
Trebler's Farm
River Rother
Lodge Wood
Trebler's Wood
Castle Hill
Castle Wood
Steep Park
Holly Grove Farm
Turner's Wood
Rumsden Farm
Castle Wood
Marlpits Wood
Limney Farm
Great Dewlands
Derridge Farm
Streel Farm
Pinehurst Farm
Coe's Farm
Upper Wood
Stone Mill Farm
Willinghurst
Under Rockes
Walsted Wood
Stonehurst
Fox Wood
Huggett's Furnace
4
3
2
1
29
28
27
26
53
54
55

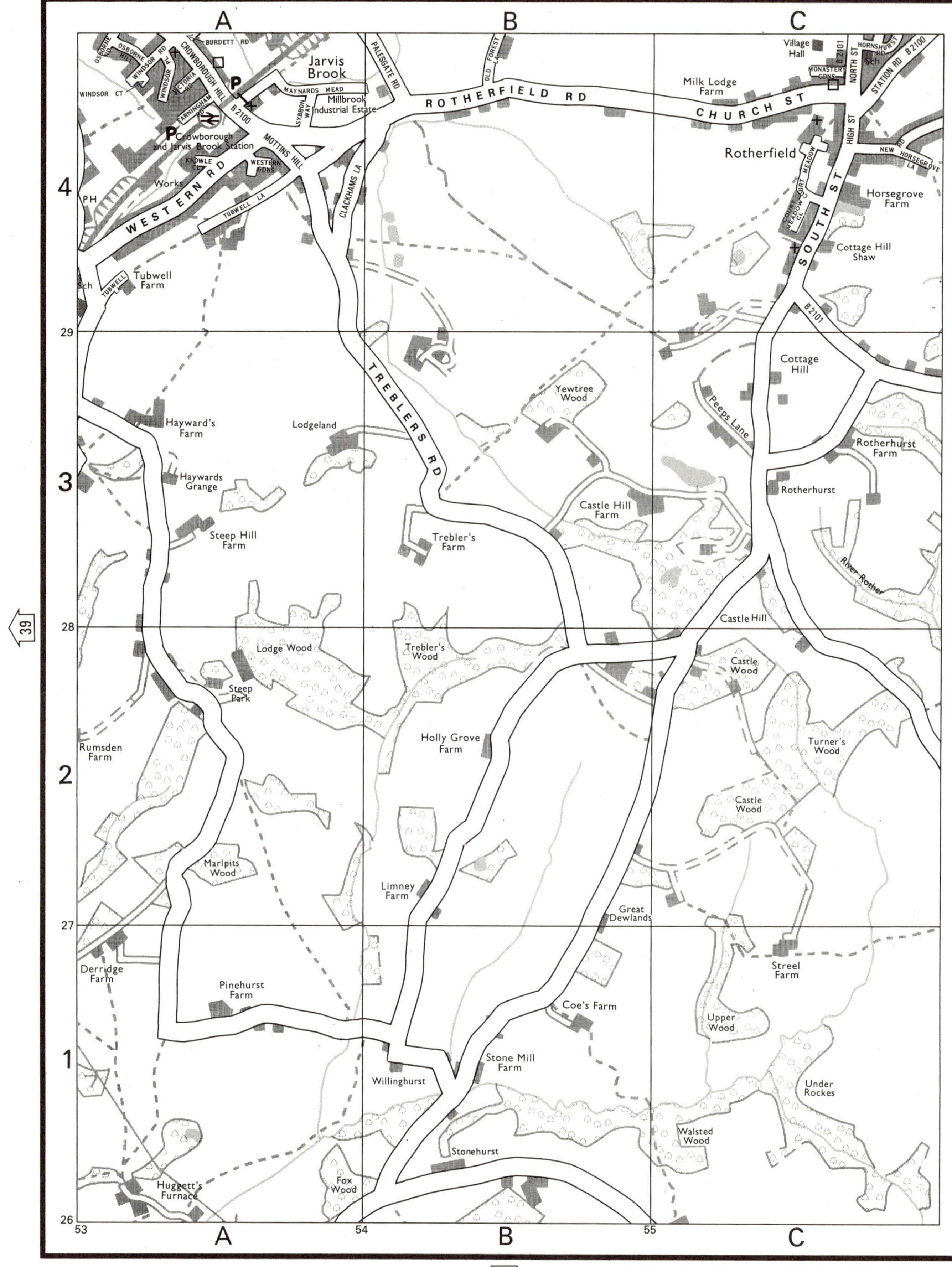

39

59

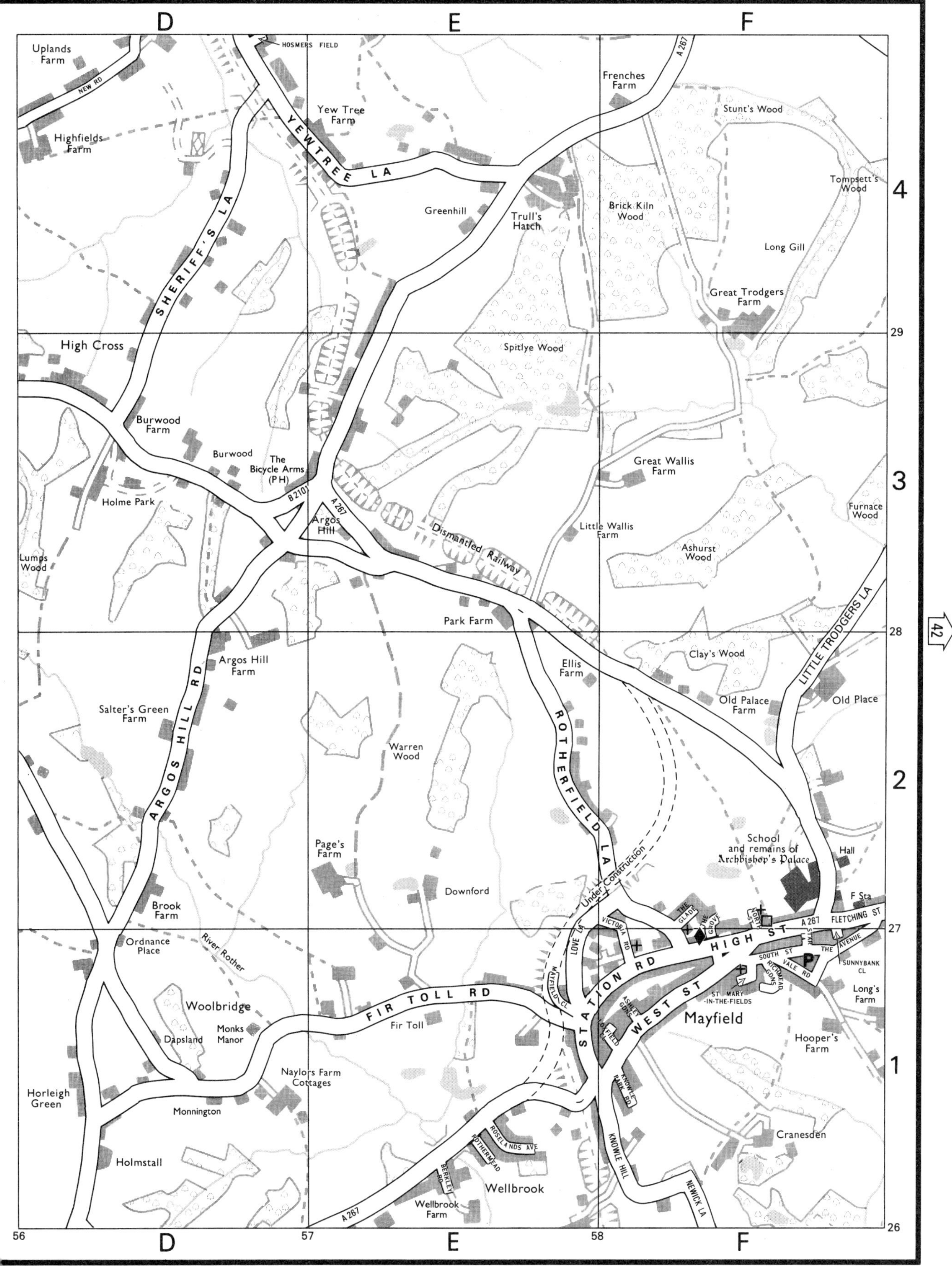
29
60
42
D
E
F
4
3
2
1
29
28
27
26
56
57
58
Uplands Farm
NEW RD
Highfields Farm
HOSMERS FIELD
Yew Tree Farm
YEWTREE LA
Frenches Farm
A 267
Stunt's Wood
Tompsett's Wood
Greenhill
Trull's Hatch
Brick Kiln Wood
Long Gill
SHERIFF'S LA
Great Trodgers Farm
High Cross
Spitlye Wood
Burwood Farm
Burwood
The Bicycle Arms (PH)
B 2101
A 267
Argos Hill
Holme Park
Great Wallis Farm
Furnace Wood
Little Wallis Farm
Dismantled Railway
Ashurst Wood
Lumps Wood
Park Farm
LITTLE TRODGERS LA
Argos Hill Farm
Clay's Wood
Ellis Farm
Old Palace Farm
Old Place
Salter's Green Farm
ROTHERFIELD LA
ARGOS HILL RD
Warren Wood
School and remains of Archbishop's Palace
Hall
Page's Farm
Under Construction
Downford
F Sta
Brook Farm
THE GLADE
THE GROVE
NORTH ST
A 267
FLETCHING ST
Ordnance Place
River Rother
VICTORIA RD
LOVE LA
HIGH ST
STAR LA
THE AVENUE
SOUTH ST
VALE RD
RICHMEAD GDNS
SUNNYBANK CL
STATION RD
MAYFIELD CL
Long's Farm
ST MARY -IN-THE-FIELDS
FIR TOLL RD
Woolbridge
ASHLEY GDNS
WEST ST
Mayfield
Fir Toll
Monks Manor
Dapsland
LOVEFIELD
Hooper's Farm
Naylors Farm Cottages
KNOWLE PARK RD
Horleigh Green
Monnington
Cranesden
ROSELANDS AVE
ROTHERMEAD
BERKLEY RD
KNOWLE HILL
Holmstall
Wellbrook
NEWICK LA
A 267
Wellbrook Farm

30

A
B
C
4
3
2
1
29
28
27
26
59
60
61
Lakestreet Wood
Newlands Farm
Towngate Farm
Tidebrook
Tidebrook Manor Farm
Tidebrook Manor
Wet Wood
Mousehall
Lakestreet Manor
Tidebrook House
Longham Wood
LAKE ST
Harewood Farm
LITTLE TRODGERS LA
Coldharbour Wood
Grubbin's Wood
Chittinghurst
Mayfield College
Rusher's Cross Farm
Rusher's Cross
Cinderhill Wood
Tide Brook
Heronry Wood
Cinderhill Farm
Sharnden
PENNYBRIDGE LA
Pennybridge Farm
Banky Wood
Combe Wood
Coggins Mill
Vicarage Wood
New House Farm
Sandpit Wood
Sharnden Old Manor Farm
Glebe Farm
COGGINS MILL RD
Six Acre Wood
Hole Wood
Rolf's Ghyll
Heron's Folly
ALEXANDRA RD
DUNSTANS CROFT
Merrieweathers
Rolf's Farm
SOUTHMEAD CL
FLETCHING ST
EAST ST
THE WARREN
Luckhurst Crouch Farm
Long's Farm
PICCADILLY LA
Sewage Works
Red House Farm
Hawksden Park Wood
Winters Farm
Old Sandalls
Great Bainden
Park Cottage
FB
Little Bainden Farm
Gillhope Farm
Amber Cottages

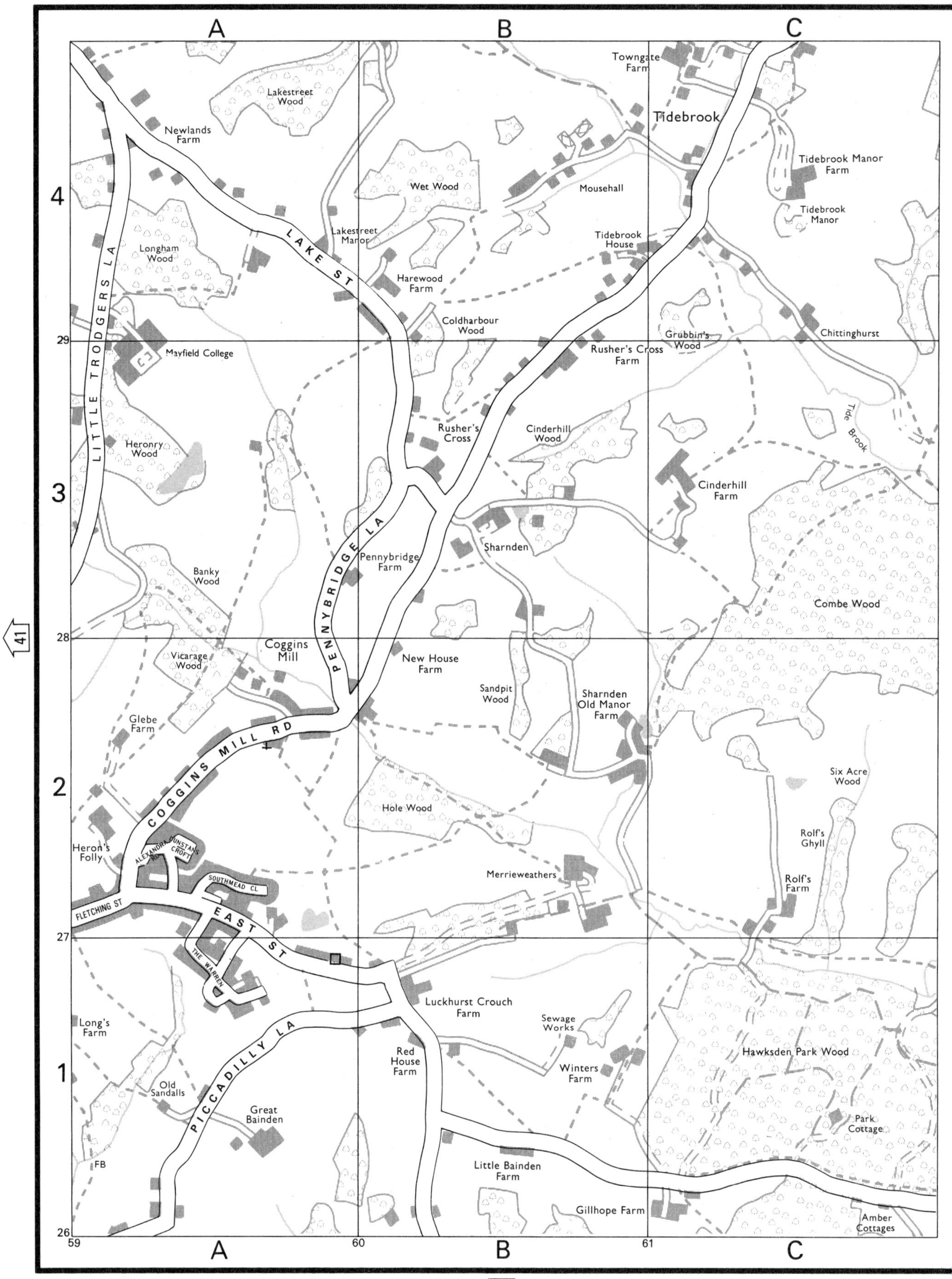

41

61

31

D
E
F
Snape Farm
Broad Shaw
Saxby Shaw
RISEDEN RD
Newland Wood
Scrag Oak
Wenbans
Poultry Farm
Butcher's Wood
Sinden Wood
4
Buttons
CHURCHSETTLE LA
Churchsettle Farm
Lodge Hill Farm
29
Railand Wood
Ashett's Wood
The Wilderness
Combe Manor Farm
3
Combe Farm
Flattenden Farm
Wadhurst Park
Dens Farm
Wadhurst Park Lake
Dens Wood
28
Doozes Gill Wood
Peartree Pit
Batt's Wood
Marchant's Wood
2
Twelve Acre Ghyll
Ten Acre Wood
Clay Wood
Batt's Wood Cottages
Newbridge Wood
27
Hampden Lodge
White's Wood
Golds Farm
Nine Acre Shaw
Bivelham Forge Farm
Hare Holt
1
River Rother
Witherenden Hill
Pound Bridge
Bedlam Wood
Bivelham Forge Bridge
Fair Oak Cottage
Bivelham Farm
Bines Farm
Fair Oak Farm
Waterloo Farm
Great Bines
62
63
64
26
D
E
F

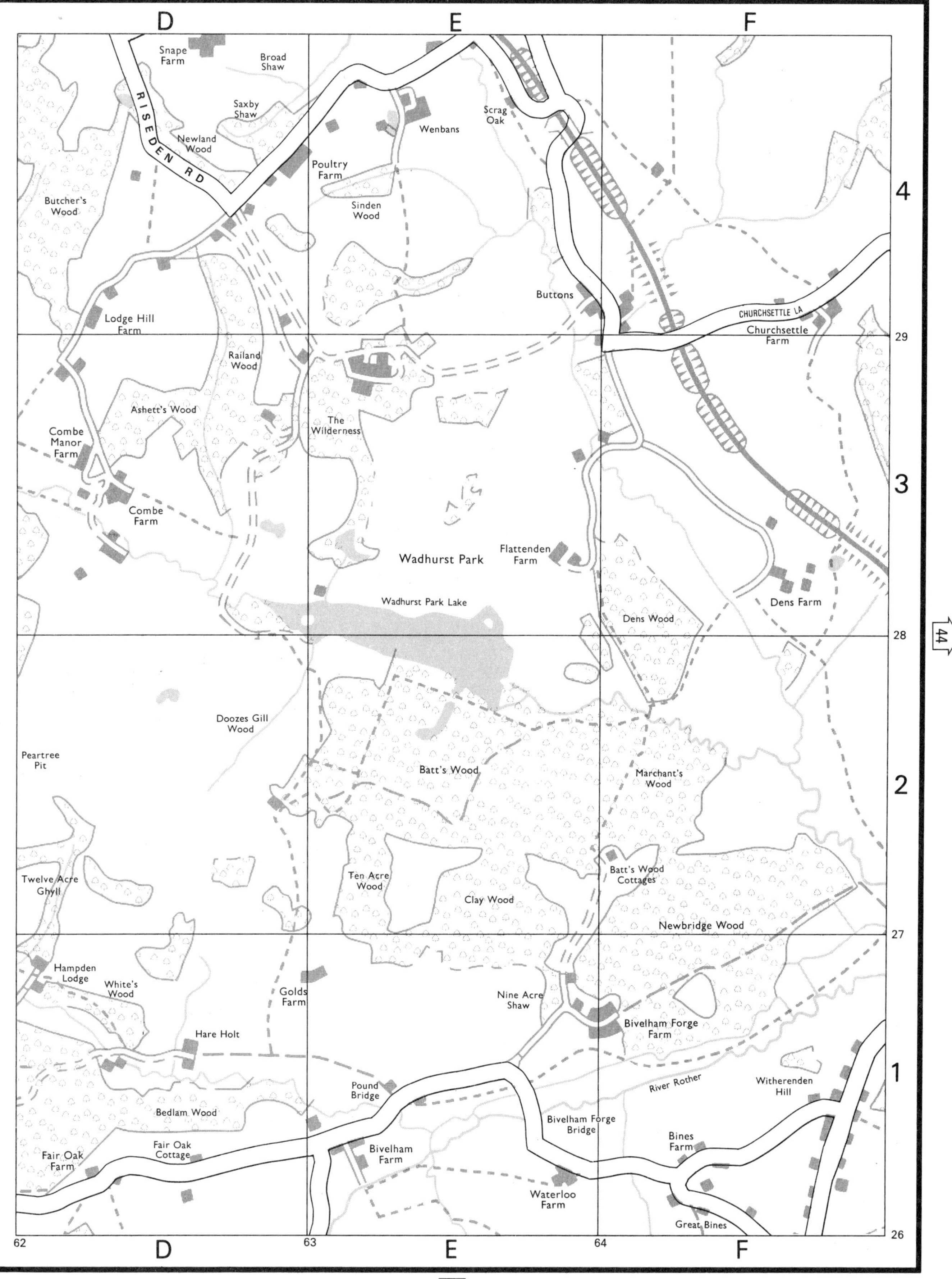

44

62

32

A
B
C
4
3
2
1
29
28
27
26
65
66
67
Slidingfield Wood
Churchsettle La
Stonegate Rd
Bricklehurst Manor
Bricklehurst Farm
Bardown
Bardown Farm
Fords
River Limden
Storrers Farm
Lymden La
Lymden Farm
Mabb's Hill Farm
Mabb's Hill
West Lymden Farm
Streak's Gill
East Lymden
Keeper's Oak Farm
Wedd's Farm
Limden Wood
Maplesden Farm
Maplesden
Coalpit Wood
Cock Farm
The Acorns
Limden Cl
Hall
Cooper's Farm
Stonegate
Sch
New House Farm
Cottenden
Cottenden Farm
Hoadley Wood
Ticehurst Rd
Bearhurst Farm
Peartree Hill
Church Wood Shaws
Battenhurst
The Bridge Inn (PH)
Witherenden Farm
Hammerden
Stonegate Station
Battenhurst Farm
Witherenden Mill
Cock's Wood
Eatonden Manor Farm
Orchard Shaw
Alder Wood
Witherenden Bridge
Upper Collingtons
Junketings
High Wood
Round Wood
River Rother
Woodknowle Farm
Wreckery Bridge

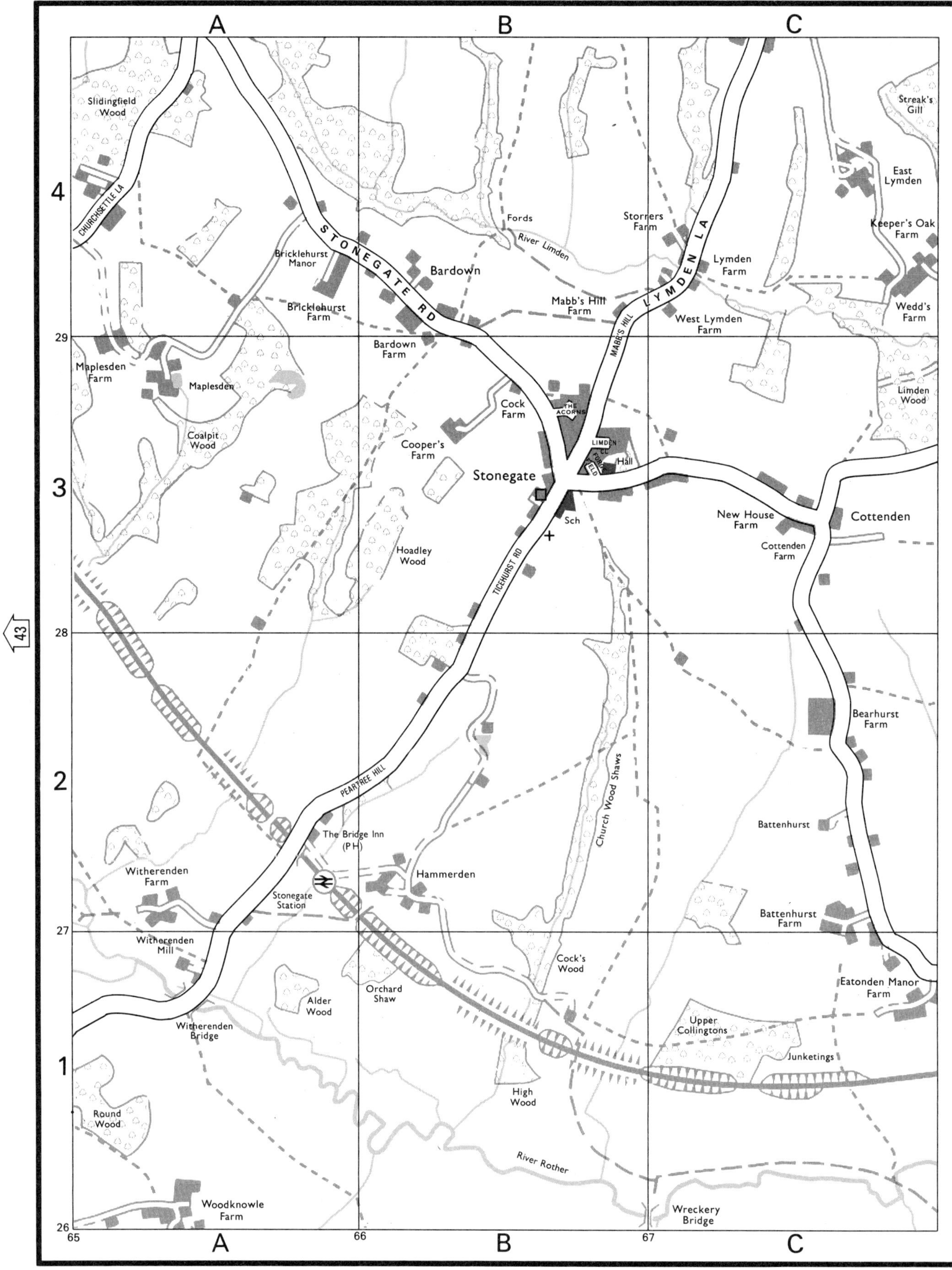

43

63

33

D
E
F
Sch
CHURCH ST
Singehurst Farm
B 2099
Devilsden Wood
Wybarnes
Birchen Wood Farm
Sheepwash Farm
Oakover
Stroodspit Wood
Parsonage Farm
Gibbs Reed Farm
Spring Wood
Bushy Wood
4
WARDSBROOK RD
Pashley Farm
Wardsbrook Farm
29
Pashley Manor
B 2099
Chestnutfield Wood
Combe Wood
Conyburrow Wood
Pashleypits Wood
Myskyns
3
Myskyns Farm
Hillside Farm
River Limden
Quarryfield Wood
Shoyswell Wood
28
Burgham
Kitchingham Farm
Fox Farm
SHEEPSTREET LA
Longdown Wood
Shoyswell Manor
Fleet Wood
2
Shortridge Farm
Foxhole Wood
Old Shoyswell Manor Farm
Shortridge Wood
Hogtrough Wood
Wellfield Shaw
New House Farm
Twenty Acre Wood
27
Shornfield Wood
CHURCH HILL
Turzes Farm
Hammer Dike
FBs
LC
1
Forge House
River Rother
Crowhurst Bridge
SHRUB LA
Crowhurst Bridge Farm
Sweetmeadow Coppice
The Ashes
The Claws
Forge Wood
26
68
69
70
D
E
F

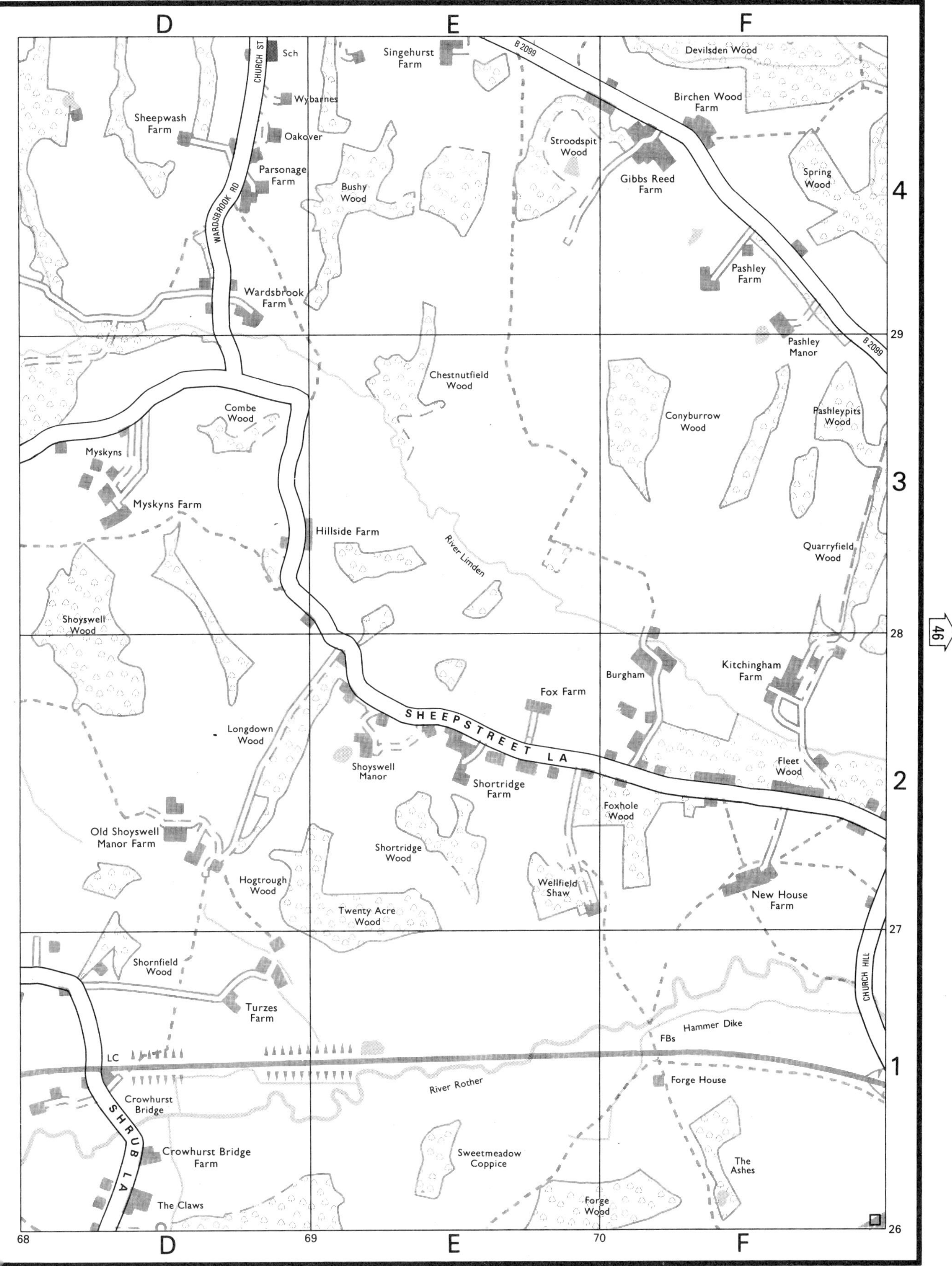

46

64

34

A
B
C
Mumpumps
Roughfield
Roughfield Farm
Hazelden Wood
Brookgate Farm
Brookgate Lane
Cedar Farm
Boundary Farm
Boggy Wood
Delmonden House
Bokes Farm
Boarzell Wood
Cox's Wood
Boarzell
Hanging Shaw
Elphicks
Kent Ditch
Winch's Plantation
Little Boarzell
Swiftsden
B 2099
Three Gates Farm
Cross Keys (PH)
Pook's Wood
Swiftsden Farm
Swanfield Farm
Eight Acre Wood
Peagle Wood
London Barn Farm
Bellhurst Wood
Wet Wood
Stone Cottages
MERRIMENTS LA
A 265
Bellhurst
Cooper's Corner
River Limden
Lodge Farm
The Lodge
Burgh Wood
PH
Hurst Green
Burgham Down Wood
CORONATION GDNS
RIDGEWAY
ACORN WAY
GREAT OAK
VICARAGE WAY
STATION RD
Driftways Farm
FYSIE LA
Fysie Bridge
Shaw Farm
Burgh Hill
LONDON RD
Park Wood
BURGH HILL
Iridge Place
Sch
HAREMERE HILL
CHURCH HILL
Etchingham
FB
Haremere Hall
Home Farm
Grovehill
Etchingham Station
CHURCH LA
LC
Church House Farm
River Rother
Sweethayes Farm
Silver Hill
Silver Hill Farm
HIGH ST
A 265
Hounsell Wood
The White Horse (PH)
A21(T)
Inn
4
3
2
1
29
28
27
26
71
72
73
45

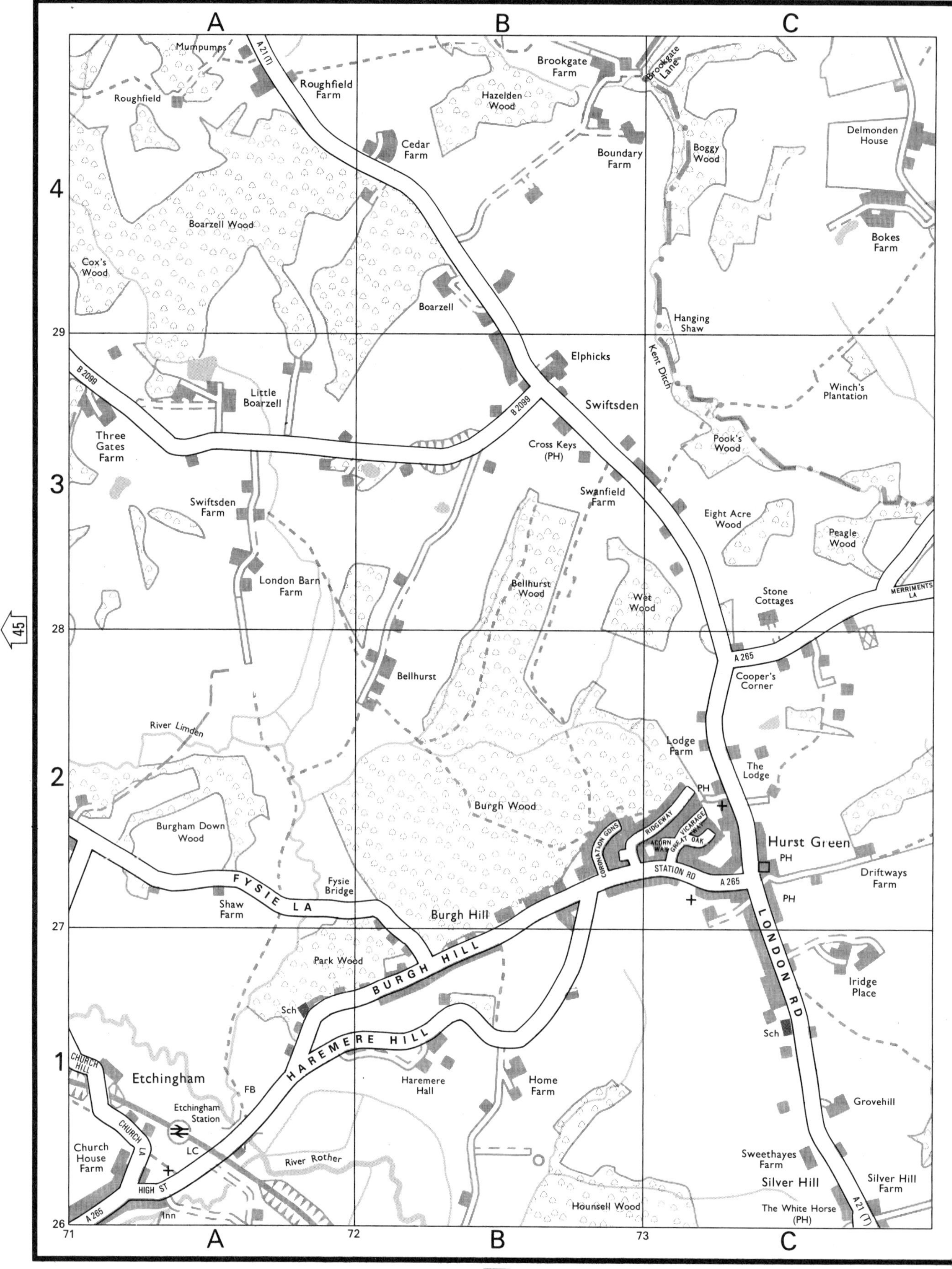

65

not continued, see key diagram

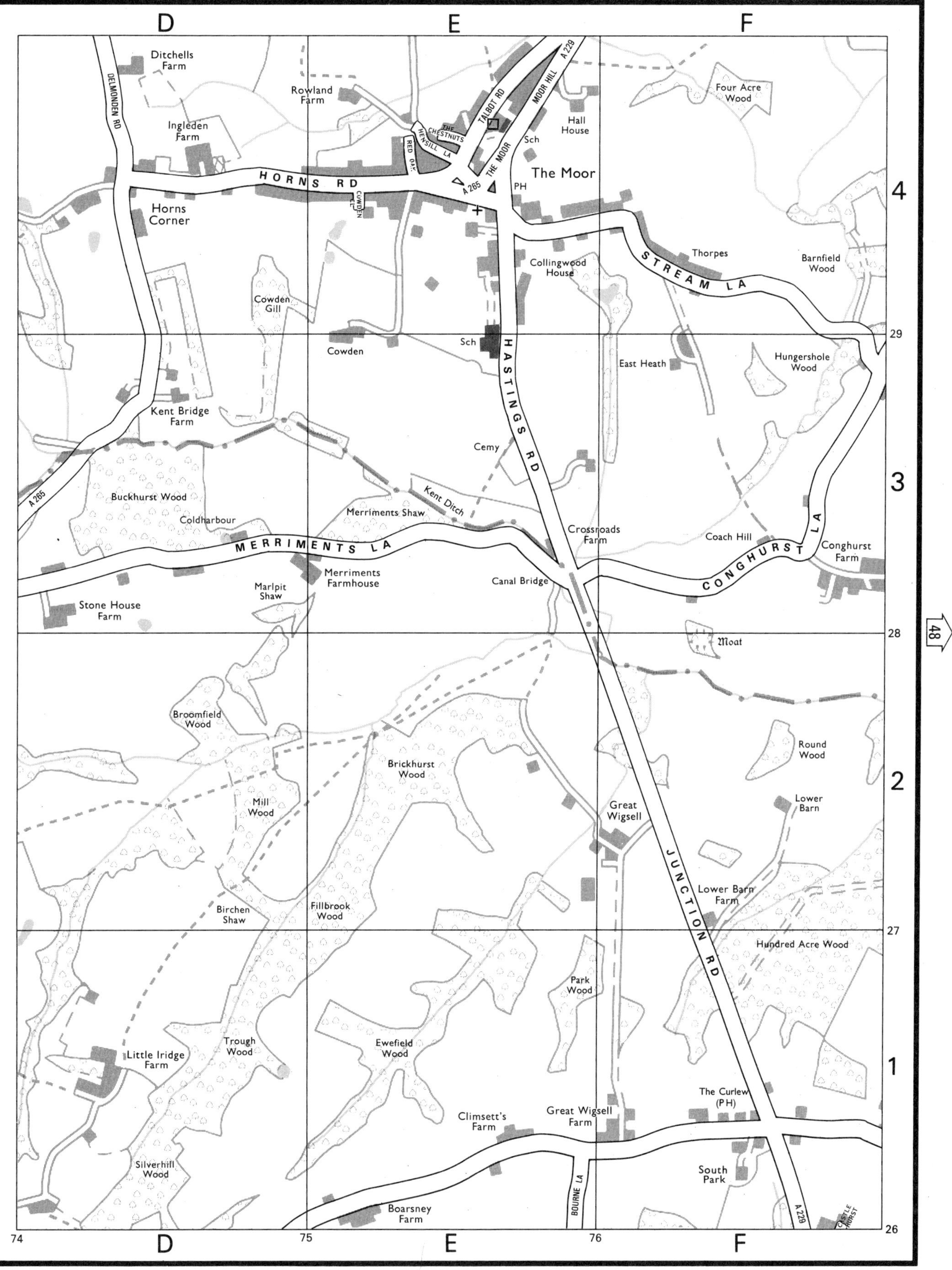

48

not continued, see key diagram

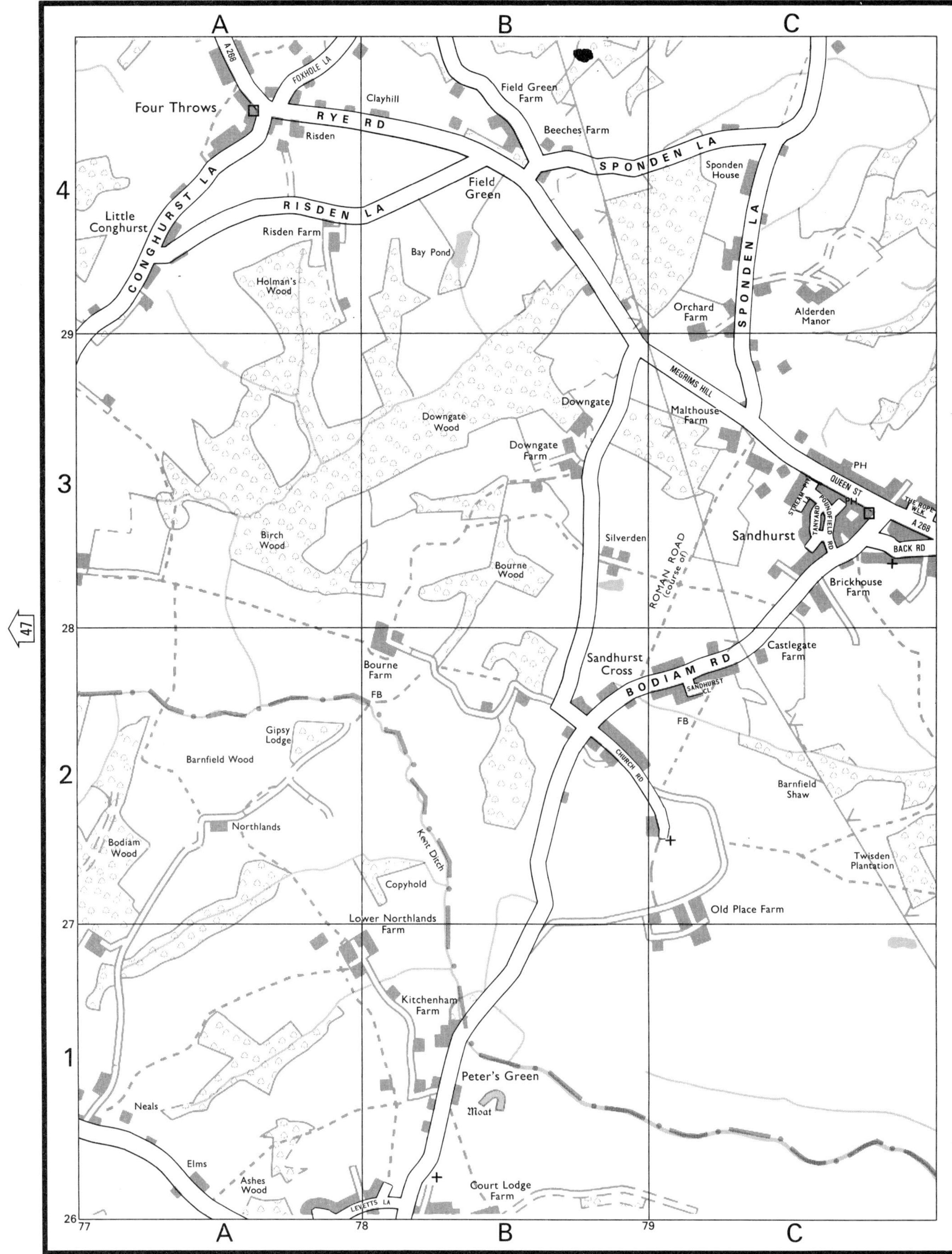

47

67

not continued, see key diagram

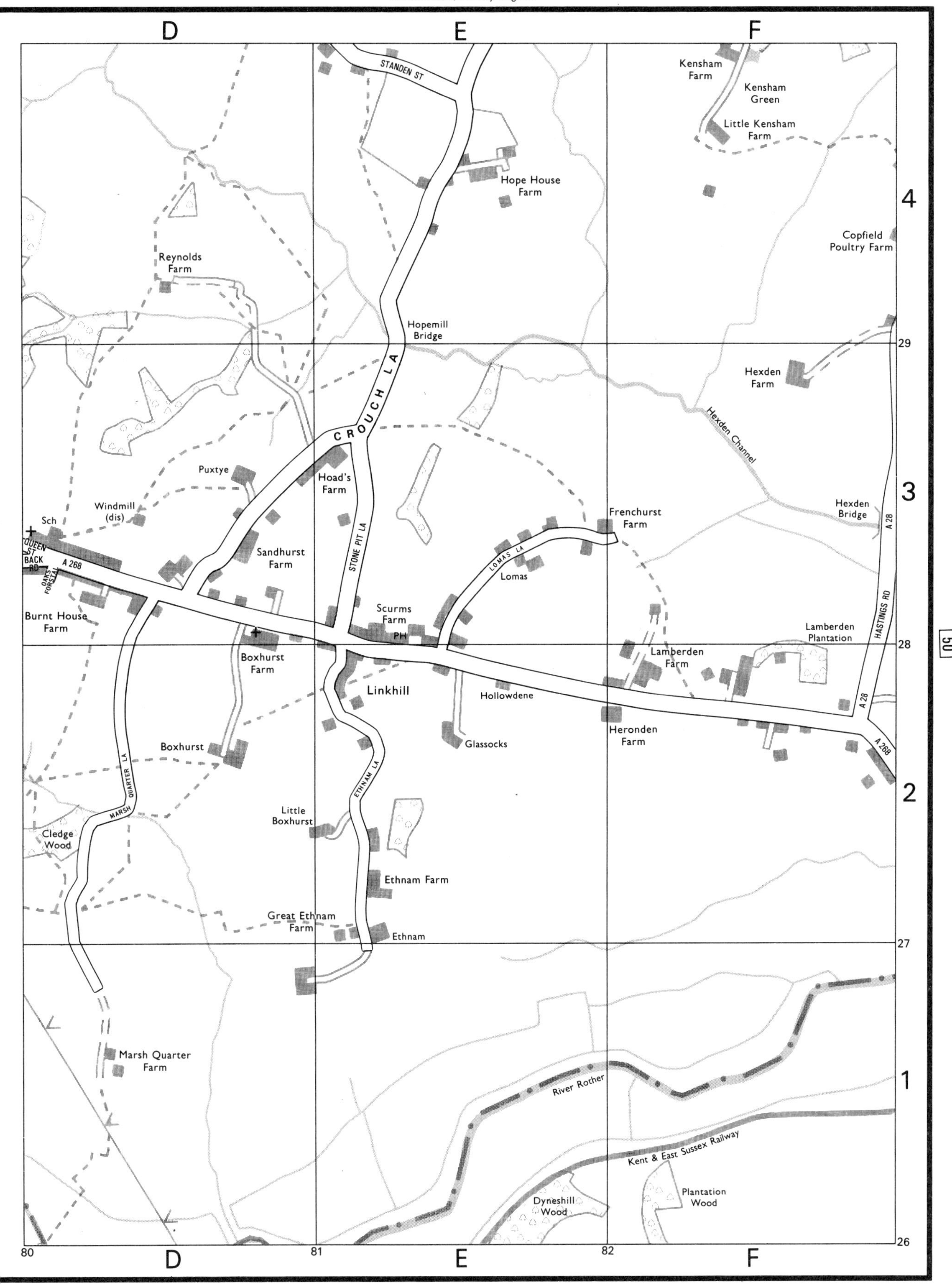

50

68

not continued, see key diagram

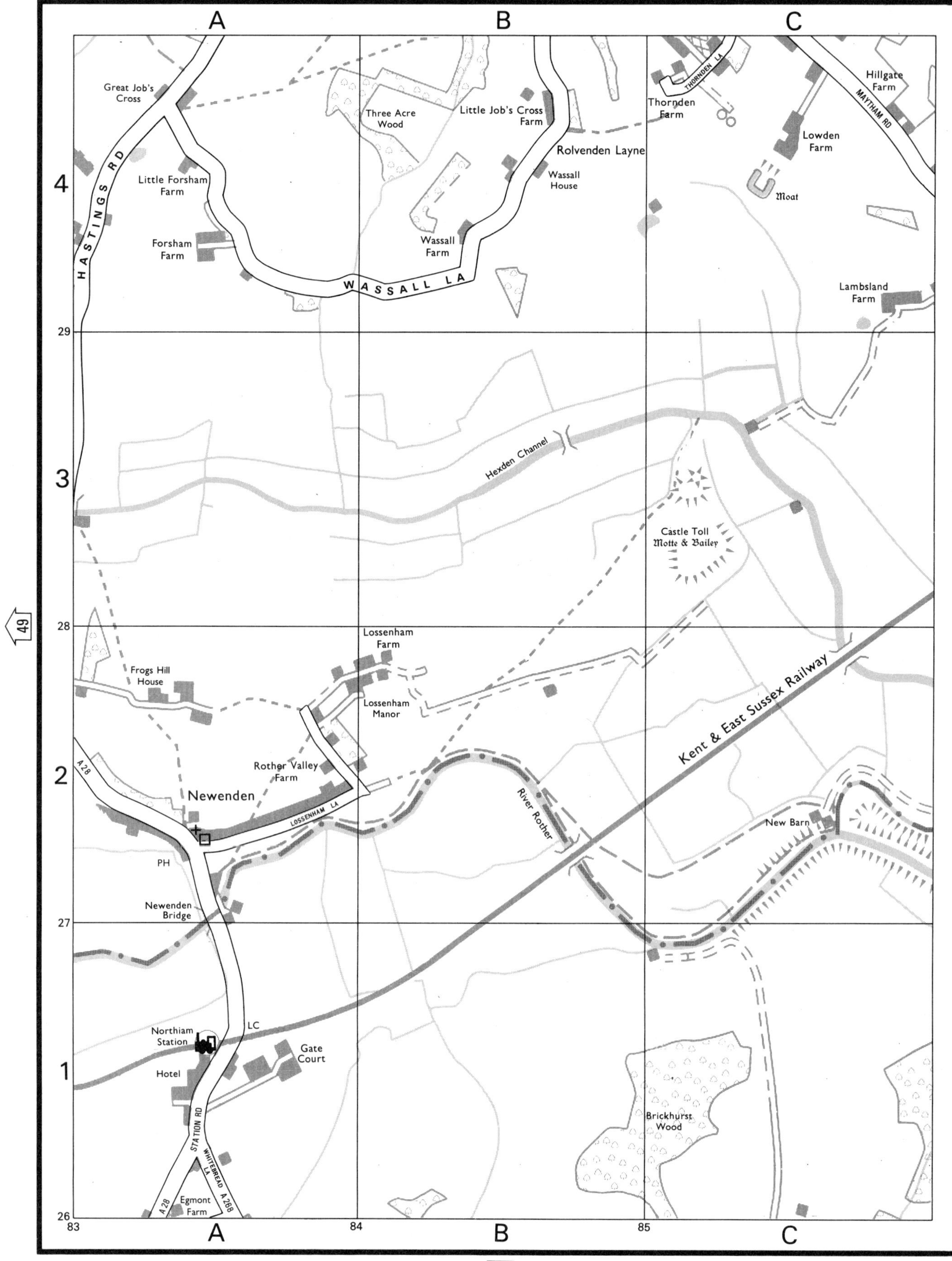

49

69

not continued, see key diagram

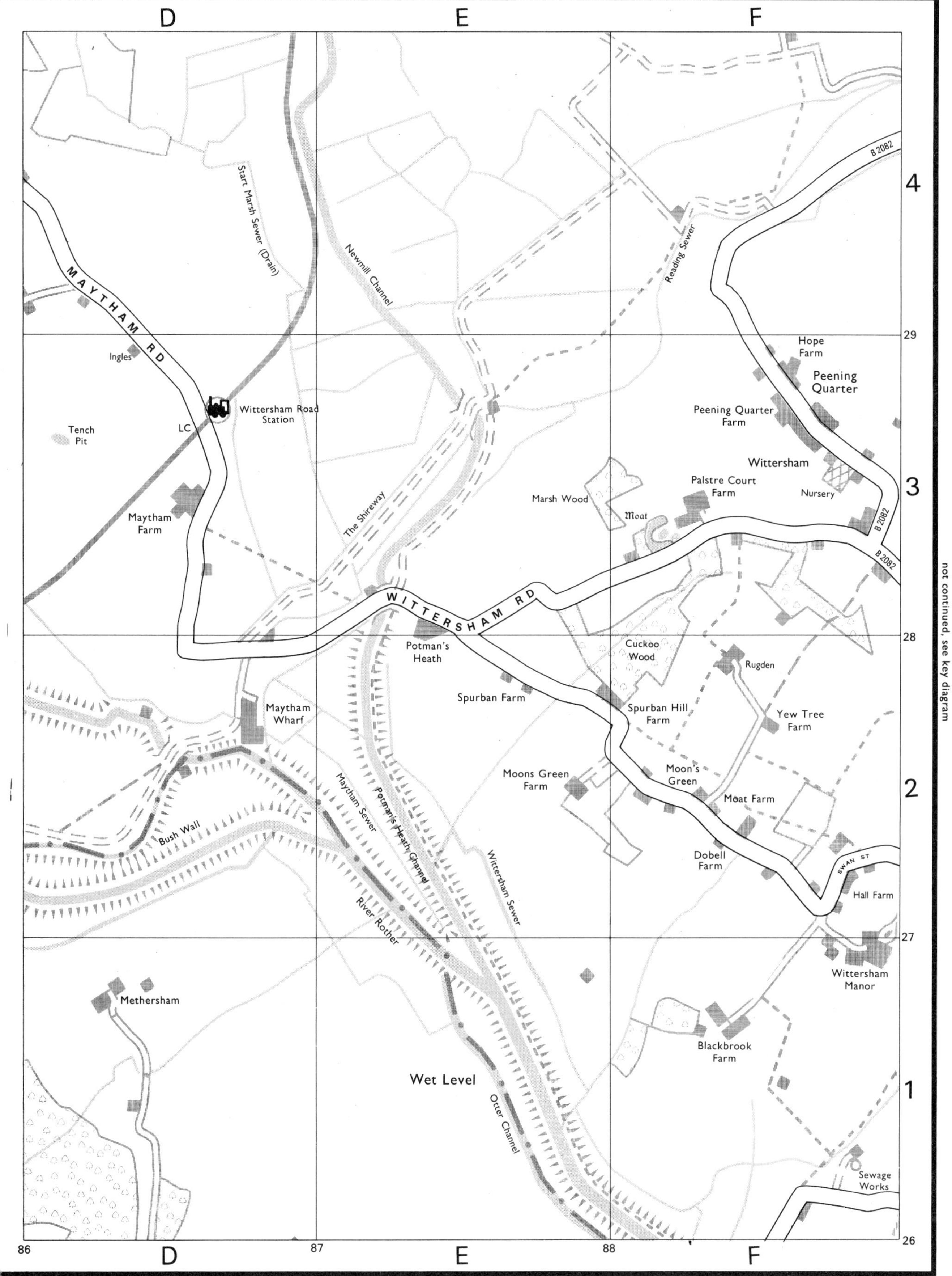

not continued, see key diagram

not continued, see key diagram

not continued, see key diagram

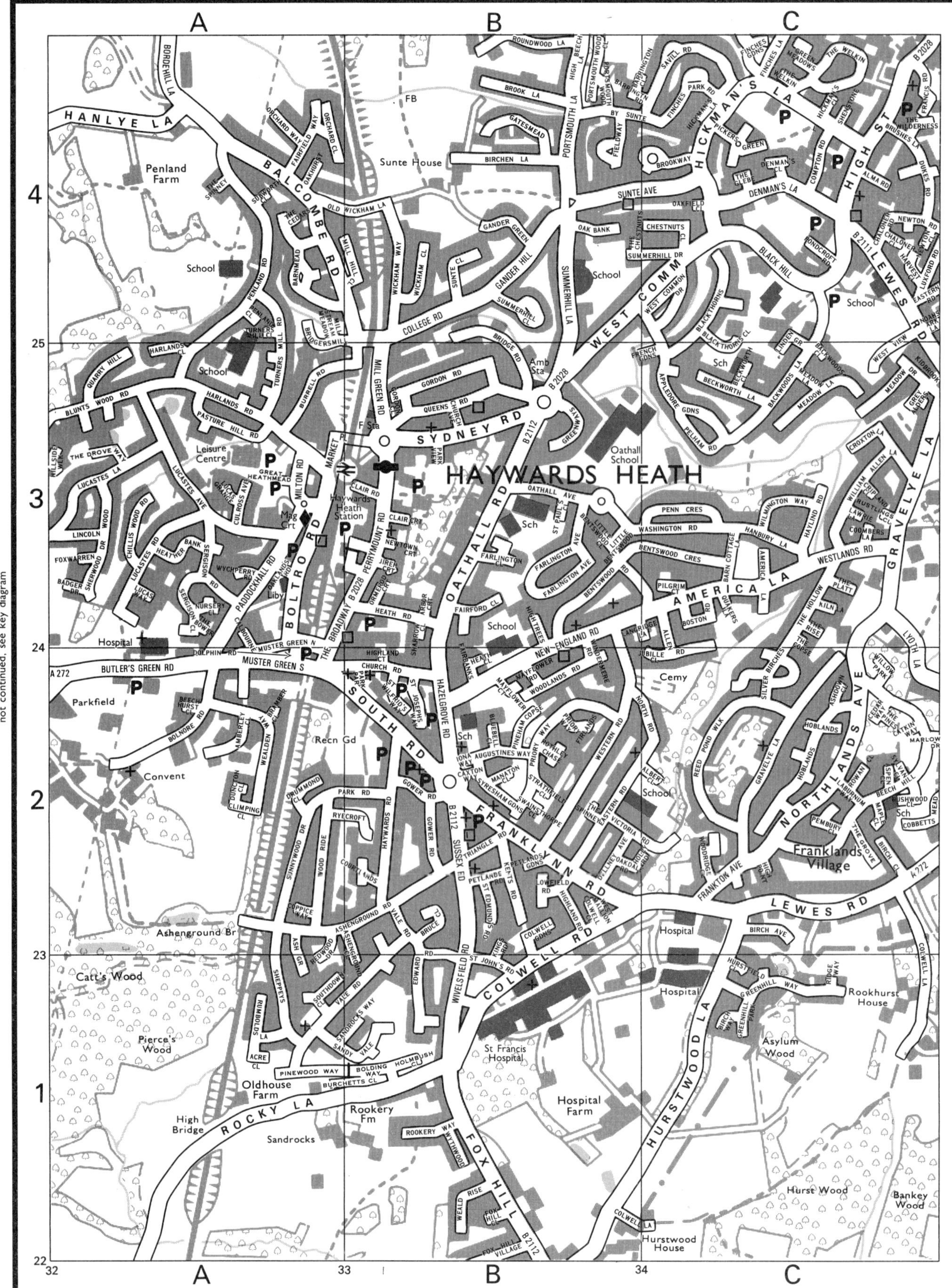

not continued, see key diagram

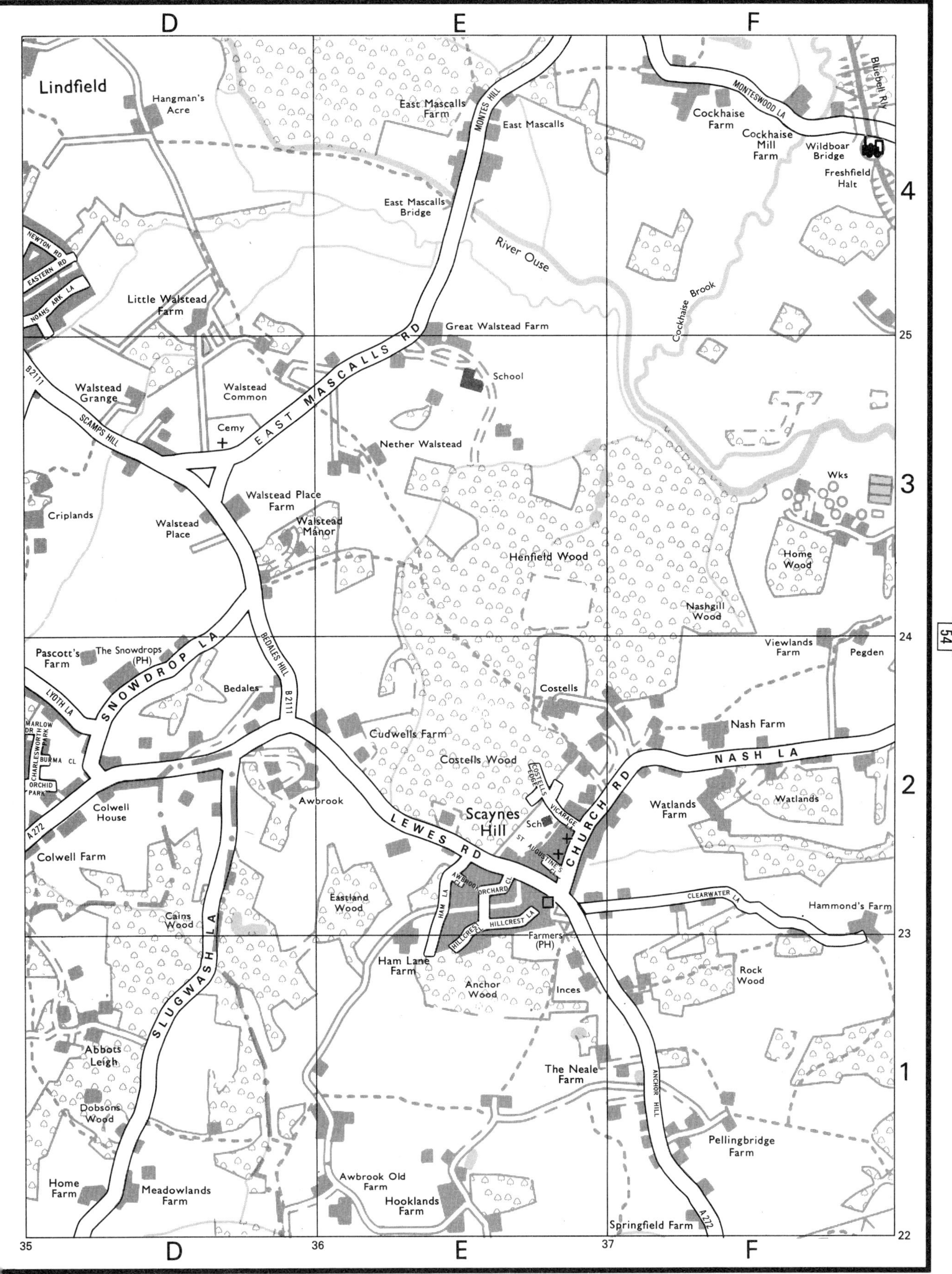

54

76

35

A
B
C
4
3
2
1
25
24
23
22
38
39
40
TREEMANS RD
FRESHFIELD LA
MONTESWOOD LA
Freshfield Crossways
Freshfields
Town Place
Town Place Farm
Town House Farm
Northland Farm
KETCHE'S LA
King's Wood
Slider's Farm
SLIDER'S LA
Glenmore Pig Farm
Sliders
Pound Wood
Pound Farm
SHEFFIELD MILL LA
TANYARD LA
A 275
Circle Wood
Sheffield Green
Round Wood
Bluebell Railway
Ketche's Farm
Coneyborough Wood
Freshfield Mill Farm
River Ouse
Old Canal
Freshfield Bridges
The Sloop Inn
Hamhouse Stud
Hammer Wood
Cole Wood
Coleham Wood
Coleham Farm
Freshfield Place
Wapsbourne Wood
NASH LA
Butterbox Farm
BUTTERBOX LA
Yew Tree Farm
Lye Wood
Sheffield Park Station
Sheffield Bridge
P
Massetts
Hunt's Gate
Wapsbourne Farm
Sennotts Farm
BLACKBROOK LA
Wapsbourne Gate
Blackbrook Bridge
Lindfield Farm
Warr's Wood
Great Wood
Clear Water
Lindfield Wood
Warr's Farm
Lane End Farm
River Farm
Rotherfield Farmhouse
Rotherfield Wood
Lane End Common
WARRS HILL LA
The Plantation
Broadwater House
Muscall's Fm
BANKS RD
Great Noven Farm
Chailey Heritage School & Hospital
REDGILL LA

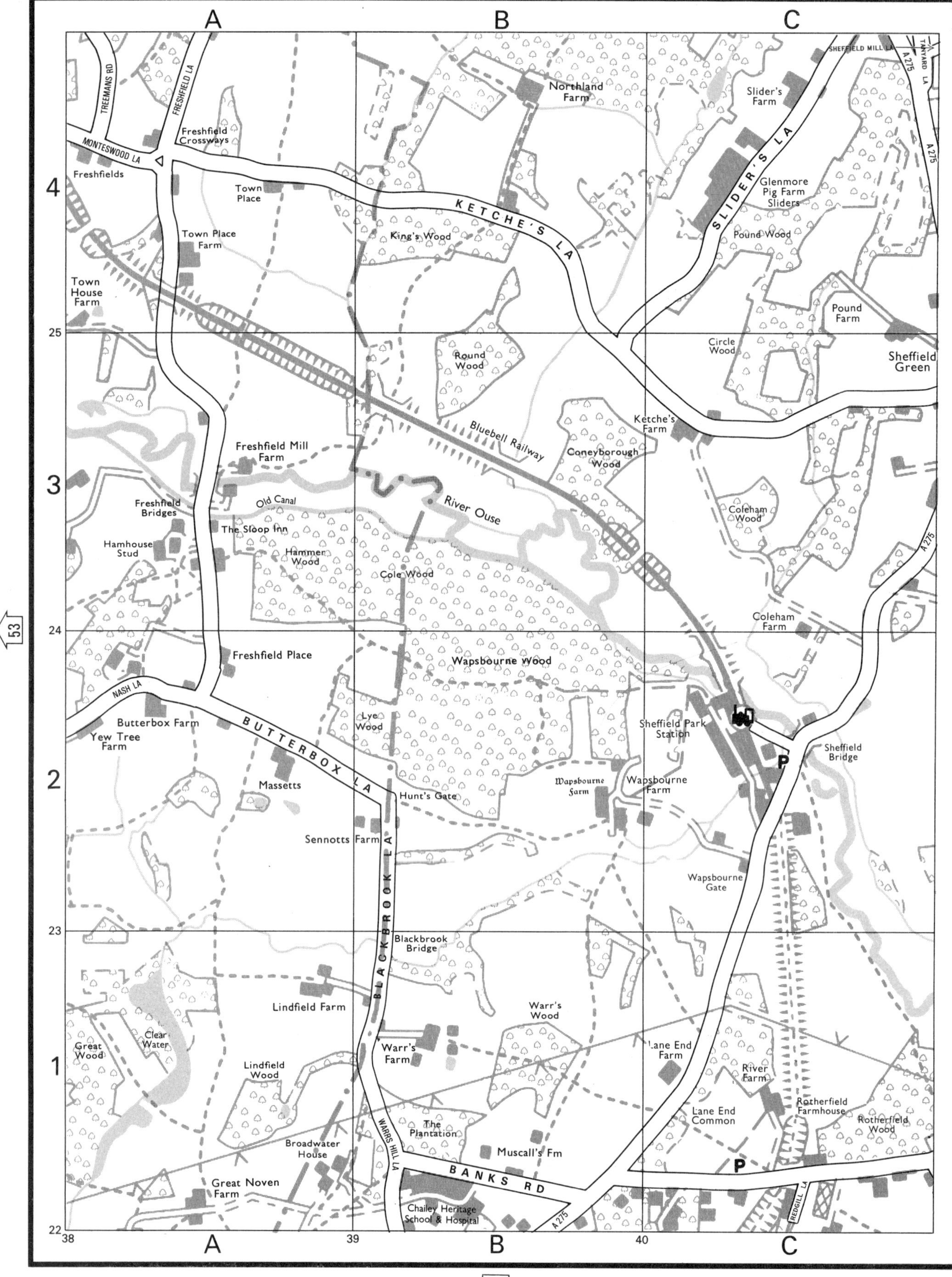

53

77

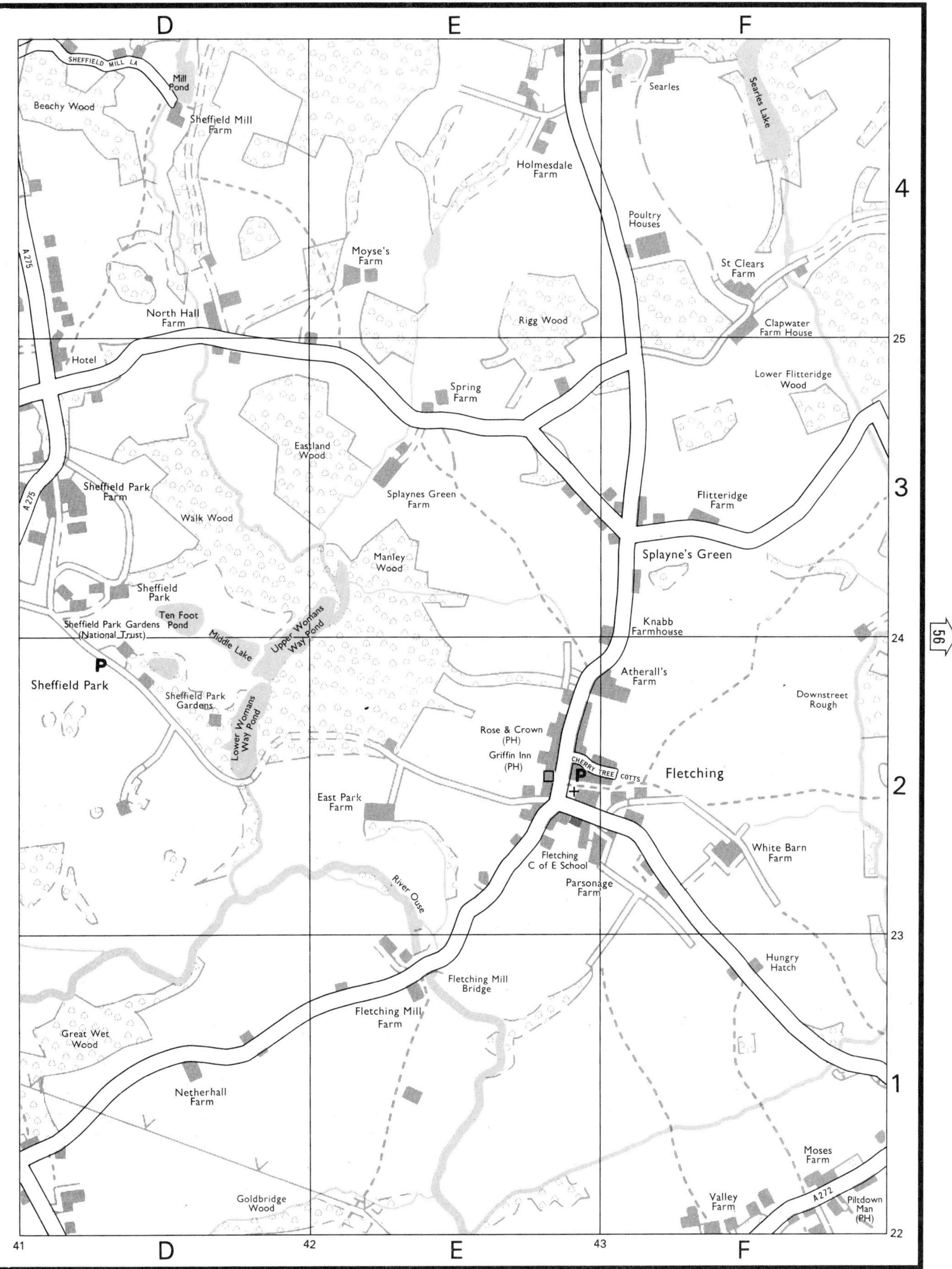
36
D
E
F
SHEFFIELD MILL LA
Mill Pond
Beechy Wood
Sheffield Mill Farm
Searles
Searles Lake
Holmesdale Farm
4
Poultry Houses
A 275
Moyse's Farm
St Clears Farm
North Hall Farm
Rigg Wood
Clapwater Farm House
25
Hotel
Spring Farm
Lower Flitteridge Wood
Eastland Wood
Sheffield Park Farm
Splaynes Green Farm
Flitteridge Farm
3
A 275
Walk Wood
Splayne's Green
Manley Wood
Sheffield Park
Ten Foot Pond
Sheffield Park Gardens (National Trust)
Middle Lake
Upper Womans Way Pond
Knabb Farmhouse
24
56
P
Sheffield Park
Atherall's Farm
Downstreet Rough
Sheffield Park Gardens
Lower Womans Way Pond
Rose & Crown (PH)
Griffin Inn (PH)
CHERRY TREE COTTS
P
Fletching
2
East Park Farm
White Barn Farm
Fletching C of E School
River Ouse
Parsonage Farm
23
Hungry Hatch
Fletching Mill Bridge
Fletching Mill Farm
Great Wet Wood
1
Netherhall Farm
Moses Farm
Goldbridge Wood
Valley Farm
A 272
Piltdown Man (PH)
22
41
42
43
D
E
F
78

37

A
B
C
Courtland Wood
Whitehouse Farm
FORGE LANE COTTS
Rock Wood
PICKETTS LA
OLD FORGE LA
B 2026
Black Ven Farm
Horney Common
Lampool Farm
Kennel Wood
Doma
Woodlands Farm
Marshall's Farm
Kingsfield Farm
Spring Wood
Marshall's Manor
Cave Wood
NURSERY LA
Reeding's Farm
THE DRIVE
Ruttingham Farm
High Wood
TOP DR
MIDDLE DR
Dairy House
Maresfield Park
STRAIGHT HALF MILE
DOWN ST
Little Brown's Wood
THE DRIVE
Down Street
Maresfield
Downstreet Farmhouse
PARKLANDS
BATTS BRIDGE RD
TOBIAN CL
QUEEN'S DR
UNDERHILL
HIGH ST
Pond Bay
THE PADDOCK
Sch
Forge Wood
SCHOOL HILL
Batt's Bridge Stream
Park Farm
Batt's Farm
Fire Brigade HQ
Mill House Farm
ROMAN ROAD (course of)
Mallingdown Farm
Batt's Wood
Sewage Works
A 22
Oak Ferrars Farm
Ruston Wood
Black Down
Park Wood
Pilt Down
Pond Bay
Shortbridge Stream
Shermanreed Wood
Thirty Acre Wood
A 272
Piltdown Pond
Golf Course
Fairhazel Wood
Piltdown
Downlands Farm
4
25
3
24
2
23
1
22
44
45
46

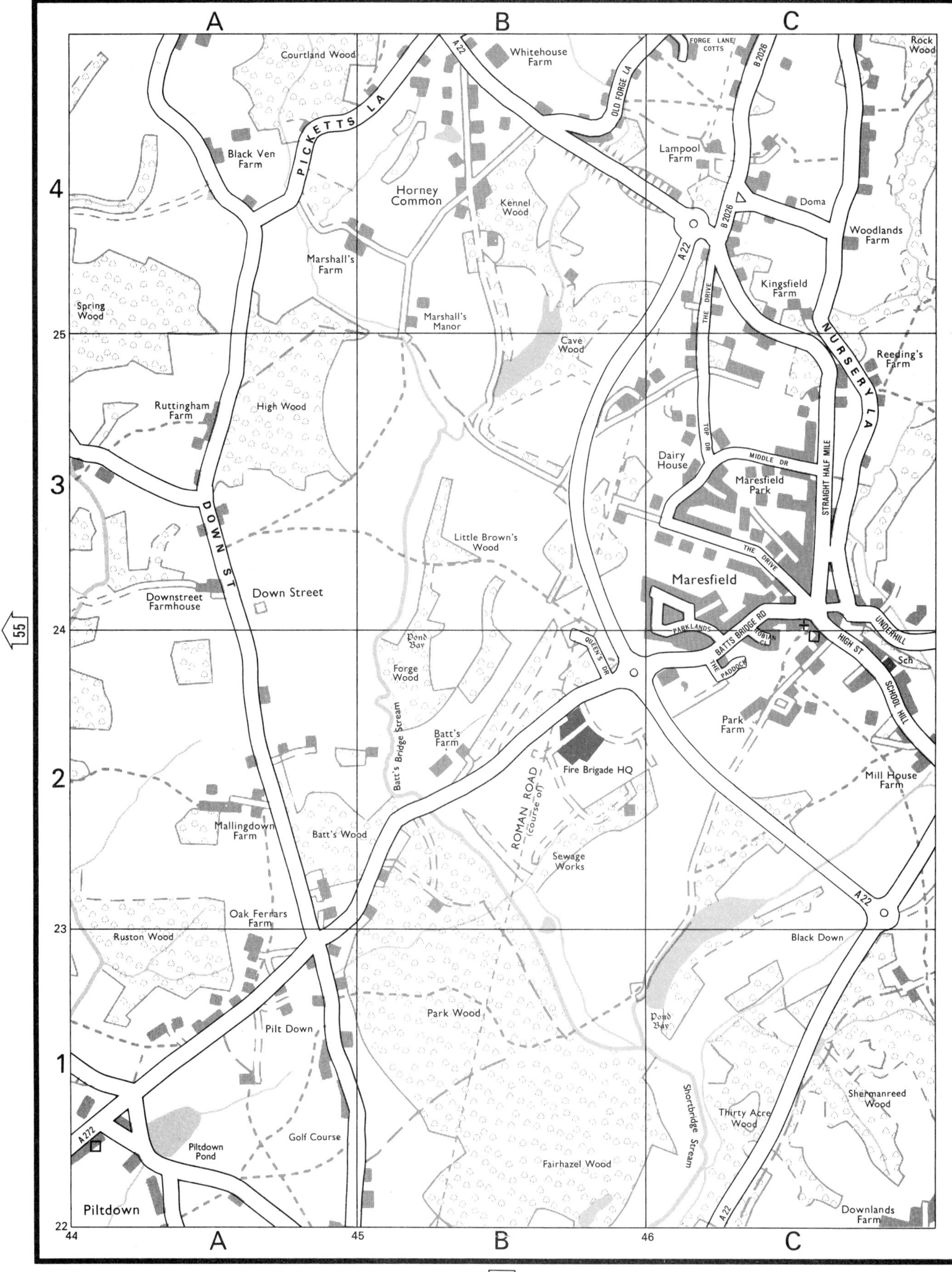

55

79

38

D
E
F
A 26
Hendall Manor Farm
Stonehouse Wood
Hendall Gate Farm
Wood Cottage
Stonehouse
Stonehouse Cottages
Stonehouse Farm
Parkhurst
Maypole Farm
MAYPOLE COTTS
CHERRY GDNS
The Maypole Inn (PH)
Nordens Green
Coxbrook
Tudor Rocks
The Hermitage
ROCKS LA
FOWLY LA
Dallings
Hendall Wood
Bevingford
Factory
Front Wood
New House Farm
Strawberry Hall
Chantlers
Olives Wood
Five Ash Down
The Oast Farm
Pig & Butcher (PH)
Lephams Bridge House
Rectory
HURSTWOOD RD
Parsonage Wood
River Uck
Sewage Works
Harrock House
MILLWOOD LA
MILLWOOD LA
A 272
Lepham's Bridge
Sch
Buxted
White Hart (PH)
Buxted Station
PARK VIEW
CHURCH RD
HIGH ST
A 272
GORDON RD
FRAMFIELD RD
Cooper's Green
Vulcan Farm
Budlett's Common
LONDON RD
White House Farm
Lower Totease Farm
Buxted Park
Deer Park
Buxted Park
Culver Wood
Ringles Cross
Views Wood
Cemy
SNATT'S RD
NEVILL GREEN
WEST VIEW
NEVILL RD
CAMBRIDGE WAY
THE GLEN
CLAREMONT RISE
CAMPBELL CL
LEA LANDS DR
THE DRIVE
VIEWS WOOD PATH
PARKVIEW RD
JEFFREYS WAY
TOWER RIDE
TOWER DENE
PATH DENE
THE DENE
QUEENS
BROWN'S LA
FIRLE GREEN
FAIR LIGHT
ARUN PATH
MICHELHAM RD
CUCKMERE PATH
TOWER RIDE
Manor Park
Tickerage Stream
4
3
2
1
25
24
23
22
47
48
49

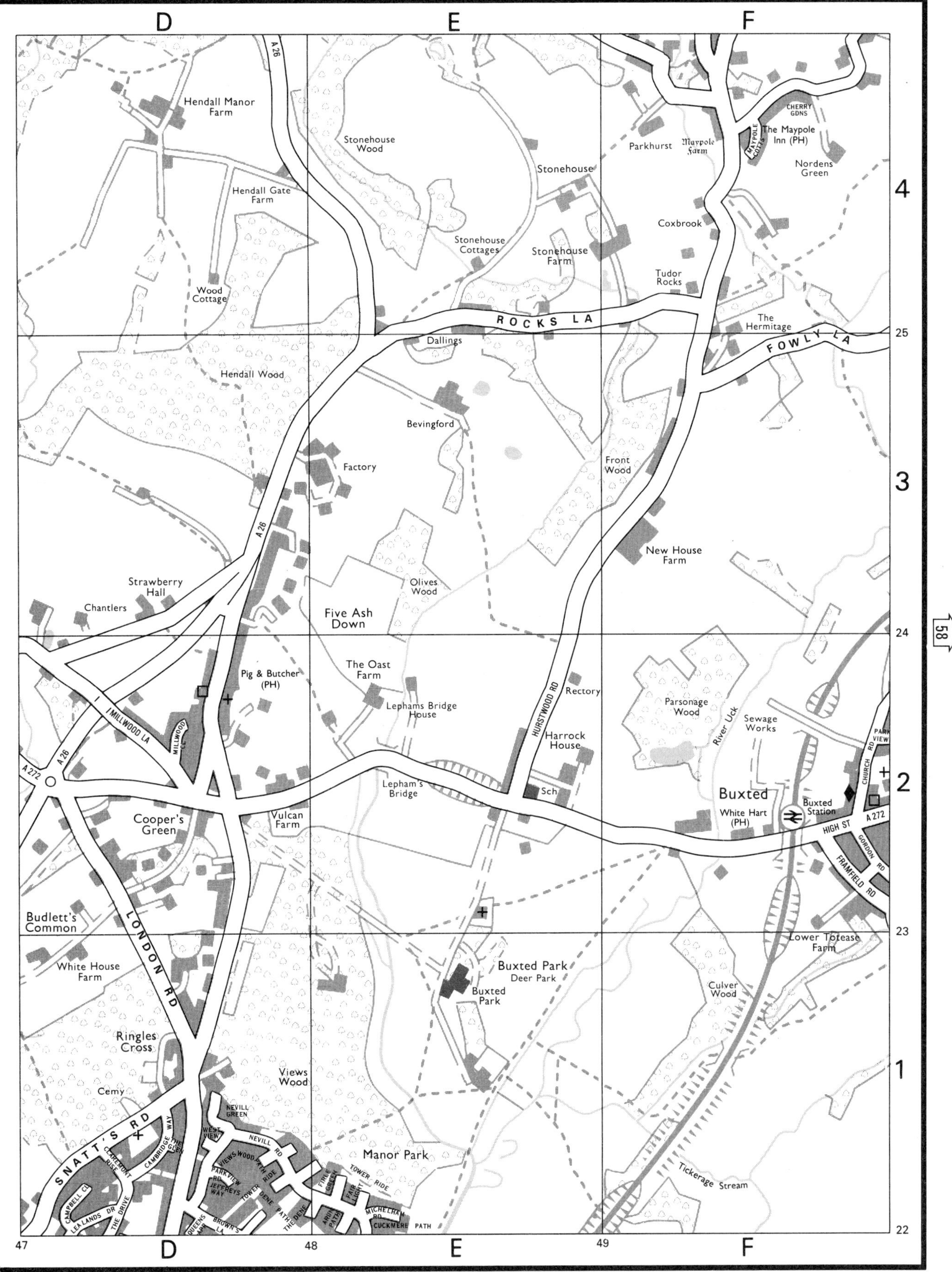

58

80

39

A
B
C
4
3
2
1
25
24
23
22
50
51
52
Buxted Wood
Sleeches
Holders Farm
Hastingford Farm
The Homestead
River Uck
FOWLY LA
Grey's Wood
Stockland Wood
Grove Wood
Greenhurst
Howbourne Farm
Huggett's Farm
Smallberry Hill
Gate House Farm
Stockland Farm
Viaduct
Foxhole Farm
Coes Rough
Stones Rough
HOWBOURNE LA
Tully's Farm
SCHOOL LA
Nashes Farm
Rosemount
BUXTED WOOD LA
CHURCH LA
SPOTTED COW LA
Five Chimneys
Upper Wood
Curtains Hill Farm
A 272
Dolloways Bank Farm
REDBROOK LA
Saxon Court
Waste Farm
CHURCH RD
Littlewood Farm
ST MARYS GARTH
Toll Farm
PARK VIEW
EIGHT BELLS
Lower Wood
Stone's Wood
Pound Green
HIGH ST
Waste Wood
A 272
LIMES LA
BRITTS FARM RD
Popeswood Farm
GORDON RD
Potter's Green
Abbotswood House
Hole Wood
NAN TUCKS LA
Bish Wood
Mascalls Farm
Warren Farm
Hole Farm
Moat
Crowpits
TANYARD COTTS
Lower Lowlands Farm
WILDERNESS LA
Tanyard Farm
Shepherd's Hill
Passalls Farm
POUND LA
Etchingwood

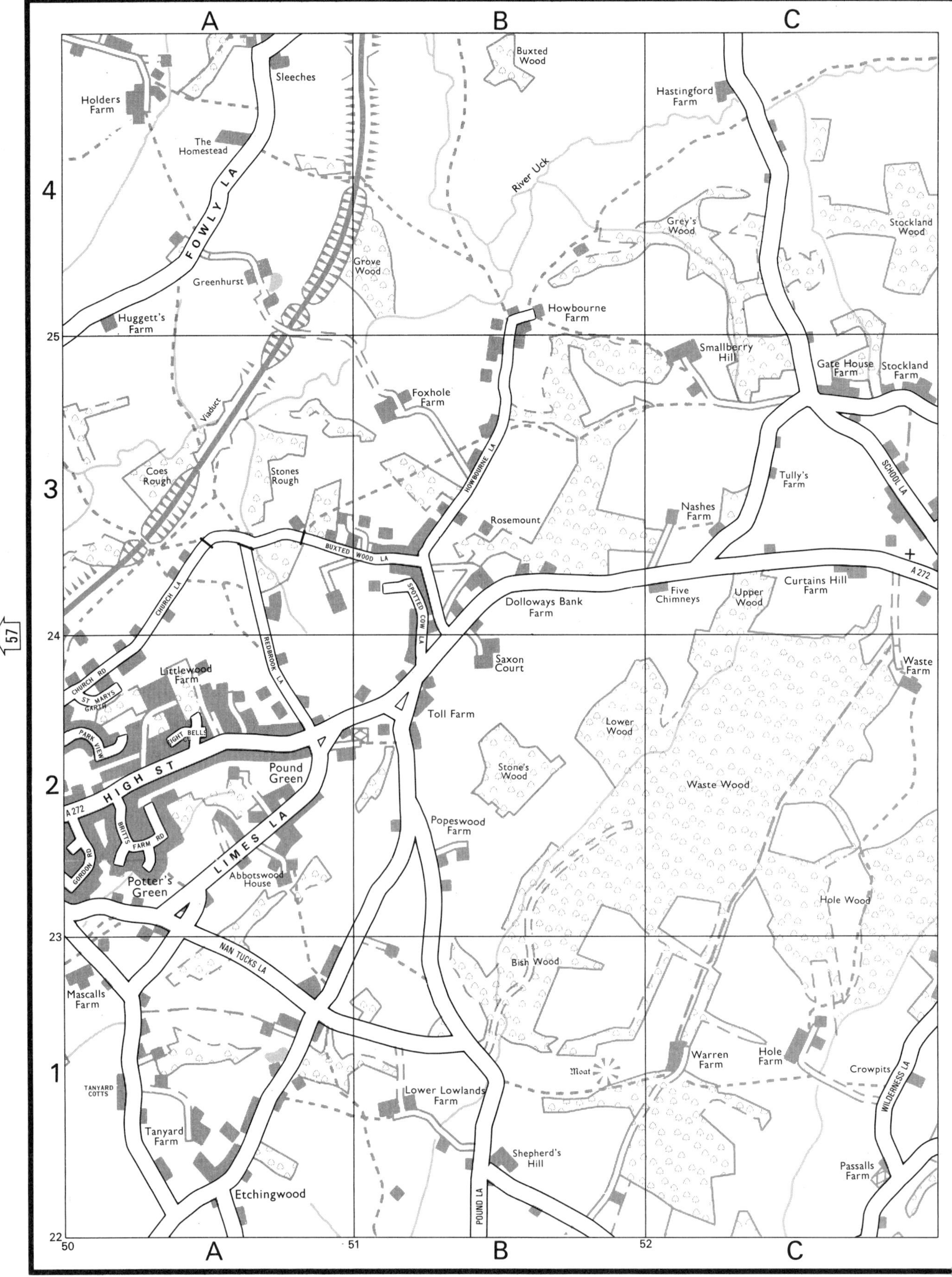

57

81

40

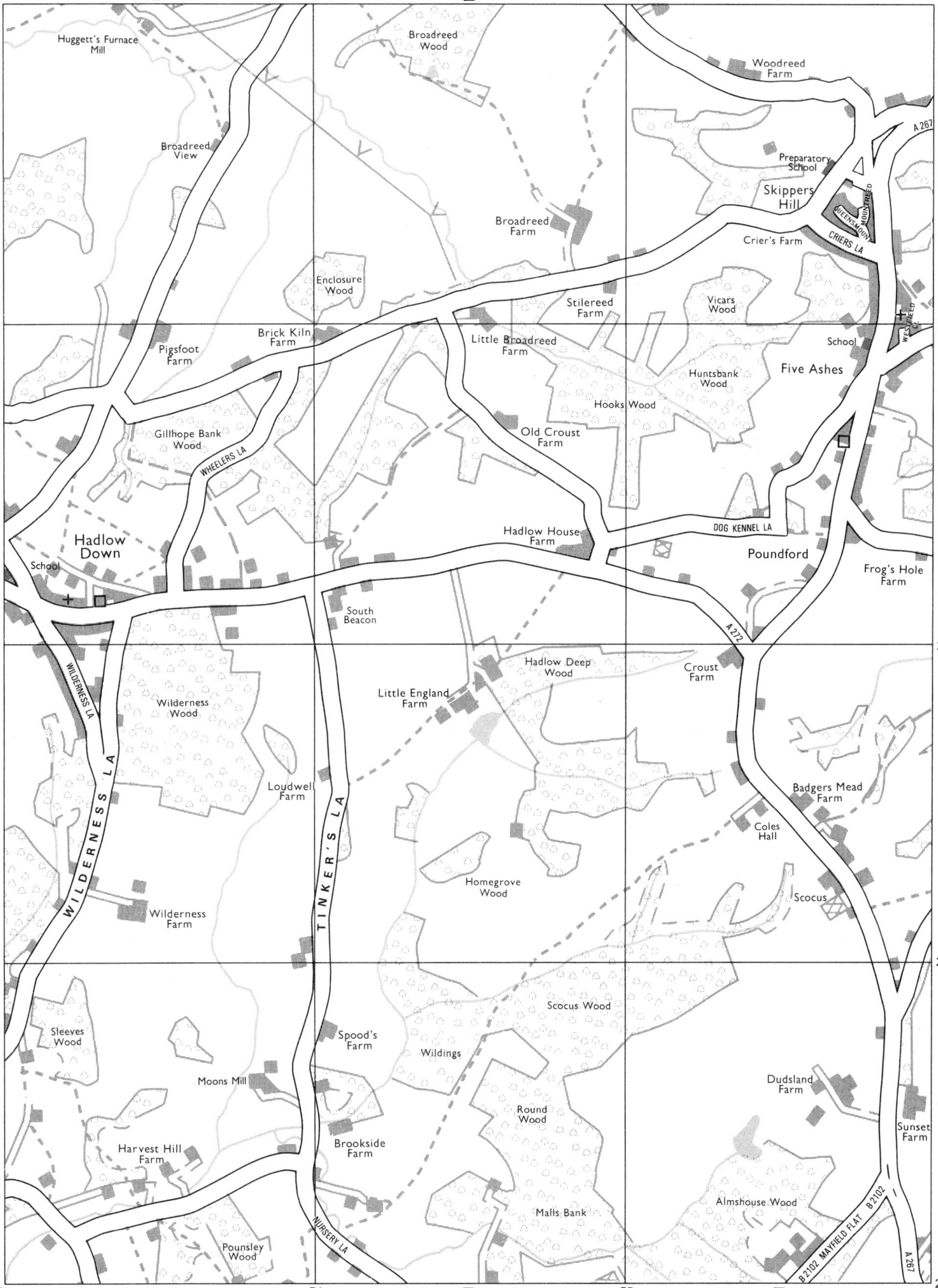

D E F

Huggett's Furnace Mill
Broadreed Wood
Woodreed Farm
A 267
Broadreed View
Preparatory School
Skippers Hill
QUEENSMOUNT
MOUNTREED
Broadreed Farm
Crier's Farm
CRIERS LA
Enclosure Wood
Vicars Wood
Stilereed Farm
WESTFIELD CL
Brick Kiln Farm
Little Broadreed Farm
School
Pigsfoot Farm
Huntsbank Wood
Five Ashes
Hooks Wood
Gillhope Bank Wood
Old Croust Farm
WHEELERS LA
DOG KENNEL LA
Hadlow House Farm
Hadlow Down
Poundford
School
Frog's Hole Farm
South Beacon
A 272
Hadlow Deep Wood
Croust Farm
WILDERNESS LA
Little England Farm
Wilderness Wood
Loudwell Farm
Badgers Mead Farm
Coles Hall
TINKER'S LA
WILDERNESS LA
Homegrove Wood
Scocus
Wilderness Farm
Scocus Wood
Sleeves Wood
Spood's Farm
Wildings
Dudsland Farm
Moons Mill
Round Wood
Sunset Farm
Harvest Hill Farm
Brookside Farm
Almshouse Wood
Malls Bank
B 2102 MAYFIELD FLAT B 2102
NURSERY LA
Pounsley Wood
A 267

4 3 2 1
25 24 23 22
53 54 55

D E F

60

82

41

A
B
C
A 267
Butcher's Cross
Cowden Farm
Crab Wood
Knowle Farm
Cranesden Farm
Clayton's Farm
PICCADILLY LA
Crabtree House
Almonds Wood
Sewage Works
River Rother
NEWICK LA
St Dunstan's Bridge
Meres Farm
Rose Meadow Farm
Allen's Farm
Old Mill Farm
Allen's Wood
Spey House
Oxen's Wood
Harlot's Farm
Northover Farm
St Quentins Farm
Northover
Cumming's Wood
Dismantled Railway
Oaken Wood
Button's Wood
Button's Farm
Herring's Farm
Quarry Wood
Furlong Wood
Isenhurst
Coalend Wood
Hog Coppice
Orchard House
Orchard Farm
Marklye Farm
Rabbit Burrow Down
Crawlsdown Wood
Markly Wood
North Down Wood
MARKLYE LA
Saw Mill
Dunly Wood
Tilsmore Wood
4
3
2
1
25
24
23
22
56
57
58

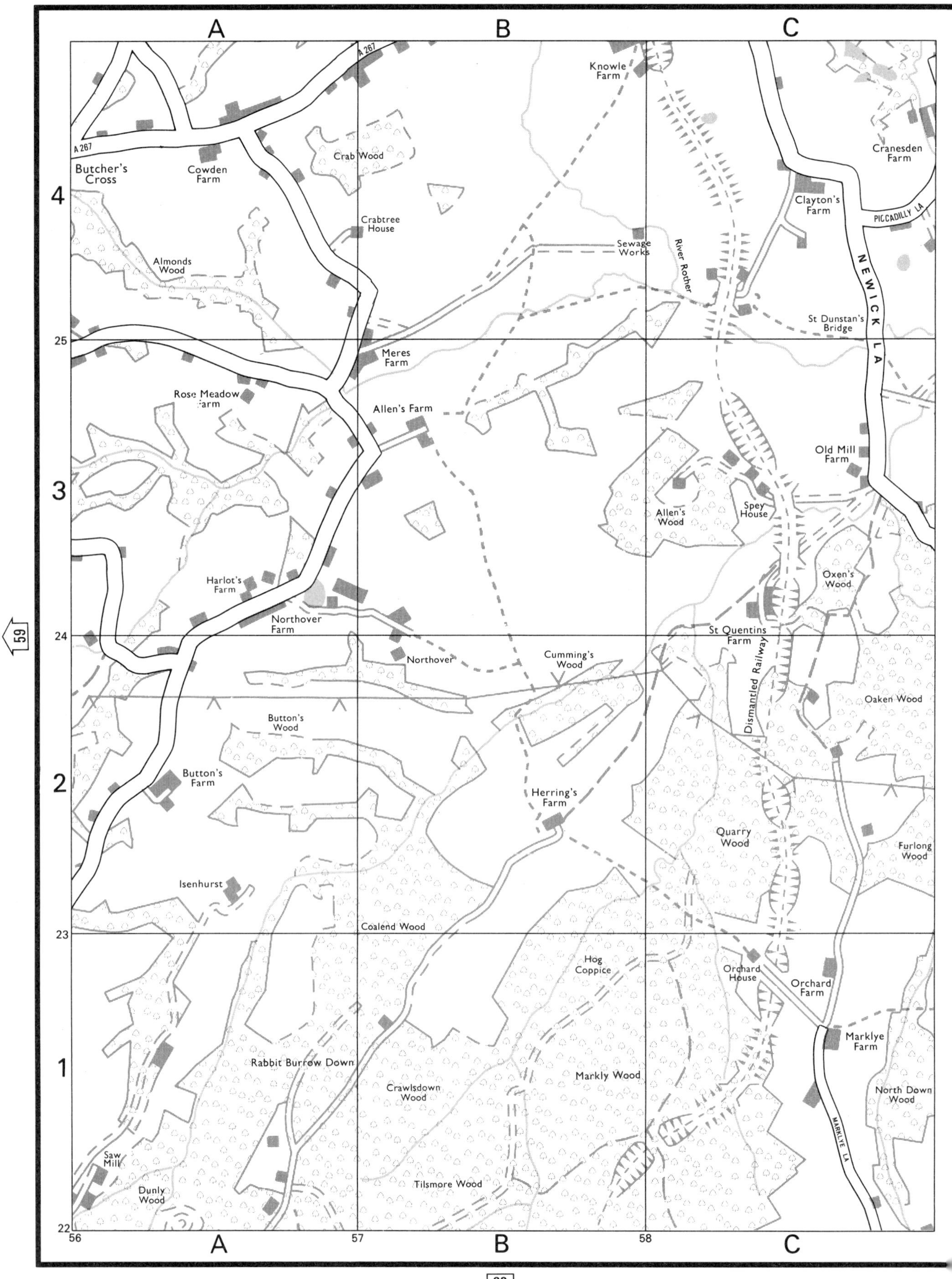

59

83

42

D
E
F
Bainden Wood
Clayland Shaw
Cookham Shaw
Great Calem Wood
Little Calem Wood
Round Wood
PICCADILLY LA
4
Scotsford Bridge
River Rother
Moat Farm
Great Pigstrood Farm
25
Moat Mill Farm
Scotsford Farm
Great Stonehurst Farm
Little Stonehurst Farm
Little Pigstrood
3
Nursements Farm
Shovels Wood
Little Furnace Wood
Bungehurst Farm
Broomhurst Farm
SCOTSFORD RD
Pottens Mill Farm
Wet Wood
Broomham
POTTENS MILL LA
Great Furnace Wood
24
Rock Farm
Pheasantry Farm
Coneyburrow Wood
Street End Farm
Baltham Wood
2
Coneyburrow Wood
NEWICK LA
Barklye Farm
Newick Wood
Prior's Farm
Holme Chase
Black Sand Wood
Olives Farm
23
Swife Wood
Cedar Swiffe Farm
Swiffes Farm
SWIFE LA
A 265
Bodell's Farm
Newick Farm
Wish End Farm
Hill Farm
Silver Birches
Sch
1
Black Wood
Tottingworth Park
STREET END LA
BROAD VIEW
GORSE HILL
HIGHFIELD RD
BROAD HILL CL
Broad Oak
Oak Hall School
UPLANDS PARK
MAYVIEW CL
BURWASH RD
HALLEY RD
Westerns Farm
IDEN'S LA
A 265
Hall
22
59
60
61
D
E
F

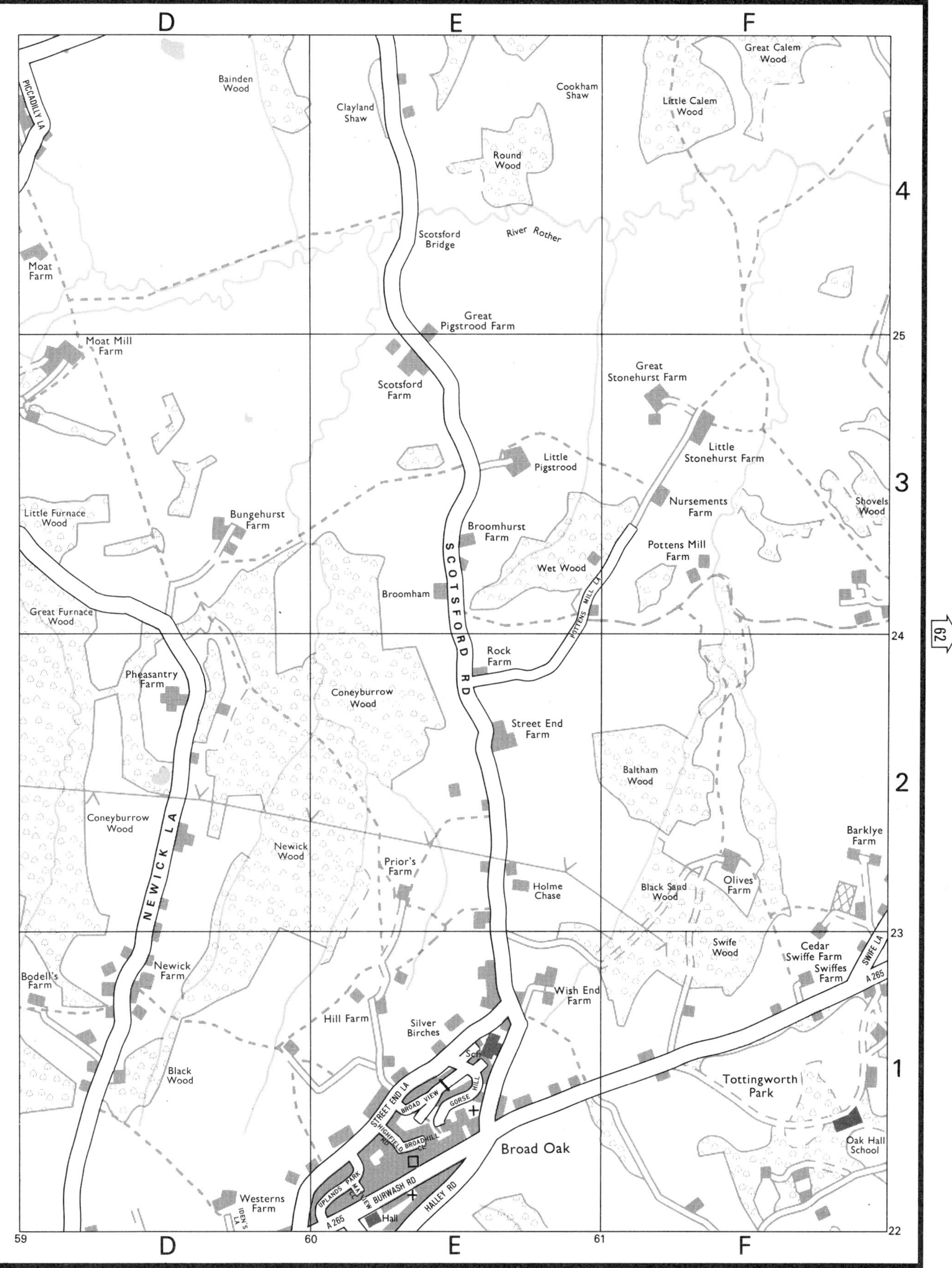

62

84

43

A
B
C
Turk's Bridge
Inn
Froghole Farm
Long Wood
4
Holmshurst
Ten Acre Wood
Holmshurst Manor Farm
Turk's Farm
Great Broadhurst Farm
Oaken Wood
Little Broadhurst Farm
Brockwood
25
Pont's Farm
Coxdown Farm
Holming Wood
Long Wood
Lakedown Farm
3
Great Bigknowle Farm
Ashen Wood
Limberlost Farm
Marlpit Shaw
Yokeing Close Wood
Broadhurst
Climshurst Wood
Knowle Farm
Schemes Wood
Blackdown Wood
Round Wood
Corner Farm
24
Foxhole Wood
Oakdown Farm
Bunker's Hill Farm
Bough Wood
Goodsoal Farm
Paine's Corner
Foxhole Farm
2
Little Park Farm
Doel Farm
Burwash Common
Burwash Weald
SWIFE LA
VICARAGE RD
Mill House Farm
Burralands
VICARAGE LA
WESTDOWN LA
A 265
FOOT'S LA
Holban's Farm
23
Luck Farm
Foot's Farm
A 265
Home Farm
Kingsdown Farm
Bohemia Farm
Spinney Farm House
Park Hill
1
Poundsford
Poundsford Farm
Parkhill Farm
Milkhurst Wood
Applebrook Farm
Stonehole Wood
Westdown Farm
Limekiln Wood
22
62
63
64

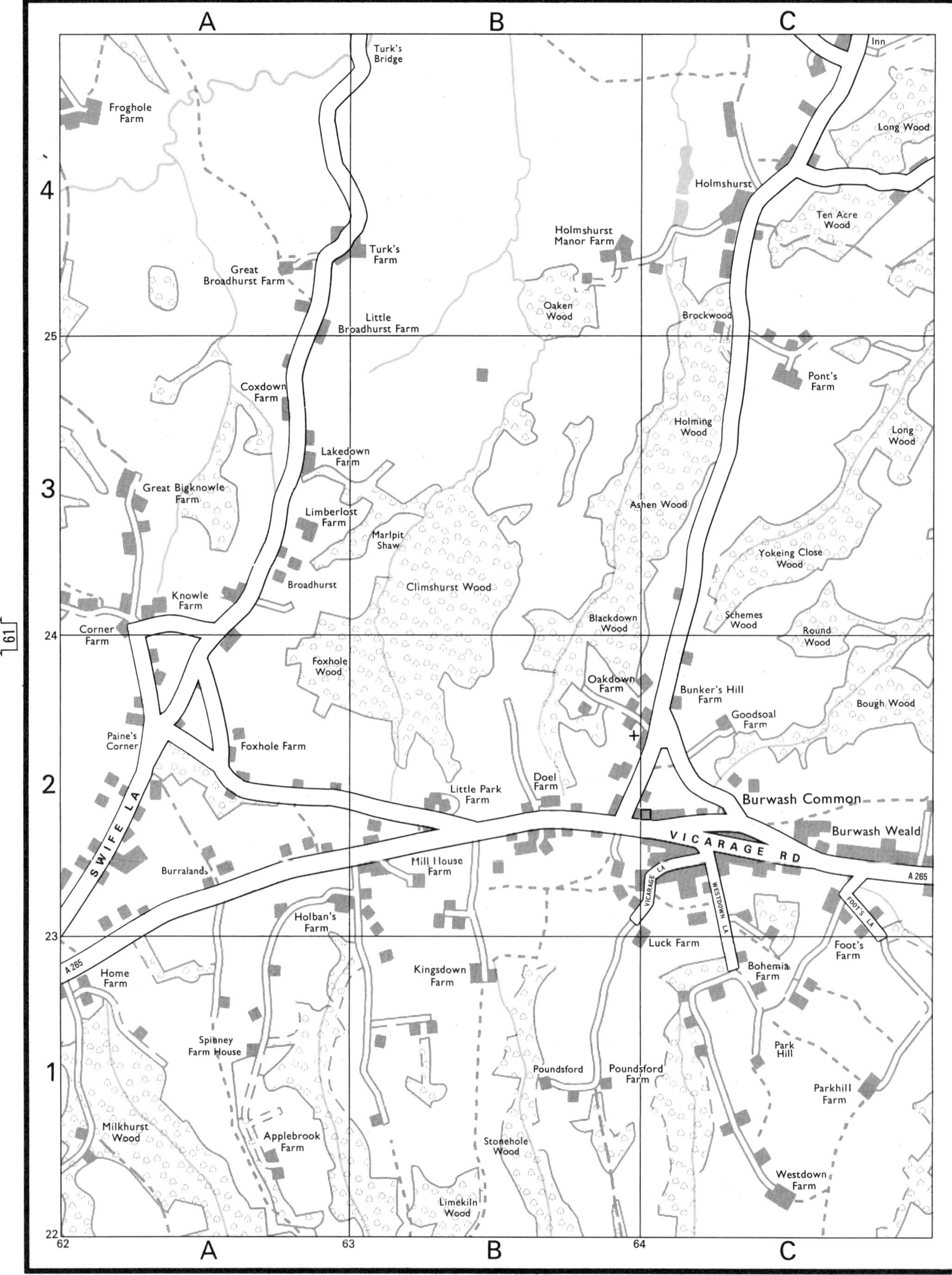

61

85

44

D
E
F
Wet Wood
Franchise Manor
Coalpit Wood
Southover
Franchise Farm
Snowdrop Copse
Honeybrook Wood
Brooksmarle
Shrub Wood
Mottynsden Manor House
Holton Farm
Holton Hill
Mottynsden Farm
Winters Farm
Outdoor Centre
Ham Lane
STRAND MEADOW
BEECHWOOD CL
HORNBEAM
SHRUB LA
Square Farm
ROTHER VIEW
WEALDEN VIEW
ROTHER CL
A 265
RECTORY CL
HAM LA
SPRING LA
Seller's Brook
Burwash
HIGH ST
Sch
Young's Wood
Hall
Motel
HIGHFIELDS
Ashlands
BELL ALLEY RD
Court Barn Farm
Pasture Wood
Alder Wood
Holton Lane
Witherhurst Farm
Furnace Gill
Woodlands Farm
COPPER'S HILL
Copper's Hill
Dudwell Farm
Highfield Shaw
BATEMAN'S LA
Dudwell Bridge
Old Dudwell Mill
Bateman's (Home of Rudyard Kipling 1902-34)
Ghyll Farm
Oakhurst Farm
Lower Bough Farm
Laurelhurst
Rye Green Farm
Magpie's Hall
River Dudwell
KING'S HILL RD
The Wheel (PH)
Burnt House Farm
Park Farm
Park Wood
Bog Wood
Mousehole Farm
WILLINGFORD LA
Forge Wood
Kemland
High Wood
Lower Leggett's Wood
Willingford Bridge
Pugshole Oast Farm
Forge Farm
Willingford Farm
Kiln Shaw
Leggett's Wood
Perch Hill Farm
Stonepetty
4
3
2
1
25
24
23
22
65
66
67

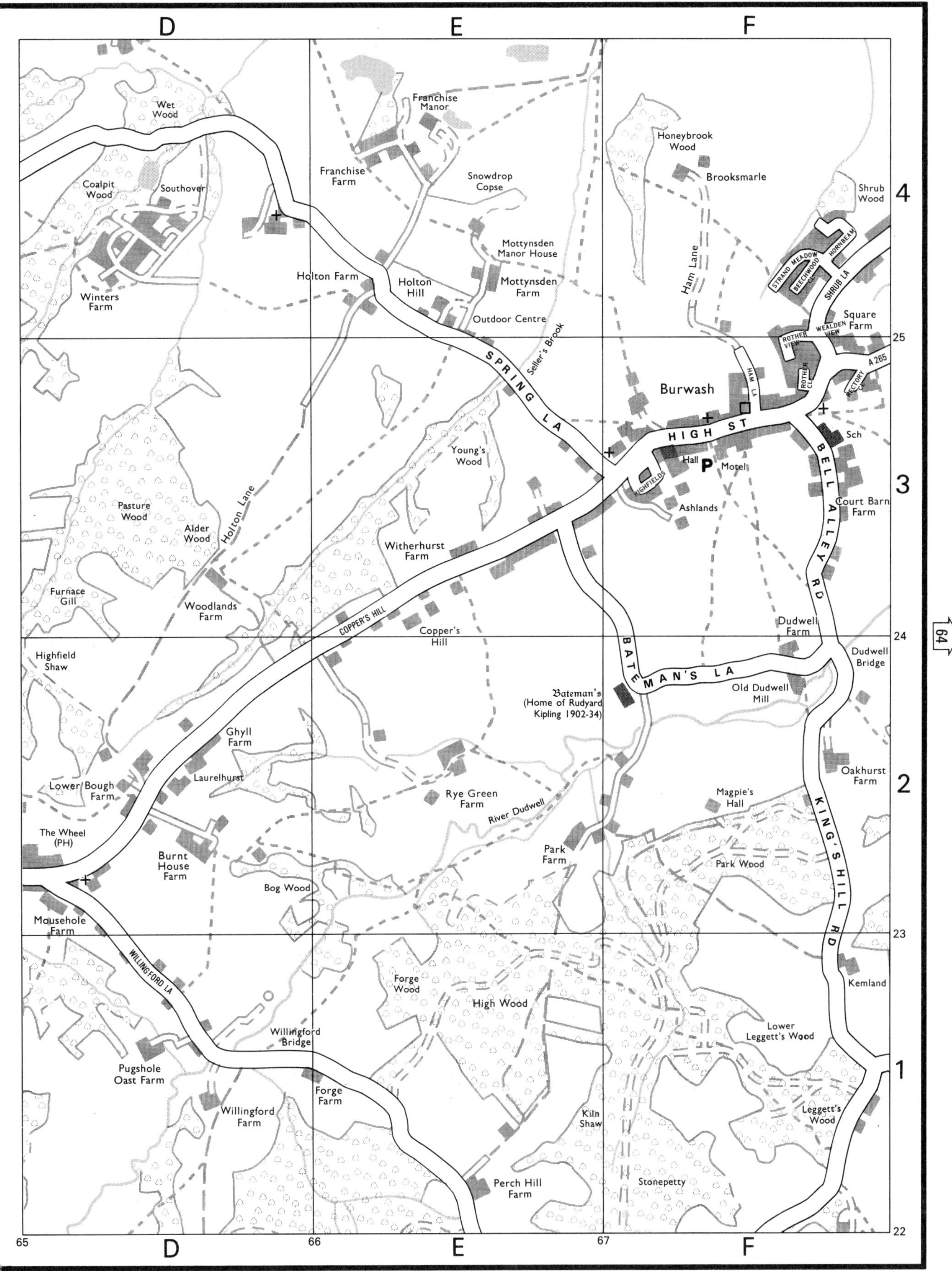

64

86

45

A
B
C
Shrubb Farm
Park Wood
Court Lodge Farm
Court Farm
HIGH ST
A265
Hall
PARK FARM CL
SHRUB LA
GREENFIELD RD
Underwood's Farm
March Farm
Little Park Wood
The Convent Dudwell St Mary
Broomwood Farm
Sores Wood
Great Tott Farm
Borders Farm
Borders
Toll Wood
Glebe House
A265
The Glebe Farm
Tott Wood
Athena Farm
Hutching's Farm
River Dudwell
Fontridge Manor
Little Grandturzel
Grandturzel
Church Wood
Fisher's Farm
Chambers Farm
Southside Farm
Nepland Pit
Old Brick Farm
Glydwish Wood
FONTRIDGE LA
Glydwish Hall
Minepit Shaw
Platt's Farm
Northgate Wood
Burgh Wood
Drive Cottage
Kemland Wood
Socknersh Manor
Park Wood
Fonthill Farm
Rabbit Wood
Furnace Wood
Barnfield Wood
Newhouse Farm
Bowman's Farm
Woodman's Farm
Mill Wood
Middle Wood
Brown's Oak Farm
Perryman's Farm
Bowden Wood
Oldhole Wood
BRIGHTLING RD
Sizzes Wood
Chilley's Wood
Perryfield Wood
Manor Farm
4
3
2
1
25
24
23
22
68
69
70

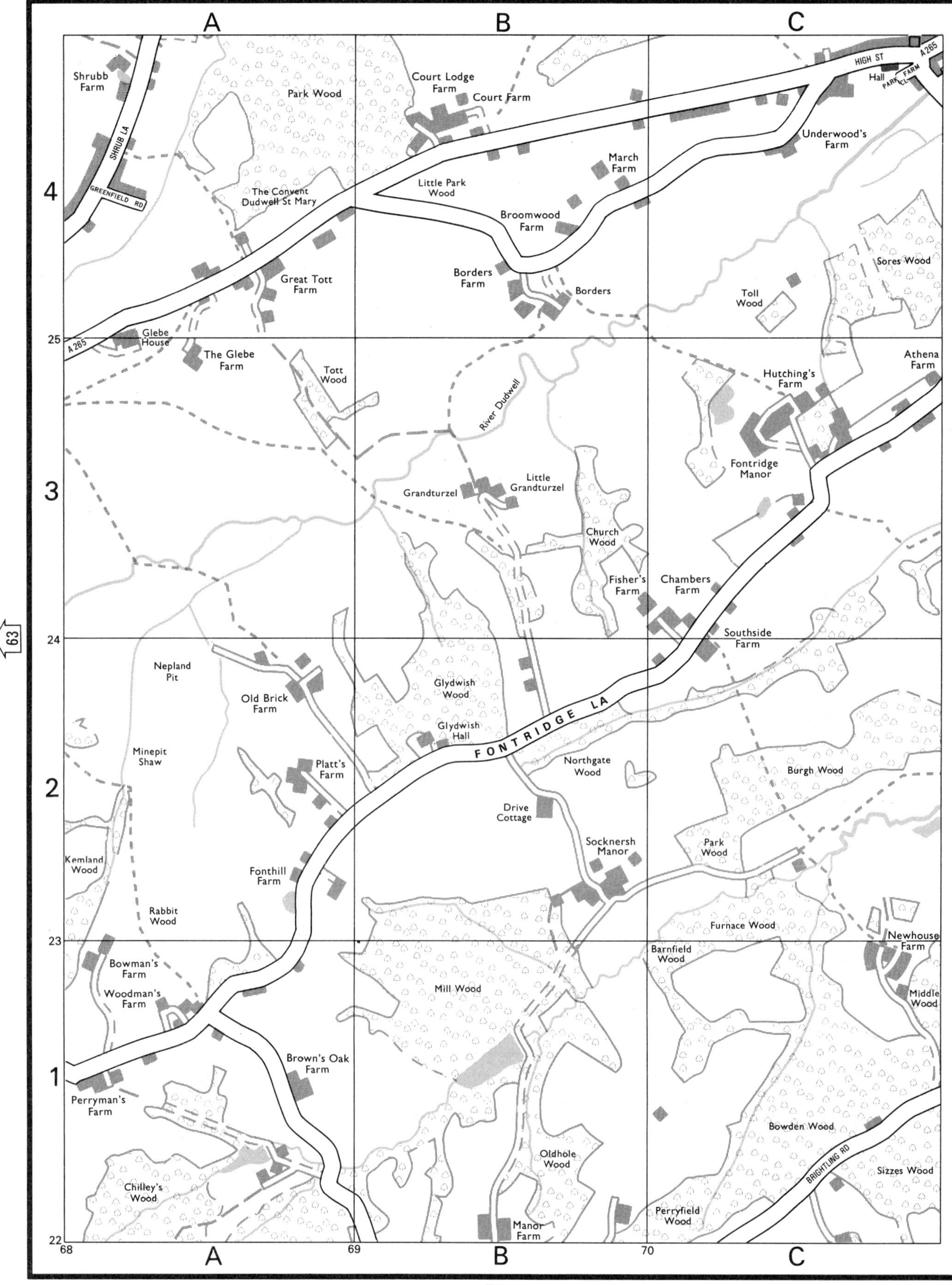

63

87

46

D
E
F
Boromead Farm
Church Wood
Lundsford Farm
Bugsell Mill Farm
Trebor Farm
Stone Rock Gill
OXENBRIDGE LA
WILLOW CL
A21(T)
Barnfield Shaw
Gigmore Wood
Ockham House
Park Wood
Bush Barn
FONTRIDGE LA
Squibs Farm
Almonds
LUDPIT LA
Hackwoods Farm
Bugsell Farm
Northbridge Street
Mill
NORTHBRIDGE ST
Willard's Hill Farm
Marlpit Shaw
Willard's Hill
Clapson's Bridge
Bugsell Wood
Beech Farm
Long Shaw
THE CLAPPERS
Robertsbridge
Column Wood
Fair Ridge Wood
School
Robertsbridge Station
FAYRE MEADOW
OAKLAND DR
HACKWOOD
BELLHURST RD
KNELLE RD
HIGH ST
FAIR LA
LANGHAM RD
THE SPINNEY
STATION RD
PIPER'S LA
BLENHEIM CT
MILL RISE
Grove Farm
Pean's Wood
Little Peans
Wyland Wood
BISHOP'S LA
GEORGE HILL
Tel Ex
Brown's Bridge
HEATHFIELD GDNS
BRIGHTLING RD
Darvell
Brownes House
JOHN'S CROSS RD
Scalands Farm
Brightling Hall
Brown's Farm
Scalands Wood
POPPINGHOLE LA
Birching Wood
Glottenham Manor
Ladds Wood
Moat
Glottenham Farm
25
24
23
22
4
3
2
1
71
72
73

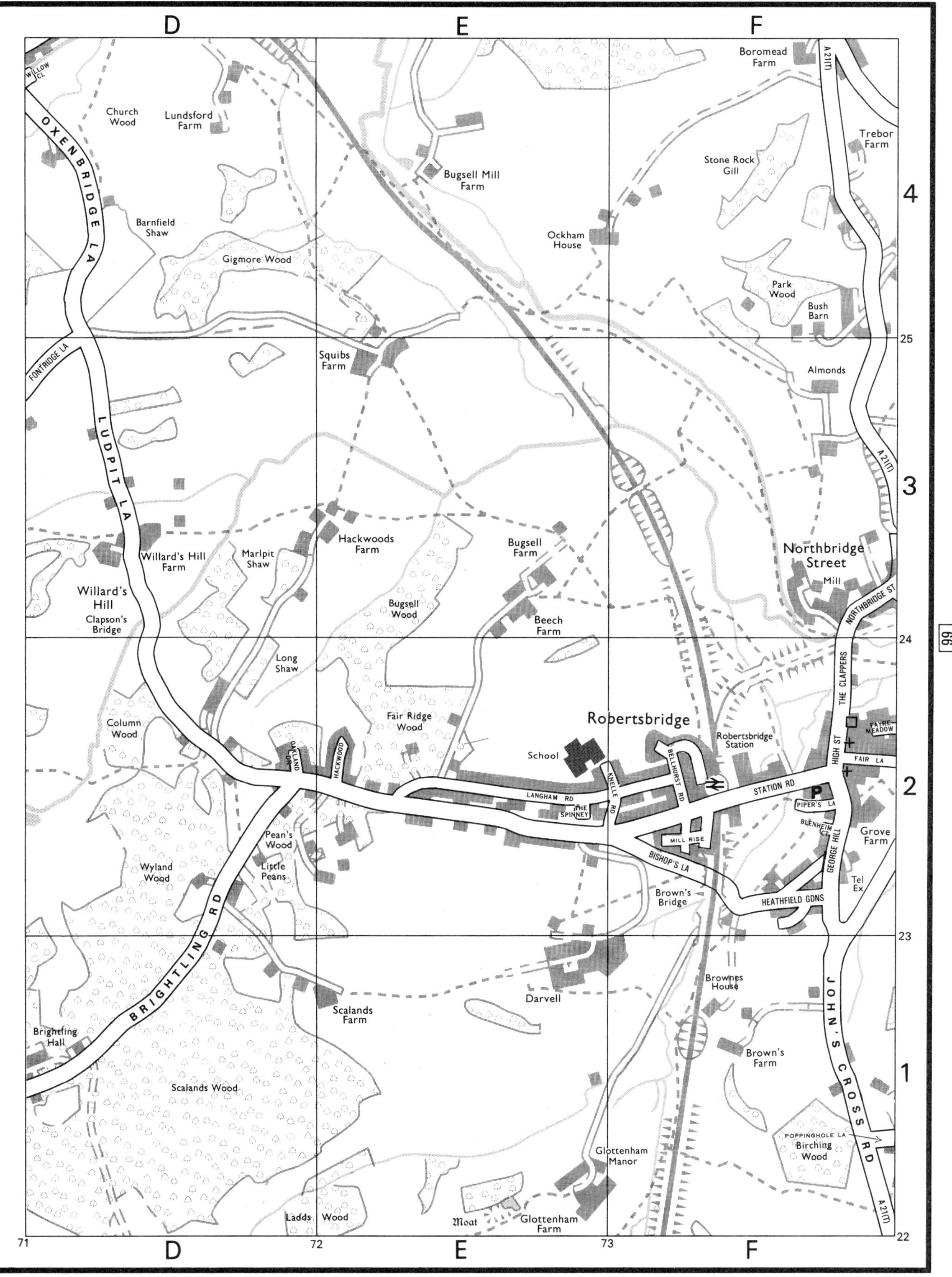

66

88

47

A
B
C
Mill Farm
Mill Farm
Seven Acre Wood
Terrace Wood
A 229
CASTLE HURST
Bushyfield Shaw
JUNCTION RD
4
Eleven Acre Shaw
Bourne Farm
BOURNE LA
Haiselman's Farm
Mayfield Farm
Silverdale
Jollie's Farm
Beech House Farm
Six Acre Wood
25
Higham House
BEECH HOUSE LA
ROCKS HILL
Bantony
3
Moat Farm
ROTHERVIEW
CORONATION COTTS
ANDREWS CL
KEMPS WAY
Salehurst
CHURCH RD
NORTHBRIDGE ST
Sch
PH
RUTLEY CL
Dismantled Railway
24
Church Bridge
River Rother
Robertsbridge Abbey
Remains of Abbey (Cistercian)
FAYRE MEADOW
FAIR LA
Redlands
Russet Farm
Fowlbrook Wood
2
Eyelids Farm
Sewage Works
Park Wood
Park Farm House
Deadman's Wood
Wellhead Wood
23
Bluebell Farm
Maynard's Wood
Keepers Cottage
Lordship Wood
1
Deadman's Wood
Wellhead Wood West
Little Deadman's Wood
POPPINGHOLE LA
Town Shaw
Walter's Farm
22
74
75
76

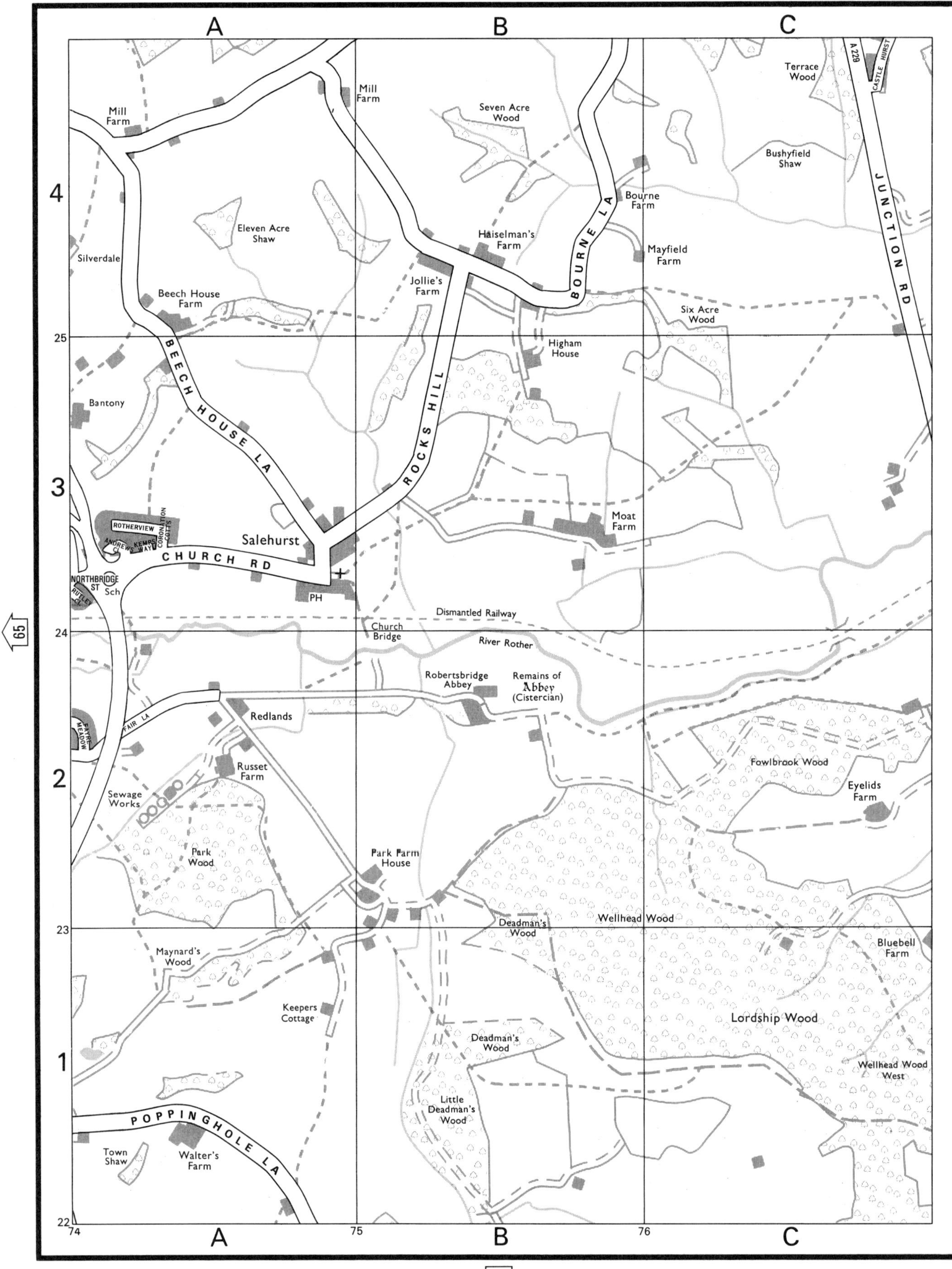

65

89

48

D
E
F
LEVETTS LA
Sch
Hotel
Court Lodge
Bodiam
Knowle Hill
Bodiam Castle
Moat
New House
The Green
Castle Inn
P
River Rother
Bodiam Bridge
Park Farm
Kent and East Sussex Railway
LC
Bodiam Station
Horselands Shaw
Ockham
PH
A 229
The Quarry
THE GREEN
Ewhurst Green
West Wood
DAGG LA
Dykes Farm
Snagshall
Udiam
Rocks Farm
Watermans Farm
Udiam Cottages
Shoreham
Sogg's House
LORDINE LA
Stumblott's Farm
Crainham Wood
Madame's Farm Oast
Udiam Lane
Stumblott's Wood
FB
Prawles Farm
Holmans Wood
Brasses Farm
Ren's Wood
JUNCTION RD
Birchin Wood
Flettice Wood
Stainsmore Wood
Hollow Wall Farm
Larkins Hollow
Crabtree Wood
Holmtree Wood
Wellhead Wood East
Sch
WEALD VIEW
Hall
Boyces
Collier's Green
Gate Farm
B 2165
FORGE LA
FORGE PL
CRICKETERS FIELD
Staplecross
B 2165
Handsel Farm
Sewage Works
Lower Morgay Farm
A 229
B 2165
Hobby Hobbs Farm
ELLENWHORNE LA
4
3
2
1
25
24
23
22
77
78
79

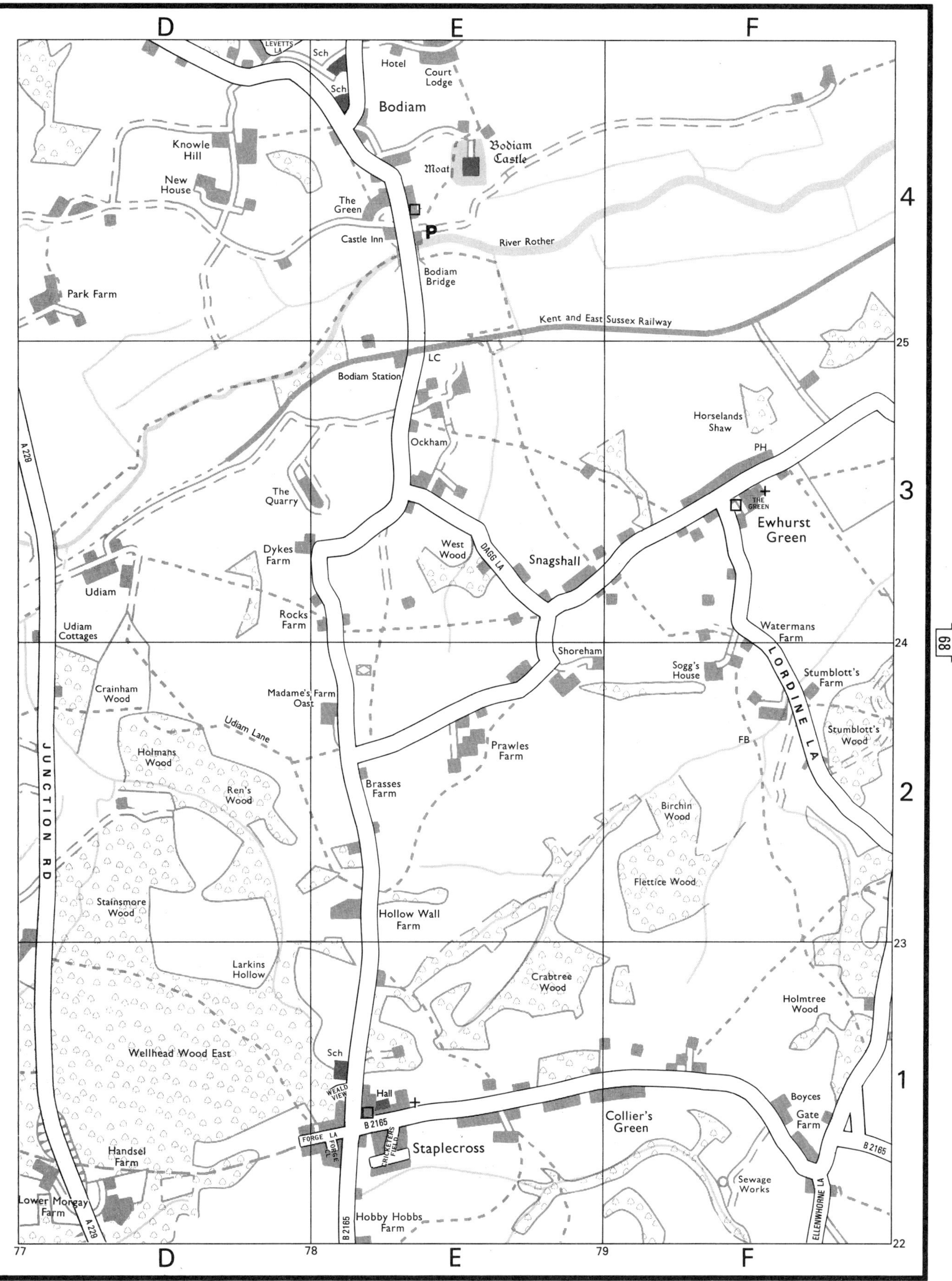

68

90

49

A
B
C
4
3
2
1
25
24
23
22
80
81
82
Kent Ditch
River Rother
Kent & East Sussex Railway
Dixter Station
Crockers
Weights Wood
Friars Cote Farm
Dixter Wood
DIXTER LA
Cantise Shaw
Padgham
Little Dixter
Great Dixter
High Park
HIGH PARK
NORTHRIDGE
COPLANDS RISE
STATION RD
MONKS WAY
GHYLL SIDE RD
GODDENS CL
GODDENS GILL
THE PADDOCK
FREWEN CL
CHAPEL FIELD
DIXTER RD
Higham Farm
BEALES LA
Northiam
Four Acre Shaw
Hall
PARK VIEW
MAIN ST
Mus
A 28
Sch
Spital Wood
Longwood
Sempstead Wood
Reach Wood
Furnace Wood
EWHURST LA
Strawberry Hole Cottage
Gusling Wood
Glebe House
Long Wood
Park Wood
Tufton Place
Coneyburrow Wood
Carriers Farm
Sempstead
Yewtree Hill
Wattshill Wood
Mill Corner
NEW RD
LORDINE LA
Martinshaw Farm
Watts Hill Farm
Brook's Farm
Ockford Farm
Sherbourne Valley
Lordine Wood
Commons Wood Farm
Spanyard's Farm
ADAMS LA
Dadland Wood
Wellhouse
Morley Farm
Lordine Court
Chantry Wood
Forstal Wood
Lawyer's Wood
Yewtree Farm
Commons Wood
B 2165
Barnwell Farm
Horns Cross
Sparks
New House Farm
Goatley Farm

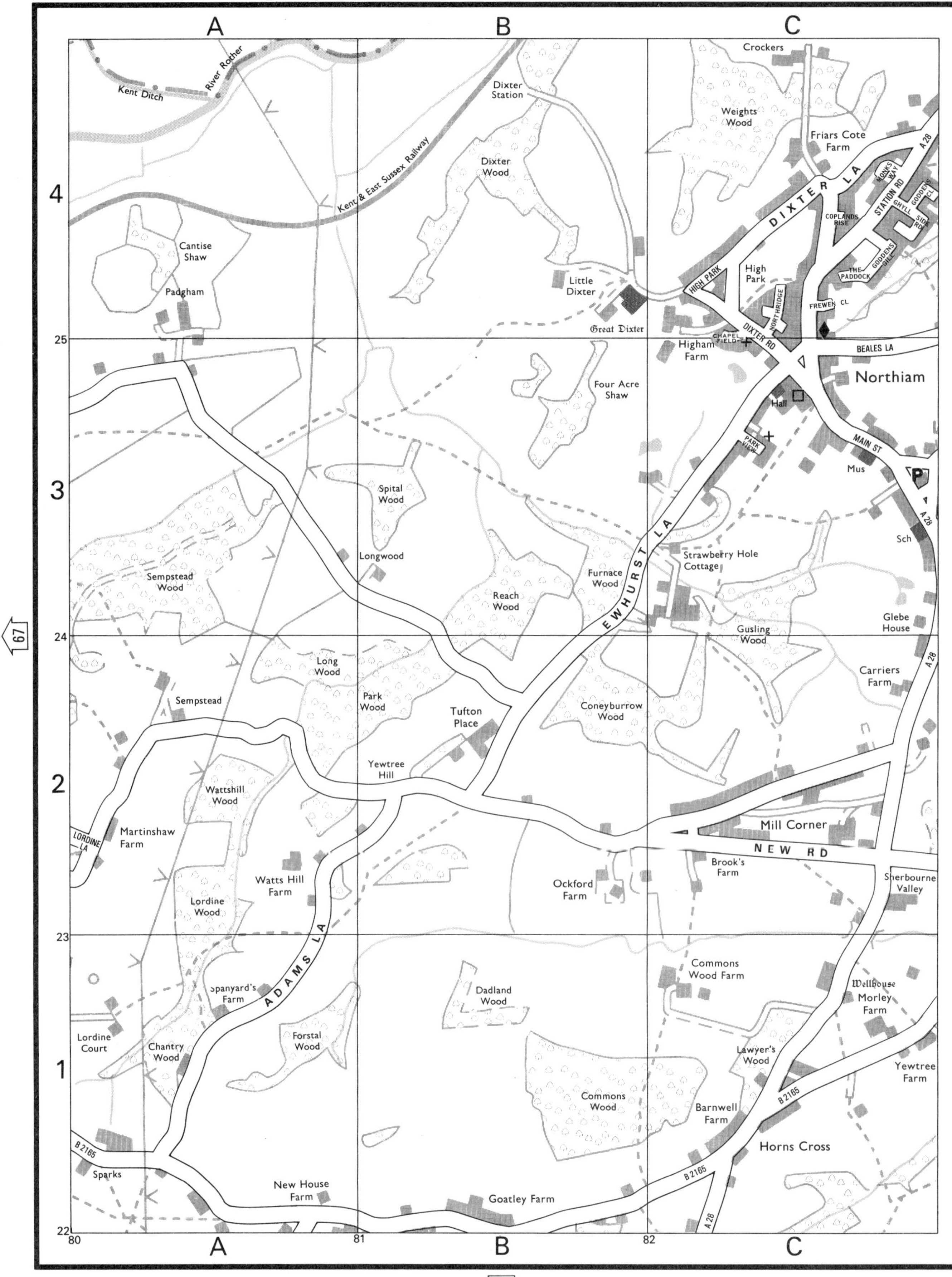

67

91

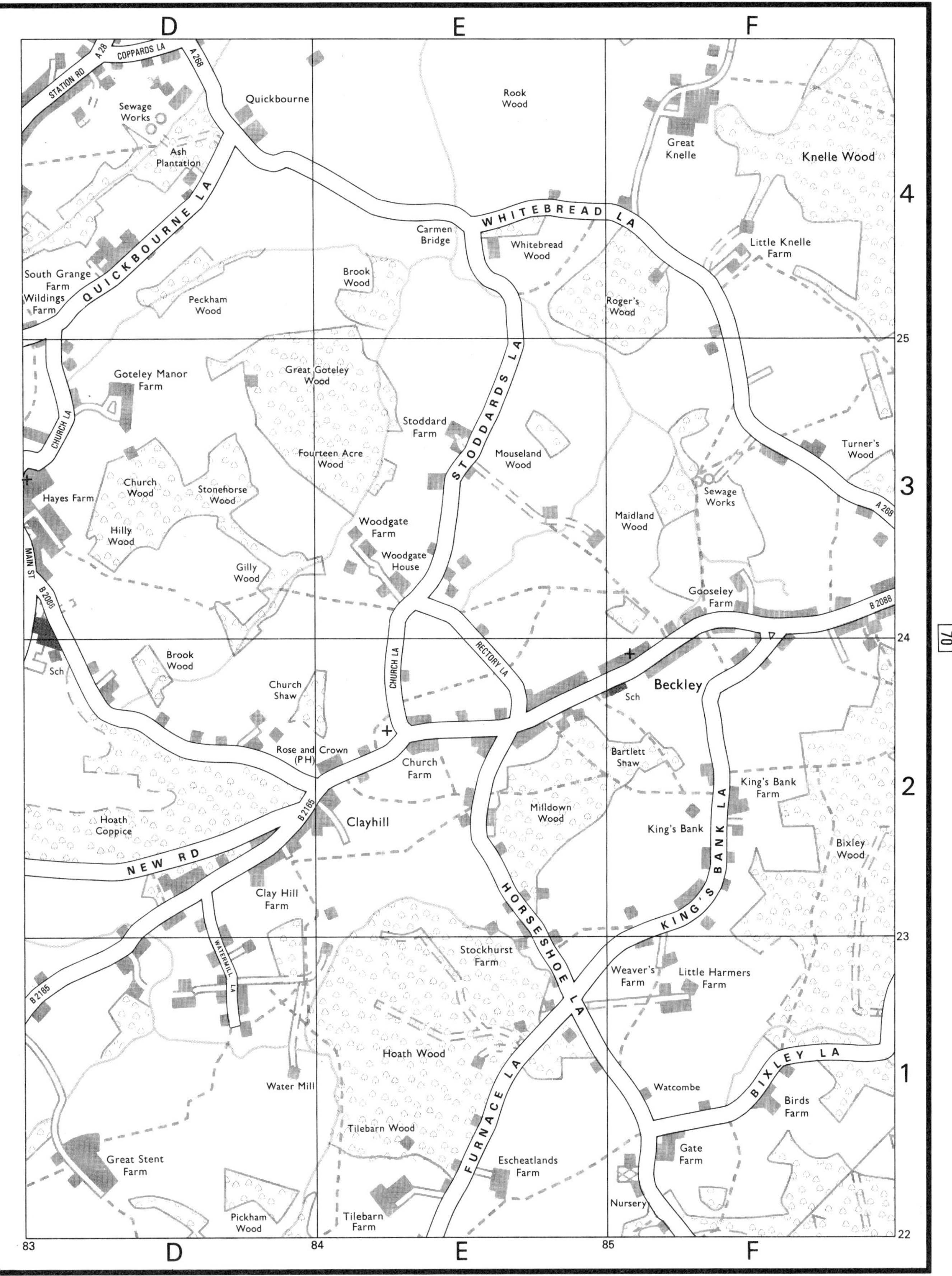
50
D
E
F
COPPARDS LA
A 28
STATION RD
A 268
Sewage Works
Quickbourne
Rook Wood
Great Knelle
Knelle Wood
Ash Plantation
4
QUICKBOURNE LA
WHITEBREAD LA
Carmen Bridge
Whitebread Wood
Little Knelle Farm
South Grange Farm
Wildings Farm
Brook Wood
Peckham Wood
Roger's Wood
25
STODDARDS LA
Goteley Manor Farm
Great Goteley Wood
CHURCH LA
Stoddard Farm
Turner's Wood
Fourteen Acre Wood
Mouseland Wood
Church Wood
Sewage Works
3
Hayes Farm
Stonehorse Wood
A 268
Maidland Wood
Hilly Wood
Woodgate Farm
MAIN ST
Woodgate House
Gilly Wood
B 2086
Gooseley Farm
B 2088
24
70
RECTORY LA
CHURCH LA
Sch
Brook Wood
Church Shaw
Beckley
Sch
Rose and Crown (PH)
Bartlett Shaw
Church Farm
2
King's Bank Farm
Milldown Wood
B 2165
Hoath Coppice
Clayhill
King's Bank
Bixley Wood
KING'S BANK LA
NEW RD
Clay Hill Farm
HORSESHOE LA
23
WATERMILL LA
Stockhurst Farm
Weaver's Farm
Little Harmers Farm
B 2165
BIXLEY LA
Hoath Wood
1
Water Mill
FURNACE LA
Watcombe
Birds Farm
Tilebarn Wood
Gate Farm
Great Stent Farm
Escheatlands Farm
Nursery
Pickham Wood
Tilebarn Farm
22
83
84
85
D
E
F
92

51

A
B
C
4
3
2
1
25
24
23
22
86
87
88
Methersham Wood
Little Bellhurst
Great Bellhurst Farm
Little Heron Farm
Hope Farm
Oxenbridge Farm
Blackwall Bridge
Otter Channel
Decoypond Ditch
Carpen Wood
Kitchenham
Swallowtail Hill
Evening Wood
Dean Wood
HOBBS LA
Hobbs' Farm
Barber's Wood
Decoypond Wood
Shepherds Farm
Spring Wood
WHITEBREAD LA
COOMBS CL
COOMBS COTTS
Streamland Wood
New House Farm
Combe Shaw
A 268
KITCHENOUR LA
Four Oaks
Kitchenour
MACKEREL HILL
OAKHILL COTTS
Hop Barn
Oaken Wood
Burnt Wood
Mill Wood
Wish Wood
Flackley Ash Farm
Two Hovens Farm
Great Dennis Wood
Cock Wood
Flackley Ash Hotel
Little Dennis Wood
Flackley Ash
BIXLEY LA
MILL LA
Flatroper's Wood (Nature Reserve)
MAIN ST
PH
Houseroper's Wood
TANHOUSE LA
Tanhouse
Peasmarsh
THE MALTINGS
The Firs
BRICKFIELD ESTATE
A 268
Fifty Acre Wood
PARK VIEW
BISKY BAR
SCHOOL LA
Cock Wood
Sch
Woodlands Farm
Rockfield Plantation
DEW LA
Van's Gill
Peasmarsh Park
Great Shelley Wood
69

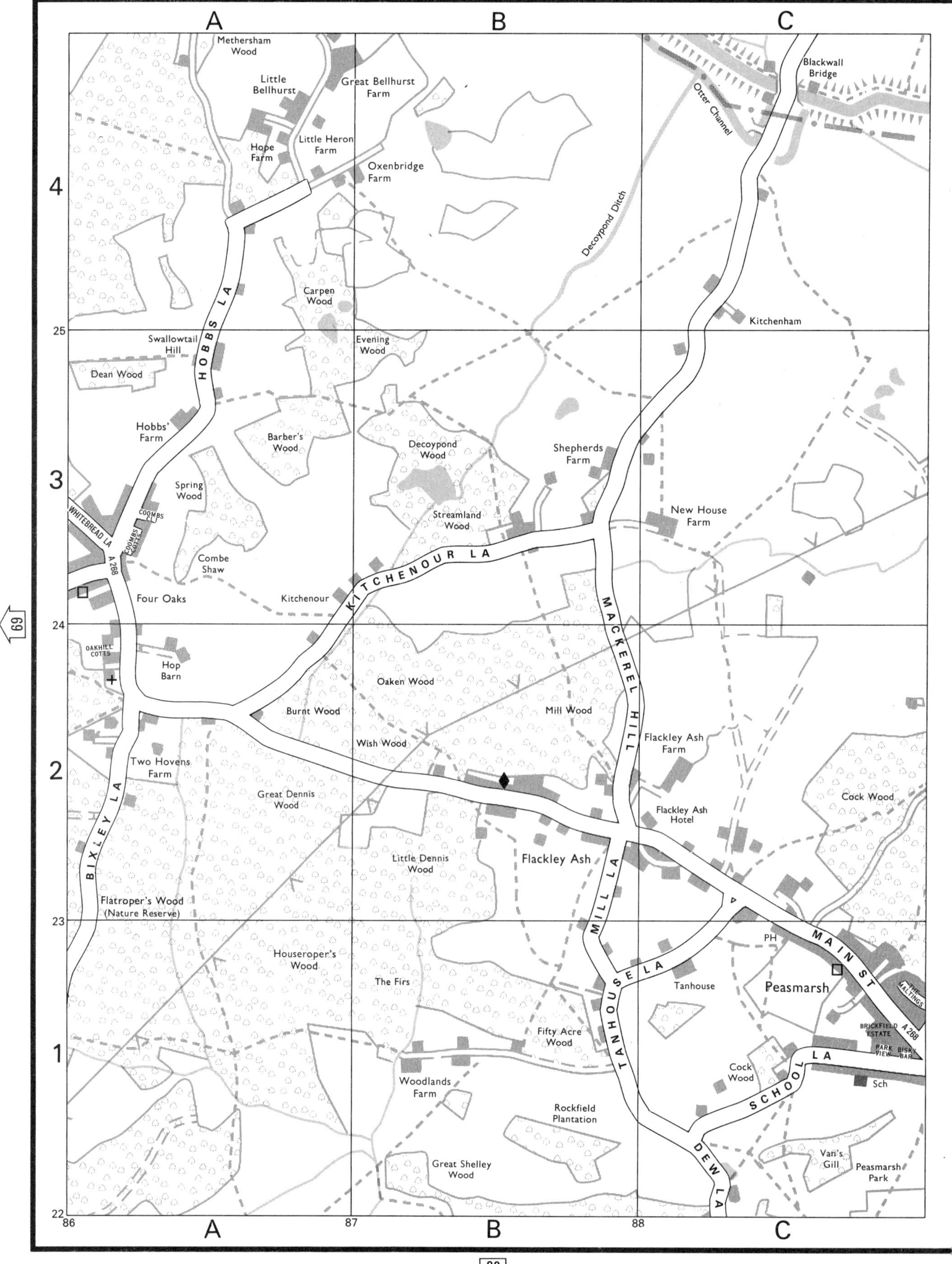

93

not continued, see key diagram

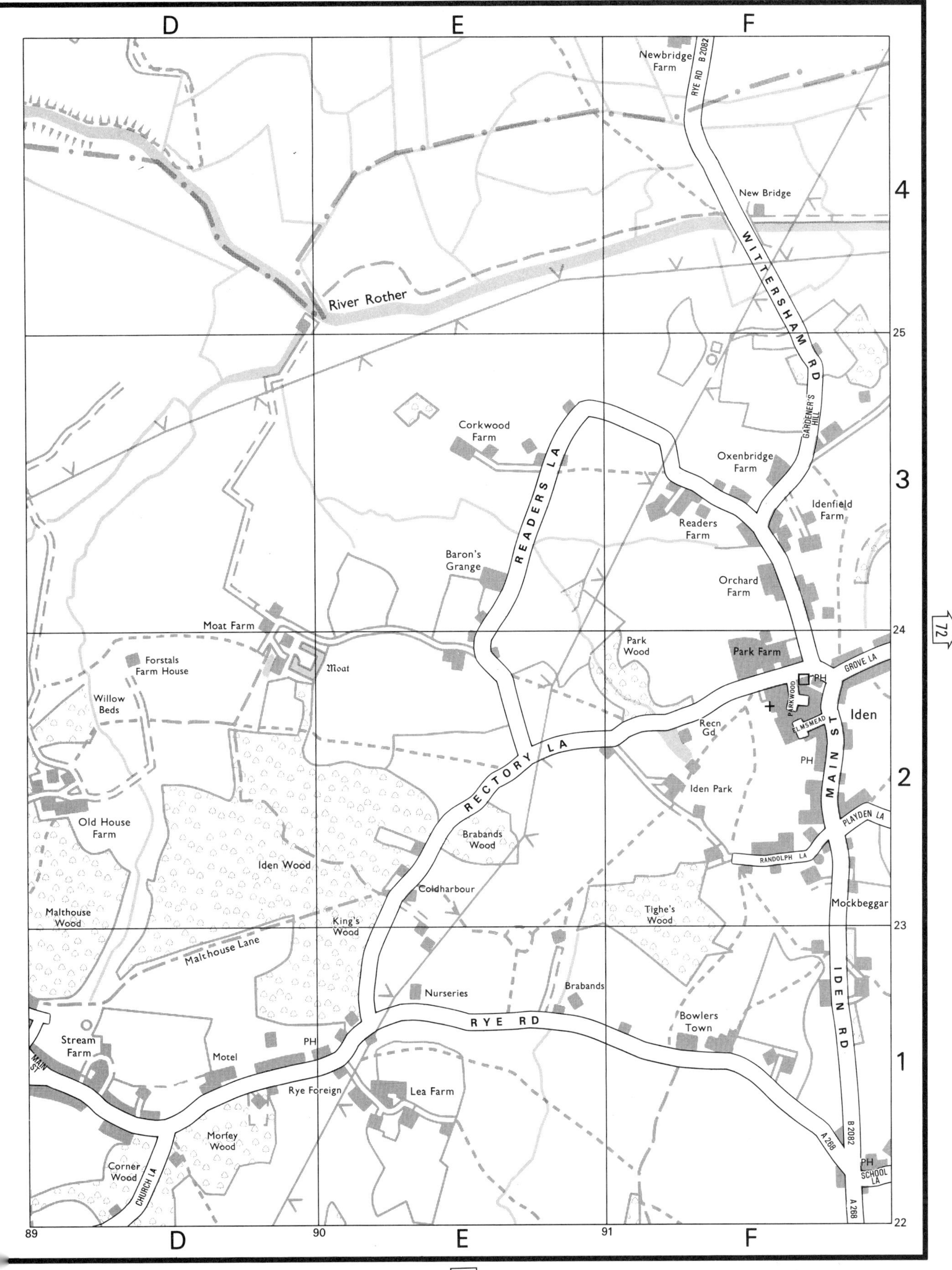

72

94

not continued, see key diagram

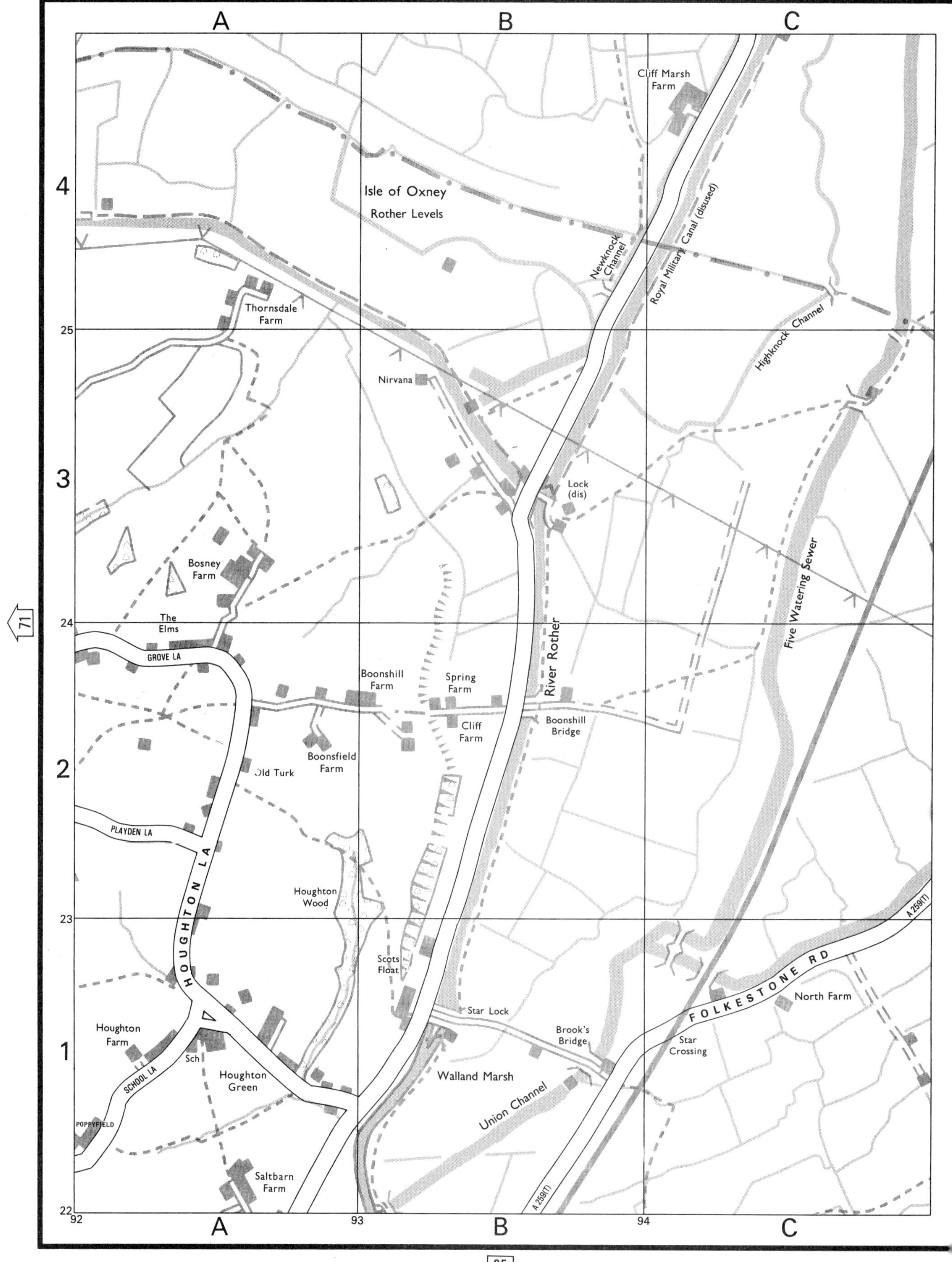

71

95

not continued, see key diagram

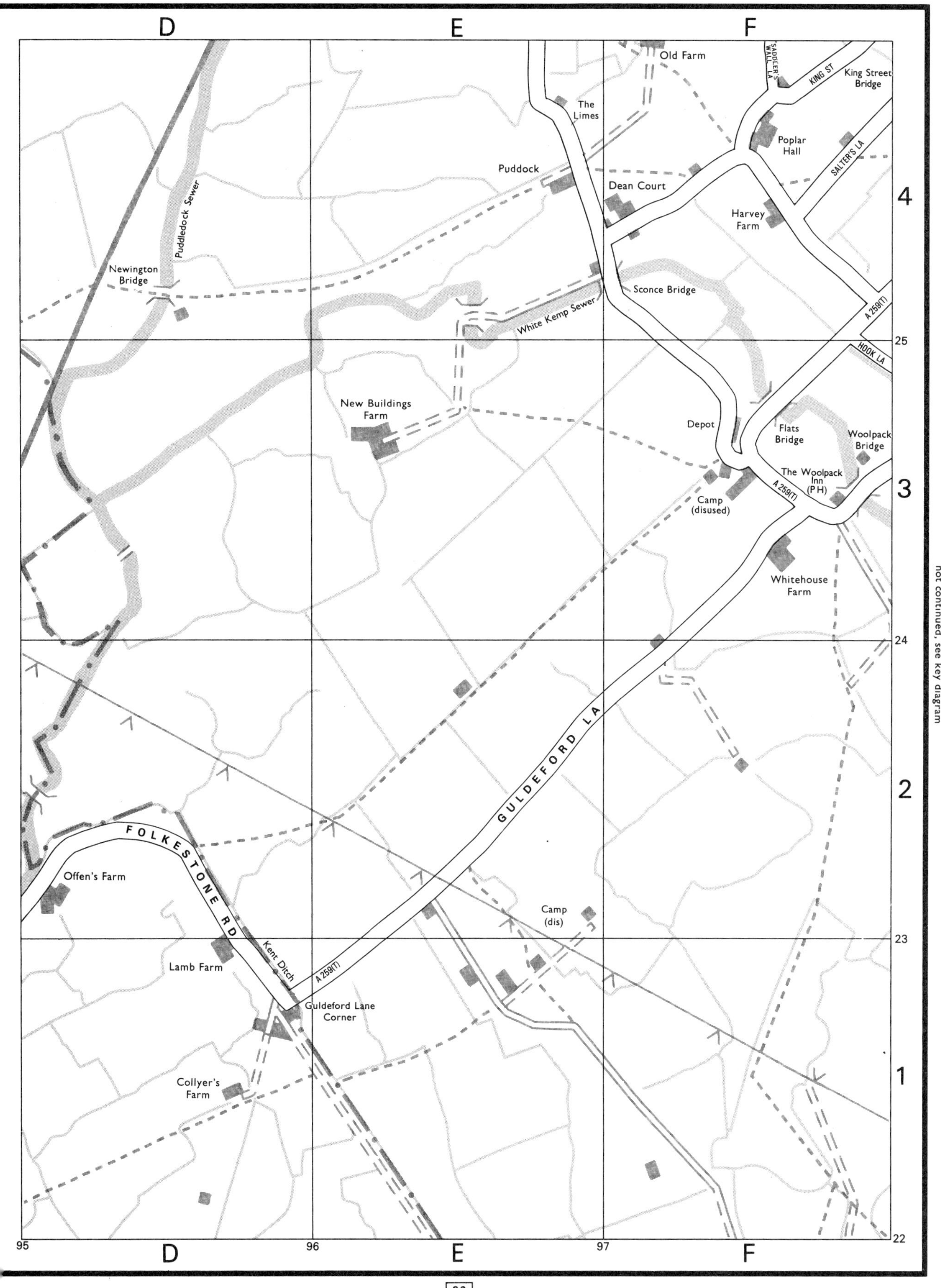

not continued, see key diagram

96

not continued, see key diagram

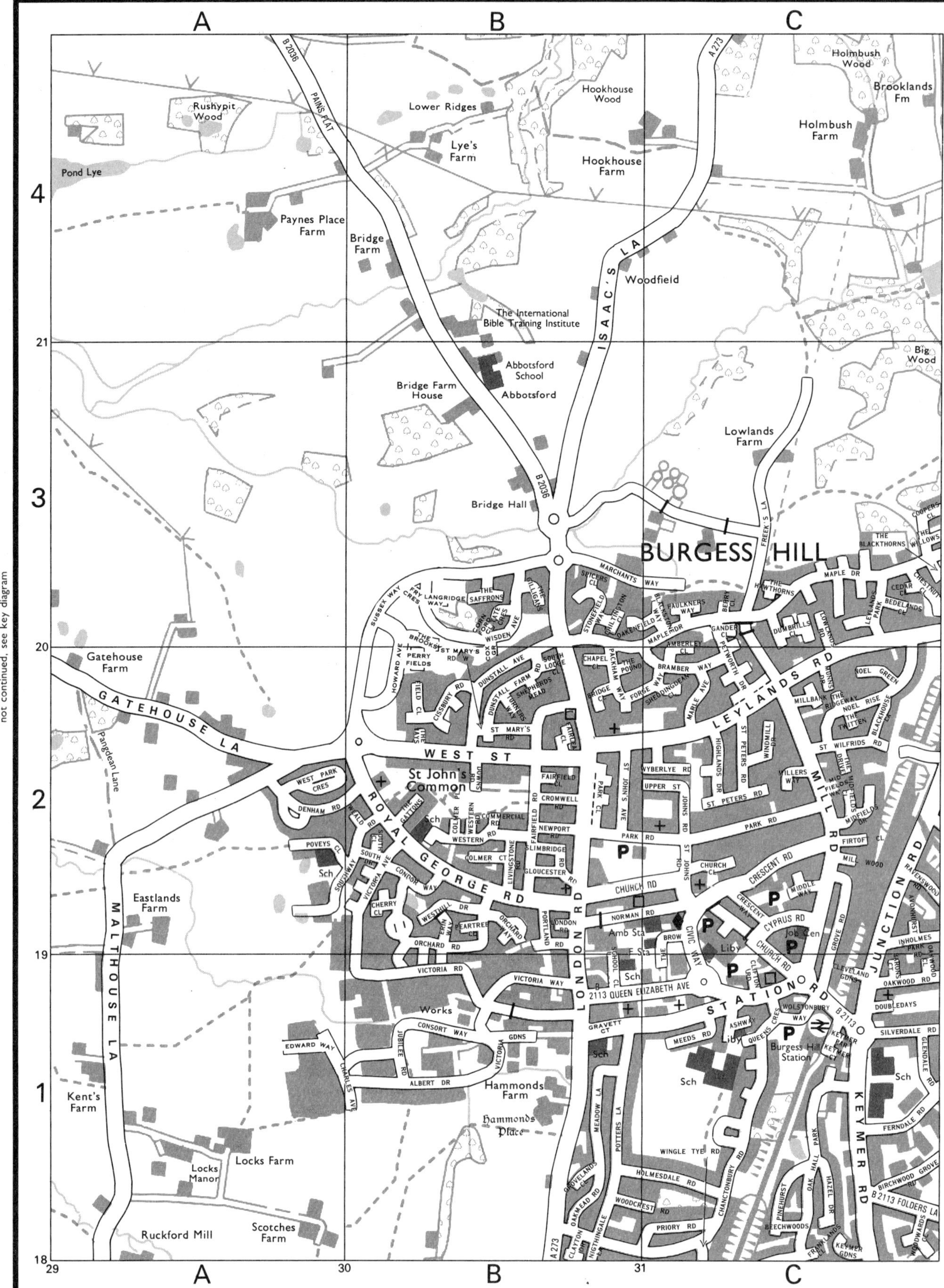

not continued, see key diagram

52

D
E
F
Folly Farm
Kiln Wood
Fox & Hounds (PH)
Clearwaters Farm
Clevewaters Farm
Lunce's Common
High Barn
Roger's Farm
Vale Bridge
Goose Pit
Tilebarn Wood
Lisnagreugh
Antye Farm
Lunces Hall
Sch
Towning Place
More House
Moat
Theobalds
Great Ote Hall
Great Otehall Wood
Wivelsfield
Sch
Ote Hall Farm
Lockstrood Farm
The Royal Oak (PH)
Wivelsfield Station
World's End
Purchase Wood
Wivelsfield Green
West Wood
Works
Hope Farm
Sawyers Land Farm
Stubs Copse
Park Farm
Freckborough Manor
Ditchling Common
North America Farm
Pollards Farm
Schs
ROCKY LA
CLEARWATER LA
VALEBRIDGE RD
THEOBALDS RD
CHURCH LA
LUNCES HILL
FOX HILL
HURSTWOOD LA
B2112
SLUGWASH LA
WIVELSFIELD GREEN RD
JANES LA
GREEN PARK CNR
EASTERN RD
Green Lane
HUNDRED ACRE LA
FOLDERS LA
B2113
B2112
B2113
P
P
4
3
2
1
21
20
19
18
32
33
34
D
E
F

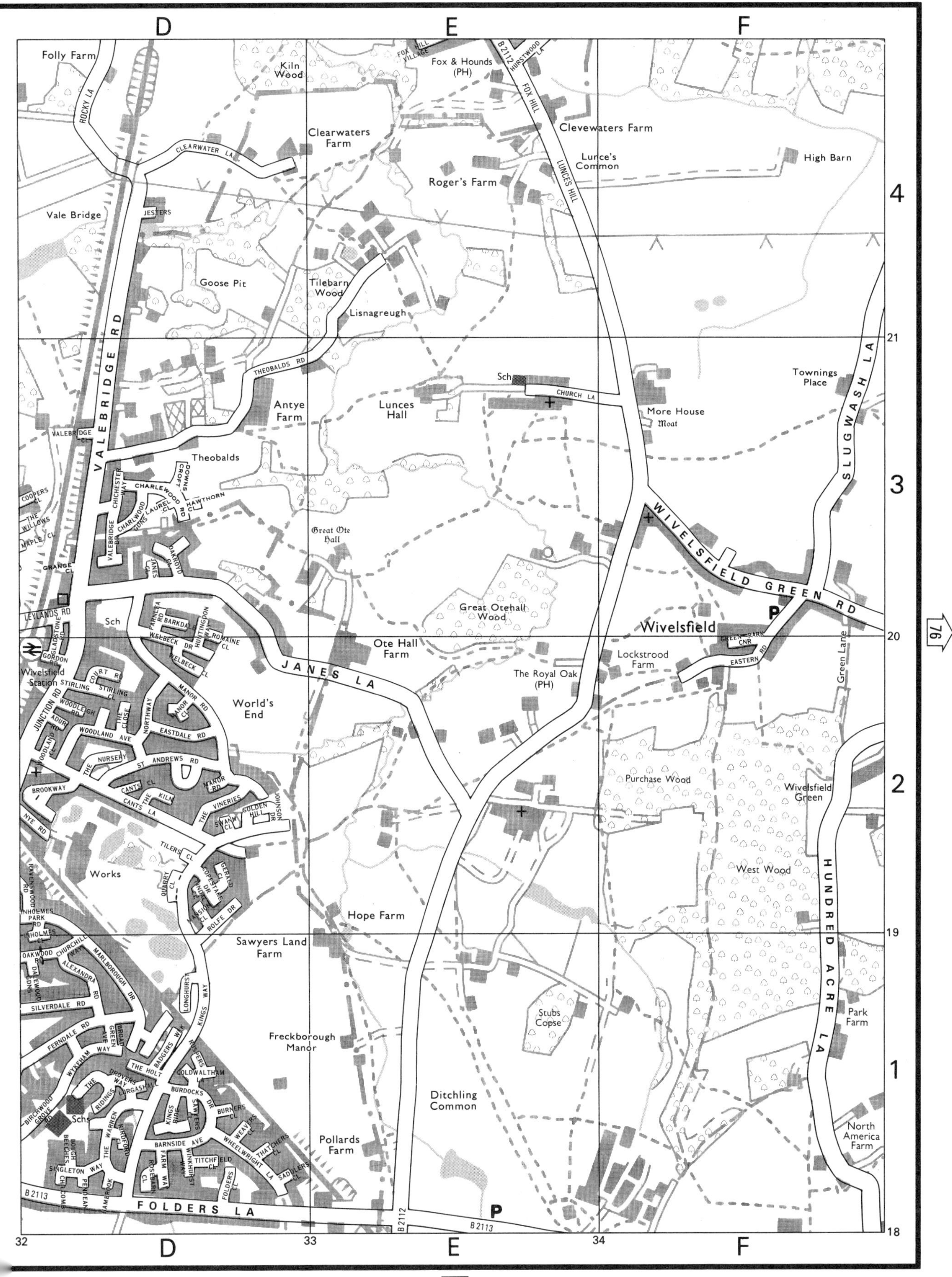

76

101

53

A
B
C
Ham Bridge
Pellingford Brook
Pelling Bridge
A 272
LEWES RD
ANCHOR HILL
Pellingford Brook
High View Farm
Teagues Fm
SLUGWASH LA
Ham Wood
Ham Lane
Tylevel Wood
Leighwood Farm
Wilderness Wood
Strood Wood
Holford Manor
A 272
B 2183
Hole Farm
Wivelsden Farm
Romany Ridge
The Hall
Newhouse Wood
Broomies
Roseland Wood
Broadstone Farm
Strood Farm
Wildfields
Newhouse Farm
NORTH COMMON RD
Mann's Farm
Roselands
Longridge
Towning's Farm
Nursery
Cock Inn (PH)
Sedgebrook Wood
WIVELSFIELD GREEN RD
FARNCOMBE CL
Godleys Green
Breens Cottages
COPPARDS CL
ALLWOOD CRES
DOWNSVIEW DR
Wivelsfield Green
Hole Farm
Longridge Wood
Sedgebrook Hostel
SOUTH RD
Cottage Wood
Grassy Wood
Alder Shaw
Lashmar Wood
Old Barn
Bower Farm
Popjoy Wood
Melbourne Farm
Lumberpits
Heath Farm
Cottage Wood
Plumpton Wood
LUMBERPIT LA
St Helena Farm
Hunt's Wood
Beresford Manor
Great Home Wood
Great Homewood Farm
Shaw Park Farm
4
3
2
1
21
20
19
18
35
36
37
A
B
C

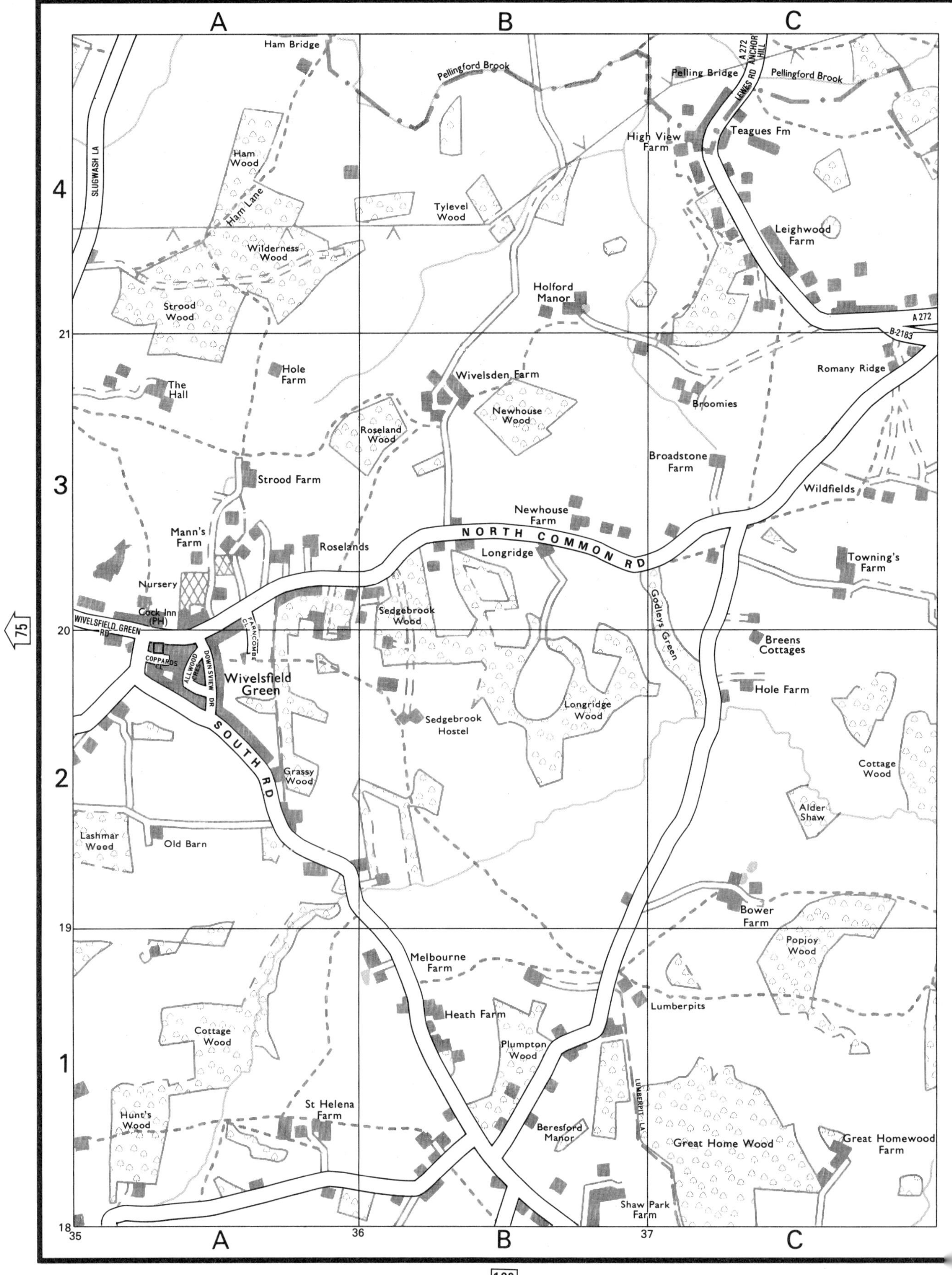

75

102

54

D
E
F
Little Noven
Warren Wood
Fletching Common
Red House
WARRS HILL LA
WARREN WAY
A 275
North Common
Bush Farm
Sch & Hospl
Leylands Fm
Neals Fm
WARREN LA
Grassington Farm
Dismantled Railway
The Warren
REDGILL LA
Cox's Farm
JACKIES LA
4
North Chailey
HAZELDENE LA
OLDHARBOUR LA
STATION RD
Reedens
A 272
Sch & Hospl
DOWNS VIEW CL
DOWNS VIEW
Frick Fm
Burchetts
WESTERN RD
ALLINGTON RD
OXBOTTOM CL
GREAT ROUGH
LOWER STATION RD
BEGGAR'S WOOD RD
Frick Wood
Great Rough
Mitchelswood Farm
Oxbottom
North Common
B 2183
3
Cronk's Wood
Bineham Wood
Vixengrove Farm
CHAILEY LA
Bineham Farmhouse
Cornwell's Bank
Roeheath
Cinder Farm
CINDER HILL
School
Chailey
Moat
2
Hickwells
Ades
Island Ponds
Wilding Farm
Cockfield Bridge (FB)
Cockfield Lane
The Five Bells (PH)
Furzegrove Farm
Long Wood
Wilding Wood
Rabbit Wood
The Hooke
Motts Wood
Markstakes Farm
1
Shelley's Farm
MARKSTAKES CNR
GREEN LA
Furzeley Farm
MARKSTAKES LA
Southam
The Horns Lodge (PH)
ST. JAMES WLK
SETFORDS FIELD
A 275
South Street
21
20
19
18
38
39
40
D
E
F

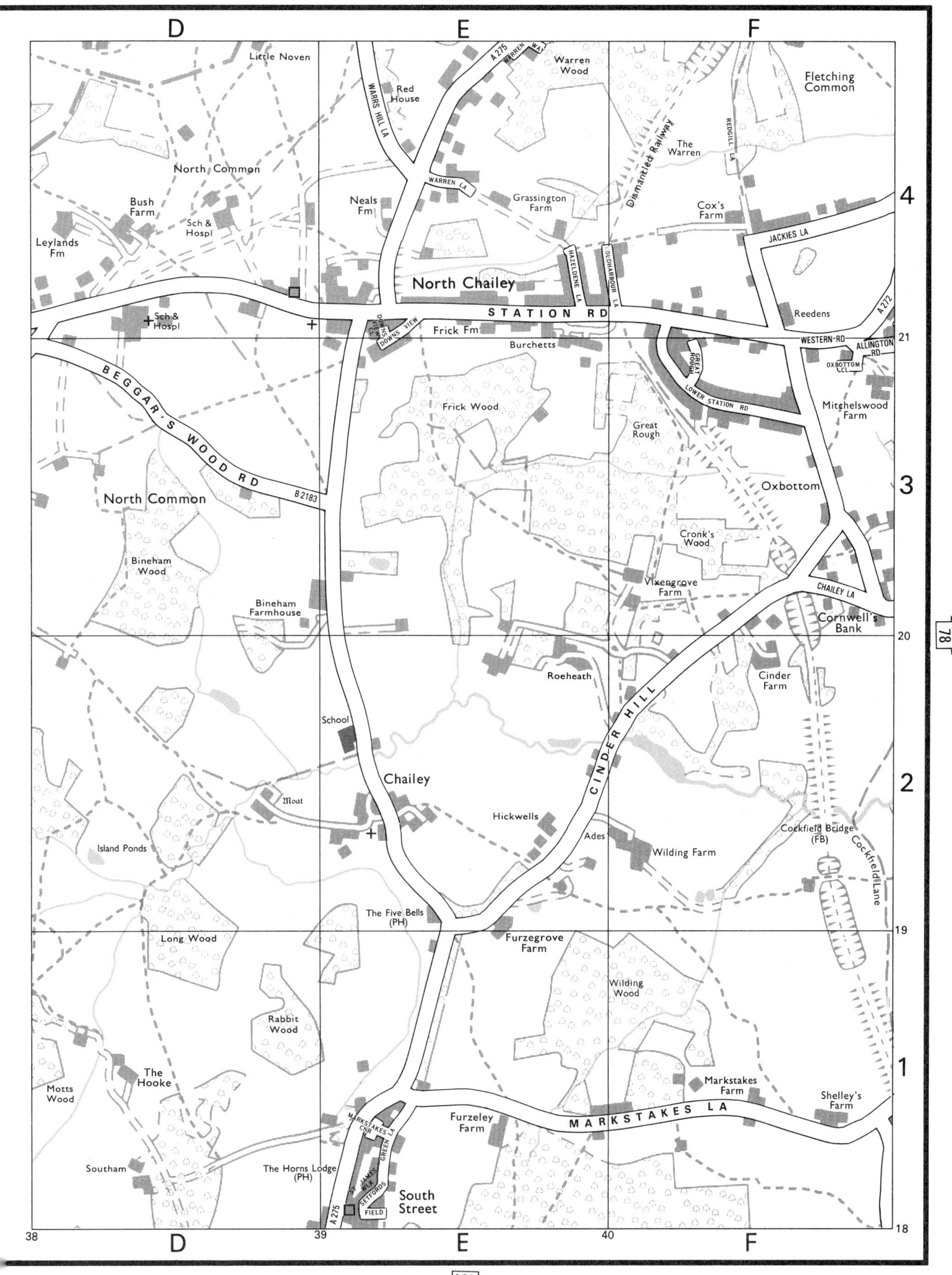

78

103

55

A
B
C
Goldstrow
Cobb's Nest
Sewage Works
Grisling Common
Argus Farm
A 272
Newick
Barkham Manor
NEWICK HILL
CRICKETFIELD
HARMERS HILL
WESTERN RD
HIGH ST
LEVELLER END
LEVELLER RD
THE PARETS
WOODBINE LA
GODDEN RD
PAYNTERS WAY
MARBLES RD
THE GREEN
OLDAKER RD
VERNONS RD
GROWERS END
THE ROUGH
POWELL RD
NEWICK DR
WESTPOINT
ALLINGTON CRES
HIGH HURST CL
BADENS CL
SOUTH ROUGH
BROOKS GDNS
THE RIDINGS
CHURCH RD
BANNISTERS FIELD
ALLINGTON RD
BLIND LA
Goldbridge Farm
GOLDBRIDGE RD
Gold Bridge
Hanger Wood
River Ouse
Eel Pot
Sharp's Bridge
Sharp's Hanger
Ketches Farm
Founthill Wood
Tilehouse Farm
Beechland
Fountill
Broomlye Wood
Sharps Farm
New Barn Farm
Schoolhouse Farm
Double Barns Farm
Broomlye
Bunce's Pit
Bunce's Farm
Ridgeland Farm
Newick Park
Vuggles Farm
Lower Park Pond
Gipp's Farm
Tutts Farm
Lodge Pond
Sutton Hall
Longford Stream
Gipp's Wood
High House Farm
Bradness Wood
Old Park
Beaks Farm
Town Littleworth
The Butletts
Longford Bridge
4
3
2
1
21
20
19
18
41
42
43

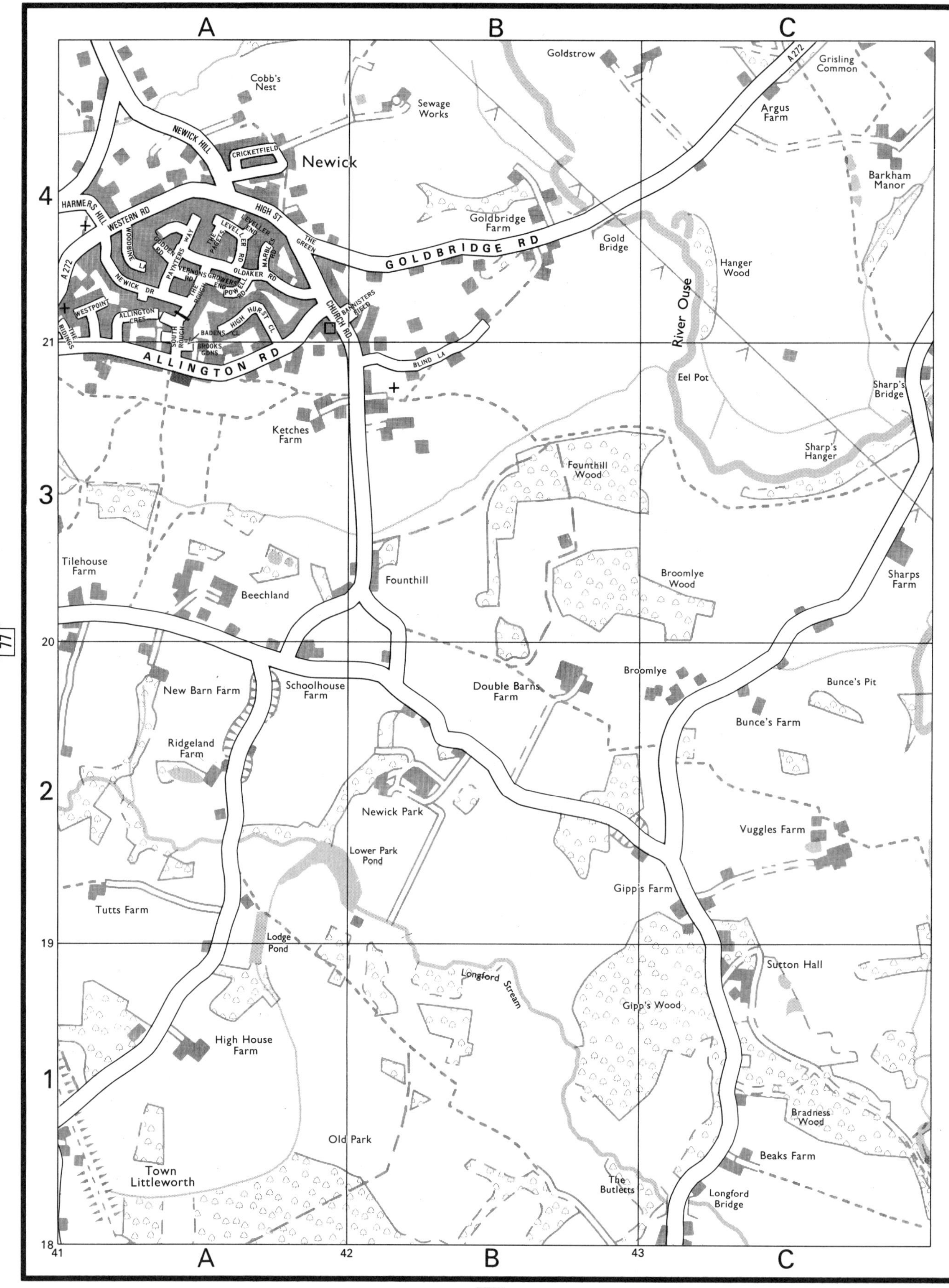

77

104

56

D
E
F
The Old Farm
Moon's Farm
The Peacock Inn (PH)
Lower Morgans Farm
Upper Morgan's Farm
Shortbridge
Shortbridge Stream
Butcher's Wood
Lake Wood
Downlands Farm
Tunnel
Sch
Rocks Park
Copwood Farm
Pierpoint's Wood
Sharpsbridge
Darvel Wood
Beeches Farm
Beechen Wood
Newbarn
B 2102
BELL LA
A 22
Sharpsbridge Farm
River Ouse
Rocky Wood
Buckham Hill
Buckham Hill House
Buckham Hill Farm
Sewage Works
Ridgewood Stream
Boothland Barn
Owlsbury Farm
ROMAN ROAD (course of)
Little Buckham Farm
Lodge Wood
Sluggs Eye Island
Dismantled Railway
FB
Foxearth Wood
River Uck
Dick's Barn
Stroodland Barn
Horsted Green
Constantia Manor
Parson's Pit
Weir
Lower Barn
New House Farm
Lower Farm
Ford
Old Rectory Farm
Isfield Place
Horsted Place Hotel
Home Farm
A 26
Lavender Line
Worth Farm
Isfield Bridge
Isfield Mill
4
3
2
1
21
20
19
18
44
45
46

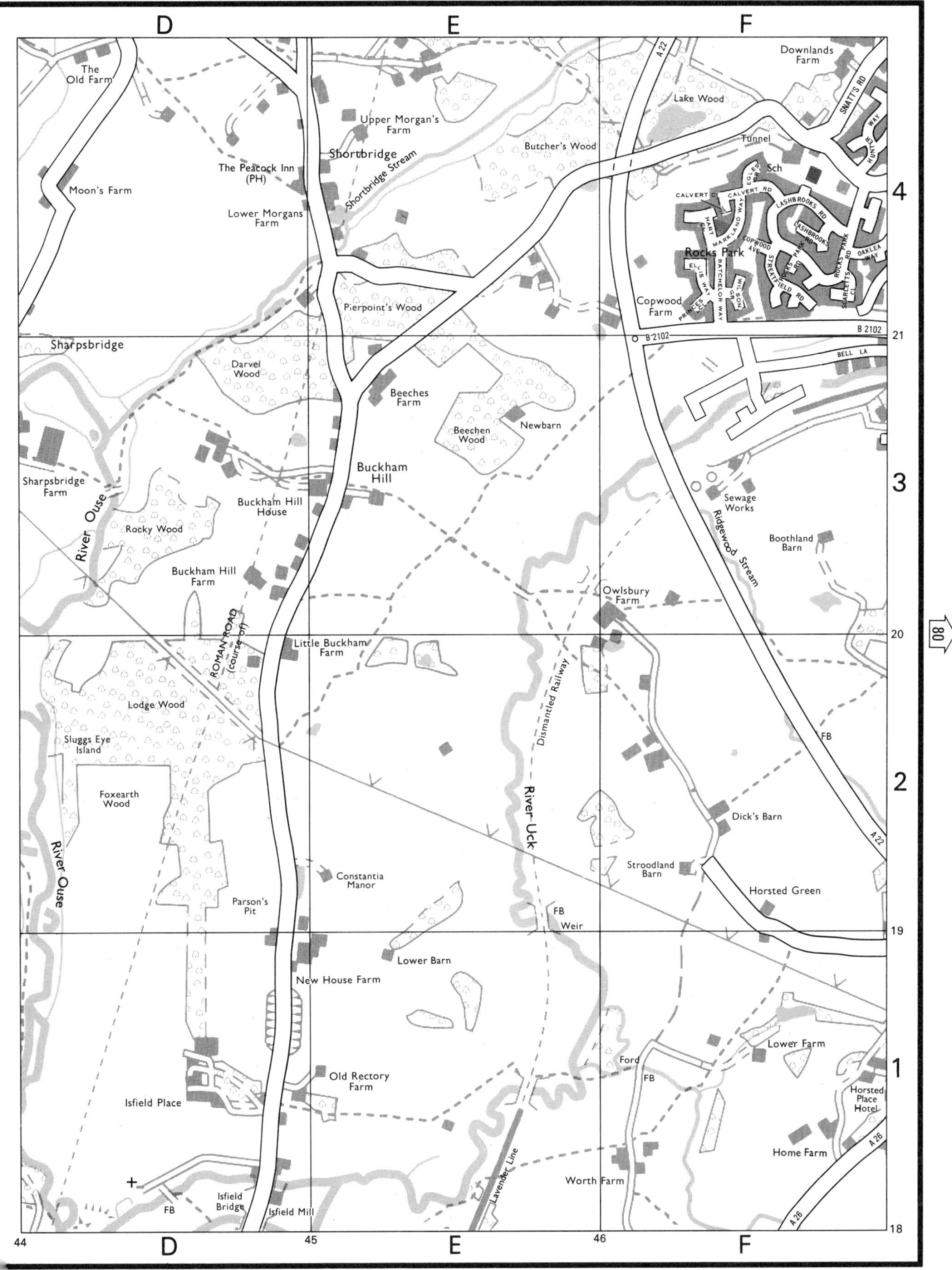

80

105

57

A
B
C
4
3
2
1
21
20
19
18
47
48
49
SNATT'S RD
Hempstead Farm Stud
Great Streele Farm
HEMPSTEAD LA
Hosp
Schools
LC
Hempstead Wood
Highlands Wood
Tickerage Stream
Highlands
Spring Barn Shaw
CHURCH ST
HEMPSTEAD RD
Liby
Town Hall
UCKFIELD
School
GRANGE RD
OLIVES MEADOW
River Uck
SANDY LA
Bretts Cottages
B 2102
HIGH ST
RIVER WAY
MILL LA
MILL DRO
ALBERT RD
KELD AVE
BIRD IN EYE HILL
Uckfield Station
MOUNT PLEASANT
FORGE RISE
FARRIERS WAY
FRAMFIELD RD
VERNON RD
SELBY RD
Bird-in-eye Farm
Hammond's Green
Framfield
FRAMELLE MT
PRESTON DR
GATEHOUSE LA
Hailwell Farm
Bird-in-eye-Shaw
School
Village Hall
The Hare and Hounds (PH)
THE STREET
BECKETS WAY
CLEVE CL
WILLOWS RISE
CHURCH APP
School
Convent
OLD TIMBERS LA
NEW PL
SELBY RISE
SELBY GDNS
New Town
Harlands Farm
Framfield Place
Sewage Works
Boothland Wood
Nightingale Wood
PH
Works
HIGHLANDS AVE
EASTBOURNE RD
The Old Laundry
Ridgewood Farm
HIGHVIEW LA
Framfield Stream
Upper Brookhouse Farm
Ridgewood
LEWES RD
NEW RD
Cysleys Farm
Brook House
Tile Barn
Well House
Ridgewood House
Barley Mow (PH)
Arches Manor
A 22
Mount Ephraim
Horstedpond Farm
A 26
Palehouse Farm
Horstedpond Wood
Park Wood
High Cross
Palehouse Common
High Cross Park
Little Horsted
Tilebarn Farm
School
High Cross Farm
High Cross Lake
High Wood
A 22

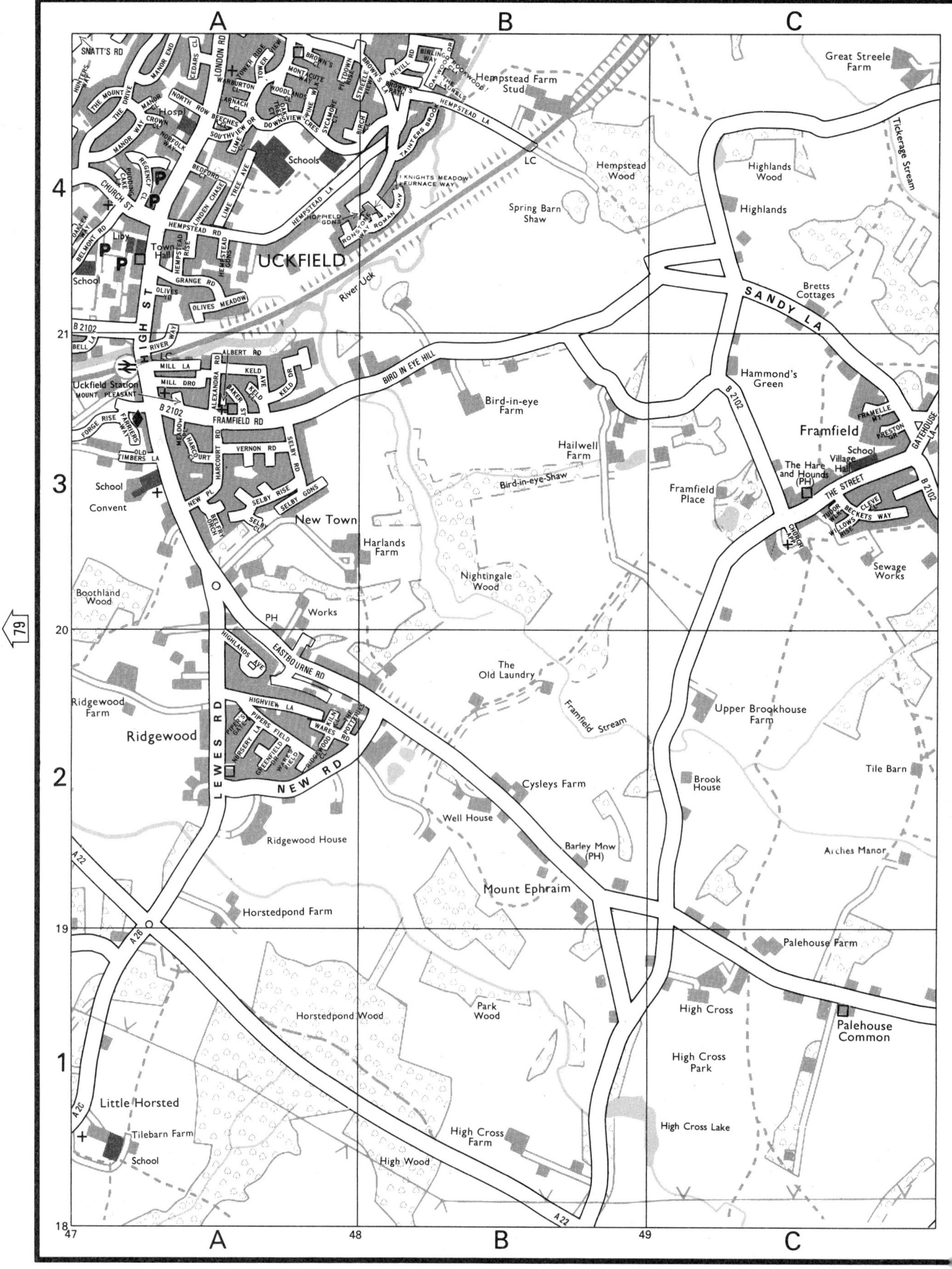

79

106

58

D
E
F
Primrose Ghyll Farm
Pounsley
Pounsley Manor
The Hundred House
Little Streele
BARN LA
Youth Hostel
Shawford Wood
Shawford Farm
4
POUND LA
Gatehouse Green Farm
Tickerage Castle
Tickerage Stream
Sewage Works
Brookhurst Farm
Mill
GATEHOUSE LA
21
Gatehouse
Tickerage Wood
TICKERAGE LA
GUN RD
Blackboys
B 2102
Upper Greatfield Farm
MOUNT PLEASANT
STAR LA
B 2192
School
THE GREEN
B 2102
3
Blackboys Inn (PH)
Framfield Grange
Kiln Wood
Old Barn
Pump Wood
Stonebridge
Browning's Wood
HOLLOW LA
20
Pembroke Manor
Little Arches Wood
Cider House Farm
Arches Farm
Newplace Farm
Newplace Wood
Borough Pit Shaw
Bushmere Stud
PUMP LA
2
Dencher Wood
Paines Place
Hawkhurst Common Wood
BUSHBURY LA
19
Scaines
Hider's Farm
Oak Tree Farm
Bushbury
Orchard Farm
Palehouse Common Farm
Twyford
Hope Farm
Works
1
Pelham's Place Farm
BEECHY RD
Little Goldsmith's Farm
Tewitts Farm
Squires
Siggs Farm
Eason's Green
Dickers Farm
Bonny's Farm
Hawkhurst Common
Durrant's Farm
Hill's Place Farm
SAND HILL LA
B 2192
18
50
51
52
D
E
F

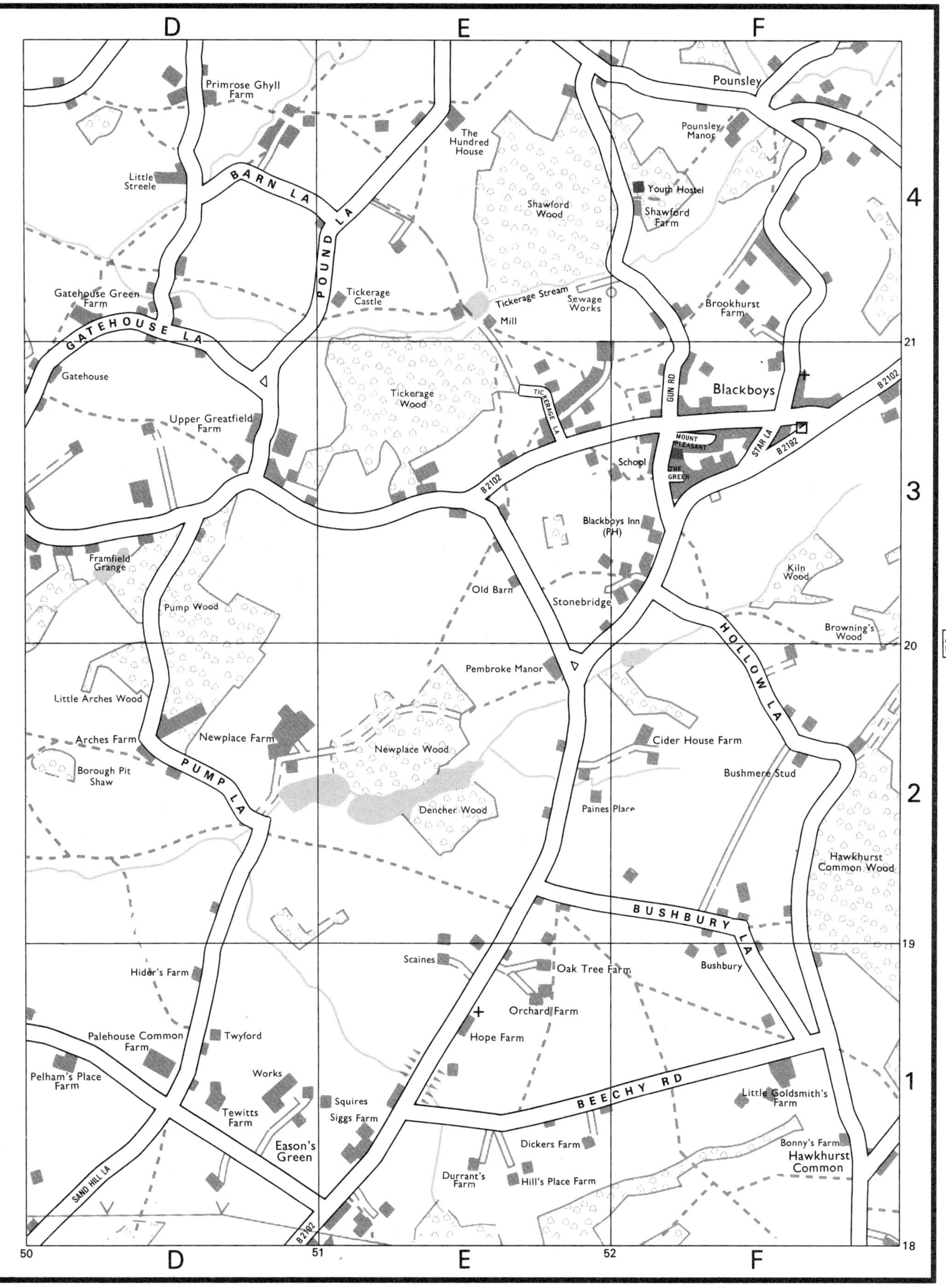

82

107

59

A
B
C
Bosmere
Sheepwash Farm
Springdene Farm
Baker's Common
Waldron Down
NURSERY LA
Mayfield Flat Farm
MAYFIELD FLAT
A 267
B 2102
B 2102
4
Burnthouse Farm
POSSINGWORTH CL
Holy Cross Priory
Beacon Down
Cross-in-Hand
Possingworth Park
WARREN LA
FIR GROVE RD
21
B 2102
Browning's Manor
WARREN CL
Firgrove Farm
FOREST PL
FOREST PL
Oxpasture Wood
Roser's Cross
Possingworth Manor House
3
Possingworth Manor Farm
Nature Reserve
BRITTENDEN LA
BRITTENDEN LA
Selwyns Wood
NORTH ST
Brittenden
Whitehouse Wood
Dower House Farm
Bryckden Place
20
Butlett's Wood
Blackdown Wood
Catts Crouch Farm
Old Glebe
2
Waldron
WHITEHOUSE LA
RAGGED DOG LA
Danesfield
Silveroaks Farm
Waldron House
Star Inn (PH)
Moat
Middle Wood
Common Wood
19
Birchlands Farm
Holms Farm
MOAT LA
Tullaghmore
Heronsdale Manor
Moat Farm
1
The Grubs
Braysland Farm
Tanyard Farm
Court Wood
Lions Green
Foxhunt Green Farm
Foxhunt Green
18
53
54
55
A
B
C

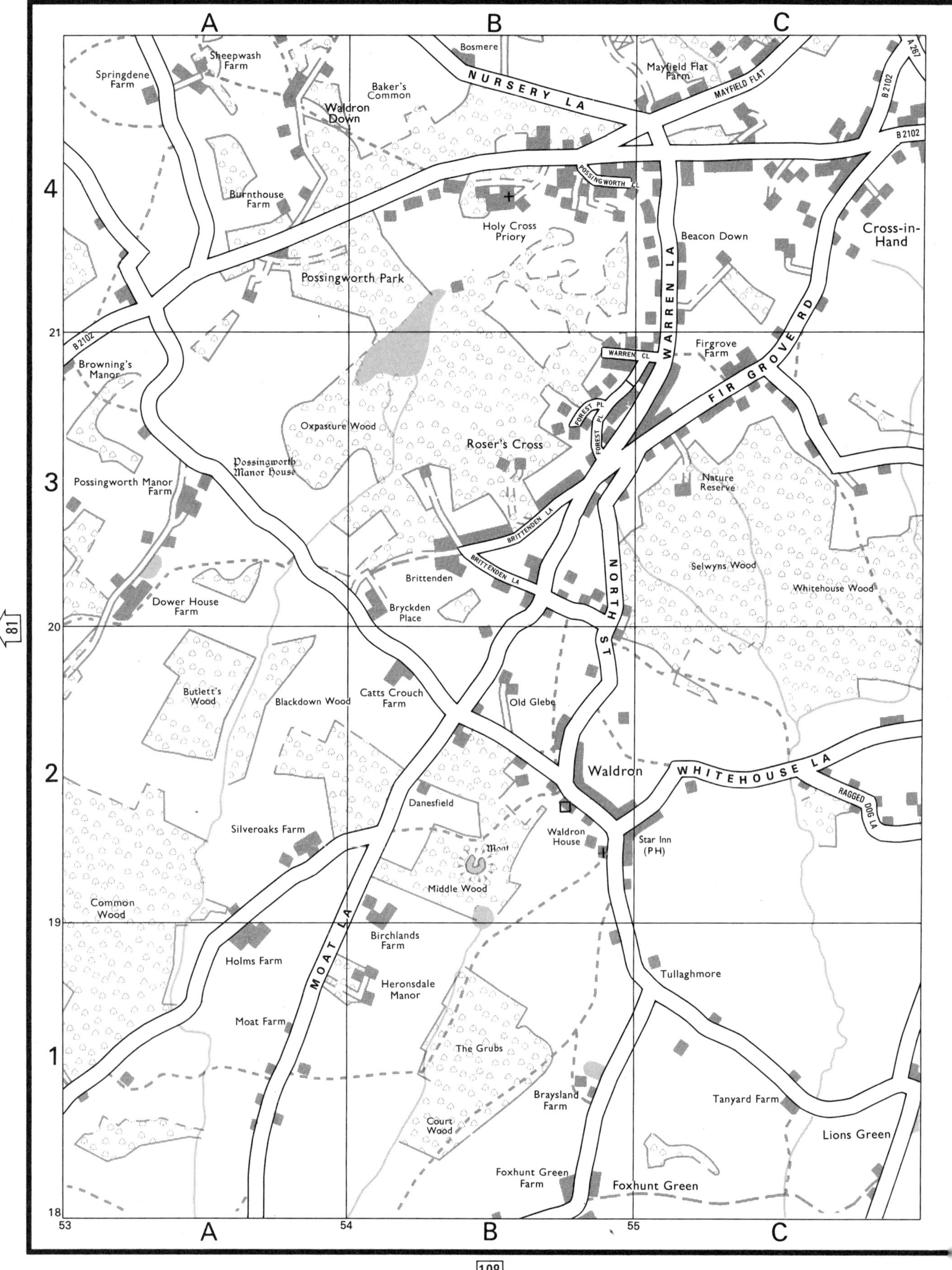

81

108

60

D
E
F
Mutton Hall
Hall
A 265
Cross-in-Hand (PH)
Heatherden
A 267
Tilsmore
Tinkers Hatch
Heatherden Wood
Holbrook House
HEATHFIELD
Gibraltar Tower
BACK LA
NEW POND HILL
New Pond Farm
POOK REED LA
GHYLL RD
HAILSHAM RD
STATION RD
HIGH ST
MUTTON HALL HILL
MUTTON HALL LANE
RIDGEWAY CL
BURWASH RD
TOWER ST
B 2203
MARSHLANDS LA
SHEEPSETTING LA
PAGES HILL
PAGES CL
WEALDVIEW RD
MILL RD
MILL CL
TILSMORE RD
WALDRON THORNS
NEWNHAM RD
SWAINES WY
CUCKOO DR
HARLEY LA
ALEXANDRA RD
PARK RD
UPPER STATION RD
WOODLANDS WAY
ELM WAY
SYCAMORE CL
HAWTHORN CL
GREEN LA
PROSPECT RD
MEADOW WAY
PINE TREE RD
CHURCHILL RD
LONGVIEW
LIMEWAY
BAY TREE CL
SANDY CROSS LA
THEOBALDS GREEN
NEW RD
FRENCHES FARM DR
ALDER CL
ROWAN CL
GEERS WOOD
COLLINGWOOD AVE
COLLINGWOOD RISE
GIBRALTAR RISE
HIGHCROFT CRES
CUCKMERE RISE
DOWNSVIEW
WALDRON CT
STATION APP
SPRINGWOOD RD
CHERWELL RD
FIRWOOD CL
FIRWOOD RISE
STREATFIELD RD
NURSERY WAY
F Sta
Sch
Crossinhand Stud
Geer's Wood
Lanrick
New Timbers Farm
Culverwood
Lower Theobalds Farm
Sandy Cross
Broadfield Wood
Theobald's Green Farm
Holms Hill Farm
Church Wood
Little London
The Runt-in-Tun (PH)
WHITEHOUSE LA
The Spinney (School)
Runtington Manor Farm
Mill Wood
Waldron Gill
Nevilles Farm
FRARY WLK
Stonelands Farm
Sapperton Wood
West Street Farm
Knabes Acre
Mepham's Farm
Maynard's Green
Huggetts Farm
WEST STREET LA
TUBWELL LA
SICKLEHATCH LA
Bray Hill
SANDY LA
HANGING BIRCH LA
Grantleys Farm
Burnt House Farm
Hendalls Farm
Stillyans Farm
Tanners Manor
Tanners Farm
Tregantle
School
21
20
19
18
4
3
2
1
56
57
58

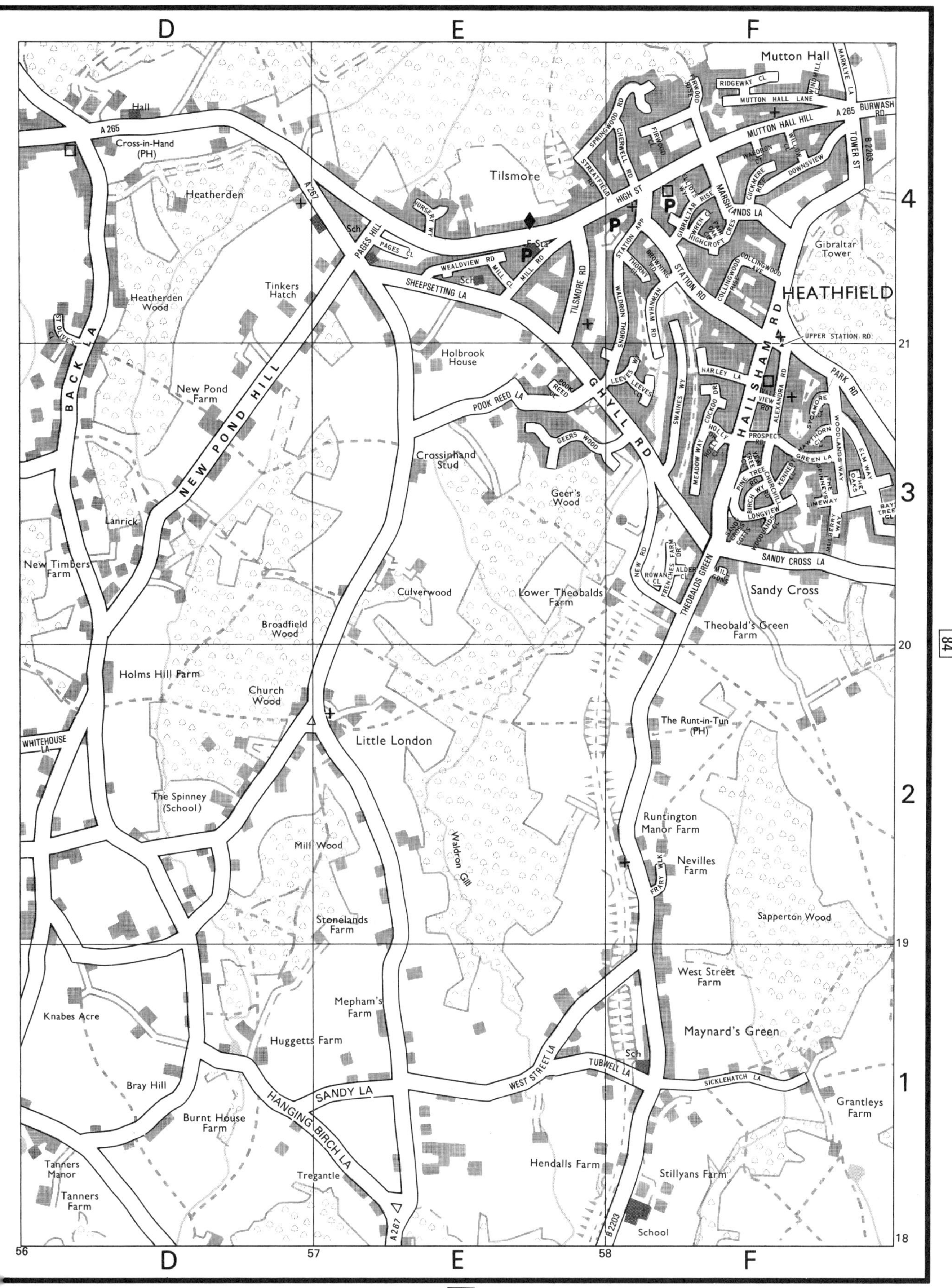

84

109

61

A
B
C
4
3
2
1
21
20
19
18
59
60
61
Crown (PH)
Amb Sta
NEWICK LA
DEN'S LA
A 265
BURWASH RD
B 2096
Satinstown Farm
HALLEY RD
Little Tottingworth Farm
Pheasant Wood
Old Tottingworth Farm
Brailsham Wood
River Dudwell
Stores Wood
Gameland Wood
Great Wood
Brailsham Farm
Rural Studies Centre
Streetfield Farm
Hugletts Farm
HUGLETTS LA
School
Jack Cade's Monument
Heathfield Park
Cade Street
Mount Pleasant Farm
Hope Farm
Sch
Chapel Cross
B 2096
Old Heathfield
PARK RD
Manor Farm
CHURCH ST
The Star (PH)
Highlands Farm
St Dunstan's Wood
Owlsbury Cross
Heathfield House
Barretts Park Farm
Walnuts Farm
Kenwards Well Farm
St Dunstan's Farm
Fountain Wood
Caller's Corner
New Sapperton Farm
Beckington Wood
Beaconland
White Birch Farm
Furnace Wood
Sapperton Manor Farm
Summerhill Farm
Wet Wood
Downgate Farm House
Nettlesworth Farm
Wayside
Nettlesworth Place
Pond Farm
Little Horeham
Beckington Bridge
FURNACE LA
Nettlesworth Wood
Chapman's Town
South Cottage
Hale Hill Farm
Warbleton
War Bill In Tun (PH)
Court Lodge Farm
Toll Wood
Kingsley Hill

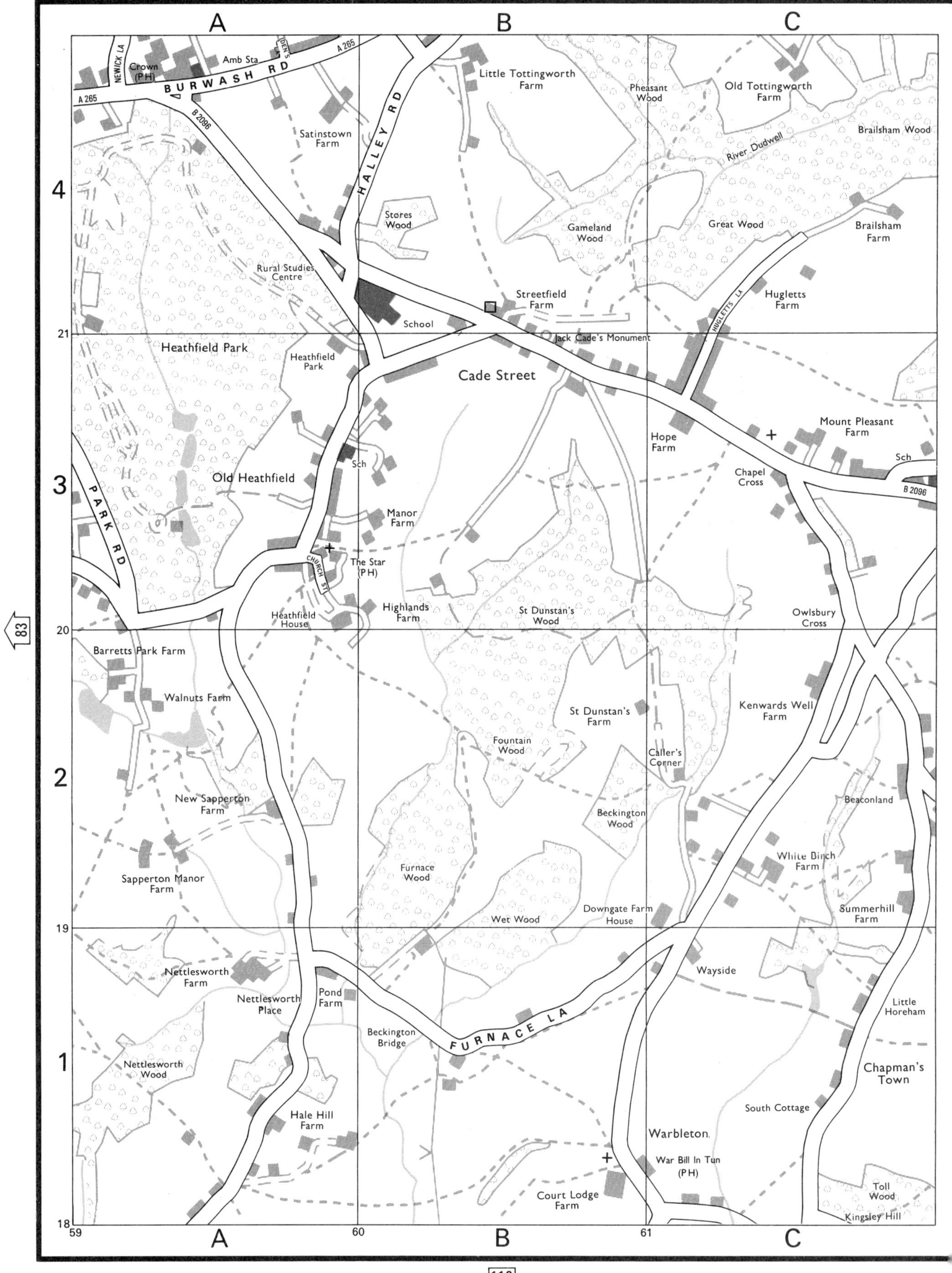

83

110

62

D
E
F
Tottingworth Wood
Hook Wood
River Dudwell
Ware's Wood
Greenwood Farm
4
Glazier's Forge Farm
Twenty Acre Wood
Green Wood
Little Poundsford Farm
Bingletts Wood
GREENWOODS LA
Stoney Wood Farm
21
Watkins Down Farm
Windmill
Dallington Forest
Punnett's Town
UPPER GREENWOODS LA
Hooksdown Farm
NORTH ST
PONT CL
3
The Barley Mow (PH)
High Holmstead Farm
Yew Tree Farm
Three Cups Corner
Rose Farm
Rigford Farm
The Three Cups (PH)
20
Rushford Farm
Oakside
FLITTERBROOK LA
Trill's Wood
Millars Farm
Willett's Farm
Coppice Farm
Turner's Green
Earl's Down
2
B 2096
Wyatts Farm
Little Marklye
Golding's Farm
Alms Wood
Bunce's Farm
Cophall Farm
19
Northfleet Farm
Stone House Farm
New Castle Farm
Marklye
Hoad's Wood
1
Christian's River
Stone House
Sand Banks
Rushlake Green
GROVELY LA
Horse & Groom (PH)
Ironworks (site of)
Great Iwood
Hotel
Grovelye Farm
BACK LA
Remains of Holy Trinity Priory
Water Mill Farm
18
62
63
64
D
E
F

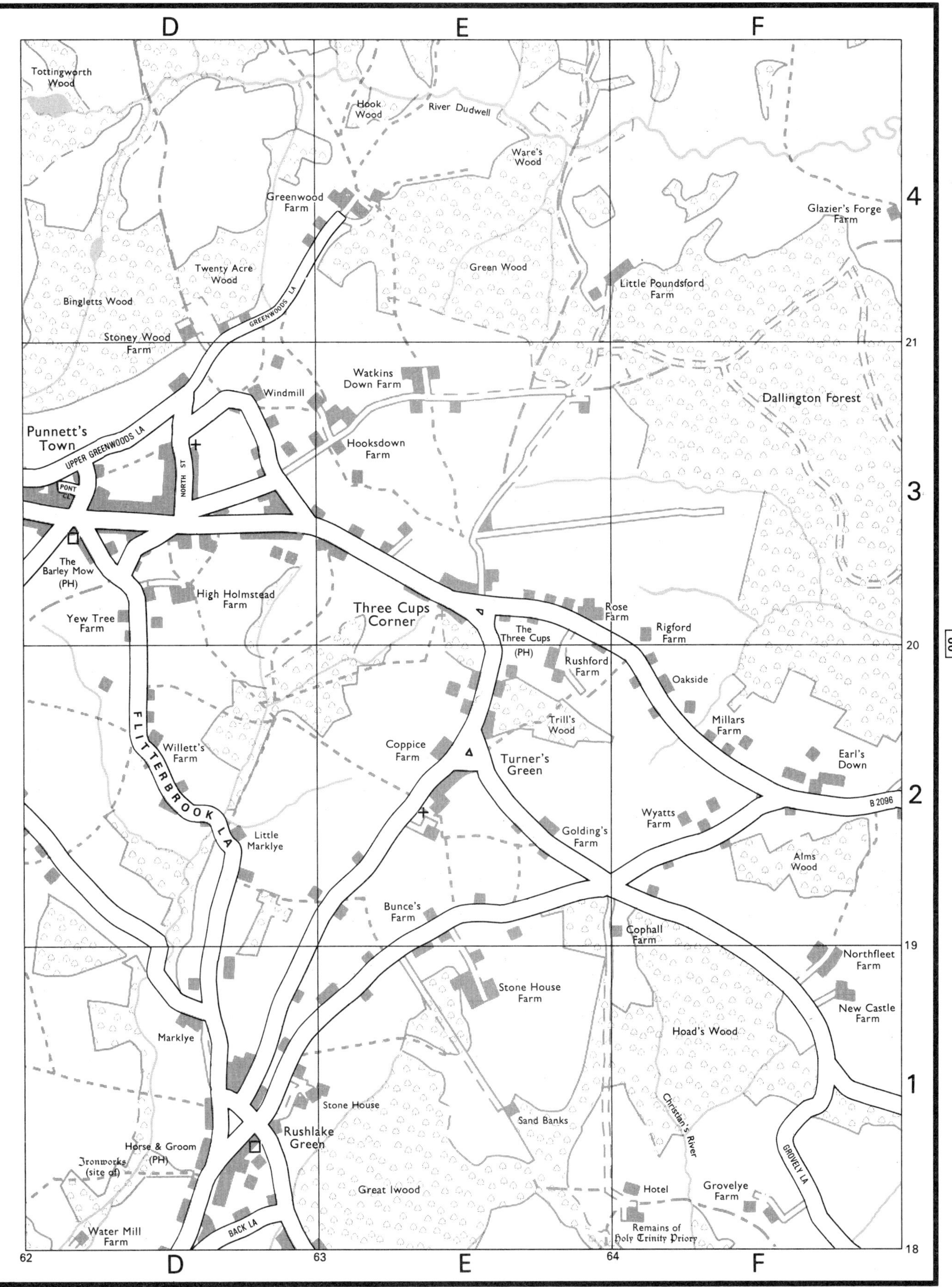

86

111

63

A
B
C
Blackbrooks
Brightling Mine (Gypsum)
Coombe Wood
Ashen Wood
4
Little Worge Farm
Glazier's Forge
Stonehouse
Mount Farm
Brightling Needle (Obelisk)
Sugarloaf Wood
Long Wood
Sheepshaw Farm
21
Great Worge
Willingford Stream
Forge Wood
Mill House Farm
The Avenue
The Observatory
Upper Plantation
3
Lower Plantation
Brightling Down
Stacey's Corner
Purchase Wood
Highlands Farm
Cox's Mill
Buckholt Farm
20
Hook's Farm House
Upper Brooklands Farm
Mansbrook Wood
Hotel
Brooklands Farm
Carrick's Hill
The Sugar Loaf
Christmas Farm
Turner's Farm
2
B 2096
Graylings
The Swan Inn (PH)
Rabbit's Farm
Wood's Corner
B 2096
Prinkle Farm
School
Haselden Farm
Old Castle
Dallington
Mine Pit Shaw
19
Griggs's Gill
Spring Wood
Acelands Farm
Haselden Gill
Uplands Farm
Willingford Stream
SOUTH LA
High Wood
Highwood Gill
Stream Farm
Haselden Wood
1
Clayton Wood
Oakland Farm
Clayton Gill
Gifford's Gill
Herring's Gill
HERRING'S RD
Parkfields Farm
Broomfield Farm
Paddock Gill
Herring's Farm
Pannelridge Wood
18
65
66
67
A
B
C

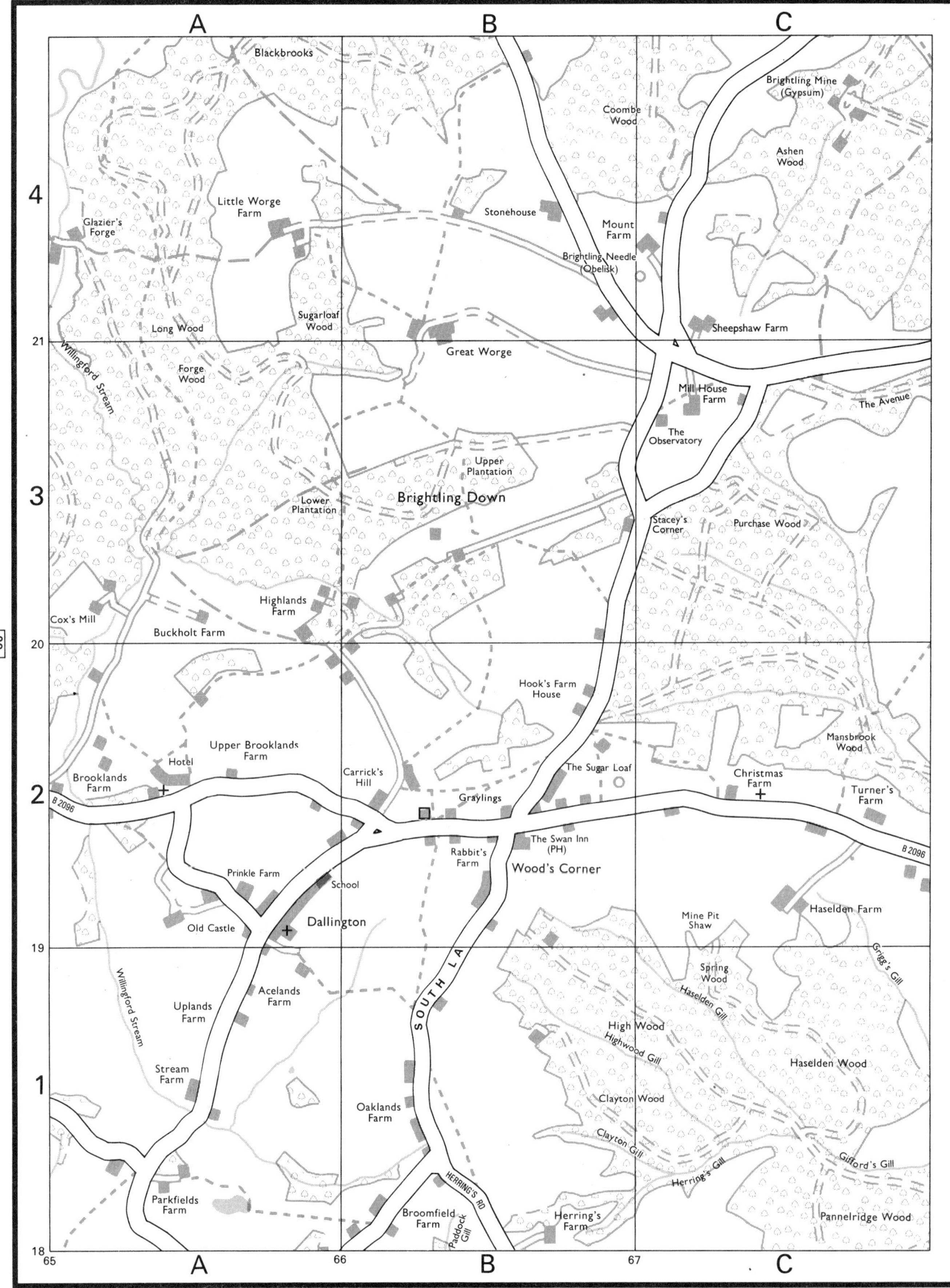

85

112

64

D
E
F
Beak's Wood
Great Wood
Perryfields
BRIGHTLING RD
Brightling Place
Oxley's Green
Rounden Wood
The Fuller's Arms (PH)
Dens Wood
Glottenham Stream
Hunter's Farm
MOUNTFIELD LA
Long Reach Farm
Aerial Ropeway
The Glebe House
Glebe Farm
Little Wood
KENT LA
Scaland Wood
Brightling Park
Brightling
Mill Wood
Hollingrove
Darwell Reservoir
Hollingrove Farm
Holman's Wood
Temple
Twelve Oaks
Birchen Wood
Saw Mill
Birchen Farm
Grants Cottages
Darwell Wood
Keepers Cottage
Darwell Stream
Cackle Street
Coblye Wood
FB
Old Stonesdown Farmhouse
Ford
Prinkle Wood
Darwell Hole
Coldharbour Farm
Gifford's Farm
Darwell Hill
Doctor's Farm
DARVEL DOWN
Waste Wood
Swaybank's Shaw
PENHURST LA
B 2096
White Hart (PH)
Homestead Farm
Long Shaw
Grigg's Gill
Musings Gill
Little Spray's Farm
Gifford's Shaw
Gifford's Gill
Musings Wood
Homestead Shaw
Sandy Wood
Bunce's Gill
Ibrook Wood
68
69
70
21
20
19
18
4
3
2
1

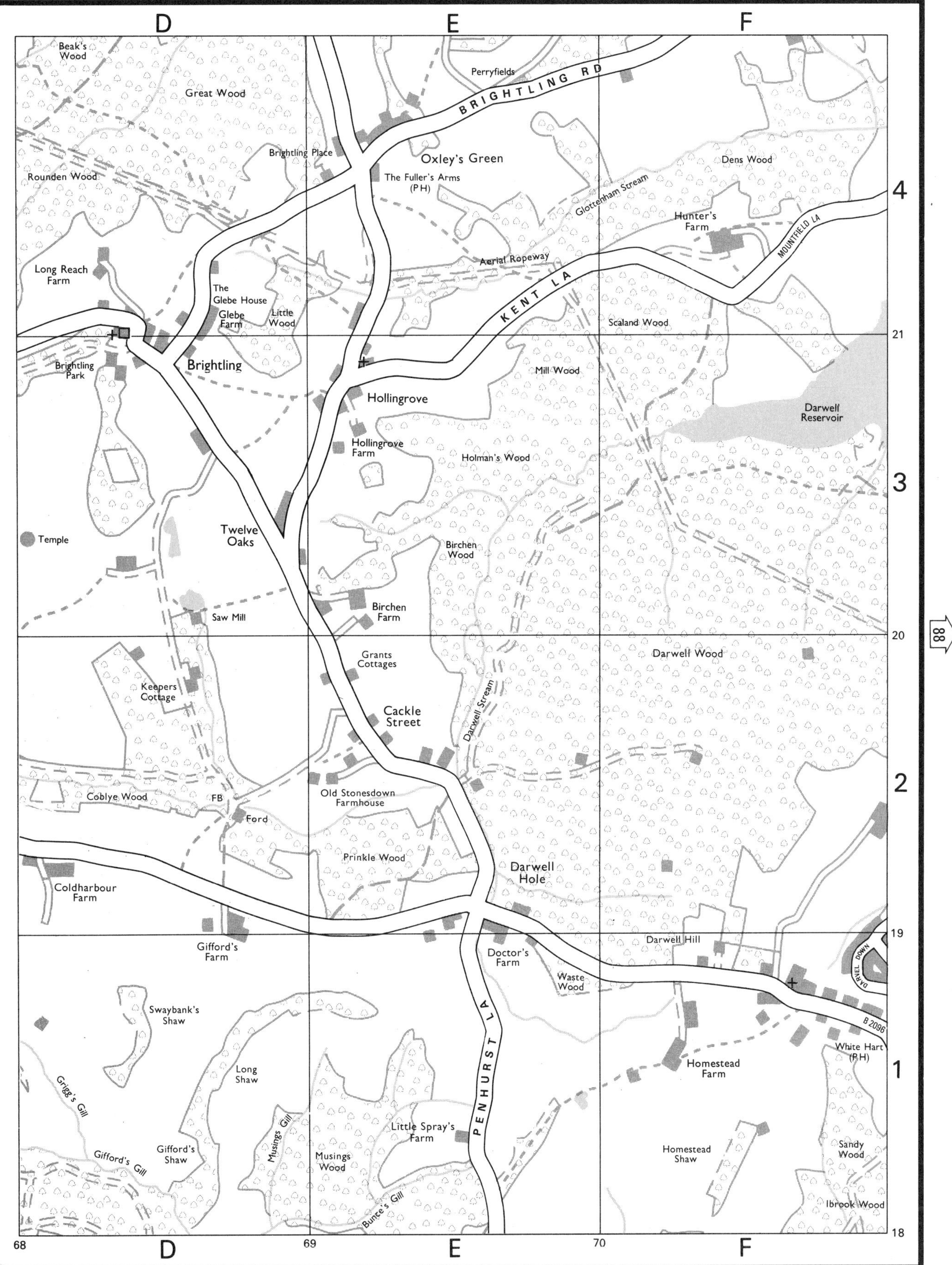

88

113

65

A
B
C
4
3
2
1
21
20
19
18
71
72
73
Mountfield Park Farm
MOUNTFIELD LA
Park Pale
Dray Shaw
Coalbridge Shaw
Darwell Stream
Clean's Wood
High Hurst Wood
Coal Bridge
Darwell Reservoir
Tunstall Farm
Bottonhold Wood
Bottonhold Brook
Temple Wood
Taylor's Cottage
Baldwin's Farm
Mountfield Court
Spring Wood
New House Farm
Mountfield
The Banks
Castle Farm
CHURCH RD
Earthwork
Limekiln Wood
Factory
Millham Wood
Lot's Wood
Aerial Ropeway
River Line
Lower Hucksteep Wood
Snep's Wood
Mountfield Mine (Gypsum)
Crowhurst Wood
Sewage Works
Great Wood
Crowhurst Farm
Upper Hucksteep Wood
DARVEL DOWN
Woodlands Farm
Netherfield
School
Brickhouse Wood
EATENDEN LA
The Netherfield Arms (PH)
Netherfield Court
NETHERFIELD WAY
The Old Rectory
B 2096
NETHERFIELD RD
Netherfield Down
Eatenden Wood
Goldspur Wood
Ivyland Farm
Toll Wood
Burnthouse Wood

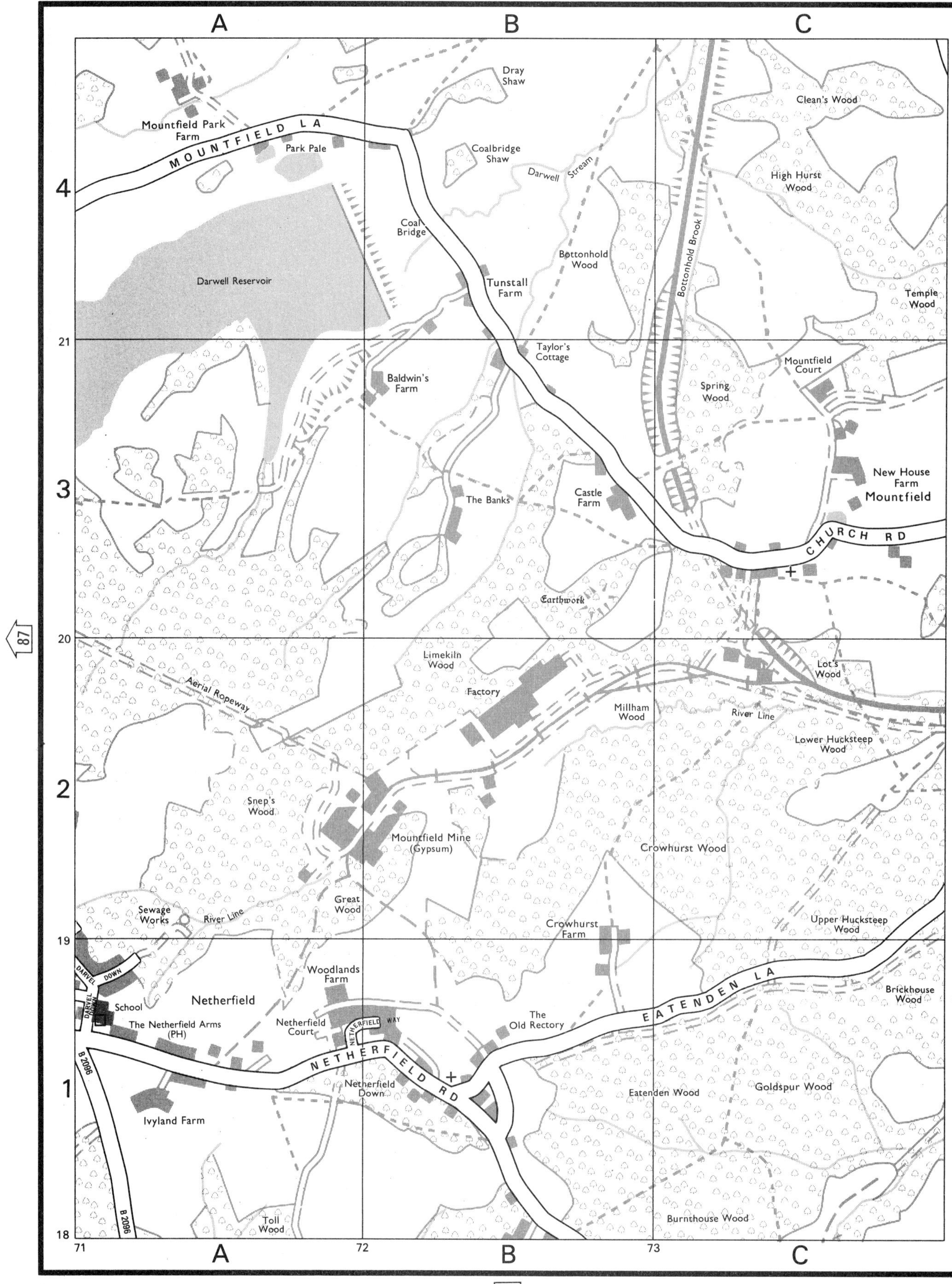

87

114

66

D
E
F
Walter's Wood
Oakey Wood
Starven Wood
Lee Bank Farm
Newpond Farm
Strawberry Hill Farm
POPPINGHOLE LA
Barne's Farm
Poppinghole Farm
JOHN'S CROSS RD
A21(T)
John's Cross Inn (PH)
John's Cross
Sch
Wimbletott's Wood
Barne's Wood
B 2089
Orchard Farm
A 2100
Vinehall Forest
Couchman Wood
VINEHALL RD
Vinehall Street
Vinehall
CHURCH RD
NEW CUT
Vinehall Farm
Footland Wood
Hoath Farm
Riverhall Farm
HOATH HILL
B 2090
PARK LA
SOLOMON'S LA
Riverhall Bridge
Line Wood
Dorrells Farm
LC
EATENDEN LA
LONDON RD
Battle Wood
Maddomswood Farm
Spring Wood
Royal Oak Inn (PH)
Woodmans Green
Hancox Farm
Footway Wood
Duke's Wood
River Line
Maddoms Wood
Burnt Oak Wood
RICCARDS LA
STREAM LA
Wood's Place
Cottage Wood
Riccards Farm
Archer Wood
Woodsdale
Mill Farm
WHATLINGTON RD
Whatlington
Plovers Mead
Eastlands Farm
4
3
2
1
21
20
19
18
74
75
76

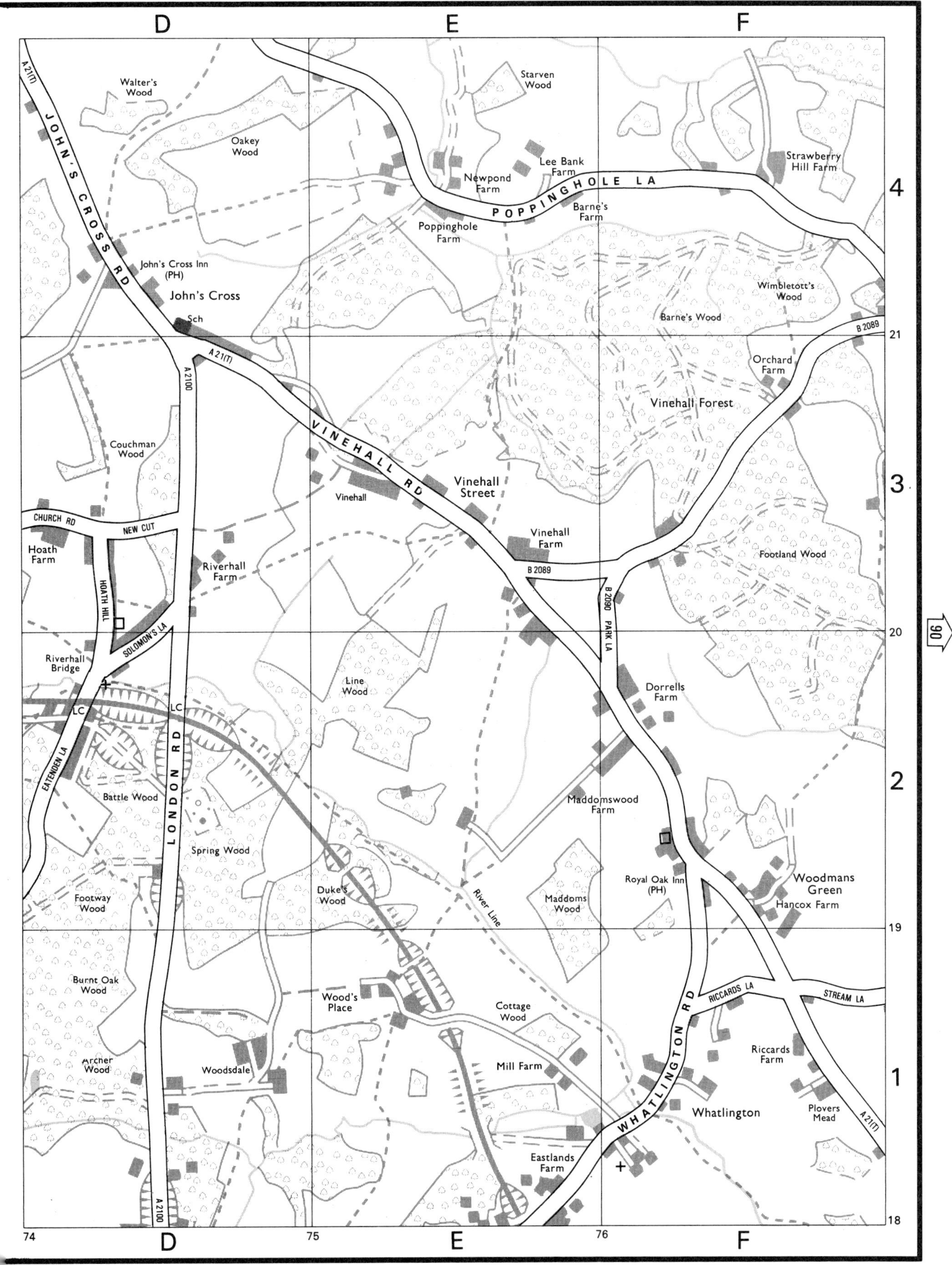

90

115

67

A
B
C
A
B
C
4
3
2
1
21
20
19
18
77
78
79
The Grange
Upper Morgay Wood
Badland Wood
Andrew's Gill
JUNCTION RD
A 229
B 2165
Wattlehill Farm
Ellenwhorne
Badland Shaw
The Beacon
Miles Farm
Stocklands Farm
ELLENWHORNE LA
Cripp's Corner
Viaduct
Whorne Wood
Swaile's Green
B 2089
Springwood Farm
Catts Green Farm
COMPASSES LA
Greenden Wood
Compasses
Brede High Wood
Streetfield Wood
Holman Wood
Footland Farm
Mill
Thorp's Wood
Long Wood
Ward's Wood
Beech Farm House
BEECH FARM RD
Powdermill Reservoir
Austford Wood
Great Sanders School
Hurst Wood
Cryalls Wood
Combe Wood
HURST LA
Killingan Wood
Churchland Lane
Jacob's Cottage
Hurst House
Moon's Wood
Jacob's Farm
POWDERMILL LA
STREAM LA
Durhamford Manor
Spilsteads Farm
Highfield
Bourne's Farm
Little Brede Wood
Balcombe Green
BREDE LA
Brede Barn Farm
Lower Jacob's Farm
Sch
LONG LA
GORSELANDS
EAST VIEW TERR
A 21(T)
THE STREET A 229
PARK SHAW
GAMMONS WAY
STREETLANDS
Sedlescombe
Sch
Sewage Works
River Brede

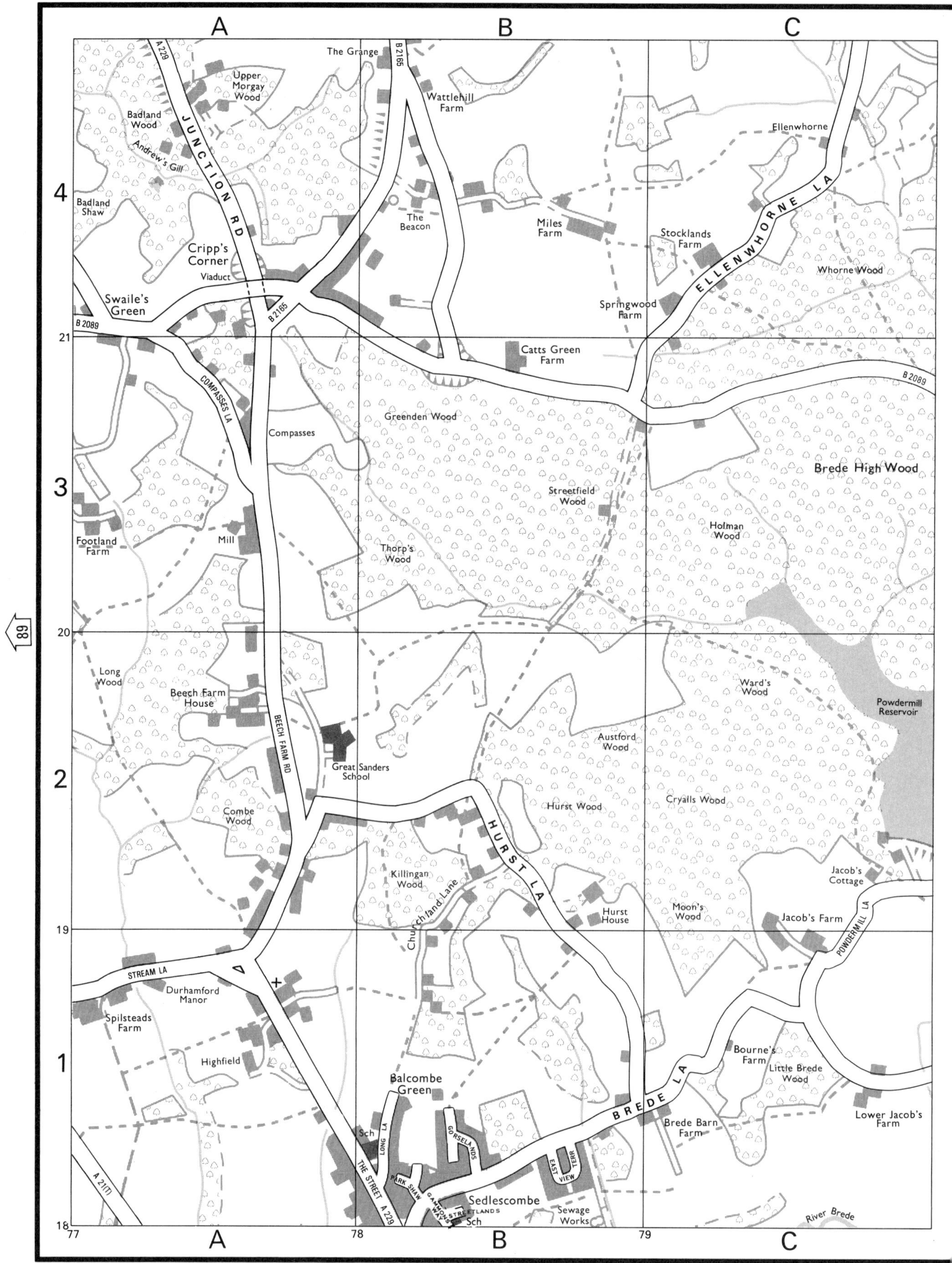

89

116

68

D
E
F
Watts' Palace Farm
Stockwood Farm
Monkings Farm
Tanhouse Farm
Doucegrove Farm
Little Doucegrove
Gilly Shaw
Bilberry Wood
WATTS' PALACE LA
Wagmire Wood
Maplestone Farm
NORTHIAM RD
A 28
River Tillingham
Arnold Bridge
Conster Manor
Chitcombe Farm
Chitcombe
Hoath Wood
Brede High Green
Austen's Wood
West Wood
FURNACE LA
Chitcombe Wood
Redland Wood
CHITCOMBE RD
Goatham Green
GOATHAM LA
Coneyburrow Wood
Granary Farm
THE TILLINGHAM VIEW
OAKHILL DR
HAWTHORNES
CHESTNUT CL
REEDSWOOD RD
FIELDWAY
THE ORCHARD
POND CL
F Sta
B 2089
Goatham Farm
Twist Wood
Cherry Tree Cottage
Broad Oak
School
Moorsholm
KING WOOD HILL
Powdermill Reservoir
Pond Wood
Lone Barn Cottage
POWDERMILL LA
Snathurst Wood
North Wood
Lone Barn Farmhouse
Plains Wood
Well Wood
Powdermill Bridge
Rafters Wood
FRYMAN'S LA
Steephill Wood
Cackle Street
CACKLE ST
Mill Wood
ST MARY'S CL
POTTERY LA
POTTERY CL
STEEP HILL
BREDE LA
Horn's Wood
Fryman's Farm
Little Park Wood
STUBB LA
Brook Lodge Farm
Park Wood
Brook Lodge House
BREDE HILL
Brede
4
3
2
1
21
20
19
18
80
81
82

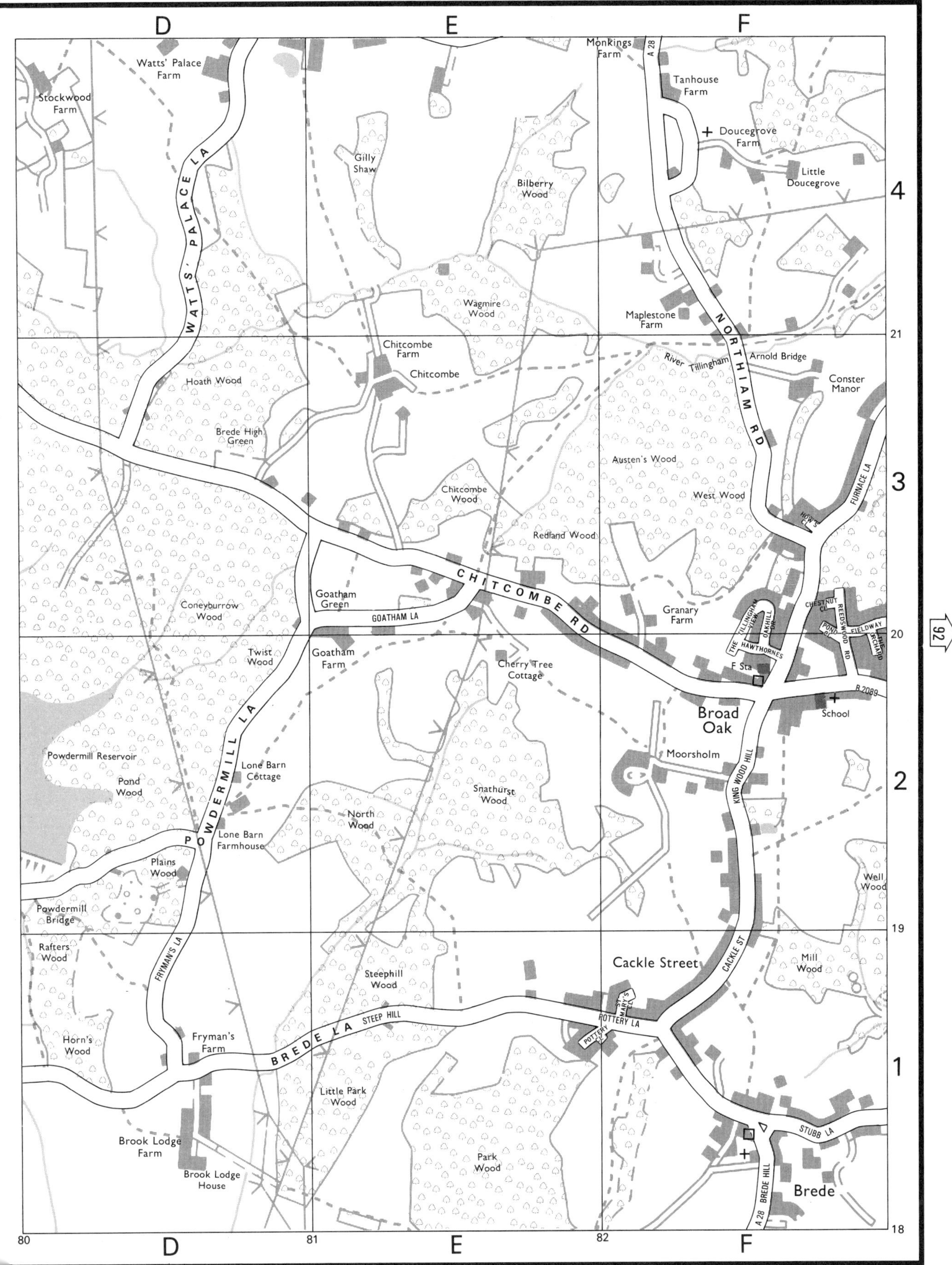

92

117

69

A
B
C
Little Gate Farm
Wharnham Wood
Garland Wood
Moore's Wood
Timber Wood
Blackland Wood
Glass Eye Farm
Greentiles Farm
Gate Cottage
Furnace Wood
Osier Gill
Sheepwash Wood
FURNACE LA
MOORE'S LA
HORSESHOE LA
Wagmary Wood
Furnace Farm
Beckley Furnace
Oak Wood
Rowland Wood
STARVECROW LA
Great Conster Farm
Burnthouse Wood
LUDLEY HILL
Alder Shaw
Ludley Farm
Kicker Wood
Heronry House Farm
River Tillingham
Birch Wood
Hayesland Farm
HAYES LA
Twist Wood
Hundredhouse Bridge
FIELDWAY
THE MARTLETS
Orchard Wood
Spring Wood
Maidlands Plantation
Maidlands Farm
B 2089
HUNDREDHOUSE LA
Gilly Wood
Great Sowdens Wood
Newman's Farm
Reysons Farm
Broadland Row
Reysons Oasts Farm
UDIMORE RD
Sowdens Farm
Broadlands Wood
The Kings Head (PH)
STUBB LA
South Sowdens Wood
Little Park Wood
Alder Wood
Great Park Wood
Hillyfield
Brede Place
Hare Cottages
Hare Farm
Pickdick Farm
Stonelink Farm
4
3
2
1
21
20
19
18
83
84
85

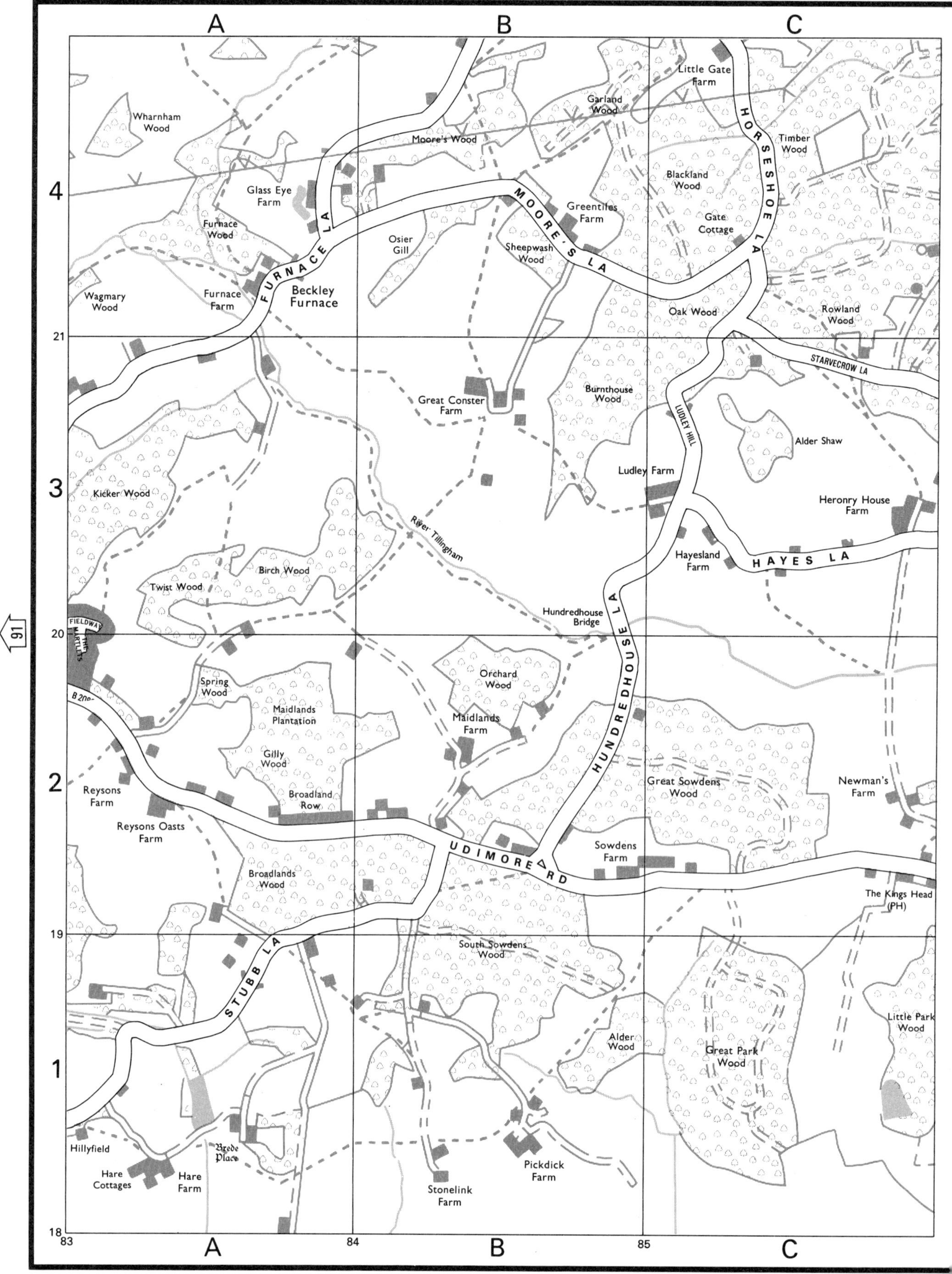

91

118

70

D
E
F
Eggshole Brook
Morebread Wood
Morebread Farm
Peasmarsh Place
CHURCH LA
Lower Gate Farm
The Hermitage
Button's Farm
DEW LA
Poplar Wood
Axletree Plantation
Waterfall Wood
Groves
STARVECROW LA
Barline Farm
Cleves Farm
Sluts Wood
Dew Farm
Pelsham
Tillingham Wood
Partridge Farm
Pelsham Farm
Ennets Wood
Coney Wood
Dinglesden Farm
TILLINGHAM LA
Pelsham Wood
Starvecrow Cottage
Hayes Farm
HAYES LA
Tillingham Farm
Hooker's Wood
River Tillingham
Tillingham Bridge
Billingham Farm
Billingham Wood
Wick Farm
Spouts Wood
BILLINGHAM LA
The Hammonds
B 2089
Stocks Wood
Parsonage Farm
Udimore
Tibbs Farm
Cock Marling
B 2089
Court Lodge
UDIMORE RD
The Plough (PH)
Knellstone
Lord's Wood
Nicholls Cottages
Roadend
Beauchamps
WINCHELSEA LA
Float Farm
River Brede
4
3
2
1
21
20
19
18
86
87
88
94

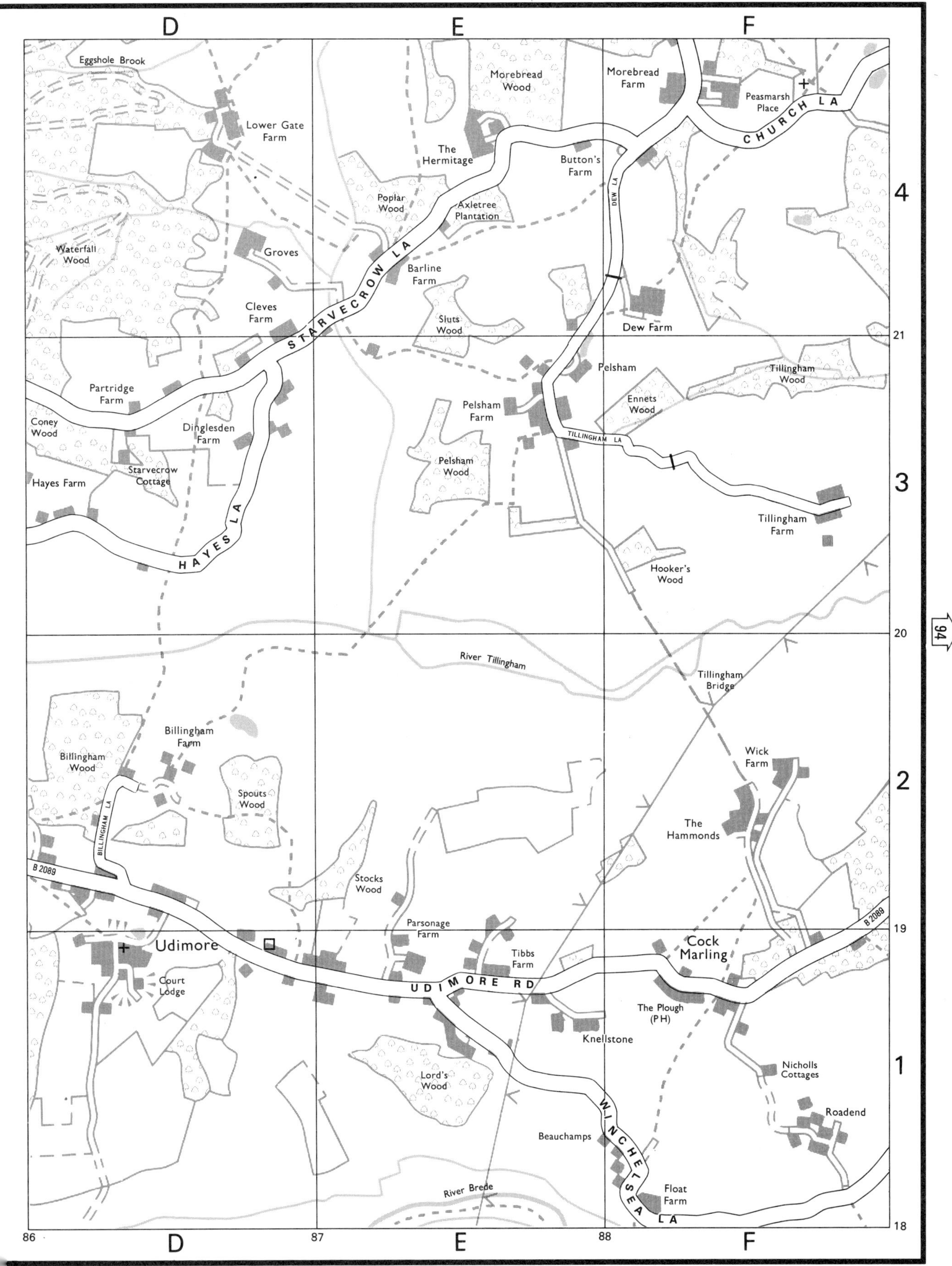

119

71

A
B
C
CHURCH LA
Norland Wood
Clayton Farm
Leasam Wood
Leasam House
Secret Wood
Springfield
A 268
LEASAM LA
THE OAKFIELD
Hospl
Hospl
Rovindene
Cockney Hill Wood
Leasam Hill
Rolvendene Farm
Cemy
LOVE LA
Sch
Cottage Shaw
River Tillingham
HENLEY CL
DENTON CL
THE CLOSE
POTTINGFIELD RD
FERRING CL
LEA AVE
NUTLEY CL
MARLEY RD
THE LINK
COOPER RD
MASON RD
Sch
TILLINGHAM AVE
Rye Station
Sch
F Sta
B 2089 FERRY RD
Offices
LC
CYPRUS PL
WISH ST
CINQUE PORTS ST
WISH WARD
THE DEALS
THE MINT
MERMAID ST
STRAND
WINCHELSEA RD
ST MARGARETS TERR
ASHENDEN AVE
WEST UNDERCLIFF
Gibbet Marsh
Calves Field Wood
Wks
Martello Tower
HARBOUR RD
Brede Sluice
CADBOROUGH CLIFF
Gillshaw Farm
Schoolhouse Farm
Cadborough Farm
Oaklands
UDIMORE RD
Turnpike Wood
Cadborough Cliff
Wick Wood
Watlands
Knellstone Wood
NEW WINCHELSEA RD
DUMB WOMAN'S LA
Farthing Wood
B 2089
River Brede
WINCHELSEA LA
Padiam Sewer
LC
Newhouse Sewer
Winchelsea Station
ROYAL MILITARY RD
STATION RD
Brede Level
Station Cottages
A 259(T)
4
3
2
1
21
20
19
18
89
90
91
A
B
C

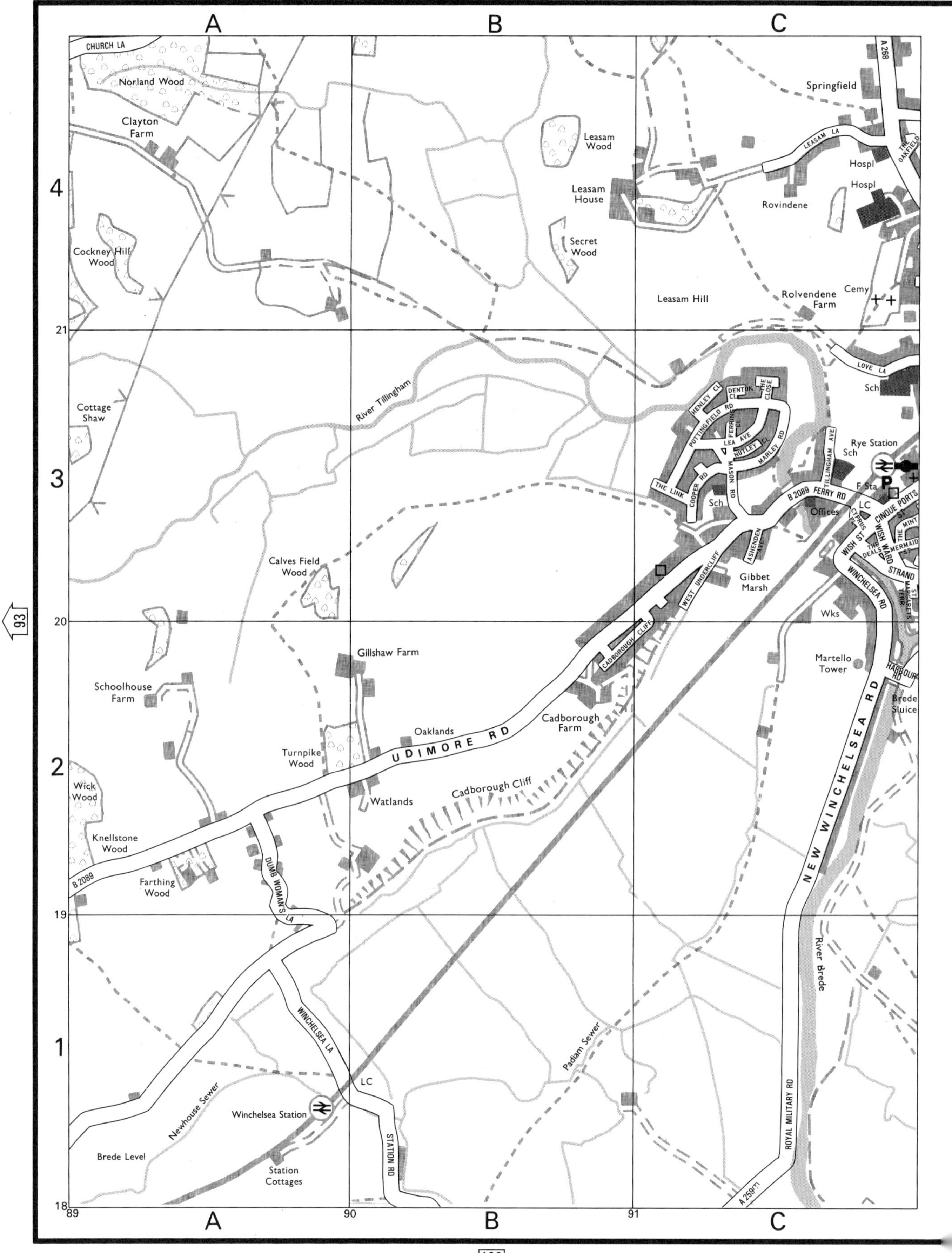

93

120

72

D
E
F
Playden
RECTORY LA
SALTCOTE ST
MILITARY RD
A 268
MILL RD
FAIR MEADOW
Point Hill
Rye Hill
NORTH SALTS
THE GROVE
Middle Salts
LC
LANDGATE
BRIDGE PL
AILSWORTH LA
KING'S AVE
NEW RD
Sch
REGENT SQ
EAGLE RD
ROPE WALK
A 259(T)
LOWER ST
FISHMARKET RD
EAST CLIFF
CONDUIT HILL
RYE
MARKET RD
HIGH ST
EAST ST
LION ST
MARKET ST
Liby
SEAVIEW TERR
TH
WEST ST
CHURCH SQ
WATCHBELL ST
Ypres Tower
SOUTH UNDERCLIFF
WATCHBELL LA
River Brede
Rye Harbour
A 259(T)
Guldeford Crossing
FOLKESTONE RD
East Guldeford
Salts Farm
Hoppets Farm
GULDEFORD RD
East Guldeford Level
Moneypenny
Black House Farm
Northpoint Sewer
CAMBER RD
Northpoint Beach
River Rother
TRADING ESTATE
HARBOUR RD
Northpoint Beach
PH
MARY STAMFORD GREEN
Club House
Inshore Rescue Boat Station
TRAM RD
Rye Golf Links
Rye Harbour
Martello Tower
Caravan Park
Lime Kiln Cottage
Rye Harbour Sewer (Drain)
Camber Castle
Nook Drain
Nature Reserve
4
3
2
1
21
20
19
18
92
93
94
D
E
F

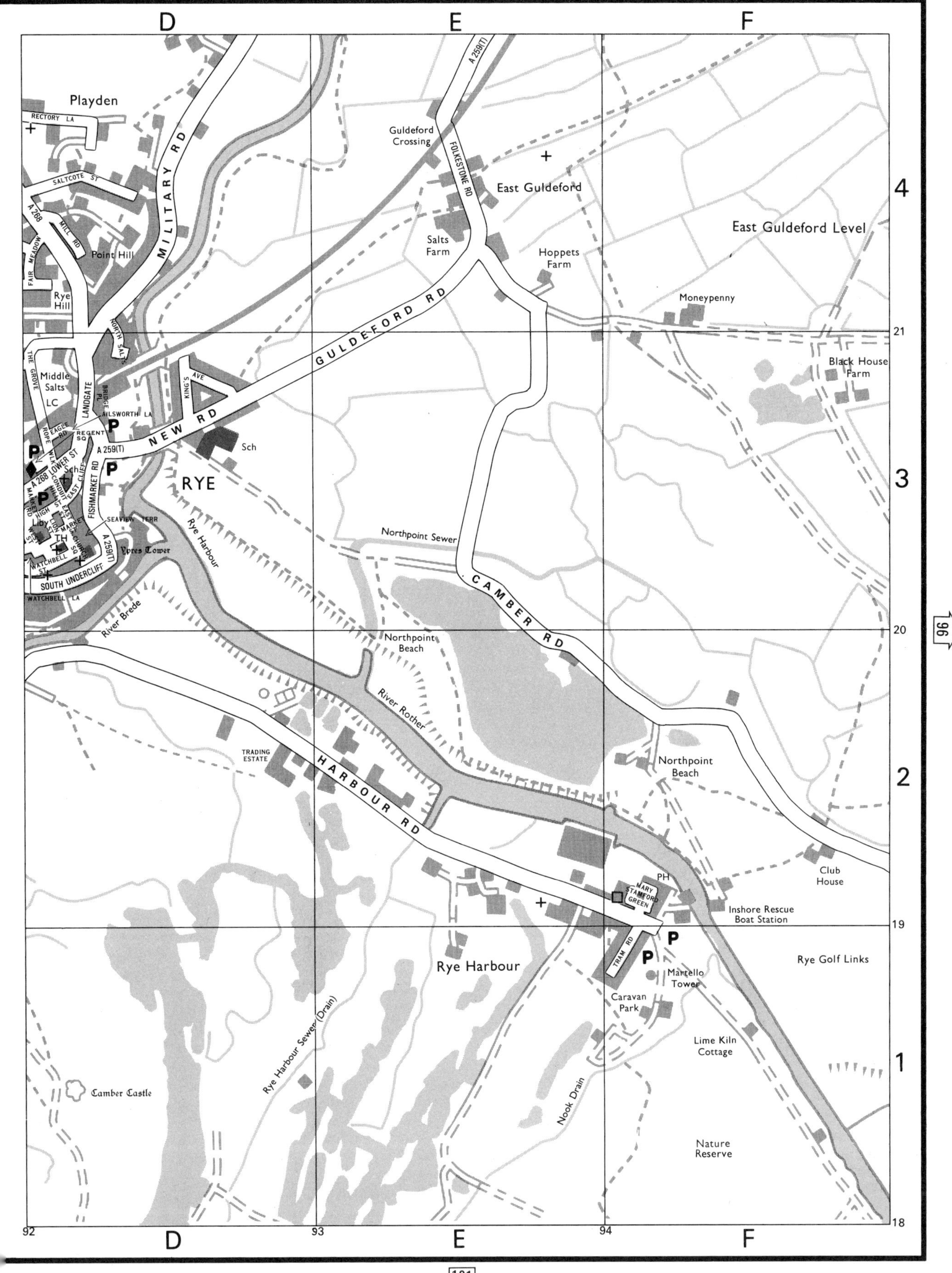

96

121

73
95
A
B
C
4
3
2
1
21
20
19
18
95
96
97
Barn Farm
Tressland
Kent Ditch
Guldeford Sewer
Wainway Wall
Wainway Wall
Guldeford Sewer
Rainbow Petty Sewer
Chittenden's Cottage
Point Farm
Pound Field Farm
FARM LA
Holiday Camps
Camber
Broomhill Creek
DRAFEIN LA
LINKS WAY
SCOTTS ACRE
Coastguard Cottages
P
PETER JAMES CL
DENHAM WAY
LYDD RD
TONBRIDGE WAY
OLD LYDD RD
MARCHANTS DR
DUNES AVE
SEA RD
FIRST AVE
SECOND AVE
LYDD RD
Caravan Park
Caravan Park
PELWOOD RD
SAUNDERS WAY
THE SUTTONS
P
Broomhill Farm
Camber Sands
East Pier

not continued, see key diagram

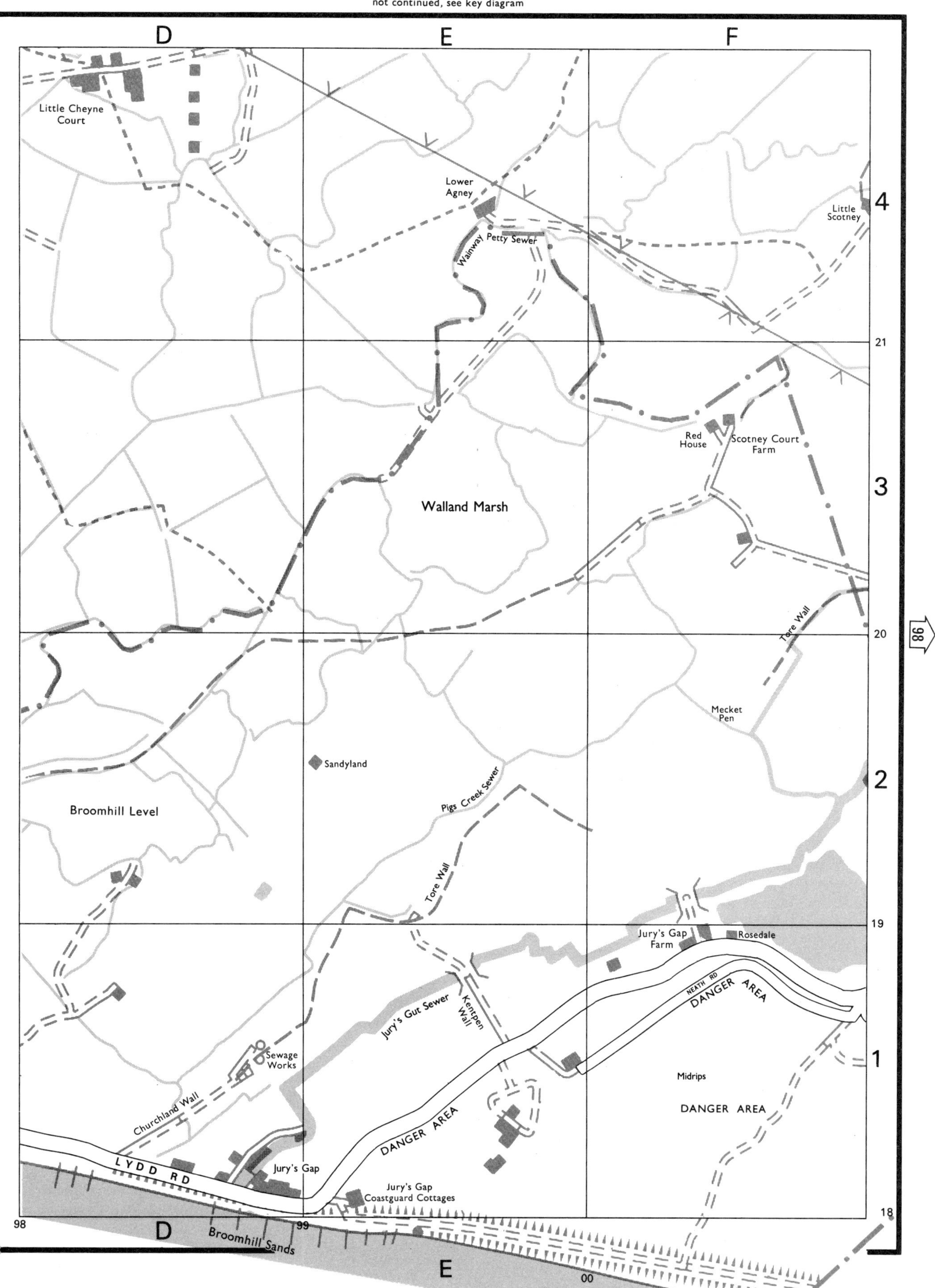

not continued, see key diagram

97

not continued, see key diagram

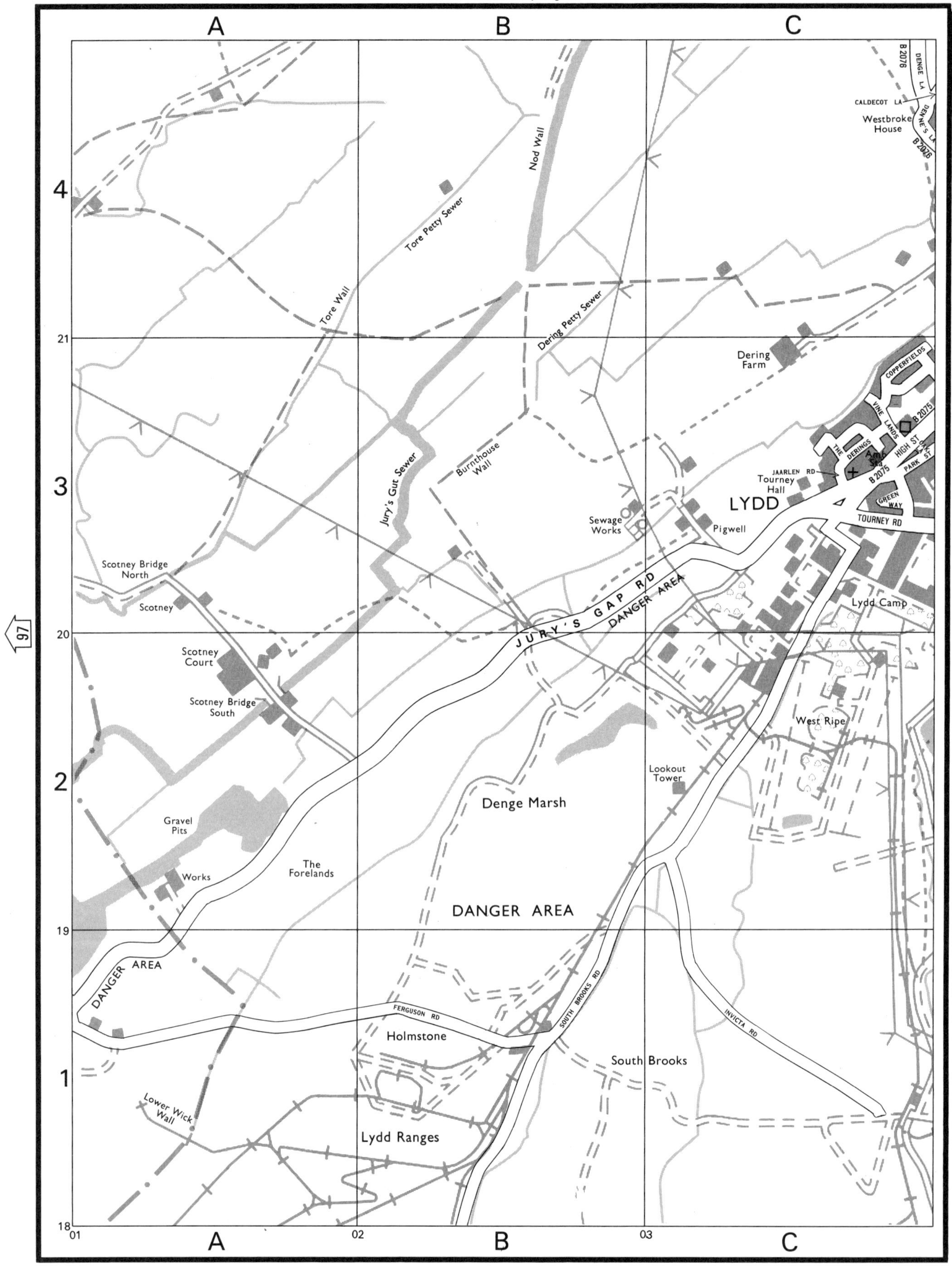

not continued, see key diagram

not continued, see key diagram

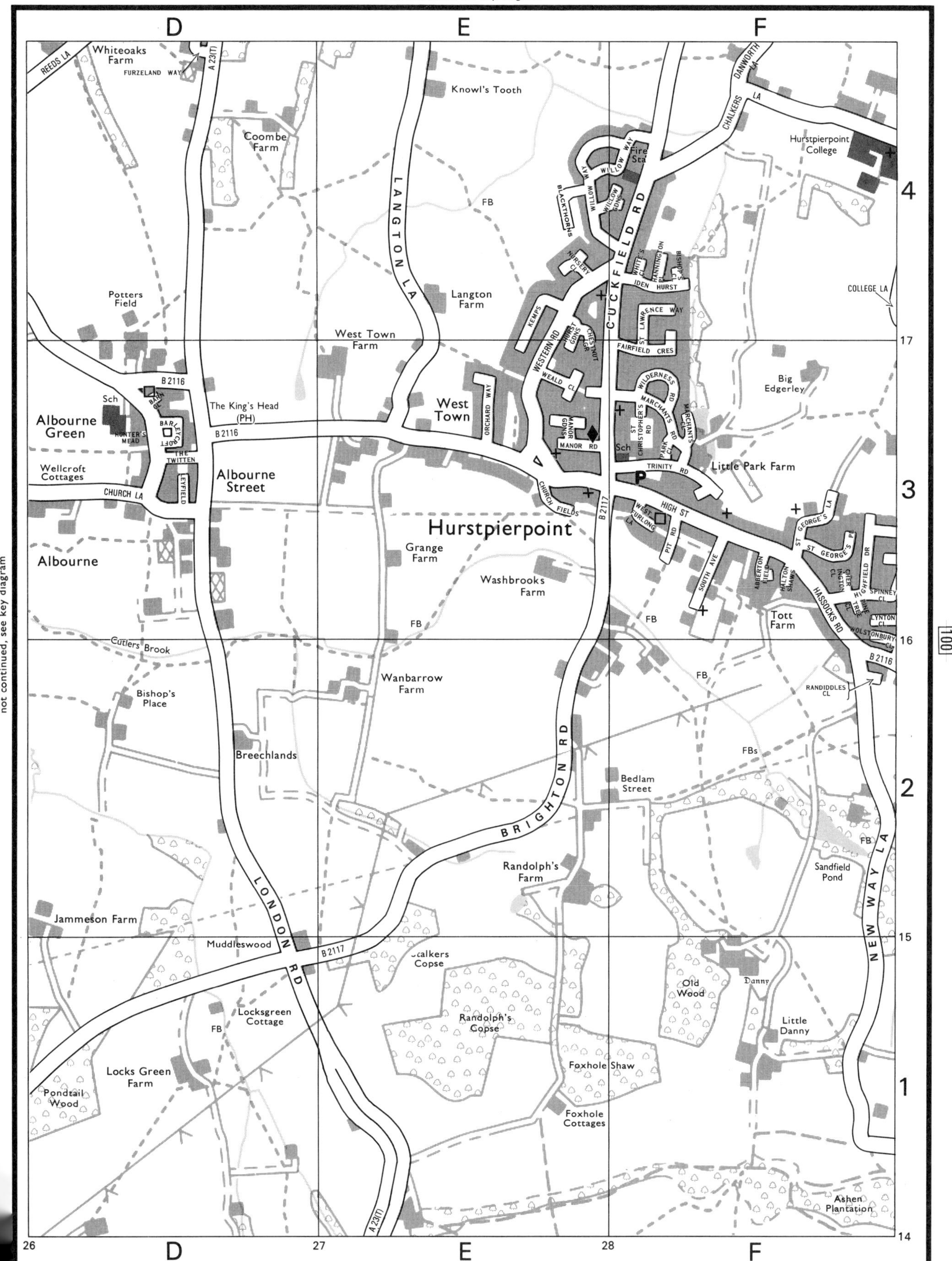

not continued, see key diagram

100

122

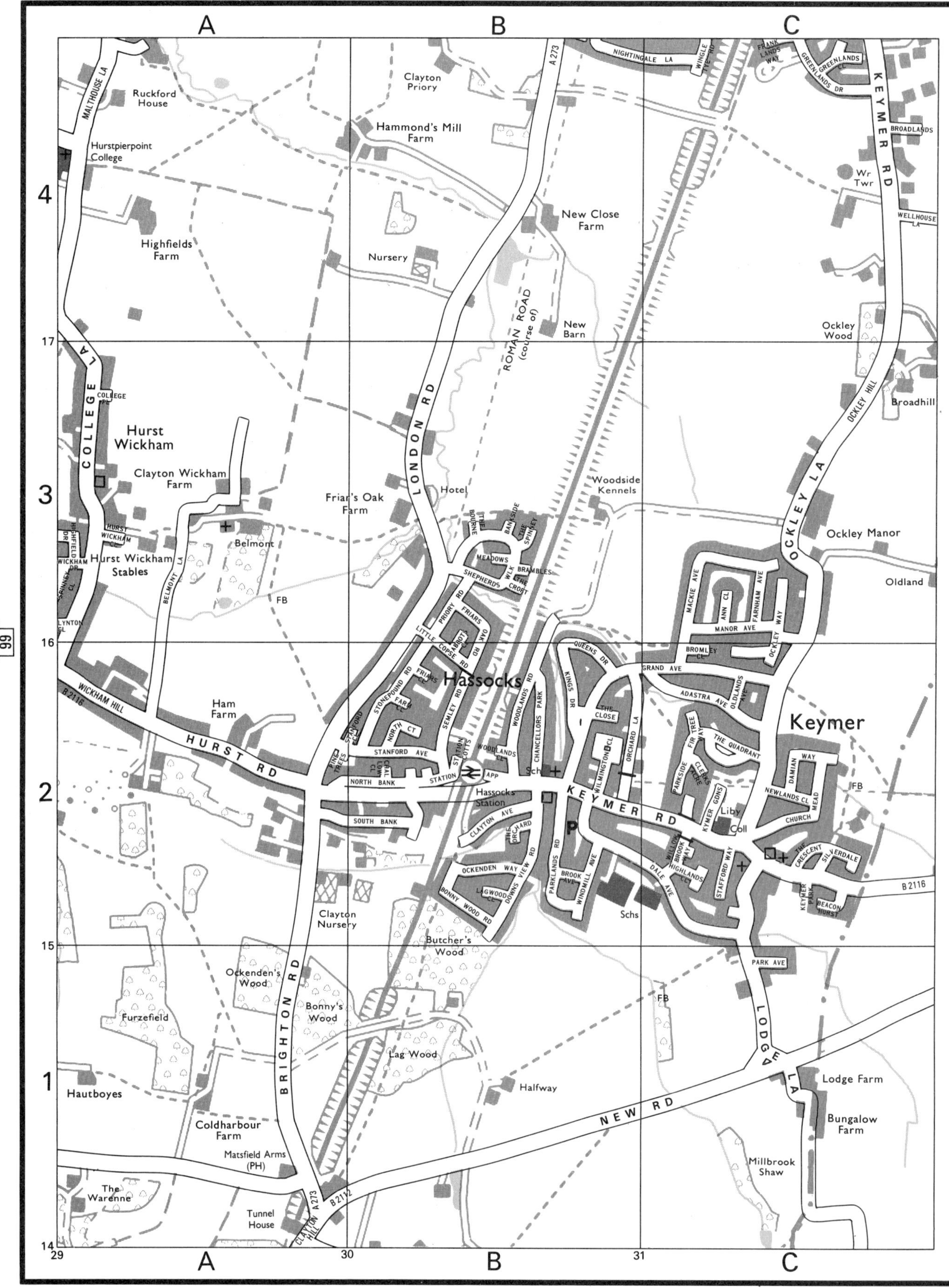
74
A
B
C
4
3
2
1
17
16
15
14
29
30
31
99
123
Ruckford House
Hurstpierpoint College
Highfields Farm
Clayton Priory
Hammond's Mill Farm
Nursery
New Close Farm
New Barn
ROMAN ROAD (course of)
LONDON RD
MALTHOUSE LA
NIGHTINGALE LA
WINGLE TYE RD
FRANKLANDS WAY
GREENLANDS DR
KEYMER RD
BROADLANDS
Wr Twr
WELLHOUSE LA
Ockley Wood
OCKLEY HILL
Broadhill
OCKLEY LA
Ockley Manor
Oldland
COLLEGE LA
COLLEGE PL
Hurst Wickham
Clayton Wickham Farm
Belmont
BELMONT LA
Hurst Wickham Stables
Friar's Oak Farm
Hotel
Woodside Kennels
Hassocks
Keymer
WICKHAM HILL
B 2116
HURST RD
Ham Farm
FB
STANFORD AVE
NORTH BANK
SOUTH BANK
Hassocks Station
KEYMER RD
Sch
Liby
Coll
Schs
MACKIE AVE
ANN CL
FARNHAM AVE
MANOR AVE
BROMLEY CL
GRAND AVE
ADASTRA AVE
OLDLANDS AVE
QUEENS DR
KINGS DR
THE CLOSE
WILMINGTON CL
ORCHARD LA
THE QUADRANT
DAMIAN WAY
NEWLANDS CL
MEAD
CHURCH
THE CRESCENT
SILVERDALE
BEACON HURST
KEYMER PARK
PARKLANDS RD
WINDMILL AVE
DALE AVE
HIGHLANDS CL
STAFFORD WAY
OCKENDEN WAY
BONNY WOOD RD
DOWNS VIEW RD
CLAYTON AVE
Clayton Nursery
Butcher's Wood
Ockenden's Wood
Bonny's Wood
Furzefield
Lag Wood
BRIGHTON RD
Hautboyes
Coldharbour Farm
Matsfield Arms (PH)
The Warenne
Tunnel House
CLAYTON HILL
A273
B2112
NEW RD
Halfway
PARK AVE
LODGE LA
Lodge Farm
Bungalow Farm
Millbrook Shaw

75

D
E
F
Hopkin's Crank
Upper Furzfield
Fragbarrow Farm
Blackbrook Wood
Gallops
WELLHOUSE LA
Wellhouse Farm
Clearview Farm
The Plantation
The Oaks Poultry Farm
LC
HUNDRED ACRE LA
B2112
The Tole
Townmead
Swansyard Farm
COMMON LA
Cottage Homes
SOUTH VIEW
Blackbrook Farm
Court Gardens Farm
SPATHAM LA
Oaktree Farm
Marchants Farm
Windmill
ORCHARD LA
Stocks Farm
NORTH END
Northend Farm
DUMBRELLS CT
LODGE HILL LA
Lodge Hill
Newtons Farm
ROMAN ROAD (course of)
Ditchling
Nurseries
BODDINGTONS LA
EAST GDNS
DYMOCK'S
THE MULBERRY
Sch
CHURCH LA
HIGH ST
THE TWITTEN
EAST END LA
KEYMER RD
WEST ST
FIELDWAY
Hayleigh Farm
SOUTH ST
Sch
FB
East End
CLAYTON RD
P
LEWES RD
BARNFIELD GDNS
Hop Garden Shaw
B2112
NEW RD
NEVILL COTTS
FB
NYE LA
LONG PARK CNR
SHIRLEYS
Sedlow Wood
Wapple Way
BEACON RD
The Nye
Molehilly Shaw
Jointer Copse
Blackdog Hill
Brocks Wood
Nye La
Nurseries
Wellcroft Shaw
Middleton Plantation
Park Barn Farm
B2116
Middleton Manor (College)
32
33
34
17
16
15
14
4
3
2
1

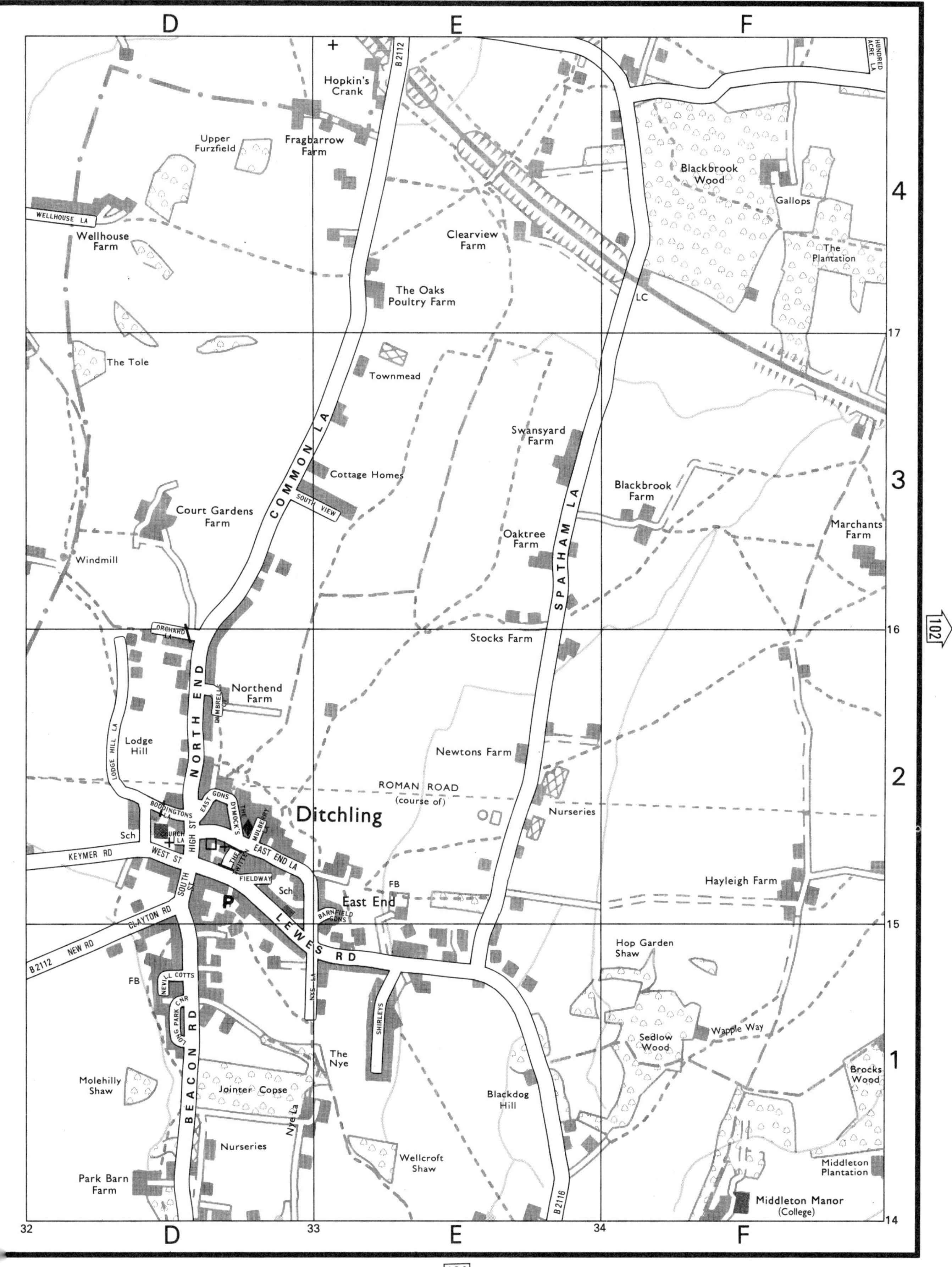

102

124

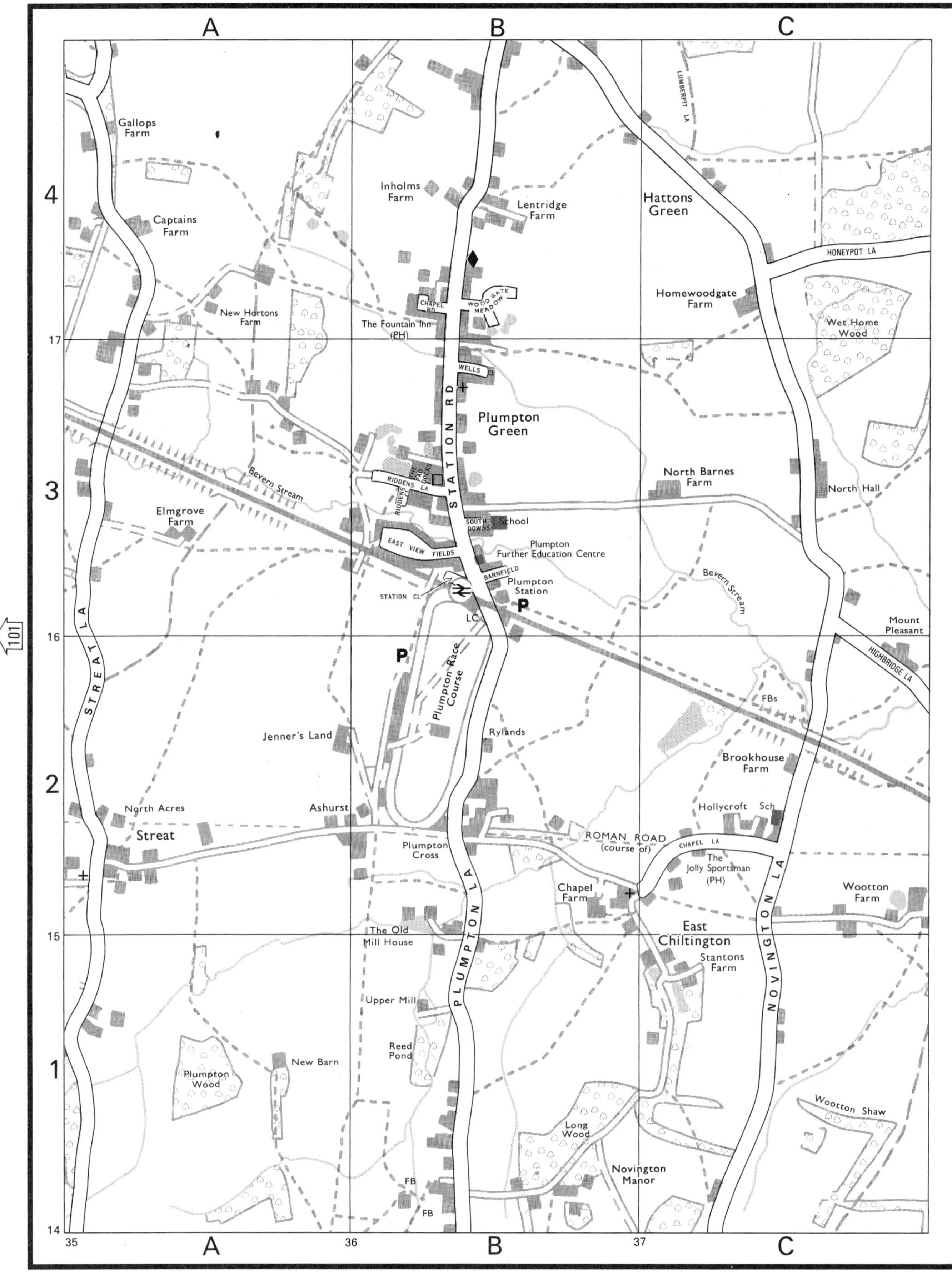
76
A
B
C
Gallops Farm
Inholms Farm
Lentridge Farm
Hattons Green
Captains Farm
LUMBERPIT LA
HONEYPOT LA
Homewoodgate Farm
Wet Home Wood
New Hortons Farm
CHAPEL RD
WOOD GATE MEADOW
The Fountain Inn (PH)
WELLS CL
Plumpton Green
STATION RD
Bevern Stream
RIDDENS LA
THE PADDOCKS
RIDDENS CL
North Barnes Farm
North Hall
Elmgrove Farm
SOUTH DOWNS
School
EAST VIEW FIELDS
Plumpton Further Education Centre
BARNFIELD
Plumpton Station
STATION CL
LC
Mount Pleasant
HIGHBRIDGE LA
Plumpton Race Course
STREAT LA
FBs
Jenner's Land
Rylands
Brookhouse Farm
North Acres
Ashurst
Hollycroft
Sch
Streat
ROMAN ROAD (course of)
CHAPEL LA
Plumpton Cross
The Jolly Sportsman (PH)
Chapel Farm
Wootton Farm
East Chiltington
The Old Mill House
Stantons Farm
PLUMPTON LA
NOVINGTON LA
Upper Mill
Reed Pond
New Barn
Plumpton Wood
Wootton Shaw
Long Wood
Novington Manor
FB
FB
4
3
2
1
17
16
15
14
35
36
37
101
125

77

D
E
F
Southam Wood
South Common
A 275
Grantham's Rough
Balneath Lane
Markstakes Common
Starvecrow Wood
Balneath Wood
Works
ST JOHN'S BANK
CAVERIDGE LA
GREEN LA
MILL LA
South Chailey
School
HONEYPOT LA
MILL CL
The Martlets
Pouchlands Hospital
KILNWOOD LA
The Swan Inn (PH)
Balneath Manor
FB
Yokehurst
Oldbarns Farm
Swan Wood
Woodbrooks Farm
Bevern Bridge Farm
Hovel Wood
Hurst Barns
Bevern Stream
Birdshole Lane
Beachy Wood
FB
HIGH BRIDGE LA
Hewenstreet Farm
Gallybird Hall
Lower Burrells
CHILTINGTON LA
LC
FB
ROMAN ROAD (course of)
Wickham Barn
WICKHAM LA
RESTING OAK HILL
Folly Wood
DEADMANTREE HILL
Blunt's Wood
Upper Burrells
Chiltington
Whitehouse Farm
Winterlands Farm
Shelley's Folly
Spooner's Farm
Over's Farm
Chapel Farm
Beechwood House
BEECHWOOD LA
Rainbow Inn (PH)
Conyboro (School)
Cooksbridge Farm
ALLINGTON LA
A 275
38
39
40
17
16
15
14
4
3
2
1

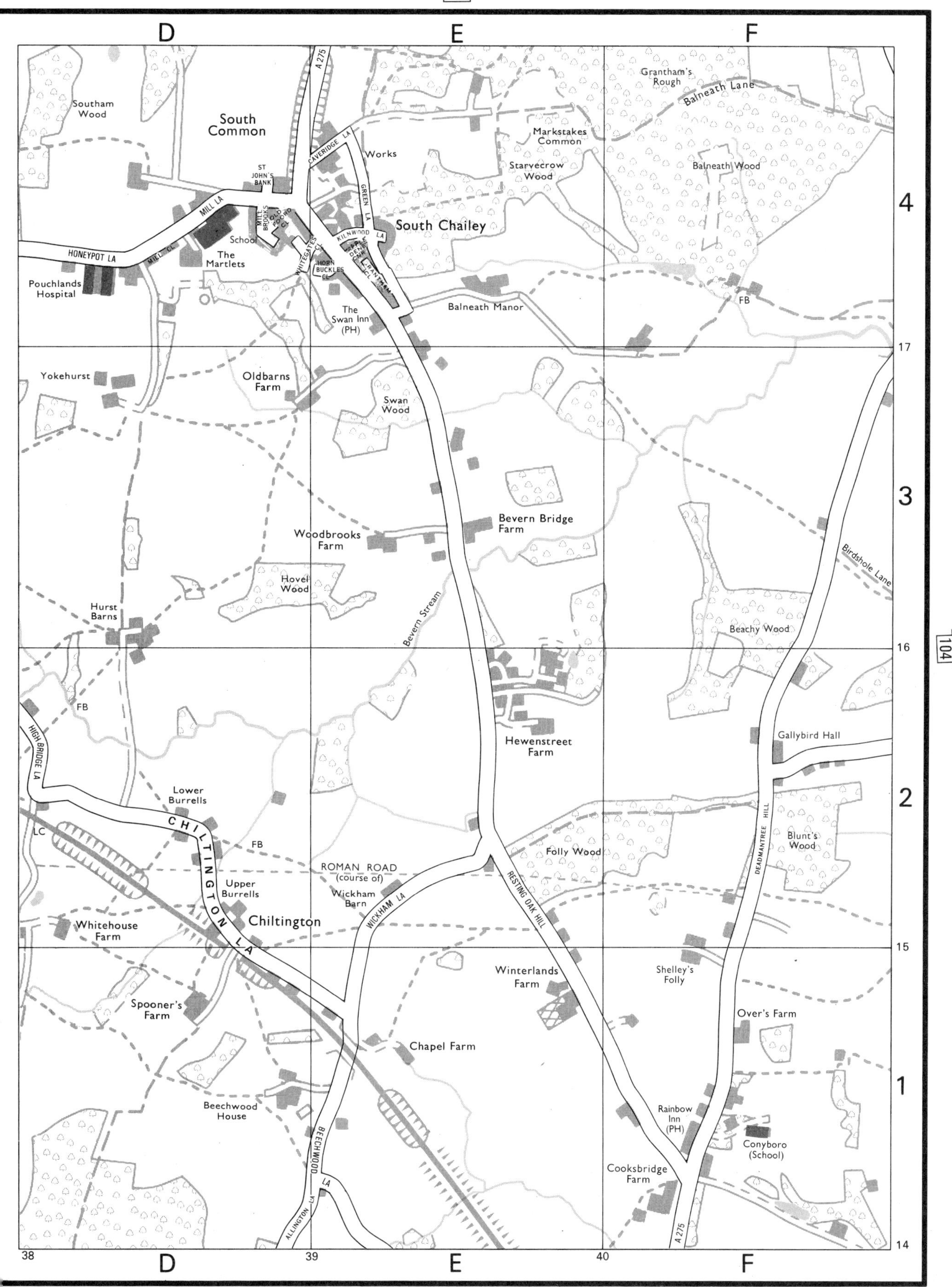

104

126

78

A
B
C
4
3
2
1
17
16
15
14
41
42
43
Oldpark Wood
Longford Farm
Church Farm
Spithurst
Spithurst House
Down Coppice
Agmond's Wood
Dallas Lane
Down View Farm
Slutsgarden Wood
Harelands Farm
Knowlands Wood
Oaktree Farm
Burtenshaw Farm
Holman's Bridge Farm
SPITHURST RD
Weir
Mount Pleasant
Sewage Works
Knowlands Farm
DALLAS LA
MOUNT PLEASANT
Scufflings
Scobell's Farm
BOAST LA
Delves Farm
ANCHOR LA
Laine Pit
Sewage Works
Dismantled Railway
Banks Farm
Clapper's Bridge
Bevern Stream
Sewell's Farm
Birdshole Lane
SCHOOL HILL
School
Barcombe Cross
HIGH ST
GRANTHAM BANK
Lower Barn Cottage
Nursery
Barcombe Place
Red Bridge
Handlye Farm
F Sta
Mongers Farm
MONGER'S MEAD
BARCOMBE MILLS RD
Half Yard Farm
Beam Bridge (FB)
Pound Corner
Camoys Court Farm
Camoys Court
CRINK HILL
Barcombe Mills
Curd's Farm
Mill Farm
River Ouse
Barcombe House
BARCOMBE MILLS RD
The Anglers Rest (PH)
The Rectory
MILL LA
CHURCH RD
Packham's Brow
FBs
FB
Pikes Bridge
Croft Ham
Barcombe
Bridge Farm
Culver Farm
Court House
Averys Farm
FB

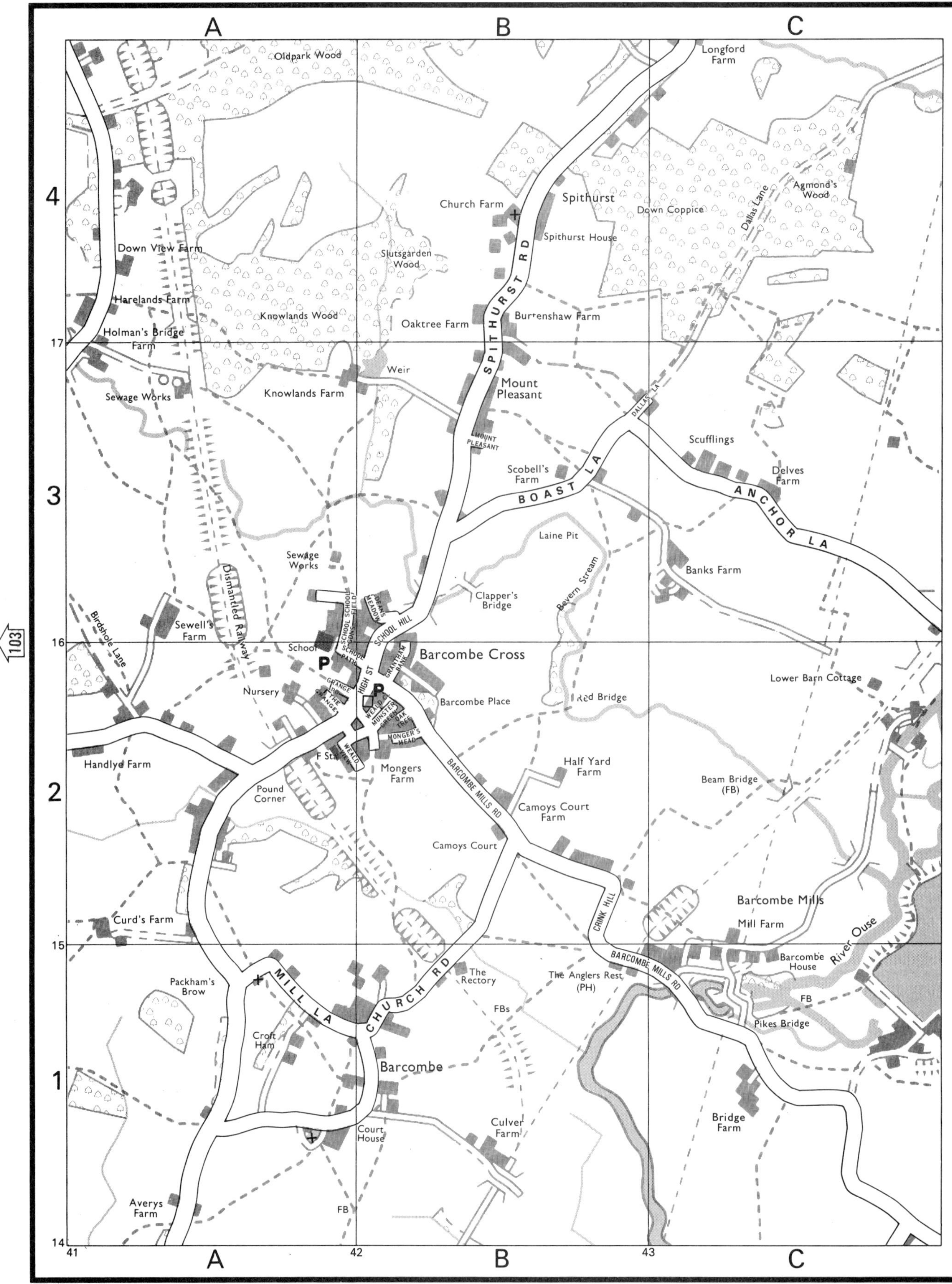

103

127

79

D
E
F
Elms Farm
Tile Barn Farm
The Lavender Line
NORTHFIELD COTTS
Isfield
Wharton's Wood
Wicklands
White Bridge
Oaks Farm
HORSTEAD LA
FB
Old Farm
Birches Farm
South Brockwell's Farm
Blunts Lane
River Ouse
Boathouse Farm
Brook Lodge Farm
Dismantled Railway
Rose Hill
Plashett Park
FB
The Halfway House (PH)
Moatpark Farm
Batchelor's Hall
Anchor Inn
ANCHOR LA
Clay Hill Wood
A 26
Plashett Wood
Barcombe Reservoir
Harvey's Gate
HARVEYS LA
Upper Clay Hill Farm
Pumping Station
Plashett Park Farm
Lower Clayhill
Clayhill House
Motte
Brickyard Farm
Old Barn Farm
GREEN LA
Little Norlington
NORLINGTON LA
BROYLE LA
Swingate
4
3
2
1
17
16
15
14
44
45
46

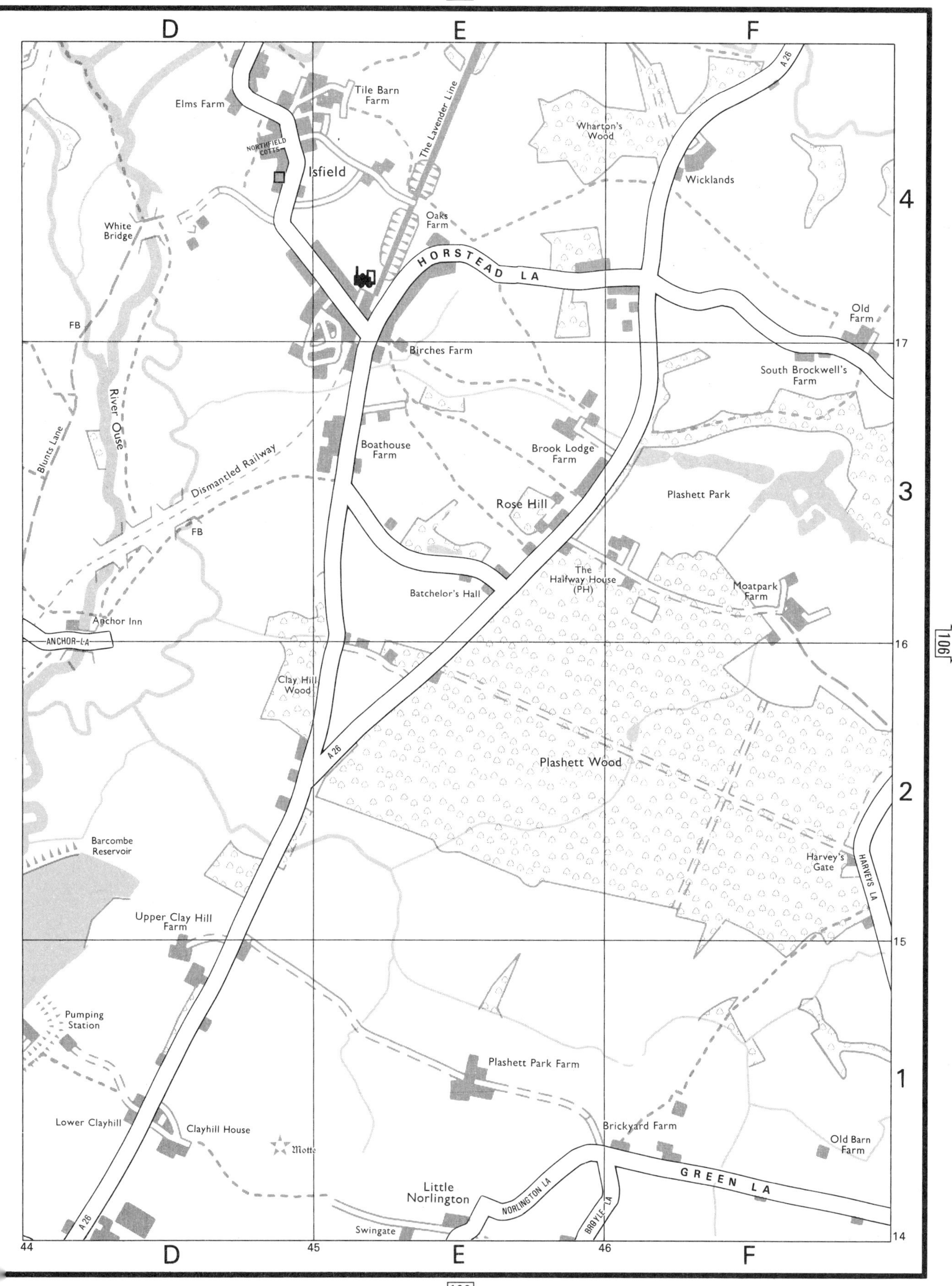

106

128

80

A
B
C
Pear Tree Farm
A22
Crockstead Farm
Hunnington's Farm
Lower Sandhill House
SAND HILL LA
Railands Wood
Crockstead Green Farm
Bradford's Farm
Sandhill
Crockstead Green
Limes Pit
FB
Whitelocks Pits
17
Bradford's Bridge
Brockwells Farm
Peckhams
Little Bentley Farm
Nursery
Crump's Corner
Crump's Wood
Bentley Wood
Vine Farm
HARVEY'S LA
Cooper's Hatch
Bentley Farm
FB
Terrible Down
White Lion Farm
Bentley Wildfowl Reserve
Mount Farm
Terrible Down Farm
Hemsley's Rough
Shortgate Manor Farm
Shortgate
15
Pingles Farm
Red Barn Farm
HARVEY'S LA
Upper Lodge Farm
Bell Farm
Little Common Wood
THE BROYLE
Middle Broyle Farm
Walls's Hawth
East Sussex Gliding Club
Laughton Common
GREEN LA
Ashreed Wood
B2192
4
3
2
1
16
14
47
48
49

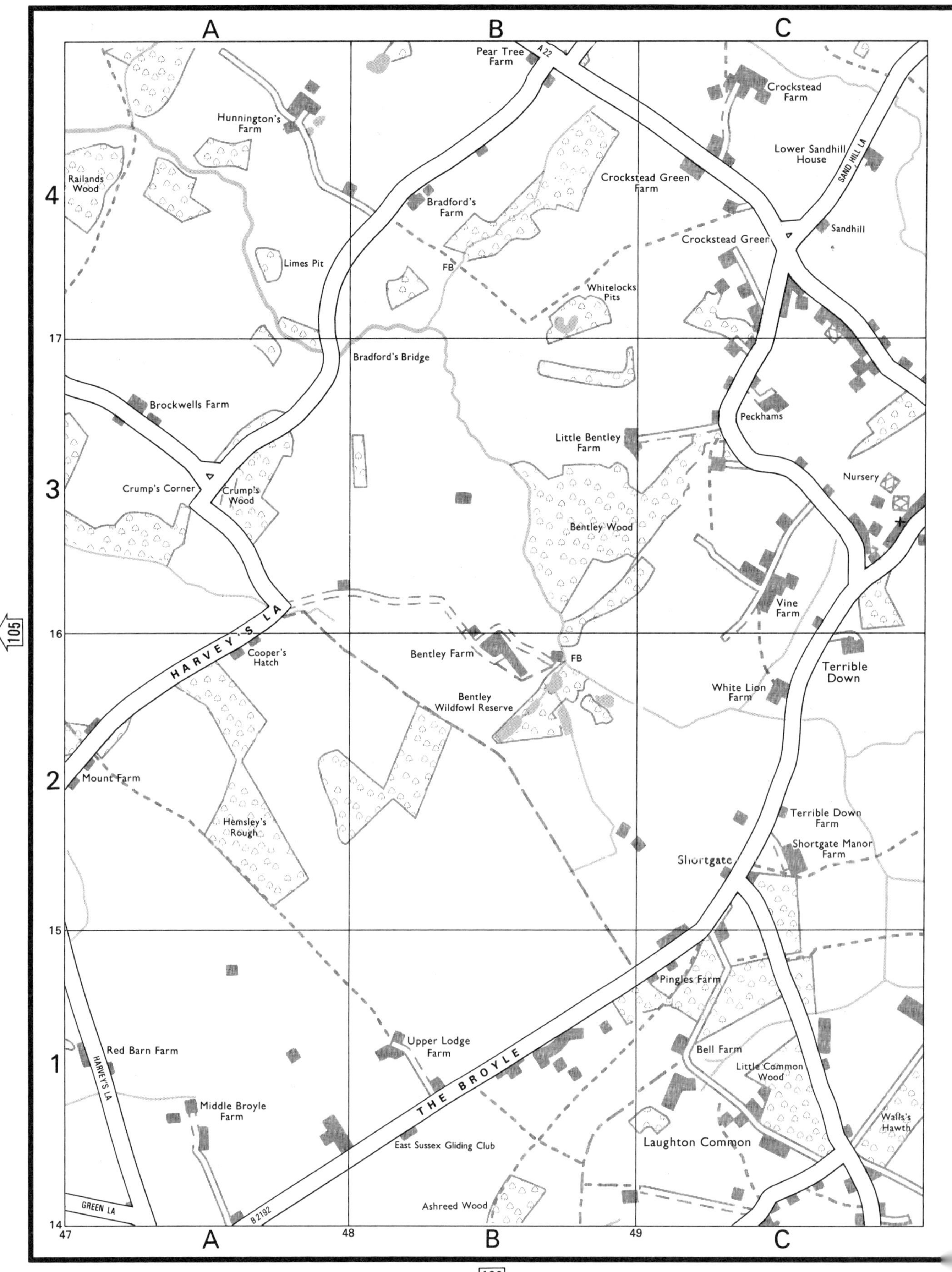

105

129

81

D
E
F
B 2192
Slay's Wood
Piper's Farm
Pilgrim Hall
Great Wood
Honey's Green
Branden Farm
4
Davis's Town
Sweetwillow Shaw
Firgrove
Barham Farm
17
FB
Jackmans Farm
Annandale Farm
Halland
Alders Wood
Old Whyly
Motel
Bentley Wood
Belmont Farm
East Hoathly
Belmont
3
CARPENTERS CROFT
THOMAS TURNER DR
WALDRON RD
Hesmonds Farm
B 2192
A 22
LONDON RD
Hartfield Farm
MILL LA
Decoy Pond
School
CIDER HOUSE WLK
HIGH ST
BUTTSFIELD LA
RECTORY CL
CHURCH MARKS LA
Godfrey Cottage
Moat Wood
THE MEWS
16
Moat
SOUTH ST
Halland Park Farm
Bog Shaw
Paine's Farm
France Wood
2
Rowland Wood
Martinland Wood
15
Laughton Park-Farm
Old Land Wood
Park Corner
Price's Farm
Bridle Gate
1
Walls Farm
The Bungalow
Upper Vert Wood
Sandpit Wood
Narvic Mink Farm
A 22
14
50
D
51
E
52
F

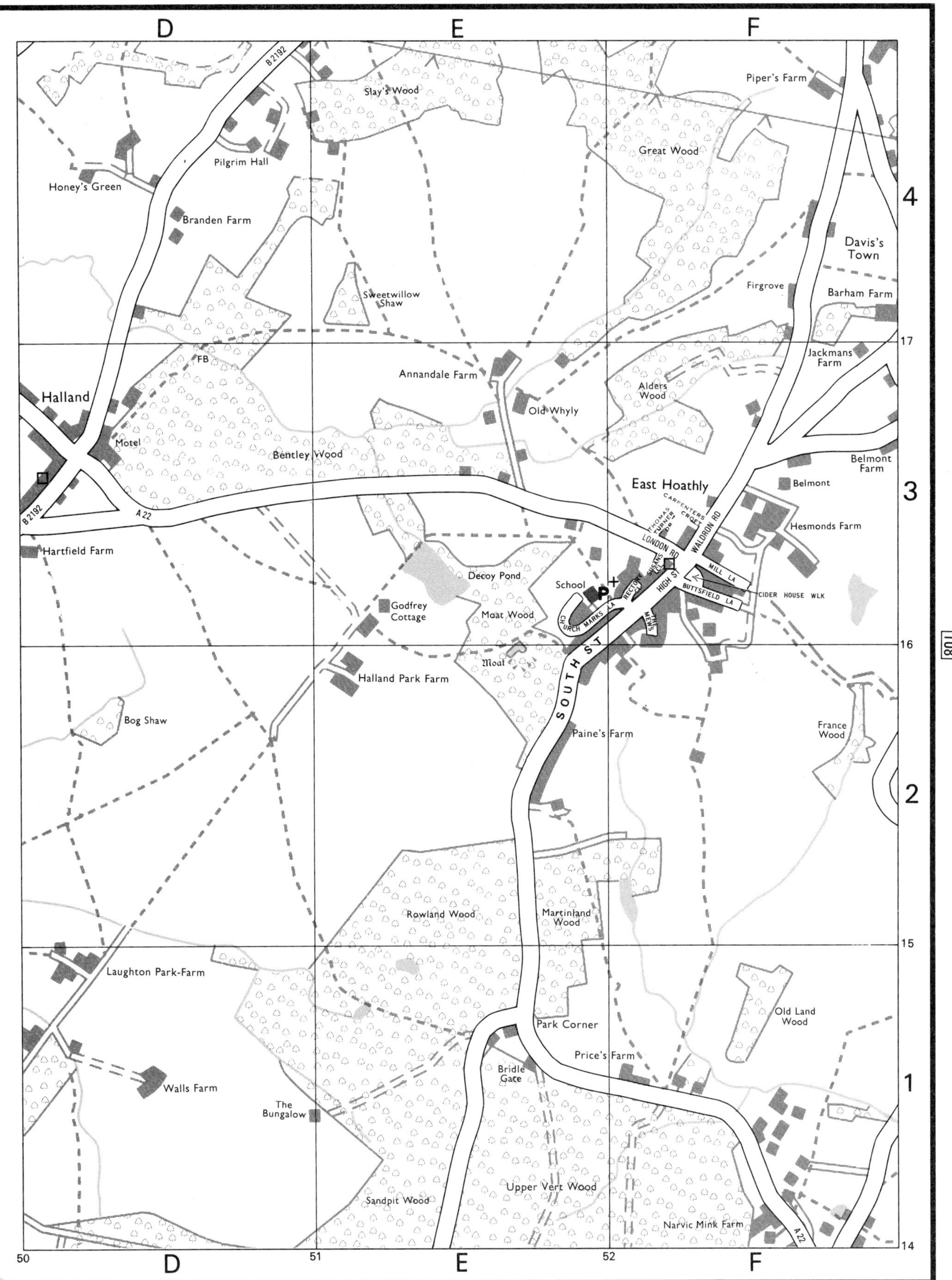

108

130

82

A
B
C
Kirby Farm
Dernlea Farm
Roughland Wood
Scallow Bridge
Hope Farm
Convent
Summersbrook Farm
Ralph Wood
Graywood Farm
Summersbrook Wood
Copford Farm
Minepit Wood
Etchingly Wood
Scotland Farm
Great Dern Wood
The Quadrangle
Broomfield Wood
Longshaw Farm
Gray Wood
Broomfield Farm
Coneyburrow Wood
Broomfield Farm Caravan Park
Great Ailies Farm
Starve Wood
Clarklye Farm
Chiswell's Farm
Stream Farm
Forge Wood
Holdens Farm
Pond Bay
Stream Mill
Mill Wood
Hilder's Court
Decoypond Wood
Smithlands Wood
Highlands Farm
Frith's Farm
Bull Bridge
Parsonage Farm
Hale Green
Hale Farm
Coneyburrow Wood
Gatehouse Wood
Latchett Wood
Chiddingly Place
Chiddingly
Hall
Little Park Farm
4
17
3
16
2
15
1
14
53
54
55
A
B
C

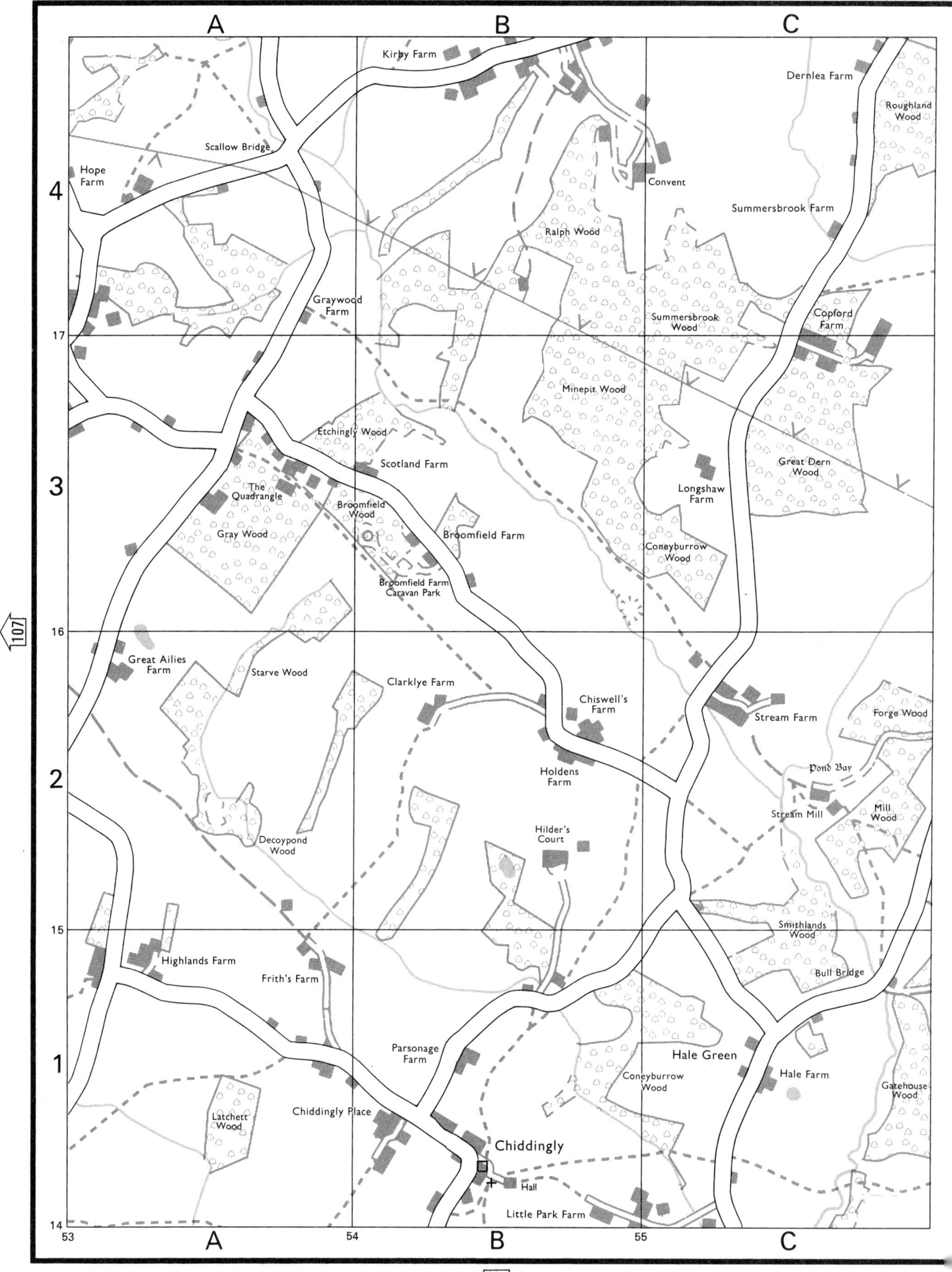

107

131

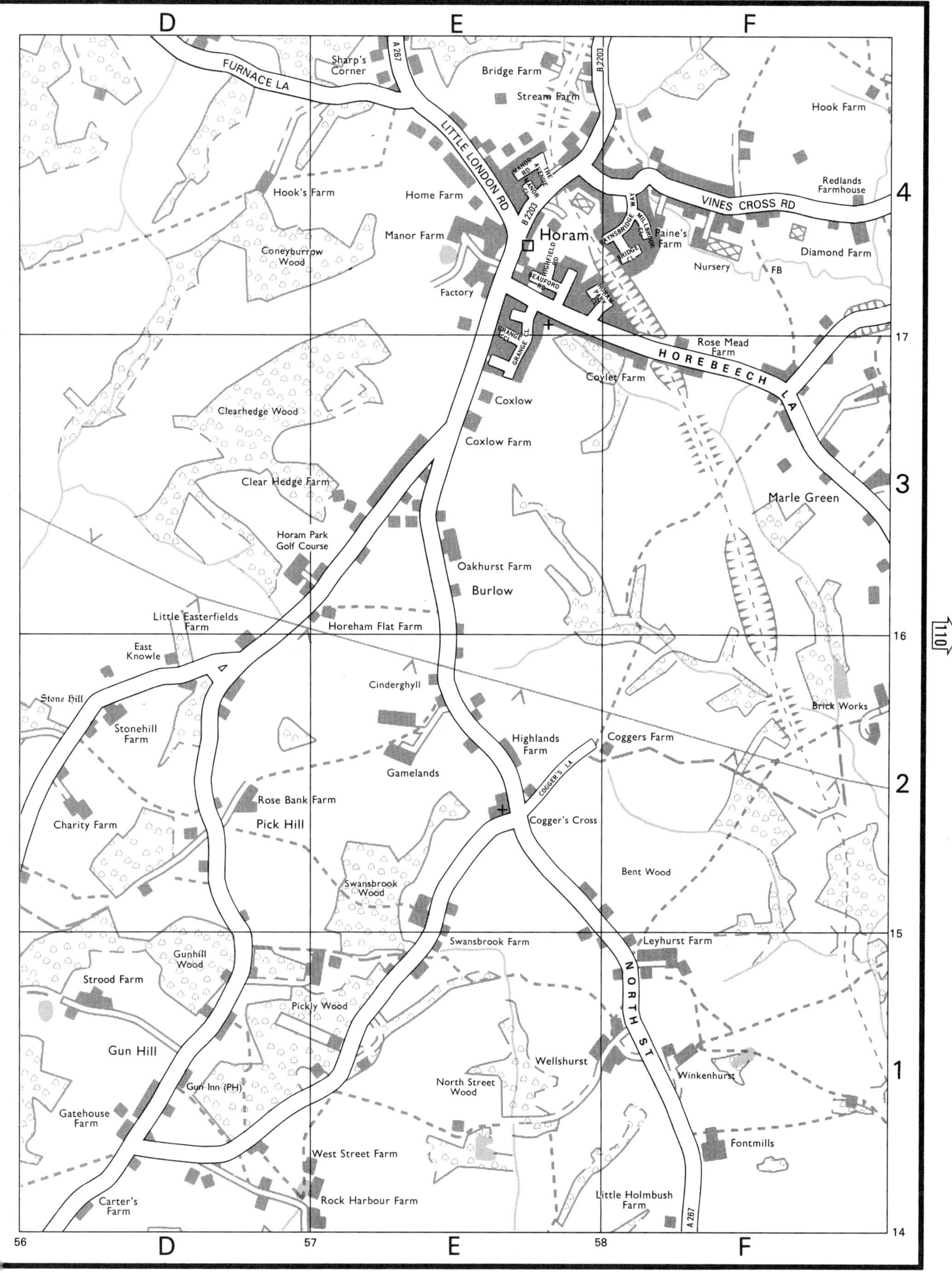
83
D
E
F
Furnace La
Sharp's Corner
A 267
Bridge Farm
Stream Farm
B 2203
Hook Farm
Little London Rd
Manor Rd
The Avenue
Manor Cl
Hook's Farm
Home Farm
Redlands Farmhouse
4
Vines Cross Rd
B 2203
Horam
Raynsbridge Way
Millbrook Cl
Paine's Farm
Manor Farm
Coneyburrow Wood
Highfield Rd
Bridge Cl
Diamond Farm
Nursery
FB
Beauford Rd
Factory
Horam Park Cl
Grange Cl
17
Rose Mead Farm
Horebeech La
Coylet Farm
Coxlow
Clearhedge Wood
Coxlow Farm
Clear Hedge Farm
3
Marle Green
Horam Park Golf Course
Oakhurst Farm
Burlow
Little Easterfields Farm
Horeham Flat Farm
16
110
East Knowle
Cinderghyll
Stone Hill
Brick Works
Stonehill Farm
Highlands Farm
Coggers Farm
Cogger's La
Gamelands
2
Rose Bank Farm
Charity Farm
Pick Hill
Cogger's Cross
Bent Wood
Swansbrook Wood
15
Swansbrook Farm
Leyhurst Farm
Gunhill Wood
Strood Farm
North St
Pickly Wood
Gun Hill
Wellshurst
1
Winkenhurst
Gun Inn (PH)
North Street Wood
Gatehouse Farm
Fontmills
West Street Farm
Carter's Farm
Rock Harbour Farm
Little Holmbush Farm
A 267
14
56
57
58
132

84

A
B
C
4
3
2
1
17
16
15
14
59
60
61
The Brewers Arms (PH)
Vine's Cross
BALLSOCKS LA
Foord's Farm
Brookside
Sewage Works
Clappers Wood
Norman Norris
Nursery
Marle Green Farm
Nurseries
New Farm
Nursery
Cowden Hall
North Corner
Cowden Hall Farm
Lewhurst Farm
Knightsbridge Farm
Grovebridge Farm
West Winds Farm
Church Wood
Tilement Farm
Causeway Wood
Ironworks (site of)
Southview Farm
Southview Nursery
Beeston's Farm
Holly Hill Nursery
Cralle Place
HAMMER LA
Cralle Bridge
Sunny Bank
Court Horeham
Sheepwash Bridge
Cuckmere River
Grove Hill House
GROVE HILL
Grove Hill
Blackford Farm
Hunton's Farm
Kingsley Hill Farm
Blackhurst Wood
Mill Wood
Mill Lane
Courtlands Farm
Burchetts Wood
Courtland Place Farm
Dowd's Wood
Gutter Wood
Forge Meadow
Heritage
Merrie Harriers (PH)
Caterman's Gill
Cowbeech
Cowbeech Farm

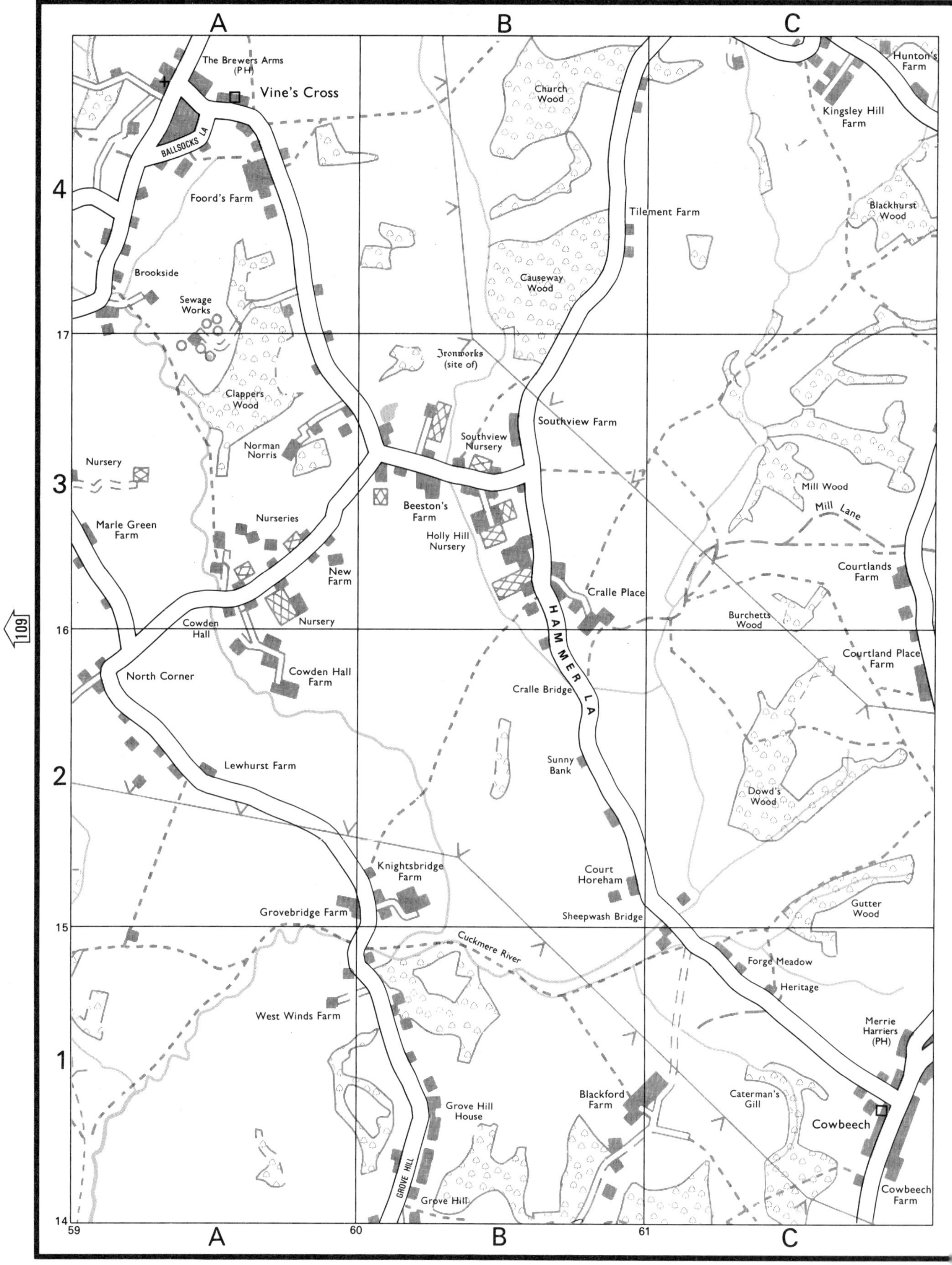

109

133

85

D
E
F
BACK LA
GROVELY LA
Little Iwood
Clapland Wood
Hugletts Wood
Little Bathurst Farm
Dean Farm
Churches Green
Round Wood
Christian's River
Ironworks (site of)
Bathurst Farm
Pilley Farm
Durrant's Pit
Hook Wood
Blackhurst Farm
Durrant's Farm
Bacon Hollow Wood
Barnfield Wood
SANDHILL LA
Iwood Place Farm
Tweazle Wood
Beech Hill Farm
Clippingham Stream
Sandhills Farm
Broadgrove Wood
Lower Sandhills Farm
Summertree Farm
Morgans Farm
Ann Wood
Batsford Farm
Egypt Farm
Thorneyfold Farm
Stonelands Farm
Red House Farm
Clippenham Wood
Foul Mile
Clippenham Farm
Furnace Brook
Tiles Farm
Broomwood Farm
Trolliloes Bridge
Attwood Farm
Hole Farm
Church Farm
Trolliloes
Trolliloes Stream
Thorndean Farm
Trolliloes Farm
Pebsham Farm
Beechcroft Farm
Bemzells Farm
CHILSHAM LA
STUDDENS LA
Beard's Farm
Studdens Farm
Pebsham Bridge
Cattle Wood
Ale House Farm
Chilsham Stream
Pebsham Stream
Merryweather's Farm
4
3
2
1
17
16
15
14
62
63
64

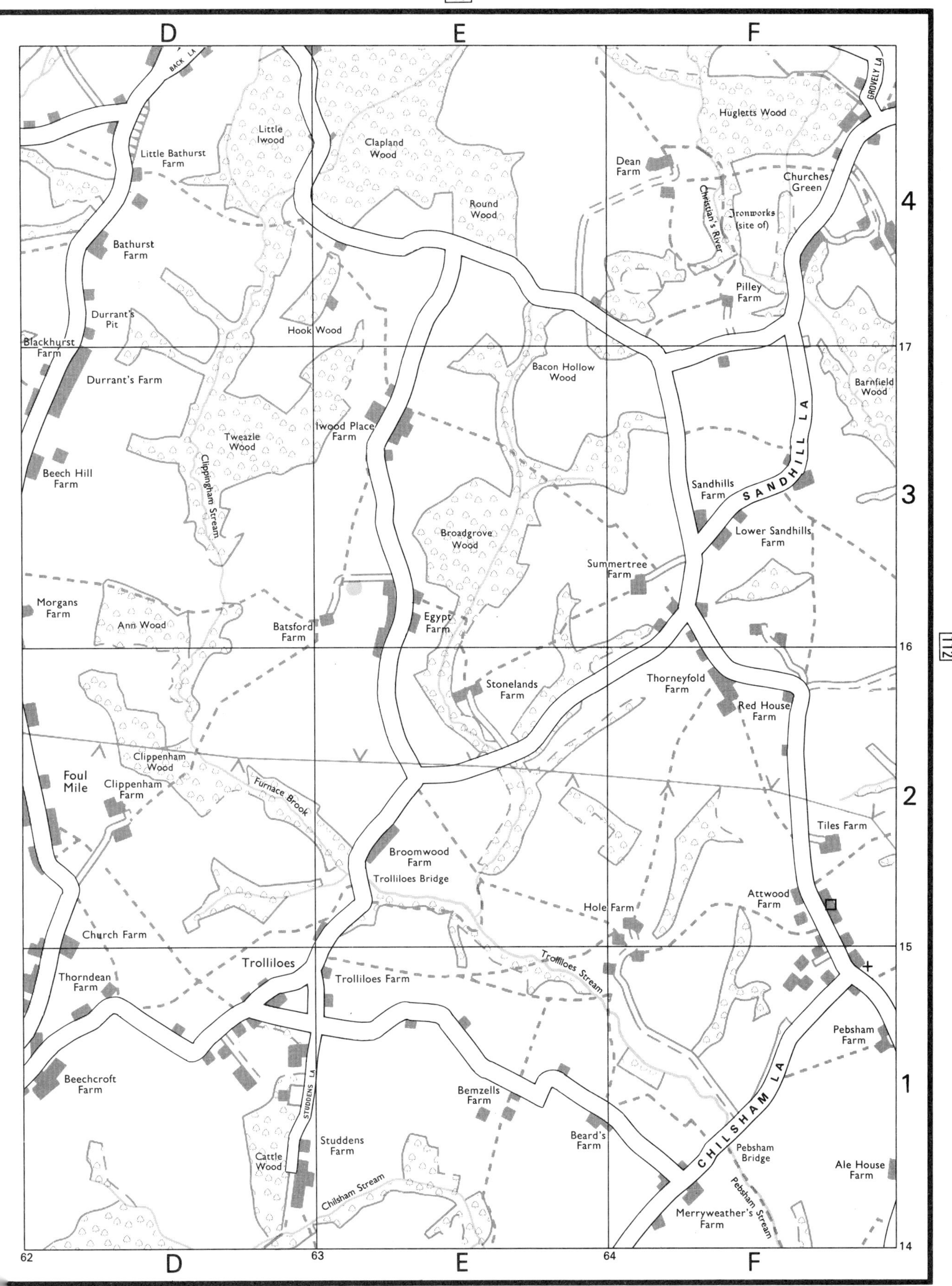

112

134

86

A
B
C
4
3
2
1
17
16
15
14
65
66
67
Padgham
Padgham Corner
PADGHAM LA
Padgham Down Farm
Little Bucksteep Farm
Coppice Farm
Little Rabbits Farm
Honey Lane
HERRING'S RD
SILVERWICK'S LA
Silvericks Farm
Butlers Wood
Wheeler's Wood
Pleasure House
LAKEHURST LA
Lakehurst
Buckwell Wood
Buckwell Gill
Buckwell Farm
Spring Gill
Little Redpale Farm
Bucksteep Wood
Marlpit Wood
Thorndale Farm
Thornden Farm
Thornden Cottages
Thornden Cottages
Lattenden Farm
Christian's River
The Stud Farm
Bucksteep Manor
Redpale Farm
Oakbank Farm
FARTHING LA
Great Buckstepe Farm
Glyde's Farm
Ponts Green
Reedlands Farm
Pear Tree Farm
Brigden Hill Farm
Water Mill Farm
Hodges
Reed Wood
Winter's Farm
The Bungalow
Ash Tree Inn (PH)
Street Farm
Brownbread Street
Brownbread Stud
NORTH RD
Bodle Street Green
The White Horse Inn (PH)
Lower Gill
Hugletts Stream
Frankwell Wood
Bray's Hill
PRINKLE LA
Prinkle Farm

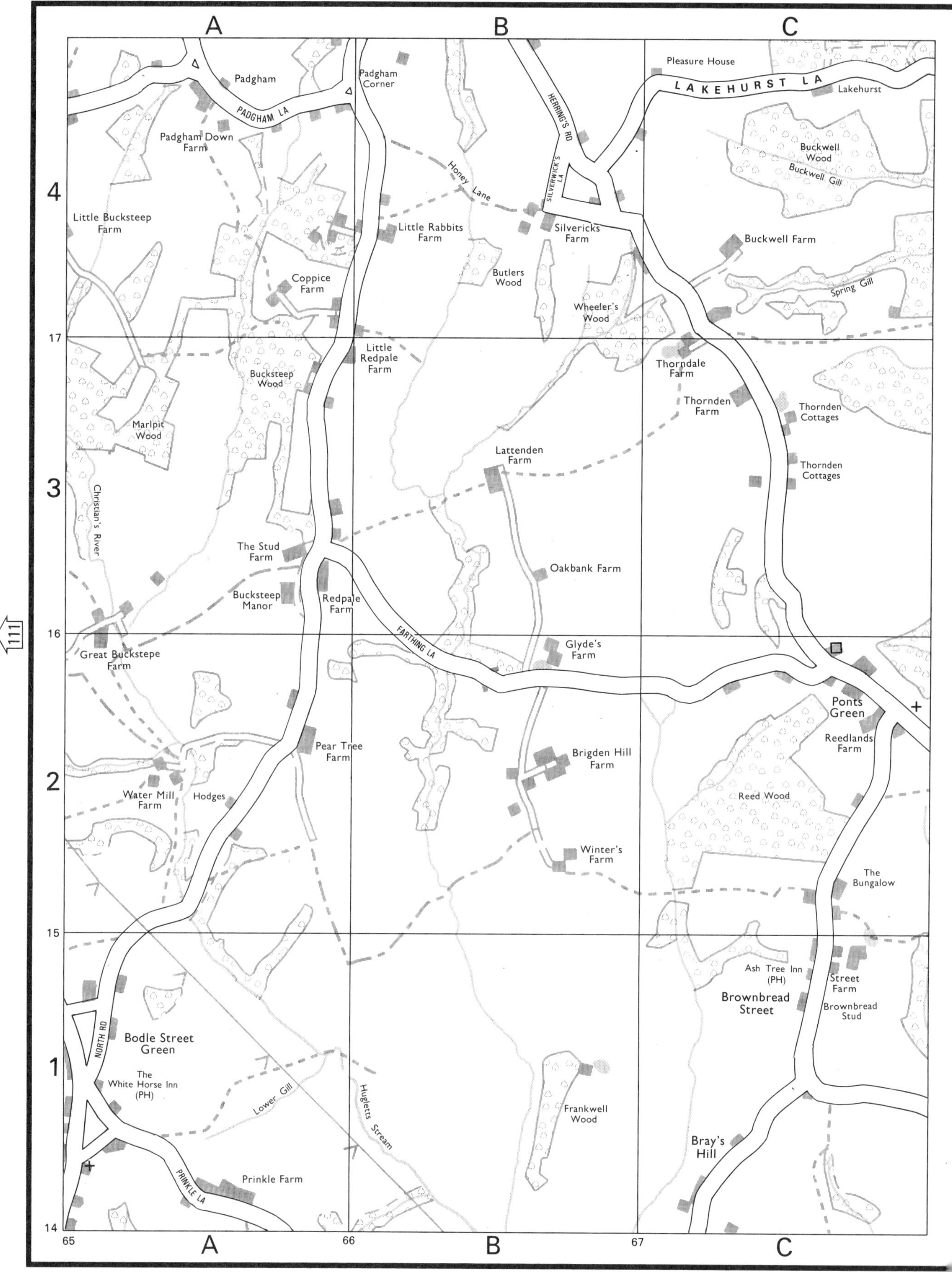

111

135

87

D
E
F
Gifford's Gill
Bunce's Farm
Link Wood
LAKEHURST LA
Buckwell Gill
Anderson's Wood
Rocks Farm
Great Spray's Farm
Atkin's Wood
Penhurst Field
Pumping Shaw
Creep Wood
Furnace Cottage
Foxearth Wood
Allfrees Wood
Hogstye Wood
Church Farm
Penhurst
Manor House
PENHURST LA
Malthouse Wood
Court Lodge
Hill Farm
Tower House
Little Beech Farm
Izlebridge Wood
Forge Cottages
Pontsgreen Wood
Peens Wood
Ash Bourne
Cowland Wood
Deer Park Lodge
Tent Hill
Ford Bridge
New Buildings Farm
Reservoir Pond
Milestone Toll
B2204
FRECKLEY HOLLOW
Pigknoll Farm
Ashburnham Place
The Grove
Front Water
The Pound
Linghams
Walk Wood
Freckley Wood
Agmerhurst Farm
Burntbarns Lane
Broad Water
Burrage Wood
Baker's Wood
Burnt Barns Farm
B2204
4
3
2
1
17
16
15
14
68
69
70

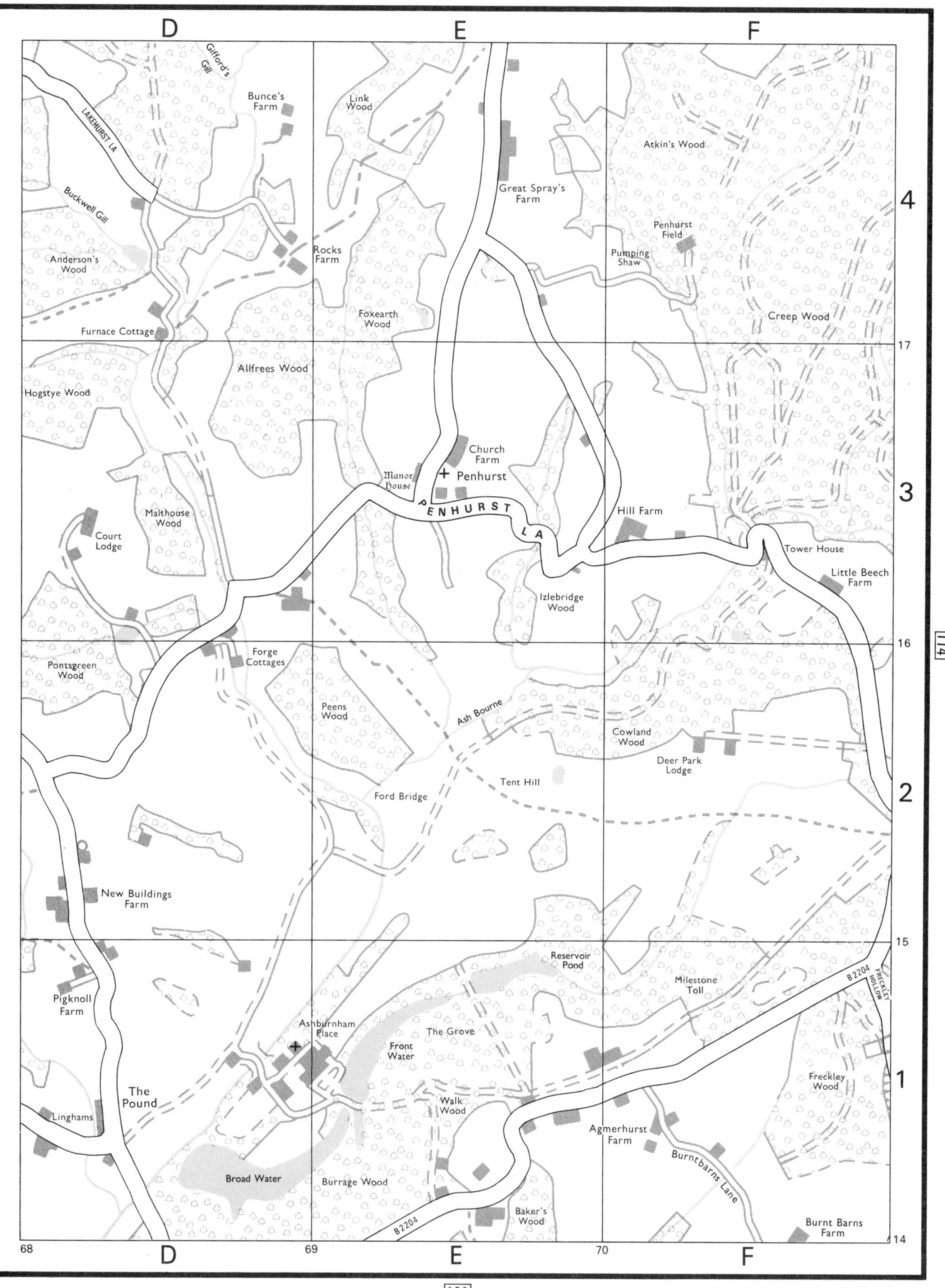

114

136

88

113

A
B
C
4
3
2
1
17
16
15
14
71
72
73
B 2096
Netherfield Place Farm
Duckreed Wood
Netherfield Place
NETHERFIELD RD
NETHERFIELD HILL
High Wood
Horseye Shaw
Pond Bay
Ashes Wood
Wadhurst Lane
Beech Wood
Foxhole Farm
Kingswell Farm
Pond Bay
Beech Farm
Beech Mill
Reeves Wood
Mill Wood
Oast Cottage
Bailiffs Cottage
Reeves Cottage
WADHURST LA
Floats Wood
Great Beech
Kelk Wood
Mile Oak Wood
North Lodge
VALE RD
Beechdown Wood
B 2096
Hospital
BATTLE GATES
A 269
NORTH TRADE RD
HAMPDEN CL
ASTEN FIELDS
A 269
The Squirrel Inn (PH)
Saxon Hill Farm
School
TOLLGATES
CLAVERHAM WAY
Saw Mill
B 2204
Birchen Shaw
Phipps's Gill
PENHURST LA
Tellis Coppice
B 2204
Model Farm
Tower Hill
The Gardens
Steven's Crouch
Farthings Farm
Redcoat Farm
Great Park Farm
Captain's Wood
Farthing Pond
Hoathybank Wood
Powdermill Lake
Bridge Lake
Parkgate Manor
Starcroft Farm
Powdermill Wood
FRECKLEY HOLLOW
The Warren
B 2095
Eight Acre Wood
POWDERMILL LA
B 2095
Upper Lake
Big Lake
A 269

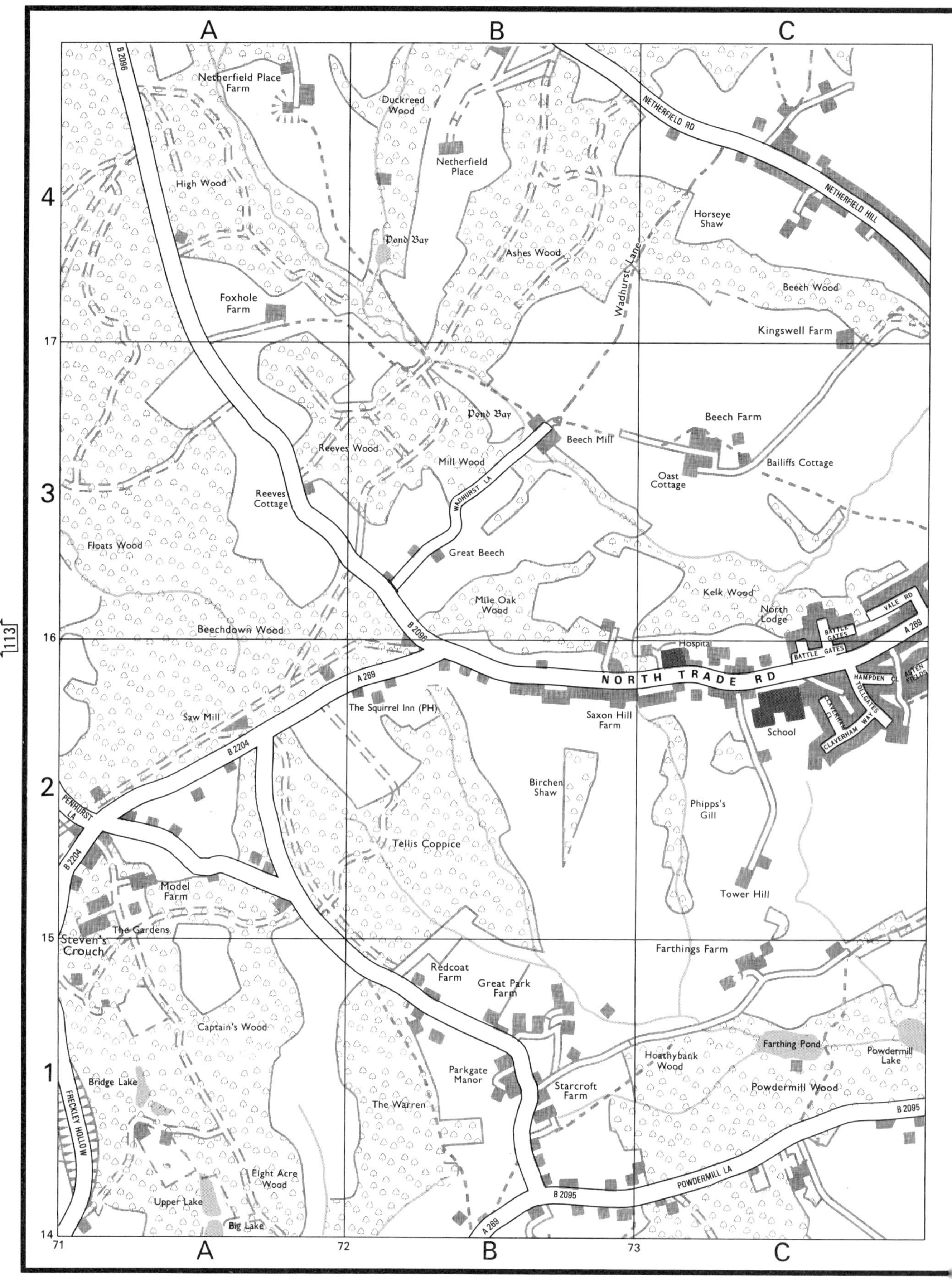

137

89

D
E
F
Riccards Wood
Lower Gate Farm
Ringlett's Farm
Canadia
Le Rette Farm
CANADIA RD
WHATLINGTON RD
Punch Bowl Farm
Petley Wood
Black Firs Farm
Somerby Farm
Loudwell Farm
LONDON RD
NETHERFIELD HILL
OAKHURST RD
VIRGIN'S CROFT
VIRGINS LA
Fuller's Farm
UCKHAM LA
Meadow View
Marley Farm
Stream Farm
BATTLE
CALDBEC HILL
Coarsebarn Farm
Marley House
Offices
Caldbec Hill
Little Park Farm
Sewage Works
CHAIN LA
WELLINGTON GDNS
MOUNT JOY
NORTH TRADE RD
A 269
HIGH ST
MOUNT ST
SAXONWOOD RD
MARLEY LA
CORONATION GDNS
NORMAN CL
MARLEY RISE
MARLEY GDNS
SWALLOW DR
PARK LA
UPPER LAKE
Sch
LC
MEADOW BANK
FALCONERS DR
HARRIER LA
Great Wood
Battle Abbey (Sch)
SHIRLEA VIEW
Blackfriars
Remains of St Martin's Abbey
LOWER LAKE
PICARDY
Battle Station
SENLAC GDNS
STATION APP
KINGSDALE
Hastings 1066
B 2095
ABBOTS CL
Starr's Green Farm
THE SPINNEY
STARRS MEAD
THE COPPICE
Horselodge Plantation
BATTLE HILL
HAROLD TERR
STARRS GREEN LA
New Pond
GLENGORSE
HASTINGS RD
Starr's Green
POWDERMILL LA
Telham Court (School)
Downbarn Farm
Powdermill Lake
Loose Farm
Telham
Powdermill House
Bushy Wood
Malthouse Wood
A 2100
Powdermill Stream
Lower Telham
TELHAM LA
Stone Cottage
74
75
76
14
15
16
17
1
2
3
4

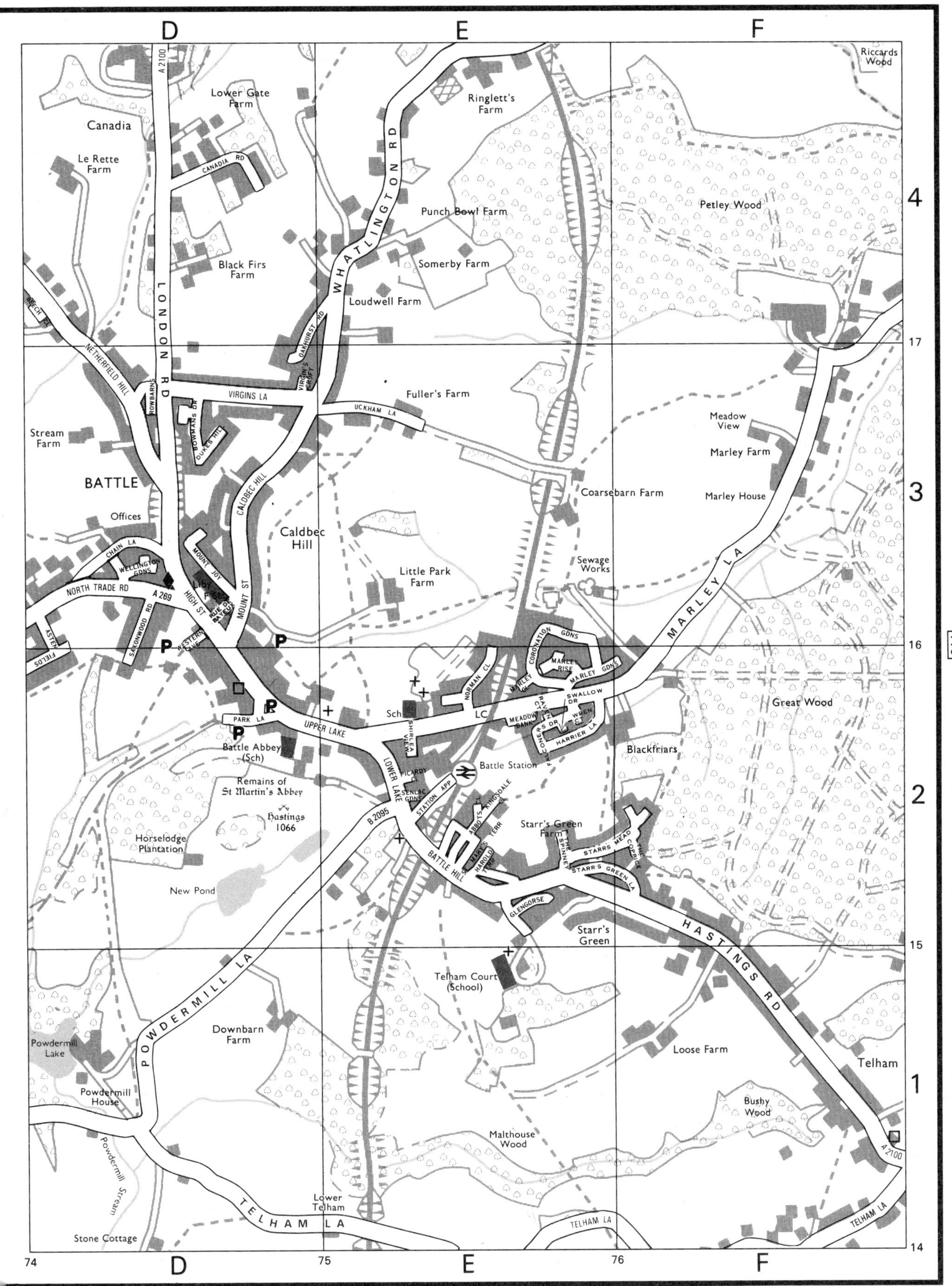

116

138

90

115

A
B
C
4
3
2
1
17
16
15
14
77
78
79
A21(T)
A229
THE GREEN
THE STREET
Catt's Shaw
River Brede
Sedlescombe Bridge
Brassets Wood
River Line
GREGORY WLK
Lower Marley Farm
Oaklands
MARLEY LA
Luff's Farm
CHAPEL HILL
PAYGATE RD
Felon Wood
Pestalozzi Children's Village
Hoads Lane
Nutkin's Wood
Magazine Farm
COTTAGE LA
CRAZY LA
Keepers Cottage
Cold Spring Shaw
Randall's Farm
Horsmans Farm
Old Horsmans
Beanford Farm
Harts Green Farm
NEW ENGLAND LA
WHYDOWN HILL
Battle Barn Farm
Platnix Farm
Oak Wood
Spray's Wood
Whitefield Wood
Fir Wood
Kent Street
Spraysbridge Farm
Great Buckhurst Farm
SPRAYS LA
Norton's Farm
BLUEMANS LA
PARSONAGE LA
Bluemans
Burnt Chimney Farm
Alder Shaw
KENT ST
Upper Morax Wood
Screen Wood
Carpenter's Barn Farm
Ireland's Farm
Branshill Farm
Duke's Wood
MOAT LA
Little Hemingfold Farm
Oak Wood
Bishop's Wood
Swan Pond
Mill Wood
Alder Wood
ROMAN BLOOMERY (site of)
STONEHOUSE DR
Babylon Wood
Hemingfold Dairy Farm
Blackhorse Hill
Stonehouse
A2100
HASTINGS RD
Black Horse (PH)
Ring Wood
Golf Course
Beauport Park
Red River
EBDEN'S HILL
Claremont School
Three Cedar Wood

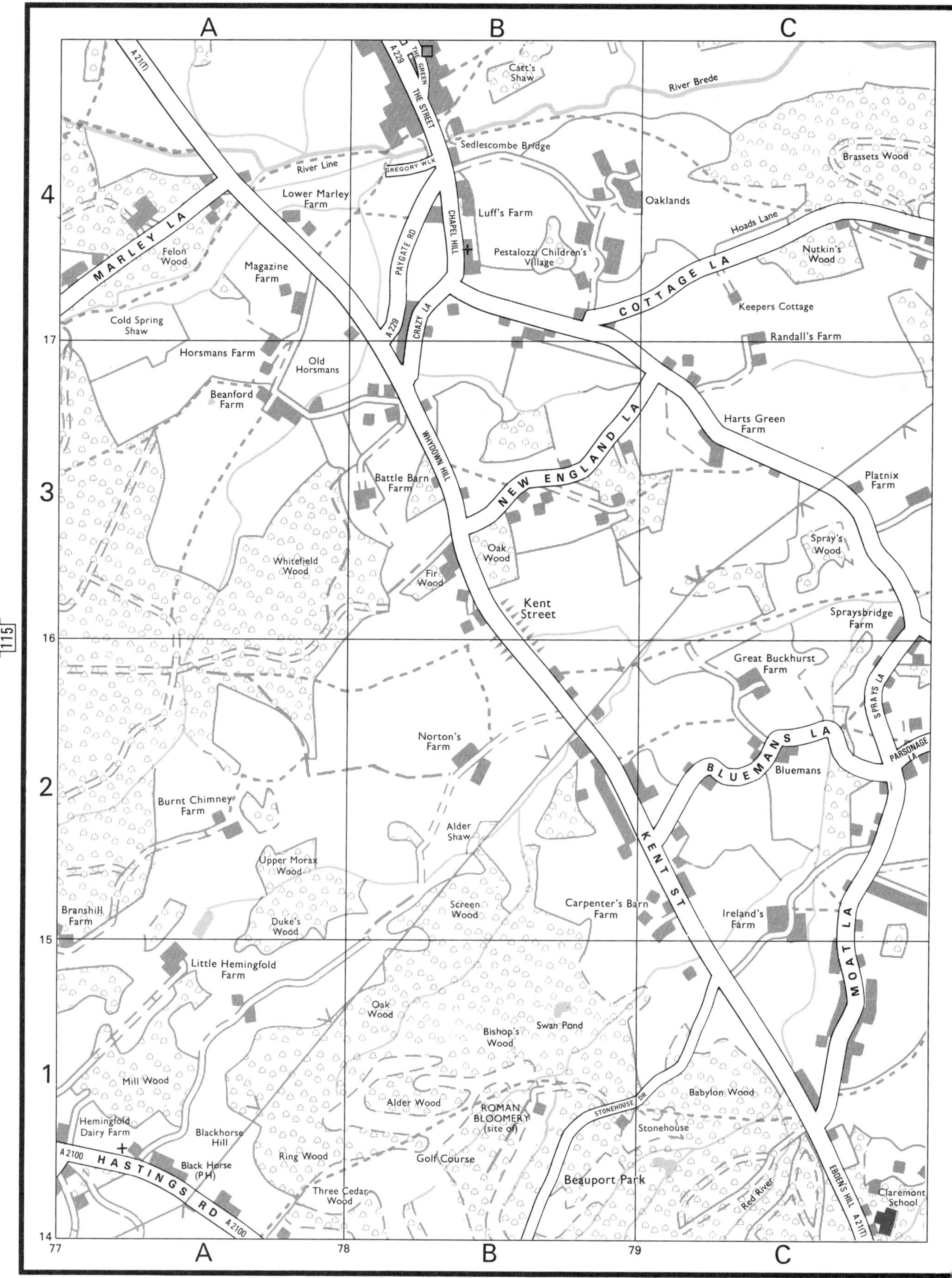

139

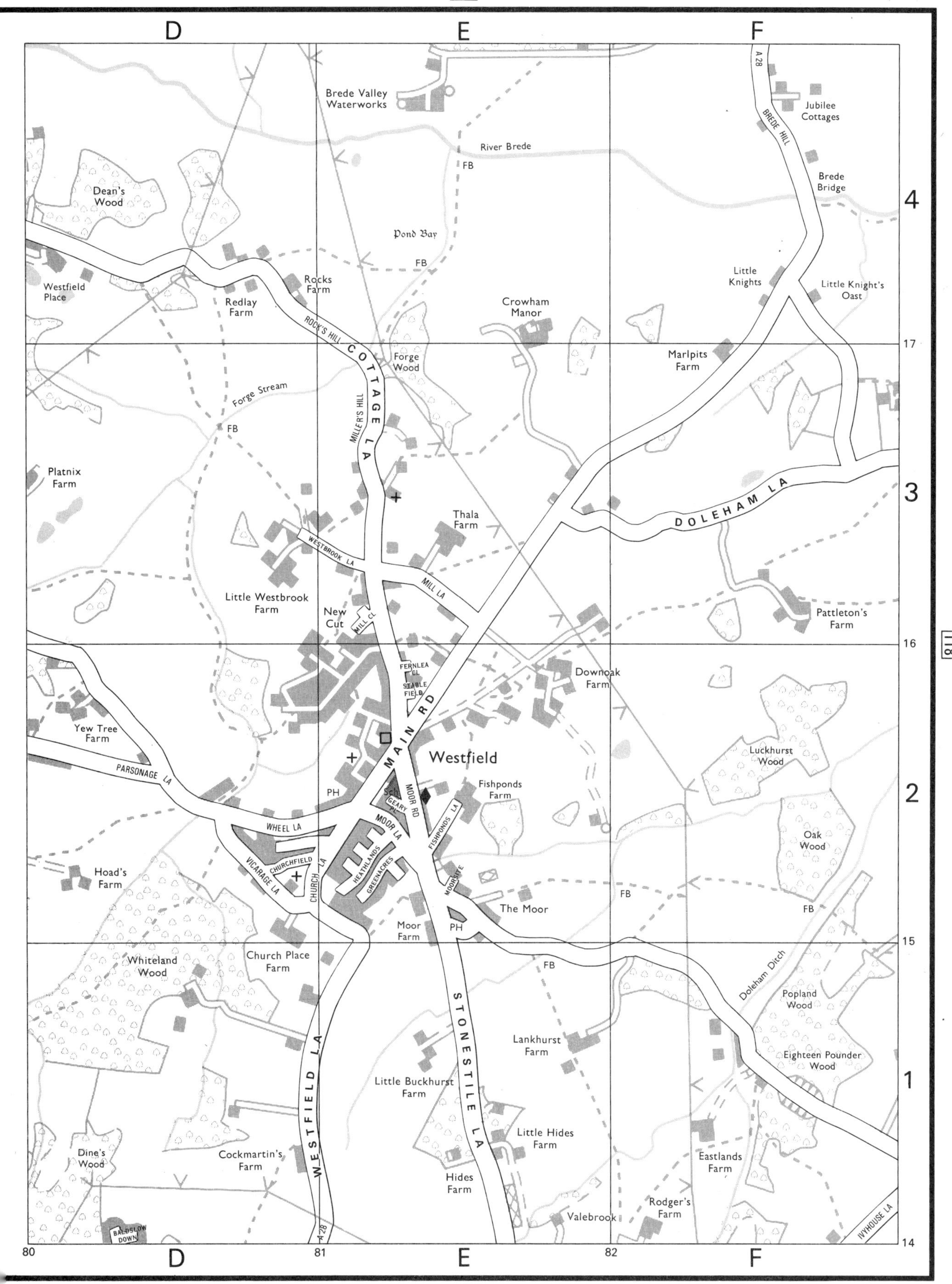
91
D
E
F
Brede Valley Waterworks
A 28
BREDE HILL
Jubilee Cottages
River Brede
FB
Brede Bridge
Dean's Wood
4
Pond Bay
FB
Westfield Place
Rocks Farm
Little Knights
Little Knight's Oast
Redlay Farm
Crowham Manor
ROCK'S HILL
COTTAGE LA
Forge Wood
Marlpits Farm
17
Forge Stream
MILLER'S HILL
FB
Platnix Farm
3
DOLEHAM LA
Thala Farm
WESTBROOK LA
MILL LA
Little Westbrook Farm
New Cut
MILL CL
Pattleton's Farm
16
118
FERNLEA CL
STABLE FIELD
Downoak Farm
MAIN RD
Yew Tree Farm
Westfield
Luckhurst Wood
PARSONAGE LA
PH
Sch
GEARY PL
MOOR RD
Fishponds Farm
FISHPONDS LA
2
WHEEL LA
MOOR LA
Oak Wood
Hoad's Farm
CHURCHFIELD
VICARAGE LA
CHURCH LA
HEATHLANDS
GREENACRES
MOORSIDE
The Moor
FB
FB
Moor Farm
PH
15
Whiteland Wood
Church Place Farm
FB
Doleham Ditch
Popland Wood
STONESTILE LA
Lankhurst Farm
Eighteen Pounder Wood
1
Little Buckhurst Farm
WESTFIELD LA
Little Hides Farm
Dine's Wood
Cockmartin's Farm
Eastlands Farm
Hides Farm
Rodger's Farm
Valebrook
IVYHOUSE LA
A 28
BALDSLOW DOWN
14
80
81
82
D
E
F
140

92

A
B
C
4
3
2
1
17
16
15
14
83
84
85
Alder Shaw
River Brede
Brede Level
Moat
Lower Snailham
Great Knight's Farm
Doleham Farm
Doleham Ditch
Lidham Hill
Snaylham Farm
Gray's Wood
Pond Wood
Doleham Halt
DOLEHAM HILL
Glover's Wood
Three Corner Wood
NORTH LA
Smith's Wood
Stocks Farm
FOURTEEN ACRE LA
North Wood
MAIN RD
Bench Wood
Stock's Green
Guestling Thorn
A 259(T)
Copshall Farm
Kitchen Wood
Little Maxfield
Great Maxfield
Broomham (School)
WILLOWSTREAM CL
Plashet Wood
Sailor's Stream
LC
MAXFIELD LA
PH
BUTCHER'S LA
Eighteen Pounder Farm
Three Oaks
Half House Farm
Church Farm
Frayslánd Wood
Three Oaks & Guestling Halt
CHURCH LA
IVYHOUSE LA
ROCK LA
EIGHT ACRE LA
Fraysland Farm
Pound Farm
Blackbrook Farm

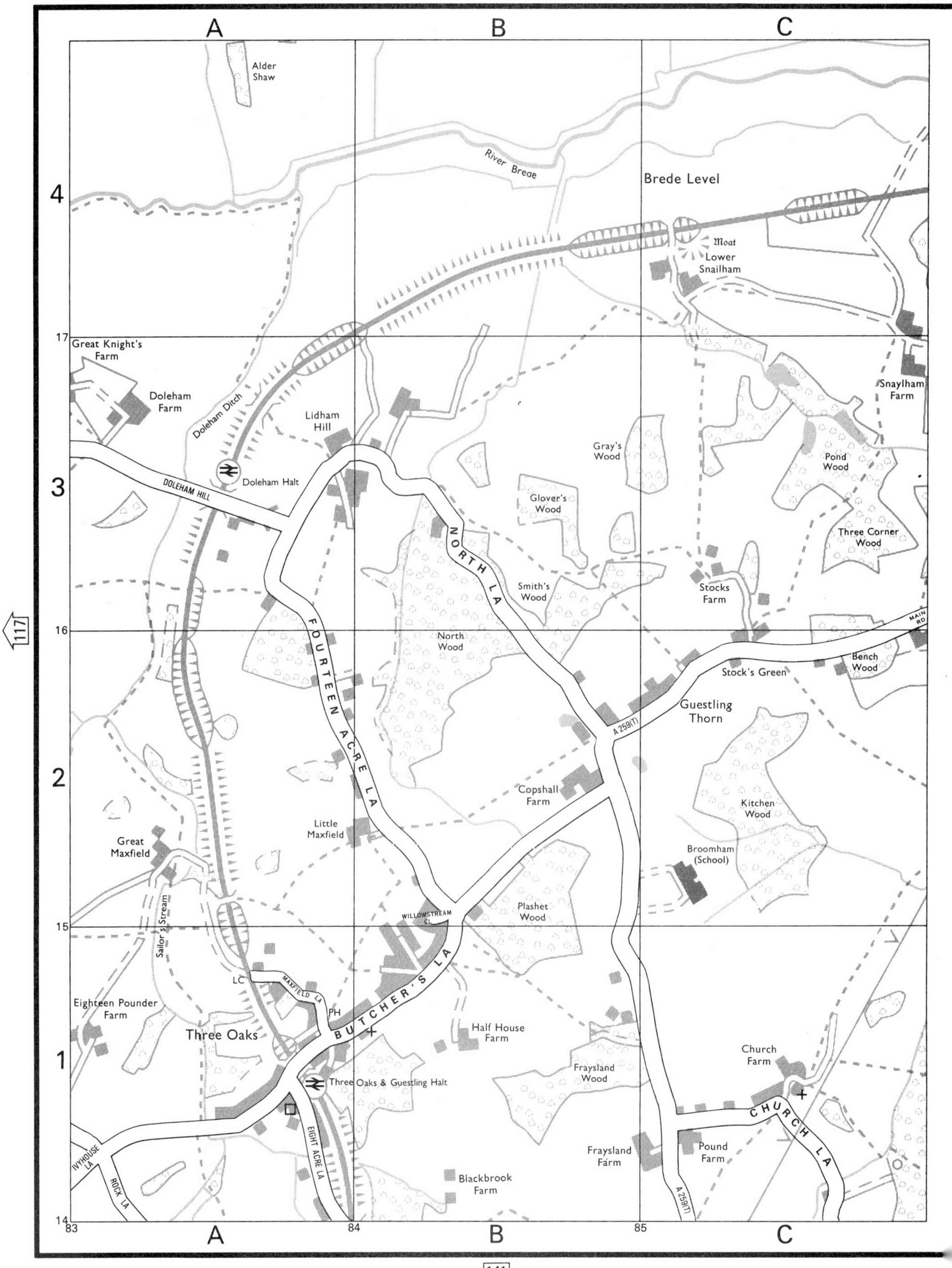

117

141

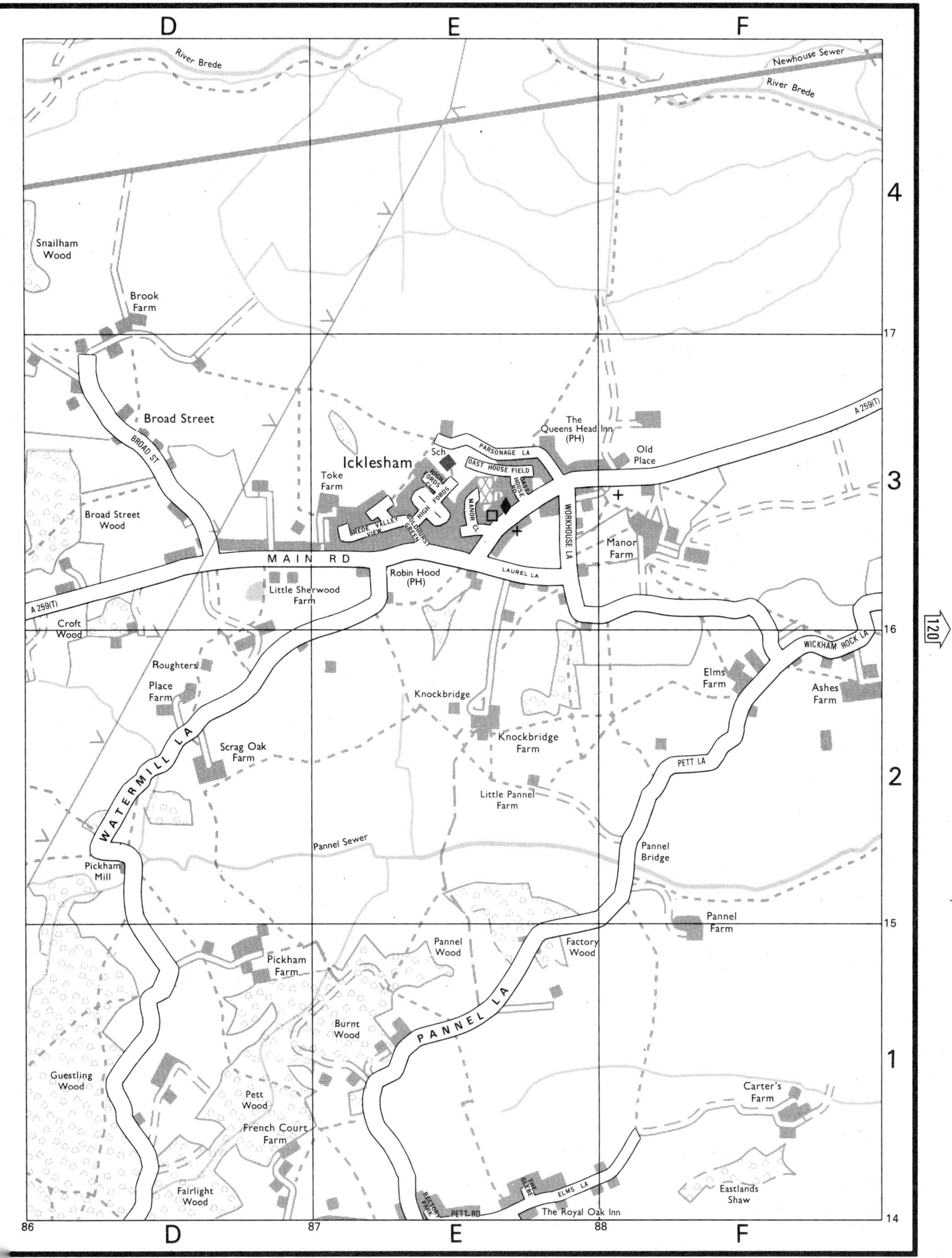

93
D
E
F
River Brede
Newhouse Sewer
River Brede
4
Snailham Wood
Brook Farm
17
Broad Street
BROAD ST
The Queens Head Inn (PH)
PARSONAGE LA
Old Place
A 259(T)
Sch
Icklesham
OAST HOUSE FIELD
OAST HOUSE RD
Toke Farm
HIGH FORDS CL
HIGH FORDS
MANOR CL
3
Broad Street Wood
BREDE VALLEY VIEW
GOLDHURST GREEN
WORKHOUSE LA
Manor Farm
MAIN RD
Robin Hood (PH)
LAUREL LA
Little Sherwood Farm
A 259(T)
Croft Wood
16
120
WICKHAM ROCK LA
Roughters
Place Farm
Knockbridge
Elms Farm
Ashes Farm
Knockbridge Farm
Scrag Oak Farm
PETT LA
2
WATERMILL LA
Little Pannel Farm
Pannel Sewer
Pannel Bridge
Pickham Mill
15
Pannel Farm
Pannel Wood
Factory Wood
Pickham Farm
PANNEL LA
Burnt Wood
1
Guestling Wood
Carter's Farm
Pett Wood
French Court Farm
Eastlands Shaw
Fairlight Wood
THE GLEBE
ELMS LA
RECTORY PARK
PETT RD
The Royal Oak Inn
14
86
87
88
D
E
F
142

94

A
B
C
4
3
2
1
17
16
15
14
89
90
91
Ferry Bridge
STATION RD
Pipewell Gate
River Brede
PH
ROYAL MILITARY RD
A 259(T)
Sewage Works
A 259(T)
FERRY HILL
TANYARD LA
Strand Bridge
Castle Farm
NORTH ST
ROBERT'S HILL
MILL RD
BARRACK SQ
STRAND HILL
Mus
CASTLE ST
WINCHELSEA
HIGH ST
GERMAN ST
ST THOMAS'S ST
ROOKERY LA
BACK LA
Strand Gate
ST GILES CL
KENT CL
FRIARS RD
SEA RD
OLD RIVER WAY
RECTORY LA
MONKS' WALK
Sch
Crutches Farm Bungalow
HOG HILL
ROUGH LA
Friary (rems of)
Crutches Farm
A 259(T)
Greyfriars
GREYFRIARS PL
MORLAIS PL
A 259(T)
Friars Cliff
PH
HARBOUR FARM
MORLAIS RIDGE
Pewis Marsh
WILLOW LA
Winchelsea Beach
Sewage Works
Wickham Manor
New Gate
Dimsdale Sewer
Wickham Manor Cottages
Caravan Park
SMEATONS LA
Jordan Farm
WICKHAM ROCK LA
DONALD WAY
VICTORIA WAY
DOGS HILL RD
THE RIDGE
Royal Military Road
Royal Military Canal (dis)
Dogs Hill
WINDSOR WAY
LB Sta
Caravan Park
Wickham Cliff
FBs
Dimsdale Sewer
Pett Level
PETT LEVEL RD
Dimsdale Sewer
Colonel Body Memorial Lakes

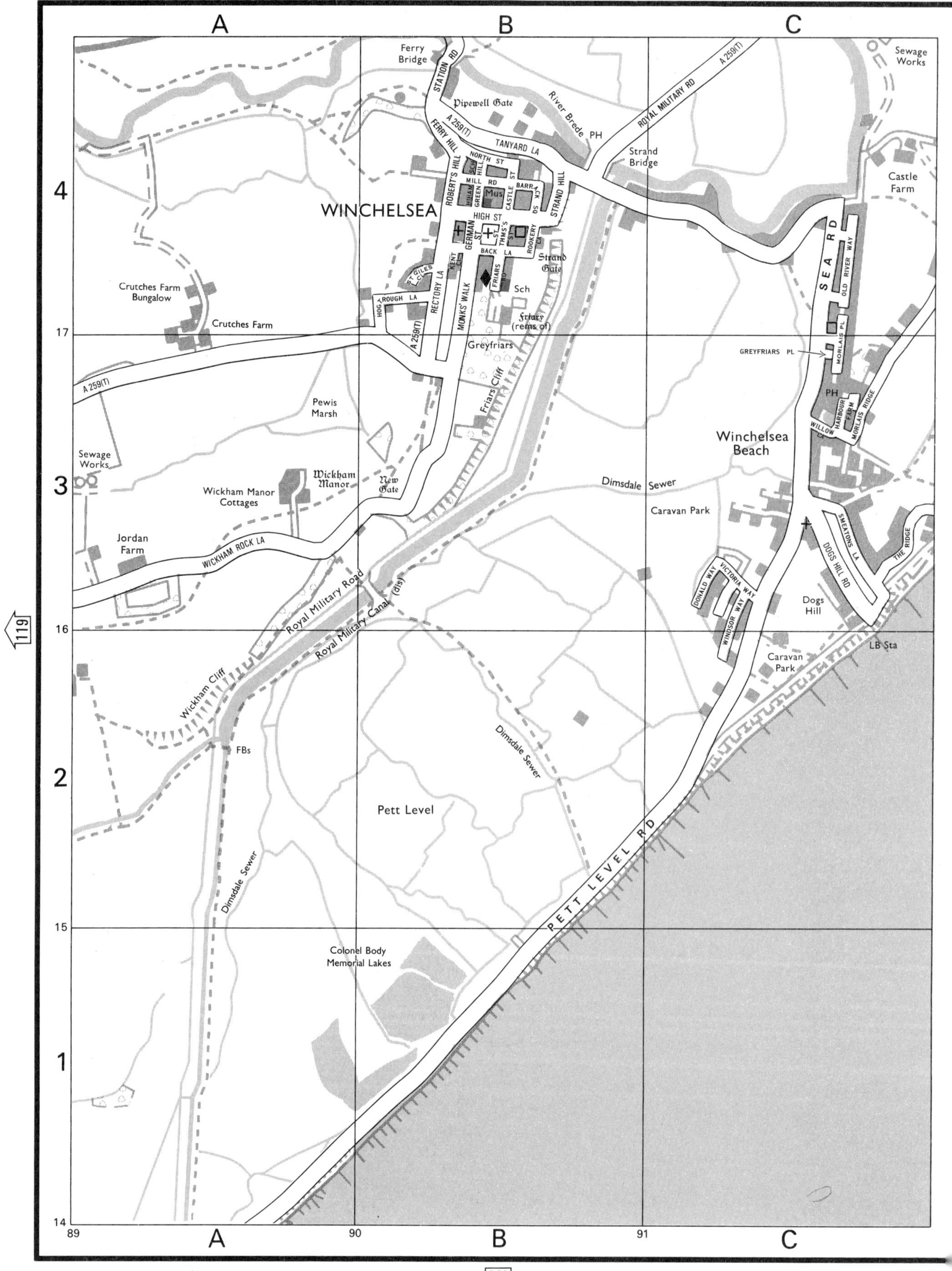

119

142

95

D
E
F
Nook Beach
The Nook
Nature
Reserve
Nook Drain
Watch
House
Rye Harbour Nature Reserve
MORLAIS RIDGE
THE RIDGE
Rye Bay
4
3
2
1
17
16
15
14
92
93
94
D
E
F

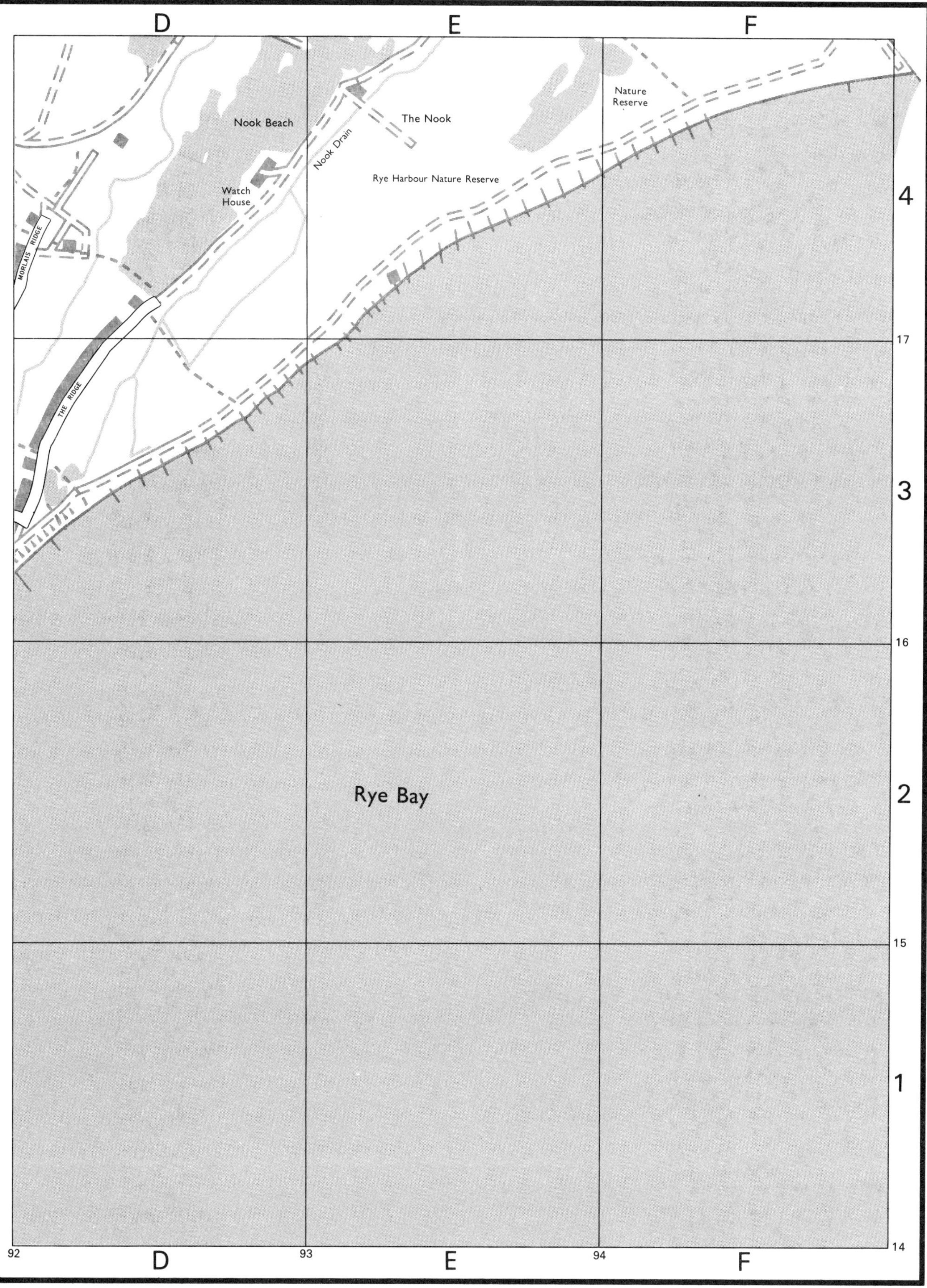

99

A
B
C
4
3
2
1
13
12
11
10
26
27
28
Park Wood
Newtimber Wood
Newtimber Place
Moat
Old Rectory
LONDON RD
A 23(T)
A 281
CHURCH LA
Round Hill
Redhouse Farm
Wolstonbury
Wolstonbury Hill
Cumulus
Chantry
WEST RD
DALE HILL
PYECOMBE ST
Cobsham Rough
Wayfield Farm
COWDOWN LA
Newtimber Holt
Pyecombe
BEGGAR'S LA
High Beeches
Newtimber Hill
HILL CL
Poynings
Cow Down
North Hill
PH
CORA'S WLK
DYKE CL
DYKE LA
Cemy
West Hill
South Downs Way
East Hill
Saddlescombe
Fort
Bostal Rd
Devil's Dyke
Summer Down
P
Tumuli
Club House
Ewe Bottom
Pond Brow
Dyke Golf Course
DEVIL'S DYKE RD
Devil's Dyke Farm
Varncombe Hill
not continued, see key diagram

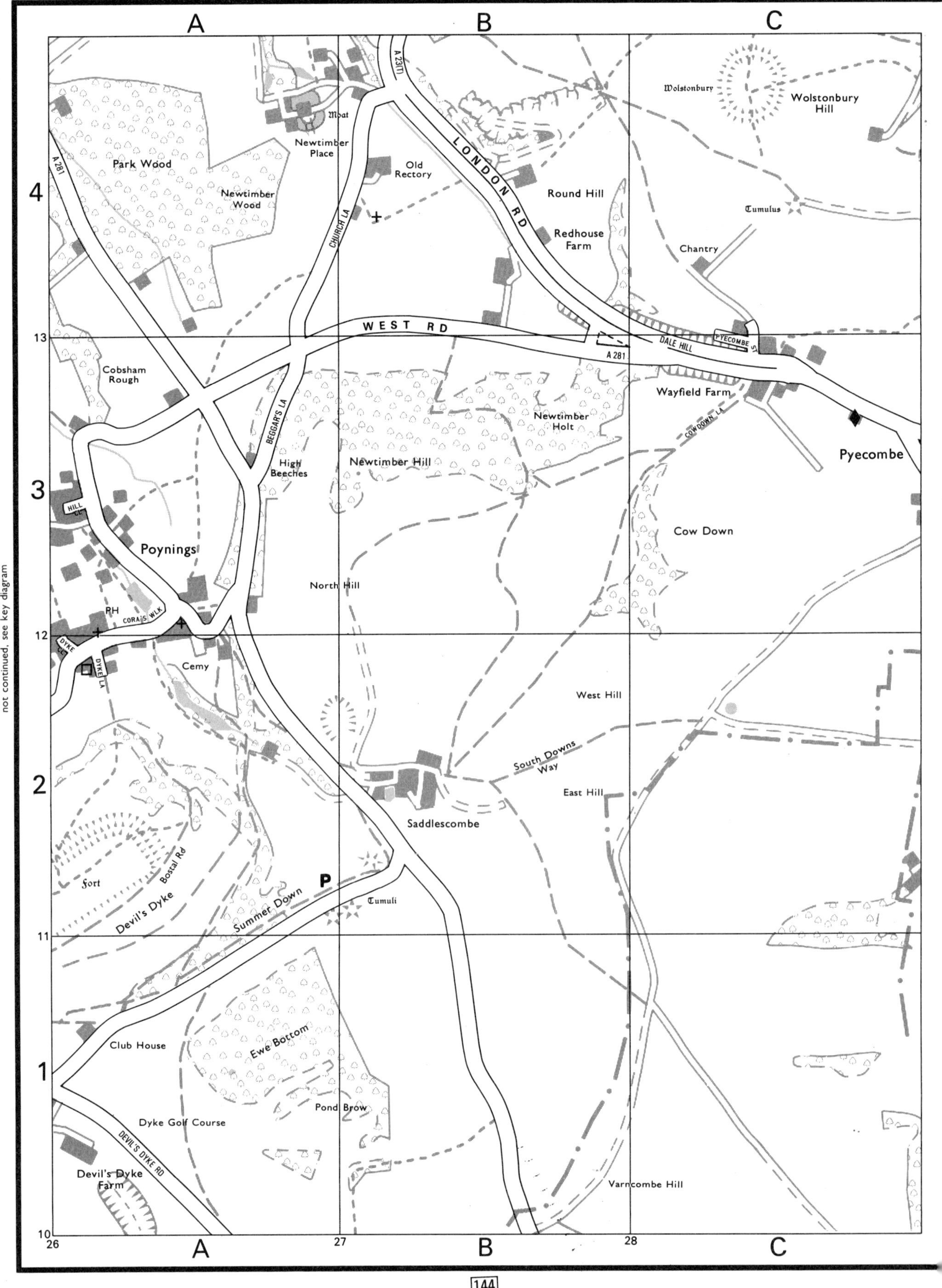

144

100

D
E
F
Clayton
SPRING LA
UNDERHILL LA
LODGE LA
Whitelands
Wellcombe Bottom
A 273
CLAYTON HILL
Clayton Holt
Coombe Bottom
Clayton Windmills
Jill
Jack
MILL LA
P
Rockrose
Clayton Tunnel
Burnthouse Bostall (Track)
New Barn Farm
South Downs Way
THE WYSHE
SCHOOL LA
Pyecombe Golf Course
Rag Bottom
The Plough Inn (PH)
A 23(T)
A 273
Dencher Bottom
Middle Brow
Pangdean Cottages
Pangdean Farm
Holt Bottom
Pangdean Holt
Lower Standean
South Hill
Holt Hill
Chattri (Indian War Memorial)
Wonderhill Plantation
Doddlis Plantation
Mid-down House
New Barn
South Hill Cottages
South Hill Barn
Poor Brow
The Pylons
Alpha Cottage
Deep Bottom
LONDON RD
Scare Hill
Tegdown Hill
Ewebottom Hill
Ewe Bottom
A 23(T)
4
3
2
1
13
12
11
10
29
30
31
D
E
F

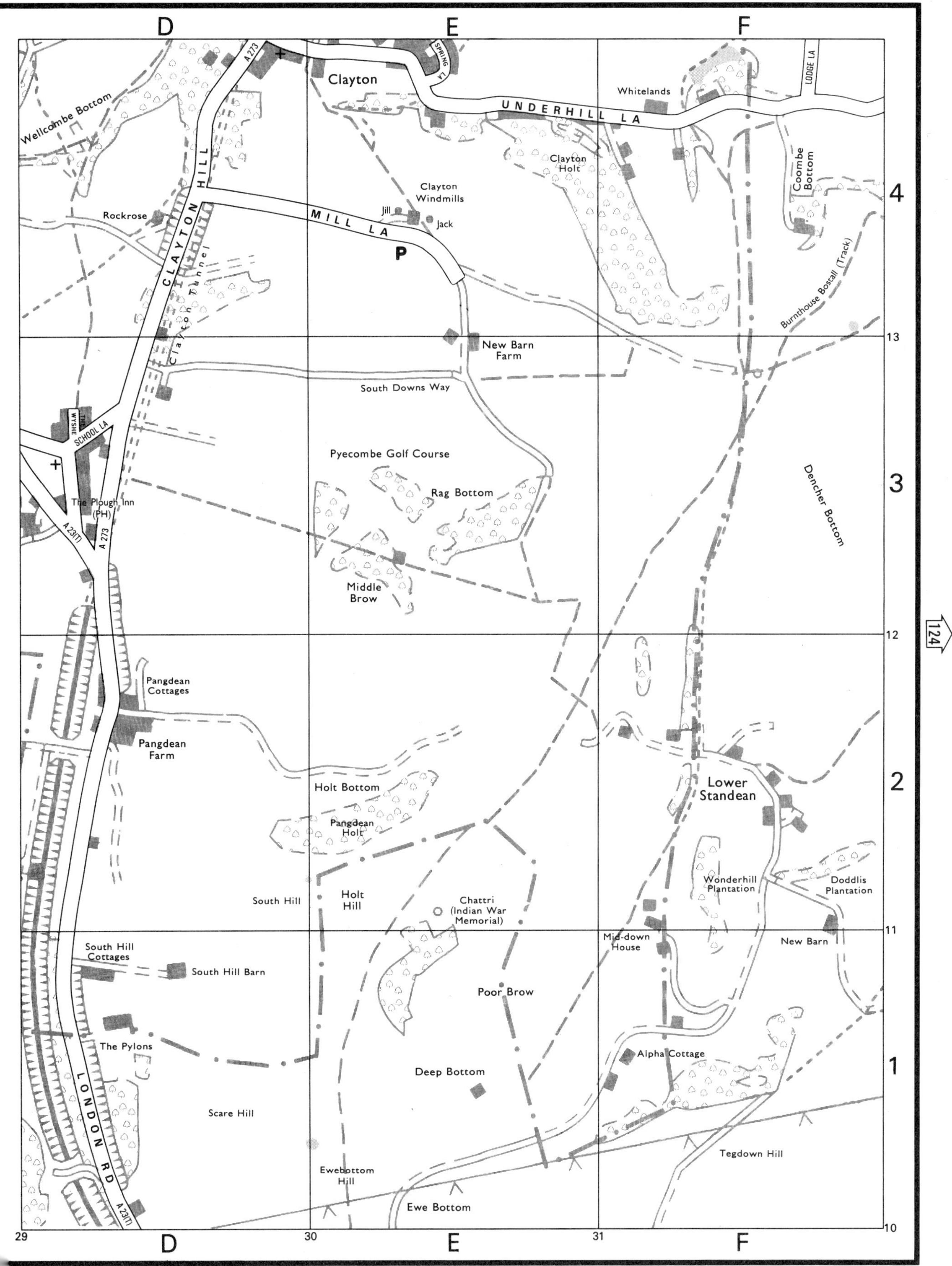

124

145

101

A
B
C
Westmeston
Beacon Rd
Nye La
B2116
Saillards
Underhill La
Wick Farm
Downsview
The Street
Lewes Rd
The Gote
Burnthouse Bostall
Ditchling Bostal
Westmeston Farm
Westmeston Bostall
Middleton (Path)
B2116
Cumulus
Cumuli
Ditchling Beacon
P
Settlement
Mound
Middleton Bostall
South Downs Way
Cumuli
Cumuli
Cumuli
Home Brow
Western Brow
Home Bottom
Field System
Tumuli
Big Bottom
Hogtrough Bottom
Heathy Brow
North Bottom
Horseshore Plantation
Ditchling Rd
Highpark Corner
High Park Farm
Highpark Wood
Bow Hill
Shambledean Bottom
Stanmer Down
Green Broom
Piddingworth Plantation
Cumulus
Moon's Bottom
St Mary's Farm
Granny's Belt
Flint Heap
Millbank Wood
Ridge Rd
Upper Lodge Wood
Limekiln Wood
Moon's Corner
4
13
3
12
2
11
1
10
32
33
34
A
B
C

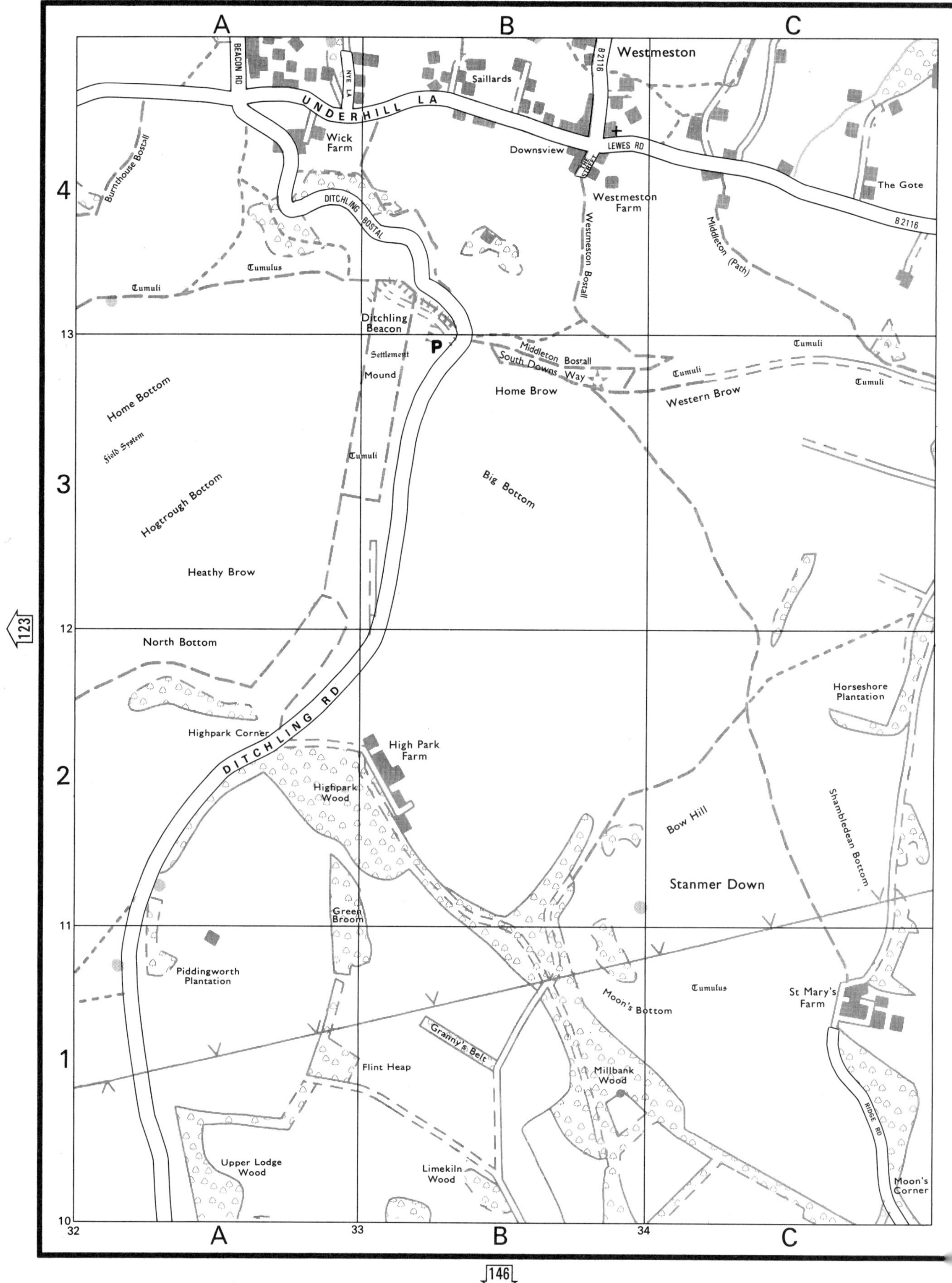

123

146

102

D
E
F
Oakwood Farm
Drews Farm
House
STREAT LA
Wales Farm
PLUMPTON LA
New Barn
Warningore Farm
NOVINGTON LA
Plumpton Place
Hackmans Farm
4
Plumpton Agricultural College
Newstead Farm
B 2116
PH
Lanes
Plumpton
Streat Bostall
B 2116
13
PLUMPTON BOSTALL
Cumuli
Cumulus
Cumulus
Mounds
The Beeches
Warningore Bostall
Cumuli
Cumuli
Cumuli
Enclosure
Plumpton Plain
Blackcap
3
Cumulus
South Downs Way
Settlement
Faulkner's Bottom
12
Ashcombe Bottom
Broad Shackles
Cumulus
2
Buckland Bank
Moustone
11
Buckland Hole
Balmer Huff
Balmer Down
South Downs Way
1
Waterpit Hill
10
35
36
37
D
E
F

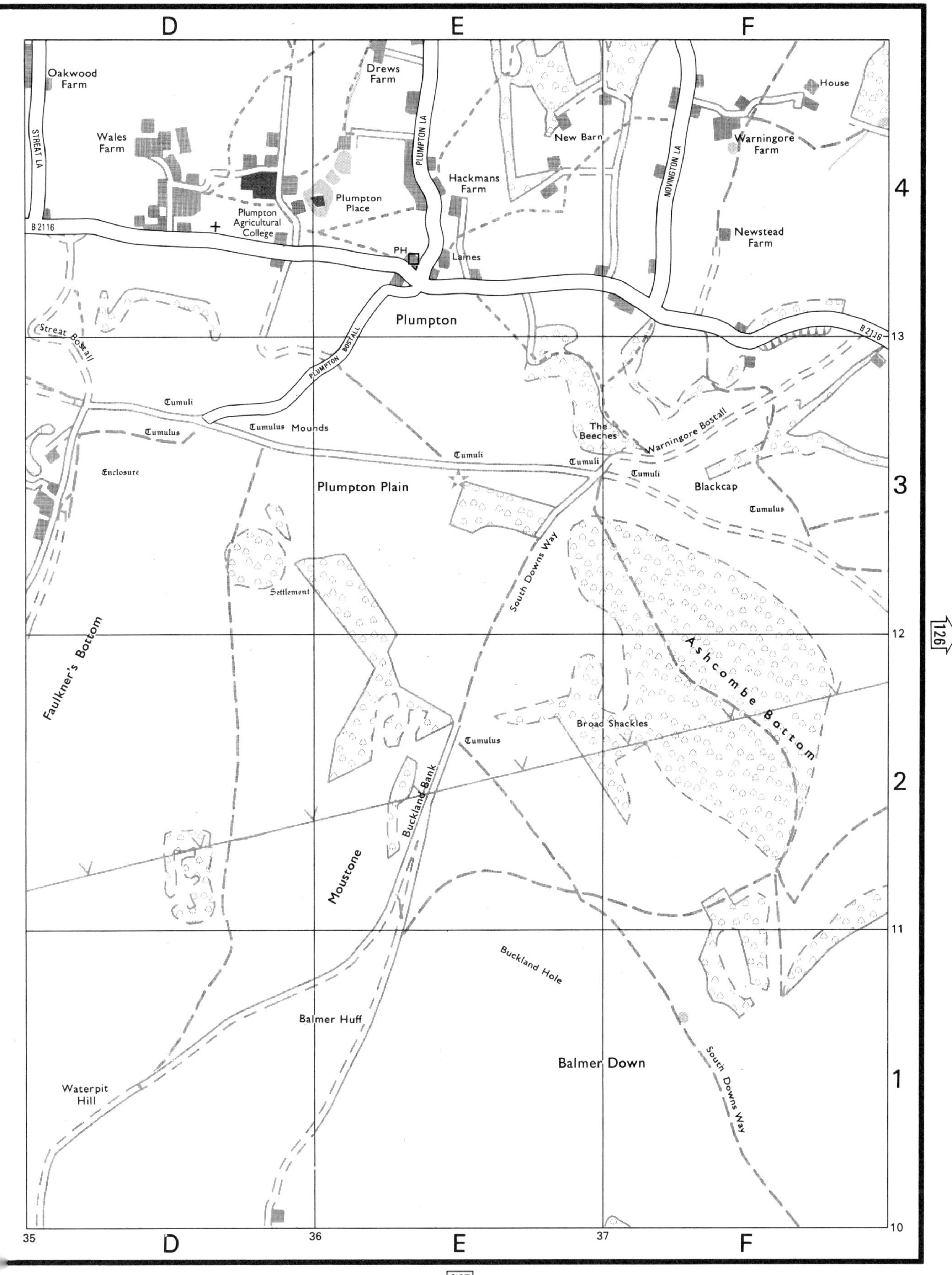

126

147

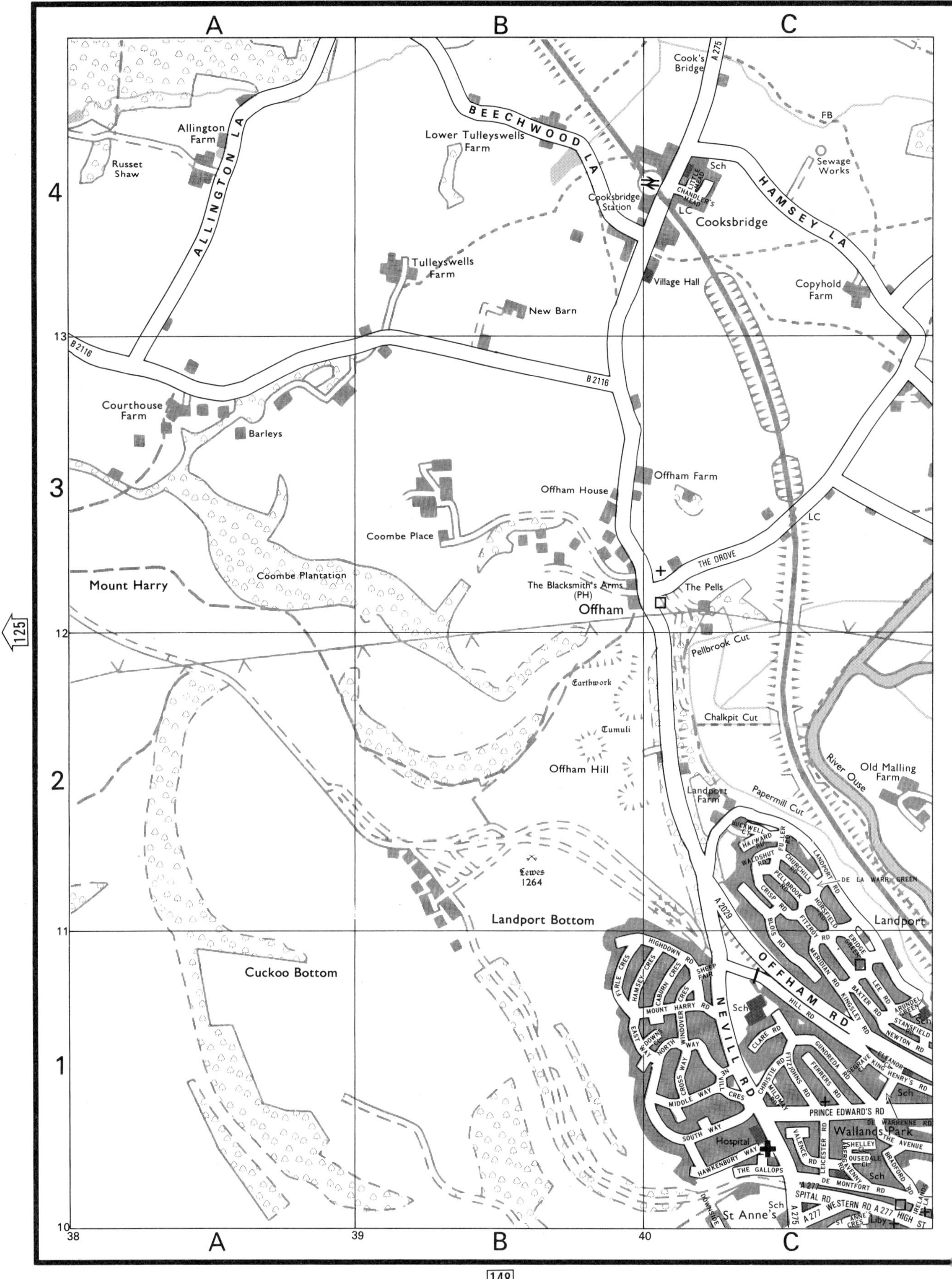
103
148
125
Allington Farm
Russet Shaw
ALLINGTON LA
BEECHWOOD LA
Lower Tulleyswells Farm
Tulleyswells Farm
New Barn
Cook's Bridge
Cooksbridge Station
Cooksbridge
HAMSEY LA
Sewage Works
Village Hall
Copyhold Farm
B2116
Courthouse Farm
Barleys
Coombe Place
Offham House
Offham Farm
THE DROVE
Mount Harry
Coombe Plantation
The Blacksmith's Arms (PH)
Offham
The Pells
Pellbrook Cut
Earthwork
Tumuli
Chalkpit Cut
Offham Hill
River Ouse
Old Malling Farm
Landport Farm
Papermill Cut
Lewes 1264
Landport Bottom
Landport
Cuckoo Bottom
OFFHAM RD
NEVILL RD
Hospital
Wallands Park
St Anne's
PRINCE EDWARD'S RD
WESTERN RD
HIGH ST
A 275
A 277
A 2029

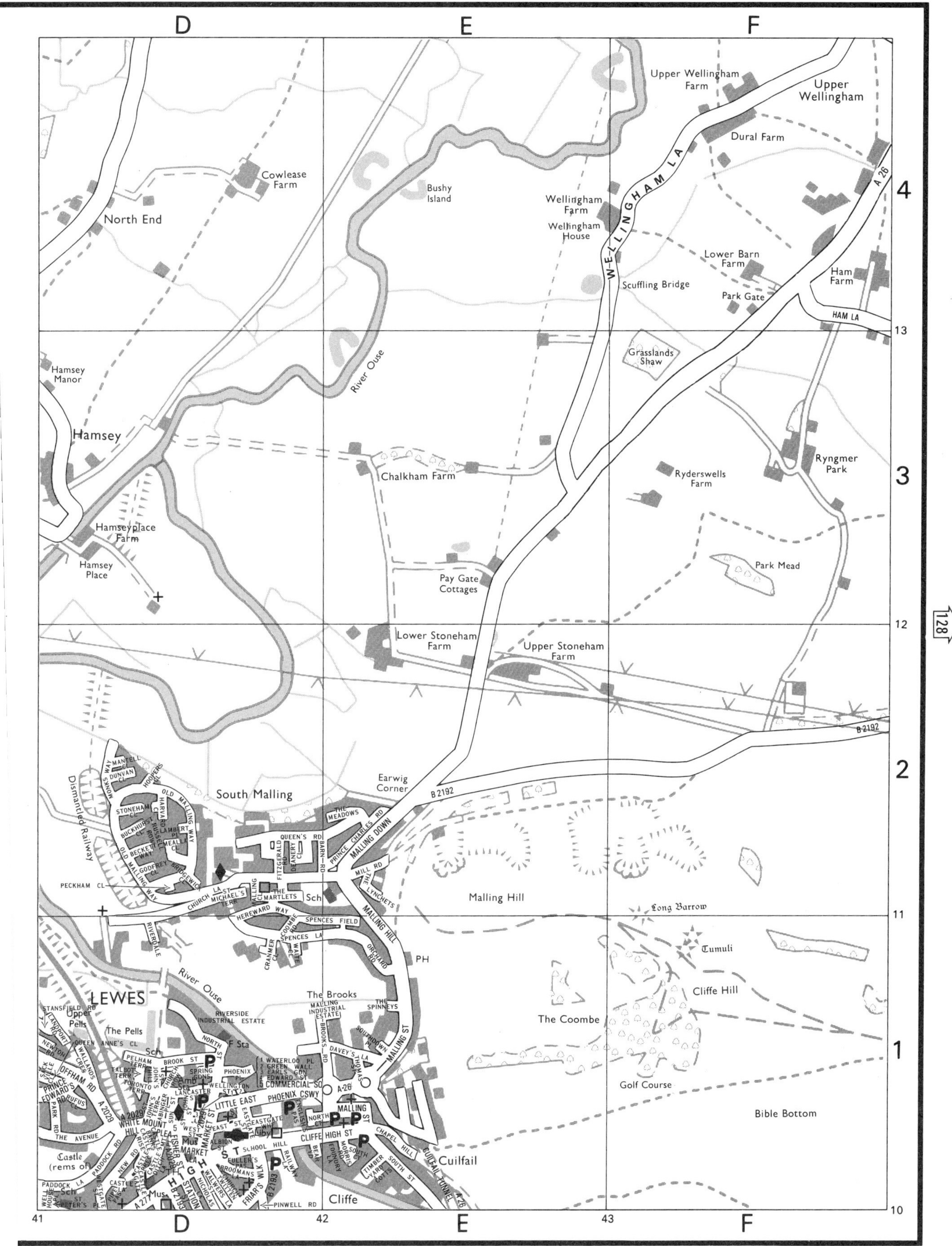
104
D
E
F
Upper Wellingham Farm
Upper Wellingham
Dural Farm
Cowlease Farm
Bushy Island
North End
Wellingham Farm
Wellingham House
WELLINGHAM LA
A 26
Lower Barn Farm
Scuffling Bridge
Park Gate
Ham Farm
HAM LA
Grasslands Shaw
Hamsey Manor
River Ouse
Hamsey
Chalkham Farm
Ryngmer Park
Ryderswells Farm
Hamseyplace Farm
Hamsey Place
Park Mead
Pay Gate Cottages
Lower Stoneham Farm
Upper Stoneham Farm
B 2192
Earwig Corner
South Malling
Dismantled Railway
Malling Hill
Long Barrow
Tumuli
Cliffe Hill
The Coombe
LEWES
The Brooks
Riverside Industrial Estate
Upper Pells
The Pells
Golf Course
Bible Bottom
Cuilfail
Castle (rems of)
Cliffe
PECKHAM CL
CHURCH LA
MALLING DOWN
MALLING ST
SPENCES FIELD
HEREWARD WAY
PINWELL RD
PH
Sch
F Sta
Mus
Liby
Amb
A 2029
A 277
B 2193
CLIFFE HIGH ST
PHOENIX CSWY
CHAPEL HILL
CUILFAIL TUNNEL
41
42
43
10
11
12
13
1
2
3
4
128
149

105

127

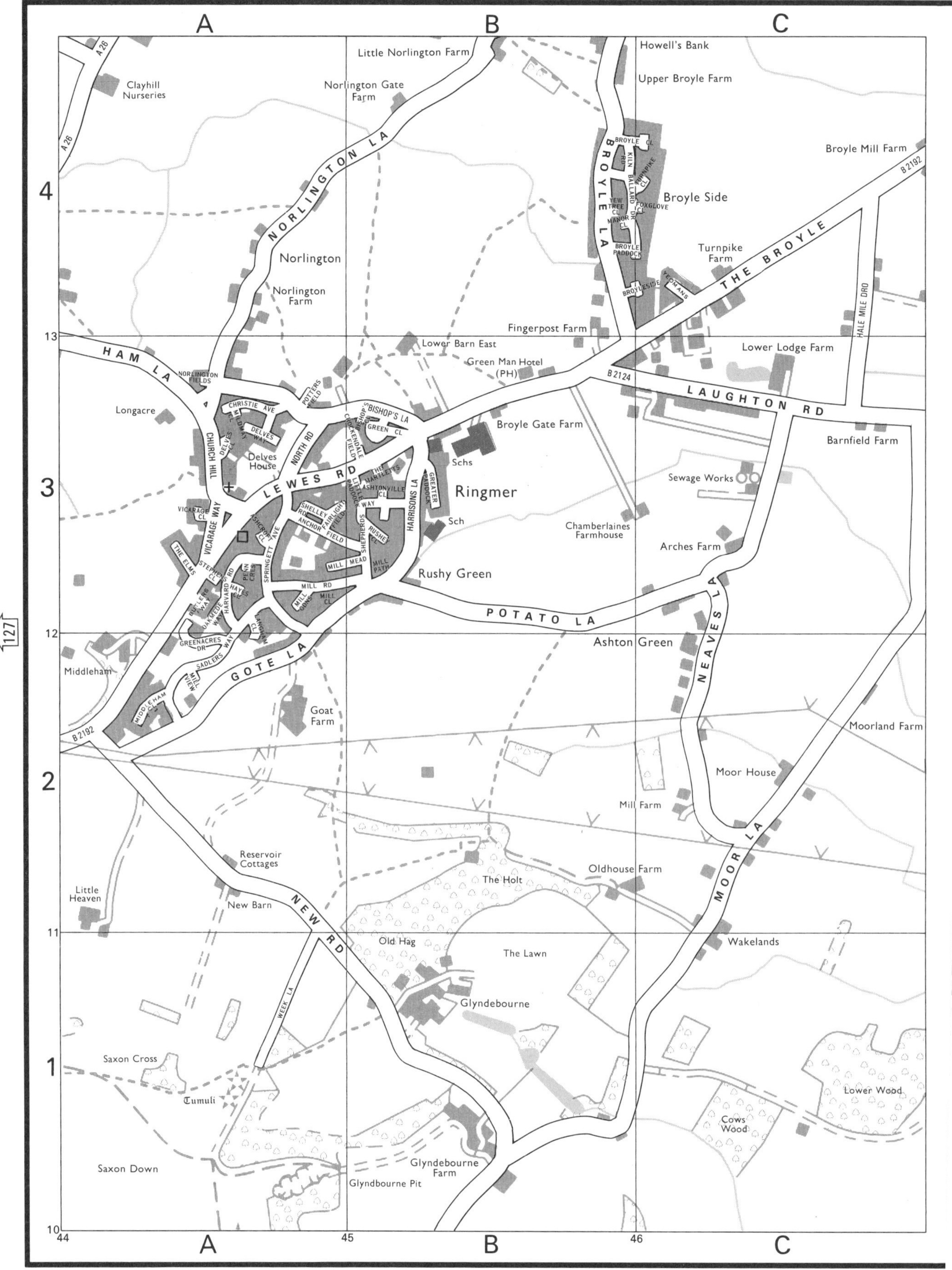

150

106

D
E
F
THE BROYLE
B 2192
HARVEY'S LA
Upper Broyle Farm
Longfield Wood
Plain Barn
Hospl
Averys Oak Farm
Wood Bungalows
Laughton Manor
4
New Barn
LAUGHTON RD
B 2124
13
Home Farm
Broyle Place
B 2124
Paygate Cottages
Colbrans Farm
Decoy Wood
Black Shaw
3
Laughton Place Farm House
Chambers Court
Old Barn
12
Willow Shaw
New Barn
Laughton Place (remains of)
2
Moat
Laughton Place Farm
Mill Farm
11
Mark Cross
Laughton Level
Glynde Reach
Totts Shaw
1
Headlee Bridge (Foot)
47
48
49
10
D
E
F

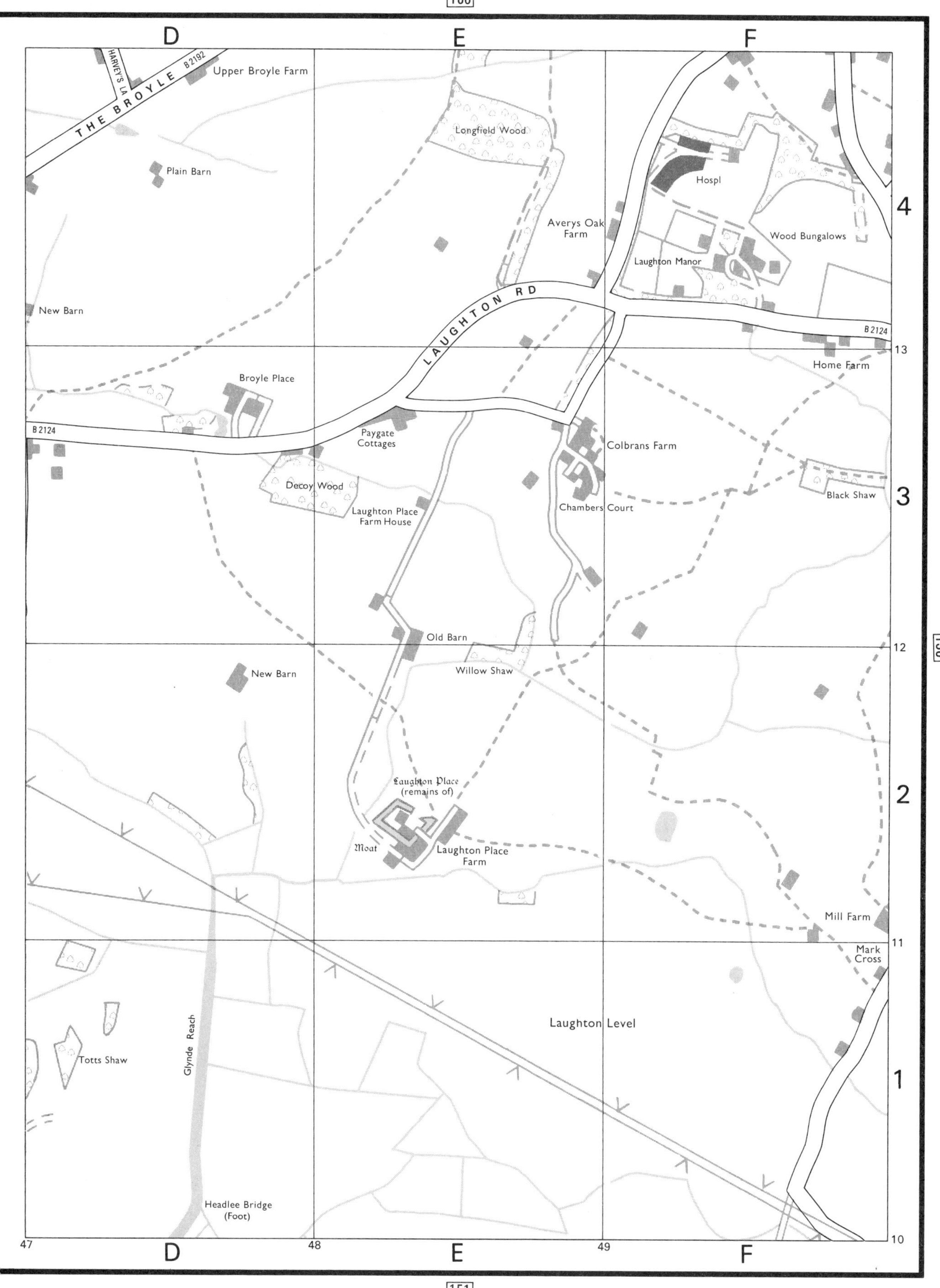

130

151

107

A
B
C
Brickhurst Wood
Brickhurst Farm
BRICKHURST LA
Laughton Common Wood
Whitesmith
A 22
Vert House
Randall's Farm
Lower Vert Wood
Saw Mill
Helouan Farm
PH
POUND LA
Laughton
ELM CL
B 2124
Vert Edge
Queeake
Bowen Wood
Broadoak Wood
Coopers Farm
Sch
Bowen Farm
Stone Cross Farm
Broomham
B 2124
Marchants Farm
Milward's Farm
Broomham Farm
New House Farm
Church Farm
Harben's Farm
Cleaver's Farm
Veals Wood
Little Stream Farm
Caravan Park
Cleggett's Farm
Martins Cottage
RIPE LA
Heathers
Green Farm
Newhouse Farm
Curls Farm
Fowler's Barn
Ripe
CHANNELERS LA
CHURCH LA
4
3
2
1
13
12
11
10
50
51
52

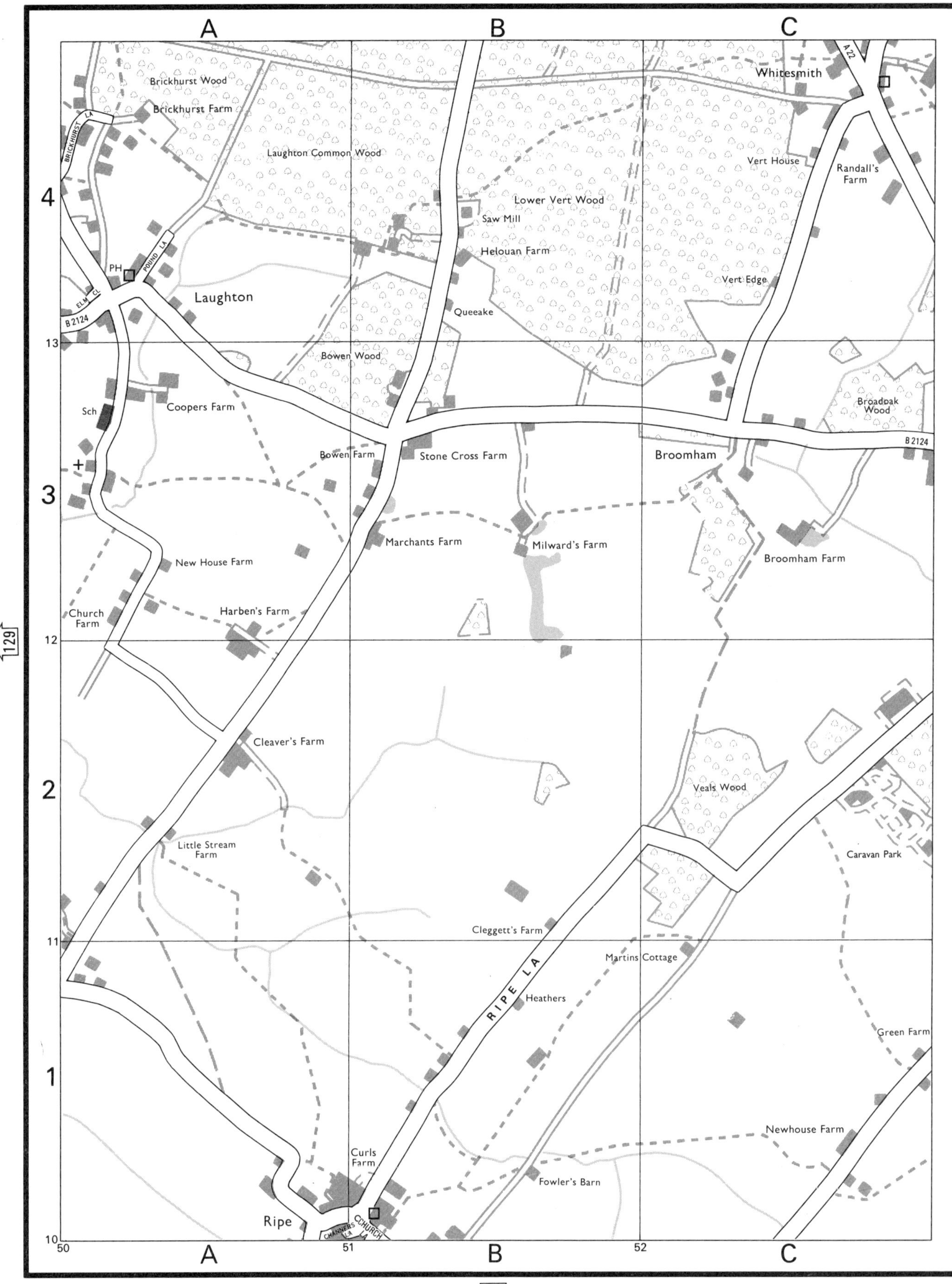

129

152

108

D
E
F
Park Bridge
Burchetts Farm
Bolt Wood
Scraper's Hill
Willetts Farm
Muddles Green
Sch
Hamly Bridge
4
Shelf Wood
Hoad's Wood
A 22
Farley Farm
Kiln Wood
Thunder's Hill
Pekes House
Pekes Farm
13
Burghill Farm
Burgh Hill
Nash Street Farm
Holmes Hill Farm
Holmes's Hill
Hazelhurst Farm
Twenty Acre Wood
B 2124
Eight Acre Wood
Golden Cross
Nash Street
3
PH
Broad Oak Farm
Brickfield's Farm
Buffcoats Farm
Marigolds Farm
12
Mill Farm
Works
Hackhurst La
Blackbarn Farm
Ivy Farm
Newhouse Farm
Nursery
A 22
2
Deanland Wood
Nickols Farm
Penny Plain Farm
Camberlot Farm
The Mount
Bridle Gate Farm
Chalvington Stud Farm
Limekiln Farm
Camberlot Wood
Camberlot Rd
11
Field House
Clover Farm
1
Coldharbour Rd
Mount Pleasant Farm
Starnash
Plenties Farm
Malvern House
Bourne Farm
Pollard's Wood
53
54
55
10
132
153

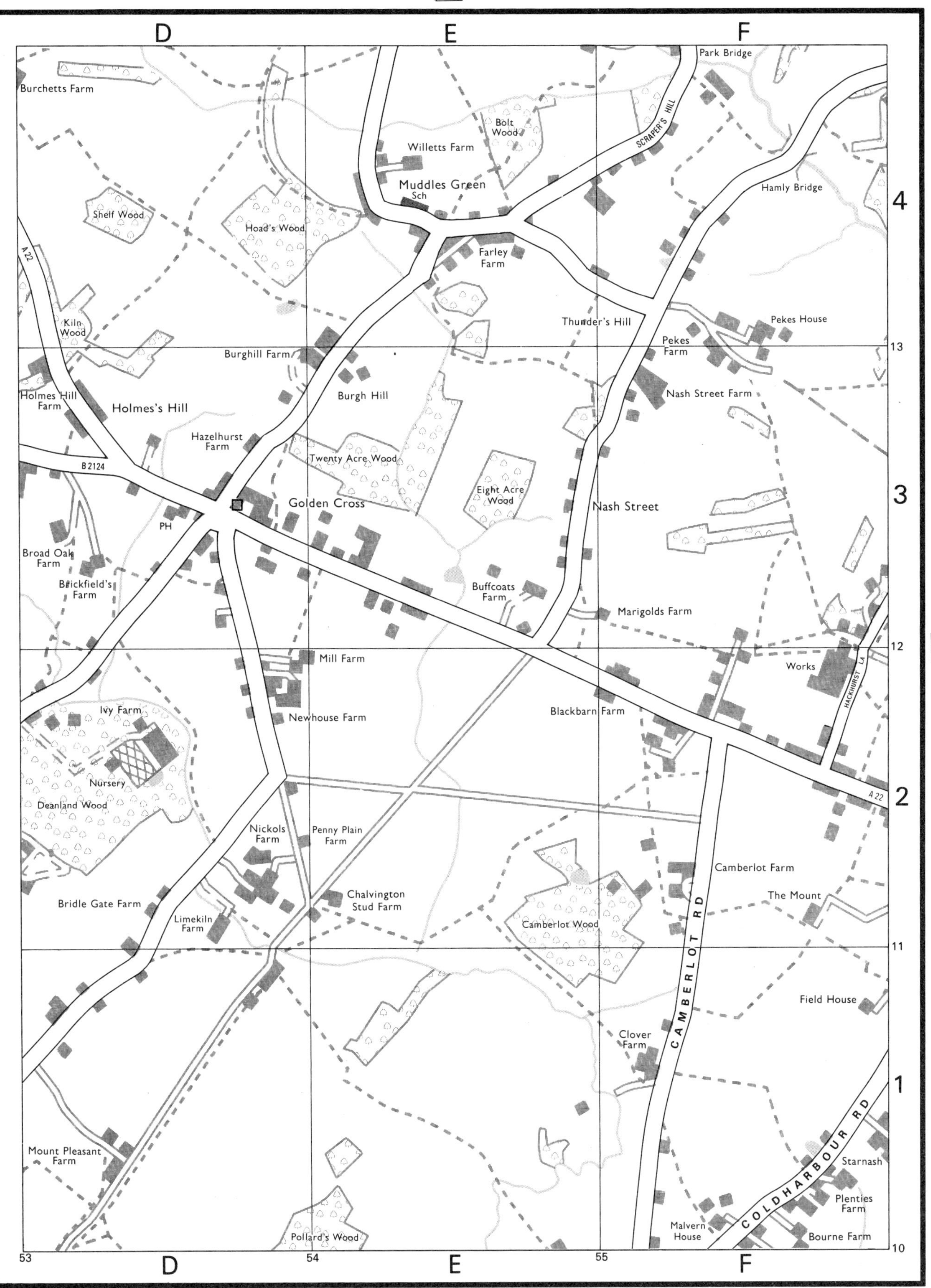

109

A
B
C
Popp's Farm
Westenden Wood
Holmbush
Westenden Farm
Mount Pleasant Cottages
Hawthbush Farm
World's End Farm
Lealands
NORTH ST
Leabridge Farm
A 267
Boggy Wood
Perryland Farm
NORTH ST
Akehurst Farm
The Golden Martlet (PH)
The Broads
CHURCH RD
HACKHURST LA
Hackhurst Farm
CHURCH PATH
Nursery
Sch
Hellingly
Horselunges
STATION RD
B 2104
NEW RD
PARK RD
Caldicott's Wood
White House
Dismantled Railway
Caldicotts Farm
CALDICOTTS LA
Lower Dicker
Lower Horsebridge
B 2104
A 22
Knight's Farm
Upper Horsebridge
HAWKSWOOD RD
A 267
A 271
UPPER HORSEBRIDGE RD
A 271
MANSERS LA
A 22
B 2104
SHEPPEY WLK
MANOR PARK CL
MANOR PARK RD
PAUL CL
LANSDOWNE WAY
LANSDOWNE CRES
UNION CL
HAREBEATING DR
BECKENHAM
FALCON WAY
Coldharbour Farm
LUNDY WK
Sch
COLDHARBOUR RD
Hatches Farm
Boship Farm Hotel
ROCKALL DR
ASHBURNHAM PL
LANSDOWNE DR
LANSDOWNE RD
HAWKS FARM CL
QUINNELL DR
HAWTHYLANDS DR
STROMA GDNS
ANGLESEY AVE
THE PADDOCKS
LONDON RD
LANSDOWNE GDNS
ARRAN CL
SOLWAY
HAWKS RD
HOWLETT DR
BEXLEY CL
Cuckmere River
The Nurseries
FARNE CL
MEDWAY
FAIRISLE CL
HAWTHYLANDS RD
HAWTHYLANDS CRES
Welbury Farm
GOODWIN CL
CROMER WAY
HARMERS HAY RD
PORTLAND CL
HEMPSTEAD LA
THE LOWLANDS
EPELAND
FERN GREEN
JASMINE GREEN
ACORN GREEN
BLOSSOM WLK
Starnash
CHESTNUT CL
OLDFIELD CRES
THE CEDARS
MILLAND RD
Woodside Farm
Chicheley Farm
Playing Field
HEMPSTEAD LA
DERWENT CL
Playing Field
Hempstead Farm
A 22
GROVELANDS RD
B 2104
Amb Sta
BATTLE RD
4
3
2
1
13
12
11
10
56
57
58

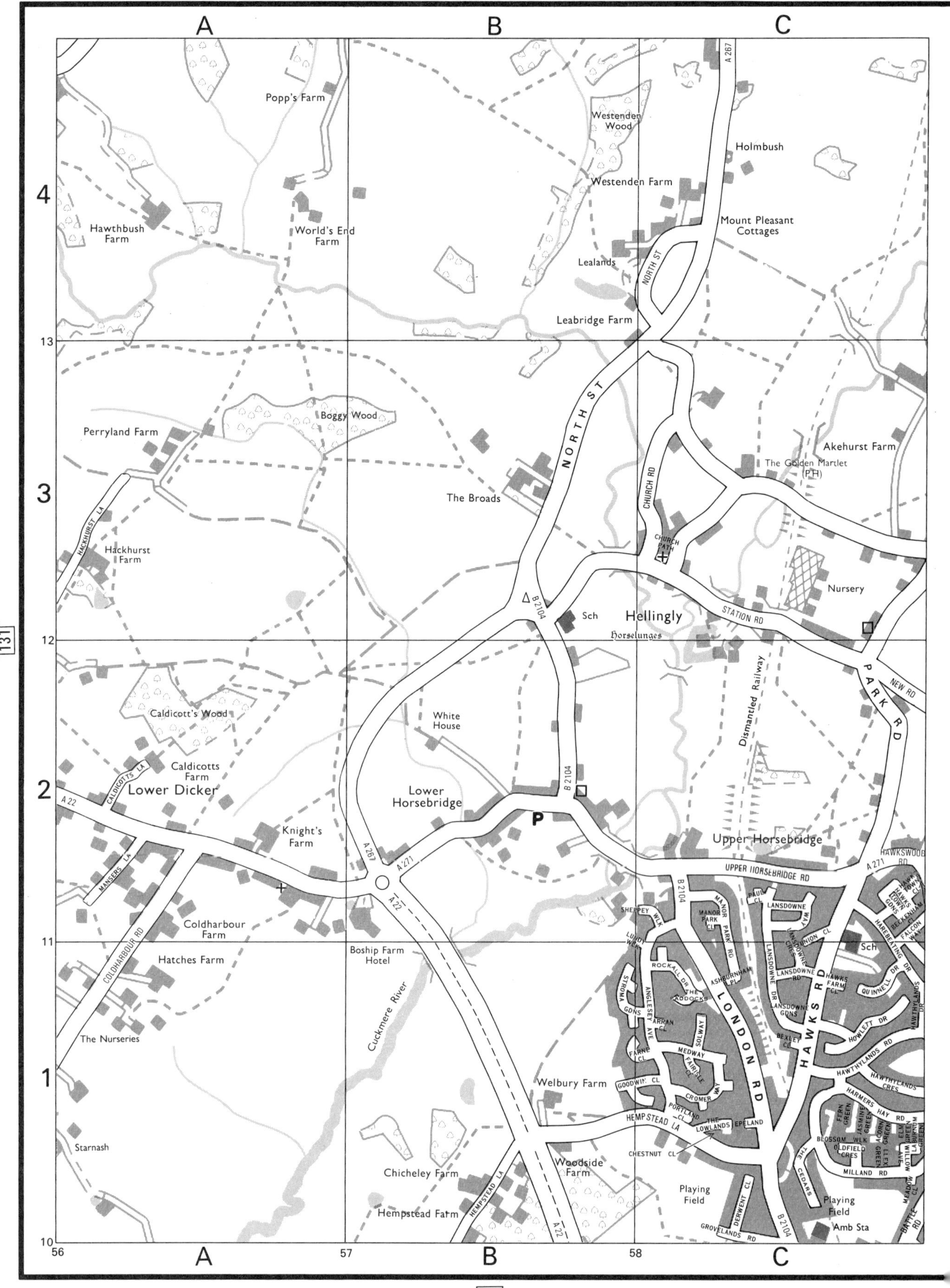

131

154

110

D
E
F
CINDERFORD LA
Old Barn Farm
Jarvis's Wood
Springham Farm
Scripp Farm
4
Nobody's Wood
Cowbeech Hill Farm
Cowbeech Hill
Blackstock Farm
GROVE HILL
Clapsons Shaw
Old Court
13
Reeves Land
Shawpits Farm
Ten Acre Wood
Oaklands
Peartree Shaw
Twelveacres
Starvecrow Wood
3
Park Wood
Carter's Corner Place
Hospital
Squirrel Lane
Park Cottage
SQUAB LA
Deudney's Farm
12
A 271
Nodes Farm
OLD RD
Park Farm
Hospital
Magham Down Farm
Harkaway
Nodes
NEW RD
Waldernheath
Magham Down
2
AMBERSTONE
A 271
UNDER RD
Amberstone Bridge
Puckridge
Gilridge Lodge
DANUM CL
HAWKSWOOD RD
HAWKSWOOD DR
PARK GATE
Amberstone Grange Farm
Puckeridge Stream
THE GREEN
A 271
HAREBEATING CL
AMBERSTONE VIEW
A 295
11
Gildridge Farm
HAWKS TOWN CRES
HAREBEATING DR
HAREBEATING GDNS
HAREBEATING CRES
OAK TREE WAY
NORTH HEATH CL
ABBEY PATH
Sewage Works
Tile Lodge Farm
WOODLANDS CL
HAWTHYLANDS RD
HAWTHYLANDS CRES
BATTLE RD
FIR TREE CL
Magham Sewer
1
Spindle Bridge (FB)
Hurst Haven
GREEN WLK
Longleys Farm
HAREBEATING LA
CORNFIELD GREEN
MILLAND RD
HARMERS HAY RD
BARN CL
A 295
Harebeating Farm
Whelpley Level
10
59
60
61

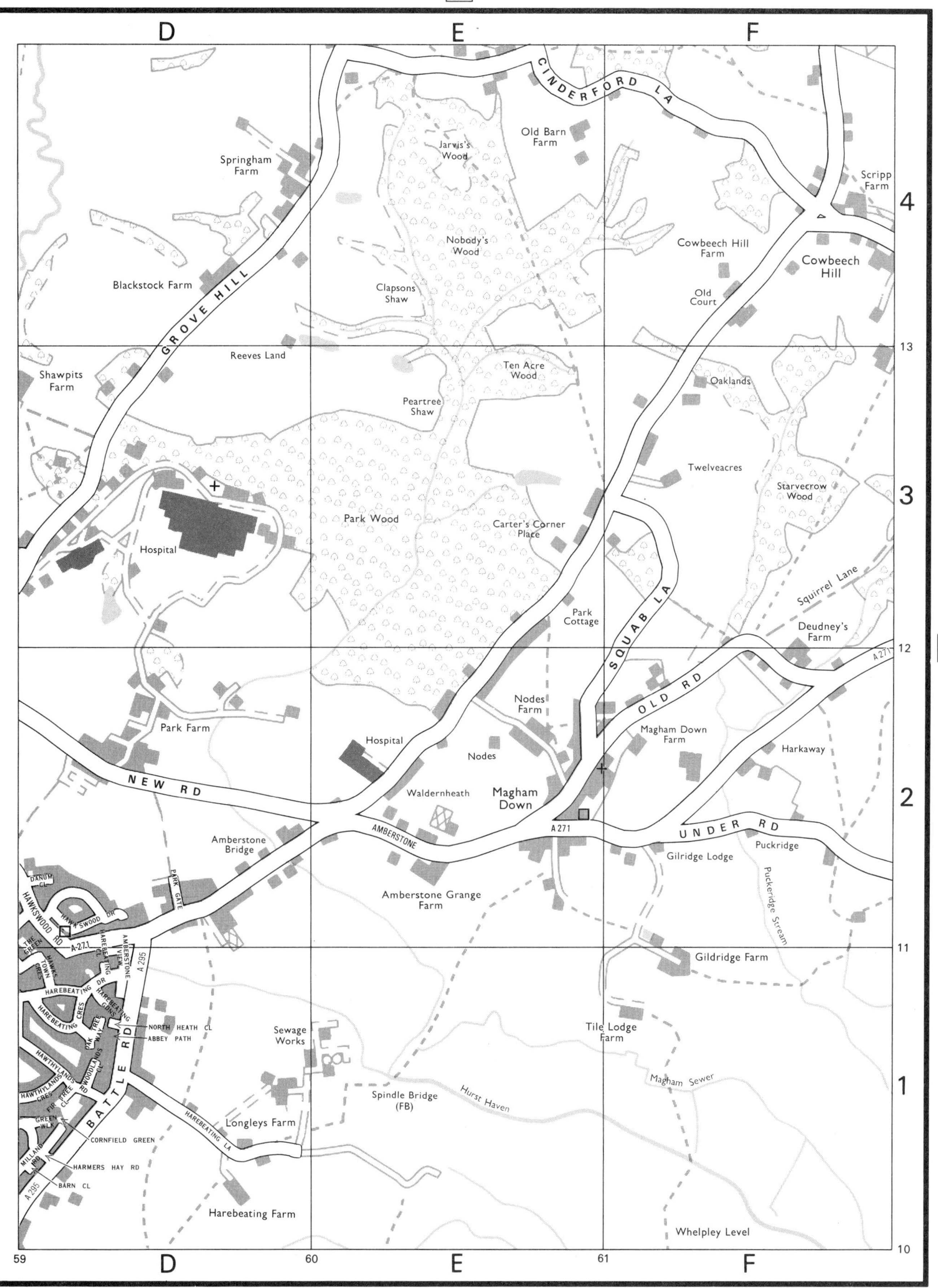

134
155

111

A
B
C
Scrip Wood
Kiln Wood
FB
Studdens Lane
Chilsham Stream
Pebsham Stream
CHILSHAM LA
Chilsham Farm
Chilsham
Greenway Fruit Farm
Calvesfield Shaw
Nunningham Stream
Stunts Green
Nunningham Farm
Hollingwood
New Barn Farm
Herstmonceux
WEST END
JAMES AVE
FAIRFIELD
MONCEUX RD
BAGHAM LA
CHESTNUT CL
THE RIDGEWAY
FAIRLAWNS DR
FIENNES RD
DACRE RD
QUEENS RD
BUCKWELL RISE
F Sta
PH
GARDNER ST
HAILSHAM RD
Ginger's Green Farm
Ginger's Green
Squirrel Lane
School
Lime Cross
Windmill Hill
Brick Farm
VICTORIA RD
COOMBE CL
MIDDLE HURST LA
WALLIS CL
NURSERY CL
HIGHVIEW CL
JOE'S LA
Buckwell Farm
The Welcome Stranger (PH)
Cooper's Croft
Lime Park
Chapel Row
Allfree Wood
A 271
Buckwell Place
Lime End Farm
Upper House Farm
CRICKETING LA
BUTLER'S LA
COMPHURST LA
Comphurst
FB
Butler's Farm
Little Comphurst
FB
Flowers Green
UNDER RD
Place Farm
Willow Farm
Chantler's Farm
LOWER RD
Herstmonceux Place
Golden Cross
Sackville Farm
Ironcroft Cottage
Cherry Croft Farm
The Park
Iron Stream
CHURCH RD
Bowley Sewer
Royal Greenwich Observatory
AIRY RD
Moat
Herstmonceux Castle
Mill Stream
Puckeridge Stream
Sackville Sewer
FLAMSTEED RD
HALLEY RD
MASKELYNE RD
Church Farm
4
3
2
1
13
12
11
10
62
63
64

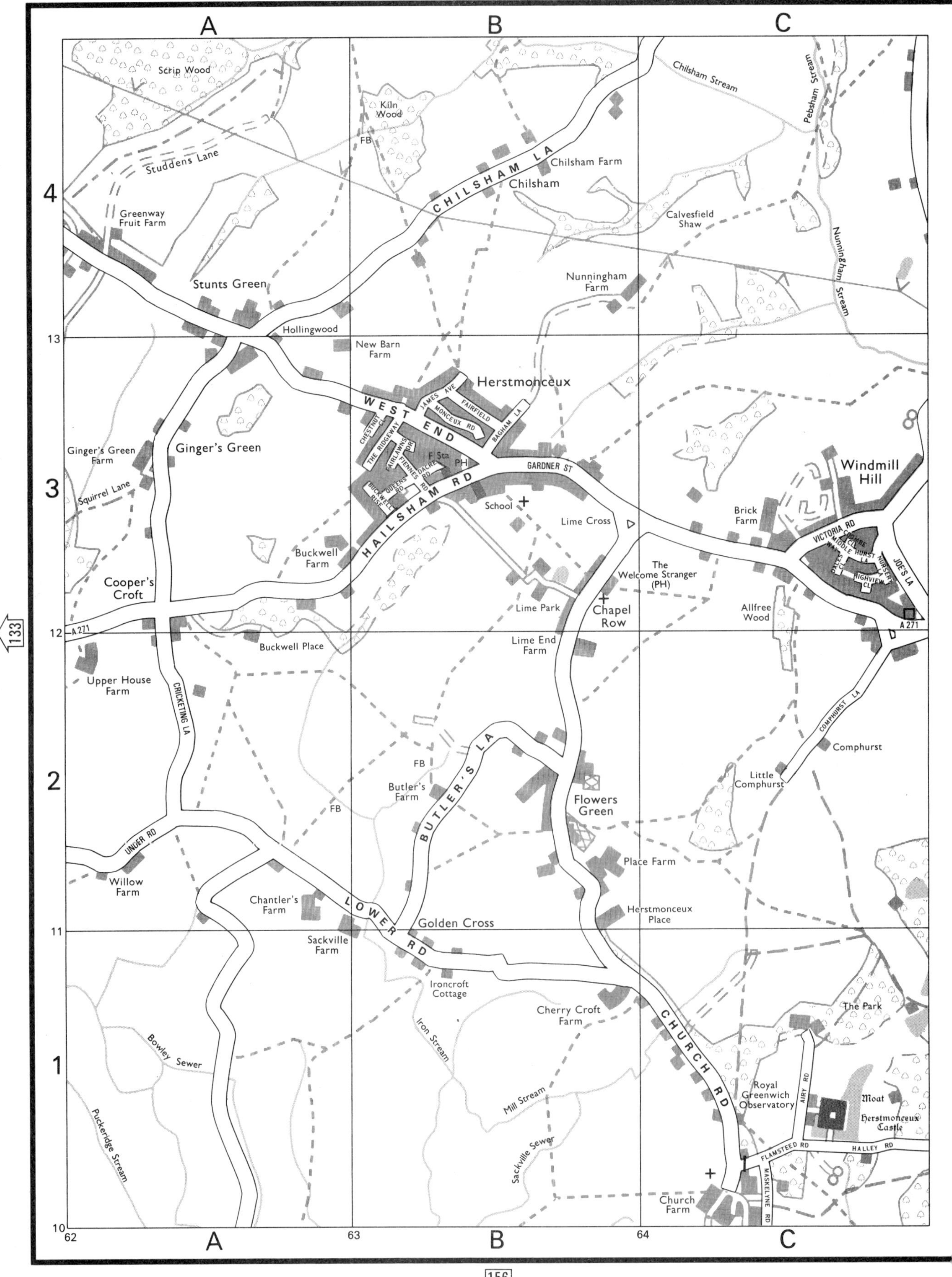

133

156

112

D
E
F
Causeway Farm
PRINKLE LA
Brownings Farm
Huggletts Stream
Henley's Bridge
HENLEY'S HILL
Cowden Wood
Breeches Wood
Wilson's Cross
4
Cowden Farm
Wilson's Farm
Ash Bourne
13
Tilley Farm
Tilley Bridge
TILLEY LA
B 2204
Fourteen Acre Wood
Works
3
Gardners Farm
Nunnington Stream
B 2204
A 271
Spinney Farm
Manor Pound
A 271
12
Boreham Bridge
Blackstock Bridge (FB)
Windmill Hill Place Tennis Centre
BOREHAM HILL
Boreham Street
2
White Friars Hotel
The Bull's Head (PH)
Boreham Farm
WARTLING RD
WOOD LA
New Barn
11
Champneys Farm
BOREHAM LA
Puddledock
Plantation Wood
Wartling Wood
1
Waller's Haven
BRADLEY RD
HALLEY RD
Rocklands Farm
Hogtrough Bridge (FB)
P
FB
The Well House
10
65
66
67

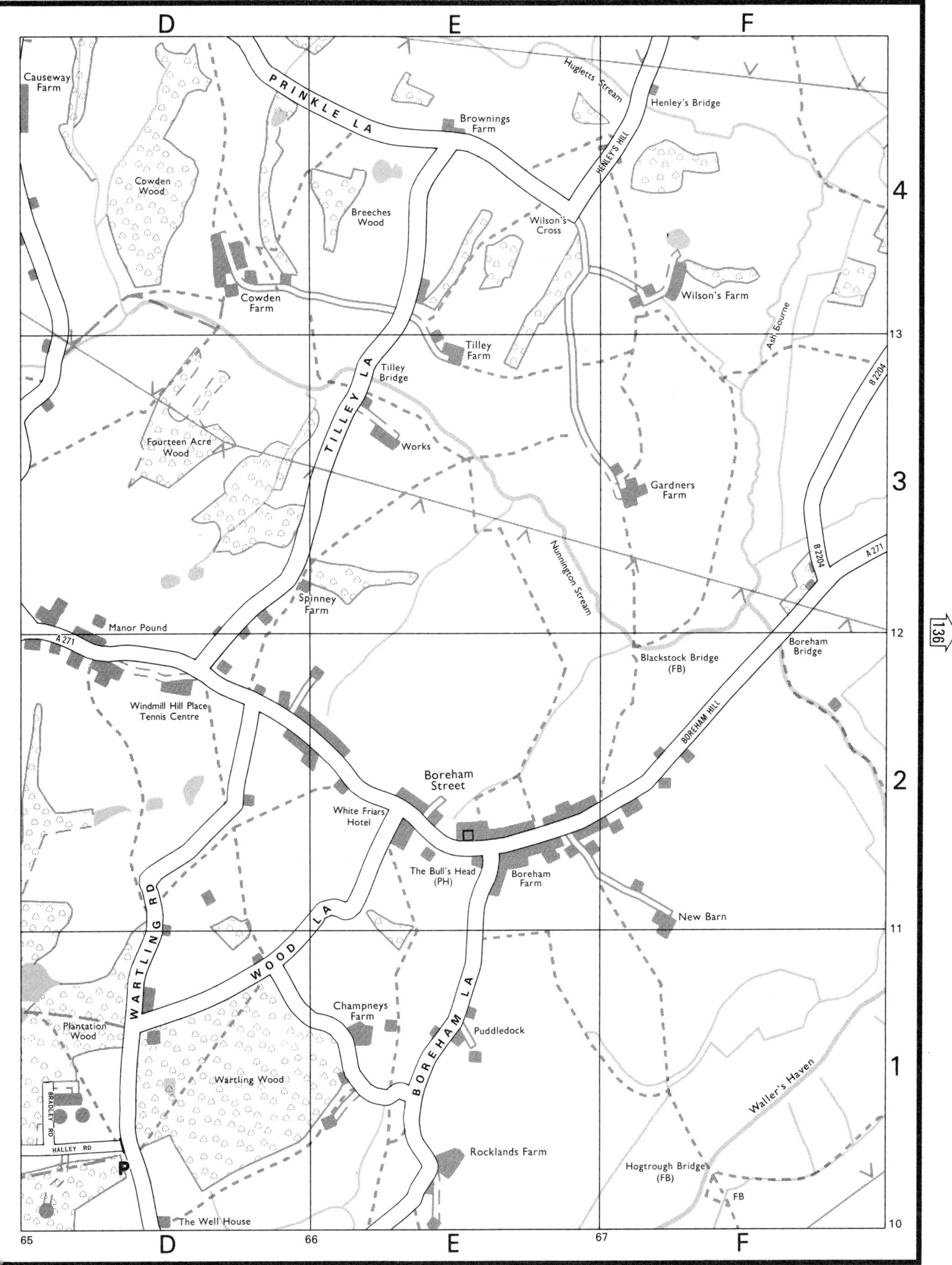

136

157

113

135

A
B
C
4
3
2
1
13
12
11
10
68
69
70
The Old Kennels
Hammer Wood
Compass Wood
Burntbarns Lane
Lower Freckley Wood
Breton's Wood
Luxford's Wood
Combe Hill Farm
Combe Hill
Wilding Wood
Combe Wood
Kitchenham Farm
Marlpits
MARLPITS LA
SKINNER'S LA
B 2204
FB
Lower Standard Hill Farm
COOMBE LA
COOMBE SHAW
CROCKSTOWN
MILLFIELD
MANCHESTER RD
HIGH ST
Ninfield
Standard Hill House
Standard Hill
THE GREEN A 271
Moor Hall Farm
A 271
Little Standard Hill Farm
Wks
Hazard's Green
DOWNS VIEW LA
CHURCH LA
Village Hall
Stocks Hotel
Sch
STOCKS MEADOW
SMITH CL
A 269
B 2095
MOORLAND CL
Hotel
Lower Street
Rough Wood
BEXHILL RD
Wet Wood
CROUCH LA
Moorhall Stream
White's Wood
Hooe Level
Waller's Haven
Russell's Green
Pashley Farm
Park Wood
Miller's Farm
Tanyard Farm
Sandhall Farm
MILL LA
Hooe Common
School Farm
Birchtree Wood
Ppg Sta
Bunts Barn
Sadlers Farm
Longdown Farm

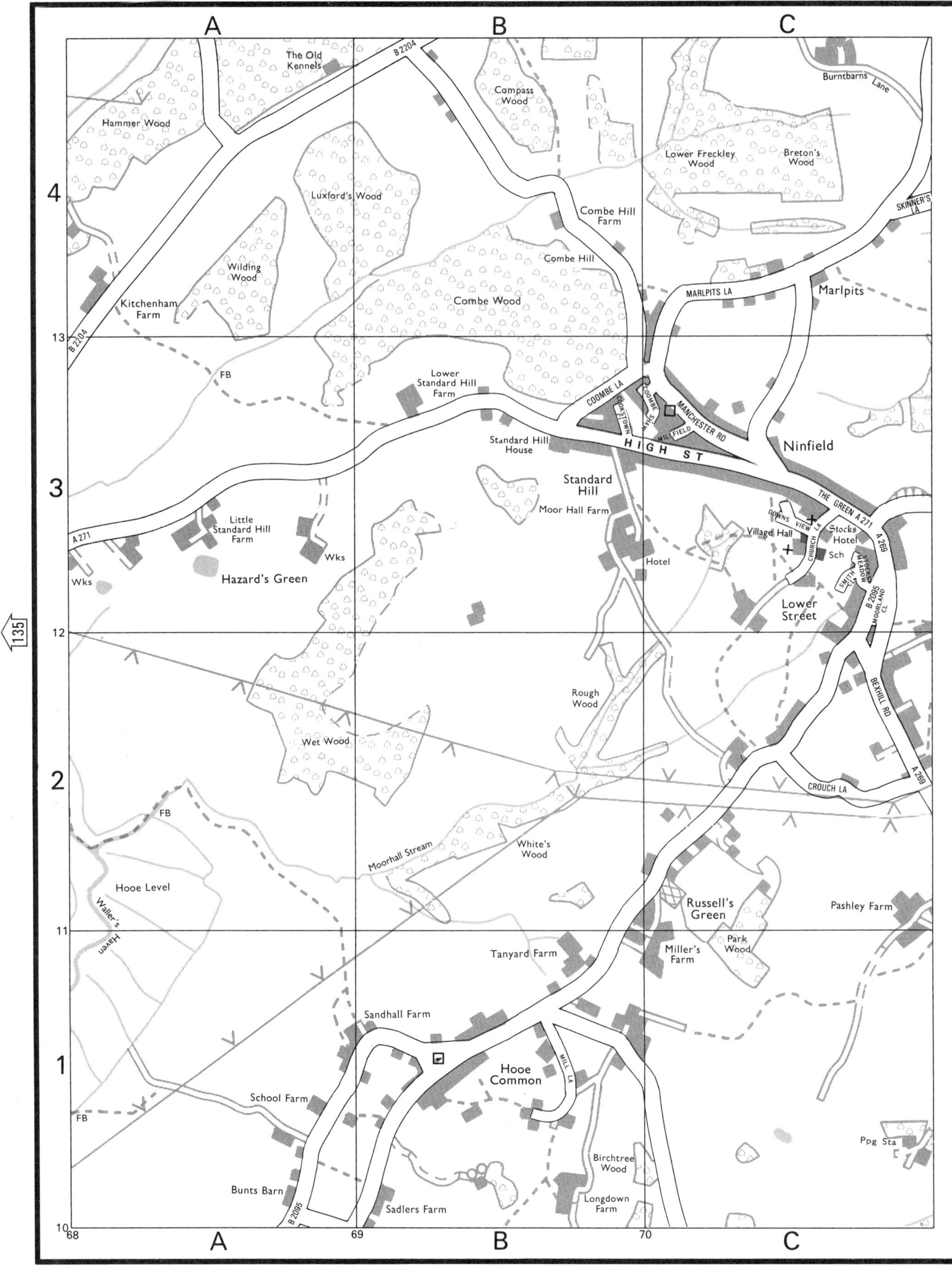

158

114

D
E
F
FRECKLEY HOLLOW
Weeks Wood
Starveswood Bank
Horse Pond
Broomham
White Hart (PH)
Hopgarden Wood
FB
THE GREEN
A 269
BLACK SMITHS LA
CHURCH LA
Catsfield
Village Hall
Sch
CHURCH RD
Catsfield Manor
Kell Wood
Wyland Farm
SKINNER'S LA
Courtlands
Catsfield Stream
The Old Rectory
Court Wood
Catsfield Bridge
Tilton
Twisly
Catsfield Place Farm
Catsfield Place (Wilton House School)
Henley's Down
Henley Down Farm
Sharpes Farm
Hurst Wood
A 269
Ingram's Farm
FB
Reed Wood
South Wood
POTMAN'S LA
Shawland Farm
Sprays Wood
New Barn Farm
Tilden's Wood
Ninfield Transforming Station
Staplehurst Wood
Potman's Place
Watermill
Kiln Wood
Francis Wood
Watermill Stream
Rushford Wood
Messens Farm
Park Wood
Shortwood
BEXHILL RD
WATERMILL LA
Thorne Farm
Sewage Works
Lunsford's Cross
Cobb's Hill Farm
FREEZELAND LA
Cockerel's Wood
The Thorne
Kiteye Wood
NINFIELD RD
Freezeland Farm
PEARTREE LA
Kiln Wood
THORNE CRES
Jack O'Boreham's Wood
ST MARY'S LA
A 269
4
13
3
12
2
11
1
10
71
72
73

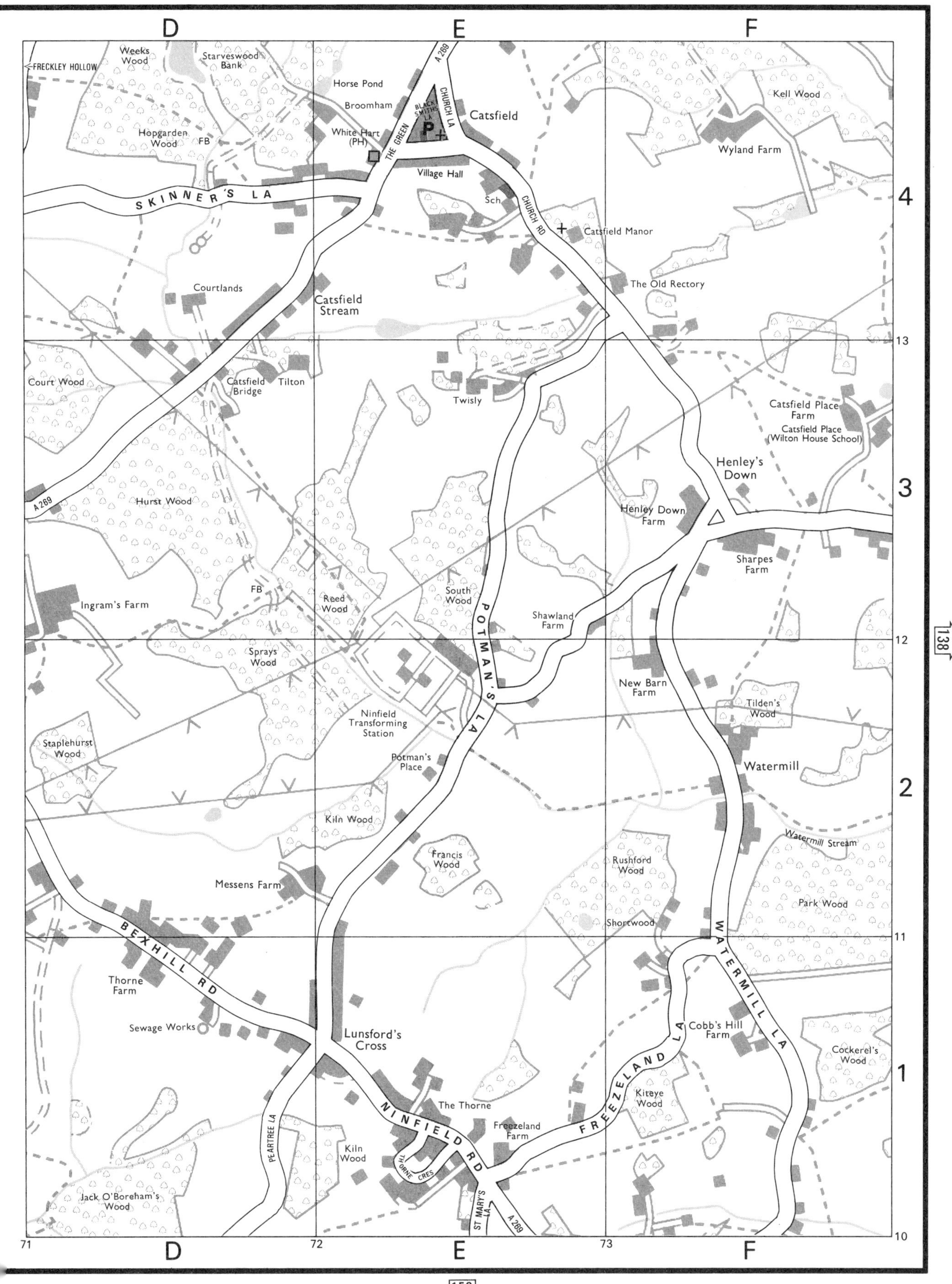

138

159

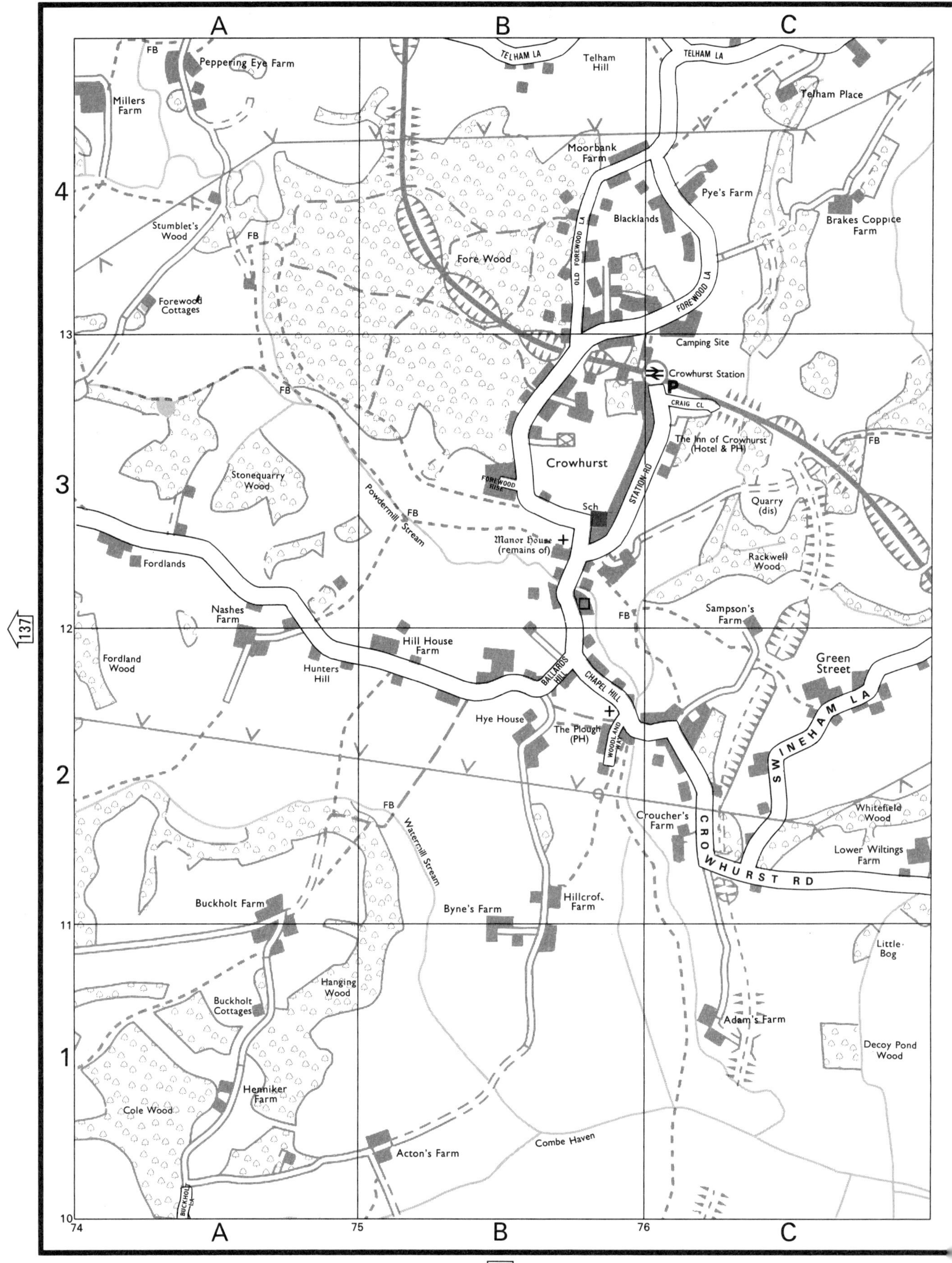
115
137
160
A
B
C
4
3
2
1
13
12
11
10
74
75
76
Peppering Eye Farm
Millers Farm
Telham Hill
TELHAM LA
Telham Place
Moorbank Farm
Pye's Farm
Blacklands
Brakes Coppice Farm
Stumblet's Wood
Fore Wood
OLD FOREWOOD LA
FOREWOOD LA
Forewood Cottages
Camping Site
Crowhurst Station
CRAIG CL
The Inn of Crowhurst (Hotel & PH)
Crowhurst
FOREWOOD RISE
STATION RD
Sch
Stonequarry Wood
Powdermill Stream
Quarry (dis)
Rackwell Wood
Manor House (remains of)
Fordlands
Nashes Farm
Sampson's Farm
Fordland Wood
Hill House Farm
Hunters Hill
BALLARDS HILL
CHAPEL HILL
Green Street
Hye House
The Plough (PH)
WOODLAND WAY
SWINEHAM LA
Croucher's Farm
Whitefield Wood
Watermill Stream
CROWHURST RD
Lower Wiltings Farm
Buckholt Farm
Byne's Farm
Hillcroft Farm
Little Bog
Hanging Wood
Buckholt Cottages
Adam's Farm
Decoy Pond Wood
Henniker Farm
Cole Wood
Combe Haven
Acton's Farm
BUCKHOLT LA
FB

116

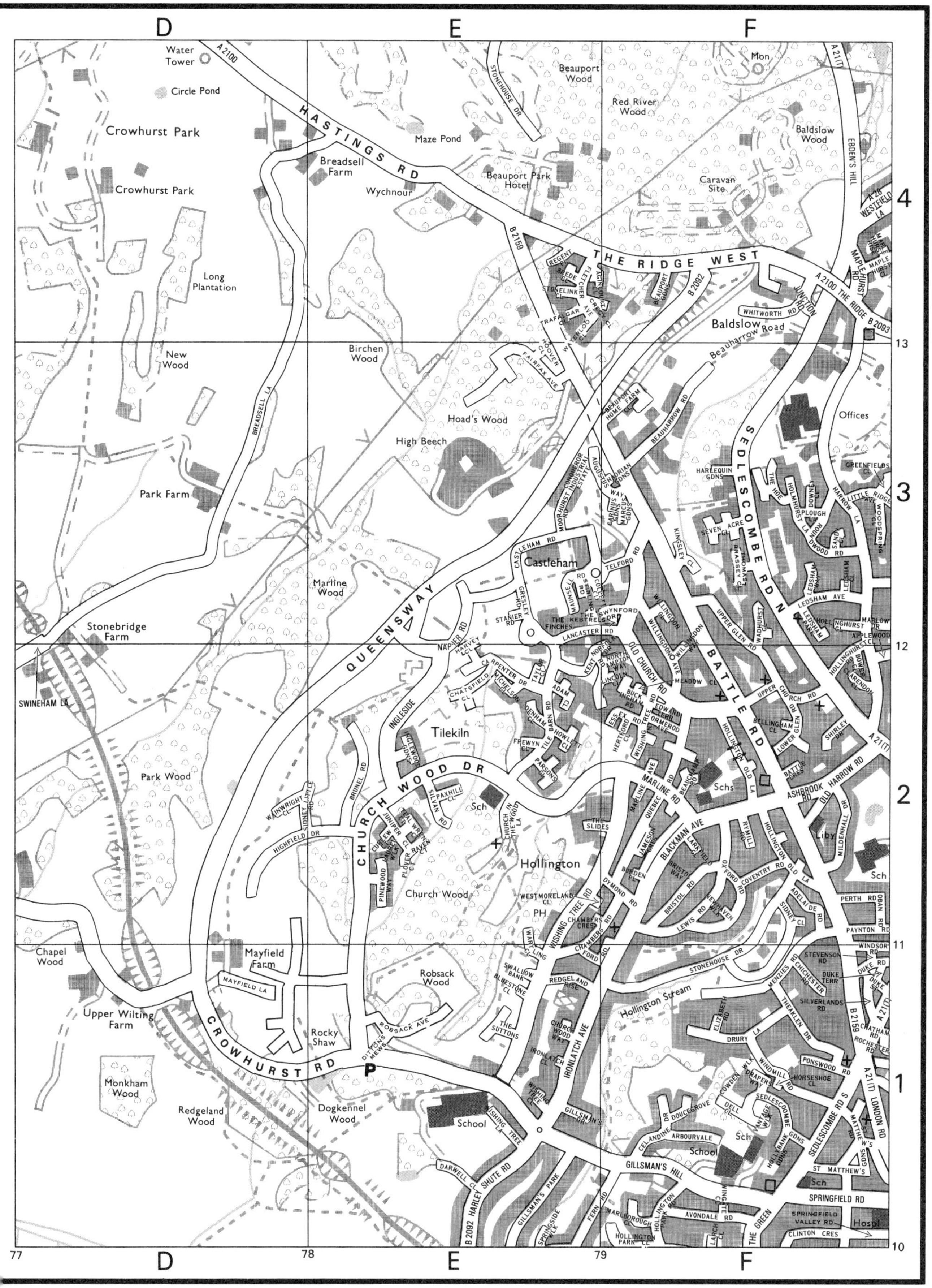

D E F

Water Tower
Circle Pond
Crowhurst Park
Crowhurst Park
Long Plantation
New Wood
Park Farm
Stonebridge Farm
SWINEHAM LA
Park Wood
Chapel Wood
Upper Wilting Farm
Monkham Wood
Redgeland Wood
HASTINGS RD
A2100
Breadsell Farm
Wychnour
Maze Pond
BREADSELL LA
Birchen Wood
High Beech
Hoad's Wood
Marline Wood
QUEENSWAY
Tilekiln
CHURCH WOOD DR
Church Wood
Mayfield Farm
MAYFIELD LA
Robsack Wood
Rocky Shaw
CROWHURST RD
Dogkennel Wood
School
Beauport Wood
Red River Wood
Beauport Park Hotel
THE RIDGE WEST
Castleham
Hollington
PH
Sch
Baldslow
Baldslow Wood
Caravan Site
Mon
Offices
SEDLESCOMBE RD N
BATTLE RD
OLD CHURCH RD
MARLINE RD
BLACKMAN AVE
Schs
Liby
Sch
Hollington Stream
GILLSMAN'S HILL
Sch
School
Sch
SPRINGFIELD RD
Hospl
A21(T) LONDON RD
A2100 THE RIDGE
B2093

4 3 2 1

13 12 11 10

77 78 79

140

D E F

161

117

A
B
C
Baldslow Wood
Hole Farm
High Lankhurst Farm
New Coghurst
WESTFIELD LANE
Maplehurst Wood
Beaney's Lane
STONESTILE LA
Baldslow
Park Wood
Hurst Farm
Beaulieu Farm
Hazel Court
Foxhole Farm
IVY HOUSE LA
Helenswood School
Holmhurst St Mary
Little Ridge Farm
CHOWNS HILL
Cold Harbour Farm
THE RIDGE
LITTLE RIDGE AVE
Cemy
Silverhill Park
Crem
St Helen's
St Helen's Park Road
Dunclutha Road
St Helen's Wood
Hillside Road
School
ELPHINSTONE RD
DOWNS RD
Silverhill
ST HELEN'S RD
Blacklands
Broomgrove
Ore Station
Alexandra Park
UPPER PARK RD
LOWER PARK RD
AMHERST RD
MOUNT PLEASANT RD
PRIORY RD
OLD LONDON RD
B 2093
A 28
A 21
A 2101
A 259
80
81
82
1
2
3
4
10
11
12
13

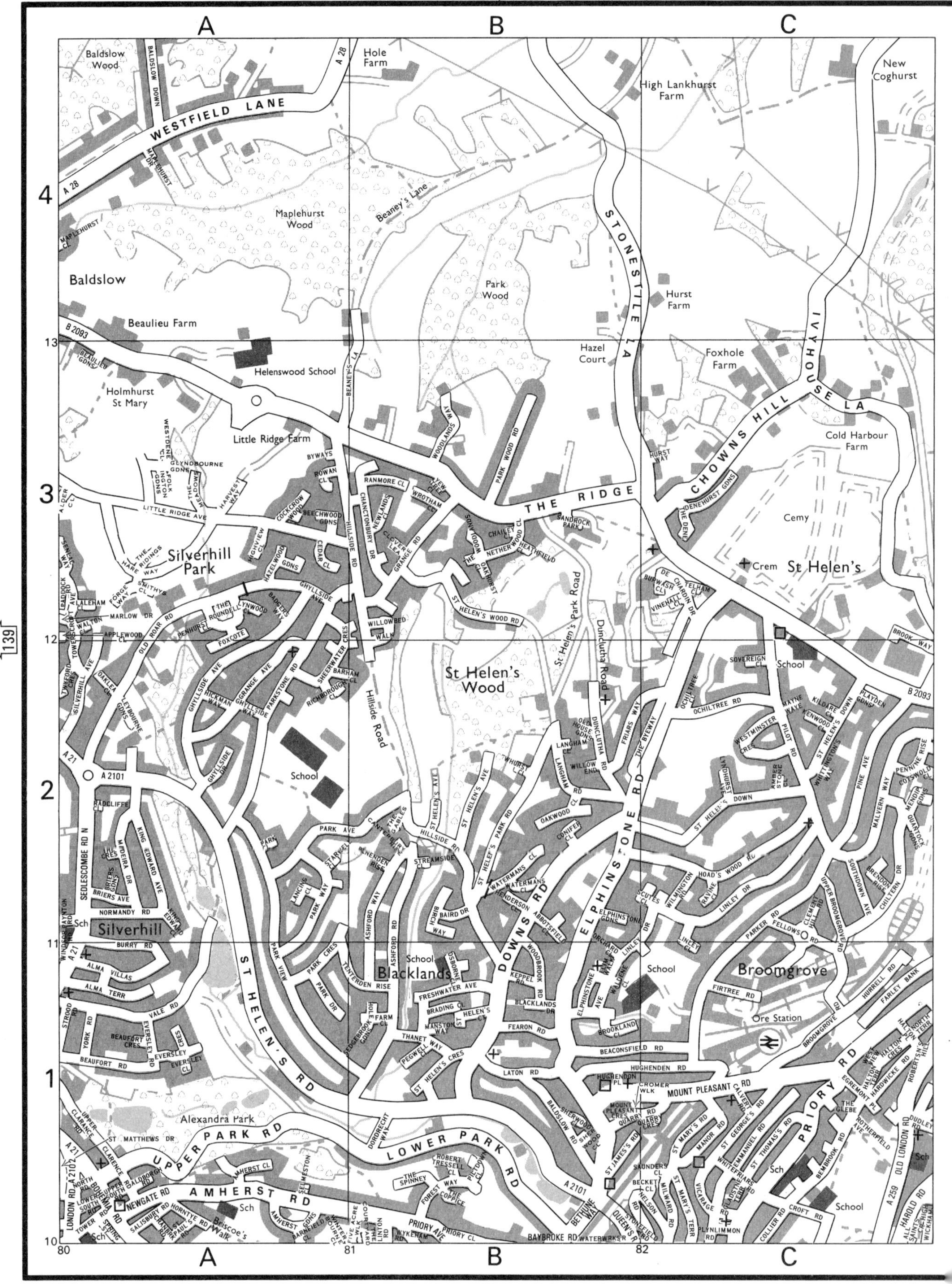

139

162

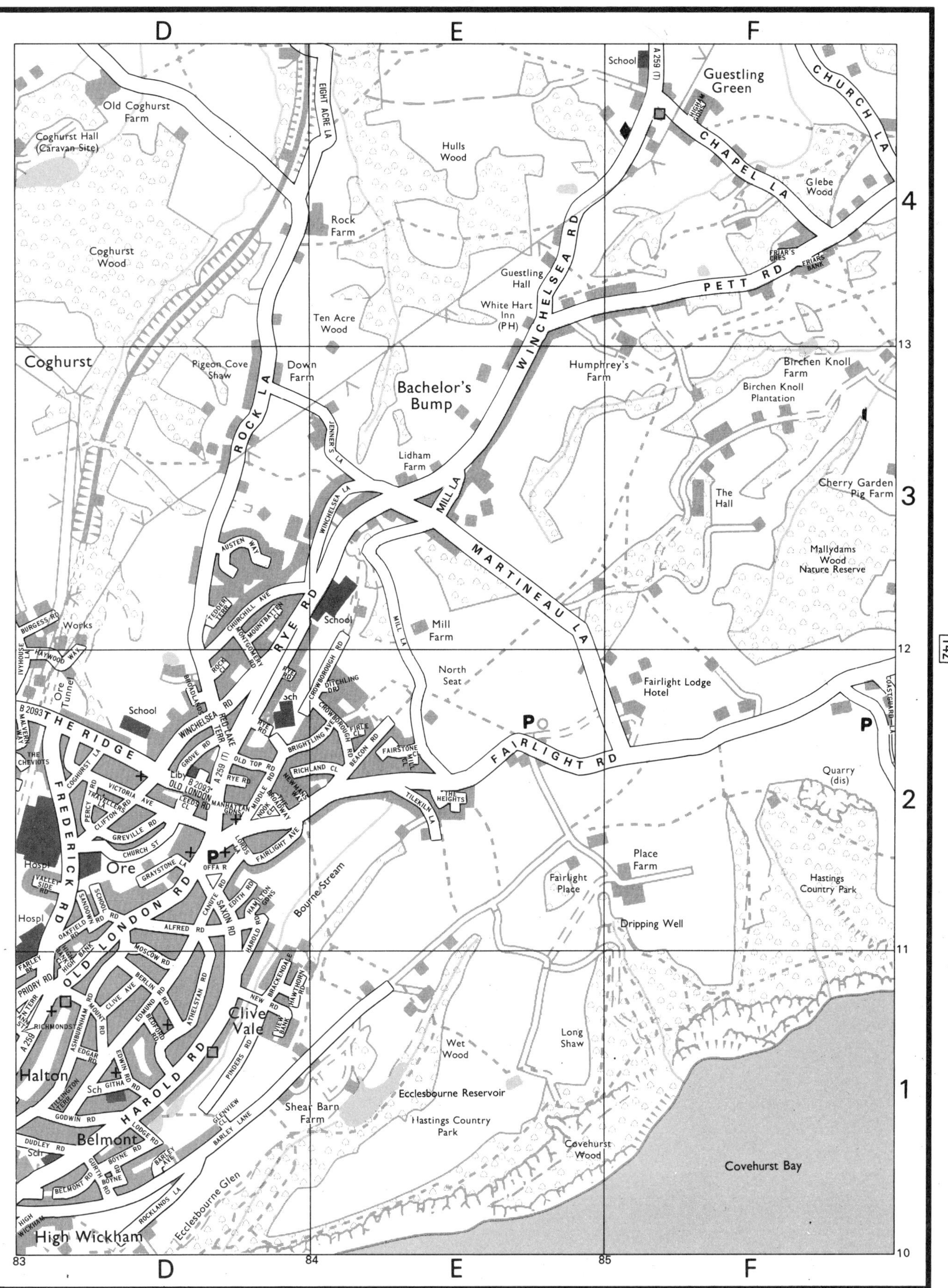
118
D
E
F
Old Coghurst Farm
Coghurst Hall (Caravan Site)
Coghurst Wood
Coghurst
Hulls Wood
Rock Farm
Ten Acre Wood
Guestling Hall
White Hart Inn (PH)
Guestling Green
School
Glebe Wood
Pigeon Cove Shaw
Down Farm
Bachelor's Bump
Lidham Farm
Humphrey's Farm
Birchen Knoll Farm
Birchen Knoll Plantation
The Hall
Cherry Garden Pig Farm
Mallydams Wood Nature Reserve
Works
School
Mill Farm
North Seat
Fairlight Lodge Hotel
Quarry (dis)
Ore
Hospl
Place Farm
Fairlight Place
Dripping Well
Hastings Country Park
Bourne Stream
Clive Vale
Halton
Belmont
Long Shaw
Wet Wood
Ecclesbourne Reservoir
Shear Barn Farm
Hastings Country Park
Covehurst Wood
Covehurst Bay
Ecclesbourne Glen
High Wickham
EIGHT ACRE LA
ROCK LA
RYE RD
WINCHELSEA RD
CHAPEL LA
CHURCH LA
PETT RD
MILL LA
MARTINEAU LA
FAIRLIGHT RD
THE RIDGE
FREDERICK RD
OLD LONDON RD
HAROLD RD
A 259 (T)
B 2093
162
142
4
3
2
1
13
12
11
10
83
84
85

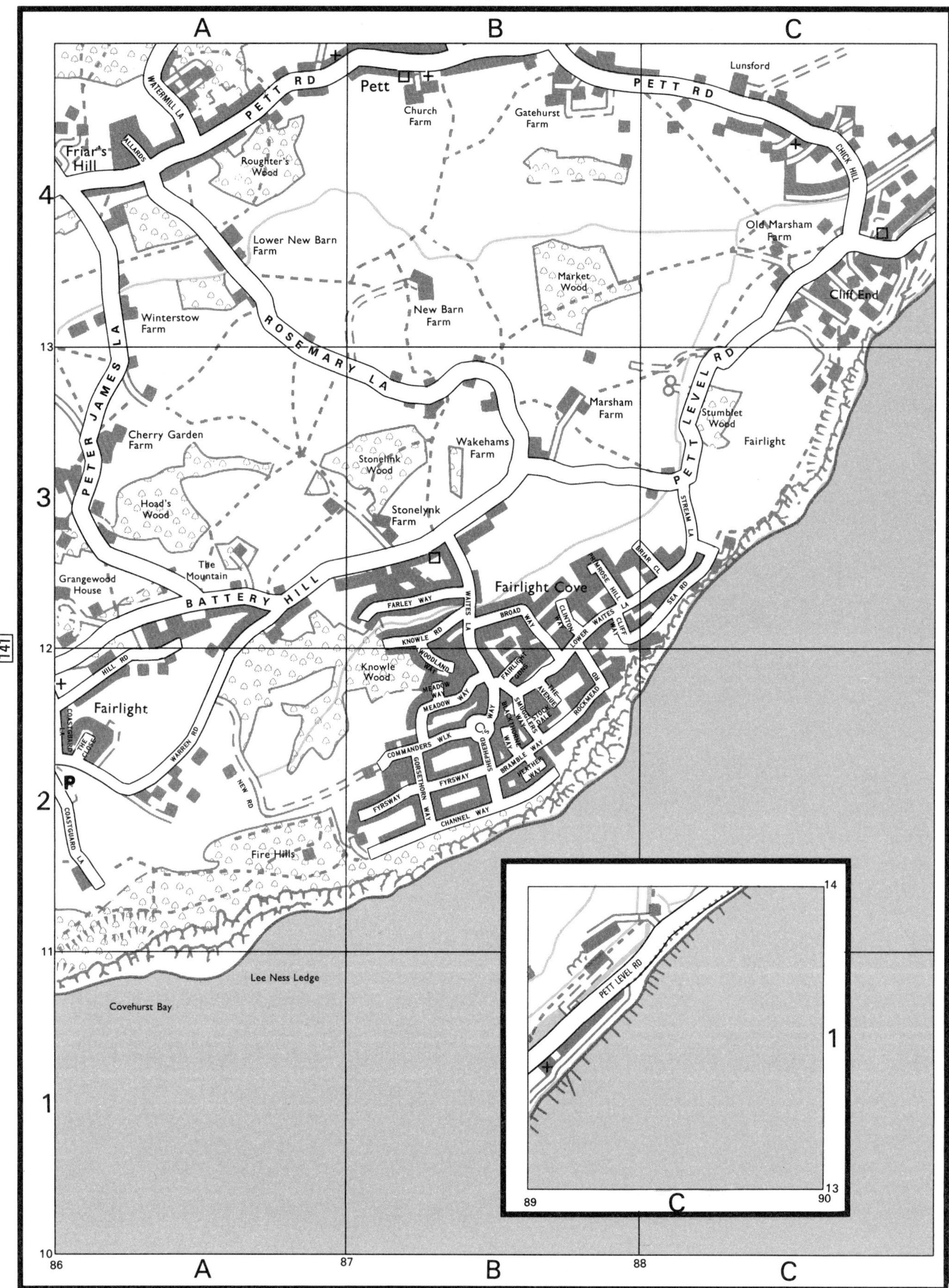

119
141
A
B
C
Pett Rd
Pett
Church Farm
Gatehurst Farm
Lunsford
Watermill La
Allards
Friar's Hill
Roughter's Wood
Chick Hill
Old Marsham Farm
Lower New Barn Farm
Market Wood
Cliff End
New Barn Farm
Winterstow Farm
Rosemary La
Peter James La
Pett Level Rd
Marsham Farm
Stumblet Wood
Fairlight
Cherry Garden Farm
Wakehams Farm
Stonelink Wood
Hoad's Wood
Stonelynk Farm
Stream La
The Mountain
Grangewood House
Battery Hill
Fairlight Cove
Farley Way
Waites La
Broad Way
Primrose Hill
Briar Cl
Sea Rd
Clinton Way
Lower Waites La
Cliff Way
Knowle Rd
Woodland Way
Hill Rd
Knowle Wood
Fairlight Gdns
The Avenue
Rockmead Rd
Meadow Way
Smugglers Way
Stockdale
Blackthorne Way
Shepherd Way
Commanders Wlk
Gorsethorn Way
Bramble Way
Heather Way
Fyrsway
Channel Way
Fairlight
Coastguard La
The Close
Warren Rd
New Rd
Fire Hills
Lee Ness Ledge
Covehurst Bay
Pett Level Rd
86
87
88
89
90
10
11
12
13
14
1
2
3
4

not continued, see key diagram

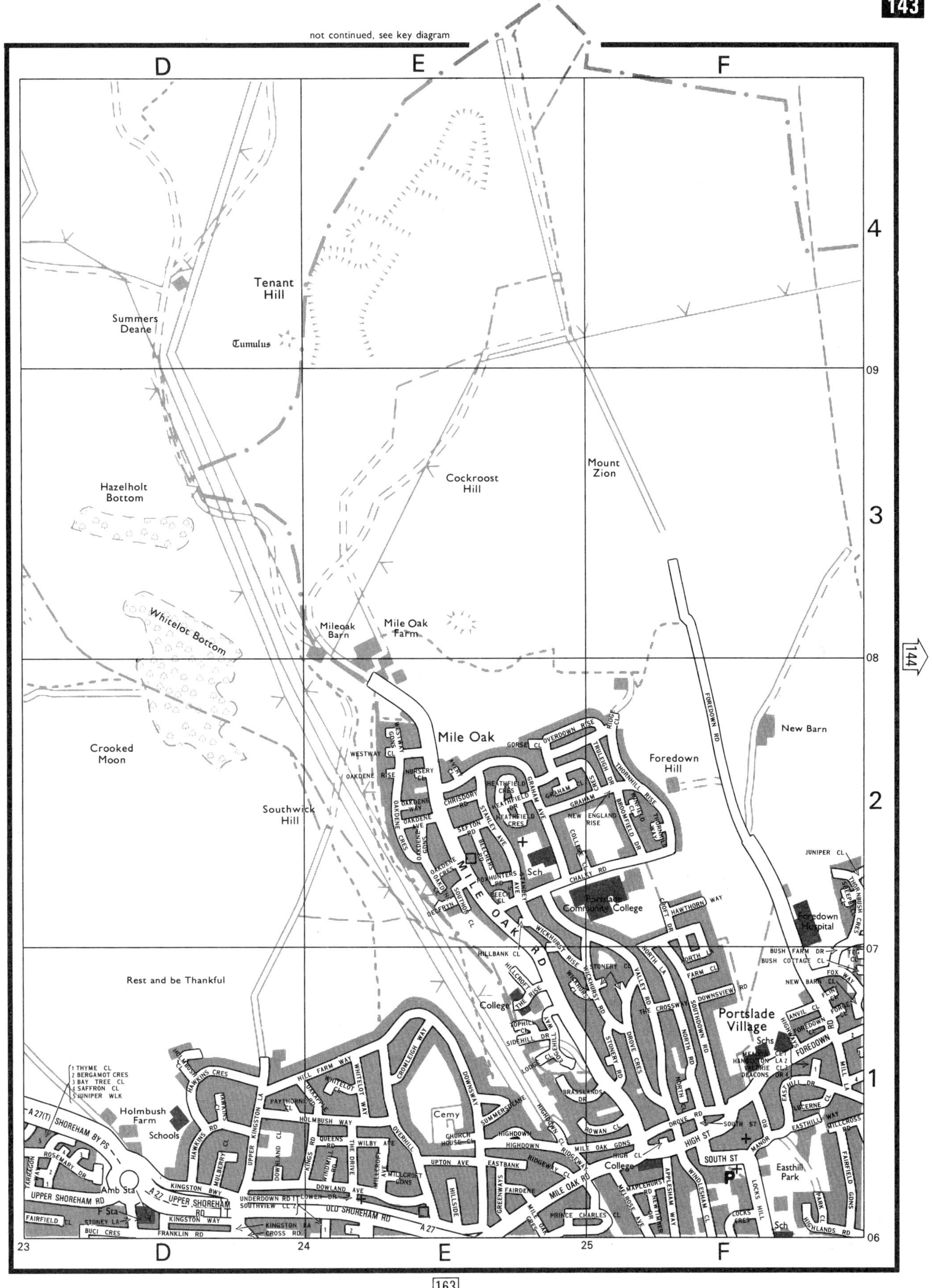

144

163

122

A
B
C
4
3
2
1
09
08
07
06
26
27
28
Waterhall Golf Course
Sweet Hill
Golf Farm
CH
Skeleton Hovel
DEVIL'S DYKE RD
Benfield Valley
Dismantled Railway
Northlane Barn
Round Hill
Brighton & Hove Golf Course
Benfield Hill
MILL RD
A 2038
Westdene
Red Hill
Schools
Hangleton Park
HANGLETON WAY
Golf Course
Benfield Farm
Park
Sch
Liby
Hangleton
Golf Course
HANGLETON RD
NEVILL AVE
West Blatchington
Schs
Mus
Brighton & Hove Stadium
Park
THE DROVEWAY
A 2023
Sch

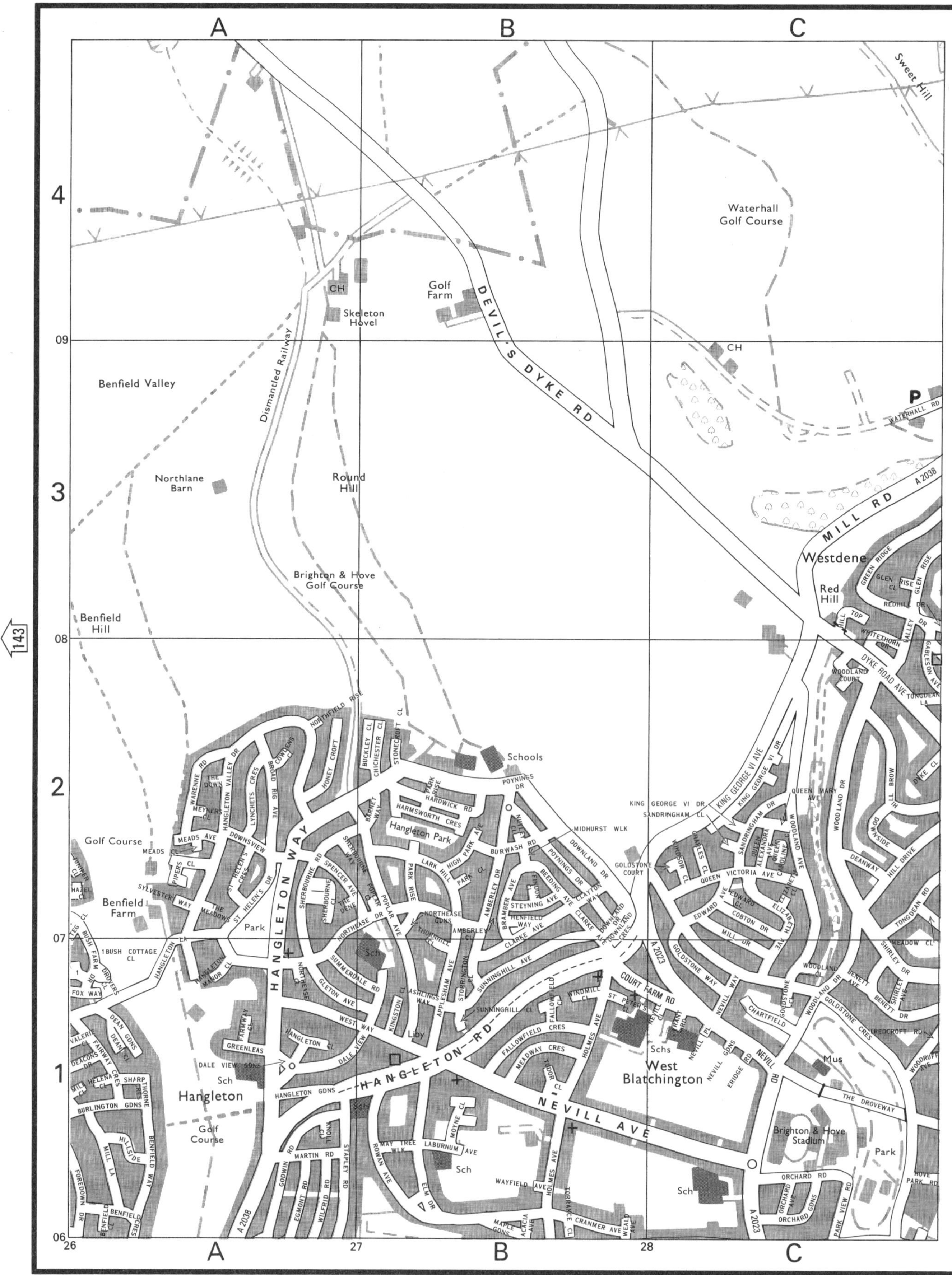

143

164

123

D
E
F
4
3
2
1
09
08
07
06
29
30
31
Sports Ground
Kennels
Field System
Eastwick Barn
Recn Gd
Recn Gd
Coney Hill
Patcham Place (Youth hostel)
Patcham
Hollingbury
Withdean Park
Upper Roedale
Roedale
Sports Arena
College
Preston Park Staion
Preston Manor (Museum)
Preston
Park
A 23(T)
A 2038
A 23
MILL RD
WATERHALL RD
WINDMILL DR
BRANGWYN CRES
PATCHAM BY PASS
LONDON RD
LADIES MILE RD
CARDEN AVE
CROWHURST RD
YOUNGSMERE CL
BRAESIDE AVE
THE DEESIDE
PEACOCK LA
TONGDEAN LA
DYKE ROAD AVE
SHIRLEY DR
DYKE RD
THE DROVEWAY
HOVE PARK RD
PRESTON DR
PRESTON RD
SURRENDEN RD
DITCHLING RD
STRINGER WAY
WOODBOURNE AVE
LARKFIELD WAY
BALFOUR RD
UPPER HOLLINGDEAN RD
HARRINGTON RD
VARNDEAN DR
VARNDEAN RD
PRESTON PARK AVE
STANFORD AVE
HOLLINGBURY PARK AVE
HOLLINGBURY RD
RUGBY RD
GRANTHAM RD
SOUTHMOUNT
HIGHCROFT VILLAS
THE MARTLET
MILLER'S RD
Sch

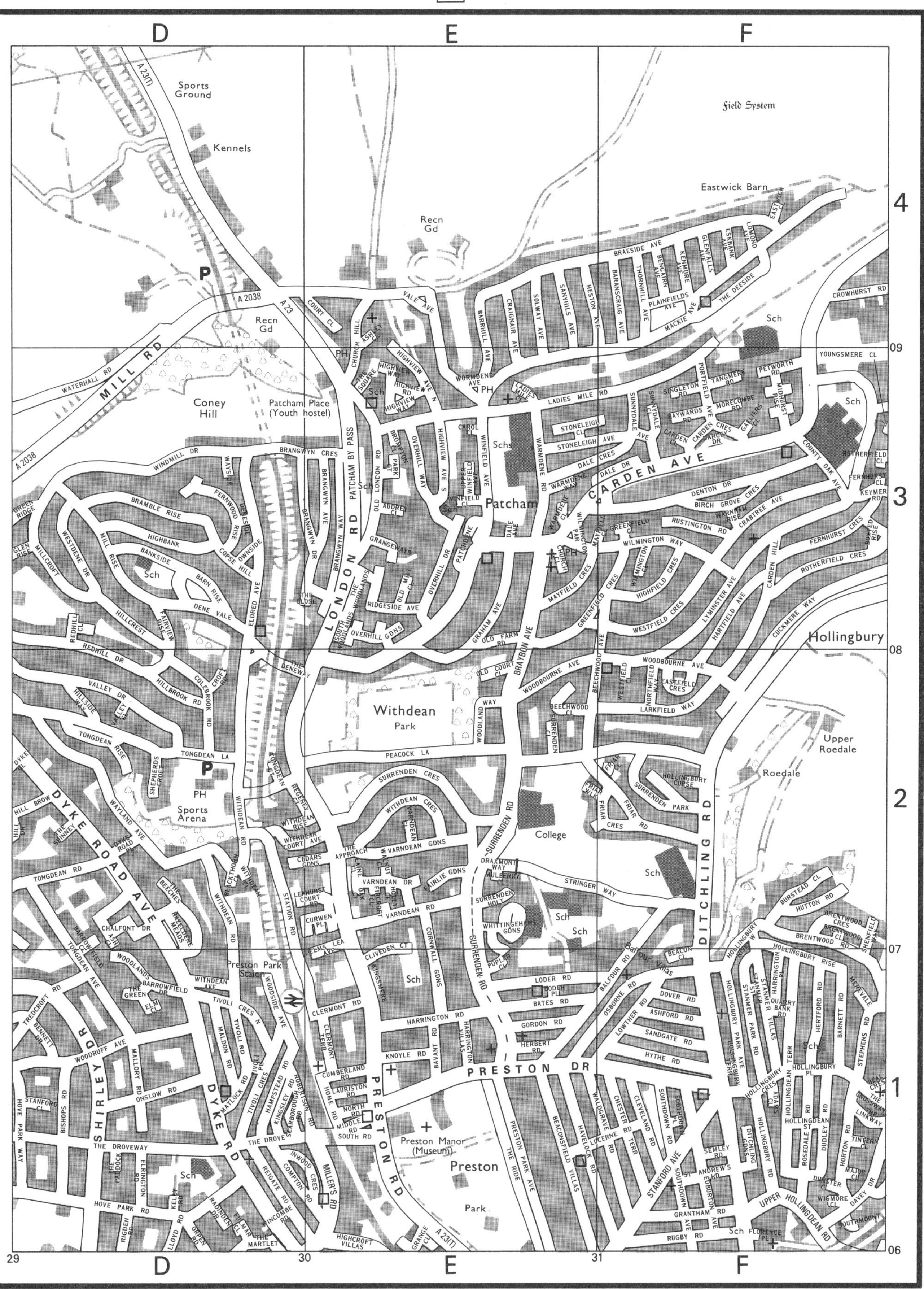

146

165

124

A
B
C
4
3
2
1
09
08
07
06
32
33
34
STANMER PARK
Upper Lodges
Stanmer
Pudding Bag
Stanmer House
Rural Museum
Grubbings
Richmond Hill
UNIVERSITY OF SUSSEX
CARDEN AVE
Old Boat Corner
CROWHURST RD
Works
DITCHLING RD
Great Wood
Milbanke's Walk
Coldean
COLDEAN LA
Coldean Wood
Marquee Brow
Lower Lodges
B2123
A27(T)
FALMER HILL
Falmer Station
TURNPIKE PIECE
Brighton Polytechnic
Westlain Plantation
Sch
Moulsecoomb Pit
Hollingbury Castle Settlement
North Moulsecoomb
Wild Park
Golf Course
Hog Plantation
East Moulsecoomb
Falmer Hill
Woodside Special School
Allot Gdns
Hollingdean
Moulsecoomb Station
Moulsecoomb
Hogtrough Bottom
Bevendean
LEWES RD
Preston Barracks
Hospl
Racehill Valley
THE HYDE
1 BROOMFIELDS
2 BROADFIELDS RD

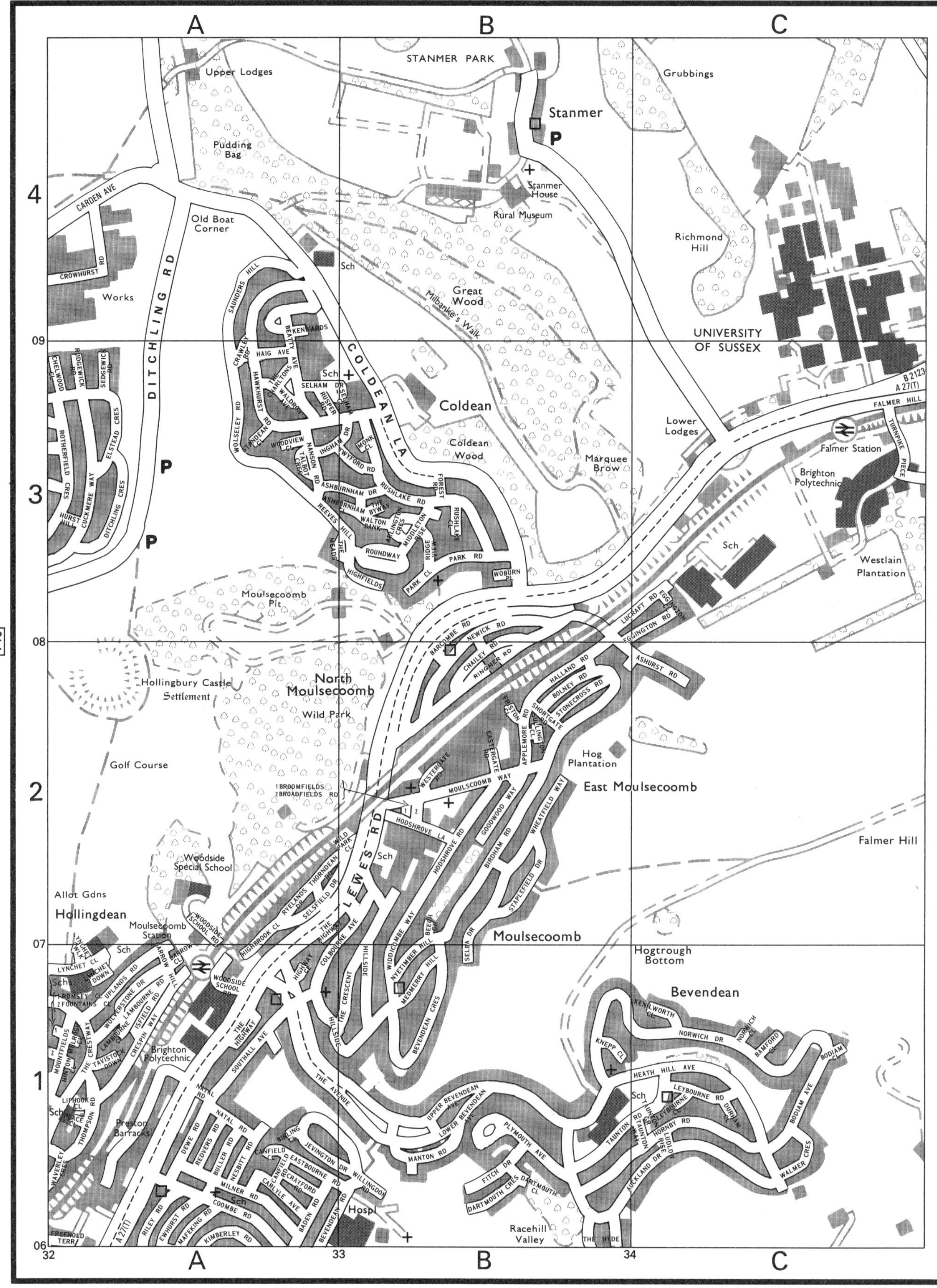

145

166

125

D
E
F
Balmer Farm
Ridge Farm
Bunkershill Plantation
South Downs Way
4
RIDGE RD
Long Hill
Housedean Farm
Housedean Cottages
FB
Old Forge Barn
The Newmarket (PH)
A 27 (T)
Knight's Gate
MILL ST
PARK ST
MIDDLE ST
09
A 27 (T)
FALMER HILL
B 2123
Cranedean Plantation
Falmer
Court Farm
SOUTH ST
EAST ST
PARK ST
New Barn
VILLAGE WAY
3
THE DROVE
Loose Bottom
Enclosure
08
Cold Coombes
South Downs Way
Jugg's Road
2
Tumulus
Newmarket Hill
FALMER RD
07
Castle Hill
Newmarket Bottom
Falmer Bottom
DROVE AVE
Tumulus
1
NORTON DRIVE
Upper Bevendean
Bullock Hill
BEXHILL RD
DROVE RD
SANDHURST AVE
LANGLEY CRES
RD
IVOR RD
MC WILLIAM RD
DOWNSWAY
HILL
VERNON AVE
HELENA RD
B 2123
THE RIDGEWAY
WARREN WAY
BALSDEAN RD
NEWELLS CL
06
35
36
37
D
E
F

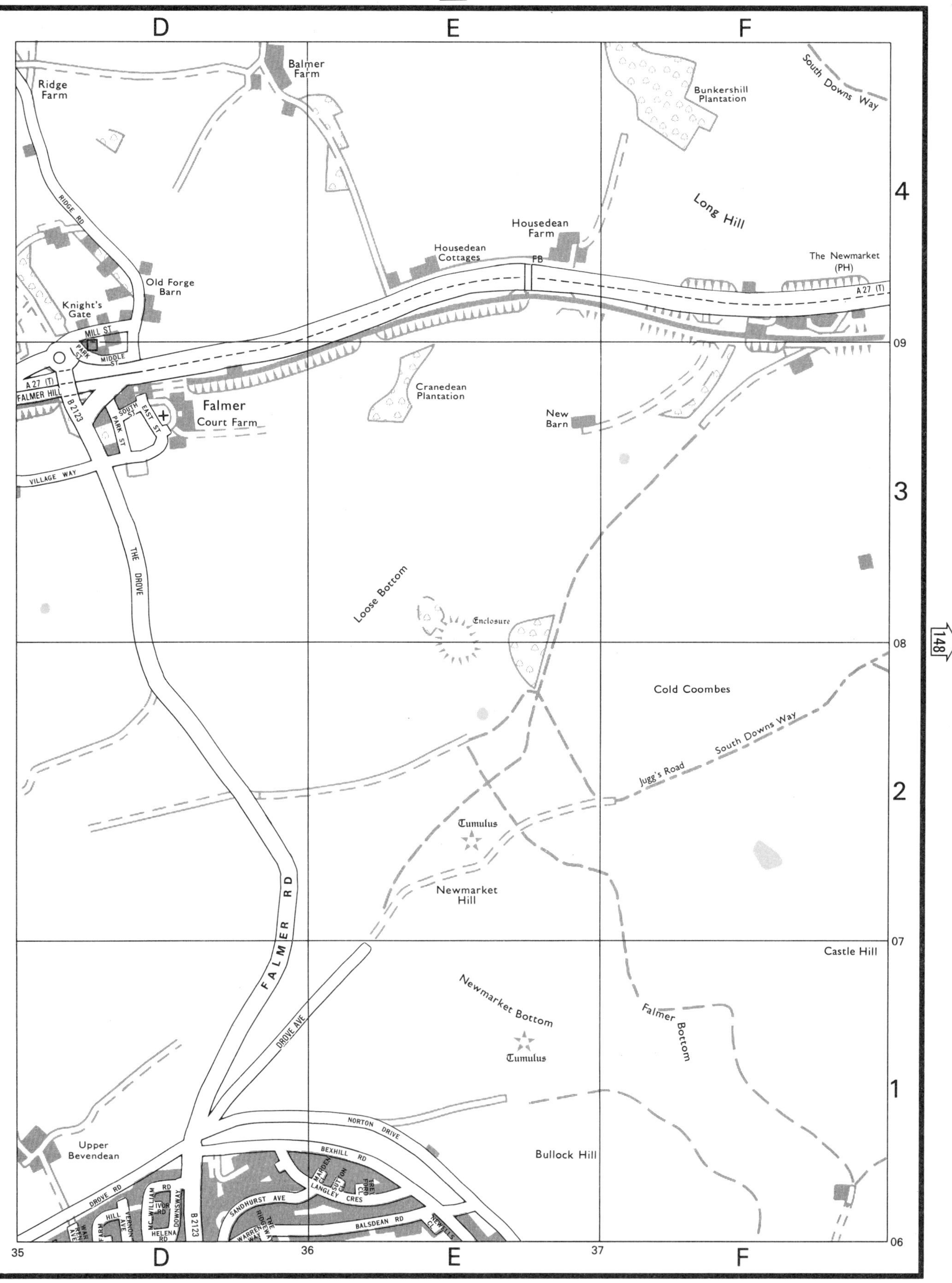

148

167

126

A
B
C
4
3
2
1
09
08
07
06
38
39
40
Ashcombe Plantation
Ashcombe Farm
South Downs Way
H M Prison
Liby
County Hall
Cemy
Sch
BRIGHTON RD
A 277
A 27(T)
Southover
JUGG'S RD
CRANEDOWN
KINGSTON RD
Sch
The Cockshut
Jugg's Road
Scabby Brow
ASHCOMBE HOLLOW
NAN KEMPS GRAVE
Kingston Hollow
KINGSTONRIDGE
Kingstonridge
ASHCOMBE LA
KENT FIELDS
Sch
SNEYDORE
WELLGREEN LA
THE STREET
Kingston near Lewes
Kingston Farm
Nurseries
Sewage Works
The Droveway
Jugg's Road
Swanborough Manor
SWANBOROUGH HOLLOW
Tumuli
Breach Road
SWANBOROUGH DRO
Iford Farm
Village Hall
Iford
South Downs Way
DENCHER RD
Stump Bottom
Bird Brow
Swanborough Hill
Balsdean Bottom
Iford Hill
Home Bottom
Long Bottom
Front Hill
White Way

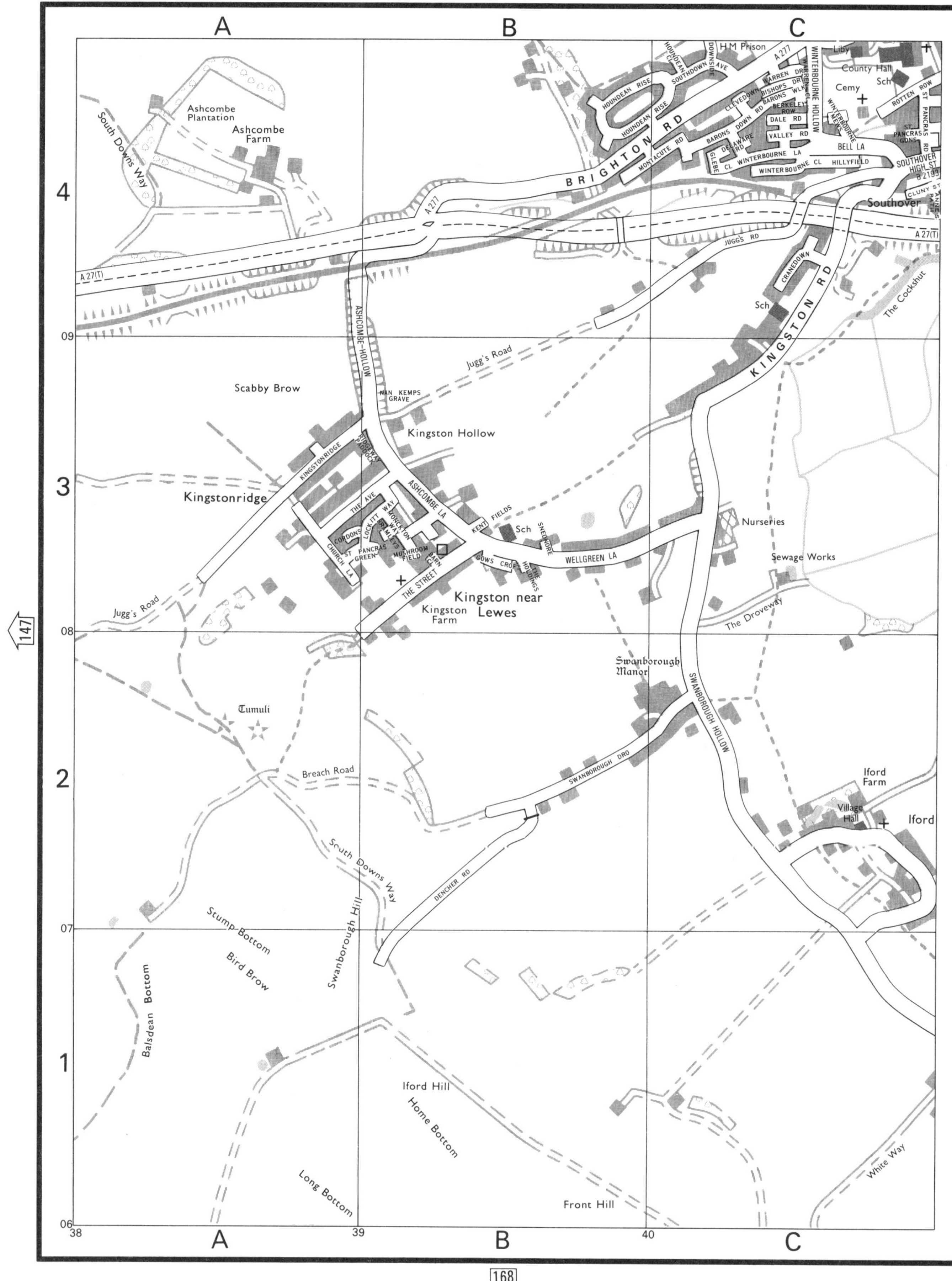

147

168

127

D
E
F
Lewes Station
Technical College
Schs
Mountfield Rd
Ham La
Priory St
The Cockshut
1 Bull La
2 St Swithun's La
3 Stewards Inn La
4 Paine's Twitten
5 St Swithun's Terr
Cliffe Industrial Estate
Southerham Farm
Machine Bottom
Oxteddle Bottom
Ranscombe Camp
Round the Down
Grey Pit
Brook Lane
Ranscombe Hill
Ranscombe La
A 27(T)
A 26
Rise Farm
Upper Rise
River Ouse
Pool Bar Wall
Celery Sewer
Norton Wall
Rise Barn
The Brooks
Lower Rise
Glynde Reach
Sutton Wall
Iford Farm
Northease Wall
Northease Manor
Northease Farm
Barley Field Cottages
Sewage Works
Rodmell
Sch
South Farm
Martens Field
Works
A 26(T)
4
3
2
1
09
08
07
06
41
42
43

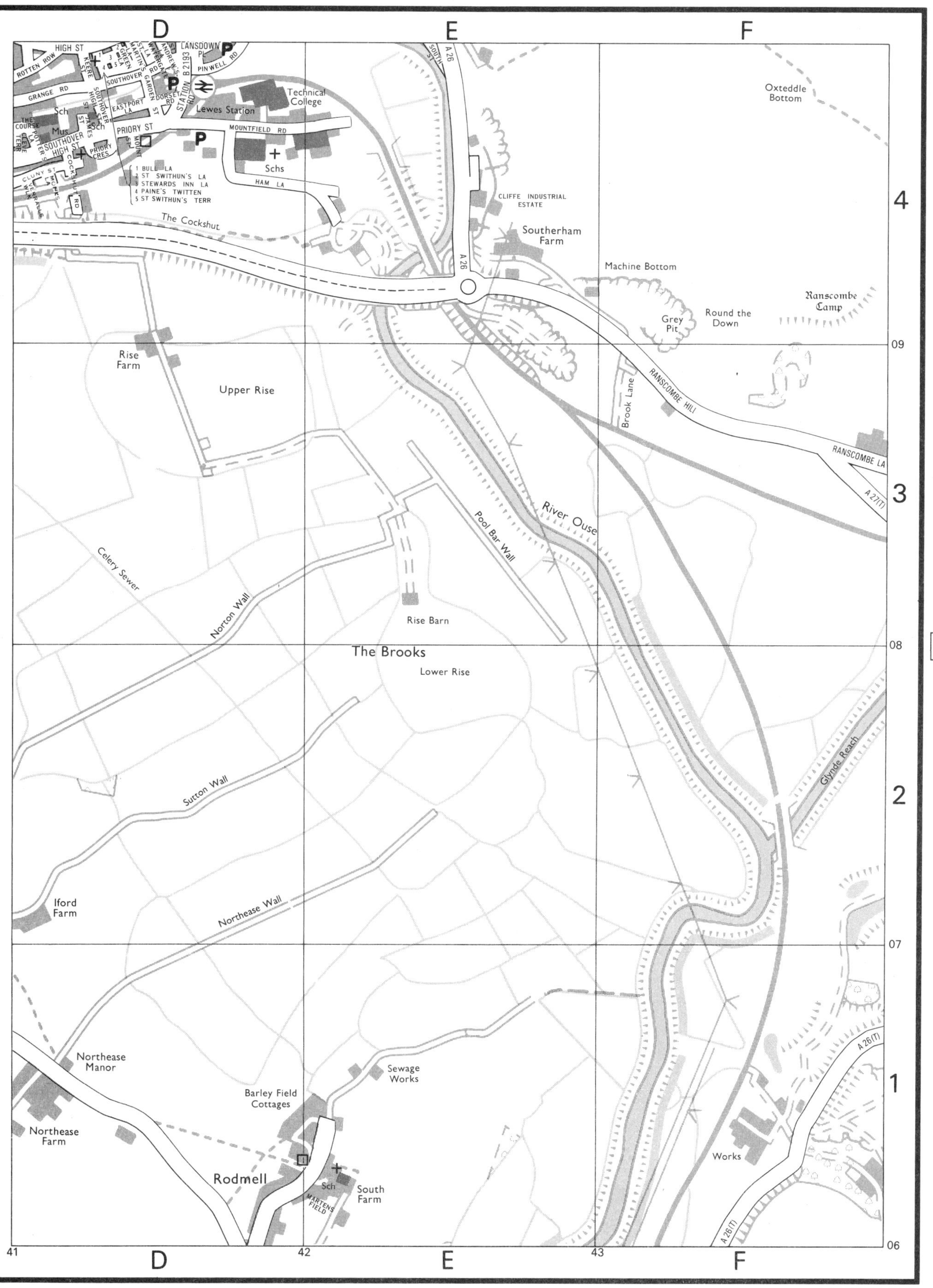

150

169

128

149

A
B
C
Tumulus
Glynde Holt
Lacys
LACYS HILL
The Park
Decoy Wood
Clay Pit (disused)
4
Caburn Bottom
Home Farm
Glynde Place
Willow Shaw
Glynde
Sch
09
Mount Caburn
Fort
Caburn Pit (disused)
Glynde Bridge
Glynde Reach
BRIGDENS HILL
Glynde Station
Loover Shaw
Brigdens
RANSCOMBE LA
PH
Trevor Gardens
Balcombe Pit (Chalk)
3
Station Farm
Loover Barn
A 27(T)
BEDDINGHAM
Beddingham Crossing
Beddingham Bridge
Spring Ditch
Garage
A 27(T)
08
A 26(T)
Preston House
Gibraltar
Courthouse Farm
Comps Farm
Beddingham
Sch
2
Cobbe Place
Narroway Buildings
Little Dene
Preston Court Farm
Ram Inn (PH)
THE STREET
FIRLE BOSTAL
Cobbe Place Farm
Newelm
Place Farm
07
The Furlongs
The Lay
A 26(T)
1
Coombe Barn
Ellman's Combe
Beddingham Hill
06
44
45
46
A
B
C

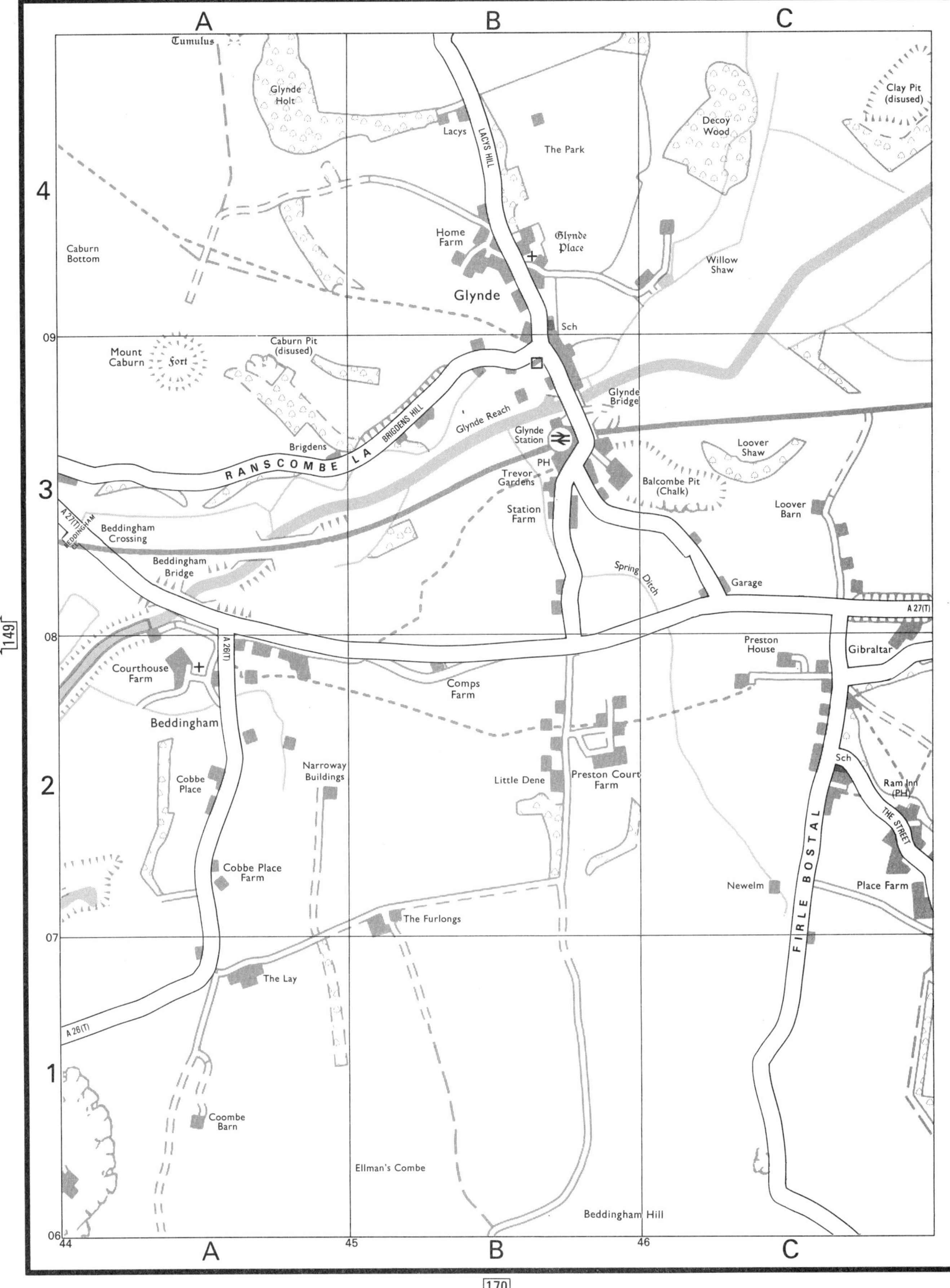

170

129

D
E
F
Glynde Reach
New Barn
Black Shaw
Lulhams Farm
4
Hall Court Farm
Barber's Wish
Burgh Shaw
09
Lower Barn
Middle Barn
Burgh Bridge
Bushy Lodge
Ripe Crossing
RAILWAY COTTS
3
Bushy Lodge Farm
Newhouse Farm
BURGH LA
Adder Wells
Stamford Buildings
Wick Street
08
Dairy Farm
Decoy Pond
Middle Farm
Pookhill Barn
Petland Barn
Firle Park
2
Swingate Cottages
Molehill Shaw
Lower Tilton Farm
West Firle
THE DOCK
Heighton Street
Compton Wood
Firle Tower
Firle Place
A 27(T)
07
Beanstalk
Charleston Farm
Tilton Farm
1
Round Hill
Pearson's Wish
Firle Plantation
Roundhill Plantation
Upper Barn
Firle Beacon
06
47
48
49
D
E
F

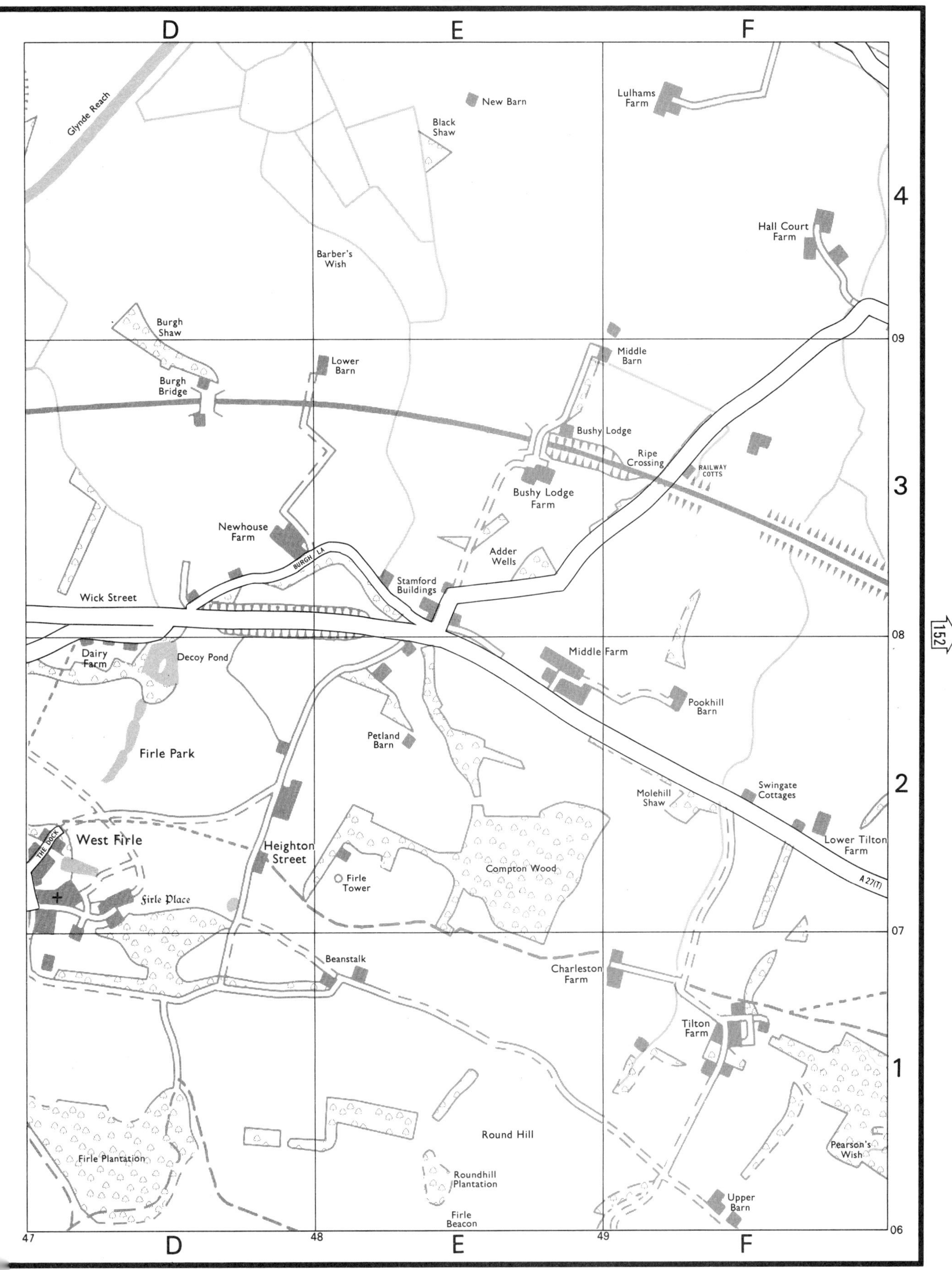

152

171

130

151

A
B
C
Roseneath Farm
Church Farm
Church La
Eckington Corner
Village Hall
Yew Farm
Yew Tree (PH)
Diplocks Farm
Lime Barnett
Darp Farm
Lovers Farm
Chalvington
Church Farm
Honey Lane
Langtye Farm
Poundfield Corner
Sheeplands Farm
Langtye La
Bungalow Farm
Meadow View Farm
Batbrook Cottages
Lower Mays
Lower Mays
Lower Claverham House
Cobb Court
Cony Hall
Mays
Mays Farm
Ludlay Coppice
Sherrington Manor
Selmeston Crossing
Ludlay
Ludlay Farm
P
A 27(T)
Selmeston
Church Farm
Carr's Barn
Selmeston House
Green House
Stonery Farm
Berwick Station
LC
Mill Hill
Hall
Barley Mow (PH)
PH
Tilton Wood
Common La
Roseland Shaw
A 27(T)
New Barn Farm
4
3
2
1
09
08
07
06
50
51
52

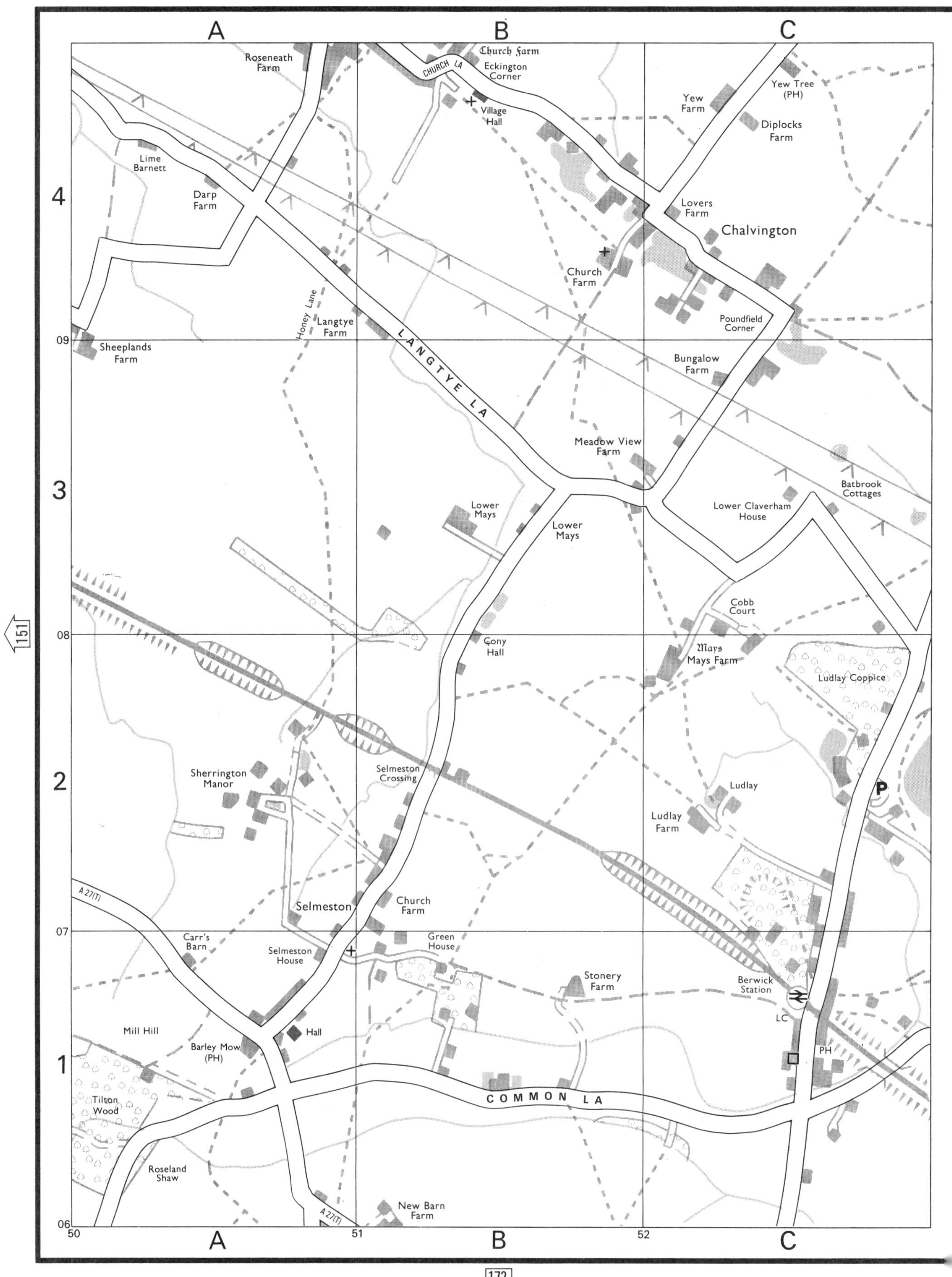

172

131

D
E
F
Selmeston Croft
Clifton Farm
The Dicker
St Bede's School
PH
CAMBERLOT RD
COLDHARBOUR RD
Upper Dicker
High Barn
Sch
Remains of Michelham Priory (Augustinian founded 1229)
Moat
Michelham Priory
4
Lower Claverham Farm
Claverham Manor
Moat
Park Wood
Parkwood Farm
09
Wickstreet Farm
Wickstreet
Winham Coppice
Mill Wood
Batbrooks Farm House
3
Fish Ponds
Sessingham Farm
Moat
08
Raylands Farm
Beaton's Wood
Primrose Farm
Tye Hill
Bate's Green Farm
Old Oak Inn (PH)
Cuckmere River
TYE HILL RD
Caneheath
Arlington
2
PH
Arlington Reservoir
P
Wilbees Farm
Moat
Placket Coppice
Stapley's
Copyhold Cottages
07
Polhill's Farm
Treatment Works
Underwood Farm
Chilverbridge House
Whiteing Lane
BAYLEY'S LA
Chilver Bridge Farm
Endlewick Cottages
1
Endlewick Farm
Moopshill Lane
Hayreed
Old Thornwell
Pickhams
ROBIN POST LA
THORNWELL RD
Moors Hill
06
53
54
55
D
E
F

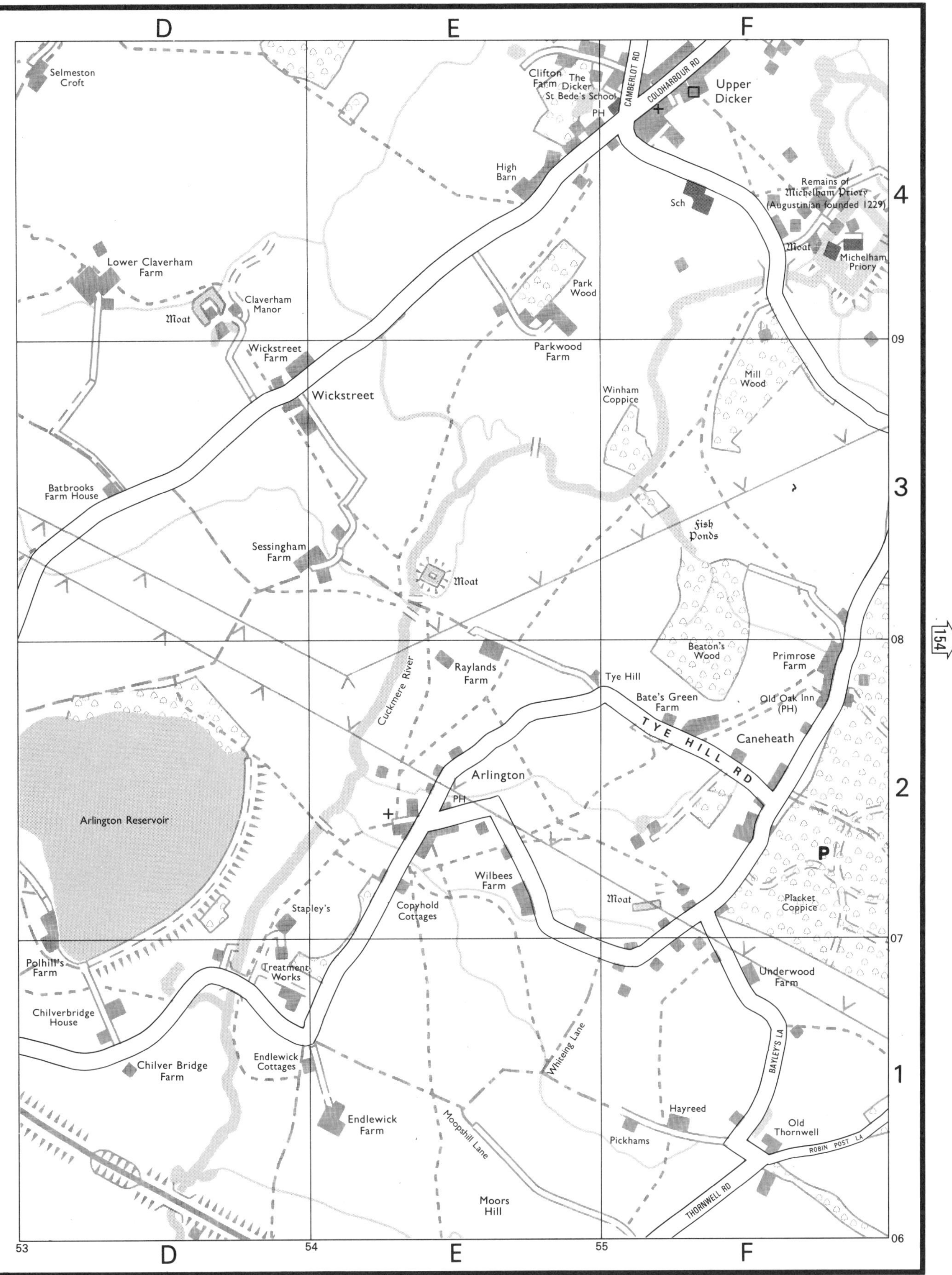

154

173

132

A
B
C
Cuckmere River
Bramble Grove
Knock Hatch Farm
Tile Hurst
Bushy Wood
Arlington Raceway
ARLINGTON RD W
ARLINGTON RD E
Robin Post
Highlands Farm
Highlands Wood
Wilmington Wood
Gillridge Wood
Robin Post Wood
Bolney's Wood
Coldthorn Wood
Folkington Wood
Abbot's Wood
Gate Wood
Robin Post Lane
Natewood Farm
Natewood Poultry Farm
Nate Wood
Cophall Wood
Ogg's Wood
New House Farm
Eastland Coppice
Cliff Combe
Nightingale Farm
Sayerland House
SAYERLAND LA
Brownings
Woodside Hall
Summer Hill
Coppards
Mulbrooks Farm
Freshfield Farm
Dismantled Railway
Oaklands
Cemy
ERSHAM RD
COLDTHORN LA
SOUTH RD
POLEGATE RD
Factory Lane
HAILSHAM INDUSTRIAL PARK
DIPLOCKS WAY
WESTERN RD
SUMMERHEATH RD
LONDON RD
HIGH ST
STATION RD
1 BELMONT CT
2 HOLYWELL WLK
3 LEAMLAND WLK
4 NURSERY PATH
5 BURTON WLK
A 22
A 295
B 2104
B 2202
FB
Sch
Amb Sta
Liby
56
57
58
09
08
07
06
1
2
3
4

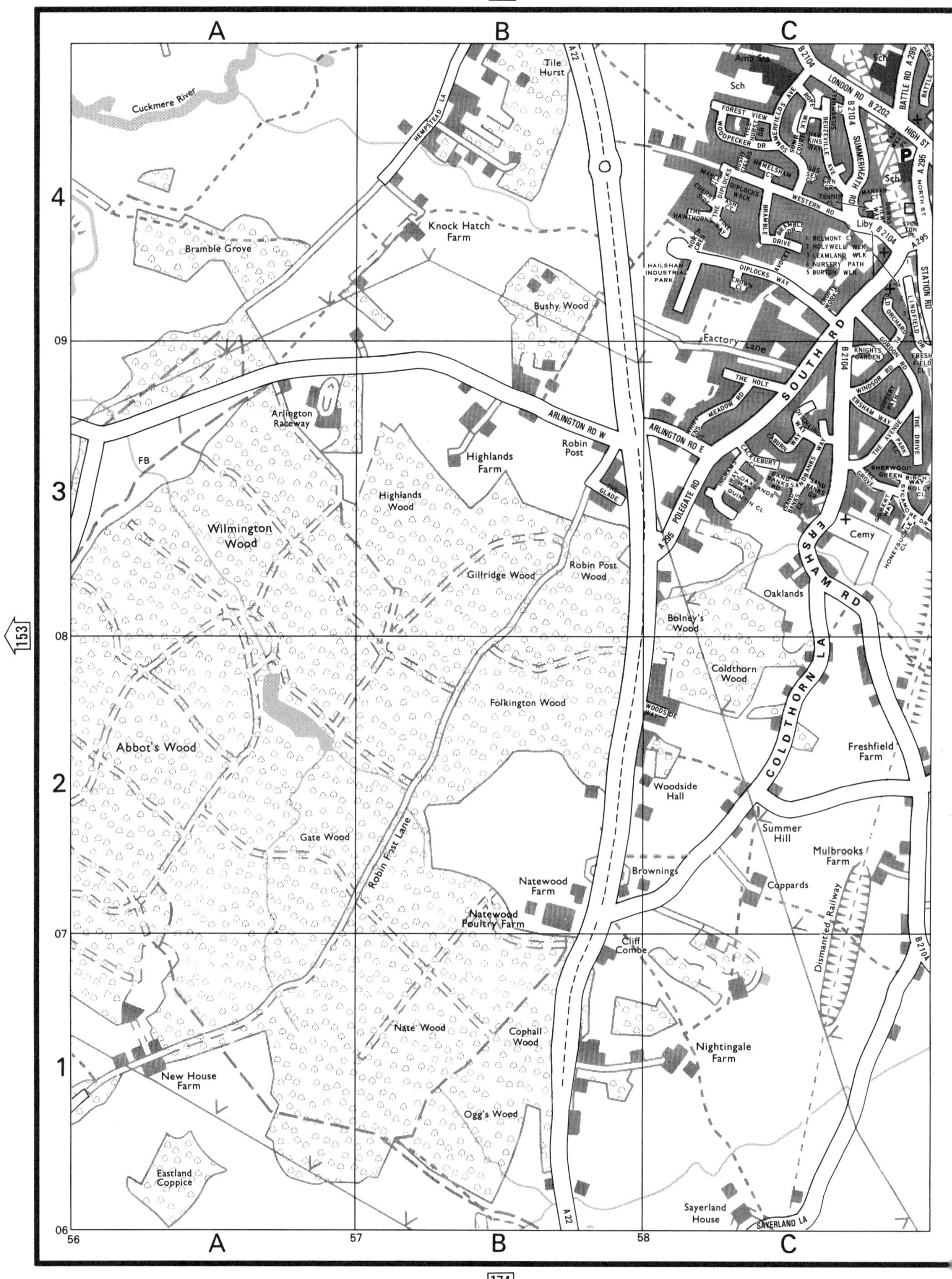

153

174

133

D
E
F
HAILSHAM
Marshfoot Farm
Old Marshfoot Farm
Seaforth Farm
Sch
Hurst Haven
Whelpley Sewer
MARSHFOOT LA
Drove Sewer
Rickney Sewer
Little Marshfoot Farm
VICARAGE LA
HIGH ST
MARKET ST
GEORGE ST
BELL BANKS RD
ST MARY'S AVE
GREENWICH RD
BAYHAM RD
OBSERVATORY VIEW
MERLIN CT
MILL RD
BOWLEY RD
SWAN RD
STATION RD
STATION RD INDUSTRIAL ESTATE
COMPTON TERR
ARCHERY WLK
PELHAM CRES
OLD SWAN LA
Snapson's Drove
Caravan Park
White Dyke Farm
White Dyke
FB
New Barn Farm
White Dyke Sewer
The Horse Eye Sewer
Lewens Sewer
Crossing Sewer
Westdown Cottages
FBs
Nursery
Downash Farm
Slyes Farm
Downash Manor Farm
Westfield Farm
Down Level
Little Downash Farm
Down Sewer
The Lewens
Honeycrock
Saltmarsh Sewer
Glynleigh Sewer
Holm Sewer
Glynleigh Level
Marland Sewer
Glyndley Manor Hotel
Drockmill Hill Gut
East Lodge
GLYNLEIGH RD
Lusteds
OTTHAM COURT LA
Duck Puddle
New Barn Farm
HAILSHAM RD
COTTAGE LA
Old Court Cottages
SHEPHAM LA
B 2104
Priesthawes Farm
Windyridge
HANKHAM ST
4
3
2
1
09
08
07
06
59
60
61

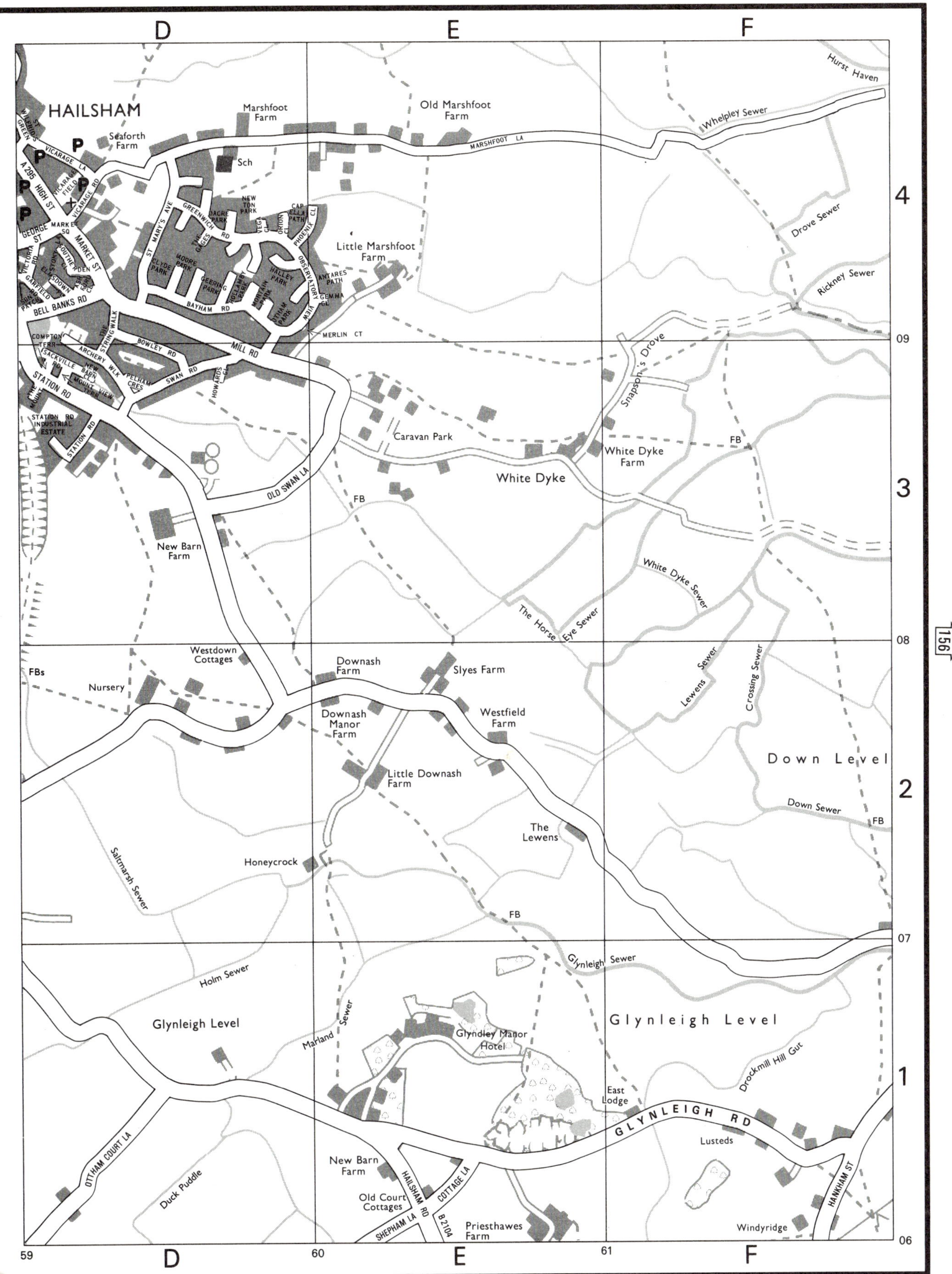

156

175

134

A
B
C
New Bridge
MASKELYNE RD
Church Farm Ditch
4
Horse Eye Level
Curteis Ditch
09
Snapson's Drove
Saltworks
3
Hurst Haven
Kentland Fleet
Sew Ditch
Horse Eye
08
Railland Ditch
Yotham
2
Church Acre Bridge
Newhouse Farm
Church Acre Drove
Pylon Cottages
Rickney Farm
Rickney
07
Elmhurst
Bridge Farm
Chilley Stream
1
Manxey Level
Hankham Gut
Chilley Green
Chilley Farm
06
62
63
64
A
B
C

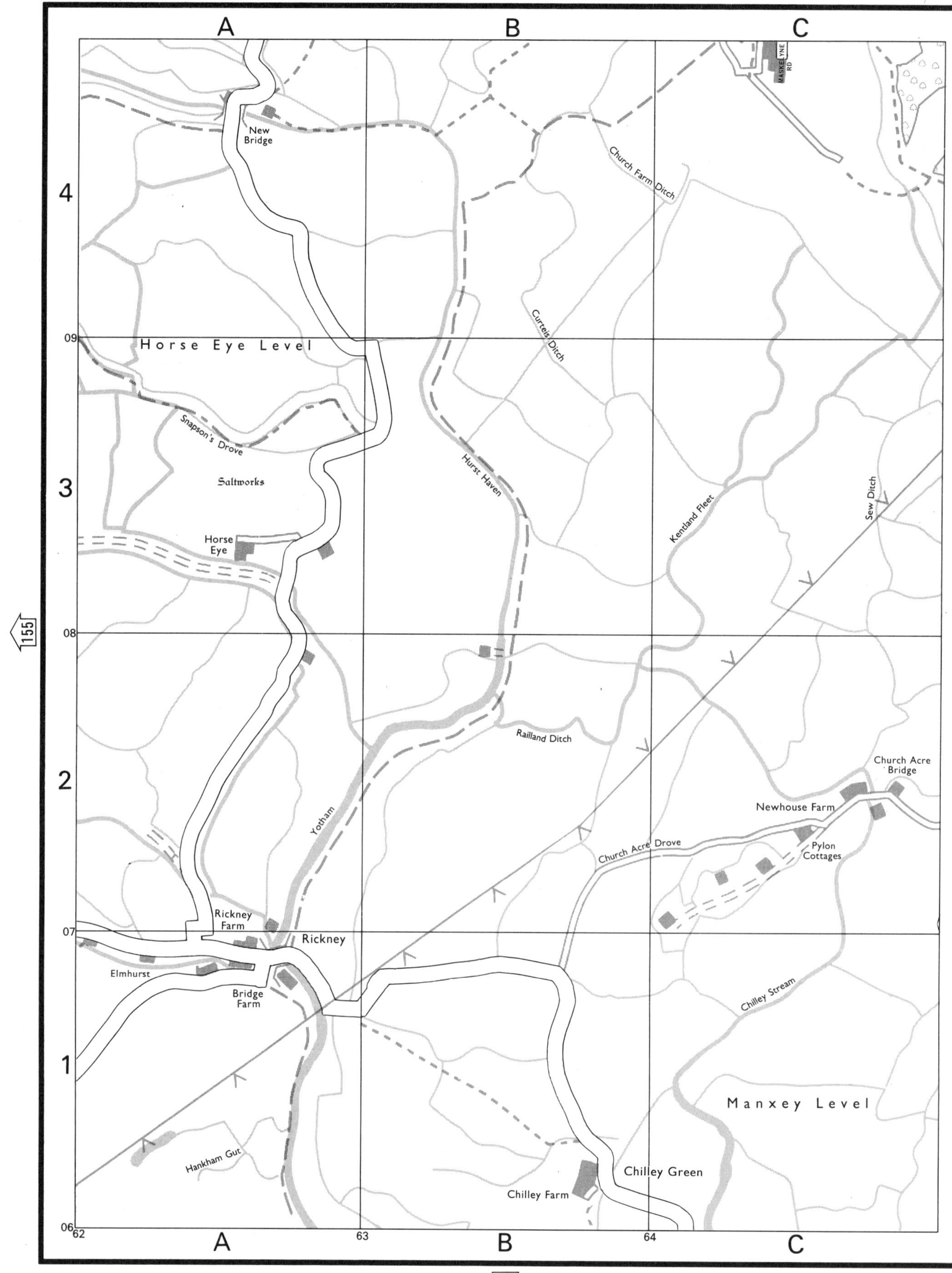

155

176

135

D
E
F
Hoads Hill Farm
The Reids
WARTLING RD
BOREHAM LA
Brooks Farm
Cooper's Farm
Wartling
PH
Waterhouse Farm
The Parsonage Farm
B 2095
Nut Brown Farm
Lord's House
HORSEWALK
Horse Bridge
KILN LA
Court Lodge Farm
Moat
Lower Barn
New Barn Farm
Waterlot Stream
Marsh Foot Farm
The Lamb (PH)
A 259(T)
B 2095
Mark Dyke
Dowle Stream
Waller's Haven
Buck's Bridge
Lampham Drove
Dowle Corner
Moat
Middle Bridge
Old Haven
Reynolds Gut
A 259(T)
4
3
2
1
09
08
07
06
65
66
67

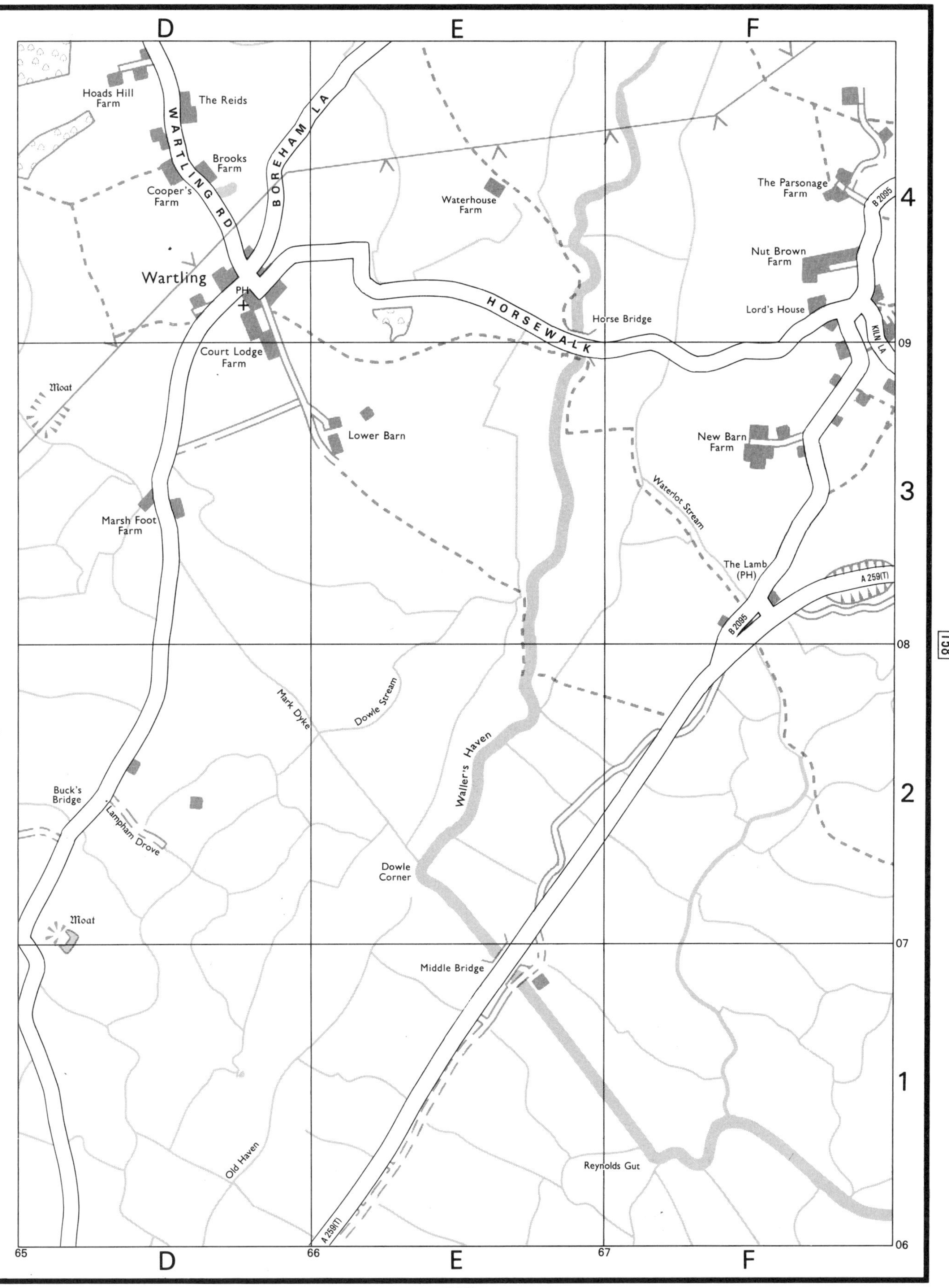

158

177

136

A
B
C
4
3
2
1
09
08
07
06
68
69
70
Oldbury Farm
Hall's Cross
Broadstreet Green
Broad Green Farm
Hooe
Grove House
Church La
B 2095
Kiln La
Court Lodge
Court Cottage
New Lodge Farm
A 259(T)
Whydown Rd
Whydown Bridge
Highwoods Farm
Holmes Farm
Holmes Lane
Whydown Farm
Whydown
Gotham Wood
Gotham
Sandhurst La
Picknill Green La
Picknill Green
Kite's Nest Wood
Coneyburrow La
HM Prison
Beeches Farm
Ticehurst Rise
Wartling Dr
Pleyden Ave
Barnhorn Rd
The Broadwalk
Hill Farm
Old Road Farm
Barnhorn Manor
Barnhorne Farm
Barnhorne Manor
Cooden Wood
Cooden Moat
Cole Stream
Maple Wlk
Clavering Wlk
Chapel Field
Hooe Level
Crooked Ditch
Nature Reserve
Cooden Sea Rd
Cooden Beach Station
Cooden Beach Golf Course
Herbrand Wlk
Groynes
Cuiver Croft Bank
LC
Ppg Sta
PH

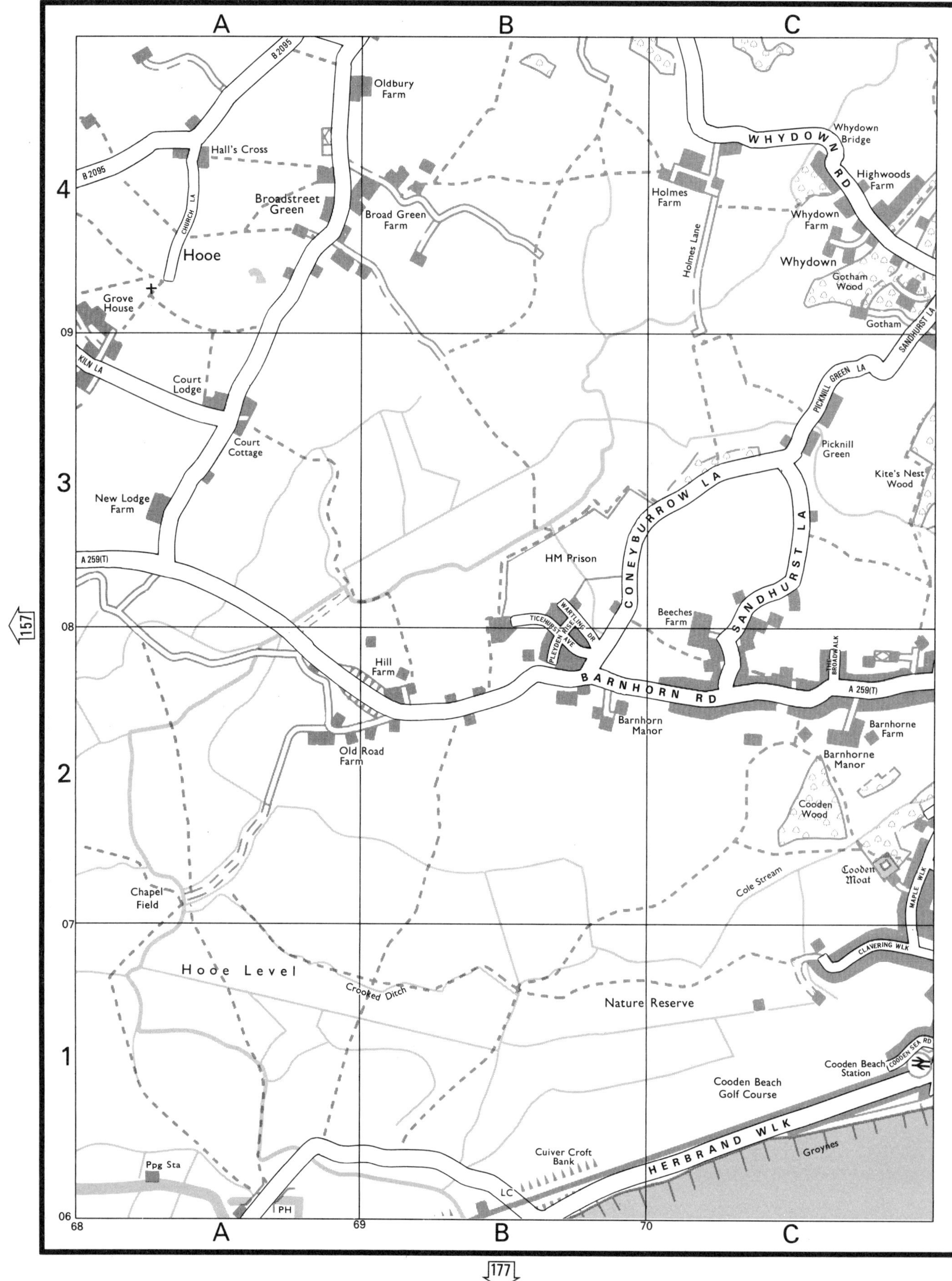

157

177

137

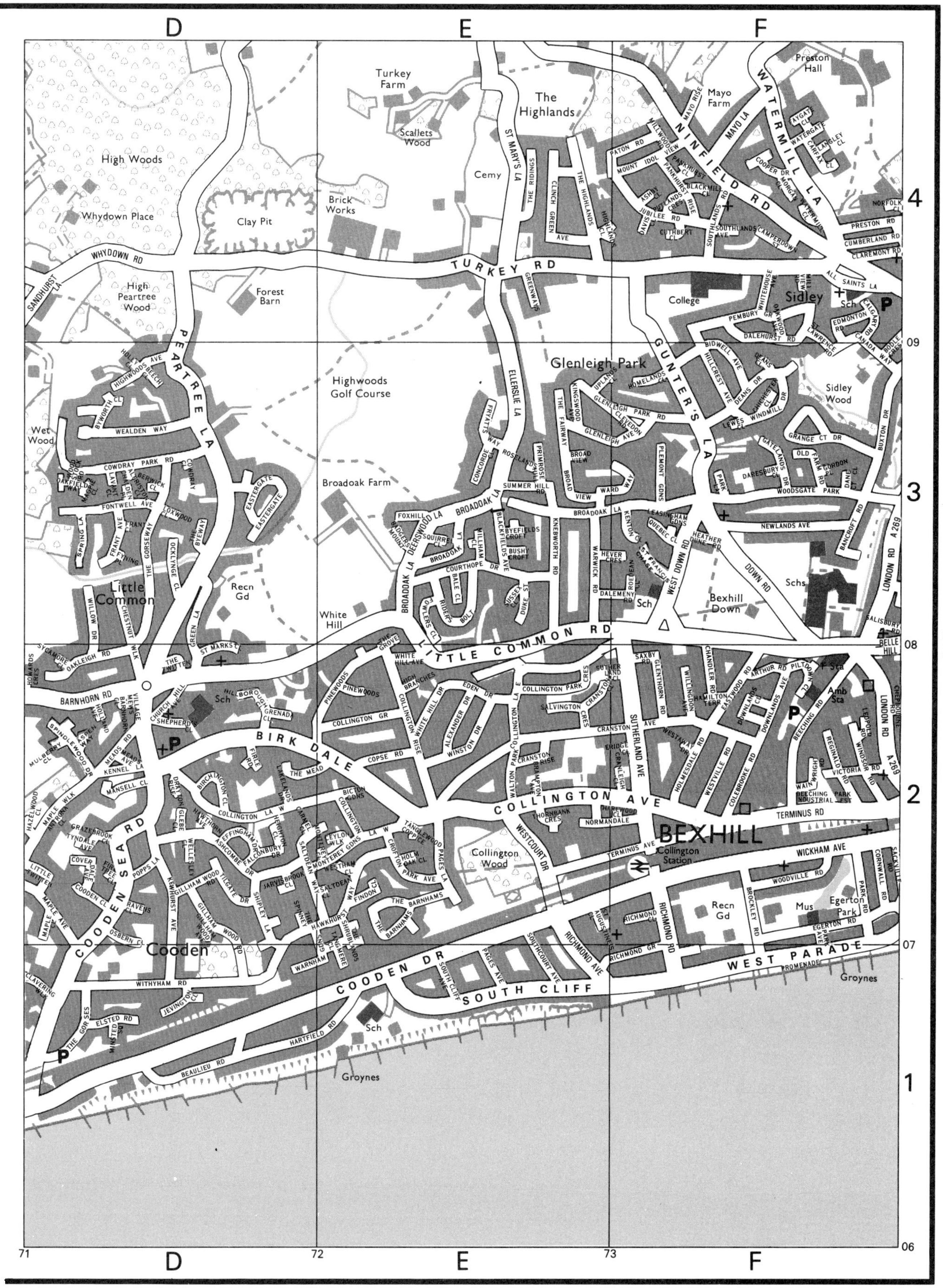
D
E
F
D
E
F
4
3
2
1
09
08
07
06
71
72
73
Turkey Farm
Scallets Wood
The Highlands
Preston Hall
Mayo Farm
High Woods
Whydown Place
Clay Pit
Brick Works
Cemy
WHYDOWN RD
TURKEY RD
SANDHURST LA
High Peartree Wood
Forest Barn
College
Sidley
Sch
PEARTREE LA
Highwoods Golf Course
Glenleigh Park
GUNTER'S LA
Sidley Wood
Wet Wood
WEALDEN WAY
COWDRAY PARK RD
FONTWELL AVE
Broadoak Farm
BROADOAK LA
Little Common
Recn Gd
White Hill
LITTLE COMMON RD
Bexhill Down
WEST DOWN RD
DOWN RD
Schs
LONDON RD
A 269
BARNHORN RD
BIRK DALE
COLLINGTON AVE
BEXHILL
Collington Station
Collington Wood
TERMINUS RD
WICKHAM AVE
Recn Gd
Mus
Egerton Park
WEST PARADE
Groynes
COODEN SEA RD
Cooden
COODEN DR
SOUTH CLIFF
Sch
Groynes
F Sta
Amb Sta
BEECHING PARK INDUSTRIAL EST
MAYO LA
NINFIELD RD
WATERMILL LA
ST MARY'S LA
ELLERSLIE LA
SUTHERLAND AVE
RICHMOND RD
WESTCOURT DR
HARTFIELD RD
BEAULIEU RD
WITHYHAM RD
BELLE HILL

160

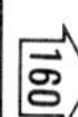

138

A
B
C
4
3
2
1
09
08
07
06
74
75
76
Dismantled Railway
Combe Wood
Worsham Farm
Glover's Farm
Worsham Farm
The Mount
Pebsham Wood
Pebsham Farm
WRESTWOOD RD
Old Town
Bexhill Hospital
Pebsham
HASTINGS RD
KING OFFA WAY
DE LA WARR RD
Glyne Gap
Galley Hill
CG Lookout
Town Hall
Bexhill Central Station
Liby
MARINA
MAGDALEN RD
Sch

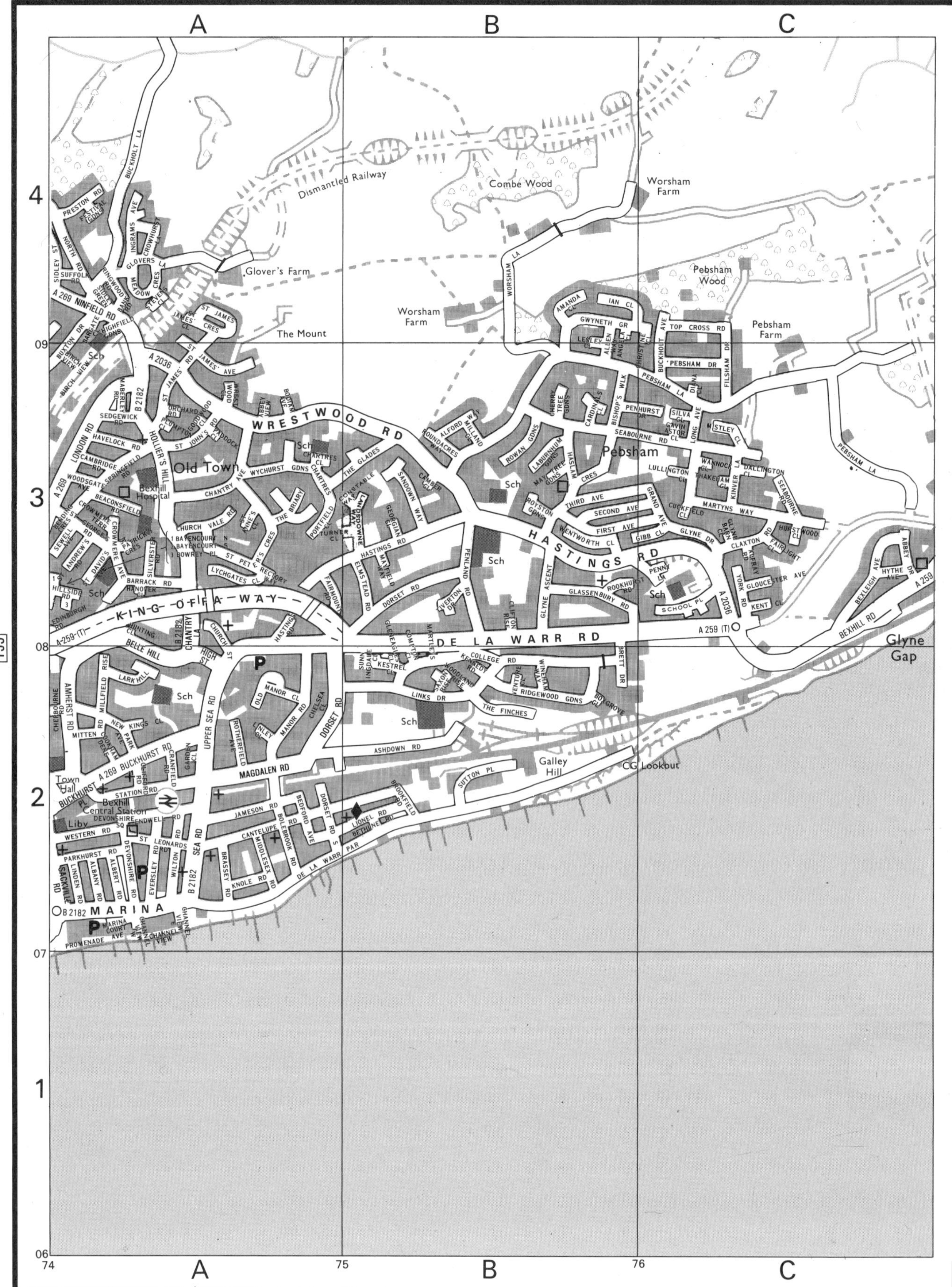

159

139

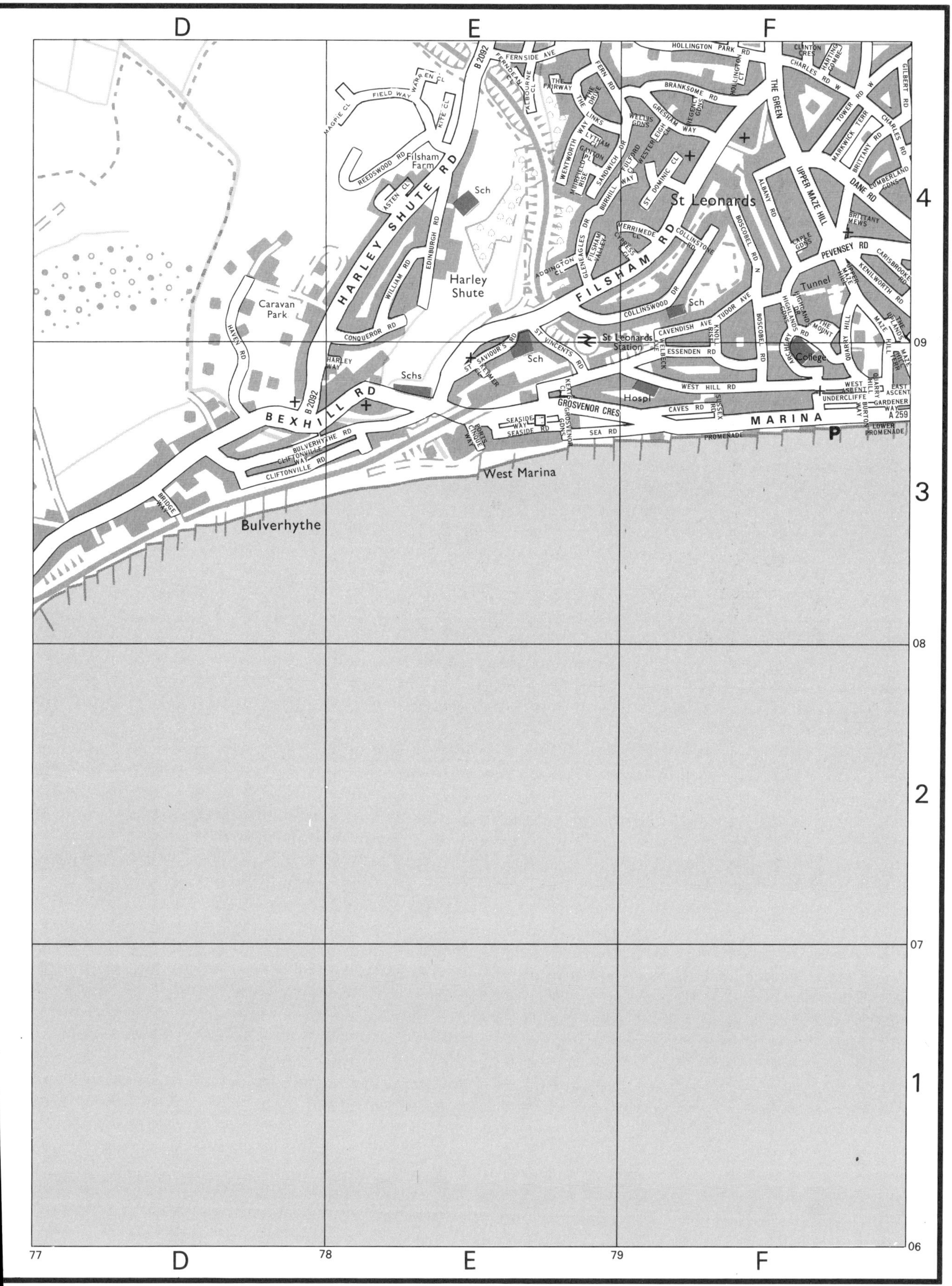

D E F

Hollington Park Rd
Clinton Cres
Harting Combe
Charles Rd W
Gilbert Rd
Fernside Ave
Ferndean
Albourne Cl
Warren Cl
Field Way
Magpie Cl
Kite Cl
The Fairway
The Drive
Fern Rd
Branksome Rd
Hollington Ct
The Green
Tower Rd W
Markwick Terr
Charles Rd
Brittany Rd
The Links
Wentworth Way
Lytham
Canton Pl
Wellis Gdns
Gresham Way
Regency Gdns
Reedswood Rd
Filsham Farm
Muirfield Rise
Sandwich Dr
Fulford Cl
Westerleigh Cl
St Dominic Cl
Burhill Way
Harley Shute Rd
Asten Cl
Sch
St Leonards
Albany Rd
Upper Maze Hill
Dane Rd
Cumberland Gdns
Brittany Mews
Edinburgh Rd
Merrimede Cl
Collinstone Rd
Boscobel Rd N
Caple Gdns
Pevensey Rd
Carisbrooke Rd
Kenilworth Rd
William Rd
Gleneagles Dr
Filsham Valley
Cypress Cl
Addington Cl
Filsham Rd
Harley Shute
Tunnel
Upper Maze Hill
Caravan Park
Collinswood Dr
Sch
Tudor Ave
Highlands Gdns
Highlands Dr
Maze Hill
The Lands
Haven Rd
Conqueror Rd
Cavendish Ave
Knoll Rise
Boscobel Rd
The Mount
Quarry Hill
St Saviour's Rd
St Vincents Rd
St Leonards Station
Welbeck Ave
Essenden Rd
Archery Rd
College
Maze Hill Terr
Harley Way
Sch
Latimer Rd
Schs
West Hill Rd
West Ascent
Quarry Hill
East Ascent
B 2092
Bexhill Rd
Kenilworth Rd
Grosvenor Cres
Hospl
Caves Rd
Sussex Rd
Undercliffe
Burton Way
Gardener Way
A 259
Seaside Way
Seaside Rd
Grosvenor Gdns
Sea Rd
Marina
Promenade
P
Lower Promenade
Bulverhythe Rd
Cliftonville Way
Cliftonville Rd
Cinque Ports Way
West Marina
Bridge Way
Bulverhythe

4 3 2 1

09 08 07 06

77 78 79

D E F

140

161

A
B
C
4
3
2
1
09
08
07
06
80
81
82
HASTINGS
Bohemia
St Leonards
Old Town
Pier
Hastings Station
Town Hall
Royal East Sussex Hospital
Museum & Art Gallery
Courts
Offices
Caves
Castle
BOHEMIA RD
LONDON RD
GRAND PAR
WARRIOR SQ
EVERSFIELD PL
VERULAM PL
WHITE ROCK
ROBERTSON ST
CARLISLE PAR
WELLINGTON PL
DENMARK PL
PELHAM PL
EAST BEACH
ROCK-A-NORE RD
A 259
A 21
1 THE LAWN
2 DECIMUS BURTON WAY
3 UNION ST
4 VALENTINE'S PAS
5 MARKET PAS
6 UNDERCLIFF TERR
7 MOUNT PLEASANT
8 MERCATORIA
9 STANHOPE PL
10 HAROLD MEWS
11 MEWS RD
1 ST MICHAEL'S PL
2 CLAREMONT
3 TRINITY ST
4 CARLISLE PAR
5 ROBERTSON PAS
6 ROBERTSON TERR
1 QUEEN'S AVE
2 YORK GDNS
3 ALBERT RD
4 WELLINGTON SQ
4 ELFORD ST
5 WELLINGTON MEWS
6 STONEFIELD PL
1 RUSSELL CT
2 CUTTER LA
3 SUN LA
4 SHELL LA
5 MARKET PAS
1 SWAN AVE
2 OAK PAS
3 POST OFFICE PAS
4 WINDING ST
5 EAST BOURNE ST
6 EAST BEACH ST
7 WELLESLEY COURT
8 SINNOCK SQ
9 PHILIP COLE CL
1 WOOD'S PAS
2 EBENEZER RD
3 HESTINGAS PLAT
4 OLD HUMPHREY AVE
STRONGS PAS
SWAINES PAS
EAST HILL PAS
Settlement
East Hill
10
83
84

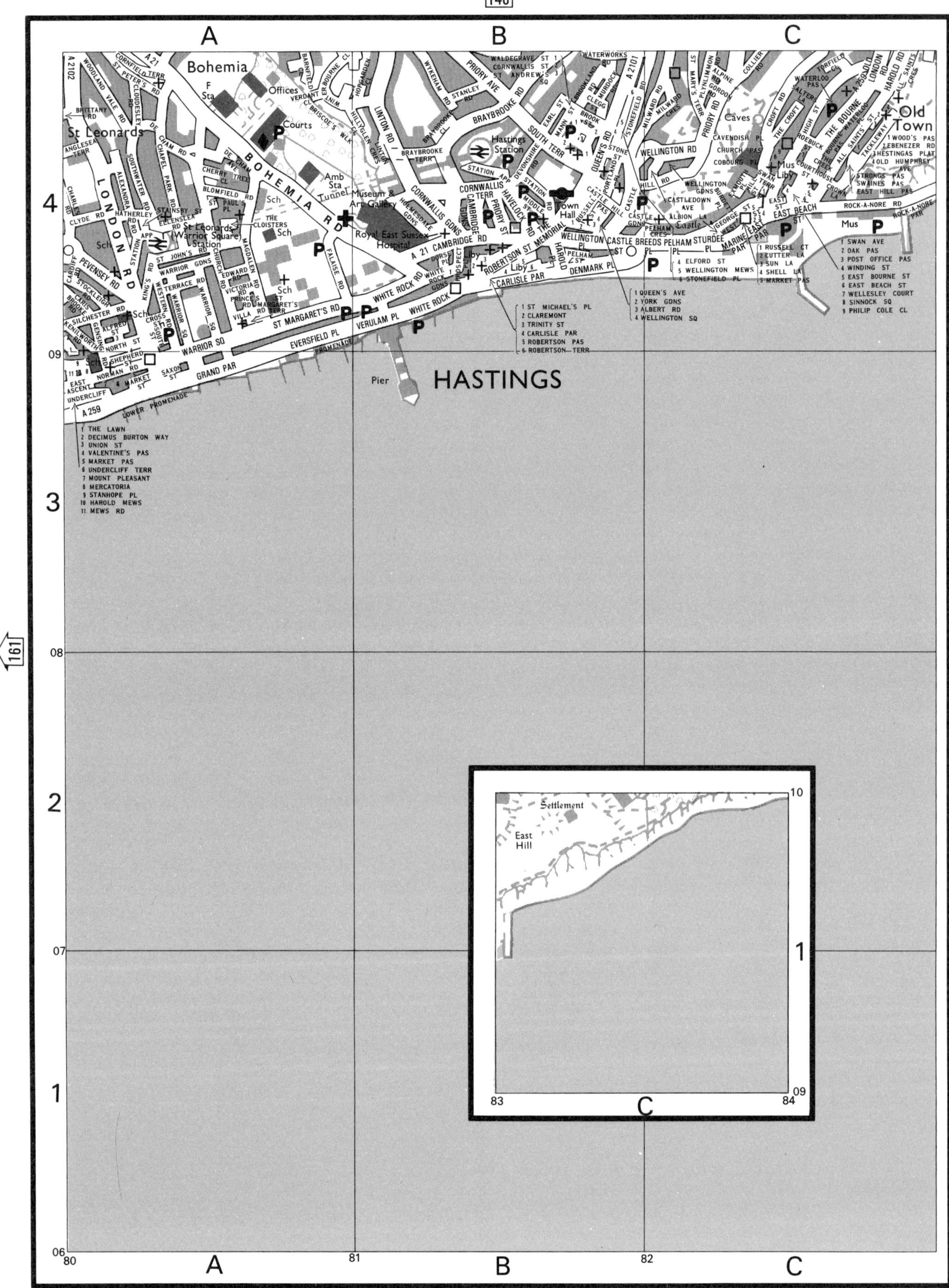

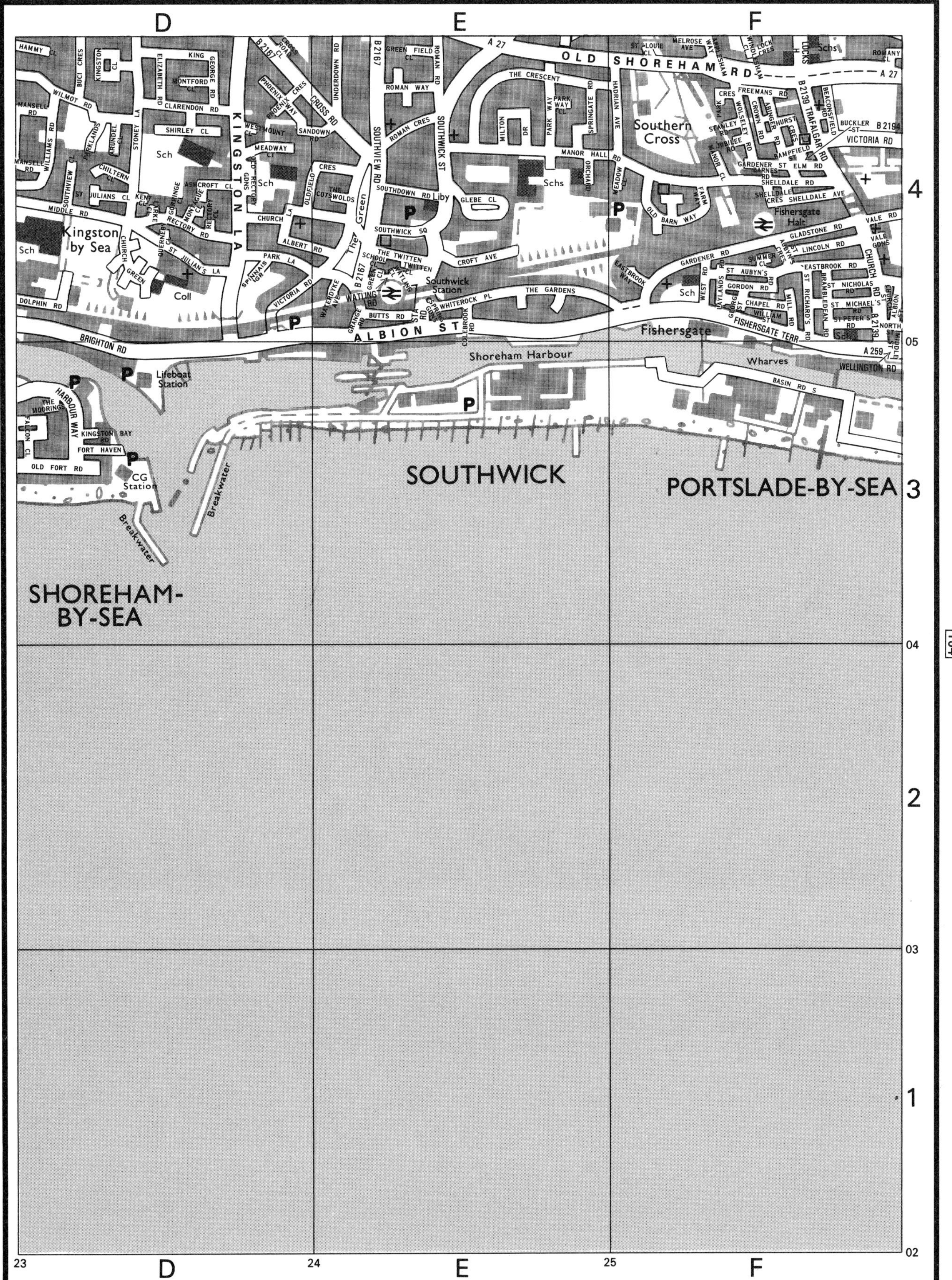

143
164
not continued, see key diagram

144

163

HOVE
OLD SHOREHAM RD
PORTLAND RD
NEW CHURCH RD
KINGSWAY
Portslade and West Hove Station
Aldrington Station
Hove Station
Aldrington
Shoreham Harbour East Arm The Canal
Lagoon
Goldstone Football Ground
Sackville Trading Estate
SACKVILLE RD
Town Hall
Fire Station
Cemy

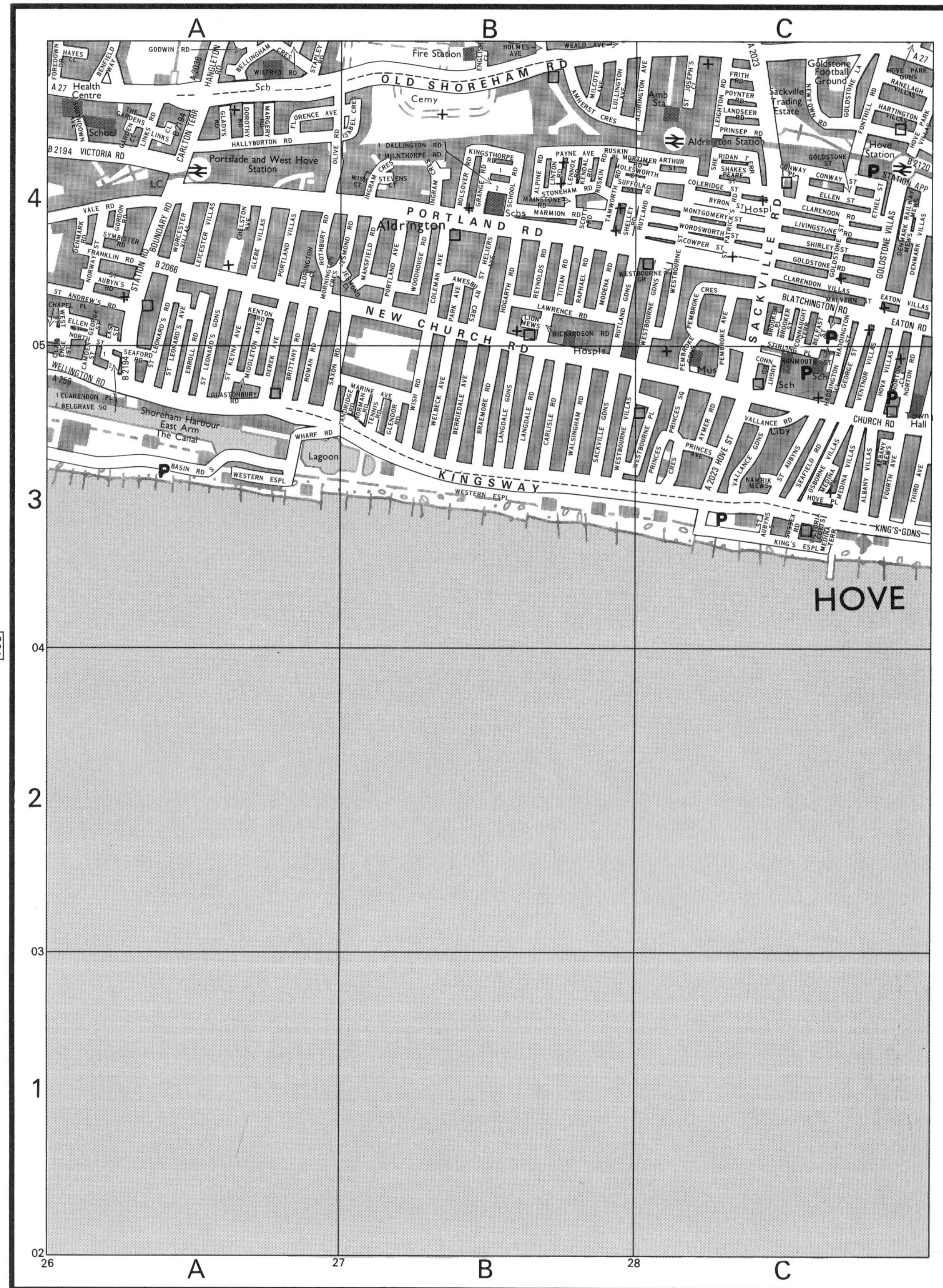

145

D
E
F
4
3
2
1
05
04
03
02
29
30
31
OLD SHOREHAM RD
THE DRIVE
DYKE RD
KINGSWAY
KING'S RD
GRAND JUNCTION RD
MARINE PAR
NEW ENGLAND RD
DITCHLING RD
LONDON RD
CROMWELL RD
EATON RD
CHURCH RD
LANSDOWNE RD
WESTERN RD
QUEEN'S RD
NORTH ST
DAVIGDOR RD
PRESTON RD
VIADUCT RD
County Cricket Ground
Magistrates Court
Hospital
College
School
Seven Dials
Brighton Station
London Road Station
Round Hill
Churchill Square
Dome
Library & Museum
Royal Pavilion
Aquarium
Information Centre
Kings Lawns
Brunswick Lawns
West Pier
Palace Pier
BRIGHTON

166

146

165

A
B
C
4
3
2
1
05
04
03
02
32
33
34
Bevendean Hospital
Cemy
BEAR RD
Cemeteries
Race Hill
TENANTRY DOWN RD
WARREN RD
Race Course
Woodingdean
Burial Ground
1 INVERNESS RD
2 ABERDEEN RD
ELM GR
Amb Sta
Brighton General Hospital
QUEEN'S PARK RD
FRESHFIELD RD
Whitehawk Camp
Whitehawk
WILSON AVE
Sheepcote Valley
Golf Course
Newhouse Farm
Blackrock Valley
Red Hill
Sports Ground
Park
Sch
Schs
Coll
Liby
Hospl
EASTERN RD
MARINE PAR
Electric Railway
Kemp Town
Bell Tower Industrial Estate
F Sta
ROEDEAN RD
Black Rock
Miniature Golf Course
MARINE DR
Undercliff Wlk
Marina
Roedean
Roedean Bottom
Roedean School
A 259
B 2118
B 2137
UPPER ST JAMES'S ST
SEYMOUR ST
SEYMOUR SQ
1 EASTERN TERR MEWS
2 EASTERN ST
Park Hill

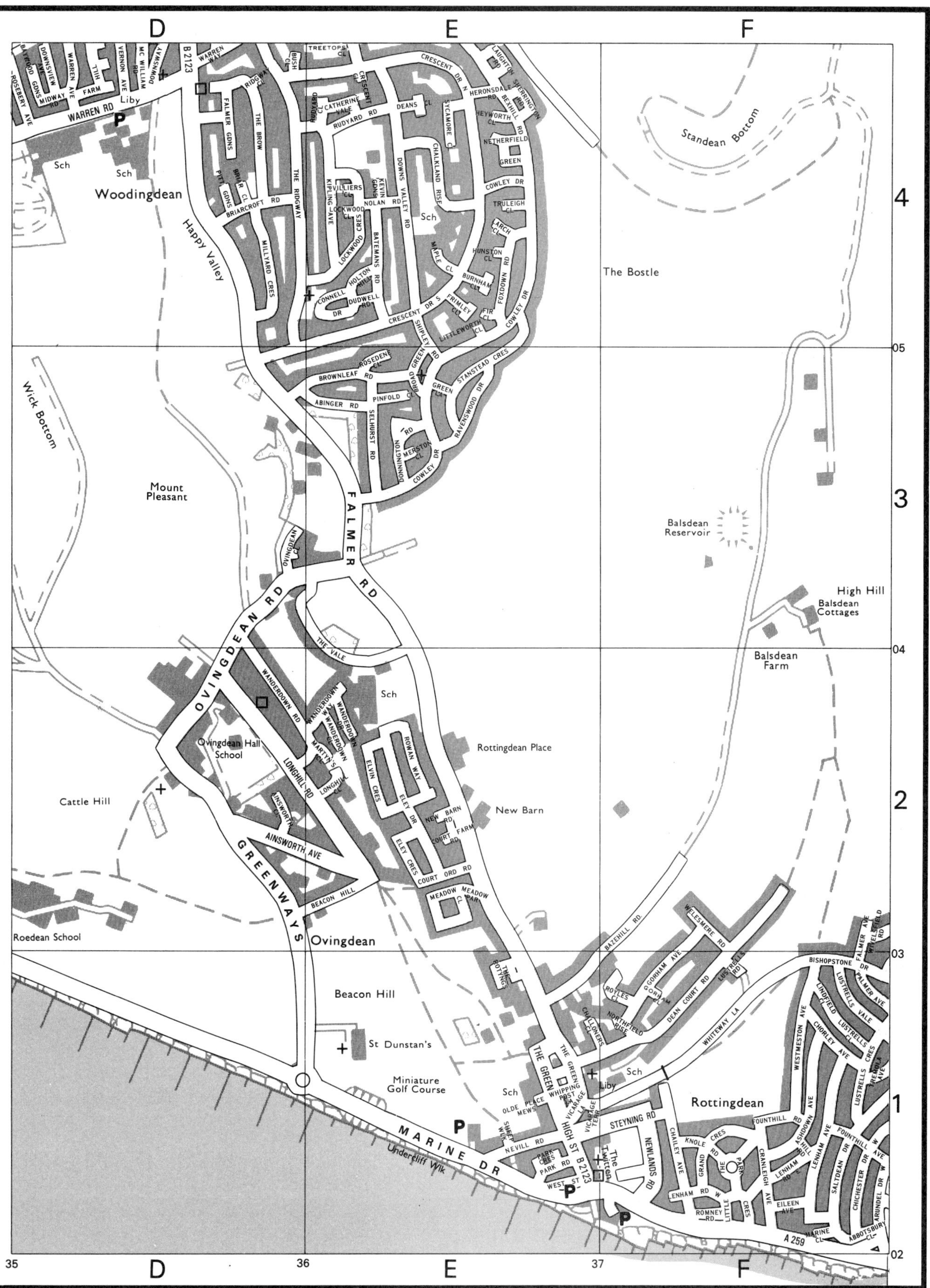
D
E
F
Woodingdean
Happy Valley
Standean Bottom
The Bostle
Wick Bottom
Mount Pleasant
Balsdean Reservoir
High Hill
Balsdean Cottages
Balsdean Farm
Rottingdean Place
New Barn
Ovingdean Hall School
Cattle Hill
Roedean School
Ovingdean
Beacon Hill
St Dunstan's
Miniature Golf Course
Rottingdean
WARREN RD
FALMER RD
OVINGDEAN RD
GREENWAYS
MARINE DR
Undercliff Wlk
HIGH ST B2123
A 259
35
36
37
4
3
2
1
05
04
03
02

148

A
B
C
4
3
2
1
05
04
03
02
38
39
40
Killall
Whiteway Bottom
Pickers Hill
Heathy Brow
South Downs Way
White Way
Breaky Bottom Farm
Breaky Bottom
Highdole Hill
Fore Hill
Tumuli
Pickers Hill Farm
Telscombe Tye
Coombe Bottom
Coombe Farm
Hillview
Telscombe
Youth Hostel
Tenant Hill
Pedlersburgh
Tumulus
Saltdean
Schs
Community Centre & Library
Hotel
Heathy Brow
SALTDEAN VALE
COOMBE VALE
WESTFIELD AVE
WESTFIELD AVE S
WESTFIELD AVE N
WESTFIELD RISE
COOMBE RISE
HOMEBUSH AVE
WIVELSFIELD RD
TUMULUS RD
PERRY HILL
RIDGEWOOD AVE
STANMER AVE
HAILSHAM AVE
HILGROVE RD
ARLINGTON GDNS
LUSTRELLS CRES
CHILTINGTON WAY
EFFINGHAM CL
MOUNT DR
GLYNDE AVE
GREENBANK AVE
HEATHFIELD AVE
WESTBROOK
CHICHESTER DR W
CHICHESTER CL
ARUNDEL DR W
ARUNDEL DR E
CHICHESTER DR E
LINCHMERE AVE
LONGRIDGE AVE
BEVENDEAN AVE
OAKLANDS AVE
WICKLANDS AVE
HAMSEY RD
BRAMBLETYNE AVE
WITHYHAM AVE
NUTLEY AVE
SHEPHAM AVE
RODMELL AVE
CISSBURY CRES
FINDON AVE
NORTHWOOD AVE
BANNINGS VALE
CHAILEY CRES
LEWES CL
IFIELD CL
RYE CL
ASHURST AVE
TELSCOMBE RD
TELSCOMBE CLIFFS WAY
HARVEST CL
BARLEY CL
LULHAM CL
SUNSET CL
THE RIDINGS
THE SWALLOWS
SHANNON CL
CHATSWORTH AVE
CHATSWORTH PARK
NORTHCOTE LA
LAURENCE CL
BERRY CL
KIRBY DR
MANOR DR
CAVENDISH CL
AMBLESIDE AVE
CAREY DOWN
STANLEY RD
RUSTIC RD
RUSTIC PARK
THE COMPTS
HEATHY BROW
FOXHILL
GLYNN RISE
PHYLLIS AVE
FIRLE RD
WARREN LODGE
WARREN WAY
TYE VIEW
PARK VIEW CL
BUSH CL
BRIDLE WAY

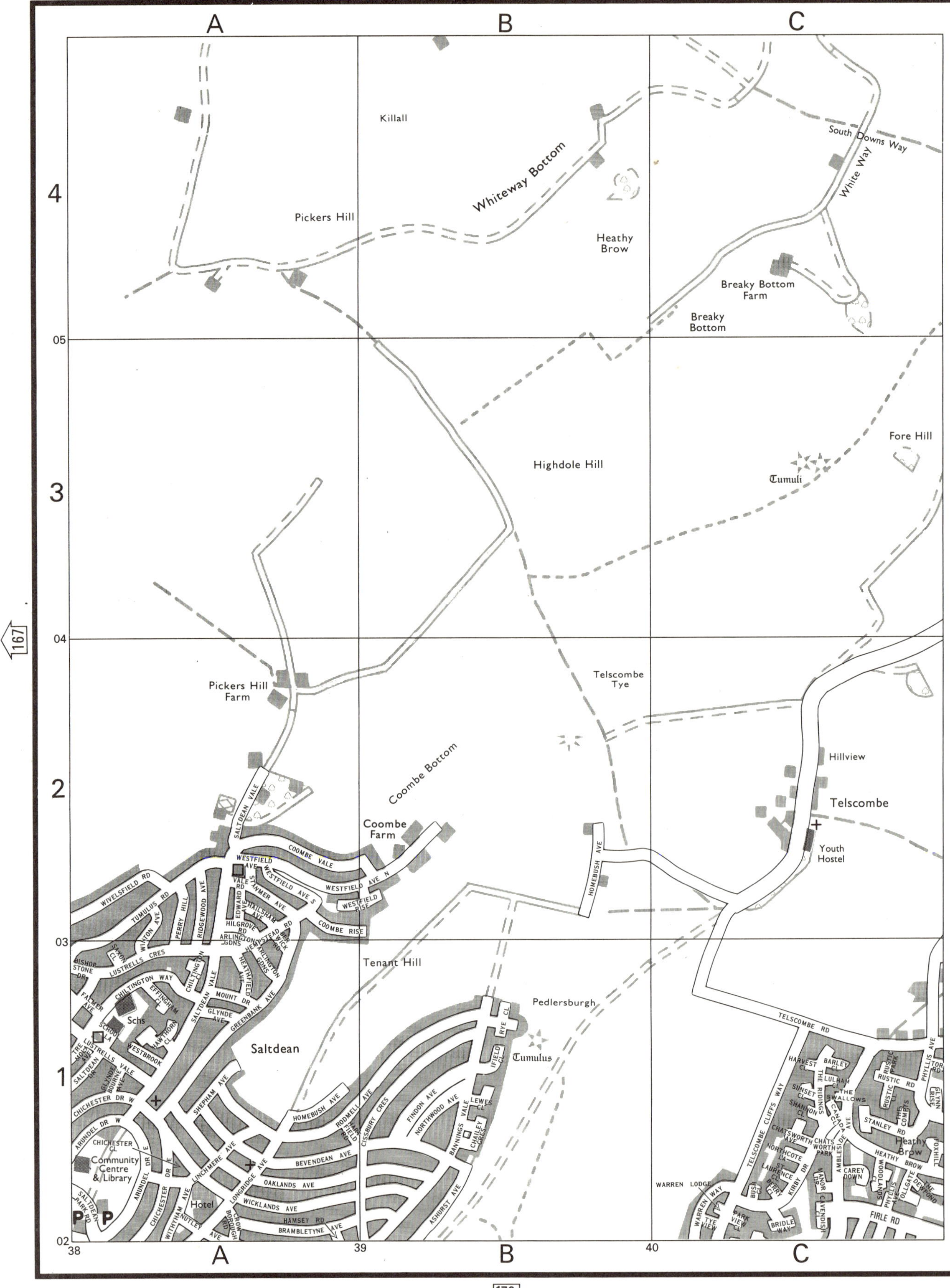

167

178

149

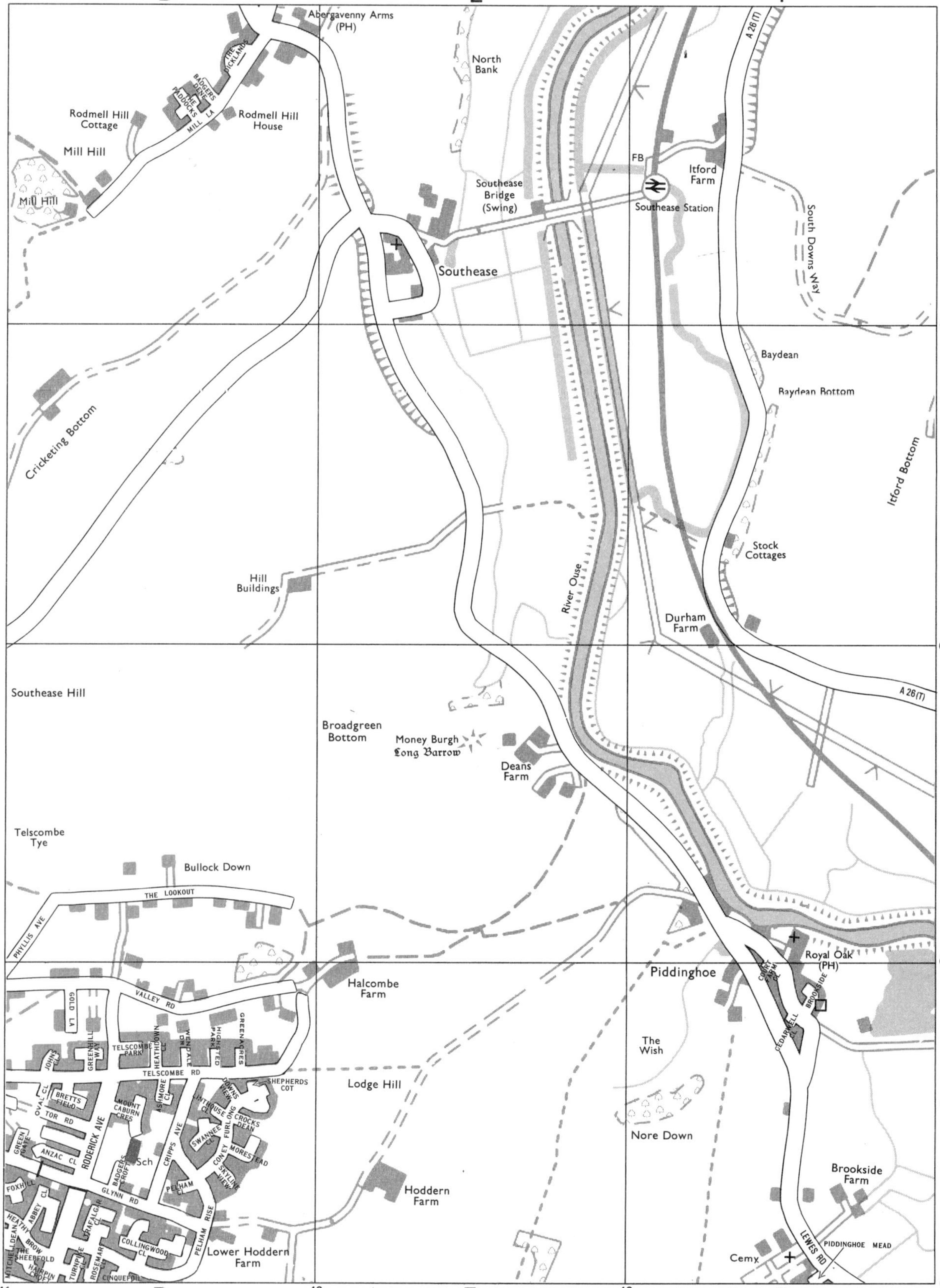

D E F

Abergavenny Arms (PH)
North Bank
Rodmell Hill Cottage
Rodmell Hill House
THE DICKLANDS
BADGERS DENE
THE PADDOCKS
MILL LA
Mill Hill
Mill Hill
Southease Bridge (Swing)
FB
Itford Farm
Southease Station
South Downs Way
Southease
A 26(T)
4
05
Baydean
Baydean Bottom
Cricketing Bottom
Itford Bottom
3
Stock Cottages
Hill Buildings
River Ouse
Durham Farm
04
Southease Hill
A 26(T)
Broadgreen Bottom
Money Burgh Long Barrow
Deans Farm
2
Telscombe Tye
Bullock Down
THE LOOKOUT
PHYLLIS AVE
Royal Oak (PH)
03
Piddinghoe
Halcombe Farm
VALLEY RD
GOLD LA
GREENHILL WAY
TELSCOMBE PARK
HEATHDOWN CL
WENDALE DR
HIGHSTED PARK
GREENACRES
COURT FARM CL
BROOKSIDE
CEDARWELL CL
The Wish
TELSCOMBE RD
SHEPHERDS COT
Lodge Hill
JOHNS CL
BRETTS FIELD
OVAL CL
TOR RD
MOUNT CABURN CRES
ASHMORE CL
LINTHOUSE CL
DOWNS VIEW
CROCKS DEAN
1
Nore Down
GREEN PARK
ANZAC CL
RODERICK AVE
CRIPPS AVE
SWANNEE CL
CONEY FURLONG
MORESTEAD
SKYLINE VIEW
Sch
BADGERS CROFT
PELHAM CL
FOXHILL
GLYNN RD
Hoddern Farm
Brookside Farm
HEATHY BROW
ABBEY CL
TRAFALGAR CL
PELHAM RISE
COLLINGWOOD CL
LEWES RD
PIDDINGHOE MEAD
MITCHELDEAN
THE SHEEPFOLD
HAIRPIN CROFT
TURNPIKE CL
ROSEMARY CL
CINQUEFOIL
Lower Hoddern Farm
Cemy
02

41 42 43

D E F

170

150

A
B
C
Tumulus
White Lion Pond
Radio Station
Males Burgh Tumulus
FIRLE BOSTAL
South Downs Way
Red Lion Pond
Itford Hill
America Farm
Blackcap Farm
Well Bottom
Cow Wish Bottom
Toy Farm
Blackcap Hill
Muggery Pope
Fore Hill
Home Bottom
Manor Farm
Tarring Court Farm
A 26(T)
Tarring Neville
Page's New Barn
Snap Hill
Caravan Park
Stump Bottom
Works
Gardener's Hill
New Barn
South Heighton Farm
South Heighton
HAMPDEN GDNS
HEIGHTON RD
River Ouse
1 PORTLAND TERR
2 FIRLE TERR
3 WEST VIEW TERR
4 MARTELLO CT
Poverty Bottom
Denton Hill Farm
Denton
THE CRESCENT
Mount Pleasant
PALMERSTON RD
HAREFIELD CL
ST LEONARD'S RD
WELLINGTON RD
THE CLOSE
THOMPSON RD
CANTERCROW HILL
PARK DR
ROOKERY CL
ROOKERY WAY
LEWIS CL
ST LEONARD'S CL
PARK DRIVE CL
HILL RISE
HILL RD
DENTON RISE
ACACIA RD
THE GROVE
RECTORY RD
VICARAGE CL
HEIGHTON CRES
GLYNDE CL
BRANDS CL
TARRING CL
ST MARTINS CRES
FORD CL
IVEAGH CRES
Sch
DENTON RD
POWELL GDNS
COTTAGE CL
B2109
NEW RD
DENTON DR
KING'S AVE
FAIRHOLME RD
CREST RD
SEAVIEW RD
CLAREMONT RD
STATION RD
BERESFORD RD
ARUNDEL RD
MOUNT RD
FALAISE RD
HOWE CL
HOLMDALE RD
AVIS RD
Amb Sta
AVIS WAY
A 26(T)
44
45
46
02
03
04
05
1
2
3
4

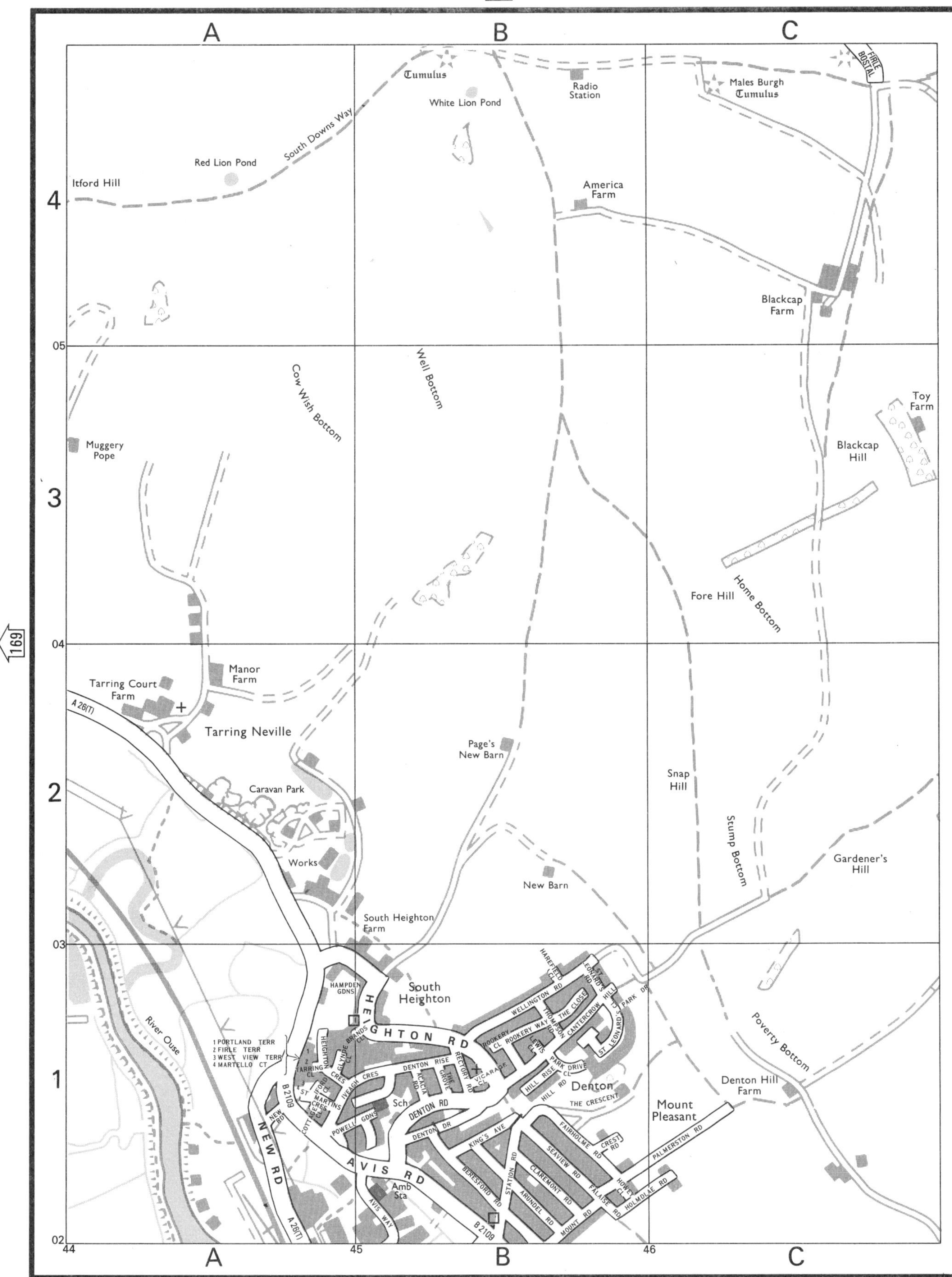

169

180

151
D 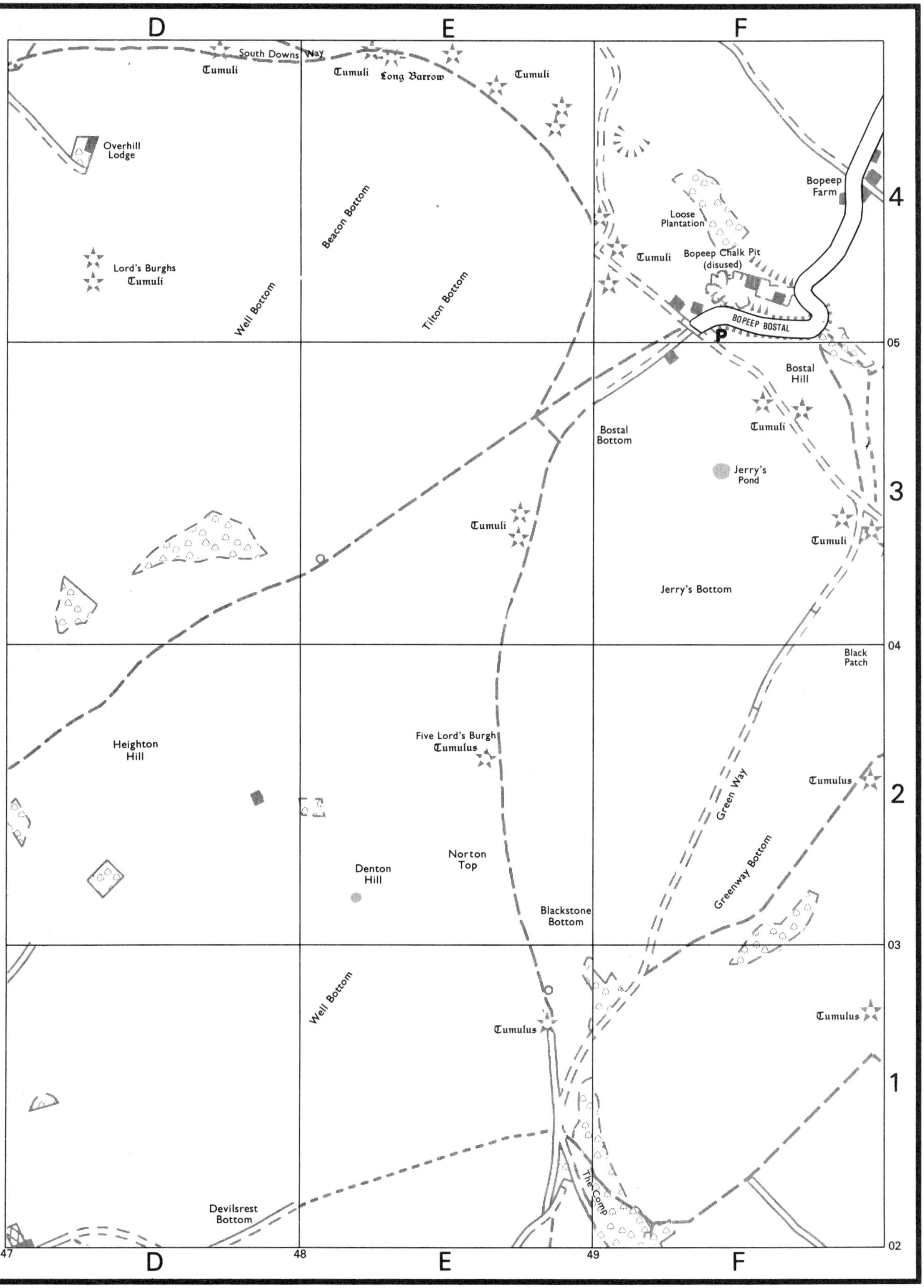
E
F
South Downs Way
Cumuli
Cumuli
Long Barrow
Cumuli
Overhill Lodge
Bopeep Farm
4
Loose Plantation
Beacon Bottom
Cumuli
Bopeep Chalk Pit (disused)
Lord's Burghs Cumuli
Tilton Bottom
Well Bottom
BOPEEP BOSTAL
P
05
Bostal Hill
Cumuli
Bostal Bottom
Jerry's Pond
3
Cumuli
Cumuli
Jerry's Bottom
04
Black Patch
172
Five Lord's Burgh Cumulus
Heighton Hill
Cumulus
2
Green Way
Norton Top
Greenway Bottom
Denton Hill
Blackstone Bottom
03
Well Bottom
Cumulus
Cumulus
1
The Comp
Devilsrest Bottom
02
47
48
49
D
E
F
181

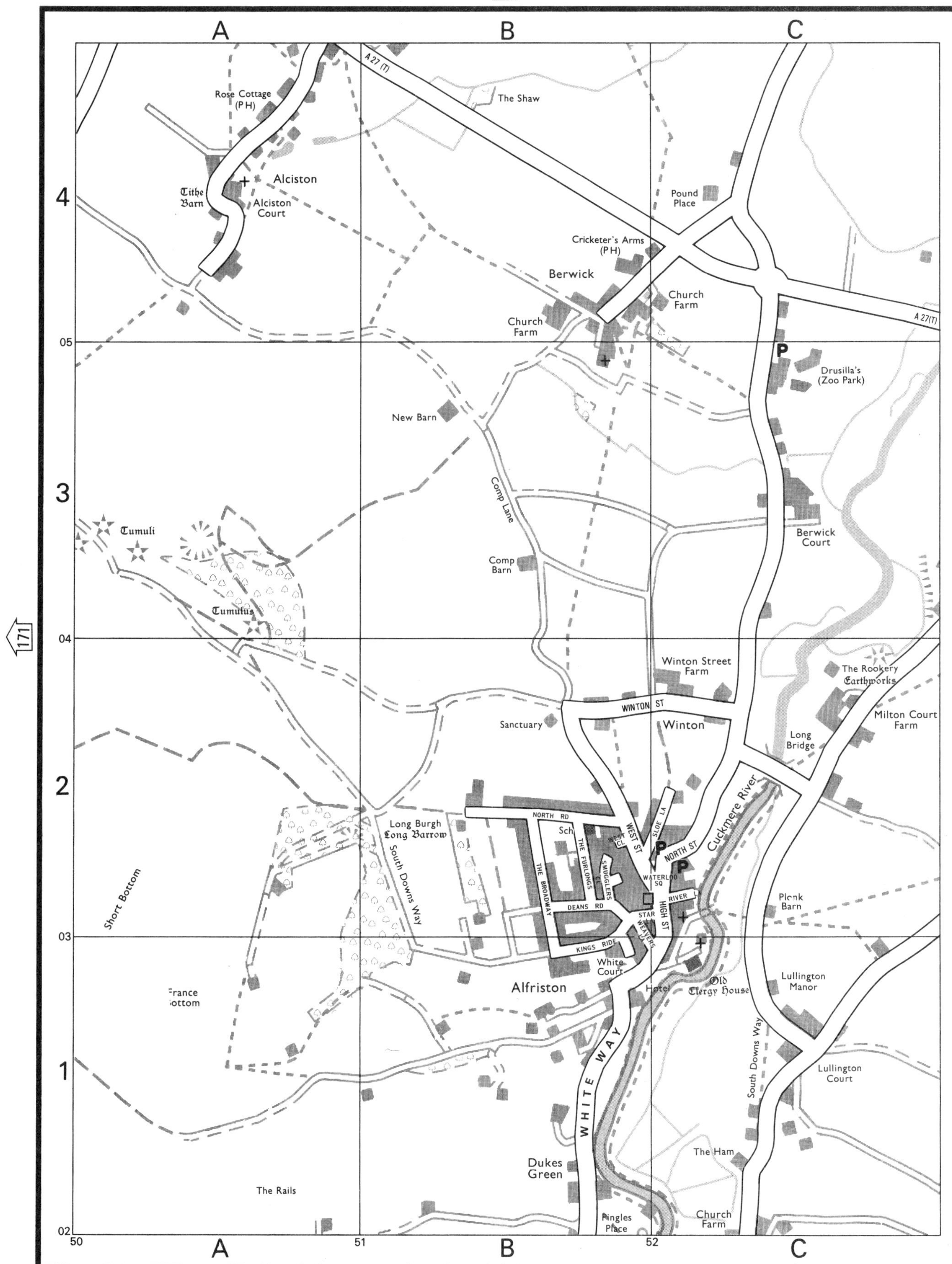
152
A
B
C
Rose Cottage (PH)
The Shaw
A 27 (T)
Alciston
Tithe Barn
Alciston Court
Pound Place
Cricketer's Arms (PH)
Berwick
Church Farm
Church Farm
A 27(T)
Drusilla's (Zoo Park)
New Barn
Comp Lane
Tumuli
Comp Barn
Berwick Court
Tumulus
171
Winton Street Farm
The Rookery
Earthworks
WINTON ST
Sanctuary
Winton
Milton Court Farm
Long Bridge
Cuckmere River
NORTH RD
Long Burgh
Long Barrow
South Downs Way
Sch
THE FURLONGS
WEST CL
WEST ST
SLOE LA
NORTH ST
SMUGGLERS CL
THE BROADWAY
WATERLOO SQ
Short Bottom
DEANS RD
STAR
RIVER LA
HIGH ST
Plonk Barn
KINGS RIDE
WEAVERS LA
White Court
Alfriston
Hotel
Old Clergy House
Lullington Manor
France Bottom
WHITE WAY
South Downs Way
Lullington Court
The Ham
Dukes Green
The Rails
Pingles Place
Church Farm
50
51
52
02
03
04
05
1
2
3
4
182

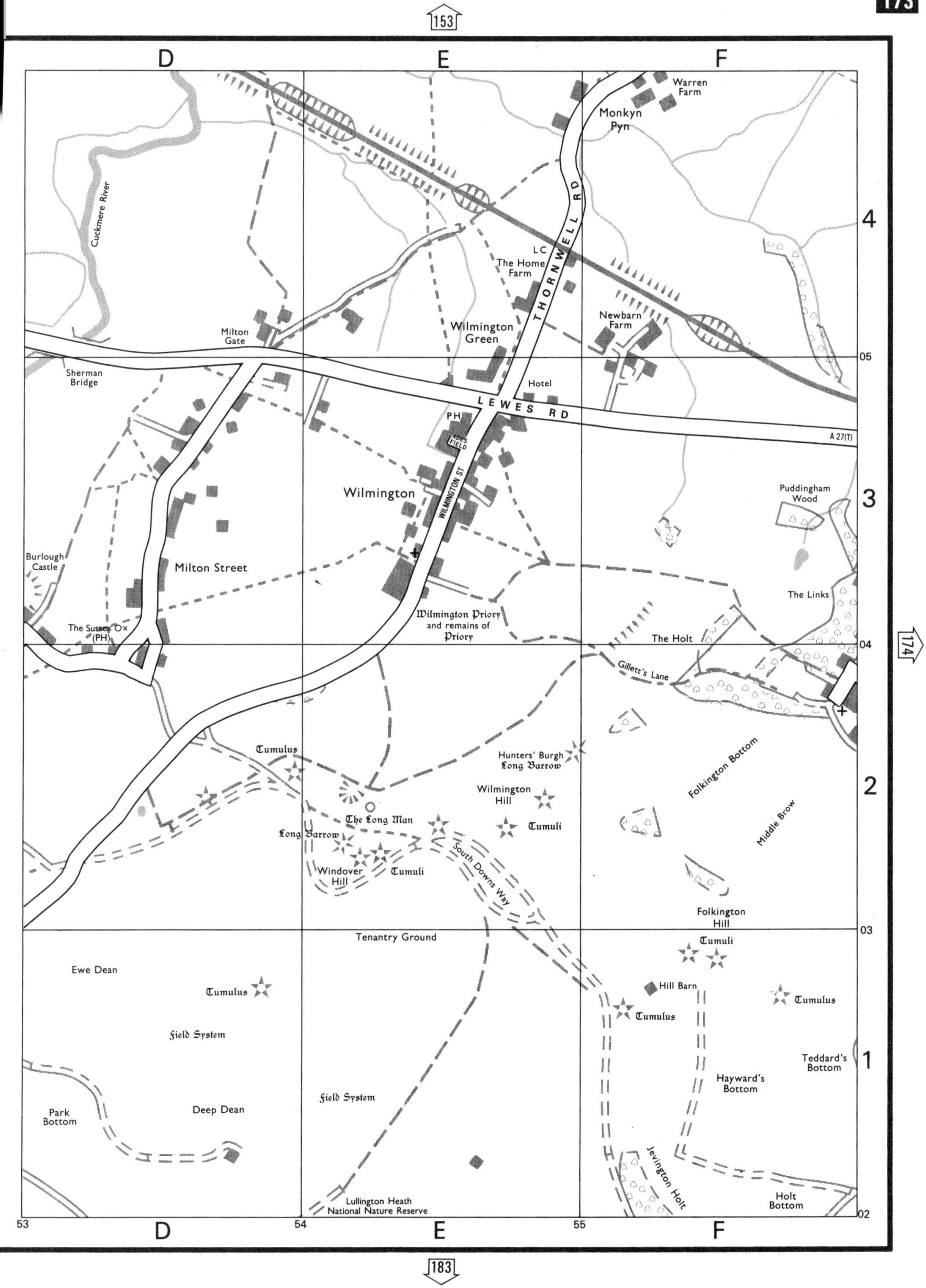

153
D
E
F
Warren Farm
Monkyn Pyn
Cuckmere River
THORNWELL RD
LC
The Home Farm
Newbarn Farm
Wilmington Green
Milton Gate
Sherman Bridge
Hotel
LEWES RD
PH
A 27(T)
Wilmington
WILMINGTON ST
Puddingham Wood
Burlough Castle
Milton Street
The Links
The Sussex Ox (PH)
Wilmington Priory and remains of Priory
The Holt
Gillett's Lane
Tumulus
Hunters' Burgh Long Barrow
Folkington Bottom
Wilmington Hill
The Long Man
Tumuli
Long Barrow
Middle Brow
Windover Hill
South Downs Way
Folkington Hill
Tenantry Ground
Ewe Dean
Field System
Hill Barn
Teddard's Bottom
Hayward's Bottom
Park Bottom
Deep Dean
Jevington Holt
Lullington Heath National Nature Reserve
Holt Bottom
53
54
55
02
03
04
05
1
2
3
4
174
183

154

A
B
C
4
3
2
1
05
04
03
02
56
57
58
Hide Farm
Bramley Farm
Cophall Farm
Cop Hall
Otteham Court
Remains of Abbey (Premonstratensian) founded 1180-7)
Wootton Manor
Polegate Honey Farm
LEWES RD
A 27(T)
The Flint House
The Stud Farm
The Rough
Folkington Manor Farm
FOLKINGTON RD
Wannock Coppice
Folkington Manor
Folkington
Windmill
Mornings Mill Farm
Foulride Green
Lower Willingdon
Wannock
School
Sch
Liby
Crane Down
Field System
Filching Manor
Dean Wood
Hanging Hill
Willingdon Links
Filching Quarry
Chalk Farm
The Combe
Tumulus
Tumuli
Tas Combe
Willingdon
Helling Down
Combe Hill
Neolithic Camp
POLEGATE BY-PS
WANNOCK RD
EASTBOURNE RD
JEVINGTON RD
HAILSHAM RD
STATION RD
PEVENSEY RD A 27(T)
HIGH ST
OTHAM COURT LA
SAYERLAND LA
BAY TREE LA
GORRINGE VALLEY RD
WANNOCK LA
HUGGETT'S LA
COOPERS HILL
CHURCH ST
BUTTS LA
A 22
Wannock Mill Stream

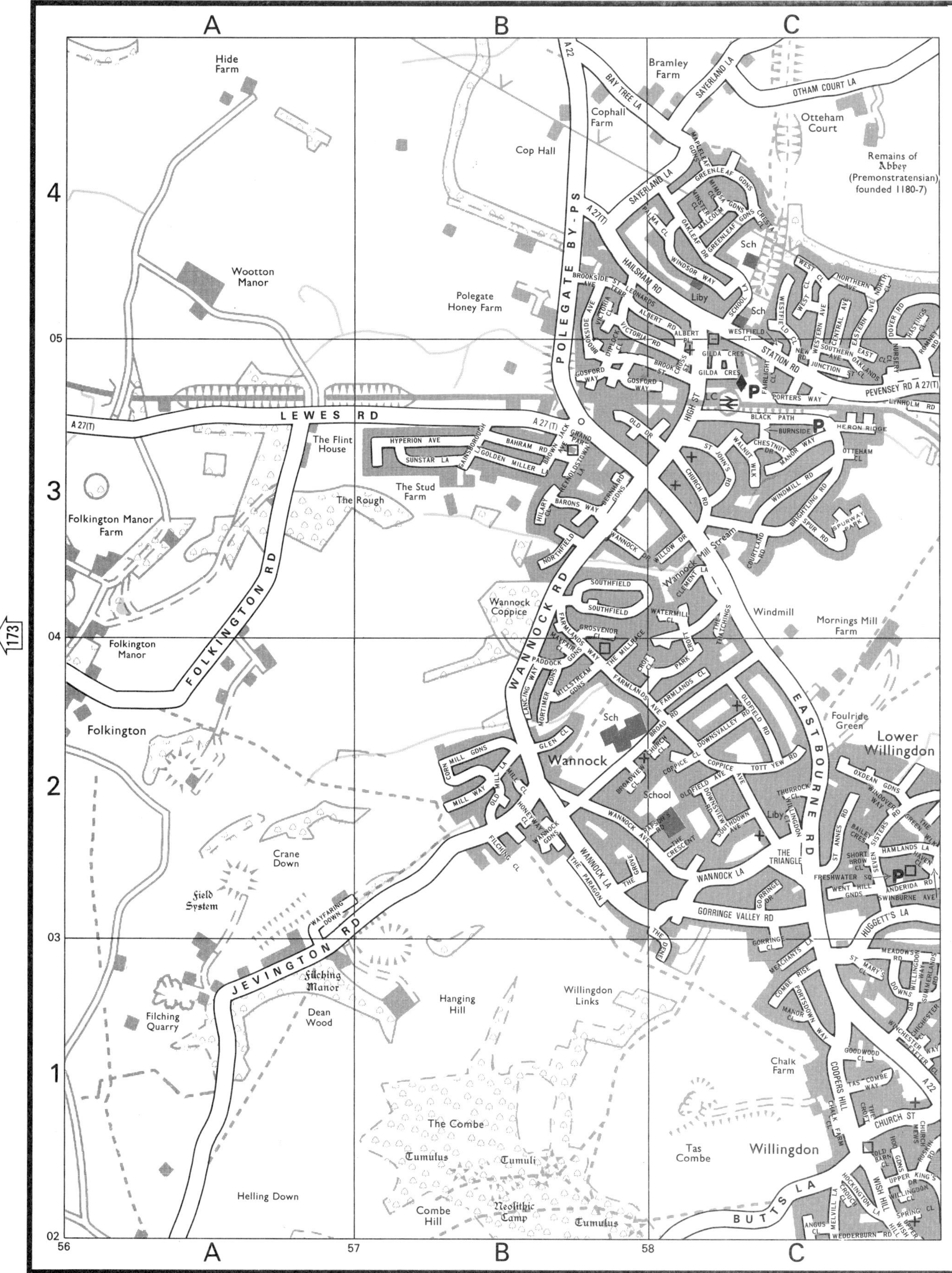

173

184

155

D
E
F
Priesthawes
Duck Puddle
SHEPHAM LA
Drockmill Hill Gut
Hankham
Hankham Cross
Nurseries
HAILSHAM RD
B2104
Sharnfold Cottages
Sharnfold
Ditton's Corner
PEVENSEY RD
Industrial Estate
Dittons
DITTONS RD
Under Construction
Blackness
Mill Ditch
Sewage Works
Dismantled Railway
Stone Cross
RATTLE RD A27(T)
The Red Lion Hotel
Hankham Place
Red Dyke House
Red Dyke Farm
Stone Cross Junction
LION HILL
New Stream Ditch
Willingdon & West Langney Sewer
Willingdon Upper
Middle Sewer
Shinewater Marsh
Friday Street
FRIDAY ST B2104
Hydneye Bridge
WILLINGDON DRO
Willingdon Levels
Willingdon Sewer
Highfield Industrial Estate (North)
Highfield Industrial Estate (South)
Hampden Park Station
Hampden Park
Schools
Sch
WILLINGDON PARK DR
EASTBOURNE RD
WILLINGDON RD A22
HUGGETTS LA
CHURCH ST
BRASSEY AVE
DECOY DR
1
2
3
4
59
60
61
02
03
04
05

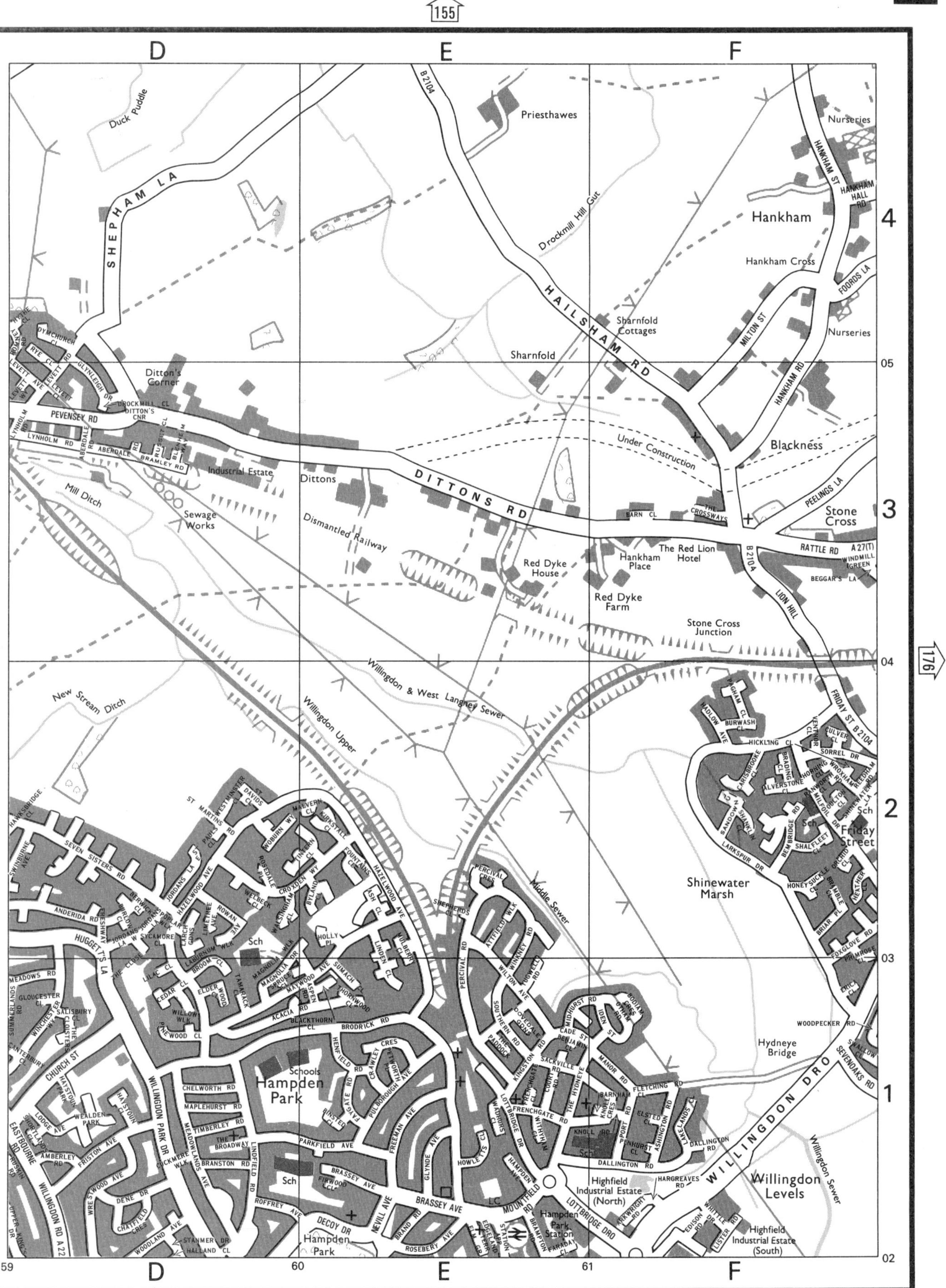

176

185

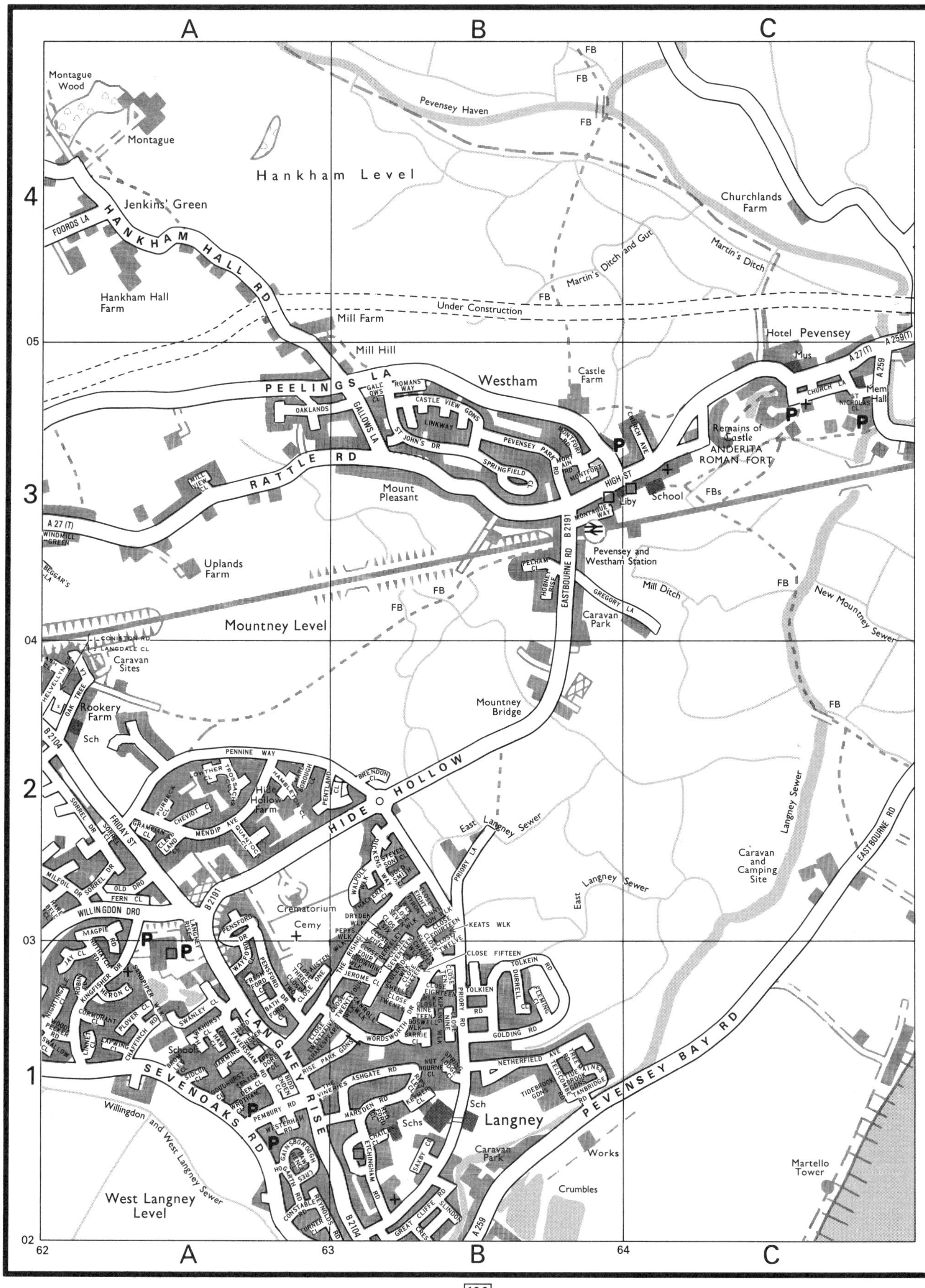
156
175
186
A
B
C
1
2
3
4
02
03
04
05
62
63
64
Montague Wood
Montague
Hankham Level
Jenkins' Green
FOORDS LA
HANKHAM HALL RD
Hankham Hall Farm
Pevensey Haven
FB
Churchlands Farm
Martin's Ditch and Gut
Martin's Ditch
Under Construction
Mill Farm
Mill Hill
Hotel Pevensey
Mus
A 259(T)
A 27(T)
A 259
CHURCH LA
Mem Hall
ST NICHOLAS CL
PEELINGS LA
GALLOWS LA
ROMANS WAY
CASTLE VIEW GDNS
LINKWAY
OAKLANDS
Westham
Castle Farm
ST JOHN'S DR
PEVENSEY PARK RD
SPRINGFIELD CL
MONTFORT RD
MONTFORT CL
CHURCH AVE
Remains of Castle
ANDERITA ROMAN FORT
RATTLE RD
MILL VIEW CL
Mount Pleasant
HIGH ST
Liby
School
FBs
MONTAGUE WAY
A 27 (T)
WINDMILL GREEN
B 2191
Pevensey and Westham Station
Uplands Farm
BEGGAR'S LA
PELHAM CL
HOBNEY RISE
EASTBOURNE RD
GREGORY LA
Mill Ditch
New Mountney Sewer
Mountney Level
Caravan Park
CONISTON RD
LANGDALE CL
Caravan Sites
HELVELLYN DR
OAK TREE LA
Rookery Farm
Sch
B 2104
Mountney Bridge
PENNINE WAY
BRENDON CL
HIDE HOLLOW
Hide Hollow Farm
PENTLAND CL
LOWTHER CL
TROSSACHS CL
PURBECK CL
CHEVIOT CL
HAMBLETON CL
GRAMPIAN CL
MENDIP AVE
QUANTOCK CL
CLEVELAND CL
SORREL DR
SORREL CL
FRIDAY ST
MILFOIL DR
OLD DRO
FERN CL
WILLINGDON DRO
B 2191
East Langney Sewer
PRIORY LA
Langney Sewer
EASTBOURNE RD
Caravan and Camping Site
Crematorium
Cemy
KEATS WLK
CLOSE FIFTEEN
TOLKEIN RD
DURRELL
FLEMING CL
PRIORY RD
TOLKIEN RD
GOLDING RD
MAGPIE
JAY CL
KINGFISHER DR
HERON CL
SANDPIPER WLK
CORMORANT CL
PLOVER CL
SWANLEY CL
CHAFFINCH RD
LAPWING CL
LINNET CL
Schools
PENSFORD DR
WAYFORD
BATH
LANGNEY RISE
THE RISING
JEROME CL
CLOSE TWENTY
WORDSWORTH DR
BOSWELL WLK
BARRIE CL
RISE PARK GDNS
NETHERFIELD AVE
TIDEBROOK GDNS
TANBRIDGE
PEVENSEY BAY RD
SEVENOAKS RD
FAVERSHAM RD
SIDCUP CL
GOUDHURST
TENTERDEN CL
WROTHAM
PEMBURY RD
THE VINERIES
ASHGATE RD
NUT BOURNE CL
MARSDEN RD
SPRING LODGE CL
Sch
Schs
Langney
Willingdon and West Langney Sewer
WESTERHAM
GAINSBOROUGH CRES
HOGARTH RD
CHAILEY
ETCHINGHAM RD
SAXBY CL
Caravan Park
Works
Martello Tower
Crumbles
West Langney Level
CONSTABLE
REYNOLDS RD
TURNER
B 2104
GREAT CLIFFE RD
SLINDON CRES
A 259
EASTBOURNE RD

157

D
E
F
Enclosure
A 259(T)
Wrenham Stream
Rockhouse Bank
Battery
Old Haven
Saltworks
Under Construction
Battery (site of)
Caravan Site
MOUNTNEY DR
TOWER CL
HAROLD CL
THE SQUARE
ARUNDEL CL
SUNSET CL
HAVEN CL
THE BOULEVARD
THE PARADE
WESTHAM DR
MARINE CL
MARINE AVE
CAMBER DR
SOUTH CL
CAMBER WAY
BROOKLAND CL
MARESFIELD DR
BEACHLANDS WAY
Beachlands
COAST RD
A 259
Pevensey Bridge Level
Pevensey Bay Station
WALLSEND RD
Salt Haven
PEBBLE RD
COBALD RD
WAVERLEY GDNS
BAY AVE
CHANNEL VIEW RD
THE PARADE
EASTBOURNE AVE
SEAVILLE DR
Pevensey Bay
PRIORY CL
BAY TERR
SEA RD
RICHMOND RD
NORTH RD
WARMINSTER RD
COLLIER RD
1 MARINE RD
2 MARINE TERR
CASTLE DR
EASTBOURNE RD
WESTERN RD
BAYTREE
PROMENADE
LEYLAND RD
ROSETTI RD
NORMAN RD
CASTLEROSS RD
VAL PRINSEPS RD
INNINGS DR
Martello Tower
GRENVILLE RD
TIMBERLAINE RD
MILLWARD RD
THE BEACHINGS
Caravan Park
GREY TOWER CARAVAN SITE
GREY TOWER BUNGALOWS
Pevensey Bay Sailing Club
Waller's Haven
Caravan Park
Normans' Bay Station
COASTGUARD COTTS
Normans' Bay
68
69
06
05
03
02
65
66
67
4
3
2
1

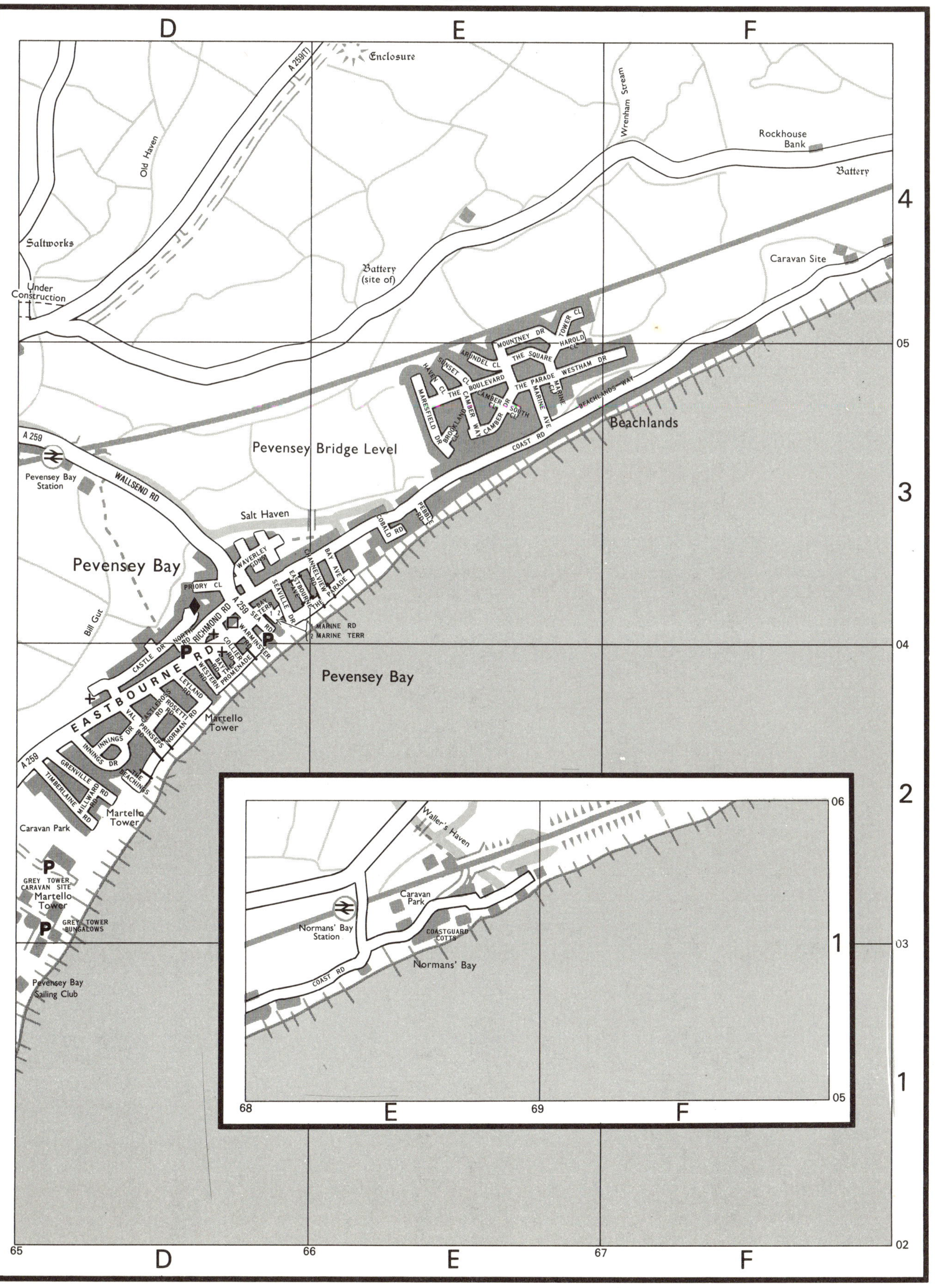

168

A
B
C
4
3
2
1
01
00
99
98
38
39
40
A 259 MARINE DR
CHICHESTER DR EAST
SALTDEAN PARK RD
UNDERCLIFF WLK
LONGRIDGE AVE
LYNWOOD RD
CROWBOROUGH RD
WALESBEECH RD
ARDINGLY RD
COWDEN RD
NUTLEY AVE
BANNINGS VALE
HAMSEY RD
ASHURST AVE
Telscombe Cliffs
SPRINGFIELD AVE
GRASSMERE AVE
GORHAM WAY
HIGHVIEW RD
TYEDEAN RD
BROOMFIELD AVE
CLIFF GDNS
FAIRLIGHT AVE
AMHURST RD
BUCKHURST RD
SOUTH COAST RD
17th Century House
SUSSEX WAY
THE ESPLANADE
TELSCOMBE CLIFFS WAY
CLIFTON WAY
CENTRAL AVE
ST PETER'S AVE
CHATSWORTH CL
AMBLESIDE AVE
PARK AVE
PARK VIEW RISE
Sch
LINCOLN AVE
THIRD RD
SECOND RD
CAIRO AVE
MALINES AVE
PHYLLIS AVE
HODDERN AVE
ROWE AVE
SUTTON AVE
BALCOMBE RD
LEA RD
LAKE DR
GREENWICH WAY
ARUNDEL RD
CAVELL AVE
RODERICK AVE
EDITH AVE
LINCOLN AVE S
CAIRO AVE S
MALINES AVE S
PROMENADE
UNDER CLIFF WLK
HORSHAM AVE
P

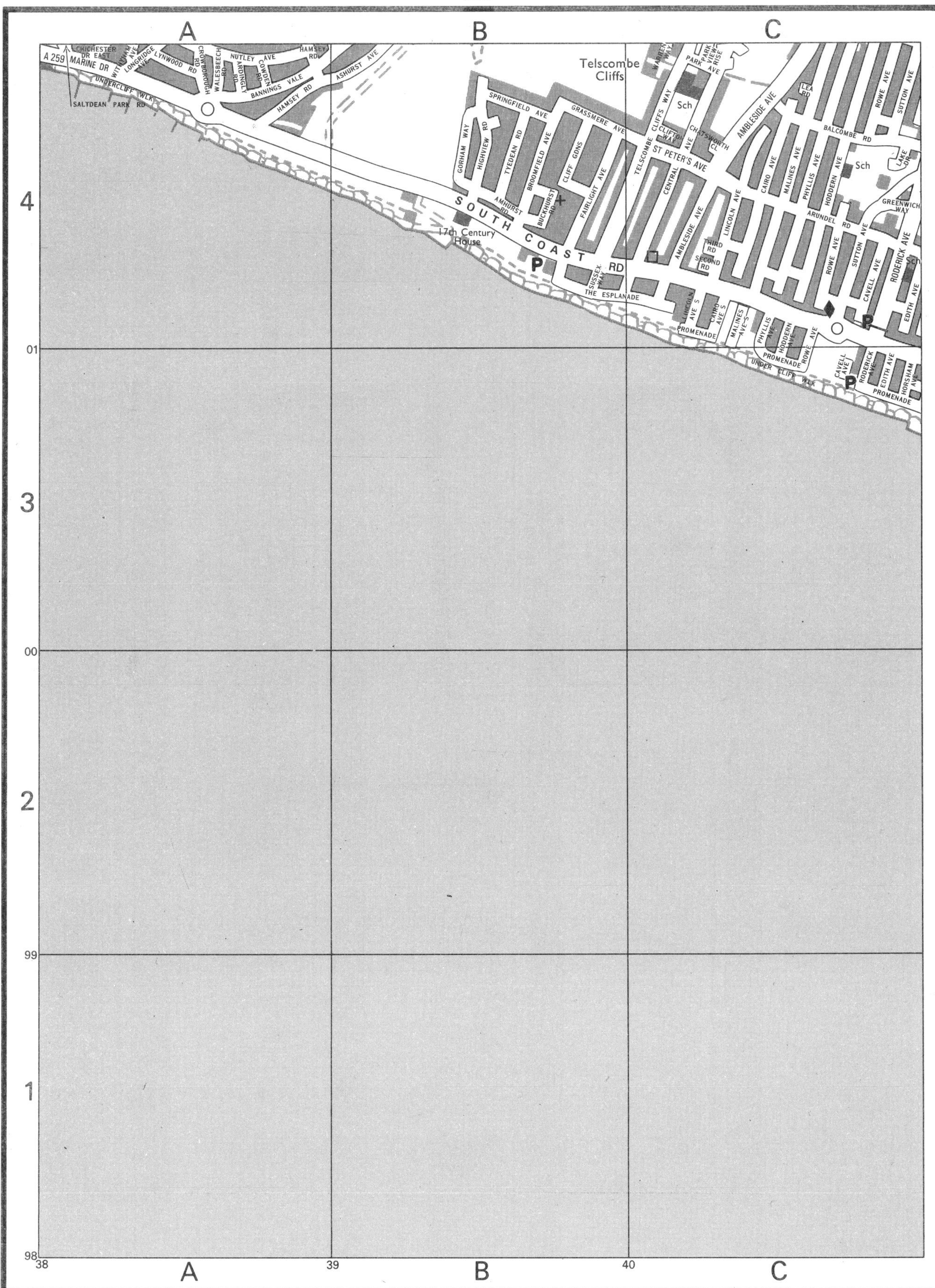

169

D
E
F
PEACEHAVEN
The Meridian Industrial Estate
Liby
Friars' Bay
Golf Course
Bollen's Bush
Sch
Hospl
Rushy Hill
Motel
Caravan Site
Peacehaven Heights
Chene Gap
Tumulus
Harbour Heights
SOUTH COAST RD
BRIGHTON RD
THE HIGHWAY
A 259
PROMENADE
LEWES RD
BUSH RD
FIRLE RD
CAVELL AVE
RODERICK AVE
EDITH AVE
HORSHAM AVE
DOROTHY AVE
BRAMBER AVE
SOUTHVIEW RD
VIEW RD
BEE RD
BRAMBER CL
NEWTON RD
HOYLE RD
GREENWICH WAY
JASON CL
DARION CL
RAYFORD CL
STEYNING AVE
VICTORIA AVE
BOLNEY AVE
CAPEL AVE
KEYMER AVE
SLINDON AVE
MAYFIELD AVE
PIDDINGHOE AVE
PIDDINGHOE CL
ARUNDEL RD
GLADYS AVE
SUNVIEW AVE
VERNON AVE
SOUTHDOWN AVE
SEAVIEW AVE
FRIARS' AVE
CORNWALL AVE
SEARLE AVE
CISSBURY AVE
HEADLAND CL
DOWNLAND AVE
CLIFF PARK CL
CHICHESTER CL
ROUNDHAY AVE
ASHINGTON GDNS
NEVILLE RD
JAY RD
YORK RD
BAYVIEW RD
WELLINGTON RD
PARK RD
LINKS AVE
CHENE RD
OUTLOOK AVE
BLAKENEY AVE
CRESTA RD
RINGMER RD
UPPER VALLEY RD
NORE RD
MARINE VIEW
NORTHDOWN RD
WESTERN RD
GIBBON RD
SOUTHDOWN CL
SOUTHDOWN RD
WILMINGTON RD
PEGLER AVE
HARBOUR VIEW RD
PENVENSEY RD
CHARLSTON AVE
CUCKMERE RD
WESTDEAN AVE
CORNELIUS AVE
HOATHDOWN AVE
VALLEY RD
CHESTNUT WAY
VALLEY DENE
ASH WLK
ELM CL
ROSE WLK
FULLWOOD AVE
KENNEDY WAY
LAPIERRE RD
METCALFE AVE
VALLEY RD
LEE WAY
VALLEY CL
41
42
43
01
00
99
98
1
2
3
4

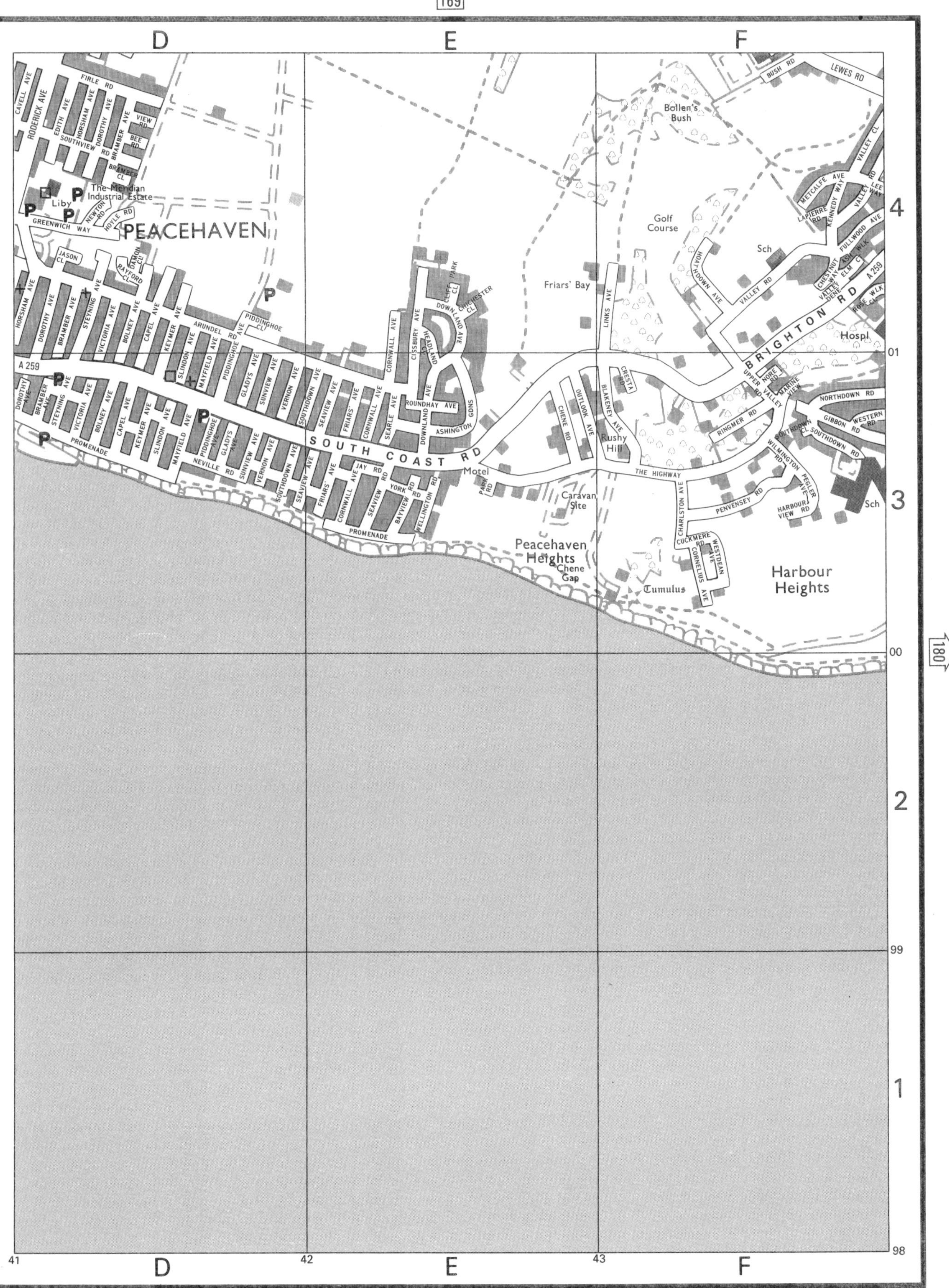

180

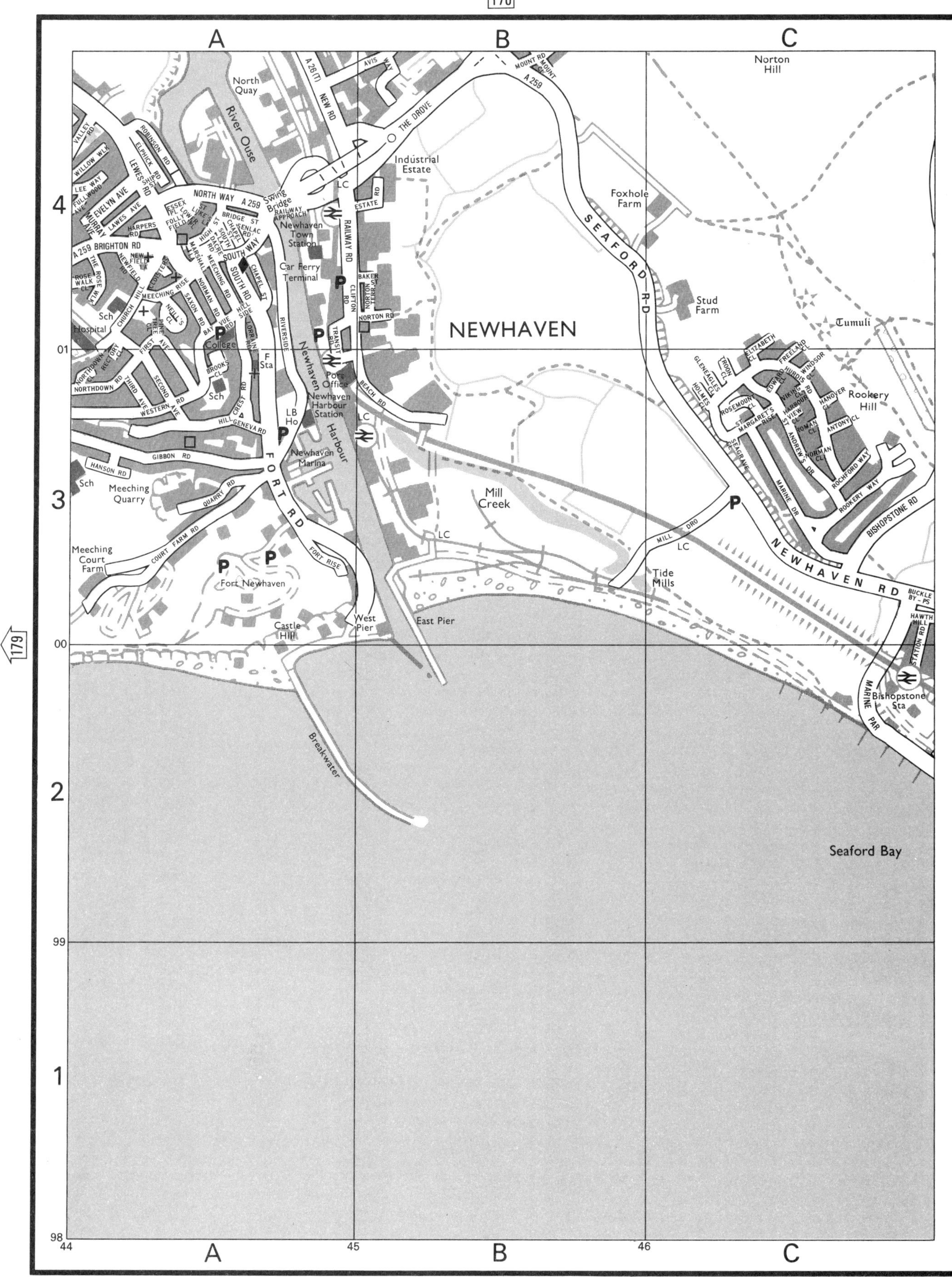
170
179
NEWHAVEN
North Quay
River Ouse
Swing Bridge
Newhaven Town Station
Car Ferry Terminal
Industrial Estate
Foxhole Farm
Stud Farm
Norton Hill
Tumuli
Rookery Hill
Newhaven Harbour Station
Newhaven Harbour
Newhaven Marina
Port Office
LB Ho
F Sta
College
Sch
Hospital
Meeching Quarry
Meeching Court Farm
Fort Newhaven
Castle Hill
West Pier
East Pier
Mill Creek
Tide Mills
Breakwater
Bishopstone Sta
Seaford Bay
SEAFORD RD
NEWHAVEN RD
FORT RD
NORTH WAY A 259
A 259 BRIGHTON RD
A 26 (T)
NEW RD
RAILWAY RD
THE DROVE
BEACH RD
MILL DRO
BISHOPSTONE RD
MARINE PAR
GIBBON RD
COURT FARM RD
HILL-GENEVA RD
LC

171

D
E
F
Norton
Beacon Hill
Norton Farm
Blackstone Barn
Golf Course
Rathfinny Farm
The Comp
Camp Hill
New Barn
Bullocks Barn
Bishopstone Manor Farm
Blatchington Reservoirs
Bishopstone
BISHOPSTONE RD
GRAND AVE
School
East Blatchington
FIRLE RD
Sch
HILL RISE
A 259
KINGSWAY
BUCKLE BY PS
CLAREMONT RD
ALFRISTON RD
Sutton
Offices
SUTTON RD
EASTBOURNE RD
SUTTON AVE
STEYNE RD
Recn Gd
Seaford Station
SEAFORD
Groynes
College
Martello Tower
Golf Links
Hawks Brow
CHYNGTON RD
F Sta
4
3
2
1
01
00
99
98
47
48
49

182

187

172

A
B
C
Rathfinny Farm House
Frog Firle
Follers Manor
Cow Lane
Litlington
PH
The Coombe
Tile Barn
Clapham Lane
Clapham House
New Bridge
Chamber's Court
Cradle Hill
Tumulus
Clapham Barn
High and Over
Alfriston Rd
Charleston Manor
South Downs Way
Brock Hole Down
Cuckmere River
Brock Hole Bottom
Westdean
Rectory
Ewe Down
Exceat
Dymock Farm
Eastbourne Rd
The Golden Galleon (PH)
A 259
Exceat Hill
Combe Bottom
Chyngton Farm
Newbarn Bottom
Seven Sisters Country Park
Walls Brow
Foxhole
Foxhole Bottom
Hard Link
South Hill
Landsdown Rd
Hillside Ave
Dymchurch Cl
Hythe Cres
Walmer Rd
Saltwood Rd
Chyngton Gdns
Chyngton La
Chyngton Way
South Way
Cuckmere Rd
Fairways Rd
Kingston Way
Ladycross Cl
Badgers Copse
Sch
Sycamore Cl
50
51
52
98
99
00
01
1
2
3
4

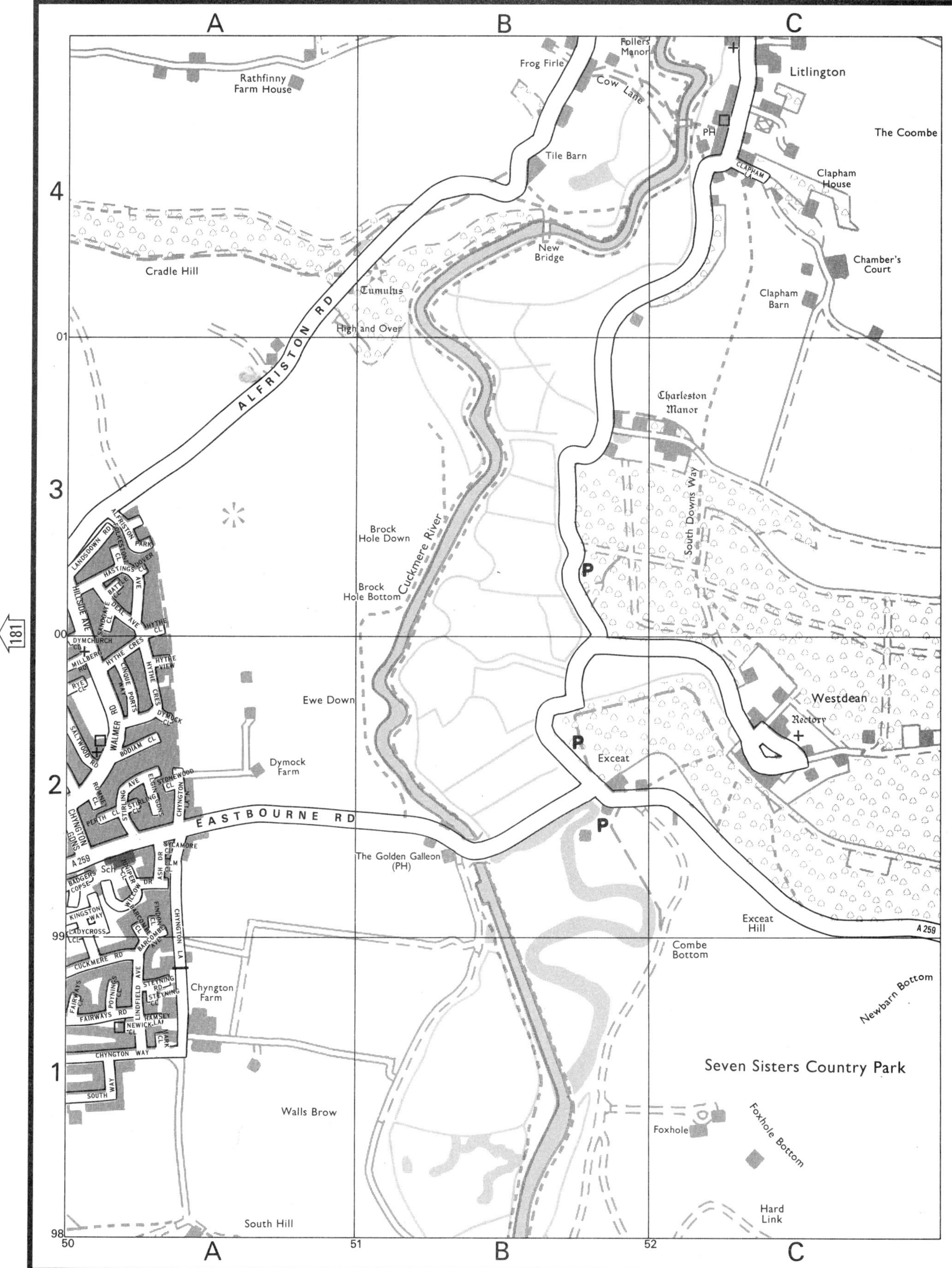

181

187

173

D
E
F
Oldkiln Bottom
South Downs Way
Tumuli
Fore Down
Lullington Heath
National Nature Reserve
4
Clay Bottom
Tumulus
Tumulus
01
Long
Barrow
Oxen Dean
3
Long Brow
Snap Hill
Charleston Bottom
00
Friston Forest
Beggar's
Croft
2
Middle Brow
Butchershole Bottom
P
New
Barn
Sewage
Works
Friston Hill
Friston Dencher
99
Friston
OLD WILLINGDON RD
FRISTON DOWNS
THE BROW
PEAKDEAN LA
Friston Place
Scabs
Island
Friston Bottom
PEAKDEAN CL
1
DENESIDE
THE RIDGEWAY
LINDON CL
WARREN CL
WARREN LA
Exceat
New Barn
Newbarn
Hill
THE OUTLOOK
ROYSTON CL
WINDMILL LA
MILL CL
FRISTON CL
DENE CL
HILLSIDE
South Hill
A 259
THE CLOSE
1 DOWNLANDS WAY
2 WENTHILL CL
MICHEL DENE RD
98
53
54
55
D
E
F

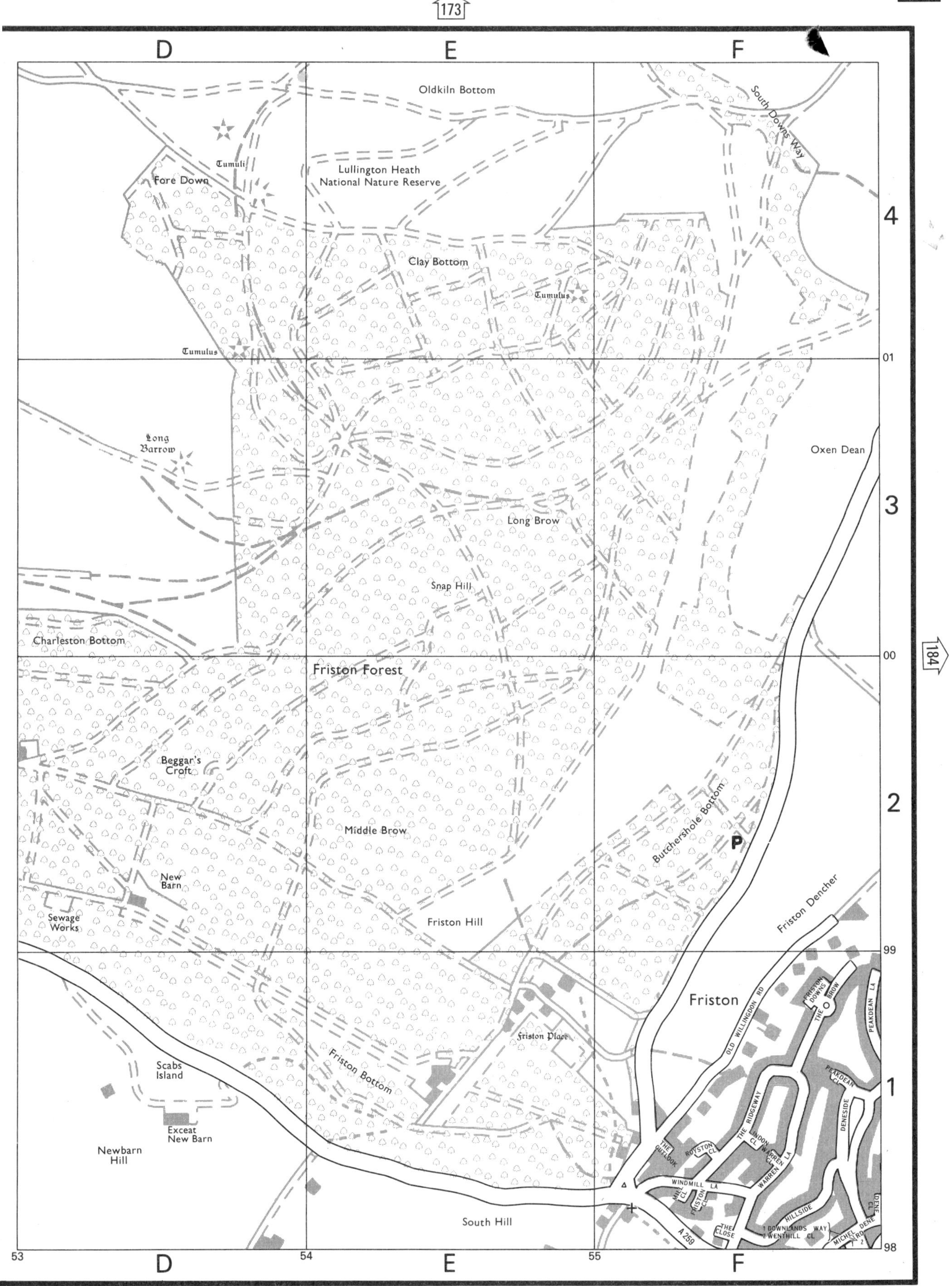

184

188

174

A
B
C
Green Lane
Home Bottom
Street Farm
The Eight Bells (PH)
Jevington Place
Jevington
JEVINGTON RD
CHURCH LA
WILLINGDON LA
P
Willingdon Bottom
Babylon Track
Field System
Cold Crouch
BUTTS LA
Babylon Down
Cumulus
Cumulus
OLD MANSION CL
DR
UPPER RATTON
MARCIA CL
BABYLON WAY
PARKWAY
BUCKHURST CL
UPPER WISH HILL
WISH HILL
MELVILL LA
THE CLOSE
WALNUT TREE WLK
MANOR WAY
THE GROVE
THE COMBE
RATTON DR
LINKWAY
Bourne Hill
Golf Course
SOUTHDOWN RD
FALMER CL
01
Harewick Bottom
Oxendean
Tumulus
Further Plantation
ROCKHURST DR
AVARD CRES
HAMSEY CL
GREENWAY
VICTORIA DR
DOWNS AVE
3
Duttle's Brow
Tumuli
Tumuli
Foxholes Brow
South Downs Way
Willingdon Hill
Duttle's Bottom
Fox Holes
HILL RD
BRACKEN RD
GORSE CL
COLWOOD CRES
MILLBROOK GDNS
FILCHING RD
LENNOX CL
PRIORY HTS
NORTH CRES
ROYAL SUSSEX CRES
CAVALRY CRES
COMMAND RD
THE CRESCENT
CENTRAL AVE
SOUTH AVE
MAYFIELD CL
BURROW DOWN CL
ABBEY RD
KIRK WAY
DEN HILL
THE SANCTUARY
BEECHY GDNS
BEECHY AVE
VICTORIA GDNS
00
Tumuli
Schs
LONGLAND RD
NORTHIAM RD
Eldon Bottom
Tumulus
2
The Peak
Beachy Brow
PEPPERCOMBE RD
OSBORNE RD
SANCROFT RD
MANVERS RD
CHERRY GARDEN RD
Crunden's Bottom
99
Golf Course
Youth Hostel
A 259
UPLAND RD
PASHLEY RD
Ringwood
Pea Down
Chapman's Bottom
1
PEAKDEAN LA
THE LINK
HIGH CL
MICHEL DENE RD
SUMMERDOWN LA
MICHEL DENE CL
MICHEL CL
ELVEN CL
ELVEN LA
WENT LA
Ringwood Bottom
New Barn
EAST DEAN RD
Pashley
B 2103
Tumuli
SUSSEX GDNS
DOWNS VIEW CL
DOWNS VIEW LA
A 259
Crapham Hill
98
56
57
58
183

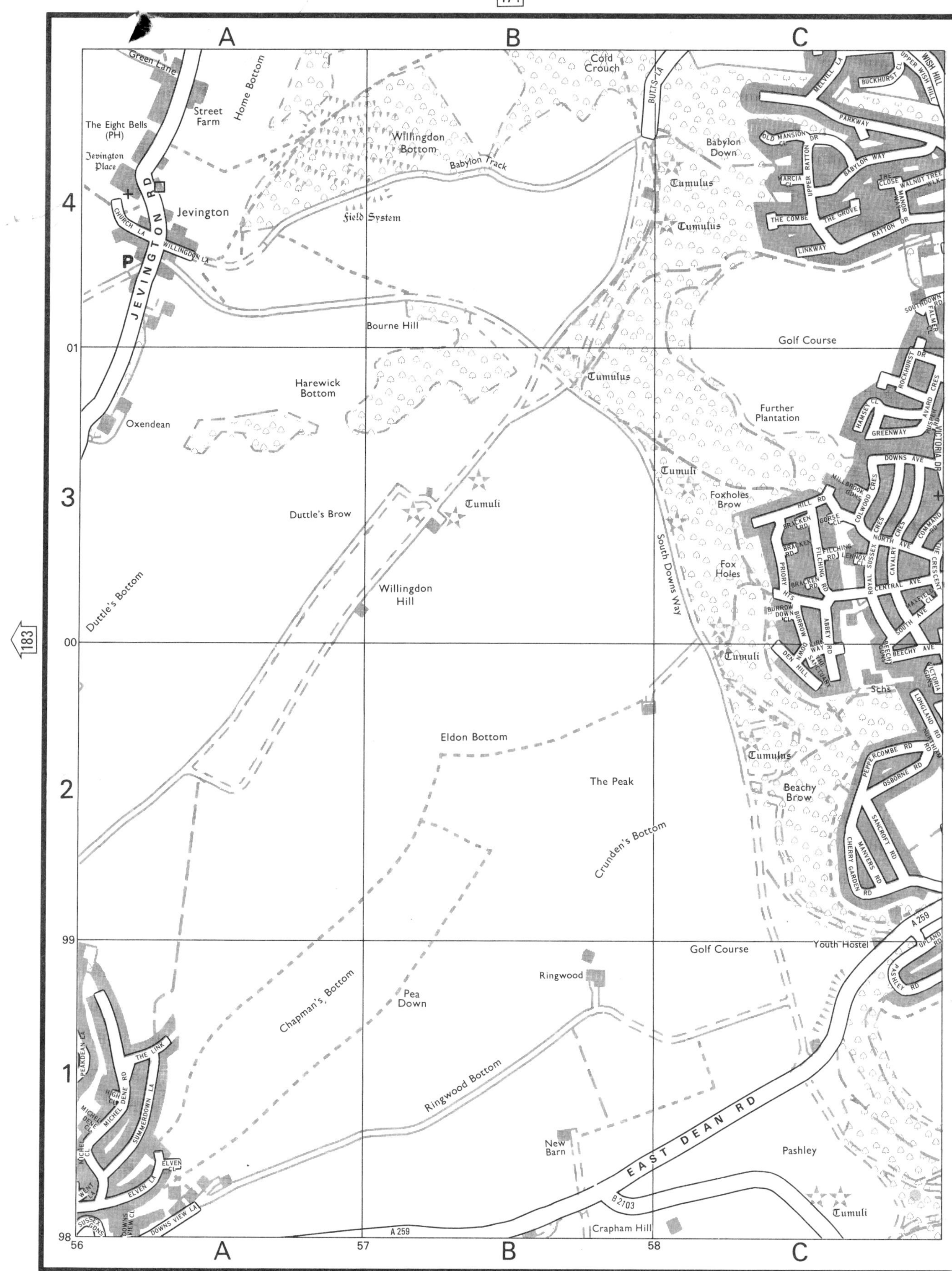

189

175

D
E
F
4
3
2
1
01
00
99
98
59
60
61
EASTBOURNE
Hampden Park
The Coppice
Ham Shaw
Indoor Tennis Centre
Brampton Road Trading Estate
Lott Bridge
LOTTBRIDGE DRO
Willingdon Sewer
Decoy Stream
Playing Fields
School
Willingdon Level
Lottbridge Sewer
College
Eastbourne Hospital
Southbourne Level
Horsey Sewer
Eastbourne Level
Upperton Farm
Schs
KING'S DR
WILLINGDON RD
VICTORIA DR
LEWES RD
Upperton
Downside
Cemy
Hospl
UPPER AVE
UPPERTON RD
THE GOFFS
Old Town
Art Gallery
Gildredge Park
Hospital
Eastbourne Station
Arndale Centre
TERMINUS RD
GRAND PARADE
MEADS RD
The Links (Golf Course)
Compton Place
Compton Park
Paradise Plantation
Tumulus
Tumuli
South Downs Way
Wish Tower (Martello Tower)
KING EDWARD'S PAR
SOUTH CLIFF
Law Courts
Coll
Sch
Liby
F Sta
Amb Sta
Wks

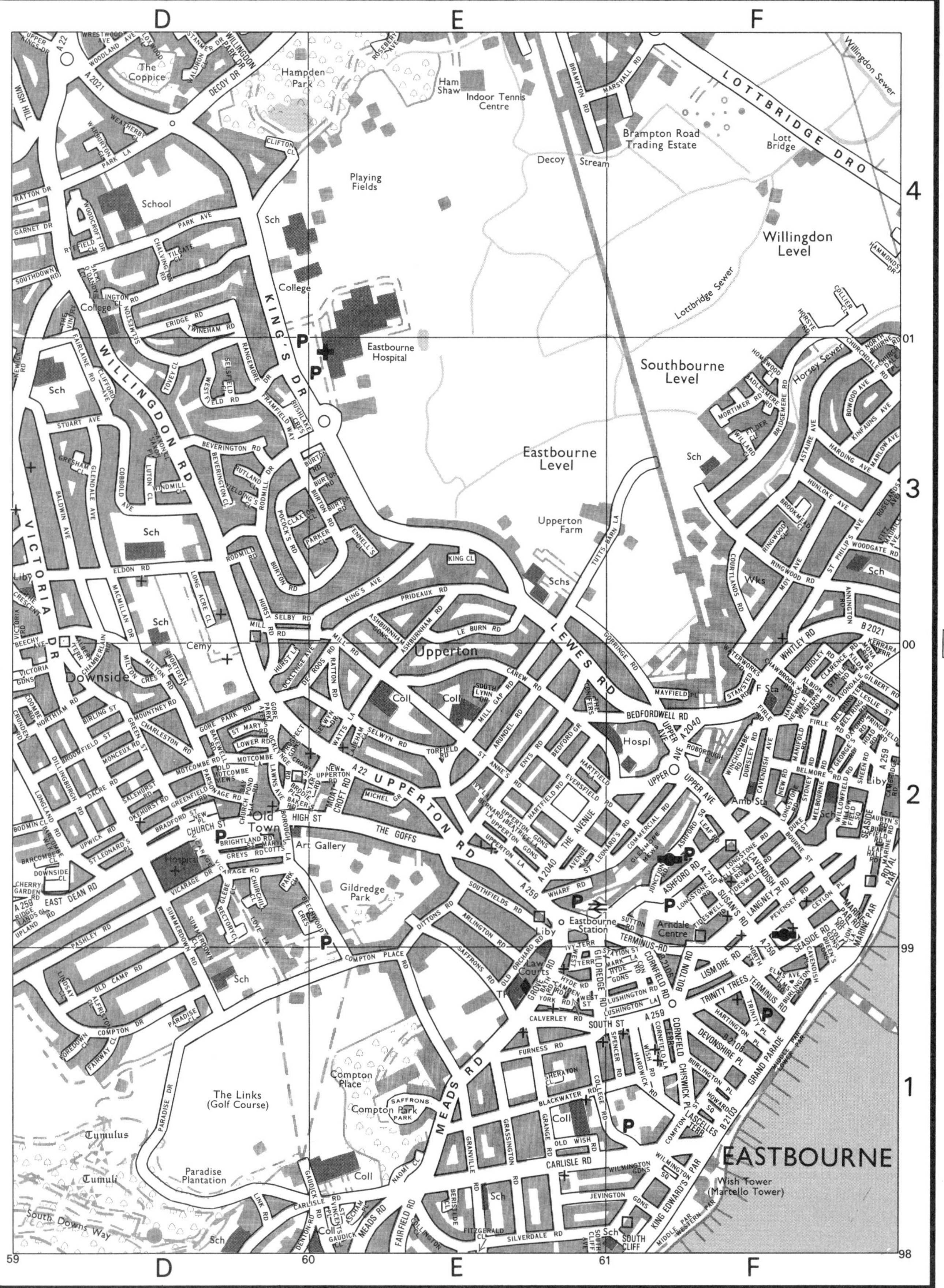

186

190

176

A
B
C
Langney Sewer
Langney Bridge
St Anthony's Hill
Holiday Park
Crumbles
Old Tollgate Bridge
Martello Tower
Langney Point
Princes Park
Roselands
The Redoubt
LB Ho
PRINCES RD
LOTTBRIDGE DRO
PRINCE WILLIAM PAR
ROYAL PAR
SEASIDE
PROMENADE
1 DELAVALL WLK
2 KEITH WLK
1 WARRIOR SQ
2 ST JAMES RD
4
3
2
1
01
00
99
98
62
63
64

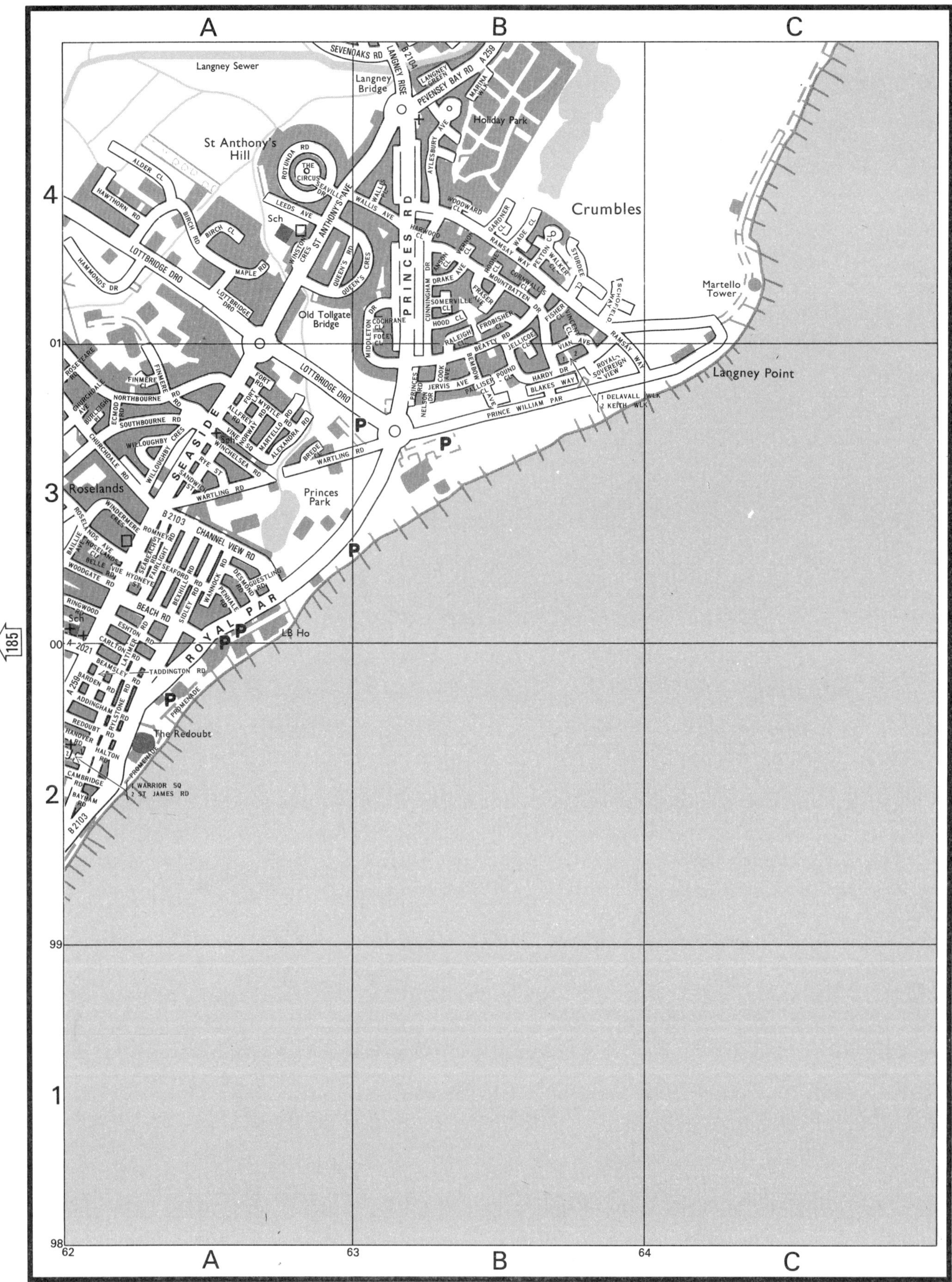

185

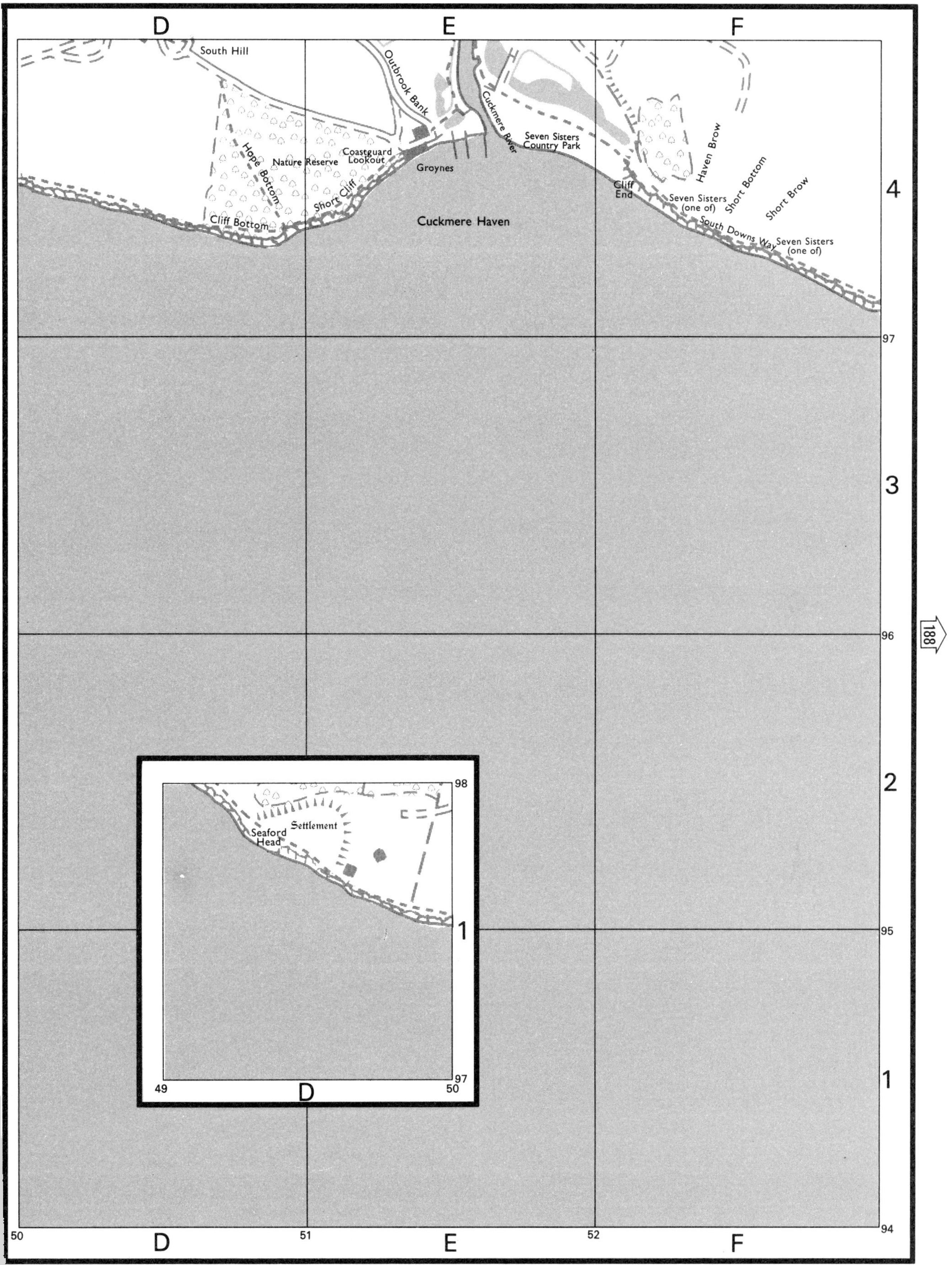
182
D
E
F
South Hill
Outbrook Bank
Cuckmere River
Seven Sisters
Country Park
Hope Bottom
Nature Reserve
Coastguard
Lookout
Groynes
Short Cliff
Cliff Bottom
Cuckmere Haven
Cliff
End
Haven Brow
Short Bottom
Short Brow
Seven Sisters
(one of)
South Downs Way
Seven Sisters
(one of)
4
97
3
96
188
2
95
1
94
Settlement
Seaford
Head
98
1
97
49
D
50
50
D
51
E
52
F

183

A
B
C
Gayles
P
A 259
Hobb's Eares
Hall
UPPER ST
WAYSIDE
WENTHILL CL
PH
LOWER ST
CHURCHFIELD
Sch
WENT WAY
The Fridays
East Dean
GILBERTS DR
Limekiln Bottom
Crowlink
4
Rough Brow
Rough Bottom
Gap Bottom
Crowlink
East Dean
Flagstaff Brow
Seven Sisters (one of)
Brass Point
97
Seven Sisters (one of)
Flagstaff Bottom
Baily's Hill
Flat Hill
Birling Farm
Went Hill
Flagstaff Point
Mon
Seven Sisters (one of)
Flathill Bottom
Tumuli
Michel Dean
BIRLING GAP RD
Seven Sisters (one of)
Mon
3
Seven Sisters (one of)
South Downs Way
The Wish
Birling Gap
Hotel
96
P
Coastguard Station
Tumulus
2
95
1
94
53
54
55
A
B
C

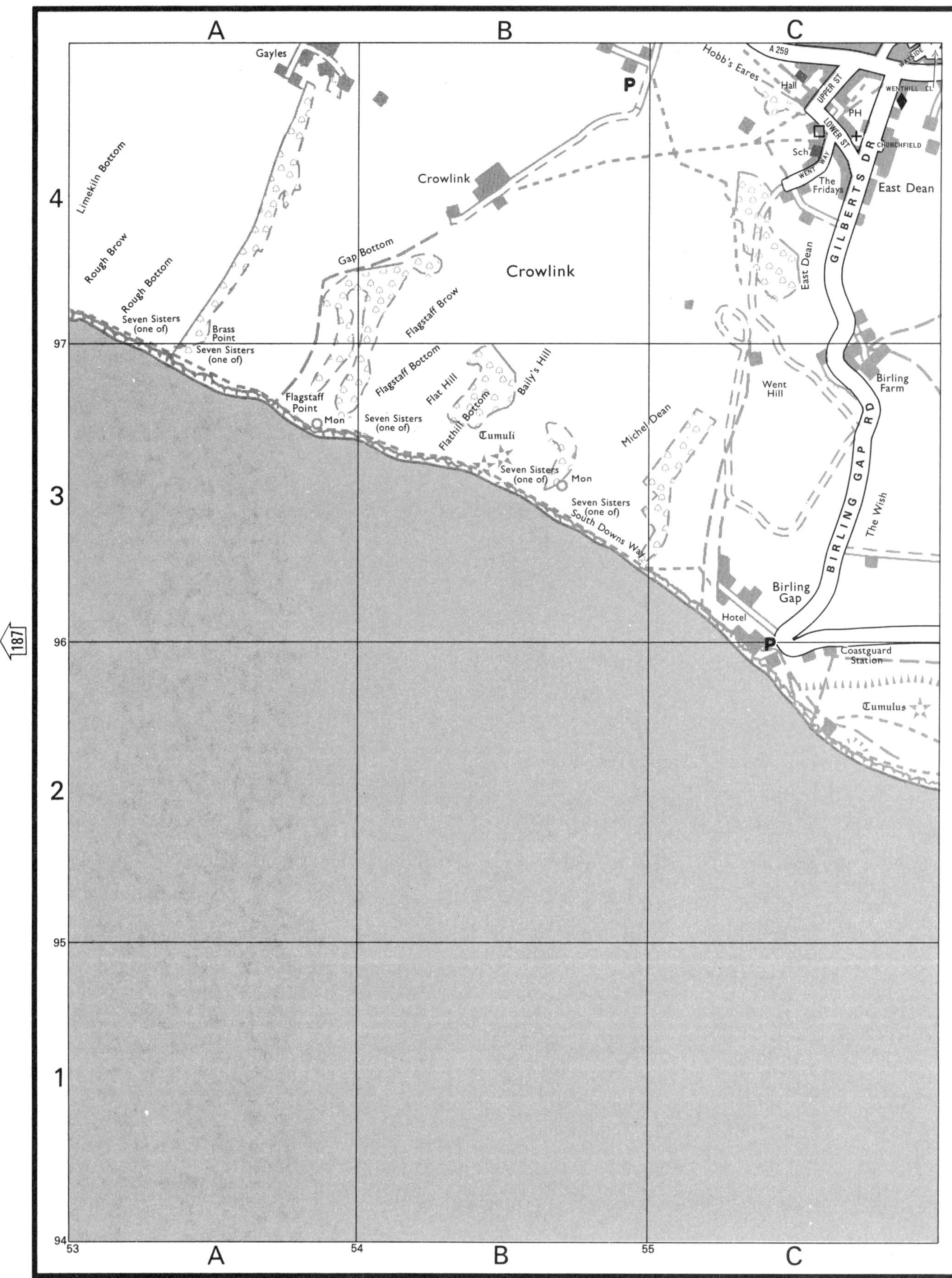

187

184

D
E
F
WENTHILL CL
DOWNS VIEW LA
A 259
EAST DEAN RD
A 259
Eastdean Down
Field System
Mill Down
New Barn
Bramble Bottom
Crapham Barn
Crapham Down
Crapham Bottom
B 2103
P
Warren Hill
Middle Brow
Black Robin Farm
Black Robin Bottom
East Hale Bottom
Wigden's Bottom
Long Down
Tumulus
Kiln Combe
Cornish Farm
Bullockdown Farm
Bullock Down
Sweet Brow
Heathy Brow
Bulling Dean
Frost Hill
Field System
West Brow
Horseshoe Plantation
Tumulus
Hod Combe
Hodcombe Farm
The Beachy Head (PH)
The Chalet Natural History Centre
Belle Tout
Shooters' Bottom
South Downs Way
4
97
3
96
2
95
1
94
56
57
58

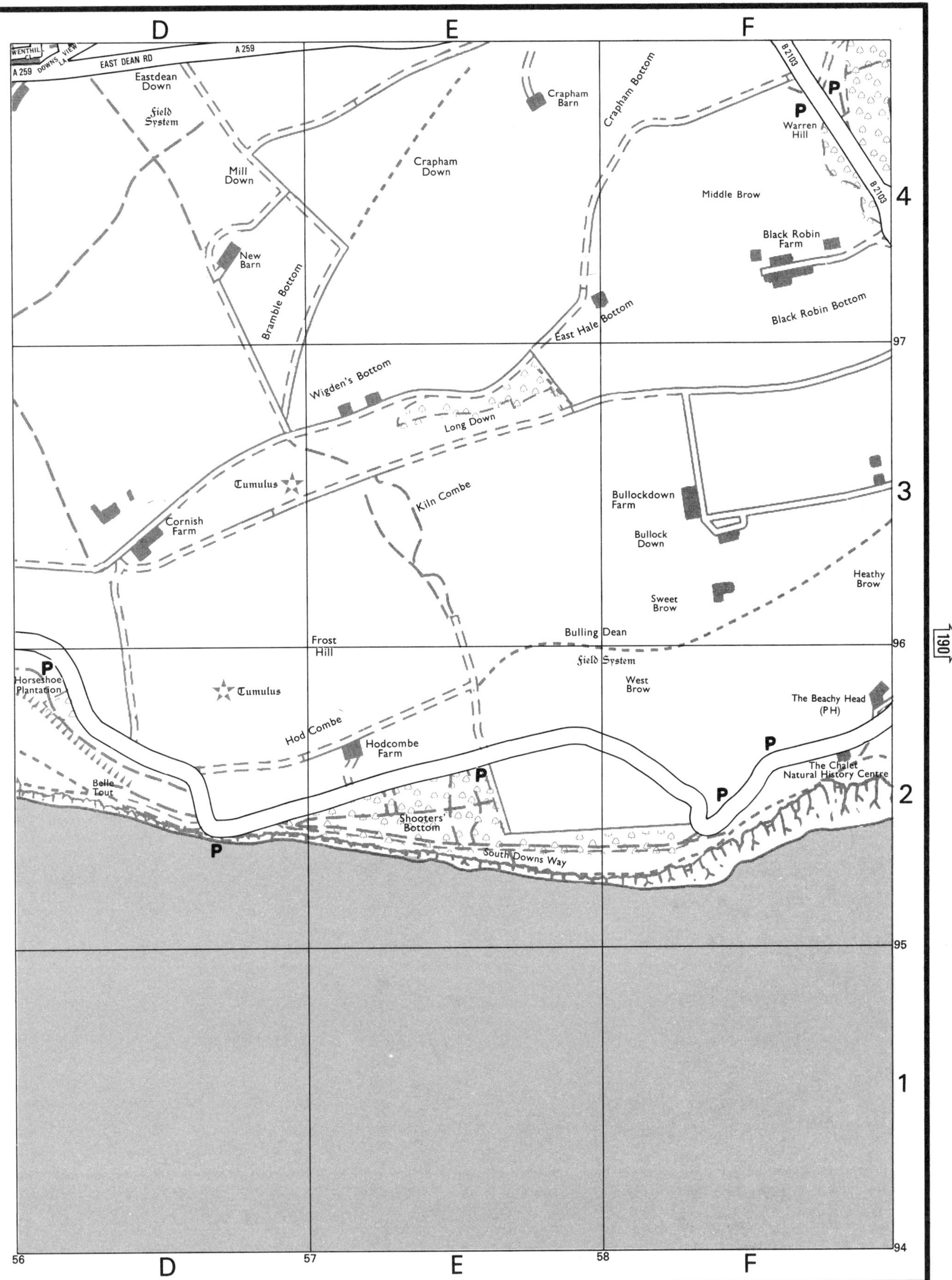

190

185

189

A
B
C
School
Warren
Meads
Beachy Head Rd
B 2103
Brighton Polytechnic
Hospital
Sch
Tumulus
Well Combe
Tumili
The Helen Garden
Holywell Retreat
The Pound
Holywell
Holywell Ledge
South Downs Way
Whitebread Hole
Cow Gap
Beachy Head
Head Ledge
King Edward's Par
Duke's Dr
Foyle Way
Meads Rd
Staveley Rd
Chesterfield Rd
Darley Rd
St John's Rd
Upper Carlisle Rd
Carlisle Rd
Denton Rd
Salisbury Rd
Cranborne Ave
Warren Cl
Baslow Rd
Rowsley Rd
Edensor Rd
Wellcombe Cres
Upper Duke's Dr
Holywell Cl
Buxton Rd
Bolsover Rd
South Cliff
Fairfield Rd
Milnthorpe Rd
Dalton Rd
Derwent Rd
Matlock Rd
Coltstocks Rd
The Village
Meads Brow
Rochester Cl
Wells Cl
Lincoln Cl
Hyde Tynings Cl
St Gregory Cl
Granville Rd
Jephson Cl
Ascot Cl
Ravenscroft
Chatsworth Gdns
Holbrook Cl
Middle Western Par
Tumulus
P
4
3
2
1
97
96
95
94
59
60
61

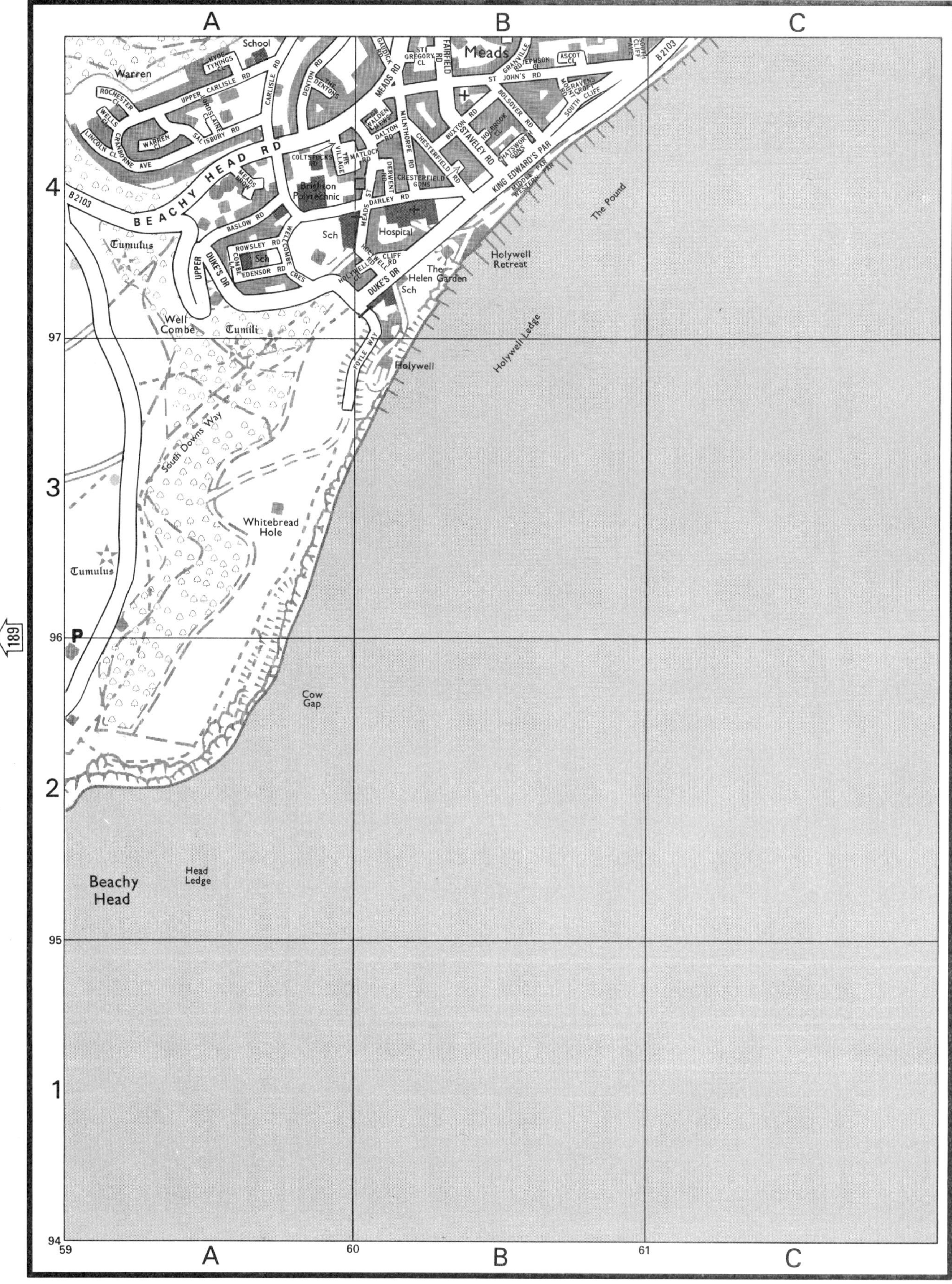

USER'S NOTES

EXPLANATION OF THE STREET INDEX REFERENCE SYSTEM

Street names are listed alphabetically and show the locality, the map page number and a reference to the square in which the name falls on the map page.

Example:	West St. Dit..*101* D2
West St.	This is the full street name, which may have been abbreviated on the map.
Dit	This is the abbreviation for the town, village or locality in which the street falls.
101	This is the page number of the map on which the street name appears.
D2	The letter and figure indicate the square on the map in which the centre of the street falls. The square can be found at the junction of the vertical column carrying the appropriare letter and the horizontal row carrying the appropriate figure.

ABBREVIATIONS USED IN THE INDEX

Road Names

Approach	App
Avenie	Ave
Broadway	Bwy
By-Pass	By-Ps
Causeway	Cswy
Common	Comm
Corner	Cnr
Cottages	Cotts
Court	Ct
Crescent	Cres
Drive	Dri
Drove	Dro
East	E
Gardens	Gdns
Grove	Gr
Heights	Hts
Lane	La
North	N
Orchard	Orch
Parade	Par
Passage	Pas
Place	Pl
Pleasant	Plea
Precinct	Prec
Promenade	Prom
Road	Rd
South	S
Square	Sq
Street, Saint	St
Terrace	Terr
Walk	Wlk
West	W
Yard	Yd

Towns, Villages and Rural Localities

Albourne Alb 99 D3
Alciston Alc 172 A4
Alfriston Alfn 172 B1
Arlington Arl 153 E2
Ashurst (Langton Green) Asht 6 A1
Ashurst Wood Ash W 13 E3
Barcombe Bar 104 B1
Barcombe Cross Bar C 104 B2
Battle Bat 115 D3
Beckley Bec 69 F2
Beddingham Bed 150 A2
Bells Yew Green Bel G 19 E3
Berwick Ber 172 B4
Bexhill Bex 159 F2
Bishopstone Bis 181 D4
Blackboys Blas 81 F3
Blackham Blam 5 F2
Boarshead Boa 28 A3
Bodiam Bod 67 E4
Bodle Street Green Bod G 112 A1
Boreham Street Bor S 135 E2
Brede Bre 91 F1
Brightling Bril 87 D3
Brighton Bri 165 F2
Broad Oak (Heathfield) Bro O 61 E1
Broad Oak (Westfield) Bro O W 91 F2
Buckland Hill Buc 20 C1
Burgess Hill Bur H 74 C3
Burwash Bur 63 F3
Burwash Common Bur C 62 C2
Buss's Green Bus G 20 C1
Buxted Bux 57 F2
Cackle Street Cac S 37 E1
Cade Street Cad S 84 B3
Camber Cam 96 B2
Catsfield Cat 137 E4
Chailey Chay 77 E2
Chalvington Chal 152 C4
Chelwood Common Che Co 36 A3
Chelwood Gate Che G 36 A4
Chiddingly Chi 108 B1
Chiddingstone Hoath Chi H 6 A4
Churches Green Chur 111 F4
Clayton Clay 123 E4
Cliff End C End 142 C4
Coghurst Cog 141 D3
Coleman's Hatch Col H 25 E4
Cooksbridge Coo 126 C4
Cousley Wood Cou W 32 A4
Cowbeech Cowb 110 C1
Cowden Cowd 4 C3
Crawley Down Cra D 11 D4
Cripp's Corner Cri C 90 A4
Cross in Hand Cro H 82 C4
Crowborough Cro 27 F1
Crowhurst Crow 138 B3
Dallington Dal 86 A2
Danehill Dan 35 F2
Ditchling Dit 101 E2
Domewood Dom 1 A3
Dormansland Dor 2 C4
Dormans Park Dor P 2 B3
Earl's Down Ear D 85 F2
Eastbourne East 185 F1
East Chiltington E Chi 102 C1
East Dean E Dean 188 C4
East Grinstead E Gri 2 B1
East Guldeford E Gul 95 E4
East Hoathly E Hoa 107 F3
Eridge Green Eri G 17 F2
Etchingham Etc 46 A1
Etchingwood Etcd 58 A1
Ewhurst Green Ewh G 67 F3
Fairlight Fai 142 B3
Fairwarp Fair 37 F1
Falmer Fal 147 D3
Felbridge Fel 1 C2
Five Ashes Five A 59 F3
Fletching Fle 55 F2
Flimwell Fli 34 A2
Folkington Fol 174 A2
Fordcombe Ford 6 C3
Forest Row For R 13 F1
Four Oaks Four O 70 A3
Four Throws Four T 48 A4
Framfield Fra 80 C3
Frant Frant 19 D2
Friar's Gate Fri G 26 C4
Friston Fri 183 F1
Glynde Gly 150 B4
Golden Cross Gol C 131 E3
Groombridge Gro 16 C4
Guestling Green Gue G 141 F4
Hadlow Down Had D 59 D3
Hailsham Hai 155 D4
Halland Hall 107 D3
Hammerwood Hamm 3 F2
Hamsey Ham 127 D3
Hankham Hank 175 F4
Hartfield Hart 15 D2
Hassocks Hass 100 B2
Hastings Hast 162 B3
Haywards Heath Hay H 52 B3
Heathfield Hea 83 F4
Hellingly Hel 132 C3
Herstmonceux Hers 134 B3
Highbrook Higk 22 B1
High Hurstwood H Hur 38 C1
Hooe Hooe 158 A4
Horam Hor 109 E4
Horsted Keynes Hor K 35 D2
Hove Hove 164 C3
Hurst Green Hur G 46 C2
Hurstpierpoint Hur 99 E3
Icklesham Ick 119 E3
Iden Iden 71 F2
Iford Iford 148 C2
Isfield Isf 105 E4
Jevington Jev 184 A4
Keymer Key 100 C2
Kingstone near Lewes Kin L 148 B3
Kipping's Cross Kip 10 C2
Lamberhurst Lam 21 F3
Langton Green Lan G 7 E2
Laughton Lau 130 A4
Lewes Lew 127 D1
Litlington Litl 182 C4
Little Bayham Lit B 20 B2
Little Horsted Lit H 80 A1
Lower Dicker Low D 132 A2
Lower Horsebridge Low H 132 B2
Lower Willingdon Low W 174 C2
Lunsford's Cross Lun C 137 E1
Lydd Lydd 98 C3
Magham Down Mag D 133 E2
Maresfield Mar 56 C3
Mark Cross Mar C 29 F2
Mayfield May 41 F1
Mill Corner Mill C 68 C2
Milton Street Milt S 173 D3
Mountfield Mou 88 C3
Netherfield Net 88 A1
New Cut New Cut 117 E3
Newenden Newd 50 A2
Newhaven Newh 180 B4
Newick Newk 78 A4
Ninfield Nin 136 C3
Normans' Bay Nor B 177 E1
Northbridge Street N St 65 F3
North Chailey N Cha 77 E4
Northiam Norm 68 C3
Norton Nort 181 D4
Nutley Nut 37 D2
Offham Off 126 B3
Ovingdean Oving 167 E2
Oxley's Green Oxl G 87 E4
Peacehaven Pea 179 D4
Peasmarsh Peas 70 C1
Pell Green Pel G 31 F4
Pembury Pem 10 A3
Penhurst Pen 113 E3
Pett Pett 142 B4
Pevensey Pev 176 C4
Pevensey Bay Pev B 177 D3
Piddinghoe Pid 169 F1
Piltdown Pil 56 A1
Plumpton Plu 125 E4
Plumpton Green Plu G 102 B3
Polegate Pole 174 C3
Ponts Green Pon G 112 C2
Portslade-by-Sea Por S 163 F3
Portslade Village Por V 143 C1
Poynings Poy 122 A3
Punnett's Town Pun T 85 D3
Pyecombe Pye 122 C3
Ridgewood Rid 80 A2
Ringmer Rin 128 B3
Ripe Ripe 130 A1
Robertsbridge Rob 65 F2
Rodmell Rod 149 D1
Rotherfield Rot 40 C4
Rottingdean Rottn 167 F1
Rushlake Green Rus 85 D1
Rye Rye 95 D3
Rye Harbour Rye H 95 E1
Salehurst Sale 66 A3
Saltdean Salt 168 A1
Sandhurst San 48 C3
Scayne's Hill Sca H 53 E2
Seaford Sea 181 D1
Sedlescombe Sed 90 B1
Selmeston Selm 152 A2
Selsfield Common Sel C 11 D1
Sharpthorne Sha 22 C3
Shoreham-by-Sea S Sea 163 D3
Shortgate Sho 106 C2
Southborough Sgh 8 C4
South Chailey S Cha 103 E4
Southease S 169 E4
South Heighton S Hei 170 B1
South Malling S Mal 127 D2
South Street S Str 77 E1
Southwick Sock 163 E3
Speldhurst Spe 7 F4
Spithurst Spi 104 B4
Staplecross Stas 67 E1
Stone Bridge St B 31 E4
Stone Cross St Cro 175 F3
Stonegate Ston 44 B3
Streat Strt 102 A2
Tarring Neville Tar N 170 A2
Telscombe Tel 168 C2
The Moor The M 47 E4
The Moor The Moor 117 E2
Three Cups Corner Thr C C 85 E3
Three Leg Cross Thr C 33 D2
Three Oaks Thr O 118 A1
Ticehurst Tic 33 E1
Tidebrook Tid 42 C4
Town Row Tow R 29 D1
Tunbridge Wells, Royal T W 8 B2
Turner's Green Tur G 85 E2
Uckfield Uck 80 A4
Udimore Udi 93 D1
Upper Dicker Upp D 153 F4
Upper Hartfield Upp H 14 C1
Vines Cross Vin C 110 A4
Wadhurst Wad 31 F2
Waldron Wald 82 B2
Wallcrouch Wal 32 B1
Warbleton War 84 C1
Wartling Wart 157 D4
Westdean Wes 182 C2
Westfield Wfd 117 E2
West Firle W Fir 151 D2
Westham Whm 176 B3
West Hoathly W Hoath 22 B3
Westmeston Wmes 124 C4
Whatlington Wha 89 F1
Whitesmith Whi 130 C4
Willingdon Willn 174 C1
Wilmington Wil 173 E3
Winchelsea Winc 120 B4
Winchelsea Beach Winc B 120 C3
Windmill Hill Win H 134 C3
Witherenden Hill Wit H 43 F1
Withyham Wit 15 F2
Wivelsfield Wiv 75 F3
Wivelsfield Green Wiv G 76 A2
Woodingdean Wood 167 D4
Wood's Green Woo G 31 E4
Wych Cross Wych C 24 B2

Abberton Field. Hur 99 F3
Abbey Cl. Pea 169 D1
Abbey Dr. Bex 160 C3
Abbey Rd. Bri 166 A2
Abbey Rd. East 184 C3
Abbey View. Bex 160 A3
Abbots Cl. Bat 115 E2
Abbots Cl. Hass 100 B2
Abbotsbury Cl. Salt 167 F1
Abbotsfield Cl. Hast 140 B2
Aberdale Rd. Pole 175 D3
Aberdeen Rd. Bri 166 A4
Abergavenny Rd. Lew 126 C1
Abinger Pl. Lew 127 D1
Abinger Rd. Por S 163 F4
Abinger Rd. Wood 167 E3
Acacia Ave. Hove 144 B1
Acacia Rd. East 175 D1
Acacia Rd. Newh 170 B1
Acer Ave. Bel G 19 D4
Acorn Cl. E Gri 12 B4
Acorn Green. Hai 132 C1
Acorn Way. Hur G 46 C2
Acorns The. Ston 44 B3
Acre Cl. Hay H 52 A1
Acres Rise. Tic 33 E1
Adam Cl. Hast 139 E2
Adams Cl. Bri 145 F1
Adams La. Ewh G 68 A1
Adams La. Mill C 68 A2
Adastra Ave. Key 100 C2
Addingham Rd. East 186 A2
Addington Cl. Hast 161 E4
Addison Rd. Hove 165 E4
Adelaide Cres. Hove 165 D3
Adelaide Rd. Hast 139 F2
Ades Field. Wil 173 E3
Admiral's Bridge La. E Gri 12 A1
Adur Rd. Bur H 75 D2
Agincourt Cl. Hast 139 E4
Agnes St. Bri 166 A4
Ailsworth La. Rye 95 D3
Ainsworth Ave. Oving 167 E2
Ainsworth Cl. Oving 167 D2
Air St. Bri 165 E3
Airy Rd. Hers 134 C1
Alan Way. Bri 166 B3
Albany Hill. T W 9 D3
Albany Mews. Hove 164 C3
Albany Rd. Bex 160 A2
Albany Rd. Hast 161 F4
Albany Rd. Sea 181 D2
Albany Villas. Hove 164 C3
Albert Cl. Hay H 52 C2
Albert Dr. Bur H 74 B1
Albert Mews. Hove 165 D3
Albert Pl. Pole 174 C4
Albert Rd. Bex 160 A2
Albert Rd. Bri 165 E3
Albert Rd. Hast 162 B4
Albert Rd. Pole 174 C4
Albert Rd. Rid 80 A3
Albert Rd. Sock 163 D4
Albert St. T W 8 C2
Albert Terr. East 185 D2
Albion Hill. Bri 165 F3
Albion La. Hast 162 C4
Albion Pl. Bri 165 F3
Albion Rd. East 185 F2
Albion Rd. T W 9 D3
Albion St. Bri 165 F3
Albion St. Lew 127 D1
Albion St. Sock 163 E4
Albourne Cl. Bri 166 B4
Albourne Cl. Hast 161 E4
Aldborough Rd. Hast 140 A1
Alder Cl. East 186 A4
Alder Cl. Hast 140 A3
Alder Cl. Hea 83 F3
Alderbrook Cl. Cro 39 F3
Alderbrook Path. Cro 39 F3
Alderbrook Way. Cro 39 F3
Alders Ave. E Gri 2 B2
Alders View Dr. E Gri 2 B2
Aldervale Cotts. Cro 39 F4
Aldrich Cl. Bri 166 B3
Aldrington Ave. Hove 164 C4
Aldrington Cl. Hove 164 A4
Alexander Dr. Bex 159 E2
Alexandra Rd. Bur H 75 D1
Alexandra Rd. East 186 A3
Alexandra Rd. Hast 162 A4
Alexandra Rd. Hea 83 F3
Alexandra Rd. May 42 A2
Alexandra Rd. Rid 80 A3
Alexandra Villas. Bri 165 E3
Alford Way. Bex 160 B3
Alfray Rd. Bex 160 C3
Alfred Rd. Bri 165 E3
Alfred Rd. Hast 141 D2
Alfred St. Hast 162 A4
Alfriston Cl. Bex 159 D3
Alfriston Cl. Bri 166 B3
Alfriston Cl. East 185 D1
Alfriston Park. Sea 182 A3
Alfriston Rd. Sea 182 A3
Alice Bright La. Cro 39 E4
Alice St. Hove 165 D3
All Saints Cres. Hast 140 C1
All Saints La. Bex 159 F4
All Saints Rd. T W 8 C3
All Saints Rise. T W 8 C3
All Saints' St. Hast 162 C4
Allan Cl. T W 8 A2
Allandale Rd. T W 9 D4
Allards. Gue G 142 A4
Allen Rd. Hay H 52 C3
Allen Way. Bex 160 B4
Allen's Cl. Ash W 13 D3
Allfrey Rd. East 186 A3
Allington Cres. Newk 78 A4
Allington La. Coo 126 A4
Allington La. Off 126 A4
Allington Rd. Newk 78 A3
Allwood Cres. Wiv G 76 A2
Alma Rd. Hay H 52 C4
Alma Terr. Hast 140 A1
Alma Villas. Hast 140 A1
Alpine Rd. Hast 162 C4
Alpine Rd. Hove 164 B4
Alverstone Cl. East 175 F2
Amanda Cl. Bex 160 B4
Amberleaze Dr. Pem 10 A3
Amberley Cl. Bur H 74 C2
Amberley Cl. Hay H 52 A2
Amberley Cl. Hove 144 B2
Amberley Dr. Hove 144 B2
Amberley Rd. East 175 D1
Amberstone. Mag D 133 E2
Amberstone Cl. Hast 140 C2
Amberstone View. Hai 133 D1
Amberstone View. Hai 133 D2
Ambleside Ave. Pea 178 C4
America La. Hay H 52 C3
Amesbury Cres. Hove 164 B4
Amherst Cl. Hast 140 A1
Amherst Cres. Hove 164 B4
Amherst Gdns. Hast 140 A1
Amherst Rd. Bex 160 A2
Amherst Rd. Hast 140 A1
Amherst Rd. T W 8 C3
Amhurst Rd. Pea 178 B4
Anchor Field. Rin 128 B3
Anchor Hill. Sca H 53 F1
Anchor La. Spi 104 C3
Anderida Rd. Willn 175 D2
Andrew Rd. Sgh 9 D4
Andrews Cl. Sale 66 A3
Andrews Cl. T W 9 D3
Angela Cl. Bex 160 B4
Anglesea Terr. Hast 162 A4
Anglesey Ave. Hai 132 C1
Angus Cl. East 174 C1
Ann Cl. Key 100 C3
Ann St. Bri 165 F4
Ann St. Hast 141 D1
Anne's Path. Lew 148 C4
Annington Rd. East 185 F3
Anson Cl. East 186 B4
Ansty Cl. Bri 166 B3
Antares Path. Hai 155 E4
Antony Cl. Sea 180 C3
Antrona Cl. Bex 159 D2
Anvil Cl. Por S 143 F1
Anzac Cl. Pea 169 D1
Apple Tree La. T W 9 D4
Appledene Cnr. S Cha 103 E4
Appledore Cl. East 176 A1
Appledore Gdns. Hay H 52 C3
Appledore Rd. Bri 146 B2
Applesham Ave. Hove 144 B1
Applesham Way. Por S 143 F1
Applewood Cl. Hast 140 A3
Approach The. Bri 145 E2
Approach The. Dor P 2 B3
Apsley St. T W 8 A2
Arbor Ct. Hay H 52 B3
Arbourvale. Hast 139 F1
Archery Rd. Hast 161 F4
Archery Wlk. Hai 155 D3
Ardingly Rd. Salt 178 A4
Ardingly St. Bri 165 F3
Argent Cl. Sea 181 F3
Argos Hill Rd. May 41 D2
Argyle Rd. Bri 165 E4
Arkwright Rd. East 175 F1
Arlington Cres. Bri 146 B3
Arlington Gdns. Salt 168 A1
Arlington Rd. East 185 E2
Arlington Rd E. Hai 154 C3
Arlington Rd W. Hai 154 B3
Arnold St. Bri 166 A4
Arnside Rd. Hast 161 E3
Arran Cl. Hai 132 C1
Arthur Rd. Bex 159 F2
Arthur St. Hove 164 C4
Arun Path. Uck 57 E1
Arundel Cl. Pev B 177 E3
Arundel Cl. S Sea 163 D4
Arundel Dr E. Salt 168 A1
Arundel Dr W. Salt 168 A1
Arundel Green. Lew 126 C1
Arundel Mews. Bri 166 B2
Arundel Mews. Bri 166 B2
Arundel Pl. Bri 166 B2
Arundel Rd. Bri 166 B2
Arundel Rd. East 185 E2
Arundel Rd. Newh 170 B1
Arundel Rd. Pea 179 D4
Arundel Rd. Sea 181 F1
Arundel Rd. T W 8 C1
Arundel St. Bri 166 B2
Arundel Terr. Bri 166 B2
Ascham Pl. East 185 E1
Ascot Cl. East 190 B4
Ash Cl. Cra D 11 D4
Ash Cl. East 175 E2
Ash Cl. Hove 145 D2
Ash Cl. Whm 176 A3
Ash Ct. Hai 154 C4
Ash Dr. Sea 182 A2
Ash Gr. Hay H 52 A1
Ashbrook Rd. Hast 139 F2
Ashburnham Cl. Bri 146 A3
Ashburnham Dr. Bri 146 A3
Ashburnham Gdns. East 185 E3
Ashburnham Pl. Hai 132 C1
Ashburnham Rd. East 185 E3
Ashburnham Rd. Hast 141 D1
Ashby Cl. Bex 159 F4
Ashcombe Dr. Bex 159 D2
Ashcombe Hollow. Lew 148 B3
Ashcombe La. Kin L 148 B3
Ashcroft Cl. Rin 128 A3
Ashcroft Cl. S Sea 163 D4
Ashdown Ave. Salt 167 F1
Ashdown Cl. For R 13 F1
Ashdown Cl. Hay H 52 C2
Ashdown Cl. T W 8 B2
Ashdown Rd. Bex 160 B2
Ashdown Rd. Bri 165 F4
Ashdown Rd. For R 13 E1
Ashdown View. E Gri 12 B4
Ashdown View. Nut 37 D3
Ashenden Ave. Rye 94 C3
Ashenden Wlk. T W 9 E4
Ashenground Cl. Hay H 52 B2
Ashenground Rd. Hay H 52 B2
Asher Reeds. Lan G 7 F2
Ashford Cl. Hai 155 D4
Ashford Rd. Bri 145 F1
Ashford Rd. East 185 F2
Ashford Rd. Hast 140 B1
Ashford Sq. East 185 F2
Ashford Way. Hast 140 B2
Ashgate Rd. East 176 B1
Ashington Gdns. Pea 179 E3
Ashley Cl. Bri 145 E4
Ashley Gdns. May 41 F1
Ashley Gdns. T W 8 A3
Ashley Park. T W 8 A3
Ashley Park Cl. T W 8 A3
Ashlings Way. Hove 144 B1
Ashmore Cl. Pea 169 D1
Ashton Rise. Bri 165 F3
Ashtonville Cl. Rin 128 B3
Ashurst Ave. Salt 168 B1
Ashurst Rd. Asht 6 B2
Ashurst Rd. Bri 146 C2
Ashurst Rd. Lan G 7 D1
Ashurst Rd. Sea 181 E1
Ashway. Bur H 74 C1
Aslington Rd. East 175 F1
Aspen Cl. Hay H 52 C2
Aspen Rd. East 175 E1
Aspen Way. Bex 159 D2
Astaire Ave. East 185 F3
Asten Cl. Hast 161 E4
Asten Fields. Bat 115 D3
Athelstan Rd. Hast 141 D1
Atlingworth St. Bri 165 F2
Attfield Wlk. East 175 E2
Attree Dr. Bri 166 A3
Auckland Dr. Bri 146 C1
Auckland Rd. T W 9 D3
Audrey Cl. Bri 145 E3
Augustines Way. Hay H 52 B2
Augustus Way. Hast 139 E3
Austen Cl. E Gri 1 C1
Austen Way. Hast 141 D3
Austen Wlk. East 176 A1
Avard Cres. East 184 C3
Avenue. Bri 165 F3
Avenue La. East 185 E2
Avenue The. Bri 146 A1
Avenue The. Dor 2 C3
Avenue The. East 185 E2
Avenue The. Fai 142 B2
Avenue The. Hai 154 C3
Avenue The. Hor 109 E4
Avenue The. Kin L 148 A3
Avenue The. Lew 126 C1
Avenue The. May 41 F1
Avery Cl. Por S 143 E2
Aviary Way. Cra D 1 A1
Aviemore Rd. Cro 27 D1
Avis Rd. S Hei 170 A1
Avis Way. Newh 180 B4
Avocet. Hai 154 C4
Avon St. T W 9 D3
Avondale Rd. East 185 F2
Avondale Rd. Hast 139 F1
Avondale Rd. Hove 165 D4
Avondale Rd. Sea 181 E2
Avonhurst. Bur H 74 C2
Awbrook Cl. Sca H 53 E2
Aylesbury Ave. East 186 B4
Aymer Rd. Hove 164 C3
Babylon Way. East 184 C4
Back La. Cro H 83 D4
Back La. Rus 85 D1
Back La. Winc 120 B4
Back Rd. San 48 C3
Backwoods Cl. Hay H 52 C3
Backwoods La. Hay H 52 C3
Baden Rd. Bri 146 A1
Badens Cl. Newk 78 A3
Badger Dr. Hay H 52 A3
Badgers Cl. Cro 27 E2
Badgers Copse. Sea 182 A2
Badgers Croft. Pea 169 D1
Badgers Dene. Rod 169 D4
Badgers Mount. Bex 159 E3
Badgers Way. Hast 140 A3
Badgers Wlk. Bur H 75 D1
Badlesmere Rd. East 185 F3
Bagham La. Hers 134 B3
Bahram Rd. Pole 174 B3
Bailey Cres. Willn 174 C2
Baillie Ave. East 186 A3
Bainbridge Cl. Sea 181 E2
Bainden Cl. Tow R 29 D1
Baird Dr. Hast 140 B2
Baker St. Bri 165 F4
Baker St. Newh 180 B4
Baker St. Rid 80 A3
Baker's Rd. East 185 D2
Bakewell Rd. East 185 D2
Balaclava La. Wad 31 F3
Balcombe La. Hor K 23 E1
Balcombe La. Sha 23 D2
Balcombe Rd. Hay H 52 A4
Balcombe Rd. Pea 178 C4
Baldslow Down. Wfd 140 A4
Baldslow Rd. Hast 140 B1
Baldwin Ave. East 185 D3
Bale Cl. Bex 159 E3
Balfour Gdns. For R 13 E1
Balfour Rd. Bri 145 F1
Ballard Dr. Rin 128 B4
Ballards Hill. Crow 138 B2
Ball's Green. Wit 15 F3
Ballsocks La. Vin C 110 A4
Balmoral. E Gri 12 C4
Balmoral Cl. Sea 181 F3
Balsdean Rd. Wood 147 E1
Bamford Cl. Bri 146 C1
Bampfield St. Por S 163 F4
Bancroft Rd. Bex 159 F3
Bank Rd. Bex 160 A4
Banks Rd. N Cha 54 B1
Bankside. Bri 145 D3
Bankside. Hass 100 B3
Bankside. Wad 31 E3
Banner Farm Rd. T W 8 C1
Bannings Vale. Salt 168 B1
Bannisters Field. Newk 78 A4
Baranscraig Ave. Bri 145 F4
Barcombe Ave. Sea 182 A1
Barcombe Cl. East 185 D2
Barcombe Cl. Sea 182 A2
Barcombe Mills Rd. Bar C 104 B2
Barcombe Rd. Bri 146 B3
Barcombe Wlk. East 185 D2
Barden Rd. East 186 A2
Barden Rd. Spe 7 F4
Bargate Cl. Bex 160 A4
Barham Cl. Hast 140 A2
Barkdale. Bur H 75 D3
Barley Ave. Hast 141 D1
Barley Cl. Pea 168 C1
Barley La. Hast 141 D1
Barleycroft. Alb 99 D3
Barming Cl. East 176 A1
Barn Cl. Alb 99 D3
Barn Cl. Hai 133 D1
Barn Cl. Kin L 148 B3
Barn Cl. Sea 181 F3
Barn Cl. St Cro 175 F3
Barn Cottage La. Hay H 52 C3
Barn La. Fra 81 D4
Barn Rd. S Mal 127 D2
Barn Rise. Bri 145 D3
Barn Rise. Sea 181 F3
Barnes Rd. Por S 163 F4
Barnet Way. Hove 144 B2
Barnett Rd. Bri 145 F1
Barnetts Way. Sgh 9 D4
Barnfield. Cro 27 F2
Barnfield. Plu 102 B3
Barnfield. T W 18 B4
Barnfield Cl. Hast 162 A4
Barnfield Gdns. Bri 166 A3
Barnfield Gdns. Dit 101 E2
Barnham Cl. East 175 F1
Barnhams The. Bex 159 E2
Barnhorn Cl. Bex 159 D2
Barnhorn Rd. Bex 158 B2
Barnmead. Hay H 52 A4
Barnside Ave. Bur H 75 D1
Barons Cl. Sea 181 D3
Barons Ct. Bur H 74 C1
Barons Down Rd. Lew 148 C4
Barons Way. Pole 174 B3
Barons Wlk. Lew 148 C4
Barrack Rd. Bex 160 A3
Barrack Sq. Winc 120 B4
Barrhill Ave. Bri 145 E4
Barrie Cl. East 176 B1
Barrington Cl. Hay H 52 B4
Barrington Rd. Hay H 52 B4
Barrow Cl. Bri 146 A1
Barrow Hill. Bri 146 A1
Barrowfield Cl. Hove 145 D2
Barrowfield Dr. Hove 145 D1
Barry Wlk. Bri 166 A3
Bartholomews. Bri 165 F3
Barton Cres. E Gri 12 C4
Basin Rd S. Hove 164 A3
Basin Rd S. Por S 164 A3
Basin Rd S. Sock 163 F3
Basinghall St. T W 8 C2
Baslow Rd. East 190 A4
Batchelor Way. Uck 79 F4
Batchelors. Pem 10 B4
Bateman's La. Bur 63 F2
Batemans Rd. Wood 167 E4
Bates Rd. Bri 145 E1
Bath Rd. East 185 E1
Bath St. Bri 165 E4
Bathford Cl. East 176 A1
Battery Hill. Fai 142 A3
Battle Cl. Sea 182 A3
Battle Cres. Hai 154 C4
Battle Cres. Hast 139 F2
Battle Gates. Bat 114 C3
Battle Hill. Bat 115 E2
Battle Rd. Hai 133 D1
Battle Rd. Hast 139 F2
Batts Bridge Rd. Mar 56 C2
Bavant Rd. Bri 145 E1
Baxter Rd. Lew 126 C1
Baxter St. Bri 166 A4
Baxters La. Che Co 36 A3
Bay Ave. Pev B 177 E3
Bay Pond Rd. East 185 D2
Bay Rd. Pev B 177 D2
Bay Terr. Pev B 177 D3
Bay Tree Cl. Hea 83 F3
Bay Tree Cl. S Sea 143 D1
Bay Tree La. Pole 174 B4
Bay Vue Rd. Newh 180 A4
Bayencourt N. Bex 160 A3
Bayencourt S. Bex 160 A3
Bayhall Rd. T W 9 D2
Bayham Rd. East 186 A2
Bayham Rd. Hai 155 D4
Bayham Rd. T W 18 C4
Bayhams Field. Sha 22 B3
Bayley's La. Wil 153 F1
Bayview Rd. Pea 179 E3
Baywood Gdns. Wood 167 D4
Bazehill Rd. Rottn 167 F2
Beach Cl. Sea 181 D2
Beach Rd. East 186 A3
Beach Rd. Newh 180 B3
Beachings The. Pev B 177 D2
Beachlands Way. Pev B 177 F3
Beachy Head Rd. East 190 A4
Beacon Cl. Bri 145 F1
Beacon Cl. Cro 27 E1
Beacon Cl. Sea 181 D3
Beacon Dr. Sea 181 E3
Beacon Gdns. Cro 27 E2
Beacon Hill. Dor 2 C4
Beacon Hill. Oving 167 E2
Beacon Hurst. Key 100 C2
Beacon Rd. Cro 27 E2
Beacon Rd. Dit 101 D1
Beacon Rd. Hast 141 E2
Beacon Rd. Sea 181 D2
Beacon Rd. Wmes 124 A4
Beacon Rd W. Cro 27 D1
Beacon The. W Hoa 22 B4
Beaconsfield Rd. Bex 160 A3
Beaconsfield Rd. Bri 165 E4
Beaconsfield Rd. Che G 78 B2
Beaconsfield Rd. Hast 140 B1
Beaconsfield Rd. Por S 163 F4
Beaconsfield Villas. Bri 145 E1
Beagles Wood Rd. Pem 10 B4
Beal Cres. Bri 145 F1
Beales La. Norm 68 C3
Beamsley Rd. East 186 A2
Beaney's La. Hast 140 B3
Beaney's La. Wfd 140 B3
Bear Rd. Bri 166 A4
Bear Yd. Lew 127 D1
Beatrice La. East 185 E2
Beatty Ave. Bri 146 A3
Beatty Rd. East 186 B4
Beauchamp Rd. Hast 139 F2
Beauford Rd. Hor 109 E4
Beaufort Cres. Hast 140 A1
Beaufort Rd. Hast 140 A1
Beaufort Terr. Bri 166 A3
Beauharrow Rd. Hast 139 F3
Beaulieu Gdns. Hast 140 A3
Beaulieu Rd. Bex 159 D1
Beauport Gdns. Hast 139 F4
Beauport Hone Farm Cl. Hast 139 F3
Beaver Cl. Cro 27 F1
Beckenham Cl. Hai 132 C2
Becket Cl. Hast 140 C1
Beckets Way. Fra 80 C3
Beckett Way. E Gri 12 B4
Beckett Way. S Mal 127 D2
Beckley Cl. Bri 166 B3
Beckworth Cl. Hay H 52 C3
Beckworth La. Hay H 52 C3
Bedales Hill. Hay H 53 D2
Beddingham Cl. Gly 150 A3
Bedelands Cl. Bur H 74 C3
Bedford Ave. Bex 160 A2
Bedford Ct. Uck 80 A4
Bedford Gr. East 185 E2
Bedford Pl. Bri 165 E3
Bedford Rd. Hast 141 D1
Bedford Sq. Bri 165 E3
Bedford St. Bri 166 A2
Bedford Terr. T W 8 C1
Bedfordwell Rd. East 185 F2
Bee Rd. Pea 179 D4
Beech Cl. Bat 115 D4
Beech Cl. Bex 159 D3
Beech Cl. Por S 143 E2
Beech Farm Rd. Sed 90 A2
Beech Fields. E Gri 2 B2
Beech Gr. Bri 146 B2
Beech Hill. Hay H 52 C2
Beech House La. Sale 66 A3
Beech Hurst. Pem 10 A4
Beech Hurst Cl. Hay H 52 A2
Beech St. T W 8 C3
Beechers Rd. Por S 143 E2
Beeches Cl. Uck 80 A4
Beeches Farm Rd. Cro 27 F1
Beeches La. Ash W 13 D3
Beeches Rd. Cro 27 F1
Beeches The. Bri 145 D2
Beeches The. Cro 27 F1
Beeching Park Industrial Estate. Bex 159 F2
Beeching Rd. Bex 159 F2
Beeching Way. E Gri 2 B1
Beechwood Ave. Bri 145 E2
Beechwood Cl. Bri 145 E2
Beechwood Cl. Bur 63 F4
Beechwood Cres. East 185 D2
Beechwood Gdns. Hast 140 A3
Beechwood La. Coo 126 B4
Beechwood Mews. T W 9 E2
Beechwoods. Bur H 74 C1
Beechy Ave. East 184 C2

Beechy Gdns. East 184 C2
Beechy Rd. Blas 81 F1
Beeding Ave. Hove 144 B2
Beggar's La. Poy 122 A3
Beggar's La. St Cro 176 A3
Beggar's Wood Rd. N Cha 77 D3
Belfast St. Hove 164 C4
Belfry Orch. Rid 80 A3
Belgrave Cres. Sea 181 E3
Belgrave Pl. Bri 166 A2
Belgrave Rd. Sea 181 E2
Belgrave Rd. T W 8 C2
Belgrave Sq. Por S 164 A3
Belgrave St. Bri 165 F3
Belgrove. T W 8 C1
Bell Alley Rd. Bur 63 F3
Bell Banks Rd. Hai 155 D4
Bell La. Lew 148 C4
Bell La. Nut 36 C2
Bell La. Uck 79 F3
Belle Hill. Bex 160 A3
Belle Vue Rd. East 186 A3
Bellevue Gdns. Bri 166 A2
Bellfield Rd. Pem 10 A3
Bellhurst Rd. Rob 65 F2
Bellingham Cl. Hast 139 F2
Bellingham Cres. Hove 164 A4
Belmont. Bri 165 E4
Belmont Ct. Hai 154 C4
Belmont La. Hur 100 A3
Belmont Rd. Hast 141 D1
Belmont Rd. Uck 80 A4
Belmont St. Bri 165 F4
Belmore Rd. East 185 F2
Belton Rd. Bri 165 F4
Beltring Rd. East 185 F2
Beltring Rd. T W 8 C3
Beltring Terr. East 185 F2
Belvedere Gdns. Cro 27 F1
Belvedere Gdns. Sea 181 F3
Bembridge Rd. East 175 F2
Bembridge St. Bri 166 A4
Bembrook Rd. Hast 140 C1
Benbow Ave. East 186 B3
Benchfield Cl. E Gri 2 C1
Bending Cres. Bex 160 A3
Benenden Cl. Sea 181 F2
Benenden Rise. Hast 140 B2
Benett Ave. Hove 144 C1
Benett Dr. Hove 144 C1
Benfield Cl. Por S 144 A1
Benfield Cres. Por S 144 A1
Benfield Way. Por S 144 A1
Bengairn Ave. Bri 145 F4
Benhall Mill Rd. Bel G 19 D4
Benhall Mill Rd. T W 19 D4
Benjamin Cl. East 175 E1
Bennett Rd. Bri 166 B2
Bentham Hill. Sgh 8 A4
Bentham Rd. Bri 166 A4
Bentswood Cres. Hay H 52 C3
Bentswood Rd. Hay H 52 B3
Berbow Ave. East 186 B3
Beresford Rd. Bri 166 A3
Beresford Rd. Newh 170 B1
Bergamot Cres. S Sea 143 D1
Beristede Cl. East 185 E1
Berkeley Rd. T W 8 C1
Berkeley Row. Lew 148 C4
Berkeley Wlk. East 176 B2
Berkley Rd. May 41 E1
Berlin Rd. Hast 141 D1
Bernard La. East 185 E2
Bernard Pl. Bri 166 A4
Bernard Rd. Bri 166 A4
Bernhard Gdns. Pole 174 B3
Berriedale Ave. Hove 164 B3
Berry Cl. Bur H 74 C3
Berry Cl. Pea 168 C1
Berwick Cl. Bex 159 D3
Berwick Cl. East 175 D2
Berwick Cl. Sea 181 D2
Berwick Rd. Salt 168 A2
Betchley Cl. E Gri 2 B2
Bethune Rd. Bex 160 B2
Bethune Way. Hast 140 B1
Beulah Rd. T W 9 D2
Beuzeville Ave. Hai 154 C4
Bevendean Ave. Salt 168 A1
Bevendean Cres. Bri 146 B1
Bevendean Rd. Bri 146 A1
Beverington Cl. East 185 D3
Beverington Rd. East 185 D3
Bewl Bridge Cl. Fli 33 F2
Bewlbridge La. Cou W 32 B4
Bexhill Rd. East 186 A3
Bexhill Rd. Hast 161 D3
Bexhill Rd. Lun C 137 D1
Bexhill Rd. Nin 137 D1
Bexhill Rd. Wood 147 E1
Bexleigh Ave. Bex 160 C3
Bexley Cl. Hai 132 C1
Bicton Gdns. Bex 159 E2
Biddenden Cl. East 176 A1
Bidwell Ave. Bex 159 F3
Bigwood Ave. Hove 165 D4
Billingham La. Udi 93 D2
Binsted Cl. East 175 E1
Birch Ave. Hay H 52 C2
Birch Cl. Cra D 11 D4
Birch Cl. East 186 A4
Birch Cl. Hay H 52 C2
Birch Cl. T W 9 D4
Birch Cl. Uck 80 B4
Birch Grove Cres. Bri 145 F3
Birch Rd. East 186 A4
Birch View. Bex 160 A3
Birch Way. Hai 154 C3
Birch Way. Hast 140 B2
Birch Way. Hay H 52 C1
Birch Way. Hea 83 F3
Birch Way. T W 9 D4
Birchen La. Hay H 52 B4
Birches Close. Cro 27 E2
Birches Industrial Estate. E Gri 1 C2
Birchetts Ave. Lan G 7 E2
Birchetts Green La. Tic 32 C2
Birchgrove La. Hor K 23 E1
Birchgrove Rd. Hor K 35 E4
Birchington Cl. Bex 159 D2
Birchwood Grove Rd. Bur H 75 D1
Bird in Eye Hill. Fra 80 B3
Bird In Hand St. Asht 16 C4
Bird La. Wad 30 C3
Birdham Rd. Bri 146 B2
Birk Dale. Bex 159 D2
Birken Rd. T W 9 D3
Birling Cl. Bri 146 A1
Birling Cl. Sea 181 D2
Birling Dr. T W 18 C4
Birling Gap Rd. E Dean 188 C3
Birling Park Ave. T W 18 C4
Birling Rd. T W 18 C4
Birling St. East 185 D2
Birling Way. Uck 80 B4
Bishop's Cl. Hur 99 F4
Bishop's Cl. Rin 128 B3
Bishops Cl. Sea 181 D2
Bishop's Down. T W 8 B2
Bishop's Down Park Rd. T W 8 A2
Bishop's Down Rd. T W 8 B2
Bishops Dr. Lew 148 C4
Bishop's La. Rin 128 B3
Bishop's La. Rob 65 F2
Bishops Rd. Hove 145 D1
Bishop's Wlk. Bex 160 B3
Bishopstone Rd. Bis 181 D4
Bisky Bar. Peas 70 C1
Bixley La. Bec 69 F1
Black Hill. Hay H 52 C4
Black Lion St. Bri 165 F3
Black Path. Pole 174 C3
Blackberry La. Dor P 2 B4
Blackberry Rd. Dor P 2 A4
Blackbrook La. N Cha 54 B2
Blackbrook La. Sca H 54 B2
Blackdon Hill. Tow R 28 C3
Blackfields Ave. Bex 159 E3
Blackhouse La. Bur H 74 C2
Blackhurst La. T W 9 E3
Blacklands Cres. For R 13 E1
Blacklands Dr. Hast 140 B1
Blackman Ave. Hast 139 F2
Blackman St. Bri 165 F3
Blackmill Cl. Bex 159 F4
Blackness Rd. Cro 39 F4
Blacksmiths La. Cat 137 E4
Blackstone Way. Bur H 74 C3
Blackthorn Cl. Bri 145 D2
Blackthorn Cl. East 175 E1
Blackthorn Way. Fai 142 B2
Blackthorns. Hay H 52 C4
Blackthorns Cl. Hay H 52 C3
Blackthorns The. Bur H 74 C3
Blackwater Rd. East 185 E1
Blackwell Farm Rd. E Gri 2 B2
Blackwell Hollow. E Gri 2 B1
Blackwell Rd. E Gri 2 B1
Blake Way. T W 9 D4
Blakeney Ave. Pea 179 F3
Blaker St. Bri 165 F3
Blakes Way. East 186 B3
Blatchington Cl. Sea 181 E2
Blatchington Hill. Sea 181 E2
Blatchington Rd. Hove 164 C4
Blatchington Rd. Sea 181 E2
Blatchington Rd. T W 8 C1
Blenheim Cl. E Gri 2 C2
Blenheim Ct. Rob 65 F2
Blenheim Pl. Bri 165 F3
Blenheim Way. Fli 34 A2
Blenheim Way. Pole 175 D3
Bletchinglye La. Tow R 29 E1
Blind La. Newk 78 B3
Blois Rd. Lew 126 C1
Blomfield Rd. Hast 162 A4
Bloomsbury Pl. Bri 166 A2
Bloomsbury St. Bri 166 A2
Blossom Wlk. Hai 132 C1
Blount Ave. E Gri 2 A1
Blowers Hill. Cowd 5 D4
Blue Haze Ave. Sea 181 F2
Bluebell Cl. Hay H 52 B2
Bluemans La. Wfd 116 C2
Bluestone Cl. Hast 139 E1
Blunt's La. Spi 105 D3
Blunts Wood Rd. Hay H 52 A3
Blytons The. E Gri 1 C1
Boarders La. Tic 33 D2
Boast La. Spi 104 B3
Boddingtons La. Dit 101 D2
Bodiam Ave. Bex 160 A3
Bodiam Ave. Bri 146 C1
Bodiam Cl. Bri 146 C1
Bodiam Cl. Sea 182 A2
Bodiam Cres. East 175 F1
Bodiam Rd. San 48 B2
Bodle Cres. Bex 159 F3
Bodmin Cl. East 185 D2
Bohemia Rd. Hast 162 A4
Bolding Way. Hay H 52 B3
Bolebrook Rd. Bex 160 A2
Bolney Ave. Pea 179 D4
Bolney Rd. Bri 146 B2
Bolnore Rd. Hay H 52 A2
Bolsover Rd. East 190 B4
Bolsover Rd. Hove 164 B4
Bolton Rd. East 185 F1
Boltro Rd. Hay H 52 A3
Bonchurch Rd. Bri 166 A4
Bond St. Bri 165 F3
Bond Street Row. Bri 165 F3
Bonfire La. Hor K 35 D3
Bonny Wood Rd. Hass 100 B2
Booker Cl. Cro 27 F1
Bopeep Bostal. Alc 171 F4
Bordehill La. Hay H 52 A4
Boreham Hill. Bor S 135 F2
Boreham La. Bor S 135 E1
Borough La. East 185 D2
Borough St. Bri 165 E3
Boscobel Rd. Hast 161 F4
Boscobel Rd N. Hast 161 F4
Boston Rd. Hay H 52 C3
Boston St. Bri 165 F4
Bough Beeches. Bur H 75 D1
Boulevard The. Pev B 177 E3
Boundary Rd. Bri 166 B2
Boundary Rd. Hove 164 A4
Boundary Rd. T W 9 D1
Boundary The. Lan G 7 F2
Bourg-de-Peage Ave. E Gri 2 C1
Bourne La. Sale 66 B4
Bourne Pas. Hast 162 C4
Bourne St. East 185 F2
Bourne The. Hass 100 B3
Bourne The. Hast 162 C4
Bowden Rise. Sea 181 E3
Bowen Rd. T W 7 F2
Bower Cl. Hast 139 F2
Bower The. Hay H 52 A3
Bowley Rd. Hai 155 D4
Bowmans Dr. Bat 115 D3
Bowood Ave. East 185 F3
Bowrey Pl. Bex 160 A3
Bowring Way. Bri 166 A3
Box La. Ash W 13 E3
Boxes La. Hor K 35 D3
Boxgrove Cl. Bex 160 B2
Box's La. Che Co 36 A3
Boyce's St. Bri 165 E3
Boyne Park. T W 8 B2
Boyne Rd. Hast 141 D1
Bracken Cl. Cro 28 A1
Bracken Cl. T W 9 E3
Bracken Rd. East 184 C3
Bracken Rd. Sea 181 F1
Bracken Rd. T W 9 E3
Brackendale. Hast 141 D1
Bradford Rd. Lew 126 C1
Bradford St. East 185 D2
Brading Cl. East 175 F2
Brading Cl. Hast 140 B1
Brading Rd. Bri 166 A4
Bradley Rd. Chid H 6 A3
Braemore Rd. Hove 164 B3
Braeside Ave. Bri 145 F4
Bramber Ave. Hove 144 B2
Bramber Ave. Pea 179 D4
Bramber Cl. Hay H 52 A2
Bramber Cl. Pea 179 D4
Bramber Cl. Sea 181 E1
Bramber La. Sea 181 E1
Bramber Rd. Sea 181 E1
Bramber Way. Bur H 74 C2
Bramble Cl. East 175 F2
Bramble Croft. Cro 27 F1
Bramble Dr. Hai 154 C4
Bramble Reed La. Kip 10 C4
Bramble Rise. Bri 145 D3
Bramble Twitten. E Gri 2 C1
Bramble Way. Fai 142 B2
Brambledean Rd. Por S 163 F4
Brambles. Hass 100 B3
Brambletyne Ave. Salt 168 A1
Bramley Rd. Pole 175 D3
Bramleys. Kin L 148 B3
Brampton Ave. Bex 159 E2
Brampton Rd. East 185 E4
Brampton Rd Trading Estate. East 185 F4
Brand Rd. East 175 E1
Brands Cl. S Hei 170 B1
Brangwyn Ave. Bri 145 E3
Brangwyn Cres. Bri 145 E3
Brangwyn Dr. Bri 145 D3
Brangwyn Way. Bri 145 E3
Branksome Rd. Hast 161 F4
Branston Rd. East 175 D1
Brassey Ave. East 175 E1
Brassey Rd. Bex 160 A2
Brasslands Dr. Por S 143 E1
Braybon Ave. Bri 145 E2
Braybrooke Cl. Hast 162 B4
Braybrooke Rd. Hast 162 B4
Braybrooke Terr. Hast 162 B4
Bread St. Bri 165 F3
Breadsell La. Crow 139 D3
Breckley Rd. Bex 159 F2
Brede Cl. Bri 166 B3
Brede Cl. East 186 A3
Brede Cl. Hast 139 E4
Brede Hill. Bre 91 F1
Brede La. Bre 91 D1
Brede La. Sed 90 C1
Brede Valley View. Ick 119 E3
Breeds Pl. Hast 162 B4
Brendon Cl. East 176 B2
Brendon Cl. T W 9 D3
Brendon Rise. Hast 140 C2
Brentwood Cl. Bri 145 F2
Brentwood Cres. Bri 145 F2
Brentwood Rd. Bri 145 F2
Bretland Rd. T W 8 A2
Brett Dr. Bex 160 B2
Bretts Field. Pea 169 D1
Brewer St. Bri 165 F4
Brewer St. Lam 21 F3
Brian Cres. Sgh 8 C4
Briar Cl. Fai 142 C3
Briar Cl. Wood 167 D4
Briar Pl. East 175 F2
Briarcroft Rd. Wood 167 D4
Briary The. Bex 160 A3
Brickfield Estate. Peas 70 C1
Brickyard La. Mar C 29 E3
Brickyard La. Tow R 29 E3
Bridge Cl. Bur H 74 B2
Bridge Cl. Hor 109 F4
Bridge Pl. Rye 95 D3
Bridge Rd. Hay H 52 B3
Bridge St. Newh 180 A4
Bridge Way. Hast 161 F4
Bridgemere Rd. East 185 F3
Bridger Way. Cro 27 F1
Bridgersmill. Hay H 52 A3
Bridgewick Cl. S Mal 127 D2
Bridle Way. Pea 168 C1
Briers Ave. Hast 140 A2
Briers Gdns. Hast 140 A2
Brigden St. Bri 165 E4
Brigdens Hill. Gly 150 B3
Bright Ridge. Sgh 8 B4
Brightland Rd. East 185 D2
Brightling Ave. Hast 141 D2
Brightling Rd. Oxl G 64 C1
Brightling Rd. Pole 174 C3
Brightling Rd. Rob 65 E2
Brighton Pl. Bri 165 F3
Brighton Rd. Alb 99 E2
Brighton Rd. Hass 100 A1
Brighton Rd. Hur 99 E2
Brighton Rd. Lew 148 C4
Brighton Rd. Newh 179 F4
Brighton Rd. S Sea 163 D3
Brighton Sq. Bri 165 F3
Brills La. Bri 165 F2
Brinker's La. Wad 31 F1
Briscoe's Wlk. Hast 162 A4
Bristol Gate. Bri 166 A2
Bristol Gdns. Bri 166 B2
Bristol Mews. Bri 166 B2
Bristol Mews. Bri 166 B2
Bristol Pl. Bri 166 B2
Bristol Rd. Bri 166 A2
Bristol Rd. Hast 139 F2
Bristol St. Bri 166 B2
Bristol Way. Hast 139 F2
Brittany Mews. Hast 161 F4
Brittany Rd. Hast 161 F4
Brittany Rd. Hove 164 A3
Brittenden La. Cro H 82 B3
Brittenden La. Wald 82 B3
Britts Farm Rd. Bux 58 A2
Broad Gr. T W 8 C1
Broad Green. Wood 167 E3
Broad Green Ave. Bur H 75 D1
Broad La. Ford 6 C2
Broad Oak. Gro 17 D3
Broad Oak Cl. T W 8 B1
Broad Rd. Willn 174 C2
Broad Rig Ave. Hove 144 A2
Broad St. Bri 165 F2
Broad St. Ick 119 D3
Broad St. Sea 181 E2
Broad View. Bex 159 E3
Broad View. Bro O 61 E1
Broad Way. Fai 142 B3
Broadcroft. T W 18 B4
Broadfield. W Hoa 22 B4
Broadfields. Bri 146 B2
Broadfields Rd. Bri 146 B2
Broadhill Cl. Bro O 61 E1
Broadlands. Bur H 100 C4
Broadlands. Hast 141 D2
Broadlands Rd. Bur H 100 C4
Broadmead. T W 18 B4
Broadmead Ave. T W 18 B4
Broadoak La. Bex 159 E3
Broadview Cl. Willn 174 B2
Broadwalk The. Bex 158 C2
Broadwater Down. T W 18 B4
Broadwater La. T W 8 B1
Broadwater La. T W 18 B4
Broadwater Rise. T W 8 B1
Broadway The. Alfn 172 B2
Broadway The. Cro 27 E2
Broadway The. East 175 D1
Broadway The. Hast 141 D2
Broadway The. Hay H 52 A3
Broadway The. Lam 21 F3
Brodie Pl. East 185 D2
Brodrick Rd. East 175 E1
Brokes Way. Sgh 8 C4
Bromley Cl. East 176 A1
Bromley Cl. Key 100 C2
Bromley Rd. Bri 165 F4
Bromley Rd. Sea 181 F2
Brompton Cl. Bri 145 E3
Brontes The. E Gri 2 A1
Brook Ave. Key 100 B2
Brook Cl. Cro 28 A1
Brook Cl. E Gri 2 C1
Brook La. Hay H 52 B4
Brook Rd. T W 9 D4
Brook St. Hast 162 B4
Brook St. Lew 127 D1
Brook St. Pole 174 C3
Brook Way. Hast 140 C3
Brooker Pl. Hove 164 C4
Brooker St. Hove 164 C4
Brookfield Rd. Bex 160 B2
Brookhouse Bottom. Che Co 36 A2
Brookland Cl. Hast 140 B1
Brookland Cl. Pev B 177 E3
Brookland Rd. Hast 162 B4
Brooklands. T W 9 D4
Brooklands Ave. Cro 39 E4
Brooklands Farm Cl. Ford 6 C3
Brooklands Way. E Gri 2 A1
Brooklyn Rd. Sea 181 E2
Brookmead Cl. East 185 F3
Brooks Cl. Newh 180 A3
Brooks Gdns. Newk 78 A3
Brooks Rd. Lew 127 E1
Brooks The. Bur H 74 B3
Brookside. Pid 169 F1
Brookside Ave. Pole 174 B4
Brookway. Bur H 75 D2
Brookway. Hay H 52 C4
Broom Cl. East 175 D1
Broom La. Lan G 7 E1
Broom Park. Lan G 7 E2
Brooman's La. Lew 127 D1
Broomfield Ave. Pea 178 B4
Broomfield Dr. Por S 143 F2
Broomfield St. East 185 D2
Broomgrove Rd. Hast 140 C1
Broomhill Park Rd. Sgh 8 B4
Broomhill Rd. T W 8 A4
Brow The. Bur H 74 C2
Brow The. Fri 183 F1
Brow The. Wood 167 D4
Brown Jack Ave. Pole 174 B3
Browning Rd. Hea 83 F4
Browning Wlk. East 176 B1
Brownings The. E Gri 2 A1
Brownleaf Rd. Wood 167 E3
Brown's Cl. Uck 80 A4
Brown's La. Uck 57 D1
Brown's Path. Uck 80 B4
Browns Wood. E Gri 2 B2
Broyle Cl. Rin 128 B4
Broyle La. Rin 128 B4
Broyle Paddock. Rin 128 B4
Broyle The. Rin 129 D4
Broyleside. Rin 128 C4
Bruce Cl. Hay H 52 B2
Brunel Rd. Hast 139 E2
Brunswick Mews. Hove 165 D3
Brunswick Pl. Hove 165 D3
Brunswick Rd. Hove 165 D3
Brunswick Row. Bri 165 F4
Brunswick Sq. Hove 165 D3
Brunswick St. Hove 165 D3
Brunswick St W. Hove 165 D3
Brunswick Terr. Hove 165 D3
Brushes La. Hay H 52 C4
Bryants Field. Cro 27 E2
Buckholt Ave. Bex 160 C4
Buckholt La. Bex 160 A4
Buckhurst Cl. E Gri 2 A2
Buckhurst Cl. East 184 C4
Buckhurst Cl. S Mal 127 D2
Buckhurst La. Wad 30 C3
Buckhurst Mead. E Gri 2 A2
Buckhurst Pl. Bex 160 A2
Buckhurst Rd. Bex 160 A2
Buckhurst Rd. Pea 178 B4
Buckhurst Way. E Gri 2 A2
Buckingham Cl. Sea 181 D2
Buckingham Dr. E Gri 12 C4
Buckingham Pl. Bri 165 E4
Buckingham Rd. Bri 165 E3
Buckingham Rd. Hast 139 F2
Buckingham Rd. T W 8 C1
Buckingham St. Bri 165 E3
Buckland Rd. Sea 181 E3
Buckle By-Ps. Sea 181 D2
Buckle Cl. Sea 181 D2
Buckle Dr. Sea 181 D2
Buckle Rise. Sea 181 D2
Buckler St. Por S 163 F4
Bucklers Cl. T W 9 D2
Buckley Cl. Hove 144 B2
Buckwell Ct. Lew 126 C2
Buckwell Rise. Hers 134 B3
Bull La. Lew 149 D4
Bulldogs Bank. W Hoa 22 B3
Buller Cl. Cro 27 F1
Buller Rd. Bri 146 A1
Bullingstone La. Ford 7 E4
Bullingstone La. Spe 7 E4
Bulls Pl. Pem 10 A3
Bulverhythe Rd. Hast 161 D3
Burchetts Cl. Hay H 52 A1
Burden Pl. Hast 139 F2
Burdett Pl. Hast 162 C4
Burdett Rd. T W 7 F2
Burdocks Dr. Bur H 75 D1
Burfield Rd. East 185 F2
Burgess Rd. Hast 141 D3
Burgh Hill. Etc 46 B1
Burgh La. W Fir 151 D3
Burhill Way. Hast 161 E4
Burleigh Pl. East 186 A3
Burlington Gdns. Por S 144 A1
Burlington Pl. East 185 F1
Burlington Rd. East 185 F1
Burlington St. Bri 166 A2
Burlow Cl. Bri 166 B3
Burlow Cl. Willn 175 D2
Burma Cl. Hay H 53 D2
Burners Cl. Bur H 75 D1
Burnham Cl. Wood 167 E4
Burns Way. E Gri 2 A1
Burnside. Pole 174 C3
Burnt House La. Lan G 7 F3
Burnt Lodge La. Wal 32 C1
Burrel Rd. Hay H 52 A3
Burrell Rd. Hay H 52 A3
Burrow Down. East 184 C3
Burrow Down Cl. East 184 C3
Burry Rd. Hast 140 A1
Burslem Rd. T W 9 E4
Burstead Cl. Bri 145 F2

Burton Rd. East 185 E3
Burton Villas. Hove 165 D4
Burton Way. Hast 161 F3
Burton Wlk. Hai 154 C4
Burwash Cl. East 175 F2
Burwash Cl. Hast 140 C3
Burwash Rd. Bro O 61 E1
Burwash Rd. Hea 83 F4
Burwash Rd. Hove 144 B2
Bush Cl. Pea 168 C1
Bush Cl. Wood 167 D4
Bush Cottage Cl. Por S 144 A1
Bush Farm Dr. Por S 144 A2
Bush Rd. Newh 179 F4
Bushbury La. Blas 81 F2
Busheyfields. Hai 154 C4
Bushy Croft. Bex 159 E3
Bushy Gill. Lan G 7 F2
Butcherfield La. Hart 14 C4
Butcher's La. Cog 118 A1
Butcher's La. Thr O 118 B1
Bute St. Bri 166 A3
Butler's Green Rd. Hay H 52 A2
Butler's La. Hers 134 B2
Butlers Way. Rin 128 A3
Butterbox La. Sca H 54 A2
Butts La. East 174 C1
Butts Rd. Sock 163 E4
Buttsfield La. E Hoa 107 F3
Buxted Rise. Bri 145 F3
Buxted Wood La. Bux 58 B3
Buxton Dr. Bex 159 F3
Buxton Rd. Bri 165 E4
Buxton Rd. East 190 B4
By Sunte. Hay H 52 B4
Bydown. Sea 181 F2
Byefields Croft. Bex 159 E3
Byeway The. Bex 159 D3
Byeway The. Hast 140 C2
Byeways The. Sea 181 E2
Byland Cl. East 175 E2
Byng Rd. T W 8 B3
Byron Gr. E Gri 2 A1
Byron St. Hove 164 C4
Byron Wlk. East 176 B2
Byway The. Bri 146 B3
Byways. Hast 140 A3
Byworth Cl. Bex 159 D3
Byworth Cl. Bri 166 B3

Cabbage Stalk La. T W 8 B1
Caburn Cres. Lew 126 C1
Caburn Rd. Hove 165 E4
Caburn Way. Hai 154 C3
Cackle St. Bre 91 F1
Cackle St. Nut 37 E1
Cacklebury Cl. Hai 154 C3
Cadborough Cliff. Rye 94 B2
Cade St. East 175 E1
Cadogan Gdns. T W 8 C2
Cairo Ave. Pea 178 C4
Cairo Ave S. Pea 178 C4
Caister's Cl. Hove 165 D4
Calbourne. Hay H 52 A3
Caldbec Hill. Bat 115 D3
Caldecot La. Lydd 98 C4
Caldicotts La. Low D 132 A2
Caledonian Rd. Bri 165 F4
Caley Rd. T W 9 D4
Calgary Rd. Bex 159 F4
Calverley Park. T W 8 C2
Calverley Park Cres. T W 8 C2
Calverley Park Gdns. T W 9 D2
Calverley Rd. East 185 E1
Calverley Rd. T W 8 C2
Calverley St. T W 8 C2
Calvert Cl. Uck 79 F4
Calvert Rd. Hast 140 C1
Calvert Rd. Uck 79 F4
Camber Cl. Bex 160 B3
Camber Cl. Bri 166 B3
Camber Cl. Pev B 177 E3
Camber Dr. Pev B 177 E3
Camber Rd. Cam 95 E3
Camber Rd. E Gul 95 E3
Camber Way. Pev B 177 E3
Camberlot Rd. Gol C 131 F1
Camberlot Rd. Upp D 131 F1
Cambrian Rd. T W 9 D4
Cambridge Gdns. Hast 162 B4
Cambridge Gdns. T W 8 C1
Cambridge Gr. Hove 165 D4
Cambridge Rd. Bex 160 A3
Cambridge Rd. East 186 A2
Cambridge Rd. Hast 162 B4
Cambridge Rd. Hove 165 D3
Cambridge St. T W 9 D2
Cambridge Way. Uck 57 D1
Camden Ave. Pem 10 A3
Camden Hill. T W 9 D1
Camden Park. T W 9 D2
Camden Rd. East 185 E1
Camden Rd. T W 8 C2
Camden St. Por S 164 A3
Camelford St. Bri 165 F2
Campbell Cl. Uck 57 D1
Campbell Cres. E Gri 1 C1
Campbell Rd. Bri 165 E4
Campbell Rd. T W 8 C3
Camperdown St. Bex 159 F4
Canada Cl. Pea 168 C1
Canada Way. Bex 159 F4
Canadia Rd. Bat 115 D4
Canfield Cl. Bri 146 A1
Canfield Rd. Bri 146 A1
Canning St. Bri 166 A3
Cannon Pl. Bri 165 E3
Cansiron La. Ash W 13 E3
Cansiron La. For R 13 F3
Cansiron La. Hart 4 B1
Cantelupe Rd. Bex 160 A2
Cantelupe Rd. E Gri 2 B1
Canterbury Cl. Willn 175 D1
Canterbury Dr. Bri 165 F4
Canterbury Rd. Pem 10 B3
Canterbury Rise. Hast 140 B2
Cantercrow Hill. Newh 170 B1
Cants Cl. Bur H 75 D2
Cants La. Bur H 75 D2
Canute Rd. Hast 141 D2
Capel Ave. Pea 179 D4
Capella Path. Hai 155 D4
Caple Gdns. Hast 161 F4
Carden Ave. Bri 145 F3
Carden Cl. Bri 145 F3
Carden Cres. Bri 145 F3
Carden Hill. Bri 145 F3
Cardiff Rd. Hast 162 A4
Cardinals Cl. Bex 160 B3
Carew Rd. East 185 E2
Carey Down. Pea 168 C1
Carfax Cl. Bex 159 F4
Carinus Gdns. Hast 139 F3
Carisbrooke Cl. East 175 F2
Carisbrooke Rd. Bri 166 A4
Carisbrooke Rd. Hast 162 A4
Carlisle Par. Hast 162 B4
Carlisle Rd. East 185 E1
Carlisle Rd. Hove 164 B3
Carlton Cl. Sea 181 D2
Carlton Cres. T W 9 D2
Carlton Hill. Bri 165 F3
Carlton Pl. Bri 165 F3
Carlton Rd. East 186 A2
Carlton Rd. Sea 181 D2
Carlton Rd. T W 9 D2
Carlton Terr. Por S 164 A4
Carlyle Ave. Bri 146 A1
Carlyle St. Bri 166 A4
Carmel Cl. Bex 159 D2
Carol Cl. Bri 145 E3
Caroline Cl. Sea 181 D3
Carpenter Dr. Hast 139 E2
Carpenters Croft. E Hoa 107 F3
Carriers Path. Hai 154 C4
Carriers Pl. Cowd 5 F2
Carroll Wlk. East 176 B1
Castle Banks. Lew 127 D1
Castle Ditch La. Lew 127 D1
Castle Dr. Pev B 177 D2
Castle Gate. Lew 127 D1
Castle Gdns. Hast 162 B4
Castle Hill Pas. Hast 162 B4
Castle Hill Rd. Hast 162 C4
Castle Hurst. Sale 66 C4
Castle La. Lew 127 D1
Castle Prec. Lew 127 D1
Castle Rd. T W 8 C2
Castle Rise. Lew 127 D1
Castle Sq. Bri 165 F3
Castle St. Bri 165 E3
Castle St. Hast 162 B4
Castle St. T W 8 C1
Castle St. Winc 120 B4
Castle View Caravan Site. Pev Bay 176 C2
Castle View Gdns. Whm 176 B3
Castle Wlk. Wad 31 E2
Castledown Ave. Hast 162 C4
Castlefields. Hart 15 E2
Castleham Rd. Hast 139 E3
Castleross Rd. Pev B 177 D2
Cat St. Upp H 14 B1
Catherine Pl. T W 8 C2
Catherine Vale. Wood 167 E4
Catkin Way. Hay H 52 C2
Catt's Hill. Tow R 29 E1
Causeway The. Sea 181 E1
Cavalier Way. E Gri 12 B4
Cavalry Cres. East 184 C3
Cavell Ave. Pea 178 C4
Cavendish Ave. East 185 F2
Cavendish Ave. Hast 161 F4
Cavendish Cl. Pea 168 C1
Cavendish Dr. T W 8 C1
Cavendish Pl. Bri 165 E3
Cavendish Pl. East 185 F2
Cavendish Pl. Hast 162 C4
Cavendish St. Bri 165 F3
Caveridge La. S Cha 103 E4
Caves Rd. Hast 161 F3
Caxton Way. Hay H 52 B2
Cedar Cl. Bur H 74 C3
Cedar Cl. East 175 D1
Cedar Cl. Hast 140 A3
Cedar Ct. T W 8 C3
Cedar Ridge. T W 9 D3
Cedar Way. Hay H 52 C2
Cedars Cl. Uck 80 A4
Cedars Gdns. Bri 145 E2
Cedars The. Hai 132 C1
Cedars The. Hay H 52 A4
Cedarwell Cl. Pid 169 F1
Celandine Dr. Hast 139 F1
Central Ave. East 184 C3
Central Ave. Pea 178 C4
Central Ave. Pole 174 C4
Centurion Rd. Bri 165 E3
Ceylon Pl. East 185 F2
Ceylon Wlk. Bex 159 E2
Chadborn Cl. Bri 166 A3
Chaffinch Rd. East 176 A1
Chafford La. Ford 6 B3
Chailey Ave. Rottn 167 F1
Chailey Cl. East 176 B1
Chailey Cl. Hast 140 B3
Chailey Cres. Salt 168 B1
Chailey La. Chay 77 F3
Chailey Rd. Bri 146 B2
Chain La. Bat 115 D3
Chalden Pl. Bex 159 D3
Chalfont Dr. Hove 145 D2
Chalk Farm Cl. East 174 C1
Chalkers La. Hur 99 F4
Chalket La. Pem 10 A3
Chalkland Rise. Wood 167 E4
Chalky Rd. Por S 143 E2
Challoners. Hor K 35 D2
Challoners Cl. Rottn 167 F1
Challow Cl. Hass 100 B2
Chaloner Cl. Hay H 52 C4
Chaloner Rd. Hay H 52 C4
Chalvington Rd. East 185 D4
Chamberlain Rd. East 185 D2
Chambers Cres. Hast 139 E2
Chambers Rd. Hast 139 E2
Chancellors Park. Hass 100 B2
Chanctonbury Dr. Hast 140 B3
Chanctonbury Rd. Bur H 74 C1
Chanctonbury Rd. Hove 165 E4
Chandler Rd. Bex 159 F2
Chandler's Mead. Coo 126 C4
Chandos Rd. T W 9 D3
Channel View. Bex 160 A2
Channel View E. Bex 160 A2
Channel View Rd. East 186 A3
Channel View Rd. Wood 166 C4
Channel View W. Bex 160 A2
Channel Way. Fai 142 B2
Channelview Rd. Pev B 177 E3
Channers La. Ripe 130 A1
Chant La. Tow R 29 D1
Chantlers Cl. E Gri 2 A1
Chantlers Mead. Cowd 4 C3
Chantry Ave. Bex 160 A3
Chantry La. Bex 160 A3
Chapel Barn Cl. Hai 155 D4
Chapel Cl. Bur H 74 B2
Chapel Field. Norm 68 C4
Chapel Green. Cro 27 E1
Chapel Hill. Crow 138 B2
Chapel Hill. Lew 127 E1
Chapel Hill. Sed 116 B4
Chapel La. Ash W 13 D3
Chapel La. E Chi 102 C2
Chapel La. For R 13 E1
Chapel La. Gue G 141 F4
Chapel Mews. Hove 165 D3
Chapel Park Rd. Hast 162 A4
Chapel Pl. Por S 164 A4
Chapel Pl. T W 8 C1
Chapel Rd. Plu G 102 B4
Chapel Rd. Por S 164 A4
Chapel Row. W Hoa 22 B4
Chapel St. Bri 165 F3
Chapel St. Newh 180 A4
Chapel Terr. Bri 166 A2
Chapel Terr Mews. Bri 166 A2
Chapman Way. Sgh 9 D4
Chapman's La. E Gri 2 A1
Charity Farm Way. Cro 27 F2
Charles Ave. Bur H 74 B1
Charles Cl. Hove 144 C2
Charles Cl. Sea 181 D3
Charles Rd. Hast 161 F4
Charles Rd W. Hast 161 F4
Charles St. Bri 165 F2
Charles St. Sgh 8 C4
Charleston Rd. East 185 D2
Charlesworth Park. Hay H 53 D2
Charlewood Gdns. Bur H 75 D3
Charlotte St. Bri 165 F2
Charlston Ave. Newh 179 F3
Charltons The. Bri 146 A3
Charlton's Way. T W 8 B1
Charlwood Rd. Bur H 75 D3
Charlwoods Business Centre. E Gri 2 A1
Charlwoods Pl. E Gri 2 B2
Charlwoods Rd. E Gri 2 B2
Chartfield. Hove 144 C1
Chartres. Bex 160 A3
Chartres Cl. Bex 160 A3
Chase The. T W 9 D1
Chatfield Cres. East 175 D1
Chatham Pl. Bri 165 E4
Chatham Pl. Sea 181 E1
Chatham Rd. Hast 139 F1
Chatsfield Cl. Hast 139 E2
Chatsworth Ave. Pea 168 C1
Chatsworth Cl. Pea 178 C4
Chatsworth Gdns. East 190 B4
Chatsworth Park. Pea 168 C1
Chatsworth Rd. Bri 165 E4
Chaucer Ave. E Gri 2 A1
Chaucer Wlk. East 176 B2
Chawbrook Rd. East 185 F2
Cheapside. Bri 165 F3
Cheeleys. Hor K 35 D3
Chelsea Cl. Bex 160 A2
Chelston Ave. Hove 164 A4
Cheltenham Pl. Bri 165 F3
Chelwood Cl. Bri 146 A3
Chelworth Rd. East 175 D1
Chene Rd. Pea 179 E3
Chenies Cl. T W 13 C4
Chepbourne Rd. Bex 160 A2
Chequer Cl. For R 13 E1
Chequer Rd. E Gri 2 B1
Chequers Cl. Cro 27 F1
Chequers Way. Cro 27 F1
Cherington Cl. Hur 99 F3
Cherry Cl. Bur H 74 B3
Cherry Garden Rd. East 184 C2
Cherry Gdns. H Hur 57 F4
Cherry Side. Hai 154 C4
Cherry Tree Cl. Hast 162 A4
Cherry Tree Cotts. Fle 55 E2
Cherry Tree Gdns. Bex 160 B3
Cherry Tree Rd. T W 8 B1
Cherwell Rd. Hea 83 F4
Chesham Pl. Bri 166 A2
Chesham Rd. Bri 166 A2
Chesham St. Bri 166 A2
Chester Ave. T W 9 D1
Chester Terr. Bri 145 F1
Chesterfield Cl. Cra D 1 A2
Chesterfield Gdns. East 190 B4
Chesterfield Rd. East 190 B4
Chesterton Ave. Sea 181 F2
Chesterton Cl. E Gri 12 B4
Chesterton Dr. Sea 181 F2
Chestnut Ave. Sgh 8 C4
Chestnut Cl. Bro O W 91 F3
Chestnut Cl. Bur H 74 C3
Chestnut Cl. E Gri 2 C1
Chestnut Cl. Hai 132 C1
Chestnut Cl. Hers 134 B3
Chestnut Cl. Sgh 8 C4
Chestnut Dr. Pole 174 C3
Chestnut Gr. Hur 99 E4
Chestnut Way. Newh 179 F4
Chestnut Wlk. Bex 159 D3
Chestnut Wlk. Dor P 2 A4
Chestnuts Cl. Hay H 52 C4
Chestnuts The. Hay H 52 B4
Chestnuts The. The M 47 E4
Cheviot Cl. East 176 A2
Cheviots The. Hast 141 D2
Chichester Cl. Bex 159 F3
Chichester Cl. Hove 144 B2
Chichester Cl. Pea 179 E4
Chichester Cl. Salt 168 A1
Chichester Cl. Willn 174 C1
Chichester Dr E. Salt 168 A1
Chichester Dr W. Salt 167 F1
Chichester Mews. Bri 166 A2
Chichester Mews. Bri 166 A2
Chichester Pl. Bri 166 A2
Chichester Rd. Hast 139 F1
Chichester Rd. Sea 181 E2
Chichester Terr. Bri 166 A2
Chichester Way. Bur H 75 D3
Chick Hill. Pett 142 C4
Chiddingly Cl. Bri 166 B3
Chieveley Dr. T W 9 D1
Chilcomb. Bur H 75 D1
Chilham Cl. East 176 A1
Chillies La. H Hur 38 C2
Chilling St. Hor K 23 D1
Chilling St. Sha 23 D2
Chillis Wood Rd. Hay H 52 A3
Chilsham La. Bod G 111 F1
Chilsham La. Hers 111 F1
Chilston Cl. T W 8 C3
Chilston Rd. T W 8 C3
Chiltern Cl. S Sea 163 D4
Chiltern Dr. Hast 140 C2
Chiltern Wlk. T W 9 D2
Chiltington Cl. Bur H 74 B3
Chiltington Cl. Salt 168 A1
Chiltington La. Bar 103 D1
Chiltington La. E Chi 103 D2
Chiltington Way. Salt 168 A1
Chiswick Pl. East 185 F1
Chitcombe Rd. Bro OW 91 E3
Chorley Ave. Salt 167 F1
Chowns Hill. Cog 140 C3
Chrisdory Rd. Por S 143 E2
Christ Church Ave. T W 8 C1
Christie Ave. Rin 128 A3
Christie Rd. Lew 126 C1
Christies. E Gri 12 A4
Christine Cl. Bex 160 C4
Christopher Rd. E Gri 2 B1
Church App. Fra 80 C3
Church Ave. Hay H 52 B3
Church Ave. Whm 176 C3
Church Cl. Bri 145 E3
Church Cl. Bur H 74 C2
Church Cl. Willn 174 C2
Church Fields. Hur 99 E3
Church Green. S Sea 163 D4
Church Hill. Bri 145 E4
Church Hill. Etc 45 F1
Church Hill. Newh 180 A4
Church Hill. Rin 128 A3
Church Hill Ave. Bex 159 D2
Church House Cl. Sock 143 E1
Church in the Wood La. Hast 139 E2
Church La. Alb 99 D3
Church La. Bec 69 E2
Church La. Bux 58 A3
Church La. Cat 137 E4
Church La. Dan 35 F2
Church La. Dit 101 D2
Church La. E Gri 2 B1
Church La. East 185 D2
Church La. Etc 46 A1
Church La. Frant 18 C2
Church La. Gue G 141 F4
Church La. Hooe 158 A4
Church La. Hor K 35 D3
Church La. Jev 184 A4
Church La. Kin L 148 A3
Church La. Nin 136 C3
Church La. Norm 69 D3
Church La. Peas 71 D1
Church La. Pev 176 C3
Church La. Poy 122 A4
Church La. Ripe 152 B4
Church La. S Mal 127 D2
Church La. Sea 181 E1
Church La. Sock 163 D4
Church La. Wfd 117 E2
Church La. Wiv 75 E3
Church Marks La. E Hoa 107 E3
Church Mead. Key 100 C2
Church Mews. Willn 174 C1
Church Pas. Hast 162 C4
Church Path. Hel 132 C3
Church Path. Nin 136 C3
Church Pl. Bri 166 B2
Church Rd. Bar 104 B2
Church Rd. Bar C 104 B2
Church Rd. Bur H 74 B2
Church Rd. Bux 57 F2
Church Rd. Cat 137 E4
Church Rd. Cro 27 E1
Church Rd. Hast 162 A4
Church Rd. Hay H 52 B2
Church Rd. Hel 132 C3
Church Rd. Hers 134 C1
Church Rd. Hove 165 D3
Church Rd. Lam 21 F3
Church Rd. Mou 88 C3
Church Rd. Newk 78 B4
Church Rd. Pem 10 A4
Church Rd. Pole 174 C3
Church Rd. Por S 163 F4
Church Rd. Sale 66 A3
Church Rd. San 48 B2
Church Rd. Sca H 53 E2
Church Rd. T W 8 C2
Church Rd. W Hoa 22 B3
Church Row. Lew 127 D1
Church Sq. Rye 95 D3
Church St. Bex 160 A3
Church St. Bri 165 F3
Church St. Cad S 84 A3
Church St. Cowd 4 C3
Church St. East 185 D2
Church St. Hart 15 D2
Church St. Hast 141 D2
Church St. Por S 163 F4
Church St. Rot 40 C4
Church St. Sea 181 E2
Church St. Uck 80 A4
Church St. Willn 175 D1
Church Twitten. Lew 127 D1
Church Vale Rd. Bex 160 A3
Church Wood Dr. Hast 139 E2
Church Wood Way. Hast 139 E1
Churchdale Ave. East 186 A3
Churchdale Pl. East 185 F3
Churchdale Rd. East 186 A3
Churchfield. E Dean 188 C4
Churchfield. Wfd 117 D2
Churchfields. Nut 37 D2
Churchill Ave. Hast 141 D3
Churchill Cl. East 185 D2
Churchill Rd. Hea 83 F3
Churchill Rd. Lew 126 C2
Churchill Rd. Sea 181 D3
Churchill Way. Bur H 75 D1
Churchland La. Sed 90 B2
Churchsettle La. Tic 32 A1
Chyngton Ave. Sea 181 F2
Chyngton Cl. Sea 181 F1
Chyngton Gdns. Sea 181 F2
Chyngton La. Sea 182 A2
Chyngton La N. Sea 182 A2
Chyngton Rd. Sea 181 F1
Chyngton Way. Sea 182 A1
Cider House Wlk. E Hoa 107 F3
Cinder Hill. Chay 77 F2
Cinderford La. Cowb 133 F4
Cinque Ports St. Rye 94 C3
Cinque Ports Way. Hast 161 E3
Cinque Ports Way. Sea 182 A2
Cinquefoil. Pea 169 D1
Circus St. Bri 165 F3
Circus The. East 186 A4
Cissbury Ave. Pea 179 E4
Cissbury Cres. Salt 168 B1
Cissbury Rd. bur H 74 B2
Cissbury Rd. Hove 165 E4
Civic Way. Bur H 74 C1
Clackhams La. Rot 40 A4
Clair Ct. Hay H 52 B3
Clair Rd. Hay H 52 B3
Clanricarde Gdns. T W 8 C2
Clanricarde Rd. T W 8 C2
Clapham La. Litl 182 C4
Claphatch La. Tic 32 C3
Clappers The. Rob 65 F2
Clappers The. Sale 65 F2
Clare Rd. Lew 126 C1
Clare Wlk. Bri 166 A3
Claremont. Hast 162 B4
Claremont Gdns. T W 8 C1
Claremont Rd. Bex 159 F4
Claremont Rd. Newh 170 B1
Claremont Rd. Sea 181 D2
Claremont Rd. T W 8 C1
Claremont Rise. Uck 57 D1
Clarence Dr. Gri 12 B4
Clarence Rd. East 185 F2
Clarence Rd. Hast 140 A1
Clarence Rd. T W 8 C2
Clarence Row. T W 8 C2
Clarence Sq. Bri 165 E3
Clarence St. Por S 164 A3
Clarendon Cl. Hast 139 F2
Clarendon Gdns. T W 8 C1
Clarendon Pl. Bri 166 A2
Clarendon Pl. Por S 164 A3
Clarendon Rd. Hove 164 C4
Clarendon Rd. S Sea 163 D4
Clarendon Terr. Bri 166 A2
Clarendon Villas. Hove 164 C4
Clarendon Way. T W 8 C1
Clarke Ave. Hove 144 B2
Claverham Cl. Bat 114 C2
Claverham Way. Bat 114 C2
Clavering Wlk. Bex 158 C1
Claxton Cl. East 185 D3

Claxton Rd. Bex 160 C3
Clay Hill Rd. Lam 21 D3
Clays Cl. E Gri 12 B4
Clayton Ave. Hass 100 B2
Clayton Dr. Bur H 74 B1
Clayton Hill. Pye 123 D4
Clayton Rd. Bri 166 A4
Clayton Rd. Dit 101 D2
Clayton Way. Hove 144 B2
Clayton's La. Asht 6 B1
Clearwater La. Sca H 53 F2
Clearwaters La. Bur H 75 D4
Cleeve Ave. T W 9 D1
Clegg St. Hast 162 B4
Clement Hill Rd. Hast 140 C2
Clement La. Pole 174 C3
Clementine Ave. Sea 181 D3
Clerks Acre. Key 100 C2
Clermont Rd. Bri 145 E1
Clermont Terr. Bri 145 E1
Cleve Cl. Fra 80 C3
Cleve Terr. Lew 149 D4
Clevedon Rd. Bex 159 F3
Clevedown. Lew 148 C4
Cleveland. T W 9 D3
Cleveland Cl. East 176 A2
Cleveland Gdns. Bur H 74 C1
Cleveland Rd. Bri 145 F1
Cliff Approach. Bri 166 B2
Cliff Cl. Sea 181 E1
Cliff Gdns. Pea 178 B4
Cliff Gdns. Sea 181 E1
Cliff Park Cl. Pea 179 E4
Cliff Rd. Bri 166 B2
Cliff Rd. East 190 B4
Cliff Rd. Sea 181 E1
Cliff Way. Fai 142 B3
Cliffe High St. Lew 127 E1
Cliffe Industrial Estate. Lew 149 E4
Clifford Ave. East 185 D3
Clifford Rd. Bex 160 A2
Clifton Cl. East 185 D4
Clifton Hill. Bri 165 E3
Clifton Pl. Bri 165 E3
Clifton Pl. T W 8 C1
Clifton Rd. Bri 165 E3
Clifton Rd. Bur H 74 C1
Clifton Rd. Hast 141 D2
Clifton Rd. Newh 180 A4
Clifton Rd. T W 9 D4
Clifton Rise. Bex 160 B3
Clifton St. Bri 165 E3
Clifton Terr. Bri 165 E3
Clifton Way. Pea 178 C4
Cliftonville Rd. Hast 161 D3
Cliftonville Way. Hast 161 D3
Climbing Cl. Hay H 52 A2
Clinch Green Ave. Bex 159 E4
Clinton Cres. Hast 139 F1
Clinton Hill. Dor 2 C4
Clinton La. Sea 181 E2
Clinton Pl. Sea 181 E2
Clinton Way. Fai 142 B3
Clive Ave. Hast 141 D1
Cliveden Ct. Bri 145 E2
Clockhouse. T W 9 E3
Clockhouse La. Nut 37 D2
Cloisters. Newh 180 A4
Cloisters The. East 175 D1
Cloisters The. Hast 162 A4
Close Eight. East 176 B2
Close Eighteen. East 176 B1
Close Eleven. East 176 B2
Close Fifteen. East 176 B1
Close Five. East 176 B2
Close Four. East 176 B1
Close Fourteen. East 176 B2
Close Nine. East 176 B1
Close Nineteen. East 176 B1
Close One. East 176 A1
Close Seven. East 176 B2
Close Seventeen. East 176 B1
Close Six. East 176 B2
Close Sixteen. East 176 B1
Close Ten. East 176 B1
Close The. Bri 145 D3
Close The. Bur H 75 D2
Close The. Cro 27 E2
Close The. E Gri 12 A4
Close The. East 184 C4
Close The. Fai 142 A2
Close The. Fri 183 F1
Close The. Key 100 B2
Close The. Newh 170 B1
Close The. Rye 94 C3
Close The. Sea 181 E1
Close The. Willn 175 D2
Close Three. East 176 A1
Close Twelve. East 176 B1
Close Twenty. East 176 B1
Close Twentyfive. East 176 A1
Close Twentyfour. East 176 B1
Close Two. East 176 A1
Cloudesley Rd. Hast 162 A4
Cloverlea. Hast 140 B3
Cluny St. Lew 149 D4
Clyde Park. Hai 155 D4
Clyde Rd. Bri 165 F4
Clyde Rd. Hast 162 A4
Coach and Horses La. Che Co 36 A3
Coach And Horses Pas. T W 8 C1
Coach La. Che Co 36 A3
Coalbrook Rd. Bri 166 A3
Coast Rd. Nor B 177 E1
Coast Rd. Pev B 177 E3
Coastguard Cotts. Nor B 177 E2
Coastguard La. Fai 142 A2
Coastguard La. Hast 142 A2
Cob Cl. Cra D 11 D4
Cob La. Ard 22 A1
Cobald Rd. Pev B 177 E3
Cobbetts Mead. Hay H 52 C2
Cobbett's Ride. T W 8 B1
Cobbold Ave. East 185 D3
Cobden Rd. Bri 166 A4
Cobhams. Spe 7 F4
Cobourg Pl. Hast 162 C4
Cobton Dr. Hove 144 C2
Cochrane Cl. East 186 B4
Cockcrow Wood. Hast 140 A3
Cockmount La. Wad 31 E3
Cockshut Rd. Lew 149 D4
Cogger's La. Hel 109 E2
Coggins Mill Rd. May 42 A2
Coghurst La. Hast 141 D2
Colbourne Ave. Bri 146 A1
Colbourne Rd. Hove 165 E4
Colchester Vale. For R 13 E1
Coldean La. Bri 146 B3
Coldharbour Cl. Cro 27 F1
Coldharbour La. N Cha 77 F4
Coldharbour Rd. Ford 6 B4
Coldharbour Rd. Low D 132 A2
Coldharbour Rd. Upp D 131 F1
Coldthorn La. Hai 154 C2
Coldwaltham La. Bur H 75 D1
Colebrook Rd. Bri 145 D2
Colebrook Rd. Sgh 9 D4
Colebrook Rd. Sock 163 E4
Colebrooke Rd. Bex 159 F2
Coleman Ave. Hove 164 B4
Coleman St. Bri 165 F4
Coleridge St. Hove 164 C4
Coleridge Wlk. East 176 B1
Colgate Cl. Bri 166 B3
College Cl. E Gri 2 B1
College Cl. Por S 143 E2
College Dr. T W 9 D2
College Gdns. Bri 166 A2
College La. E Gri 2 B1
College La. Hur 100 A3
College Pl. Bri 166 A2
College Pl. Hur 100 A3
College Rd. Bex 160 B2
College Rd. Bri 166 A2
College Rd. East 185 E1
College Rd. Hay H 52 B4
College Rd. Sea 181 E1
College St. Bri 166 A2
College Terr. Bri 166 A3
Collett Cl. Hast 139 E3
Collier Cl. East 185 F4
Collier Rd. Pev B 177 D2
Collingford La. Dan 35 F2
Collington Ave. Bex 159 E2
Collington Cl. East 185 E1
Collington Gr. Bex 159 E2
Collington La E. Bex 159 E2
Collington La W. Bex 159 D2
Collington Park Cres. Bex 159 E2
Collington Rise. Bex 159 E2
Collingwood Ave. Hea 83 F4
Collingwood Cl. E Gri 12 B4
Collingwood Cl. Pea 169 D1
Collingwood Rise. Hea 83 F4
Collinstone Rd. Hast 161 F4
Collinswood Dr. Hast 161 F4
Colmer Ct. Bur H 74 B2
Colmer Pl. Bur H 74 B2
Colonnade Gdns. East 185 F2
Colonnade Rd. East 185 F2
Coltstocks Rd. East 190 A4
Colwell Cl. Hay H 52 B2
Colwell Gdns. Hay H 52 B2
Colwell La. Hay H 52 C1
Colwell Rd. Hay H 52 B1
Colwood Cres. East 184 C3
Combe End. Cro 39 E4
Combe La. East 190 A4
Combe Rise. Willn 174 C1
Combe The. East 184 C4
Combermere Rd. Hast 139 F1
Command Rd. East 184 C3
Commanders Wlk. Fai 142 B2
Commercial Rd. Bur H 74 B2
Commercial Rd. East 185 F2
Commercial Rd. T W 8 C3
Commercial Sq. Lew 127 D1
Common La. Ber 152 B1
Common La. Dit 101 D3
Common La. Selm 152 B1
Common View. T W 8 A2
Common Wood Rise. Cro 27 E2
Compasses La. Sed 90 A3
Compharst La. Win H 134 C2
Compton Ave. Bri 165 E4
Compton Cl. Bex 160 B2
Compton Dr. East 185 D1
Compton Place Rd. East 185 E1
Compton Rd. Bri 145 D1
Compton Rd. Hay H 52 C4
Compton St. East 185 F1
Compton Terr. Hai 155 D3
Compts The. Pea 168 C1
Concord Cl. T W 9 D2
Concorde Cl. Bex 159 E3
Condor Way. Bur H 74 B2
Conduit Hill. Rye 95 D3
Coney Furlong. Pea 169 D1
Coneyburrow La. Bex 158 B3
Coneyburrow Rd. T W 9 E3
Conghurst La. Four T 48 A4
Conghurst La. The M 47 F3
Conifer Cl. Hast 140 B2
Conifers The. East 185 E2
Coniston Ave. T W 8 B3
Coniston Rd. East 176 A2
Connaught Rd. East 185 F1
Connaught Rd. Hove 164 C3
Connaught Rd. Sea 181 D2
Connaught Terr. Hove 164 C4
Connaught Way. T W 8 B3
Connell Dr. Wood 167 E4
Conqueror Industrial Estate. Hast 139 E3
Conqueror Rd. Hast 161 E4
Consort Way. Bur H 74 B1
Constable Rd. East 176 A1
Constable Way. Bex 160 B3
Conway Pl. Hove 164 C4
Conway St. Hove 164 C4
Cooden Cl. Bex 159 D2
Cooden Dr. Bex 159 E1
Cooden Sea Rd. Bex 158 C1
Cook Ave. East 186 B3
Cookham Dene. Bex 160 A2
Cooksbridge Rd. Bri 166 B3
Cookstown Cl. Nin 136 B3
Coolham Dr. Bri 166 B4
Coombe Cl. Win H 134 C3
Coombe Hill Rd. E Gri 12 A3
Coombe La. Nin 136 B3
Coombe Rd. Bri 146 A1
Coombe Rd. East 185 D2
Coombe Rd. S Mal 127 D1
Coombe Rise. Salt 168 A2
Coombe Shaw. Nin 136 C3
Coombe Vale. Salt 168 A2
Coombers La. Hay H 52 C3
Coombs Cl. Four O 70 A3
Coombs Cotts. Four O 70 A3
Cooper Dr. Bex 159 F4
Cooper Rd. Rye 94 C3
Coopers Cl. Bur H 74 C3
Coopers Hill. Willn 174 C1
Coopers La. Cro 27 D2
Coopers La. Ford 7 D4
Coopers Wood. Cro 27 D2
Copestake Dr. Bur H 75 D2
Coplands Rise. Norm 68 C4
Coppards Cl. Wiv G 76 A2
Coppards La. Norm 69 D4
Copperfields. Lydd 98 C3
Copper's Hill. Bur 63 E3
Coppice Ave. Willn 174 C2
Coppice Cl. Willn 174 C2
Coppice The. Bat 115 F2
Coppice The. Hast 140 B1
Coppice The. Pem 10 A4
Coppice Way. Hay H 52 A2
Copse Cl. E Gri 2 C2
Copse Hill. Bri 145 D3
Copse Rd. Bex 159 E2
Copse The. Hay H 52 C3
Copthorne Rd. Fel 1 B2
Copwood Ave. Uck 79 F4
Copyhold Rd. E Gri 12 A4
Cordons. Kin L 148 A3
Cormorant Cl. East 176 A1
Cornelius Ave. Newh 179 F3
Cornfield Cl. Sea 181 E2
Cornfield Green. Hai 133 D1
Cornfield La. East 185 F1
Cornfield Rd. East 185 F1
Cornfield Rd. Sea 181 E2
Cornfield Terr. East 185 F1
Cornfield Terr. Hast 162 A4
Cornford Cl. Bur H 74 B3
Cornford Cl. Cro 27 F1
Cornford Cl. Pem 9 F3
Cornford La. T W 9 F2
Cornmill Gdns. Willn 174 B2
Cornwall Ave. Pea 179 E3
Cornwall Gdns. Bri 145 E1
Cornwall Rd. Bex 159 F2
Cornwallis Cl. East 186 B4
Cornwallis Gdns. Hast 162 B4
Cornwallis St. Hast 162 B4
Cornwallis Terr. Hast 162 B4
Coronation Cotts. Sale 66 A3
Coronation Gdns. Bat 115 E3
Coronation Gdns. Hur G 46 B2
Coronation Rd. E Gri 12 B4
Coronation St. Bri 166 A4
Corseley Rd. Gro 17 D3
Corsica Cl. Sea 181 E1
Corsica Rd. Sea 181 F1
Costells Edge. Sca H 53 E2
Cotswold Cl. Hast 140 C2
Cotswolds The. Sock 163 E4
Cottage Cl. S Hei 170 A1
Cottage La. Hank 155 E1
Cottage La. Sed 116 C4
Cottage La. Wfd 117 E3
County Oak Ave. Bri 145 F3
Course The. Lew 149 D4
Court Cl. Bri 145 E4
Court Cl. E Gri 2 B1
Court Cres. E Gri 2 B1
Court Farm Cl. Pid 169 F1
Court Farm Rd. Hove 144 C1
Court Farm Rd. Newh 180 A3
Court Farm Rd. Rottn 167 E2
Court Meadow. Rot 40 C4
Court Meadow Cl. Rot 40 C4
Court Ord Rd. Rottn 167 E2
Court Rd. East 175 E1
Court Rd. T W 8 A2
Courtenwell. Lan G 7 E2
Courthope Ave. Wad 31 E2
Courthope Dr. Bex 159 E3
Courthouse St. Hast 162 C4
Courtland Rd. Pole 174 C3
Courtlands. Hay H 52 B2
Courtlands. Nut 37 D1
Courtlands Rd. East 185 F3
Courtyard The. E Gri 2 C1
Courtyard The. Hast 140 B1
Cousley Wood Rd. Cou W 32 A4
Cousley Wood Rd. Wad 31 F3
Coventry Rd. Hast 139 F2
Coventry St. Bri 165 E4
Coverdale Ave. Bex 159 D2
Cowden Cl. The M 47 E4
Cowden Rd. Salt 178 A4
Cowden Wlk. Hast 139 F1
Cowdens Cl. Hove 144 A2
Cowdray Cl. Bex 159 D3
Cowdray Park Rd. Bex 159 D3
Cowfold Rd. Bri 166 B3
Cowley Dr. Wood 167 E4
Cowper St. Hove 164 C4
Cox Gr. Bur H 74 B2
Crabtree Ave. Bri 145 F3
Cradle Hill Industrial Estate. Sea 181 F3
Cradle Hill Rd. Sea 181 F3
Craig Cl. Crow 138 C3
Craignair Ave. Bri 145 E4
Cranborne Ave. East 190 A4
Cranbourne St. Bri 165 E3
Cranbrook Rd. Hast 140 A1
Cranedown. Lew 148 C4
Cranfield Rd. Bex 160 A2
Cranleigh Ave. Salt 167 F1
Cranleigh Cl. Bex 159 F2
Cranmer Ave. Hove 144 B1
Cranmer Cl. S Mal 127 D1
Cranston Ave. Bex 159 E2
Cranston Cl. Bex 159 E2
Cranston Rd. E Gri 2 B1
Cranston Rise. Bex 159 E2
Cranwell Rd. T W 8 A2
Craven Rd. Bri 166 A3
Crawford Way. E Gri 2 B2
Crawley Cres. East 175 E1
Crawley Down Rd. Fel 1 B2
Crawley Rd. Bri 146 A3
Crayford Rd. Bri 146 A1
Crazy La. Sed 116 B4
Crecy Cl. Hast 139 E4
Creek The. Hast 162 C4
Crendon Park. Sgh 8 C4
Crescent Cl. Wood 167 E4
Crescent Dr N. Wood 167 E4
Crescent Dr S. Wood 167 E4
Crescent Pl. Bri 166 A2
Crescent Rd. Bri 165 F4
Crescent Rd. Bur H 74 C2
Crescent Rd. E Gri 2 A1
Crescent Rd. T W 8 C2
Crescent The. Bri 146 B1
Crescent The. Dor P 2 A4
Crescent The. East 184 C3
Crescent The. Hast 140 A2
Crescent The. Key 100 C2
Crescent The. Newh 170 B1
Crescent The. Sock 163 E4
Crescent The. Willn 174 C2
Crescent Way. Bur H 74 C2
Crespin Way. Bri 146 A1
Crest Rd. Newh 170 B1
Cresta Cl. Pole 174 C4
Cresta Rd. Newh 179 F3
Crestway The. Bri 146 A1
Cricketers Field. Stas 67 E1
Cricketfield. Newk 78 A4
Cricketfield Rd. Sea 181 E1
Cricketing La. Hers 134 A2
Criers La. Five A 59 F4
Crink Hill. Bar C 104 B2
Cripland Cl. Hay H 52 C3
Cripps Ave. Pea 169 D1
Crisp Rd. Lew 126 C2
Crittle's Ct. Wad 134 B2
Crockendale Field. Rin 128 B3
Crockers Hatch Cnr. Lan G 7 D1
Crocks Dean. Pea 169 D1
Croft Ave. Sock 163 E4
Croft Cl. Pole 174 B2
Croft Dr. Por S 143 F2
Croft La. Sea 181 E2
Croft Rd. Bri 145 D2
Croft Rd. Cro 27 E1
Croft Rd. Hast 162 C4
Croft The. Hass 100 B3
Croft The. Hast 162 C4
Croft The. Willn 174 C1
Croft Works. Hai 154 C4
Crofton Park Ave. Bex 159 E2
Croham Rd. Cro 27 E2
Cromer Way. Hai 132 C1
Cromer Wlk. Hast 140 B1
Cromleigh Way. Sock 143 E1
Cromwell Pl. E Gri 12 B4
Cromwell Rd. Bur H 74 B2
Cromwell Rd. Hove 165 D4
Cromwell Rd. T W 9 D2
Cromwell St. Bri 166 A4
Crooked La. Sea 181 E1
Cross La. Tic 33 D1
Cross Rd. Sock 163 D4
Cross Road Cl. Sock 163 D4
Cross St. Bri 165 F4
Cross St. Hast 162 A4
Cross St. Hove 165 D3
Cross St. Pole 174 C3
Cross Way. Lew 126 C1
Crossbush Rd. Bri 166 B3
Crossway The. Bri 145 F1
Crossway The. Por S 143 F1
Crossway The. T W 8 A1
Crossways Ave. E Gri 2 A1
Crossways The. St Cro 175 F3
Crouch Cl. East 174 C1
Crouch La. Nin 136 C2
Crouch La. San 49 E4
Crouch La. Sea 181 E1
Crowborough Hill. Cro 40 A4
Crowborough Rd. Hast 141 E2
Crowborough Rd. Salt 168 A1
Crowhurst La. Bex 160 A4
Crowhurst Rd. Bri 146 A4
Crowhurst Rd. Crow 138 C2
Crowhurst Rd. Hast 139 D1
Crowmere Ave. Bex 160 A3
Crowmere Terr. Bex 160 A3
Crown Cl. Hai 154 C4
Crown Cl. Uck 80 A4
Crown Gdns. Bri 165 E3
Crown La. Hast 162 C4
Crown Rd. Por S 163 F4
Crown St. Bri 165 E3
Crown St. East 185 D2
Croxden Wy. East 175 E2
Croxton La. Hay H 52 C3
Crunden Rd. East 185 D2
Cuckfield Cl. Bex 160 C3
Cuckfield Rd. Hur 99 F4
Cuckmere Path. Uck 57 E1
Cuckmere Rd. Newh 179 F3
Cuckmere Rd. Sea 181 F1
Cuckmere Rise. Hea 83 F4
Cuckmere Way. Bri 145 F3
Cuckmere Wlk. East 175 D1
Cuckoo Dr. Hea 83 F3
Cuilfail Tunnel. Lew 127 E1
Culross Ave. Hay H 52 A3
Culver Cl. East 175 F2
Culverden Ave. T W 8 C3
Culverden Down. T W 8 B3
Culverden Park. T W 8 B3
Culverden Park Rd. T W 8 B3
Culverden Sq. T W 8 C3
Culverden St. T W 8 C2
Cumberland Gdns. Hast 161 F4
Cumberland Gdns. T W 8 C1
Cumberland Rd. Bex 159 F4
Cumberland Rd. Bri 145 E1
Cumberland Wlk. T W 8 C1
Cumberland Yd. T W 8 C1
Cumbrian Cl. East 176 A2
Cunningham Dr. East 186 B4
Cunningham Rd. T W 8 C4
Curlew Ct. Hast 139 E2
Currie Rd. T W 8 C3
Curwen Pl. Bri 145 E2
Cuthbert Cl. Bex 159 F4
Cuthbert Rd. Bri 166 A3
Cutter La. Hast 162 C4
Cuttinglye Rd. Cra D 1 A1
Cypress Cl. Hast 161 F4
Cypress Gr. Bel G 19 D4
Cyprus Pl. Rye 94 C3
Cyprus Rd. Bur H 74 C2

Dacre Park. Hai 155 D4
Dacre Rd. East 185 D2
Dacre Rd. Hers 134 B3
Dacre Rd. Newh 180 A4
Dagg La. Ewh G 67 E3
Dale Ave. Bri 145 E3
Dale Ave. Key 100 C2
Dale Cres. Bri 145 E3
Dale Dr. Bri 145 F3
Dale Hill. Pye 122 C3
Dale Rd. For R 13 E1
Dale Rd. Lew 148 C4
Dale St. T W 8 C2
Dale View. Hove 144 B1
Dale View Gdns. Hove 144 A1
Dalehurst Rd. Bex 159 F4
Dalemeny Rd. Bex 159 F3
Dales Cl. Win H 134 C3
Dalewood Gdns. Bur H 75 F1
Dallas La. Spi 104 B3
Dallaway Gdns. E Gri 2 B1
Dallington Cl. Bex 160 C3
Dallington Rd. East 175 F1
Dallington Rd. Hove 164 B4
Dalton Rd. East 190 B4
Damian Way. Key 100 C2
Damon Cl. Pea 179 D4
Dane Cl. Sea 181 D1
Dane Ct Cl. Bex 159 F3
Dane Rd. Hast 161 F4
Dane Rd. Sea 181 E2
Danehill La. Hor K 35 E3
Danehill Rd. Bri 166 B3
Danum Cl. Hai 133 D2
Darby's La. Wad 31 F1
Darcey Dr. Bri 145 F3
Daresbury Cl. Bex 159 F3
Darley Rd. East 190 B4
Dartmouth Cl. Bri 146 B1
Dartmouth Cres. Bri 146 B1
Darvel Down. Net 88 A1
Darwall Dr. Sea 181 F2
Darwell Cl. Hast 139 E1
D'aubigny Rd. Bri 165 F4
Davey Dr. Bri 145 F1
Davey's La. Lew 127 E1
Davigdor Rd. Hove 165 E4
Davis Cl. Bex 159 F4
Dawson Terr. Bri 166 A3
De Cham Ave. Hast 162 A4
De Cham Rd. Hast 162 A4
De Chardin Dr. Hast 140 C3
De Courcel Rd. Bri 166 B2
De La Warr Green. Lew 126 C2
De La Warr Par. Bex 160 B2
De La Warr Rd. Bex 160 B3
De La Warr Rd. E Gri 2 B1
De Monkfort Rd. Bri 166 A4
De Montfort Rd. Lew 126 C1
De Roos Rd. East 185 E2
De Walden Mews. East 190 B4

De Warrenne Rd. Lew 126 C1
Deacons Dr. Por S 144 A1
Deadmantree Hill. Bar 103 F2
Deadmantree Hill. Bar C 103 F2
Deal Ave. Sea 182 A3
Deals The. Rye 94 C3
Dean Cl. Por S 144 A1
Dean Ct Rd. Rottn 167 F1
Dean Gdns. Por S 144 A1
Dean Rd. Sea 181 E1
Dean St. Bri 165 E3
Deanery Cl. S Mal 127 D2
Deans Cl. Bex 159 F3
Deans Cl. Wood 167 E4
Deans Dr. Bex 159 F3
Deans Meadow. Bar C 104 B3
Deans Rd. Alfn 172 B2
Deanway. Hove 144 C2
Decimus Burton Way. Hast 162 A4
Decoy Dr. East 175 E1
Deepdene. Wad 31 E3
Deerswood La. Bex 159 E3
Deeside The. Bri 145 F4
Delavall Wlk. East 186 B3
Delaware Rd. Lew 148 C4
Delfryn. Por S 143 E2
Dell Cl. Hast 139 F1
Dell Dr. T W 9 D2
Dell The. E Gri 2 C1
Dellney Ave. Hay H 52 B2
Delmonden Rd. Fli 34 C1
Delves Ave. T W 9 D1
Delves Cl. Rin 128 A3
Delves Way. Rin 128 A3
Den Hill. East 184 C2
Denbigh Rd. T W 9 D4
Dencher Rd. Iford 148 B2
Dene Cl. Fri 183 F1
Dene Dr. East 175 D1
Dene Path. Uck 57 D1
Dene The. Hast 140 C3
Dene The. Hove 144 A2
Dene The. Uck 57 D1
Dene The. Willn 174 C2
Dene Vale. Bri 145 D3
Denehurst Gdns. Hast 140 C3
Deneside. Bri 145 D3
Deneside. Fri 183 F1
Deneway. Spe 7 F4
Deneway The. Bri 145 D2
Denge La. Lydd 98 C4
Denham Cl. Hast 139 E2
Denham Rd. Bur H 74 A2
Denham Way. Cam 96 B1
Denman's Cl. Hay H 52 C4
Denman's La. Hay H 52 C4
Denmark Mews. Hove 164 C4
Denmark Pl. Hast 162 B4
Denmark Rd. Por S 164 A4
Denmark Terr. Bri 165 E3
Denmark Villas. Hove 164 C4
Denne's La. Lydd 98 C4
Denton Cl. Rye 94 C3
Denton Dr. Bri 145 F3
Denton Dr. Newh 170 B1
Denton Rd. East 190 A4
Denton Rd. Newh 170 B1
Denton Rise. Newh 170 B1
Dentons The. East 190 A4
Derek Ave. Hove 164 A3
Derings The. Lydd 98 C3
Derwent Cl. Hai 132 C1
Derwent Dr. T W 8 B3
Derwent Rd. East 190 B4
Desmond Rd. East 186 A3
Desmond Way. Bri 166 B3
Devil's Dyke Rd. Hove 144 B3
Devil's Dyke Rd. Poy 122 A1
Devonshire Cl. T W 18 B4
Devonshire Pl. Bri 165 F3
Devonshire Pl. East 185 F1
Devonshire Rd. Bex 160 A2
Devonshire Rd. Hast 162 B4
Devonshire Sq. Bex 160 A2
Dew La. Peas 70 C1
Dewe Rd. Bri 146 A1
Dewpond The. Pea 168 C1
Diana Cl. Bex 160 C3
Dickens Cl. E Gri 2 A1
Dickens Way. East 176 B2
Dicklands The. Rod 169 D4
Dillingburgh Rd. East 185 D2
Dillon Way. T W 9 D3
Diplock Cl. Pole 174 B3
Diplocks The. Hai 154 C4
Diplocks Way. Hai 154 C4
Diplocks Wlk. Hai 154 C4
Dirty La. Ash W 13 E3
Dirty La. Hamm 13 D3
Ditchling Bostal. Wmes 124 A4
Ditchling Cres. Bri 146 A3
Ditchling Dr. Hast 141 E2
Ditchling Gdns. Bri 145 F1
Ditchling Rd. Bri 145 F2
Ditchling Rd. Wmes 124 A2
Ditchling Rise. Bri 165 F4
Ditchling Way. Hai 154 C3
Ditton's Cnr. Pole 175 D3
Dittons Mews. Hast 139 E1
Dittons Rd. East 185 E2
Dittons Rd. St Cro 175 E3
Dixter La. Norm 68 C4
Dixter Rd. Norm 68 C3
Dock The. W Fir 151 D2
Dodshill. Cro 27 F1
Dog Kennel La. Five A 59 F3
Dogs Hill Rd. Winc B 120 C3
Doleham Hill. Thr O 118 A3
Doleham Hill. Wfd 118 A3
Doleham La. Wfd 117 F3
Dolphin Rd. Hay H 52 A2
Donald Hall Rd. Bri 166 A3
Donald Way. Winc B 120 C3
Donkey Mews. Hove 165 D3
Donnington Rd. Wood 167 E3
Dordrecht Way. Hast 140 B1
Dorking Rd. T W 9 D3
Dormans Cl. Dor 2 C4
Dormans Gdns. Dor P 2 B3
Dormans High St. Dor 2 C4
Dormans Park Rd. Dor P 2 B3
Dormans Park Rd. E Gri 2 A2
Dormans Station Rd. Dor 2 B4
Dornden Dr. Lan G 7 F2
Dornden Park. T W 7 F2
Dorothy Ave. Pea 179 D4
Dorothy Rd. Hove 164 A4
Dorset Ave. E Gri 2 A2
Dorset Gdns. Bri 165 F3
Dorset Pl. Bri 165 F3
Dorset Pl. Hast 162 B4
Dorset Rd. Bex 160 B3
Dorset Rd. Lew 149 D4
Dorset Rd. T W 9 D1
Dorset Rd S. Bex 160 A2
Dorset St. Bri 165 F3
Doubledays. Bur H 74 C1
Doucegrove. Hast 139 F1
Douglas Rd. Tow R 29 D1
Dovedale Gdns. East 175 E1
Dover Cl. Sea 182 A3
Dover Rd. Bri 145 F1
Dover Rd. Pole 174 C4
Dowland Ave. Sock 143 E1
Down Ave. Lam 21 F2
Down La. Frant 18 C1
Down Rd. Bex 159 F3
Down St. Mar 56 A3
Down St. Nut 37 D1
Down Terr. Bri 166 A3
Down The. Hove 144 A2
Downash Cl. Bri 166 B3
Downey Cl. Hast 139 F3
Downland Ave. Pea 179 E3
Downland Cl. Sock 143 D1
Downland Cl. Wood 166 C4
Downland Cres. Hove 144 B2
Downland Dr. Hove 144 B2
Downland Rd. Wood 166 C4
Downlands Ave. Bex 159 F2
Downlands Cl. Bex 159 F2
Downlands Way. Fri 183 F1
Downs Ave. East 184 C3
Downs Cl. Lew 126 C1
Downs Rd. Bur H 74 B2
Downs Rd. Hast 140 B2
Downs Rd. Sea 181 F2
Downs Rd. Willn 174 C1
Downs Valley Rd. Wood 167 E4
Downs View. N Cha 77 E4
Downs View. Nin 136 C3
Downs View. Pea 169 D1
Downs View Cl. Fri 184 A1
Downs View Cl. N Cha 77 E4
Downs View La. Fri 184 A1
Downs View Rd. Hass 100 B2
Downs View Rd. Sea 181 F2
Downs Way. Sock 143 E1
Downscroft. Bur H 75 D3
Downside. Hove 144 C2
Downside. Lew 148 C4
Downside Cl. East 185 D2
Downsvalley Rd. Willn 174 C2
Downsview. Hea 83 F4
Downsview. Hove 144 A2
Downsview Ave. Wood 167 D4
Downsview Cres. Uck 80 A4
Downsview Dr. Wiv G 76 A2
Downsview Rd. Por S 143 F1
Downsview Rd. Willn 174 C2
Downsview Way. Hai 154 C4
Downsway. Wood 147 D1
Draffin La. Cam 96 A2
Drake Ave. East 186 B4
Drapers Way. Hast 139 F1
Draxmont Way. Bri 145 E2
Drayton Rise. Bex 159 D2
Drive The. Bur H 74 C2
Drive The. Cro 27 D1
Drive The. Hai 154 C3
Drive The. Hast 161 E4
Drive The. Hove 165 D4
Drive The. Mar 56 C3
Drive The. Sock 143 E1
Drive The. T W 8 C1
Drive The. Uck 80 A4
Drockmill Cl. Pole 175 D3
Drove Ave. Kin L 147 D1
Drove Ave. Wood 147 D1
Drove Cres. Por S 143 F1
Drove Rd. Por S 143 F1
Drove Rd. Wood 166 C4
Drove The. Bri 145 D1
Drove The. Fal 147 D3
Drove The. Newh 180 B4
Drove The. Off 126 C3
Drovers Cl. Por S 144 A1
Drovers Way. Bur H 75 D1
Droveway The. Hay H 52 A3
Droveway The. Hove 145 D1
Drummond Cl. Hay H 52 A2
Drury La. Hast 139 F1
Dryden Wlk. East 176 B2
Dudley Rd. Bri 145 F1
Dudley Rd. East 185 F2
Dudley Rd. Hast 141 D1
Dudley Rd. T W 8 C2
Dudwell Rd. Wood 167 E4
Duke Rd. Hast 139 F1
Duke St. Bex 159 E3
Duke St. Bri 165 E3
Duke St. East 185 F2
Duke St. Hast 139 F1
Duke Terr. Hast 139 F1
Dukes Cl. Sea 181 D2
Duke's Dr. East 190 B4
Dukes Hill. Bat 115 D3
Dukes La. Bri 165 E3
Duke's Mound. Bri 166 A2
Duke's Pas. Bri 165 E3
Dukes Rd. Hay H 52 C4
Dukes Rd. T W 9 D3
Dulwich Cl. Sea 181 F2
Dumb Woman's La. Udi 94 A2
Dumbrells Ct. Dit 101 D2
Dumbrills Cl. Bur H 74 C3
Dunclutha Rd. Hast 140 B2
Duncton Cl. Hay H 52 A2
Dundale Rd. Bel G 10 C1
Dundale Rd. Kip 10 B1
Dunes Ave. Cam 96 B1
Dunning's Rd. E Gri 12 B4
Dunstall Ave. Bur H 74 B2
Dunstall Farm Rd. Bur H 74 B2
Dunstan Gr. T W 8 C3
Dunstan Rd. T W 8 C3
Dunstans Croft. May 42 A2
Dunster Cl. Bri 145 F1
Dunvan Cl. S Mal 127 D2
Durham Cl. Bri 146 C1
Durkins Rd. E Gri 2 A2
Durrell Cl. East 176 B1
Dursley Rd. East 185 F2
Dyke Cl. Hove 144 C2
Dyke Cl. Poy 122 A2
Dyke La. Poy 122 A2
Dyke Rd. Bri 165 E4
Dyke Road Ave. Hove 145 D2
Dyke Road Dr. Bri 165 E4
Dyke Road Mews. Bri 165 E4
Dyke Road Pl. Bri 145 D2
Dymchurch Cl. Pole 175 D4
Dymchurch Cl. Sea 182 A2
Dymock Cl. Sea 182 A2
Dymock's The. Dit 101 D2
Dymond Rd. Hast 139 F2
Dynevor Rd. T W 9 D4

Eagle Rd. Rye 95 D3
Earl St. Hast 162 B4
Earls Cl. Sea 181 D3
Earls Gdn. Lew 127 D1
Earl's Rd. T W 8 A2
East Albany Rd. Sea 181 E2
East Ascent. Hast 162 A3
East Beach St. Hast 162 C4
East Beeches Rd. Cro 27 F1
East Bourne St. Hast 162 C4
East Cl. Pole 174 C3
East Cliff. Rye 95 D3
East Cliff Rd. T W 8 C3
East Dean Rd. East 184 C1
East Dean Rise. Sea 181 F2
East Dr. Bri 166 A3
East End La. Dit 101 D2
East Gdns. Dit 101 D2
East Hill. Dor P 2 B3
East Hill Pas. Hast 162 C4
East Mascalls Rd. Hay H 53 E3
East Par. Hast 162 C4
East Park La. Dom 1 A4
East St. Bri 165 F2
East St. Fal 147 D3
East St. Hast 162 C4
East St. Lew 127 D1
East St. May 42 A2
East St. Por S 164 A4
East St. Rye 95 D3
East St. Sea 181 E2
East St. Tur H 11 D2
East View Fields. Plu 102 B3
East View Terr. Sed 90 B1
East Way. Lew 126 B1
Eastbank. Sock 143 E1
Eastbourne Ave. Pev B 177 D3
Eastbourne Rd. Bri 146 A1
Eastbourne Rd. Fel 1 B4
Eastbourne Rd. Pev B 177 D2
Eastbourne Rd. Pole 174 C3
Eastbourne Rd. Rid 80 A2
Eastbourne Rd. Sea 182 A2
Eastbourne Rd. Whm 176 B3
Eastbourne Rd. Willn 174 C2
Eastbrook Rd. Por S 163 F4
Eastbrook Way. Por S 163 F4
Eastdale Rd. Bur H 75 D2
Eastergate. Bex 159 D3
Eastergate Rd. Bri 146 B2
Eastern Ave. Pole 174 C4
Eastern Pl. Bri 166 B2
Eastern Rd. Bri 166 A2
Eastern Rd. Hay H 52 B2
Eastern Rd. Hay H 53 D4
Eastern Rd. Wiv 75 F2
Eastern St. Bri 166 A2
Eastern Terr. Bri 166 A2
Eastern Terr Mews. Bri 166 A2
Eastfield Cres. Bri 145 F2
Eastgate St. Lew 127 D1
Eastgate Wharf. Lew 127 D1
Easthill Dr. Por S 143 F1
Easthill Way. Por S 143 F1
Eastlands Cl. T W 18 B4
Eastlands Rd. T W 8 B1
Eastport La. Lew 149 D4
Eastwell Pl. Hai 154 C4
Eastwick Cl. Bri 145 F4
Eastwood Rd. Bex 159 F2
Eatenden La. Mou 88 C1
Eatenden La. Net 88 C1
Eaton Gdns. Hove 165 D4
Eaton Gr. Hove 165 D4
Eaton Pl. Bri 166 A2
Eaton Rd. Hove 165 D3
Eaton Villas. Hove 164 C4
Ebden's Hill. Hast 139 F4
Ebden's Hill. Wfd 139 F4
Ebenezer Rd. Hast 162 C4
Ecmod Rd. East 186 A3
Edburton Ave. Bri 145 F1
Eden Dr. Bex 159 E2
Eden Rd. T W 8 C1
Eden Vale. Dor P 2 B3
Eden Vale. E Gri 2 B3
Edensor Rd. East 190 A4
Edgar Rd. Hast 141 D1
Edgehill Way. Por S 143 E1
Edgeland Terr. East 175 E1
Edinburgh Rd. Bex 160 A3
Edinburgh Rd. Bri 165 F4
Edinburgh Rd. Hast 161 E4
Edinburgh Rd. Sea 181 D2
Edinburgh Way. E Gri 12 B4
Edison Rd. East 175 F1
Edith Ave. Pea 178 C4
Edith Rd. Hast 141 D2
Edmonton Rd. Bex 159 F4
Edmund Rd. Hast 141 D1
Edward Ave. Hove 144 C2
Edward Ave. Salt 168 A2
Edward Cl. Hove 144 C2
Edward Cl. Sea 180 C3
Edward Rd. Hast 162 A4
Edward Rd. Hay H 52 B1
Edward St. Bri 165 F3
Edward St. Lew 127 D1
Edward St. Sgh 8 B4
Edward St. T W 8 A2
Edward Terr. Hast 139 F2
Edward Way. Bur H 74 A1
Edwin Rd. Hast 141 D1
Effingham Cl. Salt 168 A1
Effingham Dr. Bex 159 D2
Egerton Rd. Bex 159 F2
Eggington Cl. Bri 146 C3
Eggington Rd. Bri 146 C3
Egles Gr. Uck 79 F4
Egmont Rd. Hove 144 A1
Egremont Pl. Bri 165 F3
Egremont Pl. Hast 140 C1
Eight Acre La. Thr O 118 A1
Eight Bells Cl. Bux 58 A2
Eileen Ave. Salt 167 F1
Elder Pl. Bri 165 F4
Elderwood Cl. East 175 D1
Eldon Rd. East 185 D3
Eldred Ave. Bri 145 D3
Eleanor Cl. Lew 126 C1
Eley Cres. Rottn 167 E2
Eley Dr. Rottn 167 E2
Elford St. Hast 162 B4
Elgin Gdns. Sea 182 A2
Elim Ct Gdns. Cro 27 E2
Elim Wlk. Hast 140 B1
Elizabeth Ave. Hove 144 C2
Elizabeth Cl. Hove 144 C2
Elizabeth Cl. Sea 180 C3
Elizabeth Cres. E Gri 2 B2
Elizabeth Rd. Hast 139 F1
Elizabeth Rd. S Sea 163 D4
Ellen St. Hove 164 C4
Ellen St. Por S 164 A4
Ellenslea Rd. Hast 162 A4
Ellenwhorne La. Cri C 90 C4
Ellenwhorne La. Ewh G 90 C4
Ellerslie La. Bex 159 E3
Elliots Way. Hea 83 F4
Ellis Way. Uck 79 F4
Elm Cl. Hove 145 D1
Elm Cl. Lau 130 A4
Elm Cl. Sea 182 A2
Elm Ct. Newh 179 F4
Elm Dr. E Gri 2 C1
Elm Dr. Hove 144 B1
Elm Gr. Bri 166 A4
Elm Gr. East 175 E1
Elm Green. Hai 132 C1
Elm Rd. Por S 163 F4
Elm Way. Hea 83 F3
Elmhurst Ave. Pem 10 A4
Elmore Rd. Bri 165 F3
Elms Ave. East 185 F1
Elms La. Pett 119 E1
Elms Lea Ave. Bri 145 E2
Elms Rd. East 185 F1
Elms The. Rin 128 A3
Elmsdown Pl. Hai 155 D4
Elmsmead. Iden 71 F2
Elmstead Rd. Bex 160 B3
Elphick Rd. Newh 180 A4
Elphick's Pl. T W 18 C4
Elphinstone Ave. Hast 140 B1
Elphinstone Gdns. Hast 140 B2
Elphinstone Rd. Hast 140 B2
Elrington Rd. Hove 145 D1
Elstead Cres. Bri 146 A3
Elsted Cl. East 175 F1
Elsted Rd. Bex 159 D1
Elven Cl. Fri 184 A1
Elven La. Fri 184 A1
Elvin Cres. Rottn 167 E2
Ely La. T W 8 C2
Emmanuel Rd. Hast 140 C1
Endwell Rd. Bex 160 A2
Engalee. E Gri 2 A1
English Cl. Hove 164 B4
English's Pas. Lew 127 D1
Enys Rd. East 185 E2
Epeland. Hai 132 C1
Erica Cl. East 175 F1
Eridge Cl. Bex 159 F2
Eridge Dr. Cro 27 F2
Eridge Gdns. Cro 27 F2
Eridge Green. Lew 126 C1
Eridge Rd. Boa 28 A3
Eridge Rd. Cro 27 F2
Eridge Rd. East 185 D4
Eridge Rd. Hove 144 C1
Eridge Rd. T W 18 B4
Erin Way. Bur H 74 B2
Erroll Rd. Hove 164 A3
Ersham Rd. Hai 154 C3
Ersham Way. Hai 154 C3
Esher Cl. Sea 181 E2
Eshton Rd. East 186 A3
Eskbank Ave. Bri 145 F4
Eskine Park Rd. T W 8 A2
Esplanade. Sea 181 E1
Esplanade The. Pea 178 B4
Essenden Rd. Hast 161 F3
Essex Cl. T W 18 B4
Essex Cotts. Bri 166 A2
Essex Pl. Newh 180 A4
Essex Rd. Hast 139 F2
Essex St. Bri 166 A2
Estate Rd. Newh 180 B4
Estcots Dr. E Gri 2 C1
Etchingham Rd. East 176 B1
Ethel St. Hove 164 C4
Etherington Hill. Spe 8 A4
Etherton Way. Sea 181 F2
Ethnan La. San 49 E2
Eton Cl. Sea 181 F2
Evelyn Ave. Newh 180 A4
Evelyn Rd. Lew 126 C1
Evelyn Terr. Bri 166 A3
Eversfield Pl. Hast 162 A4
Eversfield Rd. East 185 E2
Eversley Cl. Hast 140 A1
Eversley Cres. Hast 140 A1
Eversley Rd. Bex 160 A2
Eversley Rd. Hast 140 A1
Ewart St. Bri 165 F3
Ewehurst La. Spe 7 E3
Ewhurst Cl. Hast 140 B2
Ewhurst La. Mill C 68 B3
Ewhurst La. Norm 68 B3
Ewhurst Rd. Bri 146 A1
Exceat Cl. Bri 166 B3
Exeter Cl. Willn 174 C1
Exeter St. Bri 165 E4
Exmouth Pl. Hast 162 C4

Factory La. Hai 154 C3
Fair La. Rob 65 F2
Fair Meadow. Rye 95 D4
Fair Oak Cl. Hea 83 F4
Fairbanks. Hay H 52 B2
Faircrouch La. Wad 31 D3
Fairdene. Sock 143 E1
Fairfax Ave. Hast 139 E3
Fairfield. Hers 134 B3
Fairfield Ave. T W 9 D3
Fairfield Cl. Bur H 74 B2
Fairfield Cl. S Sea 143 D1
Fairfield Cres. Hur 99 F3
Fairfield Gdns. Por S 143 F1
Fairfield Rd. Bur H 74 B2
Fairfield Rd. E Gri 12 B4
Fairfield Rd. East 185 E1
Fairfield Way. Hay H 52 A4
Fairford Cl. Hay H 52 B3
Fairglen Rd. Wad 30 C2
Fairholme Rd. Newh 170 B1
Fairisle Cl. Hai 132 C1
Fairlaine Rd. East 185 D3
Fairlawn Cres. E Gri 1 C1
Fairlawn Dr. E Gri 1 C1
Fairlawns Dr. Hers 134 B3
Fairlea Cl. Bur H 74 B2
Fairley Bank. Hast 141 D1
Fairlie Gdns. Bri 145 E2
Fairlight. Uck 57 E1
Fairlight Ave. Hast 141 D2
Fairlight Ave. Pea 178 B4
Fairlight Cl. Bex 160 C3
Fairlight Cl. Pole 174 C3
Fairlight Field. Rin 128 A3
Fairlight Gdns. Fai 142 B2
Fairlight Pl. Bri 166 A4
Fairlight Rd. East 186 A3
Fairlight Rd. Hast 141 E2
Fairmile Rd. T W 9 E3
Fairmount Rd. Bex 160 A3
Fairstone Cl. Hast 141 E2
Fairview Cotts. Cro 27 E2
Fairview La. Cro 27 E2
Fairview Rise. Bri 145 D3
Fairway Cl. East 185 D1
Fairway Cres. Por S 144 A1
Fairway The. Bex 159 E3
Fairway The. Hast 161 E4
Fairways Cl. Sea 182 A1
Fairways Rd. Sea 182 A1
Fairways The. Sgh 8 C4
Falaise Rd. Hast 162 A4
Falaise Rd. Newh 170 B1
Falcon Cl. S Sea 163 D3
Falcon Way. Hai 132 C2
Falconbury Dr. Bex 159 D2
Falconers Dr. Bat 115 E2
Fallowfield Cl. Hove 144 B1
Fallowfield Cres. Hove 144 B1
Falmer Ave. Salt 168 A1
Falmer Cl. East 184 C4

Falmer Gdns. Wood 167 D4
Falmer Hill. Bri 146 C3
Falmer Hill. Fal 147 D3
Falmer Rd. Rottn 167 E2
Falmer Rd. Wood 167 D4
Faraday Ave. E Gri 12 B3
Faraday Cl. East 175 E1
Farley Bank. Hast 140 C1
Farley Way. Fai 142 B3
Farlington Ave. Hay H 52 B3
Farlington Cl. Hay H 52 B3
Farm Cl. E Gri 12 C4
Farm Cl. Hass 100 B2
Farm Cl. Por S 143 F1
Farm Cl. Sea 181 F2
Farm Hill. Wood 167 D4
Farm La. Cam 96 A2
Farm Rd. Hove 165 D3
Farm Way. Bur H 75 D1
Farm Way. Por S 163 F4
Farm Yd. Bri 165 E3
Farman St. Hove 165 D3
Farmcombe Cl. T W 8 C1
Farmcombe La. T W 8 C1
Farmcombe Rd. T W 9 D1
Farmland Way. Hai 133 D1
Farmlands Ave. Willn 174 B2
Farmlands Cl. Willn 174 C2
Farmlands Way. Pole 174 B3
Farmway Cl. Hove 144 A1
Farncombe Cl. Wiv G 76 A2
Farne Cl. Hai 132 B1
Farnham Ave. Key 100 C3
Farnham Cl. Lan G 7 F2
Farnham La. Lan G 7 F2
Farningham Rd. Cro 40 A4
Farnlea Rd. Bur H 75 D3
Farriers Way. Rid 80 A3
Farthing Hill. Tic 33 E1
Farthing La. Pon G 112 B3
Farthings The. Cro 27 F2
Faulkners Way. Bur H 74 C3
Faversham Rd. East 176 A1
Faygate Cl. Bex 159 F4
Faygate Rd. East 175 E1
Fayre Meadow. Rob 65 F2
Fearon Rd. Hast 140 B1
Felbridge Cl. E Gri 2 A2
Felbridge Ct. E Gri 1 C2
Felbridge Rd. Cra D 1 A2
Felcot Rd. Cra D 1 A2
Felcourt La. Dor P 2 A4
Felcourt Rd. Dor P 2 A4
Fellows Rd. Hast 140 C2
Fennell's Cl. East 185 E3
Ferbies. Spe 7 F4
Ferguson Rd. Lydd 98 B1
Fermor Rd. Cro 39 E4
Fermor Row. Cro 39 E4
Fermor Way. Cro 39 F4
Fern Cl. East 176 A2
Fern Green. Hai 132 C1
Fern Rd. Hast 161 E4
Ferndale. T W 9 D3
Ferndale Cl. T W 9 D2
Ferndale Rd. Bur H 75 D1
Ferndale Rd. Hove 165 D4
Ferndean Cl. Hast 161 E4
Fernhurst Cl. Bri 145 F3
Fernhurst Cres. Bri 145 F3
Fernlea Cl. Wfd 117 E2
Ferns The. T W 8 C2
Fernside Ave. Hast 161 E4
Fernwood Rise. Bri 145 D3
Ferrers Rd. Lew 126 C1
Ferring Cl. Rye 94 C3
Ferry Hill. Winc 120 B4
Ferry Rd. Rye 94 C3
Festival Gdns. Bex 160 A4
Field Cl. Bur H 74 B2
Field Cl. Sea 181 F1
Field Way. Hast 161 E4
Fielden La. Cro 27 D1
Fielden Rd. Cro 27 D1
Fieldway. Bro OW 91 F3
Fieldway. Dit 101 D2
Fieldway. Hay H 52 B4
Fiennes Rd. Hers 134 B3
Figg La. Cro 39 E4
Filching Cl. Willn 174 B2
Filching Rd. East 184 C3
Filder Cl. East 185 F3
Filsham Dr. Bex 160 C3
Filsham Rd. Hast 161 E4
Filsham Valley. Hast 161 E4
Finches Gdns. Hay H 52 C4
Finches Park Rd. Hay H 52 C4
Finches The. Bex 160 B2
Finches The. Hast 139 F3
Findon Ave. Salt 168 B1
Findon Cl. Bex 159 E2
Findon Cl. Hove 144 B2
Findon Cl. Sea 182 A2
Findon Rd. Bri 166 B3
Finmere Cl. East 186 A3
Finmere Rd. East 186 A3
Finsbury Rd. Bri 166 A3
Fir Cl. Wood 167 E4
Fir Grove Rd. Cro H 82 C4
Fir Toll Rd. May 41 E1
Fir Tree Cl. Bex 159 D2
Fir Tree Cl. Hai 133 D1
Fir Tree Rd. T W 8 B2
Fir Tree Way. Key 100 C2
Fircroft Cl. Bri 145 E2
Firlands. Hay H 52 B2
Firle Bostal. W Fir 150 C2
Firle Cl. Hast 141 E2
Firle Cl. Sea 181 E3
Firle Cres. Lew 126 B1
Firle Dr. Sea 181 E3
Firle Green. Uck 57 E1
Firle Rd. Bex 159 D2
Firle Rd. Bri 166 A3
Firle Rd. East 185 F2
Firle Rd. Pea 179 D4
Firle Rd. Sea 181 E3
Firle Terr. S Hei 170 A1
First Ave. Bex 160 B3
First Ave. Cam 96 B1
First Ave. Hove 165 D3
First Ave. Newh 180 A3
First St. Lan G 7 E2
Firtoft Cl. Bur H 74 C2
Firtree Rd. Hast 140 C1
Firwood Cl. East 175 E1
Firwood Cl. Hea 83 F4
Firwood Rise. Hea 83 F4
Fisher Cl. East 186 B4
Fisher St. Lew 127 D1
Fishmarket Rd. Rye 95 D3
Fishponds La. Wfd 117 E2
Fitch Dr. Bri 146 B1
Fitzgerald Ave. Sea 181 E1
Fitzgerald Cl. East 185 E1
Fitzgerald Park. Sea 181 E1
Fitzgerald Rd. S Mal 127 D2
Fitzjohns Rd. Lew 126 C1
Fitzmaurice Ave. East 185 F3
Fitzroy Rd. Lew 126 C1
Five Acre Wlk. Hast 140 B1
Five Ways. T W 8 C2
Flamsteed Rd. Hers 134 C1
Fleming Cl. East 176 B1
Fletcher Ave. Hast 139 E4
Fletching Cl. Bri 166 B3
Fletching Rd. East 175 F1
Fletching St. May 42 A2
Flimwell Cl. Bri 166 B2
Flimwell Cl. Fli 34 A2
Flint Cl. Por S 143 F1
Flitterbrook La. Pup T 85 D2
Flitterbrook La. Rus 85 D2
Florence Ave. Hove 164 A4
Florence Pl. Bri 145 F1
Florence Rd. Bri 165 F4
Folders Cl. Bur H 75 D1
Folders La. Bur H 75 D1
Foley Cl. East 186 B4
Folkestone Cl. Sea 182 A3
Folkestone Rd. E Gul 95 E4
Folkestone Rd. Rye 72 C1
Folkington Gdns. Hast 140 A3
Folkington Rd. Fol 174 A3
Folly Field. Newh 180 A4
Fonthill Rd. Hove 164 C4
Fontridge La. Bur 64 A2
Fontridge La. Etc 64 C3
Fontwell Ave. Bex 159 D3
Foords La. St Cro 176 A4
Foot's La. Bur C 62 C2
Ford Rd. Hast 139 E1
Fordcombe La. Ford 7 D3
Fordcombe Rd. Ford 6 C3
Fordcombe Rd. Lan G 7 D2
Foredown Cl. East 185 D1
Foredown Cl. Por S 143 F1
Foredown Dr. Por S 164 A4
Foredown Rd. Por S 143 F2
Forest Dene. Cro 28 A1
Forest Park. Cro 27 D1
Forest Pl. Cro H 82 B3
Forest Rd. Bri 146 B3
Forest Rd. For R 13 F1
Forest Rd. T W 9 D1
Forest Ridge. Sha 22 C3
Forest Rise. Cro 28 A1
Forest View. Hai 154 C4
Forest View. Nut 37 D2
Forest View Rd. E Gri 12 B3
Forest Way. Hast 140 B1
Forest Way. Pem 10 A4
Forest Way. T W 9 D1
Forewood La. Crow 138 C4
Forewood Rise. Crow 138 B3
Forge Cl. Por S 143 F1
Forge Cl. Stas 67 E1
Forge Field. Ston 44 B3
Forge La. Stas 67 E1
Forge Lane Cotts. Mar 56 C4
Forge Rise. Rid 80 A3
Forge Way. Bur H 74 C2
Forge Way. Hast 140 A3
Forstal The. Eri G 17 E2
Forstal The. Pem 10 B4
Forstall. Lan G 7 F2
Fort Haven. S Sea 163 D3
Fort La. East 186 A3
Fort Rd. East 186 A3
Fort Rd. Newh 180 A3
Fort Rise. Newh 180 A3
Foundry La. Lew 127 E1
Foundry St. Bri 165 F3
Fountains Cl. Bri 146 A1
Fountains Cl. East 175 E2
Founthill Ave. Salt 167 F1
Founthill Rd. Salt 167 F1
Fourteen Acre La. Thr O 118 B2
Fourth Ave. Hove 164 C3
Fowlers Cl. Bex 159 E3
Fowly La. H Hur 57 F3
Fox Hill. Hay H 52 B1
Fox Hill Cl. Hay H 52 B1
Fox Hill Village. Hay H 52 B1
Fox Way. Por S 143 F1
Foxcote. Hast 140 A3
Foxdown Rd. Wood 167 E4
Foxglove Cl. Rin 128 C4
Foxglove Rd. East 175 F2
Foxhill. Bex 159 E3
Foxhill. Pea 168 C1
Foxhole La. Four T 48 A4
Foxhole La. Wad 31 F2
Foxhunters Rd. Por S 143 E2
Foxwarren. Hay H 52 A3
Foyle Way. East 190 B3
Framelle Mount. Fra 80 C3
Framfield Rd. Bux 57 F2
Framfield Rd. Rid 80 A3
Framfield Way. East 185 D3
Francis Rd. Hay H 52 C4
Francis St. Bri 165 F4
Frankfield Rise. T W 8 C1
Franklands Cl. Bur H 74 C1
Franklands Way. Bur H 100 C4
Franklin Rd. Bri 166 A4
Franklin Rd. Por S 164 A4
Franklin Rd. S Sea 143 D1
Franklin St. Bri 166 A4
Franklynn Rd. Hay H 52 B2
Frankton Ave. Hay H 52 C2
Frant Ave. Bex 159 D3
Frant Cl. Bex 159 D3
Frant Rd. Hove 144 C1
Frant Rd. T W 8 C1
Frary Wlk. Hea 83 F2
Fraser Ave. East 186 B4
Freckley Hollow. Cat 113 F1
Frederick Gdns. Bri 165 F3
Frederick Pl. Bri 165 F3
Frederick Rd. Hast 141 D2
Frederick St. Bri 165 F3
Free Heath Rd. Lam 21 D2
Freehold Terr. Bri 146 A1
Freeks La. Bur H 74 C3
Freeland Cl. Sea 180 C3
Freeman Ave. East 175 E1
Freemans Rd. Por S 163 F4
Freezeland La. Bex 137 F1
Fremlin Cl. T W 7 F2
French Gdns. Hay H 52 C3
Frenches Farm Dr. Hea 83 F3
Frenchgate Cl. East 175 E1
Frenchgate Rd. East 175 E1
Freshfield. Bri 166 A3
Freshfield. Hai 154 C3
Freshfield Bank. For R 13 E1
Freshfield La. Dan 35 E1
Freshfield La. Hor K 35 E1
Freshfield Rd. Bri 166 A3
Freshfield St. Bri 166 A3
Freshfield Way. Bri 166 A3
Freshford Cl. East 176 A1
Freshwater Ave. Hast 140 B1
Freshwater Sq. Willn 174 C2
Freshway. Willn 175 D2
Frewen Cl. Norm 68 C4
Frewyn Cl. Hast 139 E2
Friar Cl. Bri 145 F2
Friar Cres. Bri 145 F2
Friar Rd. Bri 145 F2
Friar Wlk. Bri 145 E2
Friars' Ave. Pea 179 E3
Friars Bank. Gue G 141 F4
Friars Cl. Hass 100 B2
Friar's Cres. Gue G 141 F4
Friars Oak Rd. Hass 100 B3
Friars Rd. Winc 120 B4
Friars Way. Hast 140 B2
Friars Way. T W 9 D3
Friars' Wlk. Lew 127 D1
Friday St. East 176 A2
Fridays The. E Dean 188 C4
Friezland Rd. T W 8 A1
Frimley Cl. Wood 167 E4
Friston Ave. East 175 D1
Friston Cl. Bri 146 B2
Friston Cl. Fri 183 F1
Friston Cl. Sea 181 D2
Friston Downs. Fri 183 F1
Frith Park. E Gri 2 B2
Frith Rd. Hove 164 C4
Frobisher Cl. East 186 B4
Frog La. T W 8 C1
Fry Cres. Bur H 74 B3
Fryatts Way. Bex 159 E3
Fryman's La. Bre 91 D1
Fulford Cl. Hast 161 F4
Fuller Rd. Lew 126 C2
Fuller's Pas. Lew 127 D1
Fullwood Ave. Newh 179 F4
Fulmar Cl. Hove 145 D1
Fulmar Dr. E Gri 2 C2
Furlongs The. Alfn 172 B2
Furnace Ave. Lam 21 F2
Furnace Farm Rd. Cra D 1 A2
Furnace La. Bec 92 B4
Furnace La. Bro Ow 92 A3
Furnace La. Cad S 84 B1
Furnace La. Hor 109 D4
Furnace La. Lam 21 E2
Furnace La. War 84 B1
Furnace Way. Uck 80 B4
Furness Rd. East 185 E1
Furze Hill. Hove 165 D3
Furze La. E Gri 1 C2
Furzefield Ave. Spe 7 F4
Furzefield Chase. Dor P 2 B3
Furzefield Rd. E Gri 2 A2
Furzeland Way. Say C 99 D4
Fyning Pl. Bex 159 D3
Fyrsway. Fai 142 B2
Fysie La. Etc 46 A2
Gables The. Hast 140 B2
Gableson Ave. Bri 144 C2
Gage Cl. Cra D 1 A1
Gage Ridge. For R 13 E1
Gages The. Hai 155 D4
Gainsborough Cres. East 176 A1
Gainsborough La. Pole 174 B3
Galliers Cl. Bri 145 F3
Gallops The. Lew 126 C1
Gallows Cl. Whm 176 B3
Gallows La. Whm 176 B3
Gammons Way. Sed 90 B1
Gander Cl. Bur H 74 C3
Gander Green. Hay H 52 B4
Gander Hill. Hay H 52 B4
Ganton Pl. Hast 161 E4
Garden Cl. Bex 160 A2
Garden Cl. E Gri 12 B4
Garden Cl. Por S 164 A4
Garden House La. Gri 12 B4
Garden Mead. W Hoa 22 B3
Garden Rd. T W 8 C2
Garden St. Lew 149 D4
Garden St. T W 8 C2
Garden Wood Rd. E Gri 12 A4
Gardener Rd. Por S 163 F4
Gardener St. Por S 163 F4
Gardens The. Por S 164 A4
Gardens The. Sock 163 E4
Gardner Cl. East 186 B4
Gardner St. Bri 165 F3
Gardner St. Hers 134 B3
Gardner Way. Hast 161 F3
Gardner's Hill. Iden 71 F3
Garfield Rd. Hai 155 D4
Garland Rd. E Gri 2 A1
Garnet Dr. East 185 D4
Gatehouse La. Bur H 74 A2
Gatehouse La. Fra 81 D4
Gatelands Dr. Bex 159 F3
Gatesmead. Hay H 52 B4
Gattons The. Bur H 74 B2
Gaudick Cl. East 185 E1
Gaudick Rd. East 185 E1
Gavin Astor Cl. Bex 160 C3
Geary Pl. Wfd 117 E2
Geering Park. Hai 155 D4
Geers Wood. Hea 83 E3
Gemma Cl. Hai 155 E4
Geneva Rd. Newh 180 A3
Gensing Rd. Hast 162 A4
George Hill. Rob 65 F2
George St. Bri 165 F3
George St. Hai 155 D4
George St. Hast 162 C4
George St. Hove 164 C3
George St. Por S 163 F4
George St. Sock 164 A4
George St. T W 9 D2
George St. Wad 31 E3
Georgian Cl. Bex 160 B3
Gerald Cl. Bur H 75 D2
Gerald Rd. Sea 181 E1
Gerard St. Bri 165 F4
German St. Winc 120 B4
Ghyll Rd. Cro 27 E2
Ghyll Rd. Hea 83 E3
Ghyll Side Rd. Norm 68 C4
Ghyllside Ave. Hast 140 A2
Ghyllside Dr. Hast 140 A2
Ghyllside Way. Hast 140 A2
Gibb Cl. Bex 160 C3
Gibbetts. Lan G 7 E2
Gibbon Rd. Newh 180 A3
Gibraltar Rise. Hea 83 F4
Giffards Cl. E Gri 2 B1
Gilbert Rd. East 185 F2
Gilbert Rd. Hast 161 F4
Gilbert Way. Hai 154 C3
Gilberts Dr. E Dean 188 C4
Gilda Cres. Pole 174 C3
Gildredge Rd. East 185 E1
Gildredge Rd. Sea 181 E2
Gilham La. For R 13 E1
Gill The. Pem 10 B4
Gillham Wood Ave. Bex 159 D2
Gillham Wood Rd. Bex 159 D2
Gilligans The. Bur H 74 B3
Gillridge Green. Cro 27 E2
Gillsman's Dr. Hast 139 E1
Gillsman's Hill. Hast 139 F1
Gillsman's Park. Hast 139 E1
Gimble Way. Pem 10 A4
Gingerbread La. Fli 34 B1
Gipps Cross La. Lan G 7 E2
Githa Rd. Hast 141 D1
Glade The. Hai 154 B3
Glade The. May 41 F2
Glades The. Bex 160 B3
Glades The. E Gri 2 C1
Gladstone Pl. Bri 166 A4
Gladstone Rd. Bur H 75 D2
Gladstone Rd. Cro 27 E1
Gladstone Rd. Por S 163 F4
Gladstone Rd. T W 7 F2
Gladstone Terr. Hast 140 C1
Gladys Ave. Pea 179 D3
Gladys Rd. Hove 164 A4
Glassenbury Rd. Bex 160 B3
Glastonbury Rd. Hove 164 A3
Gleave Cl. E Gri 2 C1
Glebe Cl. Bex 159 D2
Glebe Cl. East 185 D2
Glebe Cl. Lew 148 C4
Glebe Cl. Sock 163 E4
Glebe Dr. Sea 181 E2
Glebe The. Fel 1 C2
Glebe The. Hast 140 C1
Glebe The. Hay H 52 C4
Glebe The. Pem 10 A4
Glebe The. Pett 119 E1
Glebe Villas. Hove 161 A4
Glen Cl. Willn 174 B2
Glen Rise. Bri 144 C3
Glen Rise Cl. Bri 144 C3
Glen The. Uck 57 D1
Glen Vue. E Gri 2 B1
Glendale Ave. East 185 D3
Glendale Rd. Bur H 74 C1
Glendale Rd. Hove 165 D4
Glendor Rd. Hove 164 B3
Glendyne Cl. E Gri 12 C4
Glendyne Way. E Gri 12 C4
Gleneagles Cl. Bex 160 B2
Gleneagles Cl. Sea 180 C3
Gleneagles Dr. Hast 161 E4
Glenfalls Ave. Bri 145 F4
Glengorse. Bat 115 E2
Glenleigh Ave. Bex 159 E3
Glenleigh Park Rd. Bex 159 E3
Glenmore Mews. East 185 F2
Glenmore Park. T W 18 B4
Glenmore Rd. Cro 27 D2
Glenmore Rd E. Cro 27 D2
Glenthorn Rd. Bex 159 F2
Glenview Cl. Hast 141 D1
Gleton Ave. Hove 144 A1
Gloucester Ave. Bex 160 C3
Gloucester Cl. Willn 175 D1
Gloucester Pas. Bri 165 F3
Gloucester Pl. Bri 165 F3
Gloucester Rd. Bri 165 F3
Gloucester Rd. Bur H 74 B2
Gloucester Rd. Wad 31 E3
Gloucester St. Bri 165 F3
Glovers La. Bex 160 A4
Glyndbourne Gdns. Hast 140 A3
Glynde Ave. East 175 E1
Glynde Ave. Salt 168 A1
Glynde Cl. S Hei 170 A1
Glynde Rd. Bri 166 A3
Glyndebourne Ave. Salt 168 A1
Glyne Ascent. Bex 160 B3
Glyne Barn Cl. Bex 160 C3
Glyne Dr. Bex 160 C3
Glynleigh Dr. Pole 175 D3
Glynleigh Rd. Hank 155 F1
Glynn Rd. Pea 169 D1
Glynn Rise. Pea 168 C1
Goatham La. Bro OW 91 E3
Godden Rd. Newk 78 A4
Goddens Cl. Norm 68 C4
Goddens Gill. Norm 68 C4
Godfrey Cl. S Mal 127 D2
Godwin Rd. Hast 141 D1
Godwin Rd. Hove 144 A1
Goffs The. East 185 E2
Gold La. Pea 169 D1
Goldbridge Rd. Newk 78 B4
Golden Hill. Bur H 75 D2
Golden La. Bri 165 D3
Golden Miller La. Pole 174 B3
Goldhurst Green. Ick 119 E3
Golding St. T W 8 C2
Goldring Rd. East 176 B1
Goldsmid Rd. Hove 165 E4
Goldsmith Cl. East 176 B2
Goldsmiths Ave. Cro 27 D2
Goldstone Cl. Hove 144 C1
Goldstone Cres. Hove 144 C1
Goldstone Ct. Hove 144 C2
Goldstone La. Hove 164 C4
Goldstone Rd. Hove 164 C4
Goldstone St. Hove 164 C4
Goldstone Villas. Hove 164 C4
Goldstone Way. Hove 144 C1
Goods Station Rd. T W 8 C2
Goodtrees La. Hart 4 C1
Goodwin Cl. Hai 132 B1
Goodwins Cl. E Gri 2 A2
Goodwins The. T W 8 B1
Goodwood Cl. Bex 160 A3
Goodwood Cl. Willn 174 C1
Goodwood Way. Bri 146 B2
Gordon Cl. Hay H 52 B3
Gordon Pl. Bex 159 F3
Gordon Rd. Bri 145 E1
Gordon Rd. Bur H 75 D2
Gordon Rd. Bux 57 F2
Gordon Rd. Cro 27 E1
Gordon Rd. Hai 154 C4
Gordon Rd. Hast 162 C4
Gordon Rd. Hay H 52 B3
Gordon Rd. Por S 163 F4
Gordon Rd. Sgh 9 D4
Gordon Rd. Sock 164 A4
Gore Park Ave. East 185 D2
Gore Park Rd. East 185 D2
Gorham Ave. Rottn 167 F1
Gorham Cl. Rott 167 F1
Gorham Way. Pea 178 B4
Gorringe Cl. S Sea 163 D4
Gorringe Cl. Willn 174 C2
Gorringe Dr. Willn 174 C2
Gorringe Rd. East 185 F2
Gorringe Valley Rd. Willn 174 C2
Gorse Cl. East 184 C3
Gorse Cl. Por S 143 E2
Gorse Dr. Sea 181 E3
Gorse Hill. Bro O 61 E1
Gorse Rd. T W 9 E3
Gorselands. Sed 90 B1
Gorses The. Bex 159 D1
Gorsethorn Way. Fai 142 B2
Gorseway The. Bex 159 D3
Gosford Way. Pole 174 B3
Gote La. Rin 128 A2
Goudhurst Cl. East 176 A1
Gower Rd. Hay H 52 B2
Gows Croft. Kin L 148 B3
Graffham Cl. Bri 166 B3

Grafton St. Bri 165 F2
Graham Ave. Bri 145 E3
Graham Ave. Por S 143 E2
Graham Cl. Por S 143 E2
Graham Cres. Por S 143 E2
Grampian Cl. East 176 A2
Grampian Cl. T W 9 D3
Grand Ave. Bex 160 C3
Grand Ave. Hove 165 D3
Grand Ave. Key 100 C2
Grand Ave. Sea 181 D3
Grand Cres. Rottn 167 F1
Grand Junction Rd. Bri 165 F2
Grand Par. Bri 165 F3
Grand Par. East 185 F1
Grand Par. Hast 162 A3
Grand Par. Pole 174 B3
Grange Ave. Hast 140 A2
Grange Cl. Bri 145 E1
Grange Cl. Bur H 75 D3
Grange Cl. Cro 27 D1
Grange Cl. Hor 109 E3
Grange Ct Dr. Bex 159 F3
Grange Gdns. T W 8 A2
Grange Rd. Bar C 104 A2
Grange Rd. East 185 E1
Grange Rd. Hast 140 B3
Grange Rd. Hove 164 B4
Grange Rd. Lew 149 D4
Grange Rd. Sock 163 E4
Grange Rd. T W 8 A2
Grange Rd. Uck 80 A4
Grange The. Bar C 104 A2
Grangeways. Bri 145 E3
Granston Way. Cra D 11 D4
Grant St. Bri 165 F4
Grantham Bank. Bar C 104 B2
Grantham Cl. S Cha 103 E4
Grantham Rd. Bri 145 F1
Granville Rd. East 185 E1
Granville Rd. Hove 165 E4
Granville Rd. T W 9 D3
Grassington Rd. East 185 E1
Grassmere Ave. Pea 178 B4
Gravelye La. Hay H 52 C3
Gravett Ct. Bur H 74 B1
Graycoats Dr. Cro 27 E1
Graystone La. Hast 141 D2
Grazebrook Cl. Bex 159 D2
Great Brooms Rd. Sgh 9 D4
Great Cliffe Rd. East 176 B1
Great College St. Bri 166 A2
Great Courtlands. Lan G 7 F2
Great Footway. Lan G 7 E2
Great Hall Arc. T W 8 C2
Great Heathmead. Hay H 52 A3
Great Oak. Hur G 46 C2
Great Rough. Chay 77 F3
Greater Paddock. Rin 128 B3
Grecian Rd. T W 8 C1
Green Cl. Rin 128 B3
Green Cl. Sock 163 E4
Green Field Cl. Sock 163 D4
Green Gate. Pea 169 D1
Green Gr. Hai 154 C4
Green Hedges Ave. E Gri 2 A1
Green Hedges Cl. E Gri 2 A1
Green La. Bex 159 D3
Green La. Cro 27 F1
Green La. Hea 83 F3
Green La. Jev 184 A4
Green La. Lew 149 D4
Green La. Rin 105 F1
Green La. S Cha 103 E4
Green La. S Str 77 E1
Green La. Sea 181 E1
Green La. Wood 167 E3
Green Meadows. Hay H 52 C4
Green Park Cnr. Wiv 75 F2
Green Ridge. Bri 144 C3
Green Sq. Wad 31 E3
Green St. East 185 D2
Green The. Blas 81 F3
Green The. Cat 137 E4
Green The. Hai 133 D1
Green The. Hast 139 F1
Green The. Hove 145 D1
Green The. Lan G 7 E2
Green The. Newk 78 A4
Green The. Nin 136 C3
Green The. Rottn 167 E1
Green The. Stas 67 F3
Green Wall. Lew 127 D1
Green Way. Lydd 98 C3
Green Way. T W 9 E4
Green Wlk. Hai 133 D1
Green Wlk. Sea 181 F1
Green Wlk The. Willn 174 C2
Greenacres. Pea 169 D1
Greenacres. Wfd 117 E2
Greenacres Dr. Hai 155 D4
Greenacres Dr. Rin 128 A2
Greenbank Ave. Salt 168 A1
Greenfield Cl. Bri 145 F3
Greenfield Cl. T W 8 A3
Greenfield Cres. Bri 145 F3
Greenfield Dr. Rid 80 A2
Greenfield Rd. Bur 64 A4
Greenfield Rd. East 185 D2
Greenfields Cl. Hast 139 F3
Greenhill Park. Hay H 52 C1
Greenhill Way. Hay H 52 C1
Greenhill Way. Pea 169 D1
Greenlands Cl. Bur H 100 C4
Greenlands Dr. Bur H 100 C4
Greenleaf Gdns. Pole 174 C4
Greenleas. Hove 144 A1
Greenleas. Pem 10 A3
Greenstede Ave. E Gri 2 B1
Greenway. East 184 C3
Greenways. Bex 159 E4
Greenways. Hay H 52 B3
Greenways. Oving 167 D2
Greenways. Sock 143 E1
Greenwell Cl. Sea 181 F2
Greenwich Rd. Hai 155 D4
Greenwich Way. Pea 179 D4
Greenwoods La. Pun T 85 D4
Greggs Wood Rd. T W 9 E4
Gregory La. Whm 176 B3
Gregory Wlk. Sed 116 B4
Grenada Cl. Bex 159 D2
Grenville Rd. Pev B 177 D2
Grenville St. Bri 165 E3
Gresham Cl. East 185 D3
Gresham Way. Hast 161 F4
Gresley Rd. Hast 139 E3
Greville Rd. Hast 141 D2
Grey Alders. Hay H 52 C3
Grey Tower Bungalows. Pev B 177 D2
Grey Tower Caravan Site. Pev B 177 D2
Greyfriars Pl. Winc B 120 C3
Greys Rd. East 185 D2
Grinstead La. Sha 23 D4
Gromenfield. Gro 17 D4
Groombridge Hill. Lan G 7 D1
Groombridge Rd. Asht 6 C1
Grosvenor Bridge. T W 8 C3
Grosvenor Cl. Pole 174 B3
Grosvenor Cres. Hast 161 E3
Grosvenor Gdns. Hast 161 E3
Grosvenor Park. T W 8 C3
Grosvenor Rd. E Gri 2 A1
Grosvenor Rd. Sea 181 E2
Grosvenor Rd. T W 8 C2
Grosvenor St. Bri 165 F3
Grosvenor Wlk. T W 8 C2
Grove Ave. T W 8 C1
Grove Hill. Bri 165 F3
Grove Hill. Hel 110 B1
Grove Hill Gdns. TW 8 C1
Grove Hill Rd. T W 8 C2
Grove La. Rye 72 A2
Grove Rd. Bur H 74 C2
Grove Rd. Chid H 6 A4
Grove Rd. East 185 E1
Grove Rd. Hast 141 D2
Grove Rd. Sea 181 E2
Grove St. Bri 165 F3
Grove The. Bex 159 E3
Grove The. Cro 27 E1
Grove The. East 184 C4
Grove The. Hai 154 C3
Grove The. Hay H 52 C2
Grove The. May 41 F1
Grove The. Newh 170 B1
Grove The. Pem 10 A4
Grove The. Rye 95 D3
Grove The. Willn 174 B2
Grovelands Cl. Bur H 74 B1
Grovelands Rd. Hai 132 C1
Grovely La. Chur 85 F1
Grover St. T W 8 C2
Growers End. Newk 78 A4
Guardswell Pl. Sea 181 E2
Guestling Rd. East 186 A3
Guildford Rd. Bri 165 E3
Guildford Rd. T W 8 C2
Guildford St. Bri 165 E3
Guldeford La. Brok 73 E2
Guldeford Rd. E Gul 95 E3
Gun Rd. Blas 81 F3
Gundreda Rd. Lew 126 C1
Gunters La. Bex 159 F3
Gurth Rd. Hast 141 D1
Gwyneth Gr. Bex 160 B4
Gwynne Gdns. E Gri 2 A1

Hackenden Cl. E Gri 2 B2
Hackenden La. E Gri 2 B2
Hackhurst La. Low D 132 A3
Hackwood. Rob 65 E2
Haddington Cl. Hove 164 C3
Haddington St. Hove 164 C4
Hadley Ct. T W 8 B3
Hadlow Ave. East 175 F2
Hadlow Cl. Bri 166 A3
Hadrian Ave. Sock 163 F4
Hadrian Gdns. Hast 139 F3
Haig Ave. Bri 146 A3
Hailsham Ave. Salt 168 A2
Hailsham Industrial Park. Hai 154 C4
Hailsham Rd. Hank 175 E4
Hailsham Rd. Hea 83 F3
Hailsham Rd. Hers 134 B3
Hailsham Rd. Pole 174 B4
Hairpin Croft. Pea 169 D1
Half Mile Dro. Rin 128 C4
Halland Cl. East 175 D1
Halland Rd. Bri 146 B2
Hallett Rd. Bri 166 A4
Halley Park. Hai 155 D4
Halley Rd. Bro O 84 B4
Halley Rd. Cad S 84 A4
Halley Rd. Hers 134 C1
Hall's Hole Rd. T W 9 E2
Hallsland. Cra D 11 D4
Hallyburton Rd. Hove 164 A4
Halsford Green. E Gri 1 C2
Halsford La. E Gri 1 C1
Halsford Park Rd. E Gri 2 A1
Halton Cres. Hast 140 C1
Halton Pl. Hast 140 C1
Halton Rd. East 186 A2
Halton Shaws. Hur 99 F3
Halton Terr. Hast 140 C1
Ham La. Bur 63 F4
Ham La. Lew 149 D4
Ham La. Rin 128 A3
Ham La. Sca H 53 E2
Hambleton Cl. East 176 A2
Hambrook. Bur H 75 D1
Hamelsham Ct. Hai 154 C4
Hamilton Gdns. Hast 141 D2
Hamilton Rd. Bri 165 E4
Hamilton Terr. Bex 159 F2
Hamlands La. Willn 174 C2
Hammer La. Cowb 110 B2
Hammer La. War 110 B2
Hammerwood Rd. Ash W 13 D3
Hammingden La. W Hoa 22 B2
Hammonds Dr. East 185 F4
Hammy Cl. S Sea 163 D4
Hampden Ave. East 175 E1
Hampden Cl. Bat 114 C2
Hampden Gdns. S Hei 170 A1
Hampden Rd. Bri 166 A4
Hampshire Ct. Bri 166 A2
Hampstead Rd. Hove 145 D1
Hampton Pl. Bri 165 E3
Hampton St. Bri 165 E3
Hampton Way. E Gri 12 B4
Hamsey Cl. Bri 166 B3
Hamsey Cl. East 184 C3
Hamsey Cres. Lew 126 B1
Hamsey La. Coo 126 C4
Hamsey La. Ham 126 C4
Hamsey La. Sea 182 A1
Hamsey Rd. Salt 178 A4
Hamsey Rd. Sha 22 C3
Hamsland. Hor K 35 D2
Hanbury La. Hay H 52 C3
Hanging Birch La. Hor 83 D1
Hangleton Cl. Hove 144 A1
Hangleton Gdns. Hove 144 A1
Hangleton La. Hove 144 A1
Hangleton Manor Cl. Hove 144 A1
Hangleton Rd. Hove 144 B1
Hangleton Valley Dr. Hove 144 A2
Hangleton Way. Hove 144 A2
Hankham Hall Rd. St Cro 176 A4
Hankham Hall Rd. Whm 176 B3
Hankham Rd. St Cro 175 F3
Hankham St. Hank 175 F4
Hanlye La. Hay H 52 A4
Hannington Pl. Hur 99 F4
Hanover Cl. Bex 160 A3
Hanover Cl. Sea 180 C3
Hanover Cres. Bri 165 F4
Hanover Rd. East 186 A2
Hanover Rd. T W 8 C2
Hanover St. Bri 165 F4
Hanover Terr. Bri 165 F4
Hanson Rd. Newh 180 A3
Harbour Farm. Winc B 120 C3
Harbour Rd. Rye 95 E2
Harbour Rd. Rye H 95 E2
Harbour View Cl. Sea 180 C3
Harbour View Rd. Newh 179 F3
Harcourt Cl. Rid 80 A3
Harcourt Rd. Rid 80 A3
Harding Ave. East 185 F3
Hardwick Rd. East 185 F1
Hardwick Rd. Hove 144 B2
Hardwicke Rd. Hast 140 C1
Hardy Dr. East 186 B3
Hare Way. Hast 140 A3
Harebeating Cl. Hai 133 D1
Harebeating Cres. Hai 133 D1
Harebeating Dr. Hai 133 D1
Harebeating Gdns. Hai 133 D1
Harebeating La. Hai 133 D1
Harebell Cl. East 176 A2
Harecombe Rd. Cro 39 E4
Harecombe Rise. Cro 39 E4
Harefield Cl. Newh 170 B1
Haremere Hill. Etc 46 A1
Harescroft. T W 18 B4
Harewood Cl. Bex 159 F2
Hargate Cl. T W 18 B4
Hargreaves Rd. East 175 F1
Harlands Cl. Hay H 52 A3
Harlands Rd. Hay H 52 A3
Harlequin Gdns. Hast 139 F3
Harlequin La. Cro 39 E4
Harlequin Pl. Cro 39 E4
Harley La. Hea 83 F3
Harley Shute Rd. Hast 161 E4
Harley Way. Hast 161 E3
Harmans Dr. E Gri 2 C1
Harmans Mead. E Gri 2 C1
Harmers Hay Rd. Hai 132 C1
Harmers Hill. Newk 78 A4
Harmony St. T W 8 A2
Harmsworth Cres. Hove 144 B2
Harold Cl. Pev B 177 E4
Harold Mews. Hast 162 A3
Harold Pl. Hast 162 B4
Harold Rd. Hast 141 D1
Harold Terr. Bat 115 E2
Harpers Rd. Newh 180 A4
Harrier La. Bat 115 E2
Harries Rd. T W 9 D4
Harrington Pl. Bri 145 F1
Harrington Rd. Bri 145 E1
Harrington Villas. Bri 145 E1
Harrison Rd. Sea 181 F2
Harrisons La. Rin 128 B3
Harrow Cl. Sea 181 F2
Harrow La. Hast 139 F3
Hart Cl. Uck 79 F4
Hartfield Ave. Bri 145 F3
Hartfield La. East 185 E2
Hartfield Rd. Bex 159 D1
Hartfield Rd. Cowd 5 D3
Hartfield Rd. East 185 E2
Hartfield Rd. For R 14 A1
Hartfield Rd. Salt 168 A1
Hartfield Rd. Sea 181 F2
Harting Combe. Hast 161 F4
Hartington Pl. Bri 166 A4
Hartington Pl. East 185 F1
Hartington Rd. Bri 166 A4
Hartington Terr. Bri 166 A4
Hartington Villas. Hove 164 C4
Harvard Cl. S Mal 127 D2
Harvard Rd. Rin 128 A3
Harvest Cl. Hay H 52 C4
Harvest Cl. Pea 168 C1
Harvest Hill. E Gri 12 B4
Harvest Way. Hast 140 A3
Harvey Cl. Hast 139 E2
Harvey's La. Fra 106 A2
Harvey's La. Rin 106 A2
Harwarden Cl. Cra D 11 D4
Harwood Cl. East 186 B4
Harwoods Cl. Gri 12 B4
Harwood's La. E Gri 12 B3
Haslam Cres. Bex 160 B3
Hasletts Cl. T W 8 C3
Hassocks Rd. Hur 99 F3
Hastings Ave. Sea 182 A3
Hastings Cl. Pole 174 C4
Hastings Rd. Bat 115 F2
Hastings Rd. Bex 160 B3
Hastings Rd. Bri 166 A4
Hastings Rd. Kip 10 C3
Hastings Rd. Newd 49 F2
Hastings Rd. Pem 10 B3
Hastings Rd. Rol L 50 A4
Hastings Rd. The M 47 E3
Hatch End. For R 13 E1
Hatherley Rd. Hast 162 A4
Havelock Rd. Bex 160 A3
Havelock Rd. Bri 145 E1
Havelock Rd. East 185 F2
Havelock Rd. Hast 162 B4
Haven Brow. Sea 181 F2
Haven Cl. Pev B 177 E3
Haven Cl. Willn 174 C2
Haven Rd. Hast 161 D4
Hawkenbury Cl. T W 9 D1
Hawkenbury Rd. T W 9 E1
Hawkenbury Way. Lew 126 C1
Hawkhurst Cl. East 176 A1
Hawkhurst Rd. Bri 146 A3
Hawkhurst Rd. Fli 34 B1
Hawkhurst Way. Bex 159 E2
Hawkins Cl. S Sea 143 D1
Hawkins Cres. S Sea 143 D1
Hawkins Rd. S Sea 143 D1
Hawkins Way. Hai 154 C4
Hawks Farm Cl. Hai 132 C1
Hawks Rd. Hai 132 C1
Hawks Town Cl. Hai 132 C2
Hawks Town Cres. Hai 133 D1
Hawks Town Gdns. Hai 132 C2
Hawksbridge Cl. Willn 175 D2
Hawkswood Dr. Hai 133 D2
Hawkswood Rd. Hai 132 C2
Hawmead. Cra D 11 D4
Hawth Cl. Sea 181 D2
Hawth Cres. Sea 181 D2
Hawth Gr. Sea 181 D3
Hawth Hill. Sea 181 D3
Hawth Park Rd. Sea 181 D2
Hawth Pl. Sea 181 D2
Hawth Rise. Sea 181 D3
Hawth Way. Sea 181 D2
Hawthorn Ave. Bex 159 D2
Hawthorn Cl. Bur H 75 D3
Hawthorn Cl. Hea 83 F3
Hawthorn Cl. Salt 168 A1
Hawthorn Rd. East 186 A4
Hawthorn Rd. Hast 141 D1
Hawthorn Way. Por S 143 F2
Hawthorn Wlk. T W 9 E4
Hawthornes The. Bro OW 91 F2
Hawthorns The. Bur H 74 C3
Hawthorns The. Hai 154 C4
Hawthylands Cres. Hai 132 C1
Hawthylands Dr. Hai 132 C1
Hawthylands Rd. Hai 132 C1
Hayes Cl. Por S 164 A4
Hayes Cl. Rin 128 A3
Hayes La. Bec 92 C3
Hayes La. Peas 93 D3
Hayland Green. Hai 133 D1
Haylind Rd. Hay H 52 C3
Haystoun Cl. East 175 D1
Haystoun Park. East 175 D1
Hayward Rd. Lew 126 C2
Haywards Rd. Bri 145 F3
Haywards Rd. Hay H 52 B2
Haywood Way. Hast 141 D2
Hazel Cl. Cra D 11 D4
Hazel Cl. Por S 144 A2
Hazel Dr. Bur H 74 C1
Hazel Gr. Willn 174 C2
Hazel Way. Cra D 11 D4
Hazelbank. Lan G 7 E2
Hazeldene. Sea 181 F2
Hazeldene Meads. Bri 145 D2
Hazeledene La. N Cha 77 E4
Hazelgrove Rd. Hay H 52 B2
Hazelwood Ave. East 175 D2
Hazelwood Cl. Bex 159 D2
Hazelwood Cl. T W 9 D4
Hazelwood Gdns. Hast 140 A3
Headland Ave. Sea 181 F2
Headland Cl. Pea 179 E3
Heath Cl. Hay H 52 B2
Heath Hill Ave. Bri 146 C1
Heath Rd. Hay H 52 B3
Heathcote Dr. E Gri 2 A1
Heathdown Cl. Pea 169 D1
Heather Bank. Hay H 52 A3
Heather Cl. East 175 F2
Heather Wlk. Fai 142 B2
Heather Wlk. Cro 28 A1
Heatherdune Rd. Bex 159 F3
Heatherway. Fel 1 B4
Heathfield Ave. Salt 168 A1
Heathfield Cl. Hast 140 B3
Heathfield Cres. Por S 143 E2
Heathfield Dr. Por S 143 E2
Heathfield Gdns. Rob 65 F2
Heathfield Rd. Sea 181 E2
Heathlands. Wfd 117 E2
Heathy Brow. Pea 168 C1
Heavegate Rd. Cro 39 D4
Heighton Cl. Bex 159 D2
Heighton Cres. S Hei 170 A1
Heighton Rd. S Hei 170 B1
Heights The. Hast 141 E2
Helena Cl. Por S 144 A1
Helena Rd. Wood 147 D1
Hellingly Cl. Bri 166 B3
Helvellyn Dr. East 176 A2
Hempstead Gdns. Uck 80 A4
Hempstead La. Hai 132 B1
Hempstead La. Uck 80 A4
Hempstead Rd. Salt 168 A2
Hempstead Rd. Uck 80 A4
Hempstead Rise. Uck 80 A4
Henderson Cl. Hast 140 B2
Hendon St. Bri 166 A3
Henfield Cl. Bri 166 B3
Henfield Rd. East 175 E1
Henfield Way. Hove 144 B2
Henley Cl. Rye 94 C3
Henley Cl. T W 9 D3
Henley Rd. Bri 166 B2
Henley's Hill. Pon G 135 F4
Henshill La. The M 47 E4
Henwood Cres. Pem 10 A3
Henwood Green Rd. Pem 10 A3
Henwoods Mount. Pem 10 B3
Herbert Rd. Bri 145 E1
Herbrand Wlk. Bex 158 C1
Hereford St. Bri 166 A3
Hereward Way. S Mal 127 D2
Hermitage La. E Gri 12 B4
Hermitage Rd. E Gri 2 A2
Herne Down. Cro 39 F4
Herne Rd. Cro 39 E4
Heron Cl. East 176 A1
Heron Pl. E Gri 12 B4
Heron Ridge. Pole 174 C3
Herons Way. Pem 10 B4
Heronsdale Rd. Wood 167 E4
Herontye Dr. E Gri 12 B4
Herring's Rd. Dal 86 B1
Herring's Rd. Pon G 112 B4
Hertford Cl. Hast 139 F2
Hertford Rd. Bri 145 F1
Heskett Park. Pem 10 A3
Hestingas Plat. Hast 162 C4
Heston Ave. Bri 145 E4
Hever Cl. East 176 A1
Hever Cres. Bex 159 F3
Heyworth Cl. Wood 167 E4
Hickling Cl. East 175 F2
Hickman Way. Hast 140 A2
Hickman's Cl. Hay H 52 C4
Hickman's La. Hay H 52 C4
Hide Hollow. East 176 B2
High Bank. Hast 141 D1
High Bank Cl. Hast 141 D1
High Beeches. T W 9 D3
High Branches. Bex 159 E2
High Broom La. Cro 39 E4
High Broom Rd. Cro 39 E4
High Brooms Rd. Sgh 9 D4
High Cl. Fri 184 A1
High Cl. Por S 143 F1
High Cross Fields. Cro 27 E2
High Fords. Ick 119 E3
High Fords Cl. Ick 119 E3
High Hurst Cl. Newk 78 A4
High Park. Norm 68 C4
High Park Ave. Hove 144 B2
High Point. Hay H 52 C2
High Rocks La. T W 8 A1
High St. Alfn 172 C2
High St. Bar C 104 A2
High St. Bat 115 D3
High St. Bex 160 A3
High St. Bri 165 F3
High St. Bur 63 F3
High St. Bux 57 F2
High St. Cowd 4 C3
High St. Cro 27 E2
High St. Dit 101 D2
High St. E Gri 12 B4
High St. E Hoa 107 F3
High St. East 185 D2
High St. Etc 64 C4
High St. Fli 34 A2
High St. Frant 19 D2
High St. Hai 155 D4
High St. Hart 15 D2
High St. Hast 162 C4
High St. Hay H 52 C4
High St. Hea 83 F4
High St. Hur 99 F3
High St. Lam 21 F3
High St. Lew 149 D4
High St. Lydd 98 C3
High St. Mar 56 C2
High St. May 41 F1
High St. Newh 180 A4
High St. Newk 78 A4
High St. Nin 136 C3

High St. Nut 37 D2
High St. Pem 10 A3
High St. Pole 174 C3
High St. Rid 80 A3
High St. Rob 65 F2
High St. Rot 40 C4
High St. Rottn 167 E1
High St. Rye 95 D3
High St. Sea 181 E1
High St. T W 8 C1
High St. Uck 80 A3
High St. Wad 31 E2
High St. Wal 32 C1
High St. Whm 176 B3
High St. Winc 120 B4
High Trees. Hay H 52 B3
High Wickham. Hast 140 C1
High Woods La. T W 9 E1
Higham Gdns. Gue G 141 F4
Highbank. Bri 145 D3
Highbridge La. E Chi 102 C2
Highbrook Cl. Bri 146 A2
Highcroft Cres. Hea 83 F4
Highcroft Rd. Sha 22 C3
Highdown. Sock 143 E1
Highdown Cl. Sock 143 E1
Highdown Rd. Hove 165 E4
Highdown Rd. Lew 126 C1
Highfield Cl. Pem 10 A3
Highfield Cres. Bri 145 F3
Highfield Dr. Hast 139 D2
Highfield Dr. Hur 99 F3
Highfield Gdns. Bex 160 A4
Highfield Rd. Bro O 61 E1
Highfield Rd. E Gri 2 A2
Highfield Rd. Hor 109 E4
Highfield Rd. Sgh 9 D4
Highfields. Bri 146 B3
Highfields. Bur 63 F4
Highfields. For R 13 E1
Highgate Rd. For R 13 E1
Highgrove. T W 18 C4
Highland Ct. Hay H 52 B2
Highland Rd. Hay H 52 B2
Highlands Ave. Rid 80 A2
Highlands Cl. Bex 159 E4
Highlands Cl. Cro 27 E2
Highlands Cl. Key 100 C2
Highlands Dr. Bur H 74 C2
Highlands Dr. Hast 161 F4
Highlands Gdns. Hast 161 F4
Highlands Rd. Por S 143 F1
Highlands Rd. Sea 181 E2
Highlands The. Bex 159 E4
Highsted Park. Pea 169 D1
Highview Ave N. Bri 145 E3
Highview Ave S. Bri 145 E3
Highview Cl. Hast 140 A3
Highview Cl. Win H 134 C3
Highview La. Rid 80 A2
Highview Rd. Bri 145 E3
Highview Rd. Pea 178 B4
Highview Way. Bri 145 E3
Highway Cl. Bri 146 A1
Highway The. Bri 146 B2
Highway The. Newh 179 F3
Highway The. Pea 179 F3
Highways. Por S 143 F1
Highwoods Ave. Bex 159 D3
Hiham Green. Winc 120 B4
Hilary Cl. Pole 174 B3
Hilbert Cl. T W 9 D3
Hilbert Rd. T W 9 D3
Hilders Farm Cl. Cro 27 F1
Hilgrove Rd. Salt 168 A2
Hill Brow. Hove 144 C2
Hill Cl. Cro 27 E1
Hill Cl. Poy 122 A3
Hill Crest. Dor P 2 B3
Hill Crest. Sgh 8 C4
Hill Crest Rd. Newh 180 A3
Hill Dr. Hove 144 C2
Hill Farm Way. Sock 143 E1
Hill Mead. Nut 37 D2
Hill Rd. East 184 C3
Hill Rd. Fai 142 A2
Hill Rd. Lew 126 C1
Hill Rd. Salt 167 F1
Hill Rise. Newh 170 B1
Hill Rise. Sea 181 D3
Hill Side. Newh 180 A4
Hill St. Hast 162 C4
Hill St. T W 8 C3
Hill Top. Bri 144 C3
Hill View Rd. T W 8 A2
Hillary Cl. E Gri 2 C2
Hillbank Cl. Por S 143 E2
Hillborough Cl. Bex 159 D2
Hillbrow Rd. Bri 145 D2
Hillbury Gdns. Tic 33 D1
Hillcrest. Bri 145 D3
Hillcrest Ave. Bex 159 F3
Hillcrest Cl. Sca H 53 E2
Hillcrest Dr. T W 9 D4
Hillcrest La. Sca H 53 E2
Hillcroft. Por S 143 E1
Hillgarth. Sgh 8 C4
Hillrise. Cro 27 F1
Hillside. Bri 146 B1
Hillside. For R 13 E2
Hillside. Fri 183 F1
Hillside. Por S 144 A1
Hillside. Sock 143 E1
Hillside Ave. Sea 182 A3
Hillside Cl. E Gri 2 B2
Hillside Rd. Bex 160 A3
Hillside Rd. Hast 140 B3
Hillside Way. Bri 145 D2
Hillside Wlk. Hay H 52 A3
Hilltop Rd. W Hoa 22 B3
Hillview Rd. Wood 166 C4
Hillyfield. Lew 148 C4
Hillyglen Cl. Hast 162 B4
Hindover Cres. Sea 181 F2
Hindover Rd. Sea 181 F2
Hinton Cl. Bri 146 A1
Hither Chantlers. Lan G 7 F1
Hoad Rd. East 185 F2
Hoadleys La. Cro 27 D3
Hoad's Wood Rd. Hast 140 C2
Hoath Hill. Mou 89 D3
Hoathdown Ave. Newh 179 F4
Hobbs Industrial Estate. Fel 1 A4
Hobbs La. Four O 70 A3
Hoblands. Hay H 52 C2
Hobney Rise. Whm 176 B3
Hockington La. East 174 C1
Hoddern Ave. Pea 178 C4
Hodshrove La. Bri 146 B2
Hodshrove Rd. Bri 146 B2
Hoe The. Hast 139 F3
Hogarth Rd. East 176 A1
Hogarth Rd. Hove 164 B4
Hoghole La. Lam 21 E1
Hogtrough La. Winc 120 B4
Holbrook Cl. East 190 B4
Holden Park Rd. Sgh 8 B4
Holdings The. Kin L 148 B3
Hole Farm Cl. Hast 140 B1
Hollamby Park. Hai 155 D4
Holland Ave. Bex 159 D2
Holland Mews. Hove 165 D3
Holland Rd. Hove 165 D3
Holland St. Bri 165 F3
Hollands Way. E Gri 2 C2
Holliers Hill. Bex 160 A3
Hollin Cl. T W 8 A2
Hollingbury Copse. Bri 145 F2
Hollingbury Cres. Bri 145 F1
Hollingbury Park Ave. Bri 145 F1
Hollingbury Pl. Bri 145 F1
Hollingbury Rd. Bri 145 F1
Hollingbury Rise. Bri 145 F1
Hollingbury Rise W. Bri 145 F1
Hollingbury Terr. Bri 145 F1
Hollingdean Rd. Bri 166 A4
Hollingdean St. Bri 145 F1
Hollingdean Terr. Bri 145 F1
Hollinghurst Cl. Hast 139 F3
Hollinghurst Rd. Hast 139 F2
Hollington Ct. Hast 161 F4
Hollington Old La. Hast 139 F2
Hollington Park Cl. Hast 139 F1
Hollington Park Rd. Hast 139 F1
Hollow La. Blas 81 F2
Hollow La. Dor 3 D3
Hollow The. Hay H 52 C3
Hollow The. W Hoa 22 B3
Holly Cl. Bex 159 D3
Holly Cl. Bri 145 E2
Holly Cl. Hai 154 C3
Holly Cl. Hea 83 F3
Holly Dr. Hea 83 F3
Holly Pl. East 175 E2
Holly Rd. Hay H 52 C2
Hollybank Gdns. Hast 139 F1
Hollydene Rd. Wad 31 E3
Hollyshaw Cl. T W 9 D1
Holm Oak Cl. Bex 159 E2
Holmbush Cl. Hay H 52 B1
Holmbush Cl. S Sea 143 D1
Holmbush Way. Sock 143 E1
Holmdale Rd. Newh 170 B1
Holmes Ave. Hove 164 B4
Holmes Cl. Sea 180 C3
Holmesdale Cl. Wad 31 E3
Holmesdale Gdns. Hast 162 B4
Holmesdale Rd. Bex 159 F2
Holmesdale Rd. Bur H 74 C1
Holmewood Rd. Lan G 7 E2
Holmewood Rd. T W 9 D4
Holmhurst La. Hast 139 F3
Holt The. Bur H 75 D1
Holt The. Hai 154 C3
Holt The. Sea 181 E3
Holters Way. Sea 181 E3
Holton Hill. Wood 167 E4
Holtview Rd. Wood 166 C4
Holtye Ave. E Gri 2 C2
Holtye Rd. E Gri 2 C2
Holyrood. E Gri 12 C4
Holywell Cl. East 190 B4
Holywell Rd. East 190 B4
Holywell Wlk. Hai 154 C4
Home Farm Ct. Frant 19 D2
Home Farm La. T W 9 E4
Home Platt. Sha 22 C3
Home Rd. Bri 145 E1
Homebush Ave. Salt 168 A1
Homebush Ave. Salt 168 B2
Homefield Cl. Sea 181 E2
Homefield Rd. Sea 181 E2
Homelands Cl. Bex 159 F3
Homewood Cl. East 185 F3
Homewood Ridge. Lan G 7 E2
Honey Croft. Hove 144 A2
Honeypot La. E Chi 102 C4
Honeysuckle Cl. East 175 F2
Honeysuckle Cl. Hai 154 C3
Honeyway Cl. Willn 174 B2
Hoo Gdns. East 174 C1
Hood Cl. East 186 B4
Hook Hill. Tic 32 C3
Hook La. Brok 73 F4
Hook La. W Hoa 22 A2
Hookswood Cl. Cro 27 F2
Hoopers Cl. S Mal 127 D2
Hoover Cl. Hast 139 E3
Hop Gdns. Fair 38 A1
Hopfield Gdns. Uck 80 A4
Hopgarden Cl. Hast 162 B4
Hophurst Hill. Cra D 1 A1
Hophurst La. Cra D 1 A1
Hopwood Gdns. T W 8 C3
Horam Park Cl. Hor 109 F4
Horebeech La. Hor 109 F3
Horley Pl. Bri 166 B3
Hornbeam. Bur 63 F4
Hornbuckles Cl. S Cha 103 E4
Hornby Rd. Bri 146 C1
Horning Cl. East 175 F2
Horns Rd. The M 47 D4
Hornshurst Rd. Rot 40 C4
Horntye Rd. Hast 140 A1
Horsegrove Ave. Tic 33 E1
Horsegrove La. Rot 40 C4
Horseshoe Cl. Hast 139 F1
Horseshoe La. Bec 92 C4
Horsewalk. Hooe 157 E4
Horsewalk. Wart 157 E4
Horsfield Rd. Lew 126 C2
Horsham Ave. Pea 179 D4
Horsham Cl. Bri 166 B3
Horsted La. Dan 35 F2
Horsted La. Isf 105 E4
Horsted La. Lit H 105 F4
Horsted La. Sha 22 C2
Horsye Rd. East 185 F4
Horton Rd. Bri 145 F1
Hoskins Pl. E Gri 2 C2
Hosmers Field. Tow R 41 D4
Houghton La. Rye 72 A1
Houndean Cl. Lew 148 C4
Houndean Rise. Lew 148 B4
Hova Villas. Hove 164 C3
Hove Park Gdns. Hove 164 C4
Hove Park Rd. Hove 145 D1
Hove Park Villas. Hove 164 C4
Hove Park Way. Hove 145 D1
Hove Pl. Hove 164 C3
Hove Sea Wall. Hove 165 D3
Hove St. Hove 164 C3
Howard Ave. Bur H 74 B2
Howard Gdns. T W 8 C1
Howard Pl. Bri 165 E4
Howard Rd. Bri 166 A4
Howard Sq. East 185 F1
Howard Terr. Bri 165 E4
Howards Cl. Hai 155 D3
Howards Cres. Bex 159 D2
Howbourne La. Bux 58 B3
Howey Cl. Newh 170 B1
Howlett Cl. Hast 139 E2
Howlett Dr. Hai 132 C1
Howletts Cl. East 175 E1
How's Cl. Bro O W 91 F3
Hoyle Rd. Pea 179 D4
Hudson Rd. Hay H 52 B3
Huggett's La. Willn 174 C2
Hughenden Pl. Hast 140 B1
Hughendon Rd. Hast 140 C1
Hugletts La. Cad S 84 C3
Humboldt Ct. T W 9 D3
Hundred Acre La. Dit 75 F1
Hundred Acre La. Wiv G 75 F2
Hundredhouse La. Bec 92 B3
Hundredhouse La. Bro O W 92 B2
Hungershall Park. T W 8 B1
Hunloke Ave. East 185 F3
Hunston Cl. Wood 167 E4
Hunter's Mead. Alb 99 D3
Hunters Way. T W 8 B1
Hunters Way. Uck 79 F4
Hunting Cl. Bex 160 A3
Huntingdon Rd. Cro 39 E4
Huntingdon Way. Bur H 75 D3
Huntley Mill Rd. Tic 33 E2
Hurdis Rd. Sea 180 C3
Hurrell Rd. Hast 140 C1
Hurst Cres. Por S 163 F4
Hurst Farm Rd. E Gri 12 A4
Hurst Gdns. Hur 99 E4
Hurst Hill. Bri 146 A3
Hurst La. East 185 D2
Hurst La. Sed 90 B2
Hurst La. Win H 134 C3
Hurst Rd. East 185 D3
Hurst Rd. Hass 100 A2
Hurst The. T W 9 E4
Hurst Way. Wfd 140 C3
Hurst Wickham Cl. Hur 100 A3
Hurstfield Cl. Hay H 52 C1
Hurstwood Cl. Bex 160 C3
Hurstwood La. Hay H 52 C1
Hurstwood La. Hor K 23 D1
Hurstwood La. T W 8 B2
Hurstwood Rd. H Hur 57 E2
Hurstwood Rd. Uck 57 E2
Hurtis Hill. Cro 39 E4
Hutton Rd. Bri 145 F2
Hyde Gdns. East 185 F1
Hyde Rd. East 185 E1
Hyde The. Bri 166 B4
Hyde Tynings Cl. East 190 A4
Hydehurst Cl. Cro 27 E1
Hydneye St. East 186 A3
Hydneye The. East 175 E1
Hylden Cl. Wood 166 C4
Hyperion Ave. Pole 174 B3
Hythe Ave. Bex 160 C3
Hythe Cl. Pole 175 D4
Hythe Cl. Sea 182 A3
Hythe Cres. Sea 182 A2
Hythe Rd. Bri 145 F1
Hythe View. Sea 182 A2

Ian Cl. Bex 160 B4
Iden Cl. Bri 166 B3
Iden Hurst. Hur 99 F4
Iden Rd. Rye 71 F1
Iden St. East 175 F1
Iden's La. Bro O 84 A4
Ifield Cl. Salt 168 B1
Iford Cl. S Hei 170 A1
Ilex Green. Hai 132 C1
Imberholme La. E Gri 1 C1
Imberhorne La. E Gri 11 F4
Imberhorne Way. E Gri 1 C2
Impala Gdns. T W 8 C3
Imperial Arc. Bri 165 E3
Ingham Dr. Bri 146 A3
Ingleside. Hast 139 E2
Ingleside Dr. Cro 27 E1
Inglewood Gdns. Hast 139 E2
Ingram Cres. Hove 164 B4
Ingrams Ave. Bex 160 A4
Ingrams Way. Hai 154 C3
Inholmes Cl. Bur H 75 D2
Inholmes Park Rd. Bur H 74 C2
Ink Pen La. For R 13 E1
Innham's Wood. Cro 27 E2
Innings Dr. Pev B 177 D2
Institute Wlk. E Gri 2 B1
Inverness Rd. Bri 166 A4
Invicta Rd. Lydd 98 C1
Inwood Cres. Bri 145 E1
Iona Way. Hay H 52 B2
Irelands La. Lew 126 C1
Ironlatch Ave. Hast 139 E1
Ironlatch Cl. Hast 139 E1
Ironstone Way. Uck 80 A4
Ironstones. Lan G 7 F2
Isaac's La. Bur H 74 B4
Isaac's La. Hay H 52 A2
Isabel Cres. Hove 164 B4
Isfield Rd. Bri 146 A1
Islingwood Pl. Bri 166 A3
Islingword Rd. Bri 165 F4
Islingword St. Bri 165 F3
Iveagh Cres. S Hei 170 B1
Ivor Rd. Wood 147 D1
Ivory Pl. Bri 165 F3
Ivy Dene La. Ash W 13 D3
Ivy La. East 185 E2
Ivy Pl. Hove 165 D3
Ivy Terr. East 185 E1
Ivyhouse La. Cog 140 C4
Ivyhouse La. Hast 140 C3

Jaarlen Rd. Lydd 98 C3
Jack O'Dandy Cl. East 185 D4
Jackies La. Chay 77 F4
Jackson St. Bri 165 F4
James Ave. Hers 134 B3
Jameson Cres. Hast 139 F2
Jameson Rd. Bex 160 A2
Janes Cl. Bur H 75 D3
Janes La. Bur H 75 D3
Janes La. Wiv 75 E2
Jarvisbrook Cl. Bex 159 D2
Jasmine Green. Hai 132 C1
Jason Cl. Pea 179 D4
Jay Cl. East 176 A1
Jay Rd. Pea 179 E3
Jays The. Bur H 74 B2
Jefferies Way. Cro 27 E2
Jeffreys Way. Uck 57 D1
Jellicoe Cl. East 186 B4
Jenner's La. Hast 141 E3
Jephson Cl. East 190 B4
Jerome Cl. East 176 B1
Jersey St. Bri 165 F3
Jervis Ave. East 186 B3
Jesmond Cl. Hove 164 B4
Jesmond Rd. Hove 164 B4
Jesters. Bur H 75 D4
Jevington Cl. Bex 159 D1
Jevington Dr. Bri 146 A1
Jevington Dr. Sea 181 D2
Jevington Gdns. East 185 E1
Jevington Rd. Jev 184 A4
Jevington Rd. Willn 174 B2
Jew St. Bri 165 F3
Jireh Ct. Hay H 52 B3
Joe's La. Win H 134 C3
John St. Bri 165 F3
John St. T W 8 C3
Johns Cl. Pea 169 D1
John's Cross Rd. Mou 89 D4
John's Cross Rd. Rob 65 F1
Johnson Dr. Bur H 75 D2
Jonas Dr. Wad 31 E3
Jonas La. Wad 31 E3
Jordans La. East 175 D2
Jordans La E. East 175 D2
Jordans La W. East 175 D2
Jordans La W. Willn 175 D2
Jordans The. E Gri 12 B4
Jubilee Gdns. Sea 181 F3
Jubilee Rd. Bex 159 F4
Jubilee Rd. Bur H 74 B1
Jubilee Rd. Por S 163 F4
Jubilee St. Bri 165 F3
Jubille Cl. Hay H 52 C2
Juggs Rd. Lew 148 C4
Julian Rd. Hove 165 E4
Junction Rd. Bri 165 E3
Junction Rd. Bur H 74 C2
Junction Rd. Cri C 90 A4
Junction Rd. East 185 F2
Junction Rd. Hast 139 F4
Junction Rd. Sale 66 C4
Junction Rd. Stas 67 D2
Junction St. Pole 174 C3
Juniper Cl. Hast 139 E2
Juniper Cl. Por S 143 F2
Juniper Cl. Sea 182 A2
Juniper Wlk. S Sea 143 D1
Jury's Gap Rd. Lydd 98 B3

Kammond Ave. Sea 181 F3
Katherine Way. Sea 181 E3
Keats Cl. Hast 161 E3
Keats Pl. E Gri 2 A1
Keats Wlk. East 176 B2
Kebworth Cl. Bex 159 E3
Kedale Rd. Sea 181 E2
Keel Gdns. Sgh 8 B4
Keere St. Lew 149 D4
Keith Wlk. East 186 B3
Keld Ave. Rid 80 A3
Keld Cl. Rid 80 A3
Keld Dr. Rid 80 A3
Kelly Rd. Hove 145 D1
Kemble Cl. T W 9 E4
Kemp St. Bri 165 F3
Kemp Town Pl. Bri 166 A2
Kemps. Hur 99 E4
Kemps Farm Rd. Cro 27 F1
Kemps Way. Sale 66 A3
Kendal Park. T W 8 B3
Kendal Rd. Hove 164 B4
Kenilworth Cl. Bri 146 C1
Kenilworth Rd. Hast 161 F4
Kenmure Ave. Bri 145 F4
Kennedy Ave. E Gri 2 A2
Kennedy Cl. Hea 83 F3
Kennedy Rd. Bex 160 B2
Kennedy Way. Newh 179 F4
Kennel La. Bex 159 D2
Kensington Gdns. Bri 165 F3
Kensington Pl. Bri 165 F3
Kensington St. Bri 165 F3
Kensington St. T W 8 C2
Kent Cl. Bex 160 C3
Kent Cl. S Sea 163 D4
Kent Cl. Winc 120 B4
Kent Fields. Kin L 148 B3
Kent La. Bril 87 E4
Kent Rd. Hast 139 E2
Kent Rd. T W 8 C3
Kent St. Sed 116 B3
Kent St. Wfd 116 C2
Kenton Cl. Bex 159 F3
Kenton Rd. Hove 164 A4
Kents Rd. Hay H 52 B2
Kenwards. Bri 146 A4
Kenwood Cl. Hast 140 C2
Keppel Rd. Hast 140 B1
Kerrara Terr. East 185 F2
Kestrel Cl. Bex 160 B2
Kestrel Cl. Hove 165 D4
Kestrels The. Hast 139 E3
Ketches La. Fle 54 B3
Ketche's La. Hor K 54 B4
Kevin Gdns. Wood 167 E4
Kew St. Bri 165 E3
Kewhurst Ave. Bex 159 D2
Keymer Ave. Pea 179 D4
Keymer Cl. East 176 B1
Keymer Cl. Hast 161 E3
Keymer Ct. Bur H 74 C1
Keymer Gdns. Bur H 74 C1
Keymer Park. Key 100 C2
Keymer Rd. Bri 145 F3
Keymer Rd. Bur H 74 C1
Keymer Rd. Dit 101 D2
Keymer Rd. Hass 100 B2
Keymer Rd. Key 100 C2
Kibbles La. Sgh 8 B4
Kidbrook. Hay H 52 C3
Kidbrooke Rise. For R 13 E1
Kidd's Hill. Col H 25 E2
Kilda St. East 185 F2
Kildare Cl. Hast 140 C2
Kiln Cl. Rid 80 A2
Kiln La. Hay H 52 C3
Kiln La. Hooe 157 F4
Kiln Rd. Rin 128 B4
Kiln The. Bur H 75 D2
Kilnwood La. S Cha 103 E4
Kimberley Rd. Bri 146 A1
Kimberley Rd. Sea 181 D2
Kindersley Cl. E Gri 2 C2
Kinfauns Ave. East 185 F3
King Cl. East 185 E3
King Edward Ave. Hast 140 A2
King Edward Cl. Hast 140 A2
King Edward's Par. East 190 B4
King George Ave. E Gri 2 A2
King George Rd. S Sea 163 D4
King George V Hill. T W 9 D3
King George VI Ave. Hove 144 C2
King George VI Dr. Hove 144 C2
King Henry's Rd. Lew 126 C1
King Offa Way. Bex 160 A3
King Pl. Bri 165 F3
King St. Bri 165 F3
King St. Brok 73 F4
King St. E Gri 2 B1
King Wood Hill. Bro O W 91 F2
Kingfisher Dr. East 176 A1
Kingfisher Rise. E Gri 12 B4
King's Ave. East 185 E3
King's Ave. Newh 170 B1
King's Ave. Rye 95 D3
King's Bank La. Bec 69 F2
Kings Chase. Cro 27 D2
Kings Cl. Bex 160 A2
King's Cliff. Bri 166 A2
Kings Ct. Cro 27 E1
Kings Dr. Key 100 B2
King's Espl. Hove 164 C3
King's Gdns. Hove 164 C3
King's Hill Rd. Bur 63 F2

King's Mead La. Sea 181 D2
King's Mews. Hove 165 D3
King's Rd. Bri 165 E3
King's Rd. Hast 162 A4
Kings Rd. Hay H 52 B2
Kings Rd. Sock 143 E1
Kings Ride. Alfn 172 B1
Kings Ride. Bur H 75 D1
Kings Ride. Sea 181 D2
Kings Toll Rd. Pem 10 C3
Kings Way. Bur H 75 D1
Kingsbury Rd. Bri 165 F4
Kingsbury St. Bri 165 F4
Kingsdale Cl. Bat 115 E2
Kingsley Cl. Hast 139 F3
Kingsley Ct. Wad 31 F2
Kingsley Rd. Bri 145 D1
Kingsley Rd. Lew 126 C1
Kingsmead. Sea 181 E3
Kingsmead Cl. Sea 181 E2
Kingsmead Way. Sea 181 E2
Kingsmead Wlk. Sea 181 E2
Kingsmere. Bri 145 E1
Kingsthorpe Rd. Hove 164 B4
Kingston Ave. Sea 181 F2
Kingston Bay Rd. S Sea 163 D3
Kingston Bwy. S Sea 143 D1
Kingston Cl. Hove 144 B1
Kingston Cl. S Sea 163 D4
Kingston Cl. Sea 181 F2
Kingston Green. Sea 181 F2
Kingston La. S Sea 163 D4
Kingston Rd. East 175 E1
Kingston Rd. Lew 148 C4
Kingston Way. S Sea 143 D1
Kingston Way. Sea 182 A2
Kingstonridge. Kin L 148 A3
Kingsway. Hove 164 B3
Kingsway. Sea 181 D3
Kingswood Ave. Bex 159 E3
Kingswood Cl. T W 9 D2
Kingswood Rd. T W 9 D2
Kingswood St. Bri 165 F3
Kinver La. Bex 160 C3
Kipling Ave. Wood 167 E4
Kipling Way. E Gri 2 A1
Kipling Wlk. East 176 B1
Kirby Dr. Pea 168 C1
Kirdford Cl. Bur H 75 D1
Kirk Way. East 184 C2
Kirkdale Rd. T W 8 C2
Kirkstall Cl. East 175 E2
Kitchenour La. Four O 70 B3
Kitchenour La. Peas 70 B3
Kite Cl. Hast 161 E4
Knebworth Rd. Bex 159 E3
Knelle Rd. Rob 65 F2
Knepp Cl. Bri 146 B1
Knights Cl. Pem 10 A4
Knights Garden. Hai 154 C3
Knights Meadow. Uck 80 B4
Knight's Ridge. Pem 10 A4
Knightsbridge Cl. T W 8 B3
Knole Gr. E Gri 2 A2
Knole Rd. Bex 160 A2
Knole Rd. Rottn 167 F1
Knoll Cl. Hove 144 A1
Knoll Cres. East 175 F1
Knoll Rd. East 175 F1
Knoll Rise. Hast 161 F4
Knowle Cl. Cro 40 A4
Knowle Cl. Lan G 7 E2
Knowle Hill. May 41 F1
Knowle Park Rd. May 41 F1
Knowle Rd. Fai 142 B3
Knoyle Rd. Bri 145 E1
Kymer Gdns. Key 100 C2

Laburnum Ave. Hove 144 B1
Laburnum Gdns. Bex 160 B3
Laburnum Green. Hai 132 C1
Laburnum Way. Hay H 52 C2
Laburnum Wlk. East 175 D2
Lacys Hill. Gly 150 B4
Ladies Mile Cl. Bri 145 E3
Ladies Mile Rd. Bri 145 E3
Lady Oak La. Fli 34 A4
Ladycross Cl. Sea 182 A2
Lady's Gift Rd. Sgh 8 B4
Ladysmith Rd. Bri 166 A4
Lagwood Cl. Hass 100 B2
Laine Cl. Bri 145 E2
Lake Dr. Pea 178 C4
Lake Rd. T W 8 A2
Lake St. May 42 A4
Lake St. Wad 29 F1
Lake View Rd. Cra D 1 A2
Lake View Rd. Dor P 2 B3
Lakehurst La. Pon G 112 C4
Lakelands Cl. East 175 F1
Lakelands Dr. Bex 159 D2
Laleham Cl. East 185 E2
Laleham Cl. Hast 140 A3
Lambert Pl. S Mal 127 D2
Lamberts Rd. T W 9 D4
Lambourn. E Gri 2 B2
Lambourn Way. T W 9 D1
Lambourne Cl. Bri 146 A1
Lambourne Rd. Bri 146 A1
Lampington Row. Lan G 7 E2
Lancaster Dr. E Gri 2 C2
Lancaster Rd. Bri 165 E4
Lancaster Rd. Hast 139 E3
Lancaster St. Lew 127 D1
Lancing Cl. Hast 140 A2
Lancing Way. Willn 174 B2
Landgate. Rye 95 D3
Landport Rd. Lew 126 C2
Landsdown Rd. Sea 181 F3
Landsdowne Way. Bex 160 B3
Landseer Rd. Hove 164 C4
Langdale Cl. East 176 A2
Langdale Gdns. Hove 164 B3
Langdale Rd. Hove 164 B3
Langham Cl. Hast 140 B2
Langham Cl. Rin 128 A3
Langham Rd. Hast 140 B2
Langham Rd. Rob 65 E3
Langholm Rd. Lan G 7 E2
Langley Cl. Bex 159 F4
Langley Cres. Wood 147 E1
Langney Green. East 186 B4
Langney Rd. East 185 F2
Langney Rise. East 176 A1
Langridge La. Hay H 52 C3
Langridge Way. Bur H 74 B3
Langton La. Hur 99 E4
Langton Rd. Lan G 7 F2
Langton Rd. T W 8 A2
Langton Ridge. Lan G 7 F2
Langtye La. Chal 152 B3
Langtye La. Ripe 152 B3
Lansdown Pl. Lew 149 D4
Lansdowne Cres. Hai 132 C1
Lansdowne Dr. Hai 132 C1
Lansdowne Gdns. Hai 132 C1
Lansdowne Pl. Hove 165 D3
Lansdowne Rd. Hai 132 C1
Lansdowne Rd. Hove 165 D3
Lansdowne Rd. T W 8 C2
Lansdowne Sq. Hove 165 D3
Lansdowne Sq. T W 8 C2
Lansdowne St. Hove 165 D3
Lansdowne Way. Hai 132 C2
Lapierre Rd. Newh 179 F4
Lapwing Cl. East 176 A1
Larch Cl. Hast 139 F1
Larch Cl. Wood 167 E4
Larch Gdns. East 175 D2
Larches Way. Cra D 11 D4
Lark Hill. Hove 144 B2
Larke Cl. S Sea 163 D4
Larkfield Cl. Hast 139 F2
Larkfield Way. Bri 145 F2
Larkhill. Bex 160 A2
Larkspur Dr. East 175 F2
Lascelles Terr. East 185 F1
Lashbrooks Rd. Uck 79 F4
Latimer Rd. East 186 A2
Latnach Cl. Uck 80 A4
Laton Rd. Hast 140 B1
Laughton Rd. Lau 129 E4
Laughton Rd. Rin 129 E4
Laughton Rd. Wood 167 E4
Laundry La. Che G 24 A1
Laurel Bank. Sgh 8 C4
Laurel Cl. Bur H 75 D3
Laurel La. Ick 119 E3
Laurel Rd. T W 9 D4
Laurel Way. T W 9 D4
Laurel Wlk. Hast 139 E2
Laurels The. Uck 80 B4
Lauriston Rd. Bri 145 E1
Lavant Cl. Bex 159 D3
Lavender St. Bri 165 F3
Lawes Ave. Newh 180 A4
Lawn The. Hast 162 A4
Lawns Ave. East 185 D2
Lawrence Cl. East 176 A1
Lawrence Rd. Hove 164 B4
Lawrie La. Hay H 52 C3
Laylands Rd. Por S 163 F4
Le Brun Rd. East 185 E3
Lea Ave. Rye 94 C3
Lea Rd. Pea 178 C4
Leaf Hall Rd. East 185 F2
Leaf Rd. East 185 F2
Leahurst Court Rd. Bri 145 E2
Lealands Cl. Gro 17 D3
Lealands Dr. Uck 57 D1
Leamland Wlk. Hai 154 C4
Leas The. Wad 31 F3
Leasam La. Rye 94 C4
Leasingham Gdns. Bex 159 F3
Ledsham Ave. Hast 139 F3
Ledsham Cl. Hast 139 F3
Ledsham Park. Hast 139 F3
Ledsham Way. Hast 139 F3
Lee Rd. Lew 126 C1
Lee Way. Newh 179 F4
Leeds Ave. East 186 A4
Leeds Cl. Hast 141 D2
Leeves Cl. Hea 83 F3
Leeves Way. Hea 83 F3
Leggs La. Lan G 7 E3
Legsheath La. E Gri 12 A1
Legsheath La. For R 23 E4
Leicester Dr. T W 18 B4
Leicester Rd. Lew 126 C1
Leicester St. Bri 165 F3
Leicester Villas. Hove 164 A4
Leighton Cl. T W 8 C4
Leighton Rd. Hor K 35 D3
Leighton Rd. Hove 164 C4
Leneda Dr. T W 18 B4
Lenham Ave. Salt 167 F1
Lenham Rd. E. Salt 167 F1
Lenham Rd E . Rottn 167 F1
Lenham Rd W. Rottn 167 F1
Lennox Cl. East 184 C3
Lennox Rd. Hove 164 B4
Lennox St. Bri 165 F3
Leopold Rd. Bex 159 F2
Leopold Rd. Bri 165 E3
Lesley Cl. Bex 160 B4
Leslie St. East 185 F2
Leveller End. Newk 78 A4
Leveller Rd. Newk 78 A4
Levett Ave. Pole 175 D3
Levett Cl. Pole 175 D3
Levett Rd. Pole 175 D3
Levett Way. Pole 175 D3
Levetts La. Bod 48 B1
Lewes Cl. Bex 159 F3
Lewes Cl. Salt 168 B1
Lewes Cres. Bri 166 B2
Lewes Rd. Ash W 13 D3
Lewes Rd. Bri 165 F4
Lewes Rd. Dan 35 F2
Lewes Rd. Dit 101 D1
Lewes Rd. E Gri 12 C4
Lewes Rd. East 185 E2
Lewes Rd. Fol 174 A3
Lewes Rd. For R 24 B4
Lewes Rd. Hay H 52 C2
Lewes Rd. Hay H 52 C4
Lewes Rd. Hor K 35 D3
Lewes Rd. Lit H 80 A2
Lewes Rd. Newh 180 A4
Lewes Rd. Pole 174 B3
Lewes Rd. Rid 80 A2
Lewes Rd. Rin 128 A3
Lewes Rd. Sca H 53 E2
Lewes Rd. Wil 173 F3
Lewes Rd. Wmes 124 B4
Lewes St. Bri 165 F3
Lewis Cl. Newh 170 B1
Lewis Rd. Hast 139 F2
Lewis's Bldgs. Bri 165 E3
Lexden Ct. Sea 181 F2
Lexden Dr. Sea 181 F3
Lexden Rd. Sea 181 E3
Leybourne Cl. Bri 146 C1
Leybourne Gdns. Hast 140 A2
Leybourne Rd. Bri 146 C1
Leyfield. Alb 99 D3
Leyland Rd. Pev B 177 D2
Leylands Park. Bur H 74 C3
Leylands Rd. Bur H 74 C2
Lilac Cl. East 175 D1
Limden Cl. Ston 44 B3
Lime Cl. Frant 18 C2
Lime Cl. Uck 80 A4
Lime Hill Rd. T W 8 C2
Lime Tree Ave. Uck 80 A4
Limekiln Ct. Cro 28 A2
Limes La. Bux 58 A2
Limes The. Fel 1 C3
Limetree Ave. East 175 D2
Limeway. Hea 83 F3
Linchmere Ave. Salt 168 A1
Lincoln Ave. Pea 178 C4
Lincoln Ave S. Pea 178 C4
Lincoln Cl. East 190 A4
Lincoln Cl. Hast 139 F2
Lincoln Cotts. Bri 165 F3
Lincoln Rd. Por S 163 F4
Lincoln St. Bri 165 F4
Lincoln Wood. Hay H 52 A3
Linden Ave. E Gri 2 A1
Linden Chase. Uck 80 A4
Linden Cl. East 175 E1
Linden Gdns. T W 8 B1
Linden Gr. Hay H 52 C4
Linden Park Rd. T W 8 C1
Linden Rd. Bex 160 A2
Lindfield Ave. Sea 182 A1
Lindfield Cl. Rottn 167 F1
Lindfield Dr. Hai 154 C4
Lindfield Rd. East 175 D1
Lindon Cl. Fri 183 F1
Lindsay Cl. East 185 D1
Lingfield Rd. E Gri 2 A2
Link Rd. East 185 D1
Link The. Fri 184 A1
Link The. Rye 94 C3
Link Way. T W 9 E4
Links Ave. Pea 179 F4
Links Cl. Cro 27 D1
Links Cl. Por S 164 A4
Links Cl. Sea 181 F2
Links Dr. Bex 160 B2
Links Rd. Por S 164 A4
Links Rd. Sea 181 F1
Links The. Hast 161 E4
Links Way. Cam 96 B1
Linkway. East 184 C4
Linkway. Whm 176 B3
Linkway The. Bri 145 F1
Linley Cl. Bex 160 A2
Linley Cl. Hast 140 C2
Linley Dr. Hast 140 B1
Linley Dr. Hast 140 C2
Linnet Cl. East 176 A1
Linthouse Cl. Pea 169 D1
Linton Ave. Bri 166 B3
Linton Cres. Hast 162 B4
Linton Rd. Hast 162 B4
Linton Rd. Hove 164 B4
Lion Hill. St Cro 175 F3
Lion La. East 185 F2
Lion Mews. Hove 164 B4
Lion St. Rye 95 D3
Lionel Rd. Bex 160 B2
Lions Pl. Sea 181 E1
Liphook Cl. Bri 146 A1
Lipscombe Rd. T W 9 D3
Liptraps La. T W 9 D4
Lismore Rd. East 185 F1
Lister Ave. E Gri 12 B3
Lister Rd. East 175 F1
Little Bentswood. Hay H 52 B3
Little Bentswood Cl. Hay H 52 B3
Little Common Rd. Bex 159 E3
Little Copse Rd. Hass 100 B2
Little Cres. Rottn 167 F1
Little East St. Bri 165 F2
Little East St. Lew 127 D1
Little Footway. Lan G 7 E2
Little George St. Bri 165 F3
Little King St. E Gri 2 B1
Little London Rd. Hor 109 E4
Little Mallett. Lan G 7 E2
Little Mead. Coo 126 C4
Little Mount Sion. T W 8 C1
Little Paddock. Rin 128 B3
Little Preston St. Bri 165 E3
Little Ridge Ave. Hast 140 A3
Little Ridge Ave. Hast 139 F3
Little Sunnyside. Cro 27 E1
Little Trodgers La. May 42 A3
Little Twitten. Bex 159 D2
Little Western St. Hove 165 E3
Littleworth Cl. Wood 167 E4
Liverpool St. Bri 165 F3
Livingstone Rd. Bur H 74 B2
Livingstone Rd. Hove 164 C4
Livingstone St. Bri 166 A3
Lloyd Rd. Hove 165 D4
Lockitt Way. Kin L 148 B3
Locks Cres. Por S 143 F1
Locks Hill. Por S 143 F1
Lockwood Cl. Wood 167 E4
Lockwood Cres. Wood 167 E4
Loder Pl. Bri 145 E1
Loder Rd. Bri 145 E1
Lodge Ave. Willn 175 D1
Lodge Cl. E Gri 2 A1
Lodge Cl. Por S 143 E1
Lodge Hill La. Dit 101 D2
Lodge La. Key 100 C1
Lodge Rd. Hast 141 D1
Lomas La. San 49 E3
Lomond Ave. Bri 145 F4
London Rd. Alb 122 B4
London Rd. Bat 115 D4
London Rd. Bex 159 F3
London Rd. Bri 145 E3
London Rd. Bri 165 F4
London Rd. Bur H 100 B4
London Rd. Cro 27 E2
London Rd. Dan 35 F2
London Rd. E Gri 2 A1
London Rd. E Hoa 107 F3
London Rd. Fli 34 A2
London Rd. For R 13 E2
London Rd. Hai 132 C1
London Rd. Hass 100 B3
London Rd. Hast 162 A4
London Rd. Hur G 46 C1
London Rd. Mou 89 D2
London Rd. Sgh 8 C4
London Rd. T W 8 C2
London Rd. Uck 57 D1
London Terr. Bri 165 F4
Long Acre Cl. East 185 D3
Long Ave. Bex 160 C3
Long La. Sed 90 B1
Long Meads. Lan G 7 F2
Long Meads. T W 7 F2
Long Park Cnr. Dit 101 D1
Long Slip. Lan G 7 F2
Longfield Rd. T W 9 D4
Longhill Cl. Oving 167 E2
Longhill Rd. Oving 167 E2
Longhurst. Bur H 75 D1
Longland Rd. East 185 D2
Longridge Ave. Salt 168 A1
Longstone Rd. East 185 F2
Longview. Hea 83 F3
Longview Way. T W 9 D4
Lonsdale Gdns. T W 8 C2
Lookout The. Pea 169 D2
Lordine La. Ewh G 67 F2
Lords La. Hast 141 D2
Lordslaine Cl. East 190 A4
Lordswell La. Cro 39 E4
Lorna Rd. Hove 165 D4
Lorne Rd. Bri 165 F4
Lorraine Rd. Newh 180 A4
Lossenham La. New 50 A2
Lottbridge Dr. East 175 E1
Lottbridge Dro. East 185 F4
Love La. East 185 D2
Love La. May 41 E1
Love La. Rye 94 C3
Lover's Wlk. Bri 165 E4
Lowdells Dr. E Gri 2 A2
Lowdell's La. E Gri 2 A2
Lower Bevendean Ave. Bri 146 B1
Lower Chalvington Pl. Bri 166 B3
Lower Dene. E Gri 2 C1
Lower Dr. Sea 181 E3
Lower Dr. Sock 143 E1
Lower Glen Rd. Hast 139 F2
Lower Green Rd. Pem 10 A4
Lower Green Rd. Spe 8 A4
Lower Green Rd. T W 8 A2
Lower Hazelhurst. Tic 32 C2
Lower High St. Wad 31 F2
Lower Lake. Bat 115 E2
Lower Market St. Hove 165 D3
Lower Mere. E Gri 12 B4
Lower Par. East 185 F1
Lower Park Rd. Hast 140 B1
Lower Pl. Newh 180 A4
Lower Platts. Tic 33 E1
Lower Prom. Hast 161 F3
Lower Rd. East 185 D2
Lower Rd. For R 13 E2
Lower Rd. Hers 134 B2
Lower Rock Gdns. Bri 165 F2
Lower Saxonbury. Cro 27 E1
Lower South Rd. Hast 140 A1
Lower Sq. For R 13 E2
Lower St. E Dean 188 C4
Lower St. Rye 95 D3
Lower Station Rd. Chay 77 F3
Lower Waites La. Fai 142 B3
Lowfield Rd. Hay H 52 B2
Lowlands Rd. Bur H 74 C3
Lowlands The. Hai 132 C1
Lowther Cl. East 176 A2
Lowther Rd. Bri 145 F1
Loxfield Cl. May 41 F1
Loxfield Gdns. Cro 27 F1
Loxwood Cl. Bex 159 D3
Loxwood Cl. East 175 D1
Lucas. Hor K 35 D3
Lucas Cl. E Gri 2 C1
Lucas Grange. Hay H 52 A3
Lucas Way. Hay H 52 A3
Lucastes Ave. Hay H 52 A3
Lucastes La. Hay H 52 A3
Lucastes Rd. Hay H 52 A3
Lucerne Cl. Por S 143 F1
Lucerne Rd. Bri 145 F1
Lucinda Way. Sea 181 E3
Lucroft Rd. Bri 146 C3
Ludley Hill. Bec 92 C3
Ludlow Rise. Bri 146 C1
Ludpit La. Bur 65 D3
Ludpit La. Etc 65 D3
Lulham Cl. Pea 168 C1
Lullington Ave. Hove 164 B4
Lullington Cl. Bex 160 C3
Lullington Cl. East 185 D4
Lullington Cl. Sea 181 F1
Lumberpit La. E Chi 102 C4
Lunces Hill. Wiv 75 E4
Lundy Wlk. Hai 132 B1
Lurgashall. Bur H 75 D1
Lushington La. East 185 F1
Lushington Rd. East 185 F1
Lustrells Cl. Salt 167 F1
Lustrells Cres. Salt 168 A1
Lustrells Rd. Rottn 167 F1
Lustrells Vale. Salt 168 A1
Luther St. Bri 166 A4
Luton Cl. East 185 D3
Luxford Dr. Cro 39 F4
Luxford La. Cro 39 F4
Luxford Rd. Cro 39 F4
Luxford Rd. Hay H 52 C4
Luxford's La. E Gri 12 C3
Lychgates Cl. Bex 160 A3
Lydd Cl. East 176 A1
Lydd Rd. Cam 96 C1
Lymden La. Ston 44 C4
Lymden La. Wal 32 C1
Lyminster Ave. Bri 145 F3
Lynchet Cl. Bri 146 A1
Lynchet Down. Bri 146 A1
Lynchet Wlk. Bri 146 A1
Lynchets Cres. Hove 144 A2
Lynchets The. S Mal 127 E2
Lyndhurst Ave. Hast 140 C2
Lyndhurst Rd. Hove 165 D4
Lynholm Rd. Pole 175 D3
Lynton Cl. E Gri 2 C1
Lynton Cl. Hur 99 F3
Lynton Park Ave. E Gri 2 C1
Lynton St. Bri 166 A4
Lynwood Cl. Hast 140 A3
Lynwood Rd. Salt 178 A4
Lyoth La. Hay H 53 D2
Lytham Cl. Hast 161 E4

Mabb's Hill. Ston 44 B4
Maberley Rd. Bex 160 A3
Mackerel Hill. Peas 70 B2
Mackie Ave. Bri 145 F4
Mackie Ave. Key 100 C3
Macmillan Dr. East 185 D3
Madehurst Cl. Bri 166 A3
Madeira Dr. Hast 140 A2
Madeira Park. T W 8 C1
Madeira Pl. Bri 165 F2
Madeira Terr. Bri 166 A2
Mafeking Rd. Bri 146 A1
Magdalen Rd. Bex 160 A2
Magdalen Rd. Hast 162 A4
Magnolia Dr. East 175 D1
Magnolia Wlk. East 175 D2
Magpie Cl. Bex 159 D3
Magpie Cl. Hast 161 E4
Magpie Rd. East 176 A2
Maidstone Rd. Pem 10 B4
Main Rd. Ick 119 E3
Main Rd. Wfd 117 E2
Main St. Iden 71 F2
Main St. Norm 68 C3
Main St. Peas 70 C1
Mainstone Rd. Hove 164 B4
Major Cl. Bri 145 F1
Major York's Rd. T W 8 B1
Malcolm Gdns. Pole 174 C4
Maldon Rd. Bri 145 D1
Malines Ave. Pea 178 C4
Malines Ave S. Pea 178 C4
Mallard Pl. E Gri 12 B4
Malling Cl. S Mal 127 D2
Malling Down. S Mal 127 E2
Malling Hill. S Mal 127 E1
Malling Industrial Estate. Lew 127 E1
Malling St. Lew 127 E1
Mallory Rd. Hove 145 D1
Malthouse La. Bur H 74 A1
Malthouse La. Hur 100 A4
Maltings The. Peas 70 C1
Malton Way. T W 9 E3
Malvern Cl. East 175 E2
Malvern St. Hove 164 C4
Malvern Way. Hast 140 C2
Manaton Cl. Hay H 52 B2

Manchester Rd. Nin 136 C3
Manchester St. Bri 165 F2
Manhattan Gdns. Hast 141 D2
Manifold Rd. East 185 F2
Mann St. Hast 162 B4
Manning Cl. E Gri 2 A1
Manor Ave. Key 100 C3
Manor Cl. Bri 166 B3
Manor Cl. Bur H 75 D2
Manor Cl. Hor 109 E4
Manor Cl. Ick 119 E3
Manor Cl. Rin 128 B4
Manor Cl. Sea 181 F2
Manor Cl. Sock 163 F4
Manor Cl. T W 8 B2
Manor Cl. Uck 80 A4
Manor Cl. Willn 174 C1
Manor Cres. Bri 166 B3
Manor Dr. Pea 168 C1
Manor End. Uck 80 A4
Manor Gdns. Bri 166 B3
Manor Gdns. Hur 99 E3
Manor Green. Bri 166 B3
Manor Hall Rd. Sock 163 E4
Manor Hill. Bri 166 B3
Manor Paddock. Bri 166 B2
Manor Park. T W 8 B2
Manor Park Cl. Hai 132 C2
Manor Park Rd. Hai 132 C2
Manor Pl. Bri 166 B2
Manor Rd. Bex 160 A2
Manor Rd. Bri 166 B3
Manor Rd. Bur H 75 D2
Manor Rd. E Gri 2 A1
Manor Rd. East 175 F1
Manor Rd. Hast 140 C1
Manor Rd. Hor 109 E4
Manor Rd. Hur 99 E3
Manor Rd. Por S 143 F1
Manor Rd. Sea 181 F2
Manor Rd. T W 8 A2
Manor Rd N. Sea 181 F2
Manor Way. Bri 166 B3
Manor Way. Cro 39 E4
Manor Way. East 184 C4
Manor Way. Pole 174 C3
Manor Way. Uck 80 A4
Mansell Cl. Bex 159 D2
Mansers La. Low D 132 A2
Mansfield Rd. Hove 164 B4
Mansion Cl. Bur H 75 D2
Manston Way. Hast 140 B1
Mantell Cl. S Mal 127 D2
Manton Rd. Bri 146 B1
Manvers Rd. East 184 C2
Maple Ave. Bex 159 D2
Maple Cl. Bex 159 D2
Maple Cl. Bur H 75 D3
Maple Cl. Hay H 52 C2
Maple Cl. T W 8 C1
Maple Cl. Wood 167 E4
Maple Ct. Hai 154 C4
Maple Dr. Bur H 74 C3
Maple Dr. E Gri 2 C1
Maple Gdns. Hove 144 B1
Maple Rd. East 186 A4
Maple Wlk. Bex 159 D2
Maplehurst Cl. Hast 140 A4
Maplehurst Dr. Wfd 140 A4
Maplehurst Rd. East 175 D1
Maplehurst Rd. Hast 139 F4
Maplehurst Rd. Por S 143 F1
Maplehurst Rise. Hast 139 F4
Mapleleaf Gdns. Pole 174 C4
Marbles Rd. Newk 78 A4
Marchants Dr. Cam 96 B1
Marchants Rd. Hur 99 F3
Marchants Way. Bur H 74 B3
Marcia Cl. East 184 C4
Marcus Gdns. Hast 139 F3
Marden Cl. Wood 147 E1
Marden's Hill. Cro 27 D3
Marden's Hill. Fri G 26 C3
Maresfield Dr. Pev B 177 E3
Maresfield Rd. Bri 166 B3
Margaret St. Bri 165 F2
Margery Rd. Hove 164 A4
Marina. Bex 160 A2
Marina. Hast 161 F3
Marina Ct Ave. Bex 160 A2
Marina Way. Bri 166 B2
Marina Wlk. East 186 B4
Marine Ave. Hove 164 B3
Marine Ave. Pev B 177 E3
Marine Cl. Pev B 177 E3
Marine Cl. Salt 167 F1
Marine Cres. Sea 181 E1
Marine Dr. Bri 166 C2
Marine Dr. Oving 167 D1
Marine Dr. Rottn 167 E1
Marine Dr. Salt 167 E1
Marine Dr. Sea 180 C3
Marine Gdns. Bri 165 F2
Marine Par. Bri 166 A2
Marine Par. East 185 F2
Marine Par. Hast 162 C4
Marine Par. Sea 181 D2
Marine Par Rd. East 185 F2
Marine Rd. East 185 F2
Marine Rd. Pev B 177 D3
Marine Sq. Bri 166 A2
Marine Terr. Pev B 177 D3
Marine Terr Mews. Bri 166 A2
Marine View. Bri 165 F3
Marine View. Newh 179 F3
Mark Cl. Sea 182 A1
Mark La. East 185 F1
Market La. Lew 127 D1
Market Pas. Hast 162 A3
Market Pas. Hast 162 C4
Market Pl. Hai 155 D4
Market Pl. Hay H 52 B3
Market Pl. T W 8 C1
Market Rd. Rye 95 D3
Market Rd. T W 8 C2
Market Sq. Hai 155 D4
Market St. Bri 165 F3
Market St. Hast 162 A3
Market St. Lew 127 D1
Market St. Rye 95 D3
Market St. T W 8 C1
Markland Way. Uck 79 F4
Marklye La. Hea 83 F4
Markstakes Cnr. S Str 77 E1
Markstakes La. S Str 77 F1
Markwick Terr. Hast 161 F4
Marlborough Cl. East 176 A2
Marlborough Cl. Hast 139 F1
Marlborough Cl. T W 8 A2
Marlborough Dr. Bur H 75 D1
Marlborough Pl. Bri 165 F3
Marlborough St. Bri 165 E3
Marle Ave. Bur H 74 C2
Marley Cl. Bat 115 E2
Marley Gdns. Bat 115 E2
Marley La. Bat 115 F3
Marley La. Sed 116 A4
Marley Rd. Rye 94 C3
Marley Rise. Bat 115 E2
Marline Ave. Hast 139 F2
Marline Rd. Hast 139 F2
Marlow Ave. East 185 F3
Marlow Dr. Hast 139 F3
Marlow Dr. Hay H 52 C2
Marlow Dr. Hay H 53 D2
Marlow Rd. Bri 166 B2
Marlpit Cl. E Gri 2 B2
Marlpit Rd. Sha 22 C3
Marlpit The. Wad 31 E3
Marlpits La. Nin 136 C4
Marmion Rd. Hove 164 B4
Marsden Rd. East 176 B1
Marsh Quarter La. San 49 D2
Marshall La. Newh 180 A4
Marshall Rd. East 185 F4
Marshalls Row. Bri 165 F4
Marshfoot La. Hai 155 D4
Marshlands La. Hea 83 F4
Martello Ct. S Hei 170 A1
Martello Rd. East 186 A3
Martello Rd. Sea 181 E1
Martens Field. Rod 149 E1
Martin Rd. Hove 144 A1
Martineau La. Hast 141 E3
Martins The. Cra D 11 D4
Martlet Ct. Cro 27 E1
Martlets The. Bro Ow 92 A2
Martlets The. Cro 27 E1
Martlets The. S Mal 127 D2
Martletts. Bex 160 B3
Martletts The. Rin 128 B3
Martyn's Cl. Oving 167 E2
Martyns Pl. E Gri 12 B4
Martyns Way. Bex 160 C3
Mary Stamford Green. Rye H 95 F2
Maryan Ct. Hai 154 C4
Maryland Rd. T W 9 D1
Maskelyne Rd. Hers 134 C1
Mason Cl. E Gri 2 B1
Mason Rd. Rye 94 C3
Mason Rd. Sea 181 E2
Matlock Rd. East 190 B4
Matlock Rd. Hove 145 D1
Maunsell Rd. Hast 139 E3
Maurice Rd. Sea 181 E1
Maxfield Cl. East 184 C3
Maxfield La. Thr O 118 A1
May Rd. Bri 166 A4
May Tree Gdns. Bex 160 B3
May Tree Wlk. Hove 144 B1
Mayfair Cl. Pole 174 B2
Mayfield Ave. Pea 179 D3
Mayfield Cl. Bri 145 F3
Mayfield Cl. May 41 E1
Mayfield Cres. Bri 145 E3
Mayfield Flat. Blas 82 C4
Mayfield Flat. Five A 59 F1
Mayfield La. Hast 139 D1
Mayfield La. Wad 31 D2
Mayfield Park. Wad 31 D3
Mayfield Pl. East 185 F2
Mayfield Rd. T W 8 B2
Mayfield Way. Bex 160 B3
Mayflower Ct. Hay H 52 B2
Mayflower Rd. Hay H 52 B2
Mayflower Sq. Bri 165 F4
Maynards Mead. Cro 40 A4
Mayne Waye. Hast 140 C2
Mayo La. Bex 159 F4
Mayo Rd. Bri 165 F4
Mayo Rise. Bex 159 F4
Maypole Cotts. H Hur 57 F4
Maypole Rd. Ash W 13 E3
Maypole Rd. E Gri 2 A1
Maytham Rd. Rol L 51 D4
Mayview Cl. Bro O 61 E1
Maywood Ave. East 175 D1
Maze Hill. Hast 161 F4
Maze Hill Terr. Hast 161 F4
Mc Indoe Rd. E Gri 2 A2
Mc William Rd. Wood 147 D1
Meachants La. Willn 174 C1
Mead The. Bex 159 D2
Meadow Bank. Bat 115 E2
Meadow Cl. Hai 132 C1
Meadow Cl. Hast 139 F2
Meadow Cl. Hove 144 C2
Meadow Cl. Por S 143 F1
Meadow Cl. Rottn 167 E2
Meadow Cl. Sock 163 F4
Meadow Cres. Bex 160 A4
Meadow Dr. Hay H 52 C3
Meadow Hill Rd. T W 8 C2
Meadow La. Bur H 74 B1
Meadow La. Hay H 52 C3
Meadow Par. Rottn 167 E2
Meadow Pl. Rid 80 A3
Meadow Rd. Gro 17 D4
Meadow Rd. Hai 154 C3
Meadow Rd. T W 8 C2
Meadow The. Pem 10 B4
Meadow Way. Fai 142 B2
Meadow Way. Hea 83 F3
Meadow Way. Sea 181 F2
Meadowcroft Cl. E Gri 2 A1
Meadowlands Ave. East 175 D1
Meadows. Hass 100 B3
Meadows Rd. Willn 174 C1
Meadows The. Cro 27 E1
Meadows The. Hast 140 A3
Meadows The. Hove 144 A2
Meadows The. S Mal 127 E2
Meads Ave. Bex 159 D2
Meads Ave. Hove 144 A2
Meads Brow. East 190 A4
Meads Cl. Hove 144 A2
Meads Rd. Bex 159 D2
Meads Rd. East 185 E1
Meads Rd. Sea 181 E2
Meads St. East 190 B4
Meads The. Bri 146 A3
Meads The. E Gri 12 B4
Meads The. T W 9 D1
Meadway Cres. Hove 144 B1
Meadway Ct. Sock 163 D4
Meadway The. Bri 166 B3
Mealla Cl. S Mal 127 D2
Medina Pl. Hove 164 C3
Medina Terr. Hove 164 C3
Medina Villas. Hove 164 C3
Medmerry Hill. Bri 146 B1
Medway. Cro 28 A1
Medway. Hai 132 C1
Medway Dr. E Gri 12 A3
Medway Dr. For R 13 F1
Medway Rd. T W 8 C3
Meeching Rd. Newh 180 A4
Meeching Rise. Newh 180 A4
Meeds Rd. Bur H 74 C1
Meeting House La. Bri 165 F3
Megrims Hill. San 48 C3
Melbourne Rd. East 185 F2
Melbourne St. Bri 166 A4
Melfort Rd. Cro 27 D1
Melrose Ave. Por S 143 F1
Melrose Cl. Bri 146 A1
Melvill La. East 174 C1
Melville Rd. Hove 165 E4
Memorial The. Hast 162 B4
Mendip Ave. East 176 A2
Mendip Gdns. Hast 140 C2
Mendip Wlk. T W 9 D3
Mendow Rd. T W 8 A2
Menzies Rd. Hast 139 F1
Mercatoria. Hast 162 A3
Mercer St. T W 8 C3
Mercers. Lan G 7 F2
Mercread Rd. Sea 181 E2
Merevale. Bri 145 F1
Mereworth Rd. T W 8 C3
Meridian Rd. Lew 126 C1
Meridian Way. E Gri 2 B2
Merlin Cl. Hove 165 D4
Merlin Ct. Hai 155 E4
Merlin Way. E Gri 2 C2
Mermaid St. Rye 94 C3
Merrimede Cl. Hast 161 F4
Merriments La. Hur G 47 E3
Merrion Cl. T W 8 C4
Merrion Way. T W 8 C4
Merston Cl. Wood 167 E3
Metcalfe Ave. Newh 179 F4
Mews Rd. Hast 162 A3
Mews The. E Hoa 107 F3
Meyners Cl. Hove 144 A2
Michael Fields. For R 13 E1
Michel Cl. Fri 184 A1
Michel Dene Cl. Fri 184 A1
Michel Gr. East 185 E2
Michele Cl. Hast 139 F1
Michelham Rd. Uck 57 E1
Michelson Cl. Hast 139 E2
Middle Dr. Mar 56 C3
Middle Field. Pem 10 B4
Middle Furlong. Sea 181 E2
Middle Par. East 185 F1
Middle Rd. Bel G 19 F3
Middle Rd. Bri 145 E1
Middle Rd. Hast 141 D2
Middle St. Bri 165 E3
Middle St. Fal 147 D3
Middle St. Hast 162 B4
Middle St. Por S 163 F3
Middle Way. Bur H 74 C2
Middle Way. Lew 126 C1
Middle Wlk. T W 9 E4
Middleham Cl. Rin 128 A2
Middlesex Rd. Bex 160 A2
Middleton Ave. Hove 164 A3
Middleton Dr. East 186 B4
Middleton Rise. Bri 146 B3
Middleway. Win H 134 C3
Midfield Cl. Bur H 74 C2
Midfield Dr. Bur H 74 C2
Midfields Wlk. Bur H 74 C2
Midhurst Rd. East 175 E1
Midhurst Rise. Bri 145 F3
Midhurst Wlk. Hove 144 B2
Midway Rd. Wood 167 D4
Midway The. T W 8 A1
Mighell St. Bri 165 F3
Milcote Ave. Hove 164 B4
Mildenhall Dr. Hast 139 F2
Mildmay Cl. Rin 128 A3
Mildmay Rd. Lew 126 C1
Mile Oak Cres. Sock 143 E1
Mile Oak Gdns. Por S 143 F1
Mile Oak Rd. Por S 143 E2
Mile Oak Rd. Sock 143 E1
Milfoil Dr. East 175 F2
Military Rd. Iden 72 B3
Military Rd. Rye 95 D4
Mill Brooks. S Cha 103 D4
Mill Cl. E Gri 12 B4
Mill Cl. Fri 183 F1
Mill Cl. Hast 141 E2
Mill Cl. Hea 83 E4
Mill Cl. Por S 144 A1
Mill Cl. Rin 128 B3
Mill Cl. S Cha 103 D4
Mill Cl. Wfd 117 E3
Mill Cl. Willn 174 B2
Mill Cres. Cro 27 E2
Mill Dr. Cro 27 E2
Mill Dr. Hove 144 C1
Mill Dr. Sea 181 F2
Mill Dro. Rid 80 A3
Mill Dro. Sea 180 C3
Mill Gap Rd. East 185 E2
Mill Gdns. Hea 83 F3
Mill Gdns. Rin 128 A3
Mill Green Rd. Hay H 52 B3
Mill Hill Cl. Hay H 52 B4
Mill La. Bar 104 A1
Mill La. Clay 123 E4
Mill La. Cro 27 E1
Mill La. Dor 2 B4
Mill La. E Hoa 107 F3
Mill La. Fel 1 B3
Mill La. Hast 141 E3
Mill La. Hooe 136 B1
Mill La. Peas 70 B2
Mill La. Por S 144 A1
Mill La. Pye 123 D4
Mill La. Rid 80 A3
Mill La. Rod 169 D4
Mill La. S Cha 103 D4
Mill La. Wfd 117 E3
Mill Mead. Rin 128 B3
Mill Path. Rin 128 B3
Mill Rd. Bri 145 D3
Mill Rd. Bur H 74 C2
Mill Rd. East 185 D3
Mill Rd. Hai 155 D3
Mill Rd. Hea 83 E4
Mill Rd. Rin 128 A3
Mill Rd. Rye 95 D4
Mill Rd. S Mal 127 E2
Mill Rd. Sock 163 F4
Mill Rd. Winc 120 B4
Mill Rise. Bri 145 D3
Mill Rise. Rob 65 F2
Mill St. Fal 147 D4
Mill Stream Meadow. Hay H 52 A4
Mill View. Rin 128 A2
Mill View Cl. Whm 176 A3
Mill View Rd. Bex 159 F4
Mill Way. E Gri 12 B4
Mill Way. Willn 174 B2
Mill Wood. Bur H 74 C2
Milland Cl. Bex 160 B3
Milland Rd. Hai 132 C1
Millbank. Bur H 74 C2
Millberg Rd. Sea 182 A2
Millbrook Cl. Hor 109 F4
Millbrook Gdns. East 184 C3
Millbrook Rd. Cro 27 F2
Millcroft. Bri 145 D3
Millcroft Ave. Sock 143 E1
Millcroft Gdns. Sock 143 E1
Millcross Rd. Por S 143 F1
Milldown Rd. Sea 181 E2
Miller's Hill. Wfd 117 E3
Miller's Rd. Bri 145 E1
Millers Way. Bur H 74 C2
Millfield. Nin 136 C3
Millfield Cl. Sea 181 F2
Millfield Cotts. Bri 166 A2
Millfield Rise. Bex 160 A2
Millham Cl. Bex 159 E3
Millrace The. Pole 174 B2
Millstream Cl. Asht 6 A1
Millstream Gdns. Willn 174 B2
Millward Rd. Pev B 177 D2
Millwood Cl. Uck 57 D2
Millwood La. Mar 57 D2
Millwood La. Uck 57 D2
Millwood Rd. Bex 159 F4
Millyard Cres. Wood 167 D4
Milner Rd. Bri 146 A1
Milnthorpe Rd. East 190 B4
Milnthorpe Rd. Hove 164 B4
Milton Cres. E Gri 12 A4
Milton Cres. East 185 D2
Milton Dr. Sock 163 E4
Milton Dr. T W 9 D4
Milton Rd. Bri 165 F4
Milton Rd. East 185 D2
Milton Rd. Hay H 52 A3
Milton St. Hank 175 F4
Milward Cres. Hast 162 C4
Milward Rd. Hast 162 C4
Mimosa Cl. Pole 174 C4
Minstead Sq. Bex 159 D1
Minster Cl. Pole 174 C4
Mint The. Rye 94 C3
Mistley Cl. Bex 160 C3
Mitchelldean. Pea 169 D1
Mitten Rd. Bex 160 A2
Moat Croft Rd. East 185 E2
Moat Farm. T W 18 C4
Moat La. Wald 82 A1
Moat La. Wfd 116 C2
Moat Rd. E Gri 2 B1
Modena Rd. Hove 164 B4
Molesworth St. Hove 164 B4
Molyneux Almshouses. T W 7 F2
Molyneux Park Rd. T W 8 B2
Mona Rd. East 185 F2
Monarch Gdns. Sea 181 F3
Monastery Gdns. Rot 40 C4
Monceux Rd. East 185 D2
Monceux Rd. Hers 134 B3
Monckton Way. Kin L 148 B3
Monger's Mead. Bar C 104 B2
Monk Cl. Bri 146 A3
Monks La. Lew 149 D4
Monks La. Wad 31 F4
Monks Walk. Winc 120 B4
Monks Way. Norm 68 C4
Monks Way. S Mal 127 D2
Monmouth St. Hove 164 C4
Monson Rd. T W 8 C2
Montacute Gdns. T W 8 B1
Montacute Rd. Lew 148 C4
Montacute Rd. T W 8 B1
Montacute Way. Uck 80 A4
Montague Cl. S Sea 163 D4
Montague Pl. Bri 166 A2
Montague St. Bri 166 A2
Montague Way. Whm 176 B3
Montargis Way. Cro 27 F1
Montefiore Rd. Hove 165 E4
Monteith Cl. Lan G 7 F2
Monterey Cl. Bex 159 E2
Monterey Gdns. Bex 159 E2
Montes Hill. Hay H 53 E4
Monteswood La. Hay H 53 F4
Monteswood La. Hor K 53 F4
Montford Cl. S Sea 163 D4
Montfort Cl. Whm 176 B3
Montfort Rd. Whm 176 B3
Montgomery Rd. Hast 141 D3
Montgomery Rd. T W 8 C4
Montgomery St. Hove 164 C4
Montpelier Cres. Bri 165 E3
Montpelier Pl. Bri 165 E3
Montpelier Rd. Bri 165 E3
Montpelier St. Bri 165 E3
Montpelier Terr. Bri 165 E3
Montpelier Villas. Bri 165 E3
Montreal St. Bri 165 F3
Moon's La. Dor 3 D4
Moor La. Gly 128 C2
Moor La. Rin 128 C2
Moor La. Wfd 117 E2
Moor Pl. E Gri 2 A1
Moor Rd. Wfd 117 E2
Moor The. The M 47 E4
Moore Park. Hai 155 D4
Moore's La. Bec 92 B4
Moorhurst Rd. Hast 139 E3
Moorings The. S Sea 163 D3
Moorland Cl. Nin 136 C3
Moorsite. Wfd 117 E2
Morecambe Rd. Bri 145 F3
Morestead. Pea 169 D1
Morgan Cl. Bex 159 F4
Morlais Pl. Winc B 120 C3
Morlais Pl. Winc B 120 C3
Morlais Ridge. Winc B 120 C3
Morland Dr. Lam 21 F3
Morley St. Bri 165 F3
Morningside Cl. Sea 181 E2
Mornington Cres. Hove 164 A4
Morris Rd. Lew 127 E1
Mortain Park. Hai 175 D4
Mortain Rd. Whm 176 B3
Mortimer Gdns. Willn 174 B2
Mortimer Rd. East 185 F3
Mortimer Rd. Hove 164 B4
Morton Rd. E Gri 12 B4
Moscow Rd. Hast 141 D1
Motcombe La. East 185 D2
Motcombe Rd. East 185 D2
Motte Field. Hart 15 E2
Mottins Hill. Cro 40 A4
Moulsecoomb Way. Bri 146 B2
Mount Caburn Cres. Pea 169 D1
Mount Cl. Newh 180 B4
Mount Dr. Salt 168 A1
Mount Edgcumbe Rd. T W 8 C2
Mount Ephraim. T W 8 C2
Mount Ephraim Rd. T W 8 C2
Mount Harry Rd. Lew 126 C1
Mount Idol View. Bex 159 F4
Mount Joy. Bat 115 D3
Mount Pl. Lew 127 D1
Mount Pleasant. Blas 81 F3
Mount Pleasant. Bri 165 F3
Mount Pleasant. Cro 40 A4
Mount Pleasant. Hast 162 A3
Mount Pleasant. Lam 21 E3
Mount Pleasant. Lew 127 D1
Mount Pleasant. Rid 80 A3
Mount Pleasant. Spi 104 B3
Mount Pleasant. Wad 31 E3
Mount Pleasant Ave. T W 8 C2
Mount Pleasant Cres. Hast 140 B1
Mount Pleasant La. Lam 21 F3
Mount Pleasant Rd. Hast 140 C1
Mount Pleasant Rd. T W 8 C2
Mount Rd. East 190 B4
Mount Rd. Hast 141 D1
Mount Rd. Newh 170 B1

Mount Sion. T W 8 C1
Mount St. Bat 115 D3
Mount St. Lew 149 D4
Mount The. Hai 155 D3
Mount The. Hast 161 F4
Mount The. Uck 80 A4
Mount View Terr. Hai 155 D3
Mount Zion Pl. Bri 165 E3
Mountbatten Cl. Hast 141 D3
Mountbatten Dr. East 186 B4
Mountfield Gdns. T W 8 C2
Mountfield La. Mou 88 A4
Mountfield Rd. East 175 E1
Mountfield Rd. Lew 149 D4
Mountfield Rd. T W 8 C2
Mountfields. Bri 146 A1
Mountney Dr. Pev B 177 E4
Mountney Rd. East 185 D2
Mountreed. Five A 59 F4
Moy Ave. East 185 F3
Moyne Cl. Hove 144 B1
Muirfield Rise. Hast 161 E4
Mulberry Cl. Bex 159 D2
Mulberry Cl. Bri 145 E2
Mulberry Cl. East 175 E2
Mulberry Cl. S Sea 143 D1
Mulberry La. Dit 101 D2
Mulberry Way. Hea 83 F3
Munns Dr. Bur H 74 C2
Munster Green. Bar C 104 B2
Murdock Rd. Hast 162 B4
Murray Ave. Newh 180 A4
Musgrave Ave. E Gri 12 B4
Mushroom Field. Kin L 148 B3
Muster Green. Hay H 52 A2
Muster Green N. Hay H 52 A2
Muster Green S. Hay H 52 A2
Mutton Hall Hill. Hea 83 F4
Mutton Hall La. Hea 83 F4
Mutton Hill. Dor 2 C4
Myrtle Rd. Cro 27 E1
Myrtle Rd. East 186 A3

Namrik Mews. Hove 164 C3
Nan Kemps Grave. Kin L 148 B3
Nan Tucks La. Bux 58 A1
Nanson Rd. Bri 146 A3
Naomi Cl. East 185 E1
Napier Rd. Hast 139 E2
Napier Rd. T W 9 D1
Nash La. Sca H 53 F2
Natal Rd. Bri 146 A1
Neath Rd. Cam 97 F1
Neaves La. Rin 128 C2
Neill's Cl. Newh 180 A4
Neills Rd. Lam 21 D1
Nellington Rd. T W 7 F2
Nelson Dr. East 186 B3
Nelson Rd. Hast 140 C1
Nelson Rd. T W 9 D1
Nesbitt Rd. Bri 146 A1
Nether La. Nut 37 D2
Netherfield. East 176 B1
Netherfield Green. Wood 167 E4
Netherfield Hill. Bat 114 C4
Netherfield Rd. Net 88 B1
Netherfield Way. Net 88 A1
Netherwood Cl. Hast 140 B3
Nevill Ave. East 175 E1
Nevill Ave. Hove 144 B1
Nevill Cl. Hove 144 C1
Nevill Cotts. Dit 101 D1
Nevill Cres. Lew 126 C1
Nevill Gate. T W 8 C1
Nevill Gdns. Hove 144 C1
Nevill Green. Uck 57 D1
Nevill Park. T W 8 A2
Nevill Pl. Hove 144 C1
Nevill Rd. Cro 27 E2
Nevill Rd. Hove 144 C1
Nevill Rd. Lew 126 C1
Nevill Rd. Rottn 167 E1
Nevill Rd. Uck 57 D1
Nevill Ridge. T W 8 A2
Nevill St. T W 8 C1
Nevill Way. Hove 144 C1
Neville Rd. East 185 F2
Neville Rd. Pea 179 D4
New Barn Cl. Hai 155 D3
New Barn Cl. Por S 143 F1
New Barn Rd. Rottn 167 E2
New Church Rd. Hove 164 B4
New Cut. Mou 89 D3
New Dorset St. Bri 165 E3
New England La. Sed 116 B3
New England Rd. Bri 165 E4
New England Rd. Hay H 52 B3
New England Rd. T W 8 C4
New England Rise. Por S 143 F2
New England St. Bri 165 F4
New Farthingdale. Dor 2 C4
New Lydd Rd. Cam 96 B1
New Park Ave. Bex 160 A2
New Pl. East 185 D2
New Pl. Rid 80 A3
New Pond Hill. Hea 83 D3
New Rd. Bec 69 D2
New Rd. Bri 165 F3
New Rd. Cro 27 E2
New Rd. Dit 100 C1
New Rd. East 185 F2
New Rd. Ford 6 C4
New Rd. Gly 128 A2
New Rd. Hast 141 D1
New Rd. Hea 83 F3
New Rd. Hel 133 D2
New Rd. Key 100 B1
New Rd. Lew 127 D1
New Rd. Mag D 133 D2
New Rd. Mill C 68 C2
New Rd. Newh 180 A4
New Rd. Pole 174 C3
New Rd. Rid 80 A2
New Rd. Rin 128 A2
New Rd. Rot 40 C4
New Rd. Rye 95 D3
New Rd. Tow R 41 D4
New Steine. Bri 165 F2
New Steine Mews. Bri 165 F2
New Upperton Rd. East 185 E2
New Way La. Hur 99 F2
New Winchelsea Rd. Rye 94 C2
Newark Pl. Bri 165 F3
Newbury La. Cou W 32 A4
Newcomen Rd. T W 8 C3
Newells Cl. Wood 147 E1
Newfield La. Newh 180 A4
Newfield Rd. Newh 180 A4
Newgate Rd. Hast 140 A1
Newham Rd. Hea 83 F4
Newhaven Rd. Sea 180 C3
Newhaven St. Bri 165 F3
Newhaven Wlk. Hast 139 F2
Newick Cl. Sea 182 A1
Newick Dr. Newk 78 A4
Newick Hill. Newk 78 A4
Newick La. Hea 61 D1
Newick La. May 60 C4
Newick Rd. Bri 146 B3
Newick Rd. East 185 D3
Newlands. Lan G 7 F2
Newlands Ave. Bex 159 F3
Newlands Cl. Hast 140 B3
Newlands Cl. Key 100 C2
Newlands Cres. E Gri 2 A1
Newlands Rd. Rottn 167 F1
Newlands Rd. T W 8 C4
Newlands Rise. T W 8 C3
Newlands Way. T W 8 C4
Newmans Way. Hast 141 D2
Newmarket Rd. Bri 166 A4
Newmarket Terr. Bri 166 A4
Newport Rd. Bur H 74 B2
Newport St. Bri 165 F4
Newtimber Dr. Por S 143 F1
Newton Ave. E Gri 12 B3
Newton Park. Hai 155 D4
Newton Rd. Hay H 53 D4
Newton Rd. Lew 126 C1
Newton Rd. Pea 179 D4
Newton Rd. T W 8 C2
Newtown Cl. Hay H 52 C4
Newtown Crt. Hay H 52 B3
Newtown Rd. Hove 164 C4
Nightingale Cl. E Gri 12 A4
Nightingale Cl. East 176 A1
Nightingale La. Bur H 100 C4
Nile St. Bri 165 F3
Ninfield Pl. Bri 166 B4
Ninfield Rd. Bex 159 F4
Ninfield Rd. Lun C 137 E1
Nizells Ave. Hove 165 E4
Noahs Ark La. Hay H 53 D4
Noel Green. Bur H 74 C2
Noel Rise. Bur H 74 C2
Nolan Rd. Wood 167 E4
Nook Cl. Hast 141 D2
Norbury Cl. Cro 27 E2
Nore Rd. Newh 179 F3
Norfolk Bldgs. Bri 165 E3
Norfolk Cl. Bex 159 F4
Norfolk Dr. Hast 139 E2
Norfolk Mews. Bri 165 E3
Norfolk Pl. Bri 165 E3
Norfolk Rd. Bri 165 E3
Norfolk Rd. T W 8 C1
Norfolk Sq. Bri 165 E3
Norfolk St. Bri 165 E3
Norfolk Terr. Bri 165 E3
Norfolk Way. Uck 80 A4
Norlington Fields. Rin 128 A3
Norlington La. Rin 128 A4
Norman Cl. Bat 115 E2
Norman Cl. Sea 180 C3
Norman Rd. Bur H 74 C2
Norman Rd. Hast 162 A3
Norman Rd. Hove 164 B3
Norman Rd. Newh 180 A4
Norman Rd. Pev B 177 D2
Norman Rd. T W 8 C3
Normandale. Bex 159 F2
Normandy Rd. Hast 140 A2
Normansland. Fair 37 F1
Normanton St. Bri 166 A4
Norstead Gdns. Sgh 8 C4
North Ave. East 184 C3
North Bank. Hass 100 B2
North Beeches Rd. Cro 27 F1
North Camp La. Sea 181 E3
North Cl. Pole 174 C4
North Cl. Por S 143 F1
North Common Rd. N Cha 76 B3
North Common Rd. Plu G 76 B3
North Common Rd. Wiv G 76 B3
North Cres. Hai 154 C4
North Ct. Hass 100 B2
North Ct. Lew 127 E1
North Dr. Bri 166 A3
North End. Dit 101 D2
North Farm La. T W 9 D4
North Farm Rd. Sgh 9 D4
North Gdns. Bri 165 E3
North Heath Cl. Hai 133 D1
North La. Por S 143 F2
North La. Thr O 118 B3
North La. W Hoa 22 B3
North Pl. Bri 165 F3
North Rd. Alfn 172 B2
North Rd. Bex 160 A4
North Rd. Bod G 112 A1
North Rd. Bri 145 E1
North Rd. Bri 165 F3
North Rd. Hast 140 A1
North Rd. Hay H 52 C2
North Rd. Pev B 177 D3
North Rd. Por S 143 F1
North Rd. Rin 128 A3
North Row. Uck 80 A4
North Salts. Rye 95 D3
North St. Alfn 172 C2
North St. Bri 165 F3
North St. Cowd 4 C3
North St. Cro H 82 B3
North St. East 185 F1
North St. Hai 154 C4
North St. Hast 162 A4
North St. Hel 132 C4
North St. Lew 127 D1
North St. Low H 132 C3
North St. May 41 F2
North St. Por S 164 A4
North St. Pun T 85 D3
North St. Rot 40 C4
North St. T W 9 D2
North St. Wald 82 B2
North St. Winc 120 B4
North St Quadrant. Bri 165 E3
North Trade Rd. Bat 114 C2
North Way. Lew 126 C1
North Way. Newh 180 A4
North Way. Sea 181 E3
Northampton Way. Hast 139 F2
Northbridge. Sale 65 F3
Northcliffe Cl. Sea 181 E2
Northcote La. Pea 168 C1
Northdown Cl. Newh 180 A3
Northdown Rd. Newh 180 A3
Northease Cl. Hove 144 A1
Northease Dr. Hove 144 B2
Northease Gdns. Hove 144 B2
Northern Ave. Pole 174 C4
Northfield. Pole 174 B3
Northfield Cl. Sea 181 E3
Northfield Cotts. Isf 105 D4
Northfield Rise. Hove 144 A2
Northfield Rise. Rottn 167 F1
Northfield Way. Bri 145 F2
Northfields. Spe 7 F4
Northiam Rd. Bro O W 91 F3
Northiam Rd. East 185 D2
Northiam Rd. Mill C 91 F3
Northlands Ave. Hay H 52 C2
Northridge. Norm 68 C4
Northway. Bur H 75 D2
Northwood Ave. Salt 168 B1
Norton Cl. Hove 164 C3
Norton Dr. Wood 147 E1
Norton Rd. Hove 164 C3
Norton Rd. Newh 180 B4
Norton Terr. Newh 180 B4
Norway Rd. East 186 A3
Norway St. Por S 164 A4
Norwich Cl. Bri 146 C1
Norwich Dr. Bri 146 C1
Nottidge Rd. T W 8 A1
Novington La. E Chi 102 C2
Nunnery La. Ford 6 B4
Nursery Cl. Hay H 52 A3
Nursery Cl. Hur 99 E4
Nursery Cl. Pole 174 C3
Nursery Cl. Por S 143 E2
Nursery La. Blas 82 B4
Nursery La. Fair 37 F1
Nursery La. Had D 59 E1
Nursery La. Mar 56 C3
Nursery La. Nut 37 D2
Nursery La. Rid 80 A2
Nursery La. Win H 134 C3
Nursery Path. Hai 154 C4
Nursery Rd. Sgh 8 C4
Nursery The. Bur H 75 D2
Nursery Way. Hea 83 E4
Nutbourne Cl. East 176 B1
Nuthatch Rd. East 176 A1
Nuthurst Cl. Bri 166 B3
Nuthurst Pl. Bri 166 B3
Nutley Ave. Salt 178 A4
Nutley Cl. Hove 144 B2
Nutley Cl. Rye 94 C3
Nye Cl. Cro 27 E1
Nye La. Dit 101 E1
Nye La. Wmes 124 A4
Nye Rd. Bur H 75 D2
Nyetimber Hill. Bri 146 B1

Oak Bank. Hay H 52 B4
Oak Cl. Bri 145 E2
Oak Croft. E Gri 12 C4
Oak Hall Park. Bur H 74 C1
Oak La. Lydd 98 C3
Oak Pas. Hast 162 C4
Oak Rd. T W 9 D4
Oak Tree Cl. T W 8 C1
Oak Tree Cotts. Dan 35 F2
Oak Tree Ct. Uck 80 A4
Oak Tree La. East 176 A2
Oak Tree Way. Hai 133 D1
Oakapple Rd. Sock 143 E1
Oakdale Rd. Hay H 52 B2
Oakdale Rd. T W 8 B2
Oakdene Ave. Por S 143 E2
Oakdene Cl. Por S 143 E2
Oakdene Cres. Por S 143 E2
Oakdene Gdns. Por S 143 E2
Oakdene Rise. Por S 143 E2
Oakdene Way. Por S 143 E2
Oakenfield. Bur H 74 B3
Oakfield Cl. Hay H 52 C4
Oakfield Ct Rd. T W 9 D2
Oakfield Rd. Hast 141 D2
Oakfield The. Rye 94 C4
Oakfield Way. Bex 159 D3
Oakfield Way. E Gri 2 B2
Oakhill Cotts. Four O 70 A2
Oakhill Dr. Bro O W 91 F3
Oakhurst. Hay H 52 A4
Oakhurst Cl. Hast 140 B3
Oakhurst Dr. Cro 27 F2
Oakhurst Gdns. E Gri 2 A1
Oakhurst Rd. Bat 115 D4
Oakland Dr. Rob 65 D2
Oaklands. Whm 176 B3
Oaklands Ave. Salt 168 A1
Oaklands Cl. Pole 174 C3
Oaklands Rd. Gro 16 C3
Oaklands Rd. Hay H 52 A3
Oaklands Way. Hai 154 C3
Oaklea Cl. Hast 140 A2
Oaklea Way. Uck 79 F4
Oakleaf Dr. Pole 174 C4
Oakleigh Rd. Bex 159 D2
Oakley Cl. E Gri 12 C4
Oakmead Rd. Bur H 74 B1
Oakmede Way. Rin 128 A3
Oakroyd Cl. Bur H 75 D3
Oaks Forstal. San 49 D3
Oaks The. E Gri 12 C4
Oaks The. Hea 83 F3
Oaktree. Bar C 104 B2
Oakwood Ave. Bex 159 F4
Oakwood Cl. Bur H 74 C1
Oakwood Cl. Hast 140 B2
Oakwood Dr. Bur H 74 C1
Oakwood Dr. Uck 80 B4
Oakwood Park. Nut 37 D3
Oakwood Rd. Bur H 75 D1
Oakwood Rise. T W 9 E4
Oast Cl. T W 9 D4
Oast House Field. Ick 119 E3
Oast House Rd. Ick 119 E3
Oathall Ave. Hay H 52 B3
Oathall Rd. Hay H 52 B3
Oban Rd. Hast 139 F2
Observatory View. Hai 155 E4
Ochiltree Cl. Hast 140 C2
Ochiltree Rd. Hast 140 C2
Ockenden Way. Hass 100 B2
Ockley Hill. Key 100 C3
Ockley La. Bur H 100 C4
Ockley La. Key 100 C3
Ockley Way. Key 100 C3
Ocklynge Ave. East 185 D2
Ocklynge Cl. Bex 159 D3
Ocklynge Rd. East 185 D2
Offa Rd. Hast 141 D2
Offham Cl. Sea 181 E3
Offham Rd. Lew 126 C1
Okehurst Rd. East 185 D2
Old Barn Cl. East 174 C1
Old Barn Way. Por S 163 F4
Old Camp Rd. East 185 D1
Old Church Rd. Hast 139 F2
Old Court Cl. Bri 145 E2
Old Dr. Pole 174 B3
Old Dro. East 176 A2
Old Farm Rd. Bex 159 F3
Old Farm Rd. Bri 145 E3
Old Foord Cl. S Cha 103 D4
Old Forest La. Rot 40 B4
Old Forewood La. Crow 138 B4
Old Forge La. Fair 37 F1
Old Forge La. Mar 56 B4
Old Gardens Cl. T W 18 C4
Old Harrow Rd. Hast 139 F2
Old House Gdns. Hast 140 B2
Old House La. Ford 7 D3
Old House La. Lan G 7 D2
Old Humphrey Ave. Hast 162 C4
Old La. Cro 27 D2
Old La. Cro 27 F1
Old London Rd. Bri 145 E3
Old London Rd. Hast 141 D2
Old Lydd Rd. Cam 96 B1
Old Malling Way. S Mal 127 D2
Old Manor Cl. Bex 160 A2
Old Mansion Cl. East 184 C4
Old Mill Cl. Bri 145 E3
Old Mill La. Willn 174 B2
Old Motcombe Mews. East 185 D2
Old Orchard Pl. Hai 154 C4
Old Orchard Rd. East 185 E1
Old Rd. E Gri 2 B1
Old Rd. Hers 133 F2
Old Rd. Mag D 133 F2
Old Rectory Gdns. Sock 163 D4
Old River Way. Winc B 120 C4
Old Roar Rd. Hast 140 A2
Old Shoreham Rd. Hove 164 B4
Old Shoreham Rd. Por S 163 F4
Old Shoreham Rd. Soc 143 E1
Old Shoreham Rd. Sock 163 E4
Old Station Rd. Wad 31 E3
Old Steine. Bri 165 F3
Old Swan La. Hai 155 D3
Old Timbers La. Rid 80 A3
Old Top Rd. Hast 141 D2
Old Wickham La. Hay H 52 B4
Old Willingdon Rd. Fri 183 F1
Old Wish Rd. East 185 E1
Oldaker Rd. Newk 78 A4
Olde Place Mews. Rottn 167 E1
Oldfield Ave. Willn 174 C2
Oldfield Cres. Hai 132 C1
Oldfield Cres. Sock 163 D4
Oldfield Rd. Willn 174 C2
Oldlands Ave. Key 100 C2
Oldlands Hill. Fair 38 A1
Oldlands Hill. Uck 38 A1
Olive Rd. Hove 164 A4
Oliver Cl. Cro 27 F1
Olives Meadow. Uck 80 A4
Olives Yd. Uck 80 A4
Onslow Rd. Hove 145 D1
Orange Row. Bri 165 F3
Orchard Ave. Hove 144 C1
Orchard Cl. Hast 140 B1
Orchard Cl. Hay H 52 A4
Orchard Cl. Sca H 53 E2
Orchard Cl. Sock 163 E4
Orchard Cl. T W 9 D3
Orchard Gdns. Hove 144 C1
Orchard La. Dit 101 D2
Orchard La. Key 100 B2
Orchard Rd. Bex 160 A3
Orchard Rd. Bur H 74 B2
Orchard Rd. Hove 144 C1
Orchard Rd. S Mal 127 E1
Orchard Rise. Gro 16 C4
Orchard The. Bro O W 91 F2
Orchard The. Hass 100 B2
Orchard Way. Bur H 74 B2
Orchard Way. E Gri 2 B1
Orchard Way. Hay H 52 A4
Orchard Way. Hur 99 E3
Orchid Cl. East 175 F2
Orchid Park. Hay H 53 D2
Oriental Pl. Bri 165 E3
Orion Cl. Hai 155 D4
Ormerod Ave. Hast 139 F2
Ormerod Ct. Hay H 52 B3
Orpen Rd. Hove 145 D1
Osbern Cl. Bex 159 D2
Osborne Cl. Hast 140 B1
Osborne Hill. Cro 40 A4
Osborne Rd. Bri 145 F1
Osborne Rd. Cro 40 A4
Osborne Rd. East 184 C2
Osborne Villas. Hove 164 C3
Osmers Hill. Wad 31 E4
Osmond Rd. Hove 165 E4
Osmunda Bank. Dor P 2 B3
Otham Ct La. Pole 174 C4
Otham Park. Hai 155 D4
Otham Rd. East 175 F1
Otteham Cl. Pole 174 C3
Oulton Cl. East 175 F2
Ousedale Cl. Lew 126 C1
Outlook Ave. Pea 179 E3
Outlook The. Fri 183 F1
Oval Cl. Pea 169 D1
Over St. Bri 165 F3
Overdown Rise. Por S 143 E2
Overhill. Sock 143 E1
Overhill Dr. Bri 145 E3
Overhill Gdns. Bri 145 E3
Overhill Way. Bri 145 E3
Overton Shaw. E Gri 2 B2
Ovingdean Cl. Oving 167 D3
Ovingdean Rd. Oving 167 D3
Ownside. Bri 145 D3
Ox Lea. Lan G 7 F2
Oxbottom Cl. Chay 77 F3
Oxdean Gdns. Willn 174 C2
Oxenbridge La. Etc 65 D4
Oxford Ct. Bri 165 F4
Oxford Pl. Bri 165 F4
Oxford Rd. East 185 F2
Oxford Rd. Hast 139 F2
Oxford St. Bri 165 F4

Packham Way. Bur H 74 B2
Paddock Cl. Bex 160 A3
Paddock Cl. Ford 6 C3
Paddock Gdns. E Gri 12 B4
Paddock Gdns. Willn 174 B2
Paddock La. Lew 127 D1
Paddock Rd. Hast 140 A3
Paddock Rd. Lew 127 D1
Paddock The. East 175 E1
Paddock The. Hove 145 D1
Paddock The. Mar 56 C2
Paddock The. Norm 68 C4
Paddock The. Pem 10 A3
Paddockhall Rd. Hay H 52 A3
Paddocks The. Cowd 4 C4
Paddocks The. Hai 132 C1
Paddocks The. Plu 102 B3
Paddocks The. Rod 169 D4
Padgham La. Chur 112 A4
Pages Ave. Bex 159 E1
Pages Cl. Hea 83 E4
Pages Hill. Hea 83 E4
Pages La. Bex 159 E2
Pagets The. Newk 78 A4
Pagham Cl. East 175 F2
Paine's Twitten. Lew 149 D4
Pains Flat. Bur H 74 A4
Palace Pl. Bri 165 F3
Palesgate Rd. Cro 28 A1
Palliser Cl. East 186 B3
Palma Cl. Pole 174 C4
Palmeira Ave. Hove 165 D3
Palmeira Pl. Hove 165 D4
Palmeira Sq. Hove 165 D3
Palmerston Rd. Newh 170 C1
Pankhurst Ave. Bri 166 A3
Pankhurst Cl. Bex 159 F4
Pankhurst Rise. Bex 159 F4
Pannel La. Pett 119 E1
Pannell Cl. E Gri 2 A1
Pantiles The. T W 8 C1
Parade The. E Gri 1 C2
Parade The. Pev B 177 E3
Paradise Cl. East 185 D1
Paradise Dr. East 185 D1

Paragon The. Willn 174 B2
Parham Cl. Bri 166 A3
Park Ave. Bex 159 F2
Park Ave. East 185 D4
Park Ave. Hast 140 A2
Park Ave. Hove 164 B4
Park Ave. Key 100 C1
Park Ave. Pea 178 C4
Park Cl. Bri 146 B3
Park Cl. Bur H 74 B2
Park Cl. East 185 D2
Park Cl. Hai 154 C3
Park Cl. Hast 140 A2
Park Cl. Hove 144 B2
Park Cl. Hur 99 F3
Park Cl. Por S 143 F1
Park Cres. Cro 27 E2
Park Cres. For R 13 F1
Park Cres. Hast 140 A1
Park Cres. Por S 163 F4
Park Cres. Rottn 167 E1
Park Cres Pl. Bri 165 F4
Park Cres Rd. Bri 165 F4
Park Cres Terr. Bri 165 F4
Park Croft. Pole 174 C3
Park Croft. Willn 174 B2
Park Ct. Bri 145 E3
Park Dr. Hast 140 A1
Park Dr Cl. Newh 170 B1
Park Farm Cl. Etc 64 C4
Park Gate. Hai 133 D2
Park Hill. Bri 166 A3
Park La. Ash W 13 D3
Park La. Bat 115 D2
Park La. Bex 159 F3
Park La. Cro 27 E2
Park La. East 185 D4
Park La. Sock 163 D4
Park La. Wha 89 F3
Park Par. Hay H 52 B2
Park Rd. Bex 159 F2
Park Rd. Bri 146 B3
Park Rd. Bur H 74 C2
Park Rd. Cro 27 E2
Park Rd. Dor P 2 B3
Park Rd. E Gri 2 A1
Park Rd. For R 13 F1
Park Rd. Hai 132 C2
Park Rd. Hay H 52 B2
Park Rd. Hea 84 A3
Park Rd. Hel 132 C2
Park Rd. Lew 127 D1
Park Rd. Pea 179 E3
Park Rd. Rottn 167 E1
Park Rd. Sea 181 D2
Park Rd. T W 8 C3
Park Rise. Hove 144 B2
Park Road Terr. Bri 165 F3
Park Shaw. Sed 90 B1
Park St. Bri 166 A3
Park St. Fal 147 D3
Park St. Lydd 98 C3
Park St. T W 9 D2
Park The. Cro 27 E1
Park The. Rottn 167 F1
Park View. Bux 58 A2
Park View. Hast 140 A1
Park View. Hay H 52 B3
Park View. Norm 68 C3
Park View. Peas 70 C1
Park View Cl. Pea 168 C1
Park View Rd. Hove 144 C1
Park View Rise. Pea 178 C4
Park Way. Hast 140 A2
Park Way Cl. Sock 163 E4
Park Wood Rd. Hast 140 B3
Parker Cl. East 185 E3
Parker Rd. Hast 140 C2
Parkfield Ave. East 175 E1
Parkhurst Rd. Bex 160 A2
Parklands. Mar 56 C3
Parklands. S Sea 163 D4
Parklands Rd. Key 100 B2
Parkmore Terr. Bri 165 E4
Parkrise. Hove 144 B2
Parkside. E Gri 2 A1
Parkside. Key 100 C2
Parkside Rd. Sea 181 E2
Parkstone Rd. Hast 140 A2
Parkview Rd. Uck 57 D1
Parkway. East 184 C4
Parkwood. Iden 71 F2
Parkwood Cl. T W 9 D3
Parrock La. Col H 14 B1
Parrock La. Upp H 14 B1
Parsonage Cl. T W 7 F3
Parsonage La. Ick 119 E3
Parsonage La. Lam 21 F3
Parsonage La. Wfd 117 D2
Parsonage Rd. East 185 D2
Parsonage Rd. T W 7 F3
Parsons Cl. Hast 139 E2
Partridges La. Wad 30 B3
Pashley Rd. East 185 D1
Paston Pl. Bri 166 A2
Pasture Hill Road. Hay H 52 A3
Patcham By-Ps. Bri 145 E3
Patchdene. Bri 145 E3
Paton Rd. Bex 159 F4
Paul Cl. Hai 132 C2
Pavilion Bldgs. Bri 165 F3
Pavilion Par. Bri 165 F3
Pavilion St. Bri 165 F3
Paxhill Cl. Hast 139 E2
Paygate Rd. Sed 116 B4
Payne Ave. Hove 164 B4
Paynsbridge Way. Hor 109 F4
Paynters Way. Newk 78 A4
Paynton Rd. Hast 139 F2
Paythorne Cl. Sock 143 D1
Peace Cl. Bri 146 A1
Peacock La. Bri 145 E2
Peakdean Cl. Fri 183 F1
Peakdean La. Fri 183 F1
Pearse Pl. Lam 21 F3
Peartree Cl. Bur H 74 B2
Peartree Hill. Ston 44 B2
Peartree La. Bex 137 D1
Peartree La. Lun C 137 D1
Pebble Rd. Pev B 177 E3
Pebsham Dr. Bex 160 C3
Pebsham La. Bex 160 C3
Pebsham La. Hast 160 C3
Peckham Cl. S Mal 127 D2
Peel Rd. Bri 166 B2
Peelings La. St Cro 175 F3
Peelings La. Whm 176 A3
Pegasus Way. E Gri 2 C2
Pegler Ave. Newh 179 F3
Pegwell Cl. Hast 140 B1
Pelham Cl. Pea 169 D1
Pelham Cl. Whm 176 B3
Pelham Cres. Hai 155 D3
Pelham Cres. Hast 162 C4
Pelham Pl. Hast 162 C4
Pelham Rd. Hay H 52 C3
Pelham Rd. Sea 181 E1
Pelham Rise. Pea 169 D1
Pelham Sq. Bri 165 F3
Pelham St. Bri 165 F3
Pelham St. Hast 162 B4
Pelham Terr. Lew 127 D1
Pelham Yd. Sea 181 E1
Pell Cl. Wad 31 F3
Pellbrook Rd. Lew 126 C2
Pelwood Rd. Cam 96 C1
Pembroke Ave. Hove 164 C4
Pembroke Cres. Hove 164 C4
Pembroke Gdns. Hove 164 C3
Pembury Cl. Hay H 52 C2
Pembury Cl. Pem 10 A4
Pembury Gr. Bex 159 F4
Pembury Grange. T W 9 F3
Pembury Rd. East 176 A1
Pembury Rd. T W 9 E3
Pendean. Bur H 75 D1
Penhale Rd. East 186 A3
Penhurst Cl. East 175 F1
Penhurst Cl. Hast 140 A3
Penhurst Dr. Bex 160 C3
Penhurst La. Brill 87 E1
Penhurst La. Pen 113 E3
Penhurst Pl. Bri 166 B3
Penhurst Rd. Ford 7 E4
Penland Cl. Hay H 52 A4
Penland Rd. Bex 160 B3
Penland Rd. Hay H 52 A4
Penn Cres. Hay H 52 C3
Penn Cres. Rin 128 A3
Pennine Rise. Hast 140 C2
Pennine Way. East 176 A2
Pennine Wlk. T W 9 D3
Penny La. Bex 160 C3
Pennybridge La. May 42 A3
Pensford Dr. East 176 A1
Penshurst Rd. Spe 7 E4
Pentland Cl. East 176 B2
Penvensey Rd. Newh 179 F3
Peppercombe Rd. East 184 C2
Pepys Wlk. East 176 B1
Percival Cres. East 175 E2
Percival Rd. East 175 E1
Percival Terr. Bri 166 A2
Percy Rd. Hast 141 D2
Perry Ave. E Gri 2 B2
Perry Hill. Salt 168 A2
Perryman's La. Che Co 36 A2
Perrymount Rd. Hay H 52 B3
Perth Cl. Sea 182 A2
Perth Rd. Hast 139 F2
Pet Level Rd. Pett 120 B2
Peter James Cl. Cam 96 B1
Peter James La. Fai 142 A3
Peter James La. Gue G 142 A4
Petersfield. Pem 10 B4
Petlands Gdns. Hay H 52 B2
Petlands Rd. Hay H 52 B2
Pett Cl. Bri 166 B3
Pett La. Ick 119 F2
Pett Level Rd. Fai 142 C4
Pett Level Rd. Pett 142 C4
Pett Level Rd. Winc B 120 C2
Pett Rd. Gue G 142 A4
Pett Rd. Pett 142 B4
Petworth Dr. Bur H 74 C2
Petworth Pl. East 175 E1
Petworth Rd. Bri 145 F3
Pevensey Bay Rd 176 B1
Pevensey Cl. Sea 181 F2
Pevensey Park Rd. Whm 176 B3
Pevensey Rd. Bri 166 A4
Pevensey Rd. East 185 F2
Pevensey Rd. Hast 161 F4
Pevensey Rd. Pole 175 D3
Peyton Cl. East 186 B4
Philip Cole Cl. Hast 162 C4
Phoenix Cl. Hai 155 D4
Phoenix Cres. Sock 163 D4
Phoenix Cswy. Lew 127 D1
Phoenix La. Ash W 13 E3
Phoenix Pl. Bri 165 F3
Phoenix Pl. Lew 127 D1
Phoenix Way. Sock 163 D4
Phyllis Ave. Pea 168 C1
Picardy Cl. Bat 115 E2
Piccadilly La. May 42 A2
Pickers Green. Hay H 52 C4
Picketts La. Mar 56 B4
Pickforde La. Tic 33 D1
Picknill Green La. Bex 158 C3
Picton St. Bri 166 A4
Piddinghoe Ave. Pea 179 D3
Piddinghoe Mead. Newh 169 F1
Piddinghole Cl. Pea 179 D4
Pilgrim Ct. Hay H 52 C3
Pilmer Rd. Cro 27 E2
Pilot Rd. Hast 140 C2
Piltdown Cl. Bex 159 F2
Piltdown Cl. Hast 140 B1
Piltdown Rd. Bri 166 B3
Piltdown Rise. Uck 80 A4
Pimms Gdns. Bri 165 F3
Pinders Rd. Hast 141 D1
Pine Ave. Hast 140 C2
Pine Gr. Cro 27 E2
Pine Gr. E Gri 1 C2
Pine Tree Cl. Hur 99 F3
Pine Tree Cl. Newh 180 A4
Pine Tree Rd. Hea 83 F3
Pine Trees. Hass 100 A2
Pine Way. Hai 154 C4
Pine Way Cl. E Gri 12 B4
Pine Wlk. Uck 80 A4
Pineham Copse. Hay H 52 B2
Pinehurst. Bur H 74 C1
Pines The. Hay H 52 C2
Pinewood Cl. East 175 D1
Pinewood Cl. Sea 181 E2
Pinewood Rd. T W 9 D3
Pinewood Way. Hast 139 E2
Pinewoods. Bex 159 E2
Pinfold Cl. Wood 167 E3
Pink Alley. T W 8 C1
Pinton Hill. Tic 32 C2
Pinwell Rd. Lew 149 D4
Pipe Pas. Lew 127 D1
Pipers Cl. Hove 144 A2
Pipers Field. Rid 80 A2
Piper's Gate. Rid 80 A2
Piper's La. Rob 65 F2
Pit Rd. Hur 99 F3
Pitt Dr. Sea 181 F3
Pitt Gdns. Wood 167 D4
Place La. Sea 181 E2
Plainfields Ave. Bri 145 F4
Plaistow Cl. Bri 166 B3
Platt The. Dor 2 C4
Platt The. Hay H 52 C3
Plaw Hatch La. For R 23 E3
Plaw Hatch La. Sha 23 D3
Playden Gdns. Hast 140 C2
Playden La. Rye 72 A2
Pleasant View Rd. Cro 27 E2
Plemont Gdns. Bex 159 F3
Pleyden Cl. Bri 166 B2
Pleyden Rise. Bex 158 B2
Plough La. Hast 139 F3
Plover Cl. East 176 A1
Plover Ct. Hast 139 E2
Plumpton Bostall. Plu 125 D3
Plumpton Cl. Bex 160 A3
Plumpton La. Plu 102 B2
Plumpton Rd. Bri 166 A3
Plymouth Ave. Bri 146 B1
Pocock's Rd. East 185 D3
Polegate By-Ps. Pole 174 B4
Polegate Rd. Hai 154 C3
Polesden Rd. T W 9 D1
Pond Cl. Bro OW 91 F3
Pond Way. E Gri 2 C1
Pondcroft Rd. Hay H 52 C4
Ponswood Rd. Hast 139 F1
Pont Cl. Pun T 85 D3
Pook Reed Cl. Hea 83 E3
Pook Reed La. Hea 83 E3
Pool Valley. Bri 165 F2
Poona Rd. T W 8 C1
Poplar Ave. Hove 144 B2
Poplar Cl. Bri 145 E1
Poplar Cl. Hove 144 B2
Poplar Wlk. East 175 D2
Poppinghole La. Rob 66 A1
Poppinghole La. Sed 89 F4
Popps La. Bex 159 D2
Poppyfield. Rye 72 A1
Port Hall Ave. Bri 165 E4
Port Hall Pl. Bri 165 E4
Port Hall Rd. Bri 165 E4
Port Hall St. Bri 165 E4
Port Rd. East 175 F1
Porters Way. Pole 174 C3
Portfield Ave. Bri 145 F3
Portfield Cl. Bex 160 A3
Portland Ave. Hove 164 B4
Portland Cl. Hai 132 C1
Portland Mews. Bri 166 A2
Portland Pl. Bri 166 A2
Portland Pl. Hast 162 B4
Portland Rd. Bur H 74 B2
Portland Rd. E Gri 12 B4
Portland Rd. Hove 164 B4
Portland St. Bri 165 E3
Portland Stps. Hast 162 B4
Portland Terr. S Hei 170 A1
Portland Villas. Hove 164 A4
Portsdown. Willn 174 C1
Portsmouth La. Hay H 52 B4
Portsmouth Wood. Hay H 52 B4
Portsmouth Wood Cl. Hay H 52 B4
Possingworth Cl. Cro H 82 B4
Post Horn Cl. For R 13 F1
Post Horn La. For R 13 F1
Post Office Pas. Hast 162 C4
Potato La. Rin 128 B3
Potman's La. Cat 137 E2
Potman's La. Lun C 137 E2
Pottens Mill La. Bro O 61 E3
Potteries The. Rid 80 A2
Potters Field. Rin 128 A3
Potters La. Bur H 74 B1
Potter's La. Lew 149 D4
Pottery Cl. Bre 91 F1
Pottery La. Bre 91 F1
Pottingfield Rd. Rye 94 C3
Pound Cl. East 186 B3
Pound La. Bux 58 B1
Pound La. Fra 81 E4
Pound La. Lau 130 A4
Pound The. Bur H 74 B2
Poundfield Rd. Cro 27 F1
Poundfield Rd. San 48 C3
Poundsbridge Hill. Ford 7 D4
Poveys Cl. Bur H 74 A2
Powder Mill La. Sgh 9 D4
Powder Mill La. T W 8 C4
Powdermill Cl. Sgh 9 D4
Powdermill La. Bat 115 D1
Powdermill La. Bre 91 D2
Powdermill La. Bro O W 91 D2
Powdermill La. Cat 114 C1
Powdermill La. Sed 90 C1
Powell Gdns. Newh 170 A1
Powell Rd. Newk 78 A4
Powis Gr. Bri 165 E3
Powis Rd. Bri 165 E3
Powis Sq. Bri 165 E3
Powis Villas. Bri 165 E3
Poynings Cl. Sea 182 A1
Poynings Dr. Hove 144 B2
Poynter Rd. Hove 164 C4
Pratt's Folly La. Cro 27 E1
Preston Circ. Bri 165 F4
Preston Dro. Bri 145 E1
Preston Gr. Fra 80 C3
Preston Park Ave. Bri 145 E1
Preston Rd. Bex 159 F4
Preston Rd. Bri 145 E1
Preston St. Bri 165 E3
Prestonville Rd. Bri 165 E4
Prideaux Rd. East 185 E3
Primrose Cl. East 175 F2
Primrose Hill. Bex 159 E3
Primrose Hill. Fai 142 B3
Primrose La. For R 13 F1
Prince Albert St. Bri 165 F3
Prince Charles Cl. Sock 143 E1
Prince Charles Rd. S Mal 127 E2
Prince Edward's Rd. Lew 126 C1
Prince Regent's Cl. Bri 166 B2
Prince William Par. East 186 B3
Princes Ave. Hove 164 C3
Princes Cl. Sea 181 E3
Princes Cl. Uck 79 F4
Prince's Cres. Bri 165 F4
Princes Cres. Hove 164 C3
Princes Pl. Bri 165 F3
Prince's Rd. Bri 165 F4
Princes Rd. East 186 B4
Prince's Rd. Hast 162 A4
Princes Sq. Hove 164 C3
Prince's St. Bri 165 F3
Prince's St. T W 9 D2
Princess Dr. Sea 181 D3
Prince's Terr. Bri 166 B2
Prinkle La. Bod G 112 A1
Prinkle La. Bor S 112 A1
Prinsep Rd. Hove 164 C4
Prior's Way. Cowd 4 C3
Priory Ave. Hast 162 B4
Priory Cl. Hast 140 B1
Priory Cl. Pev B 177 D3
Priory Cres. Lew 149 D4
Priory Hts. East 184 C3
Priory La. East 176 B2
Priory Rd. Bur H 74 C1
Priory Rd. East 176 B1
Priory Rd. For R 24 A4
Priory Rd. Hass 100 B3
Priory Rd. Hast 140 C1
Priory St. Hast 162 B4
Priory St. Lew 149 D4
Priory Way. Hay H 52 B2
Prom. Bex 160 A2
Prom. East 186 A2
Prom. Hast 162 A4
Prom. Pea 179 D3
Prom. Sea 181 D2
Prom The. Pev B 177 D2
Prospect Gdns. East 185 D2
Prospect Pl. Hast 162 B4
Prospect Rd. Hea 83 F3
Prospect Rd. Sgh 8 B4
Prospect Rd. T W 9 D2
Providence Pl. Bri 165 F4
Pudding Cake La. Uck 80 A4
Pulborough Ave. East 175 E1
Pump La. Fra 81 D2
Purbeck Cl. East 176 A2
Putlands Cres. Bex 159 F4
Pyecombe St. Pye 122 C3

Quadrant The. Key 100 C2
Quakers La. Hay H 52 C3
Quantock Cl. East 176 A2
Quantock Gdns. Hast 140 C2
Quarry Bank Rd. Bri 145 F1
Quarry Cl. Bur H 75 D2
Quarry Cres. Hast 140 C1
Quarry Hill. Hast 161 F4
Quarry Hill. Hay H 52 A3
Quarry La. Sea 181 F3
Quarry Rd. Hast 140 B1
Quarry Rd. Newh 180 A3
Quarry Rd. T W 8 C3
Quarry Rise. E Gri 2 C2
Quebec Cl. Bex 159 F3
Quebec Rd. Hast 139 F2
Quebec St. Bri 165 F3
Queen Alexandra Ave. Hove 144 C2
Queen Anne's Cl. Lew 127 D1
Queen Caroline Cl. Hove 144 C2
Queen Elizabeth Ave. Bur H 74 B1
Queen Mary Ave. Hove 144 C2
Queen Sq. Bri 165 E3
Queen St. San 48 C3
Queen Victoria Ave. Hove 144 C2
Queens App. Uck 57 D1
Queen's Ave. Hast 162 B4
Queens Cotts. Wad 31 E3
Queens Cres. Bur H 74 C1
Queen's Cres. East 186 B4
Queens Dr. Key 100 B2
Queen's Dr. Mar 56 B2
Queen's Gdns. Bri 165 F3
Queen's Gdns. East 185 F2
Queen's Gdns. Hove 165 D3
Queen's Gdns. T W 8 C3
Queens Park Gdns. Sea 181 D2
Queen's Park Rd. Bri 166 A3
Queen's Park Rise. Bri 166 A3
Queen's Park Terr. Bri 166 A3
Queen's Pl. Bri 165 F4
Queen's Pl. Hove 165 D3
Queen's Rd. Bri 165 E3
Queens Rd. Cro 27 E1
Queen's Rd. E Gri 2 B1
Queen's Rd. East 186 A4
Queen's Rd. Hast 162 B4
Queens Rd. Hay H 52 B3
Queens Rd. Hers 134 B3
Queen's Rd. S Mal 127 D2
Queens Rd. Sock 143 E1
Queen's Rd. T W 8 C3
Queen's Rd Quadrant. Bri 165 E3
Queen's Wlk. E Gri 2 B1
Queensbury Mews. Bri 165 E3
Queensmount. Five A 59 F4
Queensway. Bri 166 A3
Queensway. E Gri 2 B1
Queensway. Hast 139 E3
Queensway. Sea 181 F3
Querneby Cl. S Sea 163 D4
Quickbourne La. Norm 69 D4
Quinnell Dr. Hai 132 C1
Quintin Cl. Hai 154 C3

Radcliffe Cl. Hast 140 A2
Radinden Dr. Hove 145 D1
Radinden Manor Rd. Hove 165 D4
Ragged Dog La. Hea 82 C2
Railway App. E Gri 2 B1
Railway App. Newh 180 A4
Railway Cotts. W Fir 151 E3
Railway La. Lew 127 D1
Railway Mews. Hove 164 C4
Railway Rd. Newh 180 A4
Railway St. Bri 165 E3
Raleigh Cl. East 186 B4
Ramsay Way. East 186 B4
Ramslye Rd. T W 18 B4
Randiddles Cl. Hur 99 F2
Randolph La. Rye 71 F2
Ranelagh Villas. Hove 164 C4
Rangemoor Dr. East 185 D3
Rankine Rd. T W 9 D4
Ranmore Cl. Hast 140 B3
Rannoch Rd. Cro 27 D1
Rannoch Rd W. Cro 27 D1
Ranscombe Hill. S Mal 149 F3
Ranscombe La. Gly 150 A3
Ranworth Cl. East 175 F2
Raphael Rd. Hove 164 B4
Rapson's Rd. Willn 174 C2
Rattle Rd. St Cro 175 F3
Rattle Rd. Whm 176 A3
Ratton Dr. East 184 C4
Ratton Rd. East 185 E2
Raven Ct. Bat 115 E2
Raven Ct. Hast 139 E2
Ravens Cl. Bex 159 D2
Ravens Croft. East 190 B4
Ravenswood Ave. T W 9 D3
Ravenswood Dr. Wood 167 E3
Ravenswood Rd. Bur H 74 C2
Ravine Cl. Hast 140 C2
Rayford Cl. Pea 179 D4
Raymond Cl. Sea 181 F3
Readers La. Iden 71 E3
Reading Rd. Bri 166 B2
Rectory Cl. Bur 63 F4
Rectory Cl. E Hoa 107 F3
Rectory Cl. East 185 D2
Rectory Cl. Hast 139 F1
Rectory Cl. Newh 180 A3
Rectory Cl. S Sea 163 D4
Rectory Field. Hart 15 E2
Rectory La. Bec 69 E2
Rectory La. Iden 71 E2
Rectory La. Rye 95 D4
Rectory La. Winc 120 B4
Rectory Park. Pett 119 E1
Rectory Rd. Newh 170 B1
Rectory Rd. S Sea 163 D4
Rectory Way. Bex 160 A3
Red Lake Terr. Hast 141 D2
Red Oak. The M 47 E4
Redbridge La. Cro 39 D3
Redbrook La. Bux 58 A2
Redcross St. Bri 165 F3
Redford Cl. East 176 B1
Redgeland Rise. Hast 139 E1
Redgill La. N Cha 54 C1
Redhill Cl. Bri 145 D3
Redhill Dr. Bri 145 D2
Redleaf Cl. T W 9 D3

Redoubt Rd. East 186 A2
Redvers Rd. Bri 146 A1
Redwood Dr. Hay H 52 A2
Reed Pond Wlk. Hay H 52 C2
Reedham Rd. East 175 F2
Reed's La. Alb 99 D4
Reedswood Rd. Bro O W 91 F3
Reedswood Rd. Hast 161 E4
Reeves Hill. Bri 146 A3
Regal Dr. E Gri 12 B4
Regency Cl. Uck 80 A4
Regency Ct. Bri 145 E2
Regency Gdns. Hast 161 F4
Regency Mews. Bri 165 E3
Regency Sq. Bri 165 E3
Regent Arc. Bri 165 F3
Regent Hill. Bri 165 E3
Regent Pl. Hast 139 E4
Regent Row. Bri 165 E3
Regent Sq. Rye 95 D3
Regent St. Bri 165 F3
Regents Cl. Sea 181 E3
Reginald Rd. Bex 159 F2
Reigate Rd. Bri 145 D1
Resting Oak Hill. Bar C 103 E2
Reynolds La. Sgh 8 B4
Reynolds Rd. East 176 B1
Reynolds Rd. Hove 164 B4
Reynoldstown La. Pole 174 B3
Riccards La. Wha 89 F1
Rices Hill. E Gri 2 B1
Richardson Rd. Hove 164 B4
Richardson Rd. T W 8 C3
Richborough Cl. Hast 140 A2
Richington Way. Sea 181 F2
Richland Cl. Hast 141 E2
Richmead Gdns. May 41 F1
Richmond Ave. Bex 159 E2
Richmond Cl. Bex 159 F2
Richmond Gr. Bex 159 F1
Richmond Pl. Bri 165 F3
Richmond Rd. Bex 159 F2
Richmond Rd. Bri 165 F4
Richmond Rd. Pev B 177 D3
Richmond Rd. Sea 181 D2
Richmond Sq. E Gri 2 A2
Richmond St. Bri 165 F3
Richmond St. Hast 141 D1
Richmond Terr. Sea 181 E2
Riddens Cl. Plu 102 B3
Riddens La. Plu 102 B3
Riddlesdale Ave. T W 8 C3
Ride The. Bri 145 E1
Riders Bolt. Bex 159 E3
Ridge Cl. Nut 37 D3
Ridge Cl. Por S 143 F2
Ridge Rd. Fal 147 D4
Ridge Rd. Wmes 124 C1
Ridge The. Hast 139 F4
Ridge The. Winc B 121 D3
Ridge View. Bri 146 B3
Ridge Way. Hay H 52 C1
Ridge West The. Hast 139 F4
Ridgelands Cl. East 185 D2
Ridgeside Ave. Bri 145 E3
Ridgeway. E Gri 12 B4
Ridgeway. Hur G 46 C2
Ridgeway. Pem 10 A4
Ridgeway. Sock 143 E1
Ridgeway Cl. Hea 83 F4
Ridgeway Cl. Sock 143 E1
Ridgeway Paddock. Kin L 148 B3
Ridgeway The. Bur H 74 C2
Ridgeway The. Fri 183 F1
Ridgeway The. Hers 134 B3
Ridgeway The. Sea 181 E2
Ridgewaye The. Sgh 8 C4
Ridgewick Rd. Bri 146 A3
Ridgewood Ave. Salt 168 A2
Ridgewood Cl. Rid 80 A2
Ridgewood Gdns. Bex 160 B2
Ridgway Cl. Wood 167 D4
Ridgway The. Wood 167 D4
Ridings The. Bex 159 E4
Ridings The. Bur H 75 D1
Ridings The. Hast 140 A3
Ridings The. Newk 78 A4
Ridings The. Pea 168 C1
Ridings The. Sea 181 E3
Ridings The. T W 9 E3
Ridleys. W Hoa 22 B3
Rigden Rd. Hove 145 D1
Riley Rd. Bri 146 A1
Rill Wlk. E Gri 2 C1
Ringmer Rd. Bri 146 B2
Ringmer Rd. Newh 179 F3
Ringmer Rd. Sea 181 E1
Ringwood Cl. East 185 F3
Ringwood Rd. Bex 160 A4
Ringwood Rd. East 185 F3
Ripe La. Ripe 130 B1
Ripsley Cl. East 176 B1
Risden La. Four T 48 A4
Rise Park Gdns. East 176 B1
Rise The. E Gri 12 B4
Rise The. Hay H 52 C3
Rise The. Por S 143 E1
Riseden Rd. Wad 31 D1
Rising The. East 176 B1
River La. Alfn 172 C2
River Way. Uck 80 A3
Riverdale. S Mal 127 D1
Riverside. For R 13 E2
Riverside. Newh 180 A4
Riverside Industrial Estate. Lew 127 D1
Rixons Cl. Hor K 35 D3
Rixons Orch. Hor K 35 D3
Robert St. Bri 165 F3
Robert Tressell Cl. Hast 140 B1
Robert's Hill. Winc 120 B4
Robertson Pas. Hast 162 B4
Robertson Rd. Bri 145 D1
Robertson St. Hast 162 B4
Robertson Terr. Hast 162 B4
Robertson's Hill. Hast 140 C1
Robian Cl. Mar 56 C2
Robin Cl. East 176 A1
Robin Dene. Bri 166 B2
Robin Post La. Wil 153 F1
Robinson Rd. Newh 180 A4
Roborough Cl. East 185 F2
Robsack Ave. Hast 139 E1
Rochdale Rd. T W 9 D3
Rochester Cl. East 190 A4
Rochester Gdns. Hove 165 D3
Rochester Rd. Hast 139 F1
Rochester St. Bri 166 A3
Rochester Way. Cro 27 F1
Rochford Way. Sea 180 C3
Rock Cl. Hast 141 D2
Rock Gr. Bri 166 A2
Rock La. Cog 118 A1
Rock Pl. Bri 165 F2
Rock St. Bri 166 B2
Rock Villa Rd. T W 8 C2
Rockall Dr. Hai 132 C1
Rock-a-Nore Par. Hast 162 C4
Rock-a-Nore Rd. Hast 162 C4
Rockhurst Dr. East 184 C3
Rockington Way. Cro 39 F4
Rocklands La. Hast 141 D1
Rockmead Rd. Fai 142 B2
Rocks Hill. Sale 66 B3
Rock's Hill. Wfd 117 E4
Rocks La. H Hur 57 E4
Rocks Park Rd. Uck 79 F4
Rocky La. Hay H 52 A1
Roderick Ave. Pea 178 C4
Roderick Ave. Pea 179 D4
Rodmell Ave. Salt 168 A1
Rodmell Rd. Sea 181 F1
Rodmell Rd. T W 8 C1
Rodmill Dr. East 185 D3
Rodmill Rd. East 185 D3
Rodney Cl. East 186 B4
Roebuck St. Hast 162 C4
Roedale Rd. Bri 145 F1
Roedean Cl. Bex 159 F3
Roedean Cl. Sea 181 F2
Roedean Cres. Bri 166 C2
Roedean Path. Bri 166 C2
Roedean Rd. Bri 166 C2
Roedean Rd. T W 8 C1
Roedean Vale. Bri 166 C2
Roedean Way. Bri 166 C2
Roffrey Ave. East 175 D1
Rolfe Dr. Bur H 75 D2
Romaine Cl. Bur H 75 D3
Roman Cl. Sea 180 C3
Roman Cres. Sock 163 E4
Roman Rd. Hove 164 A3
Roman Rd. Sock 163 E4
Roman Way. Sock 163 E4
Roman Way. Uck 80 B4
Romans Way. Whm 176 B3
Romany Cl. Por S 163 F4
Romford Rd. Pem 10 B4
Romney Cl. Sea 182 A2
Romney Rd. Pole 174 C4
Romney Rd. Rottn 167 F1
Romney St. East 186 A3
Romsey Cl. Bri 146 A1
Rookery Cl. Newh 170 B1
Rookery La. Winc 120 B4
Rookery Way. Hay H 52 B1
Rookery Way. Newh 170 B1
Rookery Way. Sea 180 C3
Rookhurst Rd. Bex 160 B3
Rookley Cl. T W 9 D1
Rookwood Cl. Uck 80 B4
Roopers. Spe 7 F4
Rope Wlk. Hai 154 C4
Rope Wlk. Rye 95 D3
Rope Wlk. The. San 48 C3
Roper's Gate. T W 8 B1
Rose Hill. Bri 165 F4
Rose Hill Cl. Bri 165 F4
Rose Hill Terr. Bri 165 F4
Rose Wlk. Sea 181 E2
Rose Wlk Cl. Newh 179 F4
Rose Wlk The. Newh 180 A4
Rosebarn Cl. Bur H 75 D1
Rosebery Ave. East 175 E1
Rosebery Ave. Wood 167 D4
Rosedale Pl. East 175 D2
Rosedene Cl. Wood 167 E3
Rosehill Wlk. T W 8 C2
Roselands. Bex 159 E3
Roselands Ave. May 41 E1
Roselands Cl. East 186 A3
Rosemary Cl. Pea 169 D1
Rosemary Dr. S Sea 143 D1
Rosemary La. Fai 142 A4
Rosemary La. Tic 33 F2
Rosemount Cl. Sea 180 C3
Rosetti Rd. Pev B 177 D2
Rossdale. T W 9 D3
Roswell Wlk. East 176 B1
Rothbury Rd. Hove 164 A4
Rother Cl. Bur 63 F4
Rother Cl. Cro 39 F4
Rother Rd. Sea 181 F1
Rother View. Bur 63 F4
Rotherfield Ave. Bex 160 A2
Rotherfield Ave. Hast 140 C1
Rotherfield Cl. Bri 145 F3
Rotherfield Cres. Bri 145 F3
Rotherfield La. May 41 E2
Rotherfield Rd. Cro 40 A4
Rotherfield Rd. Rot 40 B4
Rotherhill Rd. Cro 39 F4
Rothermead. May 41 E1
Rotherview. Sale 66 A3
Rothley Chase. Hay H 52 B2
Rothsay Rd. Hast 161 F4
Rotten Row. Lew 149 D4
Rotunda Rd. East 186 A4
Rotyngs The. Rottn 167 E1
Rough Brow. Sea 181 F2
Rough Field. E Gri 2 A2
Rough The. Newk 78 A4
Round Hill Cres. Bri 165 F4
Round Hill Rd. Bri 165 F4
Round Hill St. Bri 165 F4
Roundacres Way. Bex 160 B3
Roundell The. Hast 140 A3
Roundhay Ave. Pea 179 E3
Roundhill Rd. T W 9 D1
Roundway. Bri 146 B3
Roundwood La. Hay H 52 B4
Roundwood Rd. Hast 139 F3
Rowan Ave. East 175 D2
Rowan Ave. Hove 144 B1
Rowan Cl. Hast 140 A3
Rowan Cl. Hay H 52 C2
Rowan Cl. Hea 83 F3
Rowan Cl. Por S 143 F1
Rowan Gdns. Bex 160 B3
Rowan Tree Rd. T W 8 B1
Rowan Way. Rottn 167 E2
Rowan Wlk. Cra D 11 D4
Rowbarns. Bat 115 D3
Rowe Ave. Pea 178 C4
Rowplatt La. Fel 1 B2
Rowsley Rd. East 190 A4
Royal Chase. T W 8 A2
Royal Cres. Bri 166 A2
Royal Cres Mews. Bri 166 A2
Royal George Rd. Bur H 74 B2
Royal Military Rd. Winc 94 C1
Royal Par. East 186 A3
Royal Sovereign View. East 186 B3
Royal Sussex Cres. East 184 C3
Royles Cl. Rottn 167 F1
Royston Cl. Fri 183 F1
Royston Gdns. Bex 160 B3
Rudyard Cl. Wood 167 E4
Rudyard Rd. Wood 167 E4
Rue de Bayeux. Bat 115 D3
Rufus Cl. Lew 127 D1
Rugby Cl. Sea 181 F2
Rugby Pl. Bri 166 B2
Rugby Rd. Bri 145 F1
Rumbolds La. Hay H 52 A1
Rushetts. Lan G 7 E2
Rushey Cl. Rin 128 B3
Rushlake Cl. Bri 146 B3
Rushlake Cres. East 185 D3
Rushlake Rd. Bri 146 B3
Rushlye Cl. Bel G 19 E3
Rushwood Cl. Hay H 52 C2
Ruskin Pl. Hove 164 B4
Ruskin Rd. East 174 C1
Ruskin Rd. Hove 164 B4
Rusper Rd. Bri 146 A3
Rusper Rd. East 184 C3
Ruspers. Bur H 75 D1
Russell Cres. Bri 165 E4
Russell Ct. Hast 162 C4
Russell Pl. Bri 165 E3
Russell Rd. Bri 165 E3
Russell Row. S Mal 127 D2
Russell Sq. Bri 165 E3
Russell St. Hast 162 B4
Russet Cl. Pole 175 D3
Rusthall Grange. T W 8 A2
Rusthall High St. T W 8 A2
Rusthall Park. T W 8 A2
Rusthall Rd. T W 8 A2
Rustic Cl. Pea 168 C1
Rustic Park. Pea 168 C1
Rustic Rd. Pea 168 C1
Rustington Rd. Bri 145 F3
Rustlings Cl. Hay H 52 C3
Rustwick. T W 8 A2
Rutland Cl. East 185 D3
Rutland Gdns. Hove 164 B4
Rutland Rd. Hove 164 C4
Rutley Cl. Sale 66 A3
Rydal Cl. T W 8 B3
Rydal Dr. T W 8 B3
Ryde Rd. Bri 166 A4
Ryders. Lan G 7 F2
Rye Cl. Pole 175 D4
Rye Cl. Salt 168 B1
Rye Cl. Sea 182 A2
Rye Rd. Four T 48 A4
Rye Rd. Hast 141 D3
Rye Rd. Rye 71 E1
Rye Rd. Witt 71 F4
Rye St. East 186 A3
Ryecroft. Hay H 52 B2
Ryefield Cl. East 185 D4
Ryelands Dr. Bri 146 A2
Rylstone Rd. East 186 A2
Rymers Cl. T W 9 D4
Rymill Rd. Hast 139 F2
Ryst Wood Rd. For R 14 A1
Sackville Cl. Lew 127 D1
Sackville Gdns. E Gri 2 A2
Sackville Gdns. Hove 164 B3
Sackville La. E Gri 1 C2
Sackville Rd. Bex 160 A2
Sackville Rd. East 175 E1
Sackville Rd. Hai 155 D3
Sackville Rd. Hove 164 C4
Saddlers Cl. Bur H 75 D1
Saddlers Ct. Hast 161 F3
Saddler's Wall La. Brok 73 F4
Sadler Way. Bri 166 B3
Sadlers Way. Rin 128 A2
Saffron Cl. S Sea 143 D1
Saffrons Park. East 185 E1
Saffrons Rd. East 185 E1
Saffrons The. Bur H 74 B3
St Agnes Rd. E Gri 2 B1
St Andrew's Dr. Sea 180 C3
St Andrew's La. Lew 149 D4
St Andrew's Rd. Bex 160 A3
St Andrew's Rd. Bri 145 F1
St Andrews Rd. Bur H 75 D2
St Andrew's Rd. Por S 164 A4
St Andrew's Sq. Hast 162 B4
St Anne's Cl. Bex 160 A3
St Anne's Cres. Lew 126 C1
St Anne's Rd. East 185 E2
St Annes Rd. Willn 174 C2
St Anthony's Ave. East 186 A4
St Aubyns. Hove 164 C3
St Aubyn's Cres. Sock 163 F4
St Aubyn's Mead. Rottn 167 F1
St Aubyn's Rd. East 185 F2
St Aubyn's Rd. Por S 164 A4
St Aubyns Rd. Sock 163 F4
St Aubyns S. Hove 164 C3
St Augustine's Cl. Bex 159 E2
St Augustine's Cl. Sca H 53 E2
St Christopher's Rd. Hur 99 F3
St Crispians. Sea 181 D2
St Cuthmans Cl. Bri 166 B3
St David's Ave. Bex 160 A3
St Davids Cl. East 175 D2
St David's Rd. T W 8 C3
St Dominic Cl. Hast 161 F4
St Edmund's Rd. Hay H 52 B2
St Edward's Cl. E Gri 2 A1
St Francis Chase. Bex 159 F3
St George's La. Hur 99 F3
St George's Mews. Bri 165 F3
St George's Park. T W 18 B4
St George's Pl. Bri 165 F3
St George's Pl. Hur 99 F3
St George's Rd. Bex 160 A3
St Georges Rd. Bri 166 A2
St George's Rd. East 185 F2
St George's Rd. Hast 140 C1
St George's Terr. Bri 166 A2
St Giles Cl. Winc 120 B4
St Gregory Cl. East 190 B4
St Helen's Ave. Hast 140 B2
St Helen's Cres. Hast 140 B1
St Helen's Cres. Hove 144 A2
St Helen's Ct. Hast 140 B1
St Helen's Down. Hast 140 C2
St Helen's Dr. Hove 144 A2
St Helen's Park Rd. Hast 140 B2
St Helen's Rd. Bri 166 A4
St Helen's Rd. Hast 140 A1
St Helen's Wood Rd. Hast 140 B3
St Heliers Ave. Hove 164 B4
St Hill Rd. E Gri 12 A3
St James' Ave. Bex 160 A4
St James' Cl. Bex 160 A4
St James' Cres. Bex 160 A4
St James La. Nut 37 D2
St James' Park. T W 9 D3
St James' Rd. Bex 160 A3
St James Rd. E Gri 2 B1
St James Rd. East 186 A2
St James' Rd. T W 9 D3
St James St. Lew 149 D4
St James Wlk. S Str 77 E1
St James's Ave. Bri 165 F3
St James's Pl. Bri 165 F3
St James's Rd. Hast 140 B1
St James's St. Bri 165 F2
St James's St Mews. Bri 165 F3
St John St. Lew 127 D1
St John's Ave. Bur H 74 B2
St John's Bank. S Cha 103 D4
St John's Cl. E Gri 2 B1
St John's Dr. Whm 176 B3
St John's Hill. Lew 127 D1
St John's Park. T W 8 C4
St John's Pl. Bri 165 F3
St John's Pl. Hove 165 D3
St John's Rd. Bex 160 A3
St Johns Rd. Bur H 74 C2
St John's Rd. Cro 27 D2
St John's Rd. E Gri 2 B1
St John's Rd. East 190 B4
St John's Rd. Hast 162 A4
St John's Rd. Hay H 52 B1
St Johns Rd. Hove 165 D3
St John's Rd. Pole 174 C3
St John's Rd. Sea 181 E1
St John's Rd. T W 8 C3
St John's Terr. Lew 127 D1
St Joseph's Cl. Hove 164 C4
St Josephs Way. Hay H 52 B2
St Julians Cl. S Sea 163 D4
St Julian's La. S Sea 163 D4
St Keyna Ave. Hove 164 A3
St Laurence Cl. Pea 168 C1
St Lawrence Rd. Bex 159 F4
St Lawrence Way. Hur 99 F4
St Leonard's Ave. Hove 164 A4
St Leonard's Cl. Newh 170 B1
St Leonard's Gdns. Hove 164 A3
St Leonards Park. E Gri 2 B1
St Leonard's Pl. East 185 D2
St Leonards Rd. Bex 160 A2
St Leonard's Rd. Bri 166 A4
St Leonard's Rd. East 185 E2
St Leonard's Rd. Hove 164 A4
St Leonard's Rd. Newh 170 B1
St Leonards Terr. Pole 174 B4
St Louie Cl. Sock 163 F4
St Luke's La. Newh 180 A4
St Luke's Rd. Bri 166 A3
St Luke's Rd. T W 8 C3
St Luke's Terr. Bri 166 A3
St Margaret's Ave. Dor P 2 B3
St Margaret's Pl. Bri 165 E3
St Margaret's Rd. E Gri 2 B2
St Margaret's Rd. Hast 162 A4
St Margaret's Rise. Sea 180 C3
St Margaret's Terr. Hast 162 A4
St Margarets Terr. Rye 94 C3
St Marks Cl. Bex 159 D2
St Mark's Mews. Bri 166 B2
St Mark's Mews. Bri 166 B2
St Mark's Rd. T W 18 B4
St Mark's St. Bri 166 B2
St Martins Cres. S Hei 170 A1
St Martin's La. Lew 149 D4
St Martin's Pl. Bri 166 A4
St Martins Rd. East 175 D2
St Martin's St. Bri 165 F4
St Mary Magdalene St. Bri 165 F4
St Mary-In-The-Fields. May 41 F1
St Mary's Ave. Hai 155 D4
St Mary's Cl. Bre 91 F1
St Mary's Cl. Tic 33 D1
St Mary's Cl. Willn 174 C1
St Mary's Cotts. East 185 D2
St Marys Garth. Bux 58 A2
St Mary's La. Bex 159 E4
St Mary's La. Spe 7 F4
St Mary's La. Tic 33 D1
St Mary's Pl. Bri 165 F2
St Mary's Rd. Bur H 74 B2
St Mary's Rd. East 185 D2
St Mary's Rd. Hast 140 C1
St Mary's Rd W. Bur H 74 B2
St Mary's Sq. Bri 166 A2
St Mary's Sq. Bri 166 A2
St Mary's Terr. Bat 115 E2
St Mary's Terr. Hast 140 C1
St Matthew's Dr. Hast 140 A1
St Matthew's Gdns. Hast 139 F1
St Matthew's Rd. Hast 139 F1
St Michael's Cl. Cro 39 F4
St Michael's Pl. Bri 165 E3
St Michael's Pl. Hast 162 B4
St Michaels Rd. E Gri 2 B1
St Michael's Rd. Por S 163 F4
St Michael's Rd. T W 8 C4
St Michael's Terr. S Mal 127 D2
St Nicholas La. Lew 127 D1
St Nicholas Rd. Bri 165 E3
St Nicholas Rd. Por S 163 F4
St Nicolas Cl. Pev 176 C3
St Olive's Cl. Cro H 83 D4
St Pancras Gdns. Lew 148 C4
St Pancras Green. Kin L 148 B3
St Pancras Rd. Lew 148 C4
St Patrick's Cres. Bex 160 A3
St Patrick's Rd. Hove 164 C4
St Pauls Cl. East 175 D2
St Paul's Cl. Hay H 52 B3
St Paul's Pl. Hast 162 A4
St Paul's Rd. Hast 140 A1
St Paul's St. Bri 165 F4
St Paul's St. T W 8 A2
St Peter's Ave. Pea 178 C4
St Peter's Cl. Hove 144 B1
St Peter's Cl. Sea 181 E3
St Peter's Cres. Bex 160 A3
St Peter's Pl. Bri 165 F3
St Peter's Pl. Lew 127 D1
St Peters Rd. Bur H 74 C2
St Peter's Rd. Hast 162 A4
St Peter's Rd. Por S 163 F4
St Peter's Rd. Sea 181 E3
St Peters Row. Ford 6 C3
St Peter's St. Bri 165 F4
St Peter's St. T W 9 D2
St Philip's Ave. East 185 F3
St Richards Rd. Cro 39 F4
St Richard's Rd. Por S 163 F4
St Richard's Rd. Sock 163 F4
St Saviour's Rd. Hast 161 E3
St Swithun's Cl. E Gri 2 B1
St Swithun's La. Lew 149 D4
St Swithun's Terr. Lew 149 D4
St Thomas's Rd. Hast 140 C1
St Thomas's St. Winc 120 B4
St Vincents Pl. East 185 E1
St Vincents Rd. Hast 161 E4
St Wilfred's Pl. Sea 181 F2
St Wilfrid's Green. Hai 155 D4
St Wilfrids Rd. Bur H 74 C2
St Wilfrid's Way. Hay H 52 B2
Saints Hill. Ford 6 C4
Salehurst Rd. East 185 D2
Salisbury Cl. East 175 D1
Salisbury Rd. Bex 159 F3
Salisbury Rd. East 190 A4
Salisbury Rd. Hast 140 A1
Salisbury Rd. Hove 165 D3
Salisbury Rd. Lan G 7 E2
Salisbury Rd. Sea 181 E2
Salisbury Rd. Sgh 9 D4
Salomons Rd. T W 8 A2
Saltcote St. Rye 95 D4
Saltdean Cl. Bex 159 E2
Saltdean Dr. Salt 168 A1
Saltdean Park Rd. Salt 178 A4
Saltdean Vale. Salt 168 A1
Saltdean Way. Bex 159 D2
Salter's La. Brok 73 F4
Salters La. Hast 162 C4
Saltwood Rd. Sea 182 A2

Salvington Cres. Bex 159 E2
Sancroft Rd. East 184 C2
Sanctuary The. East 184 C2
Sand Hill La. Fra 106 C4
Sand Rd. Lam 21 F2
Sandbanks Cl. Hai 154 C3
Sandbanks Gr. Hai 154 C3
Sandbanks Rd. Hai 154 C3
Sandbanks Way. Hai 154 C3
Sandfield Rd. Ford 6 C4
Sandgate Cl. Sea 182 A3
Sandgate Rd. Bri 145 F1
Sandhawes Hill. E Gri 2 C2
Sandhill La. Boa 27 F4
Sandhill La. Chur 111 F3
Sandhurst Ave. Pem 10 B3
Sandhurst Ave. Wood 147 D1
Sandhurst Cl. San 48 C2
Sandhurst Cl. T W 9 D3
Sandhurst La. Bex 158 C3
Sandhurst Park. T W 9 D3
Sandhurst Rd. T W 9 D3
Sandore Cl. Sea 181 F2
Sandore Rd. Sea 181 F2
Sandown Cl. East 175 F2
Sandown Cl. T W 9 E3
Sandown Gr. T W 9 E3
Sandown Park. T W 9 E3
Sandown Rd. Bri 166 A4
Sandown Rd. Hast 141 D2
Sandown Rd. Sock 163 D4
Sandown Way. Bex 160 B3
Sandpiper Wlk. East 176 A1
Sandridge. Cro 27 E1
Sandringham Cl. E Gri 12 C4
Sandringham Cl. Hove 144 C2
Sandringham Cl. Sea 181 F3
Sandringham Dr. Hove 144 C2
Sandrock Park. Hast 140 B3
Sandrock Rd. T W 9 D2
Sandrocks Way. Hay H 52 B1
Sandwich Dr. Hast 161 E4
Sandwich St. East 186 A3
Sandy Cl. Hast 139 F3
Sandy Cross Cotts. Hea 83 F3
Sandy Cross La. Hea 83 F3
Sandy La. Col H 25 D3
Sandy La. E Gri 2 B1
Sandy La. Fra 80 C4
Sandy La. Hor 83 E1
Sandy La. W Hoa 22 B3
Sandy Vale. Hay H 52 B1
Sanyhils Ave. Bri 145 E4
Saunders Cl. Hast 140 C1
Saunders Hill. Bri 146 A4
Saunders Rd. T W 8 B1
Saunders Way. Cam 96 C1
Savill Rd. Hay H 52 C4
Sawyers Cl. Bur H 75 D1
Saxby Cl. East 176 B1
Saxby Rd. Bex 159 F2
Saxon Cl. East 185 D3
Saxon Cl. Salt 168 A1
Saxon La. Sea 181 E1
Saxon Pl. East 185 D3
Saxon Rd. Hast 141 D2
Saxon Rd. Hove 164 A3
Saxon Rd. Newh 180 A4
Saxon Rise. Bex 160 B2
Saxon St. Hast 162 A3
Saxonbury Cl. Cro 27 E1
Saxonwood Rd. Bat 115 D3
Sayerland La. Pole 174 C4
Sayers The. E Gri 2 A1
Scamps Hill. Hay H 53 D3
Scarborough Rd. Bri 145 D1
Scarletts Cl. Uck 79 F4
Schofield Way. East 186 B4
School Cl. Bur H 74 B1
School Cl. Sock 163 E4
School Field. Bar C 104 A3
School Gdns. Bar C 104 A2
School Hill. Lam 21 F3
School Hill. Lew 127 D1
School Hill. Mar 56 C2
School Hill. Winc 120 B4
School La. Ash W 13 E3
School La. Bar C 104 B3
School La. Che Co 36 A3
School La. Cro 27 E1
School La. Dan 35 F3
School La. Had D 58 C3
School La. Nut 37 D3
School La. Peas 70 C1
School La. Pole 174 C4
School La. Pye 123 D3
School La. Rye 72 A1
School La. Salt 168 A1
School Path. Bar C 104 A2
School Pl. Bex 160 C3
School Rd. Hast 141 D2
School Rd. Hove 164 B4
Scotland St. Bri 165 F3
Scotsford Rd. Bro O 61 E3
Scott Rd. Hove 164 B4
Scotts Acre. Cam 96 B1
Scotts Way. T W 18 B4
Scraper's Hill. Chi 131 F4
Scutes Cl. Hast 140 C2
Scuthview Dr. Uck 80 A4
Sea Rd. Bex 160 A2
Sea Rd. Cam 96 B1
Sea Rd. Fai 142 C3
Sea Rd. Hast 161 E3
Sea Rd. Pev B 177 D3
Sea Rd. Winc 120 C4
Sea Rd. Winc B 120 C3
Seabeach Rd. East 186 A3
Seabourne Rd. Bex 160 C3
Seafield Cl. Sea 181 F3
Seafield Rd. Hove 164 C3
Seaford Rd. East 186 A3
Seaford Rd. Hove 164 A3
Seaford Rd. Newh 180 B4
Seaford Rd. Sea 180 B4
Seagrave Cl. Sea 180 C3
Searle Ave. Pea 179 E3
Seaside. East 186 A3
Seaside Rd. East 185 F2
Seaside Rd. Hast 161 E3
Seaside Way. Hast 161 E3
Seaview Ave. Pea 179 E3
Seaview Rd. Newh 170 B1
Seaview Rd. Pea 179 E3
Seaview Rd. Wood 166 C4
Seaview Terr. Rye 95 D3
Seaville Dr. East 186 A4
Seaville Dr. Pev B 177 D3
Second Ave. Bex 160 B3
Second Ave. Cam 96 B1
Second Ave. Hove 165 D3
Second Ave. Newh 180 A3
Second Rd. Pea 178 C4
Sedgebrook Gdns. Hast 140 B1
Sedgewick Rd. Bex 160 A3
Sedgewick Rd. Bri 146 A3
Sedlescombe Rd N. Hast 140 A2
Sedlescombe Rd S. Hast 139 F1
Sedlescoombe Gdns. Hast 139 F1
Sefton Chase. Cro 27 F2
Sefton Rd. Por S 143 E2
Sefton Way. Cro 27 F2
Segrave Cl. Lew 126 C1
Selba Dr. Bri 146 B2
Selborne Pl. Hove 165 D4
Selborne Rd. Hove 165 D3
Selby Cl. Rid 80 A3
Selby Gdns. Rid 80 A3
Selby Rd. East 185 D3
Selby Rd. Rid 80 A3
Selby Rise. Rid 80 A3
Selham Cl. Bri 146 A3
Selham Dr. Bri 146 A3
Selhurst Rd. Wood 167 E3
Selmeston Cl. Hast 140 A1
Selmeston Pl. Bri 166 B3
Selmeston Rd. East 185 D4
Selsfield Cl. East 185 D3
Selsfield Dr. Bri 146 A2
Selsfield Rd. W Hoa 22 A4
Selwyn Dr. East 185 E2
Selwyn Rd. East 185 E2
Semley Rd. Bri 145 F1
Semley Rd. Hass 100 B2
Senlac Gdns. Bat 115 E2
Senlac Green. Uck 57 E1
Senlac Rd. Newh 180 A4
Senlac Way. Hast 140 A3
Sergison Cl. Hay H 52 A3
Sergison Rd. Hay H 52 A3
Setfords Field. S Str 77 E1
Seven Acre Cl. Hast 139 F3
Seven Sisters Rd. Willn 175 D2
Sevenoaks Rd. East 176 A1
Seville St. Bri 166 A4
Sewell Ave. Bex 160 A3
Seymour Sq. Bri 166 A2
Seymour St. Bri 166 A2
Shaftesbury Pl. Bri 165 F4
Shaftesbury Rd. Bri 165 F4
Shaftesbury Rd. T W 8 C3
Shakespeare St. Hove 164 C4
Shakespeare Wlk. East 176 B1
Shalesbrook La. For R 13 F1
Shalfleet Cl. East 175 F2
Shandon Cl. T W 9 D2
Shanklin Cl. East 175 F2
Shanklin Rd. Bri 166 A4
Shannon Cl. Pea 168 C1
Sharpthorne Cres. Por S 144 A1
Sharrow Cl. Hay H 52 B3
Shaw The. T W 9 D1
Shawfield. Cro 27 F1
Sheddingdean Cl. Bur H 74 C2
Sheen Rd. East 185 F2
Sheep Pen La. Sea 181 F2
Sheep Plain. Cro 39 D4
Sheep Wlk. Rottn 167 E1
Sheepbell Cl. Por S 143 F2
Sheepfair. Lew 126 C1
Sheepfold The. Pea 169 D1
Sheepsetting La. Hea 83 E4
Sheepstreet La. Etc 45 F2
Sheepstreet La. Ston 45 E2
Sheerwater Cres. Hast 140 A2
Sheffield Mill La. Che G 55 D4
Sheffield Mill La. Dan 54 C4
Sheiling Rd. Cro 27 E2
Shell La. Hast 162 C4
Shelldale Ave. Por S 163 F4
Shelldale Cres. Por S 163 F4
Shelldale Rd. Por S 163 F4
Shelley Cl. Lew 126 C1
Shelley Rd. E Gri 2 A1
Shelley Rd. Hove 164 B4
Shelley Rd. Rin 128 A3
Shelley Wlk. East 176 B1
Shenfield Way. Bri 145 F2
Shenstone. Hay H 52 C4
Shepham Ave. Salt 168 A1
Shepham La. Pole 175 D4
Shepherd St. Hast 162 A3
Shepherd's Cl. Bex 159 D2
Shepherds Cl. East 175 E2
Shepherds Cl. Rin 128 B3
Shepherds Cot. Pea 169 D1
Shepherds Croft. Bri 145 D2
Shepherd's Hill. Col H 25 D4
Shepherds Mead. Bur H 74 B2
Shepherd's Way. Fai 142 B2
Shepherds Way. Rin 128 B3
Shepherds Wlk. Cro 28 A1
Shepherds Wlk. Hass 100 B3
Shepherds Wlk. T W 9 D2
Shepherdsgrove La. Hamm 3 F2
Sheppey Wlk. Hai 132 C2
Sheppeys. Hay H 52 A1
Shepway The. Sea 181 F2
Sheraton Cl. East 185 E1
Sherborne Cl. T W 9 D1
Sherbourne Cl. Hove 144 A2
Sherbourne Rd. Hove 144 A2
Sherbourne Way. Hove 144 A2
Sheridan Cl. E Gri 2 A1
Sheridan Terr. Hove 164 C4
Sheriff's La. Tow R 41 D4
Sherrington Rd. Wood 167 E4
Sherwood Cl. Hast 140 B1
Sherwood Cl. Hast 140 B1
Sherwood Dr. Hay H 52 A3
Sherwood Green. Hai 154 C3
Sherwood Rd. Sea 181 E2
Sherwood Rd. T W 9 D3
Sherwood Rise. Sea 181 E2
Sherwood Way. T W 9 D3
Shinewater La. East 175 F2
Ship St. Bri 165 E3
Ship St. E Gri 12 B4
Ship St. Newh 180 A4
Ship St Ct. Bri 165 F3
Ship St Gdns. Bri 165 E3
Shipley La. Bex 159 D2
Shipley Rd. Wood 167 E4
Shirlea View. Bat 115 E2
Shirley Ave. Hove 144 C1
Shirley Cl. S Sea 163 D4
Shirley Dr. Hast 139 F2
Shirley Dr. Hove 145 D1
Shirley Gdns. T W 8 A3
Shirley Gr. T W 8 A3
Shirley Rd. Hove 165 D4
Shirley St. Hove 164 C4
Shirleys. Dit 101 E1
Shoreham By-Ps. S Sea 143 D1
Short Brow. Sea 181 F2
Short Brow Cl. Willn 174 C2
Shortdean Pl. East 185 D2
Shortgate Rd. Bri 146 B2
Shortlands Cl. Willn 175 D1
Showfields Rd. T W 8 B1
Shrub La. Bur 64 A4
Shrub La. Ston 45 D1
Shrublands Ct. T W 9 D2
Shrublands The. Bex 159 E2
Sicklehatch La. Hor 83 F1
Sidcup Cl. East 176 A1
Sidehill Dr. Por S 143 E1
Sidley Green. Bex 160 A4
Sidley Rd. East 186 A3
Sidley St. Bex 160 A4
Sidney Cl. Hast 139 F2
Sidney Cl. T W 18 B4
Sidney Little Rd. Hast 139 D2
Silchester Rd. Hast 162 A4
Sillwood Pl. Bri 165 E3
Sillwood Rd. Bri 165 E3
Sillwood St. Bri 165 E3
Sillwood Terr. Bri 165 E3
Silva Cl. Bex 160 C3
Silvan Rd. Hast 139 E2
Silver Birches. Hay H 52 C2
Silverdale. Key 100 C2
Silverdale Ave. Hove 165 D4
Silverdale Ct. Hai 154 C4
Silverdale La. T W 8 C3
Silverdale Rd. Bur H 75 D1
Silverdale Rd. East 185 E1
Silverdale Rd. Hove 165 D4
Silverdale Rd. T W 8 C3
Silverhill Ave. Hast 140 A2
Silverhill Ave. Hast 140 A3
Silverlands Rd. Hast 139 F1
Silverwick's La. Pon G 112 B4
Silvester Rd. Bex 160 A3
Silwood Cl. T W 9 E4
Simons Cl. Cro 27 F1
Singleton Rd. Bri 145 F3
Singleton Way. Bur H 75 D1
Sinnock Sq. Hast 162 C4
Sir David's Park. Sgh 8 B4
Skinner's La. Cat 137 D4
Skyline View. Pea 169 D1
Slade The. Lam 21 F2
Sleeches Cross. Frant 18 C1
Sleepers Stile Rd. Lam 20 C1
Slider's La. Dan 54 C4
Slider's La. Fle 54 C4
Slides The. Hast 139 E2
Slimbridge Rd. Bur H 74 B2
Slindon Ave. Pea 179 D3
Slindon Cres. East 176 B1
Slinfold Cl. Bri 166 A3
Sloe La. Alfn 172 C2
Slugwash La. Hay H 53 D1
Slugwash La. Wiv 76 A4
Smeatons La. Winc B 120 C3
Smith Cl. Nin 136 C3
Smithys Cl. Hast 140 A3
Smolletts. E Gri 12 A4
Smugglers Cl. Alfn 172 B2
Smugglers La. Cro 27 D3
Smugglers Way. Fai 142 B2
Snape View. Wad 31 E2
Snatt's Rd. Uck 79 F4
Snednore. Kin L 148 B3
Snipe Cl. Pem 10 B4
Snowdrop La. Hay H 53 D2
Solomon's La. Mou 89 D2
Solway. Hai 132 C1
Solway Ave. Bri 145 E4
Somerhill Ave. Hove 165 D4
Somerhill Rd. Hove 165 D3
Somerset Rd. T W 8 C3
Somerset St. Bri 166 A3
Somerville Cl. East 186 B4
Somerville Gdns. T W 8 B2
Sorrel Cl. East 176 A2
Sorrel Dr. East 176 A2
South Ave. Bri 166 A3
South Ave. East 184 C3
South Ave. Hur 99 F3
South Bank. Hass 100 B2
South Brooks Rd. Lydd 98 B1
South Cl. Bur H 74 B2
South Cl. Pev B 177 E3
South Cliff. Bex 159 E1
South Cliff. East 190 B4
South Cliff Ave. Bex 159 E1
South Cliff Ave. East 185 E1
South Coast Rd. Pea 179 E3
South Coast Rd. Salt 178 B4
South Ct. Lew 127 E1
South Downs. Plu 102 B3
South Dr. Bur H 74 B2
South Gr. T W 8 C1
South La. Dal 86 B1
South La. Newh 180 A4
South Lodge Cl. Bur H 74 B2
South Lynn Dr. East 185 E2
South Rd. Bri 145 E1
South Rd. Hai 154 C3
South Rd. Hay H 52 B2
South Rd. Newh 180 A4
South Rd. Plu G 76 A2
South Rd. Wiv G 76 A2
South Rough. Newk 78 A4
South St. Bri 165 E3
South St. Cro 27 E1
South St. Dit 101 D2
South St. E Hoa 107 E2
South St. East 185 E1
South St. Fal 147 D3
South St. Hast 162 A4
South St. Lew 149 E4
South St. May 41 F1
South St. Por S 143 F1
South St. Rot 40 C4
South St. Sea 181 E1
South Terr. Hast 162 B4
South Undercliff. Rye 95 D3
South View. Dit 101 E3
South View Rd. Cro 27 E1
South View Rd. Sgh 8 C4
South View Rd. Wad 31 E3
South Way. Lew 126 C1
South Way. Newh 180 A4
South Way. Sea 182 A1
South Woodlands. Bri 145 E3
Southall Ave. Bri 146 A1
Southampton St. Bri 166 A3
Southbourne Rd. East 186 A3
Southcourt Ave. Bex 159 E1
Southdown Ave. Bri 145 F1
Southdown Ave. Hast 140 C2
Southdown Ave. Lew 148 C4
Southdown Ave. Pea 179 E3
Southdown Ave. Por S 164 A4
Southdown Ave. Willn 174 C2
Southdown Cl. Hay H 52 A1
Southdown Cl. Newh 179 F3
Southdown Pl. Bri 145 F1
Southdown Pl. Lew 127 E1
Southdown Rd. Bri 145 F1
Southdown Rd. East 185 D4
Southdown Rd. Newh 179 F3
Southdown Rd. Por S 143 F1
Southdown Rd. Sea 181 F1
Southdown Rd. Sock 163 E4
Southerden Cl. Hai 155 D4
Southern Ave. Pole 174 C3
Southern Rd. East 175 E1
Southfield. Pole 174 B3
Southfield Rd. Spe 7 F4
Southfield Rd. T W 8 C3
Southfields. Wad 31 E3
Southfields Rd. East 185 E2
Southfields Way. Sgh 8 C4
Southlands. E Gri 12 B4
Southlands Ave. Bex 159 F4
Southlands Rd. Bex 159 F4
Southmead Cl. May 42 A2
Southmount. Bri 145 F1
Southon Cl. Por S 143 E2
Southover High St. Lew 149 D4
Southover Pl. Bri 165 F4
Southover Rd. Lew 149 D4
Southover St. Bri 165 F3
Southridge Rd. Cro 39 E4
Southridge Rise. Cro 39 E4
Southview Cl. Cro 27 E1
Southview Cl. S Sea 163 D4
Southview Cl. Sock 143 E1
Southview Rd. Pea 179 D4
Southview Rd. Sock 163 E4
Southwater Cl. Bri 166 A3
Southwater Rd. Hast 162 A4
Southway. Bur H 74 A2
Southwick Cl. E Gri 2 A1
Southwick Sq. Sock 163 E4
Southwick St. Sock 163 E4
Southwood Ave. T W 8 C3
Southwood Rd. T W 7 F2
Sovereign Cl. Hast 140 C2
Sovereign Cl. Sea 181 F3
Spa Industrial Park. T W 9 E4
Sparrows Green Rd. Wad 31 E3
Spatham La. Dit 101 E3
Speldhurst Hill. Spe 7 F4
Speldhurst Rd. Lan G 7 E2
Speldhurst Rd. Sgh 8 B4
Speldhurst Rd. Spe 7 E3
Spencer Ave. Hove 144 A2
Spencer Rd. East 185 F1
Spencers Field. S Mal 127 E1
Spences La. S Mal 127 D1
Spicers Cl. Bur H 74 B3
Spindewood Dr. Bex 159 D2
Spinnais Gr. Sock 163 D4
Spinnais Gr. Sock 163 D4
Spinney Cl. Cra D 11 D4
Spinney Cl. Hur 99 F3
Spinney The. Bat 115 E2
Spinney The. Bex 159 D2
Spinney The. Hass 100 B3
Spinney The. Hast 140 B1
Spinney The. Hay H 52 A4
Spinney The. Hay H 52 B2
Spinney The. Hove 145 D2
Spinney The. Rob 65 E2
Spinneys The. Hea 83 F3
Spinneys The. Lew 127 E1
Spital Rd. Lew 126 C1
Spithurst Rd. Spi 104 B3
Spode La. Cowd 4 C4
Sponden La. Four T 48 C4
Sponden La. San 48 C4
Spotted Cow La. Bux 58 B3
Spray Hill. Lam 21 F2
Sprays La. Wfd 116 C2
Spring Cl. East 174 C1
Spring Gdns. Bri 165 F3
Spring Gdns. Lew 127 D1
Spring Gdns. Sock 163 E4
Spring Hill. Ford 6 C3
Spring La. Bex 159 D3
Spring La. Bur 63 E3
Spring La. Clay 123 E4
Spring Lodge Cl. East 176 B1
Spring Meadow. For R 13 E1
Spring St. Bri 165 E3
Spring St. Hast 140 A1
Spring Way. E Gri 2 C2
Springate Rd. Sock 163 E4
Springett Ave. Rin 128 A3
Springfield. E Gri 2 A2
Springfield Ave. Pea 178 B4
Springfield Cl. Cro 27 F1
Springfield Cl. Whm 176 B3
Springfield Rd. Bex 160 A3
Springfield Rd. Bri 165 F4
Springfield Rd. East 185 F2
Springfield Rd. Gro 17 D4
Springfield Rd. Hast 139 F1
Springfield Valley Rd. Hast 139 F1
Springfield Valley Rd. Hast 139 F1
Springfields. Tic 33 E1
Springhead. T W 9 D3
Springhead Way. Cro 39 E4
Springside Wlk. Hast 139 E1
Springwood Rd. Hea 83 F4
Spruce Cl. East 175 D1
Spur Rd. Pole 174 C3
Spurway Park. Pole 174 C3
Spurway The. T W 8 A1
Squab La. Mag D 133 F3
Square The. Bri 145 E3
Square The. Cowd 4 C3
Square The. Pev B 177 E3
Square The. Wad 31 F2
Squirrel Cl. Bex 159 E3
Squirrel Way. T W 9 E3
Stabledene Way. Pem 10 A3
Stablefield. Wfd 117 E2
Stafford Rd. Bri 165 E4
Stafford Rd. Sea 181 E2
Stafford Rd. T W 9 E2
Stafford Way. Key 100 C2
Stag Rd. T W 9 D4
Stainsby St. Hast 162 A4
Stanam Rd. Pem 10 B3
Standean Cl. Bri 146 A3
Standen Cl. E Gri 1 C2
Standen St. San 49 E4
Standen St. T W 8 C3
Stanford Ave. Bri 145 F1
Stanford Ave. Hass 100 B2
Stanford Cl. Hass 100 B2
Stanford Cl. Hove 145 D1
Stanford Rd. Bri 165 E4
Stanhope Pl. Hast 162 C4
Stanhope Rd. T W 9 D3
Stanier Rd. Hast 139 E3
Stanley Ave. Por S 143 E2
Stanley Ave S. Por S 143 E2
Stanley Rd. Bri 165 F4
Stanley Rd. East 185 F2
Stanley Rd. Hast 162 B4
Stanley Rd. Pea 168 C1
Stanley Rd. Por 163 F4
Stanley Rd. T W 8 C3
Stanley St. Bri 165 F3
Stanmer Ave. Salt 168 A2
Stanmer Dr. East 185 D4
Stanmer Park Rd. Bri 145 F1
Stanmer St. Bri 145 F1
Stanmer Villas. Bri 145 F1
Stansfield Rd. Lew 126 C1
Stanstead Cres. Wood 167 E3
Stansted Rd. East 185 F2
Staplefield Dr. Bri 146 B2
Stapley Rd. Hove 144 A1
Star La. Alfn 172 C2
Star La. Blas 81 F3
Star La. May 41 F1
Star Rd. East 185 E2

Starr's Green La. Bat 115 E2
Starrs Mead. Bat 115 E2
Starvecrow La. Bec 92 C3
Starvecrow La. Peas 93 E4
Starwell Cl. Hast 140 A2
Station App. Bat 115 E2
Station App. East 175 E1
Station App. Hass 100 B2
Station App. Hast 162 A4
Station App. Hea 83 F4
Station App. Hove 164 C4
Station App. Sea 181 E2
Station Cl. Plu 102 B3
Station Cotts. Hass 100 B2
Station Rd. Bex 160 A2
Station Rd. Bri 145 D2
Station Rd. Bur H 74 C1
Station Rd. Chay 77 E4
Station Rd. Crow 138 B3
Station Rd. E Gri 2 A1
Station Rd. For R 13 E2
Station Rd. Gro 17 D4
Station Rd. Hai 155 D3
Station Rd. Hast 162 B4
Station Rd. Hea 83 F4
Station Rd. Hel 132 C3
Station Rd. Hor K 35 D3
Station Rd. Hur G 46 C2
Station Rd. Lew 149 D4
Station Rd. May 41 F1
Station Rd. N Cha 77 E4
Station Rd. Newh 170 B1
Station Rd. Norm 68 C4
Station Rd. Plu 102 B3
Station Rd. Pole 174 C3
Station Rd. Por S 164 A4
Station Rd. Rob 65 F2
Station Rd. Rot 40 C4
Station Rd. Sea 180 C2
Station Rd. Sha 22 C3
Station Rd. Sock 163 E4
Station Rd. Tow R 29 D1
Station Rd. Wad 31 D3
Station Rd. Winc 94 B1
Station Rd. Wit 15 F3
Station Rd Industrial Estate. Hai 155 D3
Station St. Bri 165 F3
Station St. East 185 F1
Station St. Lew 127 D1
Staveley Rd. East 190 B4
Steep Hill. Bre 91 E1
Steine Gdns. Bri 165 F3
Steine La. Bri 165 F3
Steine St. Bri 165 F2
Stephens Cl. Rin 128 A3
Stephens Rd. Bri 145 F1
Stephen's Rd. T W 8 C3
Stephenson Dr. E Gri 12 B4
Stevens Cl. Bex 160 A4
Stevens Ct. Hove 164 B4
Stevenson Cl. East 176 B2
Stevenson Rd. Bri 166 A3
Stevenson Rd. Hast 139 F1
Stewards Inn La. Lew 149 D4
Stewart Rd. Sgh 9 D4
Steyne Cl. Sea 181 E1
Steyne Rd. Sea 181 E1
Steyning Ave. Hove 144 B2
Steyning Ave. Pea 179 D4
Steyning Cl. Sea 182 A1
Steyning Rd. Rottn 167 F1
Steyning Rd. Sea 182 A1
Stiles The. Hai 155 D4
Stirling Ave. Sea 182 A2
Stirling Cl. Bur H 75 D2
Stirling Cl. Sea 182 A2
Stirling Ct Rd. Bur H 75 D2
Stirling Pl. Hove 164 C3
Stirling Rd. Hast 139 E3
Stock Dale. Fai 142 B2
Stockland Green Rd. Spe 8 A4
Stockleigh Rd. Hast 162 A4
Stocks Meadow. Nin 136 C3
Stockwell Rd. E Gri 12 B3
Stoddards La. Bec 69 E3
Stoke Cl. Sea 181 F2
Stoke Manor Cl. Sea 181 F2
Stone Cross Rd. Cro 39 F3
Stone Cross Rd. Wad 31 F2
Stone Ct La. Pem 10 B4
Stone Hill. E Gri 12 A2
Stone Pit La. San 49 E3
Stone Quarry Rd. Che G 36 A4
Stone St. Bri 165 E3
Stone St. Hast 162 B4
Stone St. T W 9 D2
Stonecroft Cl. Hove 144 B2
Stonecross Rd. Bri 146 B2
Stonedene Cl. For R 13 F1
Stonefield Pl. Hast 162 B4
Stonefield Rd. Hast 162 C4
Stonefield Way. Bur H 74 B3
Stonegate Rd. Ston 44 A4
Stonegate Rd. Tic 32 A1
Stoneham Cl. S Mal 127 D2
Stoneham Rd. Hove 164 B4
Stonehouse Dr. Batt 116 B1
Stonehouse Dr. Hast 139 F1
Stonehouse Dr. Wfd 116 C1
Stonehurst Ct. Bri 166 A3
Stoneleigh Ave. Bri 145 E3
Stoneleigh Cl. Bri 145 E3
Stoneleigh Cl. E Gri 2 B1
Stonelink Cl. Hast 139 E4
Stonepark Dr. For R 13 F1
Stonepound Rd. Hass 100 B2
Stonery Cl. Por S 143 F1
Stonery Rd. Por S 143 F1
Stonestile La. Wfd 140 B4
Stonewall Park Rd. Lan G 7 E2
Stonewood Cl. Sea 182 A2
Stoney La. S Sea 163 D4
Stony La. Hai 155 D4
Storrington Cl. Hove 144 B1
Straight Half Mile. Mar 56 C3
Strand. Rye 94 C3
Strand Hill. Winc 120 B4
Strand Meadow. Bur 63 F4
Stratford St. T W 9 D3
Strathfield Cl. Hay H 52 B2
Strawberry Cl. T W 18 B4
Stream La. Fai 142 C3
Stream La. Sed 90 A1
Stream La. The M 47 F4
Stream La. Wha 89 F1
Stream Park. E Gri 1 C2
Stream Pit La. San 48 C3
Streamside Cl. Hast 140 B2
Streat La. Dit 102 A2
Streat La. Strt 102 A2
Streatfield Rd. Hea 83 E4
Streatfield Rd. Uck 79 F4
Streele View. Uck 80 B4
Street End La. Bro O 61 E1
Street The. Fra 80 C3
Street The. Kin L 148 B3
Street The. Sed 116 B4
Street The. W Fir 150 C2
Street The. Wmes 124 B4
Streetlands. Sed 90 B1
Stringer Way. Bri 145 E2
Stringwalk The. Hai 155 D4
Stroma Gdns. Hai 132 B1
Strongs Pas. Hast 162 C4
Strood Rd. Hast 140 A1
Stuart Ave. East 185 D3
Stuart Cl. T W 18 B4
Stuart Way. E Gri 12 B4
Stubb La. Bre 92 A1
Stubb La. Bro Ow 92 B2
Stubpond La. Fel 1 A4
Studdens La. Cowb 111 D1
Studdens La. Hers 134 A4
Sturdee Cl. East 186 B4
Sturdee Pl. Hast 162 C4
Sturton Pl. Hai 154 C4
Subworth Cl. Hay H 52 A4
Sudeley Pl. Bri 166 A2
Sudeley St. Bri 166 A2
Sudeley Terr. Bri 166 A2
Suffolk Rd. Bex 160 A4
Suffolk St. Hove 164 B4
Sugar La. Hor K 35 D2
Sullington Cl. Bri 146 B2
Sumach Cl. East 175 E1
Summer Cl. Por S 163 F4
Summer Hill Rd. Bex 159 E3
Summercourt. Hai 154 C4
Summerdale Rd. Hove 144 A1
Summerdown Cl. East 185 D2
Summerdown La. Fri 184 A1
Summerdown Rd. East 185 D2
Summerfields Ave. Hai 154 C4
Summerheath Rd. Hai 154 C4
Summerhill Cl. Hay H 52 B4
Summerhill Dr. Hay H 52 C4
Summerhill La. Hay H 52 B4
Summerlands Rd. Willn 175 D1
Summersdeane. Sock 143 E1
Summervale Rd. T W 8 B1
Sun La. Hast 162 C4
Sun Patch. Hai 155 D4
Sun St. Lew 127 D1
Sunningdale Cl. Bex 160 B2
Sunningdale Cl. Sea 181 F1
Sunninghill Ave. Hove 144 B1
Sunninghill Cl. Hove 144 B1
Sunnybank Cl. May 41 F1
Sunnydale Ave. Bri 145 F3
Sunnydale Cl. Bri 145 F3
Sunnyside Rd. T W 8 A2
Sunnywood Dr. Hay H 52 A2
Sunset Cl. Pea 168 C1
Sunset Cl. Pev B 177 E3
Sunstar La. Pole 174 B3
Sunte Ave. Hay H 52 B4
Sunte Cl. Hay H 52 B4
Sunview Ave. Pea 179 D3
Surrenden Cl. Bri 145 E2
Surrenden Cres. Bri 145 E2
Surrenden Holt. Bri 145 E2
Surrenden Park. Bri 145 F2
Surrenden Rd. Bri 145 E2
Surrey Cl. Sea 181 D2
Surrey Cl. T W 18 B4
Surrey Rd. Sea 181 D2
Surrey St. Bri 165 E3
Susans Cl. E Hoa 107 F3
Susan's Rd. East 185 F2
Sussex Ave. Hai 154 C4
Sussex Cl. Bex 159 E3
Sussex Cl. Hai 154 C4
Sussex Cl. T W 9 D1
Sussex Gdns. Fri 184 A1
Sussex Mews. Bri 166 B2
Sussex Mews. T W 8 C1
Sussex Pl. Bri 165 F3
Sussex Rd. Hast 161 F3
Sussex Rd. Hay H 52 B2
Sussex Rd. Hove 164 C3
Sussex Sq. Bri 166 B2
Sussex St. Bri 165 F3
Sussex Terr. Bri 165 F3
Sussex Way. Bur H 74 B3
Sussex Way. Pea 178 B4
Sutherland Ave. Bex 159 F2
Sutherland Cl. Bex 159 E2
Sutherland Rd. Bri 166 A3
Sutherland Rd. T W 8 C2
Sutton Ave. Pea 178 C4
Sutton Ave. Sea 181 F1
Sutton Cl. Wood 147 E1
Sutton Croft La. Sea 181 E2
Sutton Dro. Sea 181 E2
Sutton Park Rd. Sea 181 E2
Sutton Pl. Bex 160 B2
Sutton Rd. East 185 F2
Sutton Rd. Sea 181 E2
Suttons The. Cam 96 C1
Suttons The. Hast 139 E1
Swaines Pas. Hast 162 C4
Swaines Way. Hea 83 F3
Swainsthorpe Cl. Hay H 52 B2
Swallow Bank. Hast 139 E1
Swallow Cl. East 176 A1
Swallow Dr. Bat 115 E2
Swallow Dr. T W 9 E3
Swallows The. Pea 168 C1
Swan Ave. Hast 162 C4
Swan Rd. Hai 155 D3
Swan St. Witt 51 F2
Swan Terr. Hast 162 C4
Swanborough Dr. Bri 166 B4
Swanborough Dro. Kin L 148 B2
Swanborough Hollow. Iford 148 C2
Swanborough Pl. Bri 166 B4
Swanley Cl. East 176 A1
Swann Cl. Bur H 75 D2
Swannee Cl. Pea 169 D1
Swaylands Ave. Cro 39 E4
Sweeps Hill Cl. Pem 10 A4
Sweethaws La. Cro 39 D3
Sweetings La. Cou W 21 D1
Swife La. Bro O 62 A2
Swift Cl. Cro 27 D1
Swinburne Ave. Willn 175 D2
Swineham La. Crow 138 C2
Swissland Hill. Dor P 2 B4
Swynford Dr. Hast 139 F3
Sybron Way. Cro 40 A4
Sycamore Cl. Bex 159 D2
Sycamore Cl. East 175 D2
Sycamore Cl. Hea 83 F3
Sycamore Cl. Sea 182 A2
Sycamore Cl. Wood 167 E4
Sycamore Ct. Uck 80 A4
Sycamore Dr. E Gri 2 C1
Sycamore Dr. Hai 154 C3
Sydney Rd. East 185 F2
Sydney Rd. Hay H 52 B3
Sydney St. Bri 165 F3
Sylvan Cl. Hay H 52 C2
Sylvester Way. Hove 144 A2
Symbister Rd. Por S 164 A4
Syresham Gdns. Hay H 52 B2

Tackleway. Hast 162 C4
Taddington Rd. East 186 A2
Tainters Brook. Uck 80 B4
Talbot Cres. Bri 146 A3
Talbot Park. T W 9 D3
Talbot Rd. The M 47 E4
Talbot Terr. Lew 127 D1
Tamarack Cl. East 175 D1
Tamworth Rd. Hove 164 B4
Tanbridge Rd. East 176 B1
Tandridge Rd. Hove 164 B3
Tangier La. Frant 18 C3
Tangle Oak. Fel 1 B2
Tanglewood Coppice. Bex 159 E2
Tangmere Cl. Bex 159 E2
Tangmere Rd. Bri 145 F3
Tanhouse La. Peas 70 B1
Tanners Way. Cro 27 F1
Tanyard. San 48 C3
Tanyard Ave. E Gri 12 C4
Tanyard Cotts. Bux 58 A1
Tanyard La. Che Co 36 A3
Tanyard La. Dan 35 F1
Tanyard La. Winc 120 B4
Tapsell's La. Wad 31 D3
Tarner Rd. Bri 165 F3
Tarragon Way. S Sea 143 D1
Tarring Cl. S Hei 170 A1
Tas Combe Way. Willn 174 C1
Tate Cres. Bur H 74 B3
Taunton Gr. Bri 146 C1
Taunton Rd. Bri 146 B1
Taunton Way. Bri 146 C1
Tavistock Down. Bri 146 A1
Taylor Cl. Hast 139 E2
Taylor St. Sgh 8 C4
Tea Gdn La. T W 8 A1
Teal Ct. Hast 139 E2
Teasley Mead. Wit 6 A2
Tedder Rd. T W 8 C4
Tedder Terr. Hast 141 D3
Teg Cl. Por S 144 A1
Telegraph St. Bri 166 A2
Telford Rd. Hast 139 F3
Telham Cl. Hast 140 C3
Telham La. Bat 115 D1
Telscombe Cliffs Way. Pea 178 C4
Telscombe Park. Pea 169 D1
Telscombe Rd. East 176 B1
Telscombe Rd. Pea 169 D1
Temple Gdns. Bri 165 E3
Temple St. Bri 165 E3
Tenantry Down Rd. Bri 166 B4
Tennis Cl. Hai 154 C4
Tennis Rd. Hove 164 B3
Tennyson Rise. E Gri 2 A1
Tennyson Wlk. East 176 B2
Tenterden Cl. East 176 A1
Tenterden Rise. Hast 140 B1
Terminus Ave. Bex 159 F2
Terminus Pl. Bri 165 E4
Terminus Rd. Bex 159 F2
Terminus Rd. Bri 165 E4
Terminus Rd. East 185 F1
Terminus St. Bri 165 E3
Terrace Rd. Hast 162 A4
Thackeray Cl. East 176 B2
Thakeham Cl. Bex 160 C3
Thames Cl. Bri 165 F3
Thanet Way. Hast 140 B1
Thatchers Cl. Bur H 75 D1
Thatchings The. Pole 174 C3
Theaklen Dr. Hast 139 F1
Theobalds Green. Hea 83 F3
Theobalds Rd. Bur H 75 D3
Theobalds Rd. Wiv 75 E4
Theodore Cl. T W 9 E4
Third Ave. Bex 160 B3
Third Ave. Hove 164 C3
Third Ave. Newh 180 A3
Third Rd. Pea 178 C4
Third St. Lan G 7 E2
Thirlmere Rd. T W 8 B3
Thomas Brassey Cl. Hast 139 F3
Thomas St. Lew 127 E1
Thomas St. T W 8 C3
Thomas Turner Dr. E Hoa 107 F3
Thompson Rd. Bri 146 A1
Thompson Rd. Newh 170 B1
Thorden La. Rol L 50 C4
Thornbank Cres. Bex 159 E2
Thornbush Cres. Por S 143 F2
Thorndean Rd. Bri 146 A2
Thorne Cres. Bex 137 E1
Thornfield Gdns. T W 9 E3
Thornhill Ave. Bri 145 F4
Thornhill Cl. Hove 144 B1
Thornhill Rise. Por S 143 F2
Thornhill Way. Por S 143 F2
Thornwell Rd. Wil 173 E4
Thornwood Cl. East 175 E1
Thorny Cl. Hea 83 F4
Three Leg Cross Rd. Tic 33 D1
Three Oaks La. Wad 31 D4
Thurrock Cl. Willn 174 C2
Thyme Cl. S Sea 143 D1
Tibbs Mill La. Cro 39 E1
Ticehurst Ave. Hooe 158 B3
Ticehurst Rd. Bri 166 B3
Ticehurst Rd. Ston 44 B3
Tickerage La. Blas 81 E3
Tidebrook Gdns. East 176 B1
Tideswell Rd. East 185 F2
Tidy St. Bri 165 F3
Tilbury Pl. Bri 165 F3
Tilbury Way. Bri 165 F3
Tile Barn Rd. Hast 139 E2
Tilehurst Dr. Hai 154 C4
Tilekiln La. Hast 141 E2
Tilers Cl. Bur H 75 D2
Tilgate Cl. Bri 166 A3
Tilgate Cl. East 185 D4
Tilgate Dr. Bex 159 D2
Tilley La. Bor S 135 E3
Tillingham Ave. Rye 94 C3
Tillingham La. Peas 93 E3
Tillingham View. Bro O W 91 F3
Tillington Terr. Hast 141 D1
Tillstone St. Bri 165 F3
Tilsmore Rd. Hea 83 E4
Tiltwood Dr. Cra D 1 A1
Timber Yard Cotts. Lew 127 E1
Timberlaine Rd. Pev B 177 D2
Timberley Rd. East 175 D1
Tindal Cl. Bur H 75 D2
Tinker's La. Had D 59 E2
Tinkers La. Tic 33 E2
Tintern Cl. Bri 145 F1
Tintern Cl. East 175 E2
Tisbury Rd. Hove 165 D3
Titchborne St. Bri 165 F3
Titchfield Cl. Bur H 75 D1
Titian Rd. Hove 164 B4
Tiverton Dr. Bex 160 B3
Tivoli Cres. Bri 145 D1
Tivoli Cres N. Bri 145 D1
Tivoli Pl. Hove 145 D1
Tivoli Rd. Bri 145 D1
Tolkien Rd. East 176 B1
Toll Wood Rd. Hor 109 E4
Tollgate. Pea 168 C1
Tollgates. Bat 114 C2
Tollwood Park. Cro 27 F1
Tollwood Rd. Cro 39 F4
Tompset's Bank. For R 13 E1
Tonbridge Rd. Pem 9 F4
Tonbridge Way. Cam 96 B1
Tongdean Ave. Hove 145 D1
Tongdean Ct. Bri 145 D2
Tongdean La. Bri 145 D2
Tongdean Rd. Hove 145 D2
Tongdean Rise. Bri 145 D2
Top Cross Rd. Bex 160 C4
Top Dr. Man 56 C3
Top Rd. Sha 22 C3
Tophill Cl. Por S 143 E1
Tor Rd. Pea 169 D1
Torfield Cl. Hast 162 C4
Torfield Rd. East 185 E2
Toronto Terr. Bri 165 F3
Toronto Terr. Lew 127 D1
Torrance Cl. Hove 144 B1
Totland Rd. Bri 166 A4
Tott Yew Rd. Willn 174 C2
Tourney Rd. Lydd 98 C3
Tovey Cl. East 185 D3
Tower Cl. E Gri 2 B1
Tower Cl. Pev B 177 E4
Tower Rd. Bri 166 A3
Tower Rd. Hast 140 A1
Tower Rd W. Hast 161 F4
Tower Ride. Uck 57 D1
Tower St. Hea 83 F4
Tower View. Uck 80 A4
Towerscroft Ave. Hast 140 A3
Town Hill. Lam 21 F2
Townlands Rd. Wad 31 E2
Trading Estate. Rye H 95 D2
Trafalgar Cl. Hast 139 E4
Trafalgar Cl. Pea 169 D1
Trafalgar Ct. Bri 165 F3
Trafalgar La. Bri 165 F3
Trafalgar Rd. Por S 163 F4
Trafalgar St. Bri 165 F3
Trafalgar Terr. Bri 165 F3
Tram Rd. Rye H 95 F1
Transit Rd. Newh 180 A4
Travellers La. Hast 141 D2
Treblers Rd. Rot 40 B3
Tredcroft Rd. Hove 145 D1
Treemaines Rd. East 176 B1
Treemans Rd. Hor K 54 A4
Treetops Cl. Hast 167 E4
Tremola Ave. Salt 168 A1
Trenches Rd. Cro 27 E1
Treyford Cl. Wood 147 E1
Triangle Rd. Hay H 52 B2
Triangle The. Willn 174 C2
Trinity Cl. T W 9 D2
Trinity Pas. Hast 162 B4
Trinity Pl. East 185 F1
Trinity Rd. Hur 99 F3
Trinity St. Bri 165 F4
Trinity St. Hast 162 B4
Trinity Trees. East 185 F1
Tristan Gdns. T W 8 A2
Troon Cl. Sea 180 C3
Trossachs Cl. East 176 A2
Troy Cl. Cro 27 F1
Truleigh Cl. Wood 167 E4
Truleigh Dr. Por S 143 F2
Tubwell La. Cro 40 A4
Tubwell La. Hor 83 E1
Tudor Ave. Hast 161 F4
Tudor Cl. E Gri 12 B4
Tudor Cl. Hove 144 B1
Tudor Cl. Sea 181 D2
Tudor Ct. T W 8 B1
Tudor Wlk. Fra 80 C3
Tugwell Rd. East 175 E1
Tumulus Rd. Salt 168 A2
Tunnel Rd. T W 8 C2
Turkey Rd. Bex 159 E4
Turner Cl. Bex 160 B3
Turner Cl. East 176 A1
Turner Ct. E Gri 2 C2
Turners Green La. Wad 31 E3
Turner's Hill Rd. E Gri 12 A4
Turners Mill Cl. Hay H 52 A4
Turners Mill Rd. Hay H 52 A3
Turners Way. Bur H 74 B2
Turnpike Cl. Pea 169 D1
Turnpike Cl. Rin 128 C4
Turnpike Piece. Bri 146 C3
Turton Cl. Bri 166 A3
Tutts Barn La. East 185 E3
Tuxford Rd. T W 7 F3
Twineham Rd. East 185 D4
Twitten Cl. Sock 163 E4
Twitten La. Fel 1 B2
Twitten The. Alb 99 D3
Twitten The. Bex 159 D2
Twitten The. Cro 27 E1
Twitten The. Dit 101 D2
Twitten The. Sock 163 E4
Twittens The. Bur H 74 C2
Twyford Cres. Hast 140 A2
Twyford Rd. Bri 146 A3
Tye Hill Rd. Arl 153 F2
Tye View. Pea 168 C1
Tyedean Rd. Pea 178 B4
Tylers La. Nut 37 E1
Tyndale Ave. Bex 159 D2

Uckfield Cl. Bri 166 B3
Uckfield Rd. Cro 38 C4
Uckham La. Bat 115 E3
Udimore Rd. Bro O W 92 B2
Udimore Rd. Rye 94 B2
Udimore Rd. Udi 93 E1
Under Rd. Hers 134 A2
Under Rd. Mag D 133 F2
Undercliff Terr. Hast 162 A3
Undercliffe. Hast 161 F3
Underdown Rd. Sock 163 D4
Underhill. Mar 56 C3
Underhill La. Clay 123 E4
Underhill La. Wmes 124 A4
Union Cl. Hai 132 C2
Union Rd. Bri 165 F4
Union St. Bri 165 F3
Union St. Hast 162 A4
Upland Rd. East 185 D2
Uplands Cl. Bex 159 E3
Uplands Park. Bro O 61 E1
Uplands Rd. Bri 146 A1
Uplands The. Hast 161 F4
Upper Abbey Rd. Bri 166 A2
Upper Ave. East 185 F2
Upper Bedford St. Bri 166 A2
Upper Belgrave Rd. Sea 181 E2
Upper Bevendean Ave. Bri 146 B1
Upper Broomgrove Rd. Hast 140 C2
Upper Carlisle Rd. East 190 A4
Upper Chalvington Pl. Bri 166 B3
Upper Church Rd. Hast 139 F2
Upper Chyngton Gdns. Sea 181 E1
Upper Cl. For R 13 E1
Upper Clarance Rd. Hast 140 A1

Upper Cumberland Wlk. T W 8 C1
Upper Dr The. Hove 165 D4
Upper Duke's Dr. East 190 A4
Upper Dunstan Rd. T W 8 C3
Upper Gardner St. Bri 165 F3
Upper Glen Rd. Hast 139 F3
Upper Gloucester Rd. Bri 165 E3
Upper Greenwoods La. Pun T 85 D3
Upper Grosvenor Rd. T W 8 C3
Upper Hamilton Rd. Bri 165 E4
Upper Hollingdean Rd. Bri 145 F1
Upper Horsebridge Rd. Hai 132 C2
Upper King's Dr. East 175 D1
Upper Kingston La. S Sea 143 D1
Upper Lake. Bat 115 E2
Upper Lewes Rd. Bri 165 F4
Upper Market St. Hove 165 D3
Upper Maze Hill. Hast 161 F4
Upper Nellington. Lan G 7 F2
Upper North St. Bri 165 E3
Upper Park Pl. Bri 165 F3
Upper Park Rd. Hast 140 A1
Upper Profit. Lan G 7 F2
Upper Ratton Dr. East 184 C4
Upper Rock Gdns. Bri 165 F3
Upper Sea Rd. Bex 160 A2
Upper Sherwood Rd. Sea 181 E2
Upper Shoreham Rd. S Sea 143 D1
Upper South Rd. Hast 140 A1
Upper Sq. For R 13 E2
Upper St. E Dean 188 C4
Upper St. T W 8 A2
Upper St James's St. Bri 166 A2
Upper St Johns Rd. Bur H 74 C2
Upper Station Rd. Hea 83 F4
Upper Stephens. Lan G 7 F2
Upper Sudeley St. Bri 166 A2
Upper Valley Rd. Newh 179 F3
Upper Wellington Rd. Bri 166 A4
Upper Winfield Ave. Bri 145 E3
Upper Wish Hill. East 184 C4
Upperton Gdns. East 185 E2
Upperton La. East 185 E2
Upperton Rd. East 185 E2
Upton Ave. Sock 143 E1
Upton Quarry. Lan G 7 E1
Upwick Rd. East 185 D2

Val Prinseps Rd. Pev B 177 D2
Vale Ave. Bri 145 E4
Vale Ave. T W 8 C2
Vale Cl. Sea 181 F2
Vale Gdns. Por S 163 F4
Vale Rd. Bat 114 C3
Vale Rd. Hast 140 A1
Vale Rd. Hay H 52 B1
Vale Rd. May 41 F1
Vale Rd. Por S 164 A4
Vale Rd. Salt 168 A2
Vale Rd. Sea 181 F2
Vale Rd. T W 8 C2
Vale The. Oving 167 E2
Vale View Rd. Hea 83 F3
Valebridge Cl. Bur H 75 D3
Valebridge Dr. Bur H 75 D3
Valebridge Rd. Bur H 75 D3
Valence Rd. Lew 126 C1
Valentine's Pas. Hast 162 A3
Valerie Cl. Por S 144 A1
Vallance Gdns. Hove 164 C3
Vallance Rd. Hove 164 C3
Valley Cl. Bri 145 D2
Valley Cl. Newh 179 F4
Valley Dene. Newh 179 F4
Valley Dr. Bri 145 D2
Valley Dr. Sea 181 F3
Valley Rd. Cro 27 E1
Valley Rd. Lew 148 C4
Valley Rd. Newh 179 F4
Valley Rd. Pea 169 D1
Valley Rd. Por S 143 F1
Valley Rd. T W 8 A2
Valley Rise. Sea 181 E2
Valley Side Rd. Hast 141 D2
Valley View. Cro 27 E1
Vantage Wlk. Hast 139 F1
Varndean Cl. Bri 145 E2
Varndean Dr. Bri 145 E2
Varndean Gdns. Bri 145 E2
Varndean Rd. Bri 145 E2
Varney St. T W 8 C2
Vega Cl. Hai 155 D4
Ventnor Cl. East 175 F2
Ventnor Villas. Hove 164 C3
Venture Cl. Bex 160 B2
Verdant Cl. Hast 162 A4
Vere Rd. Bri 165 F4
Vermont Rd. T W 8 A2
Vernon Ave. Pea 179 D3
Vernon Ave. Wood 167 D4
Vernon Cl. East 186 B4
Vernon Rd. Rid 80 A3
Vernon Rd. T W 9 D3
Vernon Terr. Bri 165 E4
Vernons Rd. Newk 78 A4
Veronica Way. Bri 165 F2
Verralls Wlk. Lew 149 D4
Verulam Pl. Hast 162 B4
Viaduct Rd. Bri 165 F4
Vian Ave. East 186 B4
Vicarage Cl. Newh 170 B1
Vicarage Cl. Rin 128 A3
Vicarage Cl. Sea 181 E2
Vicarage Dr. East 185 D2
Vicarage Field. Hai 155 D4
Vicarage La. Bur C 62 C2
Vicarage La. East 185 D2
Vicarage La. Hai 155 D4
Vicarage La. Rottn 167 E1
Vicarage La. Sca H 53 E2
Vicarage La. Wfd 117 D2
Vicarage Mews. Hai 155 D4
Vicarage Rd. Bur C 62 C2
Vicarage Rd. East 185 D2
Vicarage Rd. Hai 155 D4
Vicarage Rd. Hast 140 C1
Vicarage Terr. Rottn 167 E1
Vicarage Way. Hur G 46 C2
Vicarage Way. Rin 128 A3
Victor Cl. Sea 181 E3
Victoria Ave. Bur H 74 B2
Victoria Ave. Hast 141 D2
Victoria Ave. Pea 179 D4
Victoria Cl. Pole 174 B4
Victoria Cotts. Hove 164 C3
Victoria Dr. East 185 D3
Victoria Gdns. Bur H 74 B1
Victoria Gdns. East 185 D2
Victoria Gr. Hove 165 D3
Victoria Pl. Bri 165 E3
Victoria Rd. Bex 159 F2
Victoria Rd. Bri 165 E3
Victoria Rd. Bur H 74 B1
Victoria Rd. Cro 40 A4
Victoria Rd. East 185 D3
Victoria Rd. Hai 155 D4
Victoria Rd. Hast 162 A4
Victoria Rd. Hay H 52 B2
Victoria Rd. May 41 F2
Victoria Rd. Pole 174 B4
Victoria Rd. Por S 164 A4
Victoria Rd. Sock 163 D4
Victoria Rd. T W 8 C2
Victoria Rd. Win H 134 C3
Victoria St. Bri 165 E3
Victoria Way. Bur H 74 B1
Victoria Way. E Gri 12 B4
Victoria Way. Winc B 120 C3
View Bank. Hast 141 D1
View Rd. Pea 179 D4
View Terr. Dor 2 C4
Views Wood Path. Uck 57 D1
Viking Cl. Sea 180 C3
Villa Rd. Hast 162 A4
Village Mews. Bex 159 D2
Village The. East 190 A4
Village Way. Bri 147 D3
Villiers Cl. Wood 167 E4
Vincent Cl. East 186 B4
Vine Lands. Lydd 98 C3
Vine Pl. Bri 165 E3
Vine Sq. East 186 A3
Vine St. Bri 165 F3
Vinehall Cl. Hast 140 C3
Vinehall Rd. Mou 89 E3
Vineries The. Bur H 75 D2
Vineries The. East 176 A1
Vines Cross Rd. Bri 166 B4
Vines Cross Rd. Hor 109 F4
Vineyard La. Tic 33 D1
Vintry The. East 185 D4
Vintry The. Nut 37 D2
Virgin's Croft. Bat 115 D3
Virgins La. Bat 115 D3
Vowels La. Sel C 11 D1

Wade Cl. East 186 B4
Wadhurst Cl. East 175 E1
Wadhurst Cl. Hast 139 F3
Wadhurst La. Bat 114 B3
Wadhurst Par. Wad 31 E2
Wadhurst Rise. Bri 166 B3
Wadlands Brook Rd. Dor P 2 A3
Wagg Cl. E Gri 2 C1
Wainwright Cl. Hast 139 D2
Wainwright Rd. Bex 159 F2
Waite Cl. S Mal 127 D1
Waites La. Fai 142 B3
Wakefield Rd. Bri 165 F4
Waldegrave Rd. Bri 145 F1
Waldegrave St. Hast 162 B4
Waldene Cl. Hast 140 B1
Waldron Ave. Bri 146 A3
Waldron Cl. East 185 D4
Waldron Ct. Hea 83 F3
Waldron Rd. E Hoa 107 F3
Waldron Thorns. Hea 83 F4
Waldshut Rd. Lew 126 C2
Walesbeech Rd. Salt 178 A4
Walker Cl. East 186 B4
Wall Hill Rd. Ash W 13 E3
Wall Hill Rd. For R 13 E3
Wallace Cl. T W 18 C4
Wallands Cres. Lew 127 D1
Wallers. Spe 7 F4
Wallinger's Wlk. Hast 162 C4
Wallis Ave. East 186 B4
Wallis Cl. Cro 27 F1
Wallis Pl. East 186 B4
Wallsend Rd. Pev B 177 D3
Walmer Cres. Bri 146 C1
Walmer Rd. Sea 182 A2
Walnut Cl. Bri 145 E2
Walnut Tree Wlk. East 184 C4
Walnut Wlk. Pole 174 C3
Walpole Rd. Bri 166 A3
Walpole Terr. Bri 166 A3
Walpole Wlk. East 176 B2
Walshes Rd. Cro 39 F4
Walsingham Cl. East 175 D2
Walsingham Rd. Hove 164 B3
Walters Green Rd. Ford 6 B4
Walton Bank. Bri 146 B3
Walton Cl. Hast 140 A3
Walwers La. Lew 127 D1
Wanderdown Cl. Oving 167 E2
Wanderdown Rd. Oving 167 D2
Wanderdown Way. Oving 167 E2
Wannock Ave. Willn 174 B2
Wannock Cl. Bex 160 C3
Wannock Dr. Pole 174 B3
Wannock Gdns. Willn 174 B2
Wannock La. Willn 174 B2
Wannock Rd. East 186 A3
Wannock Rd. Pole 174 B3
Warbleton Cl. Bri 166 B3
Warburton Cl. E Gri 12 C4
Warburton Cl. East 185 D4
Warburton Cl. Uck 80 A4
Ward Way. Bex 159 E3
Ward's La. Wal 32 B2
Wardsbrook Rd. Tic 45 D4
Warenne Rd. Hove 144 A2
Wares Field. Rid 80 A2
Wares Rd. Rid 80 A2
Warliegh Rd. Bri 165 F4
Warmdene Ave. Bri 145 E3
Warmdene Cl. Bri 145 E3
Warmdene Rd. Bri 145 E3
Warmdene Way. Bri 145 E3
Warminster Rd. Pev B 177 D3
Warnham Gdns. Bex 159 D1
Warnham Rise. Bri 145 F3
Warren Ave. Wood 167 D4
Warren Cl. Cro H 82 B3
Warren Cl. East 190 A4
Warren Cl. Fel 1 B2
Warren Cl. Fri 183 F1
Warren Cl. Hast 161 E4
Warren Cl. Lew 148 C4
Warren Cl. Wood 166 C4
Warren Dr. Lew 148 C4
Warren Gdn. Cro 27 E1
Warren La. Cro H 82 C4
Warren La. Fri 183 F1
Warren La. N Cha 77 E4
Warren Lodge. Pea 168 C1
Warren Rd. Bri 166 B4
Warren Rd. Cro 27 D1
Warren Rd. Fai 142 A2
Warren Rd. Fri G 26 C1
Warren Rd. Wood 166 C4
Warren Ridge. Frant 19 D2
Warren Rise. Wood 166 C4
Warren The. Bur H 75 D1
Warren The. May 42 A1
Warren Way. N Cha 77 E4
Warren Way. Pea 168 C1
Warren Way. Wood 167 D4
Warrior Gdns. Hast 162 A4
Warrior Sq. East 186 A2
Warrior Sq. Hast 162 A4
Warrs Hill La. N Cha 77 E4
Wartling Cl. Hast 139 E1
Wartling Dr. Bex 158 B3
Wartling Rd. Bor S 135 D1
Wartling Rd. East 186 A3
Wartling Rd. Wart 157 D4
Warwick Park. T W 8 C1
Warwick Rd. Bex 159 E3
Warwick Rd. Sea 181 E2
Warwick Rd. T W 8 C1
Washington Rd. Hay H 52 C3
Washington St. Bri 165 F4
Washwell La. Wad 31 E2
Wassall La. Rol L 50 B4
Watchbell La. Rye 95 D3
Watchbell St. Rye 95 D3
Watermill La. Bex 137 F1
Waterdown Rd. T W 8 B1
Waterdyke Ave. Sock 163 E4
Waterfield. T W 18 C4
Watergate. Bex 159 F4
Watergate La. Lew 149 D4
Waterhall Rd. Bri 145 D3
Waterloo Cl. Hast 139 E4
Waterloo Pas. Hast 162 C4
Waterloo Pl. Bri 165 F3
Waterloo Pl. Hast 162 C4
Waterloo Pl. Lew 127 D1
Waterloo Sq. Alfn 172 C2
Waterloo St. Hove 165 D3
Watermans Cl. Hast 140 B2
Watermill Cl. Bex 159 F4
Watermill Cl. Pole 174 C3
Watermill La. Bec 69 D1
Watermill La. Gue G 119 D1
Watermill La. Ick 119 D2
Waters Cotts. Wad 31 F2
Waterside. E Gri 2 C1
Waterworks Dr. For R 13 E2
Waterworks Rd. East 185 F2
Waterworks Rd. Hast 140 B1
Watling Cl. Sock 163 E4
Watling Rd. Sock 163 E4
Watton Park. Bex 159 E2
Watts Cl. Wad 31 E2
Watts La. East 185 E2
Watts' Palace La. Ewh G 91 D4
Waverley Cres. Bri 146 A1
Waverley Dr. T W 9 E3
Waverley Gdns. Pev B 177 D3
Wayfaring Down. Jev 174 A2
Wayfield Ave. Hove 144 B1
Wayford Cl. East 176 A1
Wayland Ave. Bri 145 D2
Wayside. Bri 145 D3
Wayside. Fri 188 C4
Weald Ave. Hove 164 B4
Weald Cl. Bar C 104 B2
Weald Cl. Hur 99 E3
Weald Rd. Bur H 74 B2
Weald Rise. Hay H 52 B1
Weald The. E Gri 2 B2
Weald View. Bar C 104 B2
Weald View. Stas 67 E1
Weald View. Wad 31 E3
Wealden Cl. Cro 27 E2
Wealden Park. East 175 D1
Wealden View. Bur 63 F4
Wealden Way. Bex 159 D3
Wealden Way. Hay H 52 A2
Wealdview Rd. Hea 83 E4
Weare Rd. Sgh 9 D4
Weatherby Cl. East 185 D4
Weavers Cl. Bur H 75 D1
Weavers La. Alfn 172 B2
Wedderburn Rd. East 174 C1
Week La. Gly 128 A1
Welbeck Ave. Hast 161 F4
Welbeck Ave. Hove 164 B3
Welbeck Ave. Sgh 9 D4
Welbeck Cl. Bur H 75 D2
Welbeck Cl. East 175 D2
Welbeck Dr. Bur H 75 D2
Welesmere Rd. Rottn 167 F2
Welkin The. Hay H 52 C4
Well House Pl. Lew 127 D1
Wellcombe Cres. East 190 A4
Weller Rd. T W 8 A2
Wellesley Cl. Bex 159 D2
Wellesley Cl. Cro 27 D1
Wellesley Ct. Hast 162 C4
Wellesley Rd. East 185 F2
Wellfield. Ash W 13 D4
Wellgreen La. Kin L 148 B3
Wellhouse La. Bur H 100 C4
Wellingham La. Rin 127 F4
Wellingham La. S Mal 127 F4
Wellington Gdns. Bat 115 D3
Wellington Gdns. Hast 162 C4
Wellington Mews. Hast 162 B4
Wellington Pl. Hast 162 B4
Wellington Rd. Bri 166 A4
Wellington Rd. Hast 162 C4
Wellington Rd. Newh 170 B1
Wellington Rd. Pea 179 E3
Wellington Rd. Por S 164 A3
Wellington Sq. Hast 162 B4
Wellington St. Bri 166 A4
Wellington St. Lew 127 D1
Wellington Town Rd. E Gri 2 A1
Wellis Gdns. Hast 161 F4
Wells Cl. East 190 A4
Wells Cl. Plu G 102 B3
Wells Cl. T W 8 C2
Wells Meadow. E Gri 2 A2
Wendale Dr. Pea 169 D1
Went Hill Gdns. Willn 174 C2
Went La. Fri 184 A1
Went Way. E Dean 188 C4
Wenthill Cl. Fri 189 D4
Wentworth Cl. Bex 160 B3
Wentworth St. Bri 165 F2
Wentworth Way. Hast 161 E4
West Ascent. Hast 161 F3
West Beeches Rd. Cro 27 F1
West Cl. Alfn 172 B2
West Cl. Pole 174 C4
West Comm. Hay H 52 B4
West Comm Dr. Hay H 52 C4
West Dean Rise. Sea 181 F2
West Down Rd. Bex 159 F3
West Dr. Bri 166 A3
West End. Hers 134 B3
West Furlong La. Hur 99 F3
West Hill. Dor P 2 B3
West Hill. E Gri 12 A4
West Hill Pl. Bri 165 E3
West Hill Rd. Bri 165 E3
West Hill Rd. Hast 161 F3
West Hill St. Bri 165 E3
West Hoathly Rd. E Gri 12 A3
West La. E Gri 12 A4
West Leigh. E Gri 12 B4
West Mallion. Hay H 52 B2
West Par. Bex 159 F1
West Park Cres. Bur H 74 A2
West Park Rd. Dom 1 A4
West Rd. Por S 163 F4
West Rd. Poy 122 B4
West Rd. Pye 122 C3
West St. Alfn 172 B2
West St. Bri 165 E3
West St. Bur H 74 B2
West St. Dit 101 D2
West St. Dor 2 C4
West St. E Gri 12 B4
West St. East 185 E1
West St. Hast 162 C4
West St. Lew 127 D1
West St. May 41 F1
West St. Por S 164 A4
West St. Rottn 167 E1
West St. Rye 95 D3
West St. Sea 181 E1
West St La. Hor 83 E1
West Terr. East 185 E1
West Undercliff. Rye 94 C3
West View. Hast 140 C1
West View. Hay H 52 C3
West View. Sea 181 E1
West View. Uck 57 D1
West View Gdns. E Gri 12 B4
West View Terr. S Hei 170 A1
West Way. Hove 144 B1
Westaway Dr. Bex 159 F2
Westbourne Gdns. Hove 164 C4
Westbourne Gr. Hove 164 C4
Westbourne Pl. Hove 164 C3
Westbourne St. Hove 164 C4
Westbourne Villas. Hove 164 B3
Westbrook. Salt 168 A1
Westbrook La. Wfd 117 E3
Westbrook Terr. T W 9 D1
Westcourt Dr. Bex 159 E2
Westdean Ave. Newh 179 F3
Westdene Cl. Hast 140 A3
Westdene Dr. Bri 145 D3
Westdown La. Bur C 62 C2
Westdown Rd. Sea 181 D2
Westergate Rd. Bri 146 B2
Westerham Rd. East 176 A1
Westerleigh Cl. Hast 161 F4
Western Ave. Bat 115 D3
Western Ave. Pole 174 C4
Western Espl. Hove 164 B3
Western Gdns. Cro 40 A4
Western Par. East 190 B4
Western Rd. Bex 160 A2
Western Rd. Bri 165 E3
Western Rd. Bur H 74 B2
Western Rd. Chay 77 F3
Western Rd. Cro 40 A4
Western Rd. East 185 F2
Western Rd. Hai 154 C4
Western Rd. Hast 162 A4
Western Rd. Hay H 52 B2
Western Rd. Hur 99 E3
Western Rd. Lew 126 C1
Western Rd. Newh 180 A3
Western Rd. Newk 78 A4
Western Rd. Pev B 177 D2
Western Rd. T W 9 D3
Western Rd. Wad 31 E3
Western St. Bri 165 D3
Western Terr. Bri 165 E3
Westfield Ave. Salt 168 A2
Westfield Ave N. Salt 168 B2
Westfield Ave S. Salt 168 A2
Westfield Cl. Bri 145 F2
Westfield Cl. Five A 59 F3
Westfield Cl. Pole 174 C4
Westfield Cres. Bri 145 F3
Westfield Ct. Pole 174 C3
Westfield La. Hast 139 F4
Westfield La. Wfd 117 D1
Westfield Rd. East 185 D3
Westfield Rise. Salt 168 B2
Westgate St. Lew 127 D1
Westham Cl. Bex 159 E2
Westham Dr. Pev B 177 E3
Westhill Dr. Bur H 74 B2
Westlands Rd. Hay H 52 C3
Westmeston Ave. Salt 167 F1
Westminster Cl. East 175 D2
Westminster Cres. Hast 140 C2
Westmoreland Cl. Hast 139 E2
Westmount Cl. Sock 163 D4
Westpoint. Newk 78 A4
Westville Rd. Bex 159 F2
Westway. Pem 10 A4
Westway Cl. Por S 143 E2
Westway Gdns. Por S 143 E2
Westwood Rd. T W 8 A3
Wharf Rd. East 185 E2
Wharf Rd. Hove 164 A3
Whatlington Rd. Bat 115 E4
Whatlington Rd. Wha 89 F1
Wheatfield Way. Bri 146 B2
Wheel La. Wfd 117 D2
Wheelers La. Had D 59 D3
Wheelwright La. Bur H 75 D1
Whichelo Pl. Bri 166 A3
Whiffens Cl. Hai 154 C3
Whincroft Park. Cro 39 D4
Whipping Post La. Rottn 167 E1
Whipping Rd. Bri 166 A4
Whippingham St. Bri 166 A4
White Hill. Lew 127 D1
White Hill Ave. Bex 159 E2
White Hill Dr. Bex 159 E2
White Rock. Hast 162 B4
White Rock Gdns. Hast 162 B4
White Rock Rd. Hast 162 B4
White St. Bri 165 F3
White Way. Alfn 172 B1
Whitebread La. Bec 69 E4
Whitebread La. Four O 70 A3
Whitebread La. Norm 69 E4
Whitecross St. Bri 165 F3
Whitefield Rd. T W 8 C3
Whitefriars Rd. Hast 140 C1
Whitegates Cl. S Cha 103 E4
Whitegates La. Wad 31 D4
Whitehawk Ave. Bri 166 B4
Whitehawk Cl. Bri 166 B3
Whitehawk Cres. Bri 166 B3
Whitehawk Hill Rd. Bri 166 A3
Whitehawk Rd. Bri 166 B3
Whitehawk Way. Bri 166 B3
Whitehill Cl. Cro 27 E1
Whitehill Rd. Cro 27 E1
Whitehouse Ave. Bex 159 F4
Whitehouse La. Hea 82 C2
Whitehouse La. Wald 82 C2
Whitelot Cl. Sock 143 E1
Whitelot Way. Sock 143 E1
Whiterock Pl. Sock 163 E4
White's Cl. Hur 99 F4
Whitethorn Dr. Bri 144 C2
Whiteway La. Rottn 167 F1
Whitley Rd. East 185 F2
Whittingehame Gdns. Bri 145 E2
Whittington's Way. Hast 140 C2
Whittle Dr. East 175 F1
Whitworth Rd. Hast 139 F4
Whybourne Crest. T W 9 D1
Whydown Hill. Sed 116 B3
Whydown Rd. Bex 159 D4
Wickham Ave. Bex 159 F2
Wickham Cl. Hay H 52 B4
Wickham Dr. Hur 100 A3
Wickham Gdns. T W 8 A3
Wickham Hill. Hur 100 A2

Wickham La. Bar.....103 E1
Wickham La. Bar C.....103 E2
Wickham Rock La. Ick.....119 F2
Wickham Rock La. Winc.....120 A3
Wickham Way. Hay H.....52 B4
Wickhurst Cl. Por S.....143 E1
Wickhurst Rd. Por S.....143 F1
Wickhurst Rise. Por S.....143 E2
Wicklands Ave. Salt.....168 A1
Widbury Cl. Lan G.....7 E2
Widdicombe Way. Bri.....146 B1
Wigmore Cl. Bri.....145 F1
Wilbury Ave. Hove.....165 D4
Wilbury Cres. Hove.....165 D4
Wilbury Gdns. Hove.....165 D4
Wilbury Gr. Hove.....165 D3
Wilbury Rd. Hove.....165 D3
Wilbury Villas. Hove.....165 D4
Wilby Ave. Sock.....143 E1
Wild Park Cl. Bri.....146 B2
Wilderness La. Had D.....59 D2
Wilderness Park. Cro.....27 E1
Wilderness Rd. Hur.....99 F3
Wilderness Rise. Dor P.....2 C3
Wilderness The. Hay H.....52 C4
Wilderwick Rd. Dor.....2 C3
Wilderwick Rd. E Gri.....2 C2
Wilfred Rd. Hove.....144 A1
Willard Cl. East.....185 F3
William Allen La. Hay H.....52 C3
William Rd. Hast.....161 E4
William St. Bri.....165 F3
William St. Sock.....163 F4
William St. T W.....8 C3
Williams Rd. S Sea.....163 D4
Willingdon Ave. Bex.....159 F2
Willingdon Ave. Hast.....139 F3
Willingdon Cl. East.....174 C1
Willingdon Cl. Hast.....139 F3
Willingdon Ct. Willn.....174 C2
Willingdon Dro. East.....175 F1
Willingdon La. Jev.....184 A4
Willingdon Park Dr. East.....175 D1
Willingdon Rd. Bri.....146 B1
Willingdon Rd. East.....185 D3
Willingdon Way. Hast.....139 F3
Willingdon Way. Willn.....174 C1
Willingford La. Bur.....63 D1
Willoughby Cres. East.....186 A3
Willow Ave. Hai.....132 C1
Willow Cl. E Gri.....2 A2
Willow Cl. Etc.....64 C4
Willow Cl. Hea.....83 F4
Willow Dr. Bex.....159 D3
Willow Dr. Pole.....174 C3
Willow Dr. Sea.....182 A2
Willow End. Hast.....140 B2
Willow Gdns. Hur.....99 F4
Willow La. Winc B.....120 C3
Willow Mead. E Gri.....12 B4
Willow Park. Hay H.....52 C2
Willow Tree Rd. T W.....8 B1
Willow Way. Hur.....99 E4
Willow Wlk. East.....175 D1
Willow Wlk. Newh.....180 A4
Willow Wlk. T W.....9 E4
Willowbed Wlk. Hast.....140 B3
Willowbrook Way. Key.....100 C2
Willowfield Rd. East.....185 F2
Willowfield Sq. East.....185 F2
Willowmead. Cro.....39 E4
Willows Rise. Fra.....80 C3
Willows The. Bur H.....75 D3
Willowstream Cl. Thr O.....118 B2
Wilman Rd. T W.....8 C4
Wilmington Cl. Bri.....145 F3
Wilmington Cl. Key.....100 B2
Wilmington Gdns. East.....185 F1
Wilmington Par. Bri.....145 E3
Wilmington Rd. Hast.....140 C2
Wilmington Rd. Newh.....179 F3
Wilmington Rd. Sea.....181 D2
Wilmington Sq. East.....185 F1
Wilmington St. Wil.....173 E3
Wilmington Way. Bri.....145 F3
Wilmington Way. Hay H.....52 C3
Wilmot Rd. S Sea.....163 D4
Wilson Ave. Bri.....166 B3
Wilson Gr. Uck.....79 F4
Wilton Ave. East.....175 E1
Wilton Rd. Bex.....160 A2
Wiltshire Way. T W.....9 D4
Winchcombe Rd. East.....185 F2
Winchelsea Cl. Sea.....181 F3
Winchelsea La. Hast.....141 E3
Winchelsea La. Udi.....94 A1
Winchelsea Rd. East.....186 A3
Winchelsea Rd. Hast.....141 E4
Winchelsea Rd. Rye.....94 C3
Winchester St. Bri.....165 F4
Winchester Wy. Willn.....175 D1
Wincombe Rd. Bri.....145 D1
Windermere Cres. East.....186 A3
Windermere Rd. Hay H.....52 B2
Winding St. Hast.....162 C4
Windlesham Ave. Bri.....165 E3
Windlesham Cl. Por S.....143 F1
Windlesham Gdns. Bri.....165 E4
Windlesham Rd. Bri.....165 E3
Windmill Ave. Key.....100 B2
Windmill Cl. East.....185 D3
Windmill Cl. Hea.....83 F4
Windmill Cl. Hove.....144 B1
Windmill Dr. Bex.....159 F3
Windmill Dr. Bri.....145 D3
Windmill Dr. Bur H.....74 C2
Windmill Green. St Cro.....176 A3
Windmill La. Ash W.....13 D4
Windmill La. Cou W.....32 A4
Windmill La. E Gri.....2 A2
Windmill La. Fri.....183 F1
Windmill La. Wad.....31 D2
Windmill Rd. Hast.....139 F1
Windmill Rd. Pole.....174 C3
Windmill Rd. Sock.....143 E1
Windmill St. Bri.....165 F3
Windmill St. T W.....9 D2
Windmill Terr. Bri.....165 F3
Windover Cres. Lew.....126 C1
Windover Way. Willn.....174 C2
Windsor Cl. Hove.....144 C2
Windsor Cl. Sea.....180 C3
Windsor Ct. Cro.....40 A4
Windsor Pl. Cro.....40 A4
Windsor Pl. E Gri.....12 C4
Windsor Rd. Bex.....159 F2
Windsor Rd. Cro.....40 A4
Windsor Rd. Hai.....154 C3
Windsor Rd. Hast.....139 F2
Windsor St. Bri.....165 E3
Windsor Way. Pole.....174 C4
Windsor Way. Winc B.....120 C3
Wineham Way. Bex.....160 B2
Winfield Ave. Bri.....145 E3
Winfield Cl. Bri.....145 E3
Winfield Cl. Por S.....143 F2
Wingate Cl. Hast.....139 F1
Wingle Tye Rd. Bur H.....100 C4
Winkhurst Way. Bur H.....75 D1
Winkney Rd. East.....175 E2
Winston Cres. East.....186 A4
Winston Dr. Bex.....159 E2
Winstone Scott Ave. Lan G.....7 E2
Winterbourne Cl. Hast.....162 A4
Winterbourne Cl. Lew.....148 C4
Winterbourne Hollow. Lew.....148 C4
Winterbourne La. Lew.....148 C4
Winterbourne Mews. Lew.....148 C4
Winton Ave. Salt.....168 A2
Winton St. Alfn.....172 B2
Wire Mill La. Fel.....1 B4
Wisden Ave. Bur H.....74 B3
Wiseacre. Lam.....21 F2
Wish Ct. Hove.....164 B4
Wish Hill. East.....184 C4
Wish Rd. East.....185 F1
Wish Rd. Hove.....164 B3
Wish St. Rye.....94 C3
Wish Ward. Rye.....94 C3
Wishing Tree Cl. Hast.....139 E1
Wishing Tree La. Hast.....139 E1
Wishing Tree Rd. Hast.....139 E2
Wishing Tree Rd N. Hast.....139 F2
Wiston Rd N. Bri.....166 B4
Wiston Rd S. Bri.....166 B3
Wiston Way. Bri.....166 B4
Withdean Ave. Bri.....145 D1
Withdean Cl. Bri.....145 D2
Withdean Cres. Bri.....145 E2
Withdean Ct Ave. Bri.....145 D2
Withdean Rd. Bri.....145 D2
Withdean Rise. Bri.....145 D2
Withyham Ave. Salt.....168 A1
Withyham Cl. East.....175 E1
Withyham Rd. Bex.....159 D1
Withyham Rd. Gro.....16 C3
Wittersham Rd. Iden.....71 F4
Wittersham Rd. Rol L.....51 D3
Wittersham Rd. Witt.....51 F3
Wivelsfield Green Rd. Wiv.....75 F3
Wivelsfield Green Rd. Wiv G.....76 A3
Wivelsfield Rd. Hay H.....52 B1
Wivelsfield Rd. Salt.....168 A2
Woburn Pl. Bri.....146 B3
Woburn Wy. East.....175 D2
Wolfe Cl. Cro.....39 F4
Wolseley Rd. Bri.....146 A3
Wolseley Rd. Por S.....163 F4
Wolseley Rd. Sgh.....9 D4
Wolstonbury Cl. Hur.....99 F2
Wolstonbury Rd. Hove.....165 E4
Wolstonbury Way. Bur H.....74 C1
Wolverstone Dr. Bri.....146 A1
Wood La. Bor S.....135 D1
Wood Ride. Hay H.....52 A2
Wood St. Bri.....165 F3
Wood St. E Gri.....2 A1
Wood St. T W.....8 C2
Woodbine La. Newk.....78 A4
Woodbourne Ave. Bri.....145 F2
Woodbrook Rd. Hast.....140 B1
Woodbury Ave. E Gri.....2 C1
Woodbury Cl. E Gri.....12 C4
Woodbury Park Gdns. T W.....8 C3
Woodbury Park Rd. T W.....8 C3
Woodcock Hill. Fel.....1 B3
Woodcote Rd. For R.....13 E1
Woodcrest Rd. Bur H.....74 B1
Woodcroft Dr. East.....185 D4
Woodgate Meadow. Plu G.....102 B4
Woodgate Rd. East.....186 A3
Woodhill Park. Pem.....10 A3
Woodhouse Rd. Hove.....164 B4
Woodland Ave. Bur H.....75 D2
Woodland Ave. East.....175 D1
Woodland Ave. Hove.....144 C1
Woodland Cl. Bur H.....75 D2
Woodland Cl. Hove.....144 C1
Woodland Cl. T W.....8 C4
Woodland Ct. Hove.....144 C2
Woodland Dr. Hove.....144 C2
Woodland Rd. T W.....9 D4
Woodland Rise. Bex.....160 B2
Woodland Vale Rd. Hast.....162 A4
Woodland Way. Bri.....145 E2
Woodland Way. Cro.....39 E4
Woodland Way. Crow.....138 B2
Woodland Way. Fai.....142 B2
Woodlands. Hove.....145 D1
Woodlands. Pem.....10 B4
Woodlands Cl. Hai.....133 D1
Woodlands Cl. Hass.....100 B2
Woodlands Cl. Hea.....83 F3
Woodlands Cl. Pea.....168 C1
Woodlands Cl. Uck.....80 A4
Woodlands Rd. E Gri.....2 C2
Woodlands Rd. Hass.....100 B2
Woodlands Rd. Hay H.....52 B2
Woodlands The. Bri.....145 E3
Woodlands The. Hast.....140 B3
Woodlands Way. Hea.....83 F3
Woodleigh Rd. Bur H.....75 D2
Woodpecker Dr. Hai.....154 C4
Woodpecker Rd. East.....175 F1
Woodridge Cl. Hay H.....52 C2
Woodruff Ave. Hove.....145 D1
Woods Hill Cl. Ash W.....13 D3
Woods Hill La. Ash W.....13 D3
Wood's Pas. Hast.....162 C4
Woodsgate Ave. Bex.....160 A3
Woodsgate Park. Bex.....159 F3
Woodsgate Way. Pem.....9 F3
Woodside. Cro.....27 E1
Woodside Ave. Hove.....145 D1
Woodside Cl. Pem.....10 B3
Woodside Rd. Pem.....10 B3
Woodside Rd. T W.....8 A2
Woodside School Rd. Bri.....146 A1
Woodside Way. Hai.....154 C2
Woodspring Cl. Hast.....139 F3
Woodstock. E Gri.....2 A1
Woodstock Rd. Bex.....159 D3
Woodview Cl. Bri.....146 A3
Woodville Rd. Bex.....159 F2
Woodward Cl. East.....186 B4
Woodwards Cl. Bur H.....74 C1
Worcester Villas. Hove.....164 A4
Wordsworth Dr. East.....176 B1
Wordsworth Rise. E Gri.....2 A1
Wordsworth St. Hove.....164 C4
Workhouse La. Ick.....119 E3
Worsham La. Bex.....160 B4
Worsted La. E Gri.....12 C4
Wray Cl. Ash W.....13 D3
Wren Cl. Hea.....83 F4
Wren Ct. Bat.....115 E2
Wren Ct. Hast.....139 E2
Wrestwood Ave. East.....175 D1
Wrestwood Cl. Bex.....160 A3
Wrestwood Rd. Bex.....160 B3
Wrotham Cl. East.....176 A1
Wrotham Cl. Hast.....140 B3
Wroxham Rd. East.....175 F2
Wyatts La. Hor K.....35 D3
Wyberlye Rd. Bur H.....74 C2
Wybourne Rise. T W.....18 C4
Wychperry Rd. Hay H.....52 A3
Wychurst Gdns. Bex.....160 A3
Wykeham Rd. Hast.....162 B4
Wykeham Way. Bur H.....75 D1
Wyndham St. Bri.....165 F2
Wyshe The. Pye.....123 D3
Wythwood. Hay H.....52 B1

Yardley St. Bri.....165 F4
Yeomans. Rin.....128 C4
Yew La. E Gri.....1 C2
Yew Tree Cl. Hast.....140 B3
Yew Tree Cl. Hea.....83 F3
Yew Tree Cl. Rin.....128 B4
Yew Tree Rd. Sgh.....8 C4
Yewtree La. Tow R.....41 E4
Yielding's Cl. East.....185 D3
York Ave. Hove.....165 E3
York Gdns. Hast.....162 B4
York Gr. Bri.....165 E4
York Hill. Bri.....165 F4
York Pl. Bri.....165 F3
York Rd. Bex.....160 C3
York Rd. East.....185 E1
York Rd. Hast.....140 A1
York Rd. Hove.....165 E3
York Rd. Pea.....179 E3
York Rd. T W.....8 C2
York Villas. Bri.....165 E4
Youngsmere Cl. Bri.....145 F3

Zion Gdns. Bri.....165 E3